Power, Politics and Religion in Timurid Iran

Beatrice Forbes Manz uses the history of Iran under the Timurid ruler Shahrukh (1409–47) to analyze the relationship between government and society in the medieval Middle East. She provides a rich portrait of Iranian society over an exceptionally broad spectrum – the dynasty and its servitors, city elites and provincial rulers, and the religious classes, both ulama and Sufi. The work addresses two issues central to pre-modern Middle Eastern history: how a government without the monopoly of force controlled a heterogeneous society, and how a society with diffuse power structures remained stable over long periods. Written for an audience of students as well as scholars, this book provides the first broad analysis of political dynamics in late medieval Iran and challenges much received wisdom about civil and military power, the relationship of government to society, and the interaction of religious figures with the ruling class.

BEATRICE FORBES MANZ is Associate Professor of History at Tufts University, Massachusetts. Her previous publications include *The Rise and Fall of Tamerlane* (1989) and, as editor, *Studies on Chinese and Islamic Central Asia* (1995).

Cambridge Studies in Islamic Civilisation

Published titles in the series are listed at the back of the book

Power, Politics and Religion in Timurid Iran

BEATRICE FORBES MANZ

Tufts University

CAMBRIDGE
UNIVERSITY PRESS

CAMBRIDGE UNIVERSITY PRESS
Cambridge, New York, Melbourne, Madrid, Cape Town, Singapore, São Paulo

Cambridge University Press
The Edinburgh Building, Cambridge CB2 2RU, UK

Published in the United States of America by Cambridge University Press, New York

www.cambridge.org
Information on this title: www.cambridge.org/9780521865470

First published 2007

Printed in the United Kingdom at the University Press, Cambridge

A catalogue record for this publication is available from the British Library

ISBN-13 978-0-521-86547-0 hardback

For Eve and Ellen Manz,
with love and admiration.

Contents

List of maps — *page* x
Preface — xi
Chronology — xiii
Family tree of major Timurid princes — xviii

Introduction — 1
1 The formation of the Timurid state under Shahrukh — 13
2 Issues of sources and historiography — 49
3 Shahrukh's *dīwān* and its personnel — 79
4 Political and military resources of Iran — 111
5 Timurid rule in southern and central Iran — 146
6 Political dynamics in the realm of the supernatural — 178
7 The dynasty and the politics of the religious classes — 208
8 The rebellion of Sultan Muhammad b. Baysunghur and the struggle over succession — 245
Conclusion — 276

Bibliography — 284
Index — 296

Maps

Preface

I have profited from the support of several institutions while writing this book. A fellowship from the American Research Institute in Turkey in 1990 allowed me to begin research in the libraries of Istanbul. In the summer of 1996 I spent two months in Tashkent, Bukhara and Samarqand on a Tufts Faculty Research award. Grants from the American Council of Learned Societies and the National Endowment for the Humanities in 1991–92 and a National Council for Eurasian and East European Research Fellowship for the calendar year 1999 allowed me to take leave from teaching. Finally, in 2003–04 a membership at the School of Historical Studies, Institute for Advanced Studies, together with an American Council of Learned Societies fellowship and a Tufts Faculty Research award allowed me to finish the manuscript while beginning my next project. To all of these institutions I want to express my heartfelt thanks.

A number of individuals have also provided valuable help. Professor Bert Fragner generously facilitated a semester spent at the University in Bamberg, in spring, 1993, which provided a peaceful place to work and an introduction to several colleagues who continue to help and inspire. Leonard Lewisohn lent me his unpublished dissertation and answered a number of important questions for me. Several colleagues have read parts of the manuscript and offered valuable advice; I want to thank in particular Devin Deweese, Jo-Ann Gross, Ahmet Karamustafa, Robert McChesney, David Morgan, Johannes Pahlitsch and Jürgen Paul. Finally, I want to express my gratitude to Hesna Ergün and Hande Deniz, for their invaluable help with the index and galleys.

The work of two scholars in particular underlies much of what I have written here. The numerous articles of the late Jean Aubin provided an indispensable base and constant inspiration for me, as he has for anyone writing on this and related periods. Over the course of his long career, Professor Iraj Afshar has collected and edited an extraordinary number of medieval sources, particularly the local histories crucial to the understanding of southern and central Iran. Without his work, the sections of the book on central and southern Iran could not have been written.

Note on usage

I have tried to make this book both useful for scholars and accessible to non-specialists. My solution to the perennial problem of transcription is to use classical Arabic transcription for Arabic and Persian names and terms, but not for Turkic ones. Names of well-known cities are written with their common spelling, while less well-known ones are transcribed in classical fashion. Within the text I have omitted most diacriticals except for technical terms. In bibliographical references and the index to the book, full diacriticals are used. Dates are given first according to the Islamic calendar and then the Christian one.

Chronology

794/1391–92 Temür appoints Pir Muhammad b. Jahangir governor of Kabul and Multan.

796/1394 ʿUmar Shaykh b. Temür dies and is succeeded as governor of Fars by his son, Pir Muhammad.

799/1396–97 Shahrukh is appointed governor of Khorasan.

800/1397–98 Muhammad Sultan b. Jahangir is appointed governor of northern Transoxiana.

18 Shaʿban, 805/March 13, 1403 Muhammad Sultan b. Jahangir dies.

Winter, 806/1404–05 Temür in Qarabagh, sends out inspectors to provincial *dīwān*s.

17 or 18 Shawwal, 807/February 17 or 18, 1405 Temür dies in Otrar.

Rajab, 808/December, 1405 to January, 1406 Khorezm is taken over by the Jochids.

809/1406–07 Sayyid Fakhr al-Din Ahmad comes from Samarqand to Herat, where he is appointed to *dīwān*, and then dislodged.

Ramadan, 809/February, 1407 Pir Muhammad b. Jahangir is murdered.

Dhuʾl-Qaʿda, 810/April, 1408 Defeat of Aba Bakr and Amiranshah by the Qaraqoyunlu, death of Amiranshah.

811/1408 Vizier Ghiyath al-Din Salar Simnani is killed and Fakhr al-Din Ahmad is returned to *dīwān*.

Late winter of 811/1409 Khudaydad and Shaykh Nur al-Din invite Shahrukh to undertake a joint campaign against Khalil Sultan. Shahrukh arrives in Transoxiana in late spring.

27 Dhuʾl-Hijja, 811/May 13, 1409 Shahrukh enters Samarqand; he spends about six months there and in early 812/1409 appoints Ulugh Beg governor.

3 Muharram, 812/May 18, 1409 Murder of Pir Muhammad b. ʿUmar Shaykh; beginning of Iskandar b. ʿUmar Shaykh's rise to power in Fars.

12 Dhuʾl-Hijja, 812/April 17, 1410 Shaykh Nur al-Din defeats Ulugh Beg's army, necessitating Shahrukh's second campaign in Transoxiana.

813/1410–11 Shahrukh completes a madrasa and *khānaqāh* in Herat and appoints teachers.

Dhuʾl-Qaʿda, 813/February–March, 1411 Shahrukh declares that he has abrogated the Mongolian dynastic code, the *yasa*, and reinstated the *sharīʿa*. He has wine from the taverns publicly poured out.

813–14/1410–12 Ḥāfiẓ-i Abrū writes a continuation of Shami's *Zafarnama*; Taj al-Salmani writes *Shams al-husn*.

Last day of Rabiʿ I, 814/July 22, 1411 Shahrukh sets out against Transoxiana on threat of another attack by Shaykh Nur al-Din, backed by the eastern Chaghadayid khan. On receiving news of Shahrukh's movement, the khan deserts Shaykh Nur al-Din.

Dhuʾl-Hijja, 814/March–April, 1412 Rustam murders Qadi Ahmad Saʿidi; the population of Isfahan turns against him and soon after Iskandar b. ʿUmar Shaykh takes the city.

End of 815/spring, 1413 Successful expedition against Khorezm under Amir Shahmalik.

816/1413–14 Composition of Iskandar's history of Temür and his house, and first recension of Natanzi's *Muntakhab al-tawarikh*. Iskandar begins to use title "Sultan."

Beginning of 817/March–April, 1414 Shahrukh heads against Iskandar.

3 Jumada I, 817/July 21, 1414 Isfahan submits to Shahrukh; Iskandar flees but is captured and handed to his brother Rustam.

817/1414–15 Ibrahim Sultan b. Shahrukh is appointed governor of Fars.

Early 818/1415 Baysunghur is made governor of Mazandaran and western Khorasan.

Early 818/spring, 1415 Saʿd-i Waqqas b. Muhammad Sultan, governor of Qum, defects to the Qaraqoyunlu. Disturbances in western regions including Fars, where Bayqara b. ʿUmar Shaykh pushes Ibrahim Sultan out of Shiraz.

17 Jumadi II, 818/August 24, 1415 Shahrukh sets off against Fars.

27 Ramadan, 818/December 1, 1415 Bayqara submits to Shahrukh at the request of the population.

Spring, 819/1416 Shahrukh campaigns against Kerman, arriving at the beginning of Rabiʿ II/May–June, 1416.

819/1416–17 Amir Buhlul begins uprising against Qaydu b. Pir Muhammad b. Jahangir, governor of Kabul.

819–20/1416–18 Gawharshad builds cathedral mosques, *dār al-siyāda* and *dār al-ḥuffāẓ*, in Mashhad.

820/1417–18 Jaʿfar b. Muḥammad al-Ḥusayni Jaʿfari presents *Tarikh-i wasit* to Shahrukh.

820 Work begins on Gawharshad's complex in Herat.

820/1417 Amir Ghunashirin is appointed governor of Kerman.

Middle Rabiʿ I, 820/beginning of May, 1417 Shahrukh sets off on campaign towards Kabul to put down disturbances of Hazara and others; he winters in Qandahar.

Jumadi I, 820/June–July, 1417 Death of vizier Fakhr al-Din Ahmad.

End of 820/early 1418 Ghiyath al-Din Pir Ahmad is appointed *ṣāḥib dīwān.*

821/1418–19 Soyurghatmish replaces Qaydu as governor of Kabul.

By 823/1420 Chaqmaq has been appointed governor of Yazd.

11 Shaʿban, 823/August 21, 1420 Shahrukh leaves Herat for Azarbaijan campaign.

7 Dhuʾl Qaʿda, 823/November 13, 1420 Death of Qara Yusuf Qaraqoyunlu.

8 Dhuʾl Hijja, 823/December 14, 1420 Shahrukh reaches Qarabagh.

End of Rajab 824/late July, 1421 Qara Yusuf's sons Isfand and Iskandar meet Shahrukh's armies in Alashgird. After a hard battle Shahrukh's forces prevail.

19 Shawwal, 824/October 17, 1421 Shahrukh arrives back in Herat.

827/1423–24 Disturbance by Shaykh Ishaq Khuttalani and his disciple Nurbakhsh.

827 or 828/1423–45 Death of Rustam b. ʿUmar Shaykh. Governorship of Isfahan goes to the family of Amir Firuzshah.

829/1425–26 Baraq Khan of the Blue Horde claims Sighnaq.

Muharram, 829 to end of 830/November, 1425 to October–November, 1427 Shahrukh rebuilds the Ansari shrine at Gazurgah.

830/1426–27 Ḥāfiẓ-i Abrū completes the *Majmaʿ al-tawārīkh* and *Muʿizz al-ansāb.*

6 Muharram, 830/November 17, 1426 Death of Shahrukh's son Soyurghatmish, governor of Kabul.

23 Rabiʿ I, 830/January 22, 1427 A member of the Hurufi sect makes an attempt on Shahrukh's life. Qasim al-Anwar is banished from Herat to Samarqand.

Middle of 830/March–May, 1427 Ulugh Beg and Muhammad Juki attack Baraq and are defeated.

1 Shaʿban, 830/May 28, 1427 Shahrukh leaves Herat for Transoxiana and briefly deposes Ulugh Beg from his governorship. He returns to Herat on 14 Dhuʾl Hijja/October 6.

831/1427–28 Completion of Sharaf al-Din Yazdi's *Zafarnama.*

832/1428–29 Iskandar Qaraqoyunlu takes a number of cities, including Sultaniyya.

5 Rajab, 832/April 10, 1429 Shahrukh sets off on his second Azarbaijan campaign.

18 Dhuʾl Hijja, 832/September 18, 1429 Decisive battle at Salmas. Shahrukh defeats Iskandar and installs Qara Yusuf's youngest son, Abu Saʿid, in Azarbaijan.

833/1429–30 Shahrukh appoints Muhammad Juki to the governorship of Khuttalan.

8 Muharram, 834/September 26, 1430 Shahrukh arrives back in Herat from Azarbaijan campaign.

834/1430–31 Uzbeks, under Abu'l Khayr Khan, begin to attack the borders of Khorezm.

835/1431–32 Hurufi uprising in Isfahan.

7 Jumadi I, 837/December 20, 1433 Death of Baysunghur b. Shahrukh.

c. 838/1434–35 Eastern Chaghadayids retake Kashghar.

2 Rabiʿ II, 838/November 5, 1434 Shahrukh sets out on third Azarbaijan campaign.

Jumadi II to Rajab, 838/January to February, 1435 Outbreak of plague in Herat.

2 Shawwal, 838/May 1, 1435 Death of Zayn al-Din Khwafi.

4 Shawwal, 838/May 3, 1435 Death of Ibrahim Sultan b. Shahrukh.

Spring to summer 838/1435 Shahrukh in Azarbaijan. Iskandar Qaraqoyunlu retreats. Shahrukh receives submission of most local rulers, including Jahanshah Qaraqoyunlu. Jahanshah Qaraqoyunlu is left as vassal.

839/1435–36 Uzbeks take the northern part of Khorezm.

2 Rabiʿ II, 840/October 14, 1436 Shahrukh arrives back in Herat.

840/1436 Death of Amir Ghunashirin. Governorship of Kerman goes to his sons, notably Hajji Muhammad.

840/1436–37 Muhammad b. Falah Mushaʿshaʿ declares himself *mahdī.*

841/1437–38 Completion of mosque and madrasa of Gawharshad.

842/1438 Accession of Mamluk Sultan Chaqmaq. Relations with the Mamluks improve.

17 Jumadi I, 844/October 14, 1440 Amir ʿAlika dies.

13 Shawwal, 844/March 7, 1441 First military encounter between the Timurids and the Mushaʿshaʿ, near Wasit.

845/1441–42 Rains and floods through much of Iraq and Fars. Beginning of quarrel between Yusuf Khwaja and Malik Gayumarth of Rustamdar. Defeat of Shahrukh and Yusuf Khwaja's joint forces.

22 Rabiʿ I, 845/August 10, 1441 *Dīwān* upheaval; Pir Ahmad Khwafi is forced to accept a new partner.

Early 846/1442 Death of Yusuf Khwaja, governor of Rayy. Appointment of Sultan Muhammad b. Baysunghur as governor of northern Iran.

846/1442–43 Shahrukh sends Shah Mahmud Yasawul to assess tax arrears of ʿIraq-i ʿAjam.

847/1443–44 Return of Shah Mahmud Yasawul. News of Sultan Muhammad's ambitions. Power of Amir Firuzshah exceeds bounds. Shahrukh orders investigation into the taxes of Balkh, under Firuzshah's charge.

Late 847 through early 848/March to June, 1444 Serious illness of Shahrukh. Gawharshad makes Firuzshah swear *bayʿat* to ʿAlaʾ al-Dawla.

848/1444–45 Misappropriation of taxes of Balkh is proven, leading to the disgrace and death of Firuzshah.

848/1444–45 Death of Muhammad Juki; Khuttalan is given to his son Aba Bakr.

5 Safar, 850/May 2, 1446 Sultan Muhammad enters Isfahan at the request of its notables, an overt move against Shahrukh.

Middle of Ramadan 850/early December, 1446 Shahrukh, campaigning against Sultan Muhammad, executes several Isfahani notables at Sawa.

25 Dhu'l Hijja, 850/March 13, 1447 Shahrukh dies near Rayy.

851/1447–8 Sultan Muhammad is consolidating power in Iran.

c. Late Safar, 851/early May, 1447 Ulugh Beg takes Aba Bakr b. Muhammad Juki captive, crosses Oxus to camp at Balkh, makes peace with 'Ala' al-Dawla.

25 Rajab, 851/October 5, 1447 Sultan Muhammad defeats the army of Fars outside Shiraz.

Early 852/spring, 1448 Ulugh Beg and 'Abd al-Latif invade Khorasan, defeat 'Ala' al-Dawla in Tarnab.

Middle Ramadan, 852/mid-November, 1448 Ulugh Beg learns that Yar 'Ali has escaped and is besieging Herat.

Dhu'l Hijja, 852/February, 1449 Abu'l Qasim Babur takes Herat from Yar 'Ali, executes him.

Rabi' I, 853/April–May, 1449 Abu'l Qasim Babur offers submission to Sultan Muhammad.

Probably early summer, 853/1449 'Abd al-Latif's opposition becomes so open that Ulugh Beg has to go against him.

8 or 10 Ramadan, 853/October 25 or 27, 1449 'Abd al-Latif murders Ulugh Beg after defeating him near Samarqand.

13 Ramadan, 853/October 30, 1449 Sultan Muhammad defeats the army of Abu'l Qasim Babur near Jam.

Ramadan, 853/October–November, 1449 Sultan Muhammad pushes Abu'l Qasim Babur out of Herat.

25 Rabi' I, 854/May 8, 1450 'Abd al-Latif is killed by emirs in Samarqand.

3 Rabi' II, 854/May 16, 1450 Sultan Muhammad sends Hajji Muhammad b. Ghunashirin against Abu'l Qasim Babur; Hajji Muhammad is killed in battle.

22 Jumada I, 855/June 21 or 22, 1451 In Transoxiana Abu Sa'id seizes power from 'Abd Allah b. Ibrahim Sultan.

15 Dhu'l-Hijja, 855/January 9, 1452 Abu'l Qasim Babur defeats Sultan Muhammad near Astarabad and has him killed.

Rajab, 856/August, 1452 The Qaraqoyunlu take most of central and western Iran.

Family tree of major Timurid princes

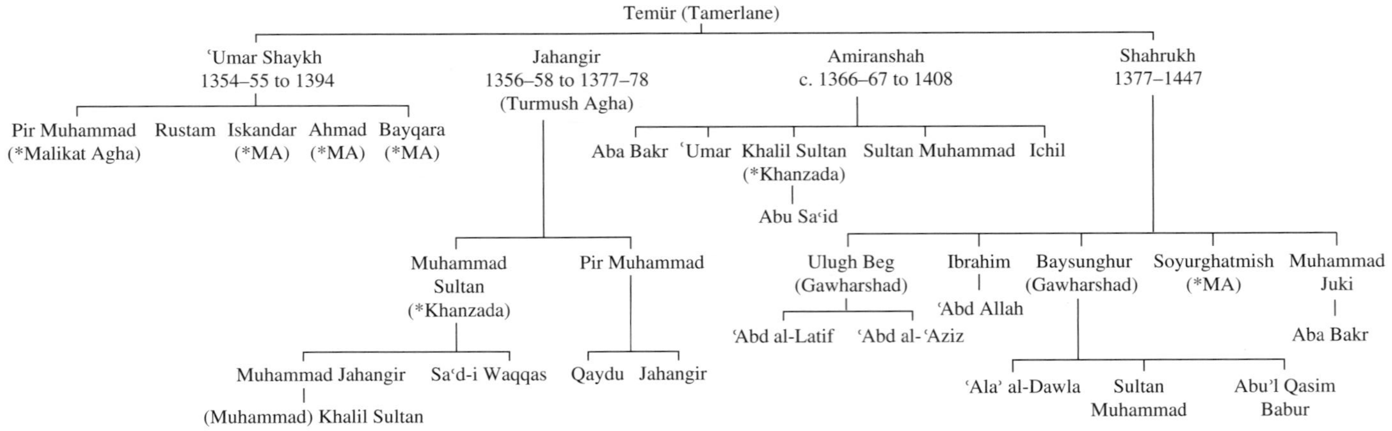

Note: The names of mothers with political or genealogical importance are given in parenthesis below the name of their sons. For reasons of space I have abbreviated the name of Malikat Agha after the first use.

* denotes a woman of Chinggisid descent.

Introduction

A scholar contemplating pre-modern government must experience a sense of wonder. How was it possible to keep control over an extensive region with so few of the tools that modern governments possess? The central administration rarely held a monopoly of force, and a message sent to the other end of the kingdom could require weeks or months to arrive. The population spoke a variety of languages and most were more firmly attached to local elites than they were to the central government. Tax collection was difficult, since both landowners and peasants attempted to thwart the process. In the medieval Middle East, the challenge was particularly great, since there were few legal entities which provided society with a formal structure or regulated relationships among its separate parts. Furthermore its inhabitants included not only urban and agricultural populations but also large numbers of mountain peoples and nomads, some of whom inhabited regions almost inaccessible to government forces. Despite all this, governments did gain and hold power in the Middle East and society remained remarkably cohesive and resilient through numerous dynastic changes.

This book is an examination of how the system worked: both how government retained control over society, and how society maintained its cohesion through periods of central rule and of internal disorder. It is also a portrait of a particular place, time and dynasty: the place is Iran, the time the first half of the fifteenth century, and the dynasty is the Timurids, founded by the Turco-Mongolian conqueror Temür, or Tamerlane (r. 1370–1405). I am examining in particular the reign of Tamerlane's son Shahrukh who ruled from 1409 to 1447. The Timurid dynasty and its military followers came from outside the Middle East, spoke a language foreign to most of the population, and depended on an army that was consciously different from their Iranian subjects. At the same time they were Muslim, literate, and for the most part fluent in Persian. Many were landowners and cultural patrons who had much in common with their subjects, and particularly with the Persian elite who made up the class of city notables. Timurid rule depended on the superiority of nomad armies, but, like all other rulers, the Timurids required some form of consent from the population.

The relationship of government to society in the medieval Middle East is a slippery question. Here, as elsewhere, the ruler was the lynchpin of government, despite his inability to monopolize coercive force. He held an ambivalent position – above his followers and subjects, but also at their mercy. Because there was no fixed system of succession, the death of a ruler often unleashed a struggle. A serious illness commonly brought disorders within the realm and death could precipitate a free-for-all, bringing with it the destruction of crops and cities and the implementation of ruinous taxes. The Sufi shaykh Khwaja Ahrar told his disciples that his family had been preparing a feast to celebrate the shaving of his head on his first birthday, when they learned the news of Temür's death in 1405. They were too frightened to eat, and so emptied the cauldrons onto the ground and fled to hide in the mountains.[1] The population's panic was fully justified. The importance of the ruler to the system did not ensure respect to central government, the ruler's possessions, or even to his corpse after death.[2]

Despite the fragility of central rule, the medieval Middle East was the locus of a stable and self-replicating society, which was based on personal ties rather than formal structures. The urban populations who depended most directly on central rule included separate and self-conscious groups: the religious classes, artisans, and merchants – none of them organized into legal corporate bodies with a fixed relationship to the ruler or the city. Major cities contained centrally appointed governors and garrison troops, but not in numbers large enough to dominate the area. The towns from which the Timurids ruled their dominions were rather like an archipelago within a sea of semi-independent regions, over which control was a matter of luck, alliance and an occasional punitive expedition. Some major cities remained under their own leaders, as vassals of the higher power. All of the local rulers, of cities, mountain regions and tribes, had their own political programs. Nonetheless the economic system remained strong enough to make the Middle East one of the most powerful and prosperous regions of the world.

I am not the first to attempt an analysis of the relationship between government and society in this area, and my study owes a great deal to those which have preceded it. Roy Mottahedeh's classic study, *Loyalty and Leadership in an Early Islamic Society*, demonstrated the importance of social and ideological loyalties in forging the bonds which fostered order in early medieval Iran. As he showed, people created loyalties in predictable ways through oaths which bound them in relationships of clientage or military service.

[1] Fakhr al-Dīn ʿAlī b. Ḥusayn Wāʾiẓ Kāshifī, *Rashaḥāt-i ʿayn al-ḥayāt*, edited by ʿAlī Aṣghar Muʿīniyān (Tehran: Bunyād-i Nīkūkārī-yi Nūriyānī, 2536/1977), 391.

[2] When Temür's grandson Pir Muhammad b. ʿUmar Shaykh was murdered by a follower in 812/1409–10, one of his followers stole the clothes from his body, leaving him naked (Tāj al-Dīn Ḥasan b. Shihāb Yazdī, *Jāmiʿ al-tawārīkh- Ḥasanī*, edited by Ḥusayn Mudarrisī Ṭabāṭabāʾī and Īraj Afshār [Karachi: Muʾassasa-i Taḥqīqāt-i ʿUlūm-yi Āsiyā-i Miyāna wa Gharbī-yi Dānishgāh-i Karāchī, 1987], 18–19).

Although such acquired loyalties did not survive the men who made them, they were often dictated or reinforced through loyalties of category based on a perception of shared self-interest among people of common family, lifestyle or profession. Almost from the beginning of Islamic history, there was a theoretical separation between the ruler and his subjects, considered necessary because only a ruler outside the groups making up society would be able to remain impartial and maintain a balance among them. The dreams which connected the ruler to the supernatural, and made his rule a compact with God rather than with man, were one mark of the ruler's separate status.[3]

More recently Jürgen Paul has presented an analysis of eastern Iran and Transoxiana up to the Mongol period emphasizing the economic and institutional aspects of government and society. He describes a division of tasks between local elites and the central government with a relationship mediated largely by the local notables and Sufi shaykhs, whose importance increased as the period progressed. What set the notables apart was their local base of power, which was independent of the central government. Both Mottahedeh and Paul stress the importance of individual loyalties to personal groupings and the ruler himself. Paul discusses a long period and suggests an increasing distance between government and society from the eleventh century, with the advent of nomad rulers who were less connected with agricultural and urban society.[4]

For the later period two scholars, Marshall G. S. Hodgson and Albert Hourani, put forward complementary theories of the relationship between government and society which have been widely accepted. Hodgson outlined a dynamic which he called the "*aʿyān-amīr* system." The landowning classes were drawn to the cities, where they exerted influence through clientship, in a social atmosphere imbued with the values of Islamic law. Order and security were assured by a garrison of military commanders – emirs – who were often foreign.[5] Hourani described the politics among the city notables, drawn from these landowning classes and dominated, usually, by the ulama. Hourani showed that the city elite could control a significant part of city life and in times of government weakness or crisis they could take over governance of the city.[6] Thus we see a separation between government and society with the

[3] Roy Mottahedeh, *Loyalty and Leadership in an Islamic Society* (Princeton, NJ: Princeton University Press, 1980), 69–71, 178–80.

[4] Jürgen Paul, *Herrscher, Gemeinwesen, Vermittler: Ostiran und Transoxanien in vormongolischer Zeit* (Beirut: F. Steiner, 1996). The two studies mentioned are of course not the only ones from which I have profited. Claude Cahen, *Mouvements populaires et autonomisme urbain dan l'Asie musulmane du moyen âge* (Leiden: Brill, 1959), Ann K. S. Lambton, *Continuity and Change in Medieval Persia* (Albany, NY: Biblioteca Persica, 1988), and more recently Michael Chamberlain, *Knowledge and Social Practice in Medieval Damascus* (Cambridge: Cambridge University Press, 1994) are among the central contributions to the discussion.

[5] Marshall G. S. Hodgson, *The Venture of Islam*, 4 vols. (Chicago and London: Chicago University Press, 1974), vol. II, 64–69.

[6] For a discussion of Hourani's theories see Boaz Shoshan, "The 'Politics of Notables' in Medieval Islam,"*Asian and African Studies* 20 (1986), 179–215.

city and its elite as the point of contact. Government and society were connected by a tacit contractual relation based on common interests in stability, the promotion of religion, and the protection of trade and agriculture. For the later period in particular, military matters are seen to be the domain of the government, largely removed from the general population. Since the central administration took limited responsibility for the daily life of the population, social cohesion is usually ascribed to the strength of social and kinship groups controlling the life of the individual.[7]

The basic schema drawn by Hourani and Hodgson has been elaborated by numerous specialized works over the last thirty years, particularly concerning the religious classes who made up the core of the city notables. In such studies, scholars draw conclusions about the general from the particular, and the choice of population studied is determined by the sources available. The middle period of Islamic history, from the Seljukid through the Mamluk and Timurid period, has provided most of the material for detailed analysis. For social history, biographical works are usually the most valuable source and studies of urban life and the activities of the ulama are most often based on material from the Mamluk Sultanate which produced rich historical literature, including voluminous biographical collections on the ulama. Studies on the composition and organization of the military have also depended heavily on the superior sources available from the Mamluk regions.[8] For Iran and Central Asia, there is much less information on ulama but we have a fund of biographical literature on Sufi shaykhs. These have strong influence over our views on Sufi society. A social history of the Middle East based on existing secondary studies is likely to depend on Mamluk material about cities and the ulama, but may favor Iranian material for Sufi circles. We should recognize however, that social norms in the two regions may not have been identical.

While studies on individual communities can provide invaluable insight into social history, they do not fit together well to produce a composite picture of the dynamics of society as a whole. The literature of the medieval period divides society into classes and types of people, and separates out the history of each. Each genre of historical compilation preserves a different type of information, and thus provides a selected and homogenized picture of the people with which it deals; together the sources serve to emphasize the peculiarities of each group and the differences between them. The picture thus presented of separate and distinct groups is misleading. Neither occupational nor kinship groups were mutually exclusive. Few people and certainly few families belonged to only one class or type; this is something we know and

[7] See Albert Hourani, *The History of the Arab Peoples* (New York: MJF Books, 1991), 98–146, and Chase F. Robinson, *Islamic Historiography* (Cambridge: Cambridge University Press, 2003), 128.

[8] See the numerous studies by David Ayalon, and more recently those of Reuven Amitai.

often acknowledge, but it is nonetheless difficult to write history in a way that fully incorporates our understanding. Furthermore, we must recognize that politics, even within a given milieu, rarely involved only internal personnel; people fighting over a common prize often reached outside their own group for allies. Just as no type of person was clearly defined and separated from others, there was no sphere of power controlled exclusively by one group of people. Rulers and military were important in the religious sphere and religious figures in the economic one. In Iran at least, the city classes, including both artisans and ulama, played an important role in regional military contests. The nomad and semi-nomad populations of mountain and steppe were connected not only to central and regional military powers, but also directly to city populations.

Most studies have focused on institutions and on the practices they engendered. In this book I attempt to analyze the relationship between government and society primarily by examining the practice of politics, seeking the dynamics that kept people together within the groups they belonged to, and connected people of different associations. I am looking for the blurred edges of groups; for the overlaps among different types of organizations and classes of people. I have chosen to concentrate on a single defined period, the reign of Tamerlane's son Shahrukh and the first years of the power struggle after his death. The place is likewise limited to Iran and Central Asia, which were the central parts of Shahrukh's domains. While the use of a limited time and region prevent me from drawing conclusions which can be confidently applied over a longer period, it does offer a number of advantages. First of all, it allows the use of a variety of interrelated sources, which make it possible to trace the activities of important people in different spheres. In this way, the action of an individual in one situation can be judged against accounts from different sources; we can discern secondary identities not mentioned in a single type of source. Secondly, it is possible in a detailed study to recognize the different affiliations contributing to the prestige of an individual or a family.

I have tried to treat individuals not as representatives of particular groups but as independent actors, using whatever affiliations were available to them. I have done the same in the case of cities and provinces. Here again, there are advantages to a study which goes beyond the individual city but remains within a contained period. It is possible both to determine something of the common political structure in Iranian cities and to discern variations in political culture. Likewise, in the case of provinces and regions, one can perceive a range of difference within the larger system. Examining a number of different Sufi affiliations, together with contemporary habits of shrine visitation, allows us to analyze the interaction among communities and to gauge their place and their role in society more fully than the study of one *ṭarīqa* over time would allow. Moreover, the detailed analysis of a particular time and place permits the historian to check the actual against the ideal. The literature of the period is liberal in its explanations of approved attitudes and the narrative is shaped to reflect them. If motives for behavior are mentioned they will fit into the categories considered appropriate, and it is thus important to keep in mind that collective memory can distort both events and conventions to fit what are perceived as the rules of society. William Lancaster has analyzed the practice of manipulation in his discussion of genealogy among the Rwala Bedouin:

> As political and economic motives change with time, so the genealogy must change to accommodate changing assets and new options and so there is no true genealogy – truth is relative to the pragmatic needs of the group involved. Thus a society that appears to be constrained by the past (for this is how we see genealogies) is in fact generating the very genealogy through which it 'explains' the present, and ... using that genealogy to generate the future.[9]

Many of our sources manipulate their material in similar ways, and while we cannot untangle relationships and motivation reliably, the use of a variety of different sources and the study of different groups does allow some correction to the picture provided.

There are two major questions posed in this study: first, how a government retained power and fulfilled its function without a monopoly of force, and second, how society maintained its cohesion. The most common answer for the functioning of government has been that the preservation of order was worth the payment of taxes. The city populations who made up urban government thus had some common interests with the ruling group.[10] Society was so frightened of disorder that any government was better than none at all, and should thus be obeyed; this maxim became a truism of premodern political thought.[11] Had obedience been only passive, this explanation would be sufficient, but in Iran at least urban elites and semi-independent rulers were actively engaged in politics and military activity. In examining the life of the cities, religious classes, and independent rulers, one sees a mass of people pursuing their interests with the tools they had at hand. Some further explanation is therefore needed. I have examined here not only the common interests which might persuade powerful, independent groups to collaborate with the government, but also the way in which their internal politics intersected with those of the central and provincial administrations.

The other major issue I address is the cohesion of society, and here a central part of the discussion is the question of how to deal with the relationship of the individual to the group. When we learn that a person was a member of a given commonality, what does that tell us? If people saw themselves less as

[9] William Lancaster, *The Rwala Bedouin Today* (Cambridge: Cambridge University Press, 1981), 35.
[10] Hourani, *Arab Peoples*, 133–37.
[11] Ira Lapidus, *A History of Islamic Societies* (Cambridge: Cambridge University Press, 1988), 182–83.

free individuals than as members of a group or community, then we must attempt to understand how a specific community affected the individual, what its internal politics were, and how it fit into society at large. We should not assume that because a group was an important factor in the life of its members it would command their full loyalty or achieve internal unity. The history of any royal lineage demonstrates that blood ties can cause as much conflict as cooperation. The extended families central to pre-modern society also fostered internal rivalry; one can argue that the more benefits the extended family offers, the more likely it is that there will be strife within it.

The central question, then, is how people coped with the constraints and possibilities of their society. Each group to which a person belonged offered both support and danger; one could hope to call on one's fellows for help, but one was very likely to be competing with them for a common set of prizes. Alliances thus often went across recognized groups, both of birth and of training. The politics of the Timurid period was highly factional, with a dynamic made up of individuals with multiple loyalties, identities and rivalries. The multiplicity of obligation gave choice back to the individual person – anyone in a position of wealth or authority had to navigate among a variety of conflicting obligations and attachments. Thus, in the end, we must assume that the individual was a key player in this society, and not always a predictable one.

The place and the period

The period I have chosen for this study is the early fifteenth century, and the dynasty that of the Timurids, who ruled Iran and Central Asia for much of the century. The founder of the dynasty was Temür, a Muslim Turk of Mongol descent who came to power in Samarqand in 1370 and spent most of his life in spectacularly successful conquest. He was succeeded by his son Shahrukh, whose reign, from 1409–47, is the focus of this study. Shahrukh was a cautious ruler who balanced the ideological and political forces of his time to consolidate control over a friable realm, and he was a man who fit the time he lived in. The fifteenth century offers us less sound and fury, and fewer outstanding personalities than the centuries which preceded and followed it. The major dynasties who controlled the Middle East after the Mongol conquests were already in power: the Ottomans in Anatolia and eastern Europe, the Mamluks in Syria and Egypt, the Timurids in Iran and Central Asia and the Delhi sultans in northern India. This was a period in which the changes of the past could be assimilated and newly won positions consolidated.

One of the great watersheds in the history of the central Islamic lands was the Mongol invasion of the early thirteenth century. The whole of the Middle East was affected by their rule, either directly or by example: their conquests and their rivalries became part of the political dynamic of the Middle East. After the death of Chinggis Khan in 1227, his empire was ruled by a supreme khan or *khaghan* and was divided into sections ruled by subordinate khans from the families of Chinggis Khan's four sons by his chief wife. The western region stretching from the steppes north of the Black Sea to the Aral Sea and into Siberia was the inheritance of the eldest son, Jochi. The family of the second son, Chaghadai,[12] held much of central Asia from Transoxiana through Turkistan and the Ili region. Chinggis's third son Ögedei became supreme khan, but the personal area of his house lay outside Mongolia, in the Altai. The youngest son Tolui inherited Mongolia itself; his descendants succeeded in taking over the position of great khan, and then in founding a separate dynasty in Iran: the Ilkhanate. After the death of the great khan Möngke in 1259, no one member of Chinggis Khan's family was able to achieve universal recognition as *khaghan*. Supreme power remained limited to the family of Chinggis Khan but each section of the empire was ruled as an independent state. By the mid-fourteenth century, the Mongol elites west of Mongolia had converted to Islam, and the Islamic and Mongol worlds had come to overlap. Despite its division, as an idea the Mongol Empire remained strong and the memory of Chinggis Khan retained a supreme place in political and cultural traditions.

In the Middle East the Mongol conquest reinforced some old political traditions and introduced new ones. The elimination of the caliphate with the fall of Baghdad in 1258 created new possibilities for rulers within the Islamic world. It became possible to claim full sovereign power within one area and to base one's legitimacy on dynastic claims unrelated to the house of the Prophet. The first to take advantage of the new situation were the Mamluks in Egypt and Syria, who based their legitimacy in part on their resistance to the Mongols and their possession of a descendant of the ʿAbbasid dynasty whom they kept in Cairo as a titular caliph. Iran and Iraq were ruled by the Mongol Ilkhans. Mongol rule brought about an ethnographic change, with the division of the region into separate culture areas. The arrival of new nomads to occupy the pastures of the eastern regions displaced Turks who had entered with the Seljukid invasions of the eleventh century. This population had already begun to move into Anatolia, and Mongol pressure completed the Turkification of the region. Mongol rule centered in Iran and did not extend beyond Iraq, thus creating a separation between these areas and the Arab cultural region of Egypt and the Levant controlled by the Mamluks. From this time on, the Middle East has retained the division into three major cultural zones, one primarily Arab, one primarily Iranian, and one primarily Turkic.

In Iran and Central Asia the impact of Mongol rule was far-reaching. Throughout their realms, the Mongols introduced a period of experimentation.

[12] Where I discuss Chinggis Khan's son, I use the Mongol version of the name, but for the people and the khanate to which he gave his name, I have chosen to use the later Turkic rendering of this name: Chaghatay.

In the realm of culture, science and daily life, they brought in changes of all sorts – new foods, new plants, new styles of art.[13] In the political sphere, they brought in traditions from earlier steppe empires and from China. In the fifteenth century many Mongol administrative traditions were still in force. There were regional armies conscripted from the population and organized in decimal units, military governors – *darughas* – in many cities, and a Turco-Mongolian military and court administration bearing Mongol titles. These two regions were part of the former Mongol Empire, just as they were part of the former caliphate.

The high culture of Iran under the Mongols was influenced by its new ruling class, and by the end of the Mongol period Iran differed markedly from the Arab regions of Egypt and Syria in literary and visual culture. The Mongols employed many Iranian bureaucrats, and, at their court, Persian became the primary language of high culture. In the visual arts they introduced significant Chinese influence and their rule oversaw the introduction of a new art form, the Persian miniature. By the Timurid period the Persian miniature was well established and buildings, decorated liberally in colored tiles, were very different from the Mamluk architecture which relied on stone for decoration.

In the fourteenth century, as the descendants of Chinggis Khan began to lose power in some of the areas they controlled, a heady period of apparently unlimited opportunity arose. In China, an indigenous dynasty took control and pushed the Mongol ruling class back into the steppe. Towards the end of the century, the Chinggisid ruler Tokhtamish reunited much of the Jochid section of the Mongol realm and revived its claims to the Transcaucasus and Khorezm. In the west, the Ottomans under Bayazid I (r. 1389–1402), decisively entered the central Islamic lands and laid claim to the whole of Anatolia. The most spectacular career was that of Temür, who undertook a symbolic recreation of the Mongol Empire. He died in his eighties on his way to reconquer China, where Mongol government had been overthrown in 1368. While he was not descended from Chinggis Khan and thus could not claim supreme power for himself, he created a structure of Mongol legitimation by marrying into the Chinggisid house and ruling formally through a puppet khan descended from Chinggis. At the same time, Temür claimed supremacy in the Islamic world and crushed the Mamluk and Ottoman rulers who dared to assert equality. In explaining the justice of his conquests, he called on both the *sharīʿa* and Mongol traditions.

The great military engagements of Temür and his contemporaries gave way after his death, in 1405, to a period of more cautious rule within most of the Islamic lands. In both the Mamluk Sultanate and the Ottoman state the first task was to repair the ravages of Temür's campaigns and to regain formal

[13] For more information on the Mongol impact on cultural exchange see Thomas T. Allsen, *Culture and Conquest in Mongol Eurasia* (Cambridge: Cambridge University Press, 2001).

independence from the Timurid dynasty. The level of ambition shown by Bayazid I was not appropriate for his immediate successors. For the Delhi Sultanate and the other Muslim dynasties of northern India, even independence was beyond reasonable expectations, and they continued as formal vassals of the Timurids to the end of Shahrukh's reign.[14] The Golden Horde of the Russian steppe could support local rulers in the Crimea or the Volga, but had lost control over the trade routes and much of their influence over the western steppe. Neither the Islamic nor the Turco-Mongolian world of the fifteenth century encouraged the adventurism shown by Temür and his contemporaries.

The choices that Temür himself had made also discouraged his successors from considering further conquest. In the last ten years of his career, he had clearly differentiated between two types of military campaign: those designed to bring land into his domains and those undertaken to display his superiority over rivals. He chose only to incorporate lands which had a strong agricultural base and had been part of the Mongol Empire; these were the regions which would accept his Mongol legitimation and could produce taxes sufficient to support a mixed army of nomad and settled forces. At the time of his death his realm was complete and further conquests would have been both costly and unprofitable.

Both Temür and his successors used Mongol legitimation and recognized their kinship with other Mongol peoples, most notably the Jochid Uzbeks and the eastern Chaghadayid Khanate, from whom they sought brides descended from Chinggis Khan. While Shahrukh discontinued the practice of ruling through a puppet khan, he himself informally adopted the Mongol supreme title of *khaghan* and in the histories written for him and his sons, the dynasty's connection to the house of Chinggis Khan became the subject of an elaborate myth. Loyalty to the Mongol heritage did not prevent the Timurids from subscribing fully to the Perso-Islamic culture of their subjects. Temür himself, though illiterate, was bilingual in Persian and Turkic and had a strong interest in intellectual questions, particularly history and religious studies. He collected at his court not only the finest craftsmen of the cities he conquered, but whatever scholars he could bring home. In religious sciences he was particularly successful; his court contained three scholars of outstanding prestige, Saʿd al-Din Taftazani, Sayyid ʿAli Jurjani, and Muhammad al-Jazari. He commissioned histories of his reign in both Persian and Turkish. What was equally important for the future course of the dynasty was Temür's active interest in the education of his descendants. According to the historians of Shahrukh's period, Temür took charge of the education of his grandchildren, personally appointing their nurses and tutors. During his lifetime, almost all his grandsons were raised in the central court

[14] Peter Jackson, *The Delhi Sultanate. A Political and Military History* (Cambridge: Cambridge University Press, 1999), 322.

by Temür's wives or sometimes those of his followers. They were to be trained in good behavior, and taught the arts and manners of rulers (*ādāb-i pādshāhī*).[15] It is clear that cultural patronage was an expected part of rule both for Temür and for his descendants. Shahrukh showed a strong interest in historical writing and many of Temür's grandsons were famous for their enthusiastic and informed patronage. They continued Temür's interest in history and religion, and added active patronage of mathematics and astronomy, and most particularly, the arts of the book.

The Timurids after Temür excelled not in military might but in cultural patronage, and this was probably not by chance. While Temür left his heirs a realm which was logically complete, his cultural legacy provided ample scope for ambition and initiative. His descendants had the advantage of inheriting the Iranian lands ruled by the Mongols, thus the area in which new ideas, techniques and art forms were still in the process of development. They were in a position to gather the calligraphers and miniature painters of Tabriz and Shiraz and the astronomers working on the rich legacy of Nasir al-Din Tusi, whose observatory at Maragha was financed by the first Ilkhan Hülegü. The active exchange of embassies with Ming China, quickly renewed after Temür's death, continued the importation of outside influences. Thus we need not be surprised to find that among Temür's successors, building and cultural production were among the first steps in the assertion of power and position.

Despite significant differences, the Timurids shared many institutions with the neighboring Muslim dynasties of their period. The Ottomans, Delhi sultans, and Mamluks were all Turks, originating from the Eurasian steppe, who ruled over the population as outsiders. Because they owed their prestige to the nomad military prowess of their armies, they preserved the foreign element, whether by upholding traditions and importing new foreign soldiers. The "middle period" of Islamic history, when rulers of nomad origin predominated, strengthened a number of institutions which were common to the central Islamic lands. While terminology differed among regions, as did the importance of individual institutions, all states in some way used the *iqtāʿ* (grants of land use for salary) and charitable *waqf* endowments, and all struggled with the resultant loss of tax revenue. They endowed similar religious establishments, the madrasa and the *khānaqāh*, sometimes organized into mausoleum complexes, and thereby created religious positions dependent on their favor. The prestige of Sufi shaykhs and the growing importance of shrines and Sufi brotherhoods was likewise a development common to all regions. Thus we can examine the Timurids as a dynasty trying to control a

[15] Ḥāfiẓ-i Abrū, *Majmaʿ al-tawārīkh*, Istanbul, Süleymaniye Library, MS Fatih 4371/1, fols. 8b–9a; see also Sharaf al-Dīn ʿAlī Yazdī, *Ẓafarnāma*, edited by Muḥammad ʿAbbāsī, 2 vols. (Tehran: Amīr Kabīr, sh. 1336/1957), vol. I, 278, 504, 515 (for Ibrahim Sultan), vol. II, 36 (for Ulugh Beg), 285 (for several princes).

society similar to that of its neighbors, with many of the same tools. On the other hand, their direct connection to the Mongols and their rule over the central Iranian lands set them apart from Mamluks and Ottomans. We can assume that their society and politics were similar to those of their western neighbors, but significant differences also existed.

The organization of the book

One basic premise of this book is that much of the political activity within the realm originated in society, and that the task of the government was less to initiate than to balance and to react. It would be logical therefore to begin my analysis from below, with the city, the countryside and the province. There is one major practical disadvantage to such a course – the narrative history of the period, to which we must refer for our framework, depends largely on the activities of the dynasty and its immediate servitors. Without introduction to the chronology and the personnel of the central government, the history of individual communities cannot be explained or related to each other. I will therefore begin where I would have liked to end, with a discussion of the history of Shahrukh's reign and the organization of the dynasty, its central army and its formal administration.

In the first chapter, I combine a brief narrative history with analysis of the rulers and their Chaghatay followers. My goal is to place events in sequence and show their impact on the dynasty and its core military command. The second chapter is a discussion of the sources and the problems they raise. The third deals with the central chancellery (*dīwān*) and its first section is largely narrative. Many of the events introduced in the first and third chapters will be analyzed in greater detail in subsequent chapters concerned with other segments of society. My fourth chapter is an analysis of the political and military dynamics of Iran, and I have followed it with a discussion of government and society in the province of Fars, since the two chapters deal with similar issues. Chapters 6 and 7 are devoted to the politics of the religious classes; in the sixth chapter I give a general analysis of the dynamics of politics in the religious sphere, and in the seventh discuss specific people, shrines and communities. The last chapter is a description of the rebellion of Shahrukh's grandson in the last years of his reign and the succession struggle after his death, which illustrate many of the political dynamics discussed throughout the book.

CHAPTER 1

The formation of the Timurid state under Shahrukh

In the years after Temür's death his youngest son, Shahrukh, succeeded in taking over Temür's central lands. Shahrukh had none of the theatrical inclination of his father and limited his military campaigns to those he considered truly necessary. He was also much more willing to share power than his father had been, and under him we find both more provincial independence and more individual power among the Persian and Turco-Mongolian elite. These traits, along with his conspicuous religious observance, have won him a reputation as a ruler who devoted himself to religion while leaving the business of governing to his officials and his powerful wife, Gawharshad.[1] This assessment appears to be based on the assumption that Temür had left an intact polity which was relatively easy to govern. Such was not the case. Shahrukh had to win the realm he ruled through battle and diplomacy; he had to balance innumerable separate centers of power – dynastic, provincial and local. While some contemporary historians of the latter part of Shahrukh's reign portray him as a distant and preoccupied ruler, those writing about his early and middle years show a man active in the affairs of army and administration. Even Shahrukh's early rival and critic, the prince Iskandar b. ʿUmar Shaykh, gives Shahrukh credit for skill in ruling. He states that he knew how to maintain the externals of religious and customary law, and although he allowed his subordinates considerable power, he himself controlled major decisions.[2]

The military and dynastic history of the Timurid period was dominated by two closely interrelated groups: the Timurid dynasty and the Chaghatay commanders – emirs – descended from Temür's highest commanders. The dynasty and emirs shared a common origin within the Ulus Chaghatay of

[1] See, for example, H. R. Roemer, "The Successors to Tīmūr," *The Cambridge History of Iran* (Cambridge: Cambridge University Press, 1986), vol. VI, 104; V. V. Bartol'd, *Ulugbek i ego vremia*, in *Sochineniia* (Moscow: Nauka, 1964), vol. II, pt. 2, 97.

[2] "Synopsis of the House of Timur," in *A Century of Princes: Sources on Timurid History and Art*, edited and translated by Wheeler Thackston (Cambridge, MA: The Aga Khan Program for Islamic Architecture, 1989), 240, 245–46.

Transoxiana and eastern Afghanistan which bound them to the history of the Mongol Empire and the charismatic figure of Chinggis Khan. They owed their position as a ruling group more immediately to Temür, who had won the realm they ruled and raised them or their fathers to power. Their descendants remained central to military power right up to the end of the Timurid dynasty. In order to attain and hold power over the Timurid realm a ruler had to dominate this group of people – both princes and emirs – who were at once his first rivals for power and his most important agents in keeping control over the populations of subject territories. The settled and nomad peoples of Timurid lands were neither powerless nor politically unimportant, but to win and keep their allegiance, a ruler had to control his own family and army.

The challenges facing Shahrukh changed over the course of his reign. During the first fifteen years after his father's death, he competed with the other members of the dynasty for power. While he struggled to achieve supremacy over his relatives, he also had to bring his Chaghatay emirs into order. The two processes were closely related since many emirs had connections to several different princes and felt free to switch allegiance. In 823/1420 Shahrukh was able to turn his attention to retaking Azarbaijan; from this time until about 835/1431–32 we find him at the head of a stable and well-functioning government, able to meet any outside challenges offered. After 835 new problems arose and from 840/1436–37 the combination of Shahrukh's increasing age and illness, the death of his most senior emirs and the early death of most of his sons led to a serious decline in the efficiency of his government.

The composition of the ruling elite

Temür had divided his realm into four sections, each governed by the family of one of his sons. Amiranshah's sons held the governorship of Azarbaijan, ʿUmar Shaykh's sons that of central and southern Iran, Pir Muhammad, the son of his senior son, Jahangir, was governor of Kabul and its region, and Shahrukh and his young sons were appointed to Khorasan and the regions surrounding Transoxiana. This arrangement appears to have been an imitation of Chinggis Khan's disposition of his realm, but it should not be seen as the acceptance of a divided state. Temür, to the end, was jealous of power and insistent on centralization. When he died, only two of his sons were still alive. The elder, Amiranshah, was thirty-seven, but had been discredited and removed from his governorship for what was probably an attempted rebellion.[3] Shahrukh was twenty-seven. In addition, there were numerous grandchildren, ranging in age from twenty-nine to newborn.

[3] John E. Woods, "Turco-Iranica II: Notes on a Timurid Decree of 1396/798," *Journal of Near Eastern Studies*, 43/4 (1984), 333–35; Yazdī, *Ẓafarnāma*, vol. II, 148–50, 406.

For the whole of the Timurid period, the Turco-Mongolian Chaghatay soldiers, who had originated as the nomad population of the Ulus Chaghatay, formed the standing army. Temür had risen to power at the head of a tribal confederation, but he had replaced tribal levies with a more centralized army commanded by men personally close to him. The majority of commanders under Shahrukh were the descendants of the men whom Temür had collected around himself as a personal following early in his career. He had connected these men closely to his family through a number of marriage alliances; their descendants were thus cousins of the princes involved in the struggle for power after his death. But, having created this ruling elite, Temür took care to control it. When he installed his sons and grandsons as governors of provinces, he appointed to each of them an army commanded largely by members of his followers' families, and made sure that members of any one family were appointed to different princes. By the time Temür died, a number of his original followers had been replaced by their sons and relatives, who were already active and experienced commanders. Although most of the original Chaghatay tribes continued to exist, the histories of Shahrukh's period rarely mention them and they seem to have played little part in politics during his reign.

Before discussing the Chaghatay emirs, it is useful to confront the question of how we delimit this group. What distinguished them as a class was neither separation from civilian society nor an exclusive hold on military power but their closeness to the dynasty and their near monopoly of the highest military commands. Despite the military activities of other populations, both the histories and the official dynastic genealogy, the *Muʿizz al-ansab*, usually omit Iranians and nomads when they discuss the central military class. When we look at the highest military command, we are dealing with a relatively small group of seventy to one hundred people, including the emirs serving under Timurid princely governors. In determining who should be counted among the Chaghatay emirs I have looked first of all at the dynastic histories, to see which figures appear consistently on campaigns and in positions of trust. I have also included the men listed under the highest offices in the *Muʿizz al-ansāb fī shajarat al-ansāb*. The central office was that of *amīr dīwān*, entailing both military and administrative responsibility. One other position seems to have conferred great power – that of *tovachi*, or troop inspector.[4] These emirs made up the backbone of the high military command, acting as leaders of *tümen*s (the largest military contingent, theoretically 10,000 troops), as governors of provinces, and as close advisors to the ruler. Most were Chaghatay, and almost all were Turkic or Turco-Mongolian.[5]

[4] Not all of the men listed were active at the same time; five or six died early in Shahrukh's reign, and about an equal number became active later (*Muʿizz al-ansāb fī shajarat al-ansāb,* MS Paris, Bibliothèque Nationale, 67, fols. 132b–33b).

[5] Under Shahrukh we have two further lists of prominent commanders: the lists of *tümen*s and their commanders for the center, left and right wings of the army, and a list appended later,

I should note that while the definitions I have applied here are those of military office, neither emirs nor princes limited themselves to activities in this sphere. The position of *amīr dīwān*, existing under both Timurid princes and the central ruler, was one which conferred wide responsibility in both the army and the administration. Princes and emirs were also involved in regional affairs, some as governors or *darughas*, others as supervisors of *dīwāns* or as holders of income-producing land grants (*soyurghals* or *tiyuls*).

Many of Temür's Chaghatay emirs were experienced older men who had served under several princes, some as guardians for the princes rather than as their servitors. They had owed their primary loyalty to Temür himself, and were often not strongly attached to the prince they had been appointed to serve; many, moreover, had remained in the central army. Like the princes, the emirs depended for their power on the continuance of the dynasty, and, for their prestige, on Temür's memory. In the first several years after Temür's death, we find emirs continually rebelling; sometimes to express disapproval of an action of the prince they served, sometimes to assert independence, and sometimes simply deserting to another potentially more rewarding ruler. What brought this activity to an end was the unification of the realm, which deprived the emirs both of places of refuge and of an alternative place to serve.

The dynastic struggle for power

Temür died in Otrar, on his way to conquer China, on 17 or 18 Shawwal, 807/February 17 or 18, 1405.[6] Although he was probably in his eighties and had been ill for several months, his death caused consternation. After a short time his descendants and emirs decided to abandon the campaign and return home to decide the question of the future. Temür's choice of successor was a problematical one, based on birth rather than position or accomplishment. In 801/1399 he had addressed the issue of succession and had chosen not one of his surviving sons, but a grandson of high lineage on his mother's side. His choice, Muhammad Sultan, was the son of Temür's second son, Jahangir, the only one born of a free wife, Jahangir's chief wife Khanzada, a woman of

entitled "past and present commanders of *tümens*." The last list contains fifty-three names, twenty-three of which are also in the other lists (*Muʿizz,* fols. 135b-137a; Shiro Ando, *Timuridische Emire nach dem Muʿizz al-ansāb. Untersuchung zur Stammesaristokratie Zentralasiens im 14. und 15. Jahrhundert* [Berlin: K. Schwarz, 1992], 120–22). In all three lists the names point to an overwhelmingly Turco-Mongolian provenance. The people mentioned as leading armies on Shahrukh's campaigns conform to the same pattern; here we find the most prominent of the men mentioned in the "Muʿizz al-ansab." See for example, Ḥāfiẓ-i Abrū, *Zubdat al-tawārīkh*, edited by Sayyid Kamāl Ḥājj Sayyid Jawādī, 2 vols. (Tehran: Nashr-i Nay, sh. 1372/1993) 363, 631, 669–71, 786–91, ʿAbd al-Razzāq Samarqandī, *Maṭlaʿ al-saʿdayn wa majmaʿ al-baḥrayn*, edited by Muḥammad Shafīʿ, 2 vols. (Lahore: Kitābkhāna-i Gīlānī, 1360–68/1941–49), vol. II, 321.

6 I give two possible dates here because the date of 18 Shawwal is preceded by the term "*shab-i,*" which can mean either the night before or the night of the actual date.

Chinggisid descent.[7] When Muhammad Sultan died on 18 Sha'ban, 805/March 13, 1403, Temür apparently did nothing to replace him as heir apparent and it was only on his deathbed that he appointed Muhammad Sultan's younger, and less well-born, brother, Pir Muhammad, as successor. This was not a choice that could work. Pir Muhammad, then twenty-nine years old, had been governor of the distant province of Kabul and Multan since 794/1391–92, a position of less prestige and power than those held by his uncle Shahrukh and many of his cousins. Judging from what we know of his actions after Temür's death, he was not a particularly forceful leader or commander. Before Pir Muhammad could even approach the capital, Samarqand was seized by Amiranshah's young and adventurous son, Khalil Sultan, who had been closer to the capital and who also had the advantage of a Chinggisid mother.[8]

The Timurid princes were in a difficult situation. While Temür had been alive, his will had been law, and it is clear that his designation of Pir Muhammad was known and considered binding.[9] While most princes succumbed to the temptation to go against Temür's testament, they still had to consider the loyalties of the emirs who had served the sovereign. It is likely that the need to retain their services was an incentive to show respect towards Temür's will. Thus everyone who claimed power had to find some way to justify his position in relation to Temür's career and his wishes. The writing of histories and genealogies became one of the first marks of aspiration to rulership.

Khalil Sultan's takeover precipitated a power struggle on two levels; one regional, largely within the members of each princely lineage, and another among the different regions. While seeking hegemony within their own close families, almost all princes aimed to increase their power at the expense of other areas. There were several men who might hope to rule and no one of them held a clear advantage. Many of Temür's grandsons had reached their early twenties, the age when ambition often flowered with little experience to check it. The recklessness and contentiousness that many displayed proved a benefit to Shahrukh, who was able to restore control over his province of Khorasan while his relatives destroyed each other.

[7] *Mu'izz*, fols. 112b, 114b; John E. Woods, *The Timurid Dynasty (Papers on Inner Asia)* (Bloomington: Indiana University, 1990), 17, 29. Temür appointed Muhammad Sultan some time before he conquered Delhi; he ordered the *khuṭba* read there in his own name and that of Muhammad Sultan as his designated successor, in Rabi' II, 801/December, 1398–January, 1399 (Niẓām al-Dīn Shāmī, *Histoire des conquêtes de Tamerlan intitulée Ẓafarnāma, par Niẓāmuddīn Šāmī*, edited by F. Tauer, 2 vols. [Prague: Oriental Institute, 1956], vol. I, 192).

[8] Khalil Sultan was the son of Khanzada, married to Amiranshah after the death of her first husband, Jahangir. Thus Khalil Sultan was Muhammad Jahangir's uncle (*Mu'izz*, fol. 122b).

[9] Since Pir Muhammad was dead by the time that the histories were written, there would have been no incentive for later historians to invent a testament in his favor (Beatrice F. Manz, "Family and Ruler in Timurid Historiography," in *Studies on Central Asian History in Honor of Yuri Bregel*, edited by Devin DeWeese (Bloomington: Indiana University, 2001), 58–61).

Map 1. The Timurid realm and neighboring powers in the fifteenth century

The region of Fars remained under Temür's oldest grandsons, the sons of ʿUmar Shaykh. These princes were Shahrukh's strongest rivals but spent the first years after Temür's death in local rivalries involving Fars, Kerman and Azarbaijan. In Azarbaijan Timurid control had been insecure even during Temür's life. Within a few years Amiranshah and his sons lost Azarbaijan and ceased to offer a significant challenge for control over the realm. Their failure was partly due to the lack of judgment they often displayed and, more immediately, to the strength of the two nomadic powers of the region, the Jalayir and the Qaraqoyunlu, who had not been significantly weakened by Temür's campaigns. Amiranshah's two older sons, Aba Bakr, then about

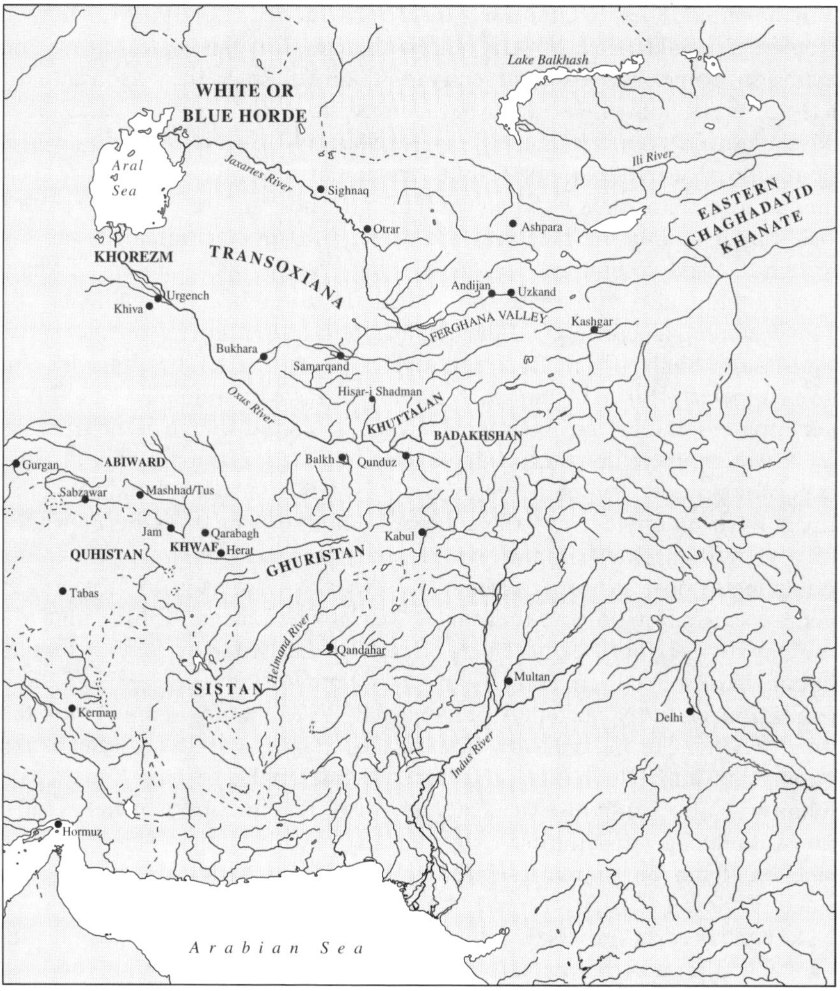

Map 1. (*cont.*)

twenty-three, and 'Umar, about twenty-two, had been appointed to governorships in the western regions of the realm, where Amiranshah remained in an ambiguous position. After Temür's death father and sons fought incessantly among themselves and with neighboring princes. Aba Bakr almost immediately lost the province of Iraq to the Jalayir and began to contest Azarbaijan with 'Umar. He succeeded in pushing out 'Umar, who died in Khorasan in 809/1407, but he and Amiranshah were decisively defeated by the Qaraqoyunlu in spring of 810/1408. Amiranshah was killed in battle, thus leaving Shahrukh as Temür's only surviving son. Aba Bakr fled first to Kerman and then to Sistan.

In the center, Khalil Sultan's seizure of Samarqand, before Pir Muhammad b. Jahangir could reach the city, threw the emirs of the central army into confusion. Some chose to swear fealty to Khalil Sultan, as the person actually in the capital, while others attached themselves to Pir Muhammad and a few, like the powerful emir Shahmalik, chose Shahrukh as a close and powerful figure who appeared to honor Temür's testament. Several emirs changed their minds more than once.[10] Khalil Sultan paid nominal respect to Temür's wishes by installing the nine-year-old prince Muhammad Jahangir, the son of Temür's first designated heir, Muhammad Sultan, as a figurehead khan. Khalil Sultan also apparently attempted to strengthen his legitimacy by commissioning a genealogy of the Timurid house stressing his own line.[11]

Although Shahrukh made a tentative peace with Khalil Sultan, he also gave support to Pir Muhammad b. Jahangir. Pir Muhammad's position as heir apparent and his age might have given him an advantage in the struggle, but he was hampered by the fact that he had to leave his own province in order to bid for power over the realm as a whole. His attacks on Khalil Sultan's forces were mounted from the Khorasan border, and thus he depended heavily on Shahrukh's support. All the other princes of Jahangir's line were too young to pose a direct challenge but they did serve as pawns for princes or emirs seeking legitimacy according to Temür's testament. Pir Muhammad's son Qaydu was about eight. There were also the two sons of Muhammad Sultan, who were still in Transoxiana: Muhammad Jahangir, age eight, and Yahya, four or five years old. As it happened, Pir Muhammad b. Jahangir did not live long. He moved with his army to Balkh, but despite Shahrukh sending his son, Ulugh Beg, and his emir Shahmalik to help him, Khalil Sultan was able to repulse their attacks. In Ramadan, 809/February, 1407, Pir Muhammad was murdered by one of his own emirs. Shahrukh had benefited from his support of Temür's testament without sacrificing his chance at power.[12]

Despite his early success, Khalil Sultan suffered from two major disadvantages. The first was that he had no history of rule in the region and no local troops he could count on; many of the regional forces had been brought in from outside and when Khalil Sultan had exhausted the treasury they were quick to leave. Furthermore, he had no historical claim either to Transoxiana or the kingdom as a whole. Khalil Sultan's actions also counted against him, particularly his failure to show proper respect for the reputation of the

[10] Ḥāfiẓ-i Abrū, *Zubdat*, 11–23, Tāj al-Salmānī, *Šams al-ḥusn: eine Chronik vom Tode Timurs bis zum Jahre 1409 von Tāğ al-Salmānī*, edited and translated by Hans Robert Roemer (Wiesbaden: F. Steiner, 1956), 40–42; Yazdī, *Ẓafarnāma*, vol. II, 482–511.

[11] John E. Woods, "Timur's Genealogy," in *Intellectual Studies on Islam, Essays Written in Honor of Martin B. Dickson*, edited by Michel M. Mazzaoui and Vera B. Moreen (Salt Lake City: University of Utah Press, 1990), 85.

[12] I have described the succession struggle elsewhere in greater detail. See Beatrice F. Manz, *The Rise and Rule of Tamerlane* (Cambridge: Cambridge University Press, 1989), 128–47.

dynasty. He is remembered particularly for his scandalous treatment of many of the widows of Temür and Muhammad Sultan, whom he married off to various emirs far below them in status. This was considered an insult to the honor of the dynastic founder and to the wives themselves. Since some of these women had raised their grandsons, the princes now fighting for power, they could not be easily discounted.

Although in his first years Khalil Sultan did have sufficient strength to repulse Pir Muhammad's invasions, he could not withstand the continuing attacks of two of Temür's closest and most powerful emirs, Khudaydad and Shaykh Nur al-Din. The success of their campaign illustrates the power that emirs could wield. Both these emirs had had connections to Muhammad Sultan and they seem to have justified their opposition to Khalil Sultan as loyalty to the line that Temür had chosen. Their platform attracted considerable local support. The northern borders of Transoxiana had been under Muhammad Sultan's governorship from 800/1397–8 to his death, and his emirs had remained in the region. His wives and children had also remained in Transoxiana, where they and their offspring continued to support Muhammad Sultan's sons. Since all Muhammad Sultan's sons were still young, support of his house offered local emirs the chance to expand their own power while promoting the legitimacy of the line that Temür had chosen. There were two centers for forces supporting this branch – the northern borders and the region of Hisar-i Shadman.[13] The presence of such strong attachment to Muhammad Sultan was probably one reason why Khalil Sultan installed his son Muhammad Jahangir as figurehead khan.

Khudaydad had been one of four emirs appointed with Muhammad Sultan to guard the northern borders of Transoxiana; the others were Shaykh Nur al-Din's brother Birdi Beg, Hajji Sayf al-Din, and Shams al-Din b. ʿAbbas, all important members or relatives of Temür's following.[14] For several years, some of these emirs challenged Khalil Sultan from their power base on the northern borders. Late in the winter of 811/1409 Khudaydad and Shaykh Nur al-Din invited Shahrukh to undertake a joint campaign against Khalil Sultan, whom they captured even before Shahrukh's arrival.[15]

Shahrukh's Chaghatay emirs

Like Khalil Sultan, Shahrukh had to struggle with rebellious emirs, but he had a considerable advantage because he had held his province steadily for six years, and thus retained the same army. Nonetheless Shahrukh lost the loyalty of several of his major emirs, particularly those who had served him during Temür's life. Of the prominent emirs who had been assigned to

[13] Yazdī, *Ẓafarnāma*, vol. II, 153; Tāj al-Salmānī, *Shams*, 97–98; Ḥāfiẓ-i Abrū, *Zubdat*, 367–68.
[14] Yazdī, *Ẓafarnāma*, vol. II, 17.
[15] Tāj al-Salmānī, *Shams*, 123–30; Ḥāfiẓ-i Abrū, *Zubdat*, 277–83, 303–15.

Shahrukh by his father, a large proportion – half or more – rose against him shortly after Temür's death. These rebellions by his emirs were a serious challenge to Shahrukh, but the harm they did was mitigated by his relative leniency towards them. While some individuals were executed or banished for their acts, Shahrukh did not discriminate against their relatives and thus he retained the services of the larger family and the overall makeup of his elite did not change significantly.

The army that Temür had assigned to Shahrukh included several personal followers and their offspring, as well as a sizeable number of emirs of the Qa'uchin, a group of Chaghatays from Transoxiana.[16] I will mention here only the most prominent commanders. The most senior was Sulaymanshah, one of Temür's closest followers, probably appointed as a watchdog over Shahrukh. Sulaymanshah had married Temür's daughter, and his son Yusuf was married to the daughter of Muhammad Sultan b. Jahangir.[17] Another emir was Midrab b. Chekü Barlas, the son of a very early follower whose family had been richly rewarded. Midrab's first cousin Edigü had married a cousin of Temür and held the governorship of Kerman, and Midrab had succeeded to his father's lands and troops in Qunduz and Baghlan.[18] Amir ʿAbd al-Samad b. Hajji Sayf al-Din also came from a follower family related to the dynasty and two of his sisters had married Timurid princes.[19] Two other emirs – ʿAli Tarkhan and Hasan Sufi Tarkhan – were sons of Ghiyath al-Din Tarkhan, a follower whose family married intensively into the dynasty. His daughter Gawharshad was Shahrukh's most powerful wife and two other daughters married sons of Temür's eldest son ʿUmar Shaykh.[20] Several emirs were sons or relatives of other followers but not related by marriage; these included Sayyid Khwaja b. Shaykh ʿAli Bahadur, Hasan Jandar, the nephew of Temür's follower Khitay, Malikat, a relative of the follower Aqtemür, and Malikat's son Jahanmalik. In addition there was an emir of unknown provenance, Pir Muhammad b. Pulad. All these men had been favored by the dynasty and had a strong interest in its continuance, but the benefits heaped on them had been given by Temür himself, not by Shahrukh.

The first rebellion was probably that of Pir Muhammad b. Pulad, appointed to govern Sari in Mazandaran. It is not clear exactly when it took place, but it was almost certainly shortly after Temür's death – and definitely before 809/1406–07 when another Timurid governor was in charge

[16] Yazdī, *Ẓafarnāma*, vol. I, 573. The Qa'uchin, though visible as a group, rarely held very high positions (Ando, *Timuridische Emire*, 157; *Muʿizz*, fols. 133b, 135b). Their origin remains obscure. For a discussion see Manz, *Rise and Rule*, 161–63, and Ando, *Timuridische Emire*, 92, 266–69.

[17] Manz, *Rise and Rule*, 78; *Muʿizz*, fol. 116a.

[18] Manz, *Rise and Rule*, 81; Ando, *Timuridische Emire*, 128; Yazdī, *Ẓafarnāma*, vol. II, 296–97.

[19] Manz, *Rise and Rule*, 186, n. 31; *Muʿizz*, fols. 108b, 110a, 125a, 129a, 130a.

[20] *Muʿizz*, fols. 103b, 104b, 106b, 132b.

of Sari.[21] The next emir to assert himself was Sulaymanshah b. Da'ud Dughlat, who left Shahrukh's service in early 808/1405. Near the end of Temür's life Sulaymanshah had been removed from Shahrukh's army to be appointed governor of Rayy and Firuzkuh. When Shahrukh refused to spare a rebellious prince on Sulaymanshah's request, he left Shahrukh to serve Khalil Sultan. We hear almost nothing of Sulaymanshah after his desertion and little of his family, except for a son, Rustam, listed among the emirs of Ulugh Beg.[22]

The uprising later that year illustrates both the slender hold that Shahrukh had over the loyalty of his emirs and his willingness to continue to favor the family of rebels. The attempt was led by Sayyid Khwaja b. Shaykh ʿAli Bahadur, and supported by several other sons of Temür's followers, notably ʿAbd al-Samad b. Hajji Sayf al-Din, connected by marriage to the family of ʿUmar Shaykh, and four sons of Uch Qara. One of these was Shams al-Din, who had been connected to Shahrukh during Temür's life.[23] For this uprising Sayyid Khwaja was executed, while his fellow conspirators fled into Fars and served ʿUmar Shaykh's sons there.[24] Despite this, other members of Sayyid Khwaja's family – the descendants of Shaykh ʿAli Bahadur – continued to enjoy Shahrukh's favor. Two of his brothers led *tümens* and served as *amīr dīwān* and as provincial governors in Iraq-i ʿAjam, positions they passed on to their children.[25] The possession of Radkan, a choice location with excellent pasture, which had been given in *soyurghal* to Shaykh ʿAli Bahadur, stayed in the family.[26] Indeed this line remained one of the most prominent Chaghatay families under Shahrukh. There was also no discrimination against Sayyid Khwaja's fellow conspirator, ʿAbd al-Samad b. Hajji Sayf al-Din, who returned to Shahrukh's service in 817/1414 after several years of conspicuous service to the sons of ʿUmar Shaykh in Fars. He held high posts in both army and administration, serving as *amir dīwān*, *tovachi*, and city governor until his death in 835/1432.[27] Shams al-Din b. Uch Qara returned earlier to Shahrukh's service, but we know nothing about his further career. His brothers served under Shahrukh and several of his sons.[28]

21 The dynastic histories do not mention the rebellion, but since we know that Pulad was executed as a result and since he appears nowhere in the histories, it is likely that this was soon after Temür's death ("Muʿizz," fol. 133a; Yazdī, *Ẓafarnāma*, vol. II, 397; Sayyid Ẓahīr al-Dīn b. Naṣīr al-Dīn Marʿashī, *Tārīkh-i Ṭabaristān wa Rūyān wa Māzandarān*, edited by Muḥammad Ḥusayn Tasbīḥī (Tehran: Sharq, 1966), 245–46.

22 Ando, *Timuridische Emire*, 168–69.

23 Manz, *Rise and Rule*, 139; Ḥāfiẓ-i Abrū, *Zubdat*, 106–08; "Muʿizz," fol. 133a; Ando, *Timuridische Emire*, 158; Tāj al-Salmānī, *Shams*, 80–81.

24 Ando, *Timuridische Emire*, 158–59; Ḥāfiẓ-i Abrū, *Zubdat*, 136.

25 Ando, *Timuridische Emire*, 133–37.

26 Aḥmad b. Jalāl al-Dīn Faṣīḥ Khwāfī, *Mujmal-i faṣīḥī*, edited by Muḥammad Farrukh, 3 vols. (Mashhad: Bāstān, 1339/1960–61), vol. III, 279.

27 *Muʿizz*, ff. 133a, 137a; Ando, *Timuridische Emire*, p. 159, *Zubdat*, 671.

28 In the *Muʿizz al-ansab* Shams al-Din is noted under Pir Muhammad b. ʿUmar Shaykh whom he served in Fars (*Muʿizz*, f. 102b). One brother, Shir ʿAli, is mentioned on Shahrukh's Transoxiana campaign of 813/1410–11 and listed in the *Muʿizz* as *amīr dīwān* for Ahmad b.

The family of Hasan Jandar, one of the emirs appointed with Shahrukh to Khorasan, also remained part of the ruler's entourage despite early disloyalty to Shahrukh. At the end of 810/1408 several members of Shahrukh's army conspired, protesting at the taxation imposed by his vizier. The uprising was led by Jahanmalik b. Malikat and included both Hasan Jandar and his son Yusuf Jalil. Jahanmalik was executed and the others fled to the welcoming arms of the Timurid princes of Fars.[29] Hasan Jandar died there but Yusuf Jalil returned to Shahrukh on Iskandar b. ʿUmar Shaykh's defeat in 817/1414 and, like ʿAbd al-Samad, gained a high position in Shahrukh's service, where he commanded a *tümen*.[30]

By 811/1408–09, when he was invited into Transoxiana, Shahrukh had put down the most serious challenges from within his own province; his realm was intact, and his treasury less depleted than those of most other princes. By this time many of his rivals had died or been unseated, with little direct action on his part. The lines of Amiranshah and Jahangir could no longer compete for central power. Shahrukh was now Temür's only surviving son, and though only twenty-seven at the time of Temür's death, he had the advantage of an established governorship in the rich province of Khorasan, to which he had been appointed in 799/1396–97. He was fortunate in having no dynastic competition within his realm, since his eldest sons, Ulugh Beg and Ibrahim Sultan, were only ten. He was in an excellent position to assert his power over a larger realm.

Shahrukh's rise to supreme power

We cannot know Shahrukh's intentions before his takeover of Transoxiana, but from this time on it is clear that he aimed at succeeding Temür and planned to reunite the whole of his father's realm. However, it proved difficult to establish solid rule over Temür's capital region, and for several years Transoxiana was the center of a conflict which involved Shahrukh himself, several of his major emirs, the Moghul khans of the eastern Chaghadayid Khanate, and emirs from the Jochid White or Blue Horde to the north.[31] Although Shahrukh had been invited into Transoxiana by Khudaydad and Shaykh Nur al-Din, when he arrived in late 811/spring, 1409, he found Khudaydad immediately opposed to him. When Khudaydad had attacked

ʿUmar Shaykh, appointed governor of Uzkand and Andijan in 812/1409–10. (Ḥāfiẓ-i Abrū, *Zubdat*, 301, 373; *Muʿizz* f. 108b.) Another of Uch Qara's sons, Jahan, is mentioned in 820/1417–18, serving Shahrukh's nephew Qaydu in Kabul. (Faṣīḥ Khwāfī, *Mujmal-i faṣīḥī* III, p. 231; Ḥāfiẓ-i Abrū, *Zubdat*, 668. Two other descendants appear only in the *Muʿizz* serving the princes Ilangir b. Aba Bakr b, Amiranshah and Ibrahim Sultan b. Shahrukh. (*Muʿizz*, ff. 125b, 141b.)

29 Manz, *Rise and Rule*, 139; *Zubdat*, 206–215.

30 Ḥāfiẓ-i Abrū, *Zubdat*, 525–27; Ando, *Timuridische Emire*, 139, 165; Faṣīḥ Khwāfī, *Mujmal-i faṣīḥī* III, 289, 748–50, *Muʿizz*, ff. 135b–137a. His death and that of his brother, both fighting the Uzbeks in Mazandaran in 844/1440–41, are highlighted in the histories. (Samarqandī, *Maṭlaʿ* II/2, 749–50.)

31 Both the primary sources and modern historians disagree on the name of the Jochid polity north of the Jaxartes.

Khalil Sultan in 811/1408–09, he had lured Muhammad Jahangir over to his side and raised him to the throne, and before handing Khalil Sultan over to Shahrukh he stipulated that the rule of Transoxiana be in the hands of Muhammad Jahangir.[32] When Shahrukh refused and headed against him, Khudaydad sought help from Muhammad Khan of the eastern Chaghadayid Khanate, who sent troops under his brother. Soon however the Moghuls decided that Shahrukh had a stronger chance, broke with Khudaydad and killed him.[33]

In the meantime Shahrukh had entered Samarqand on 27 Dhu'l-Hijja, 811/13 May, 1409. He spent about six months in the city, made Ulugh Beg governor of Transoxiana under the tutelage of Shahmalik, and appointed other princes to nearby regions. Then he returned to his own capital of Herat. These acts made two things quite clear: Shahrukh was no longer promoting the rule of Jahangir's line as he had previously claimed to do, and he intended Transoxiana to become the province of a realm centered in Khorasan. Shahrukh's actions may well have come as a surprise to the emirs of Transoxiana. It probably had not been clear that Shahrukh aspired to rule personally outside of Khorasan. Although he had for several years been minting coins in his own name and claiming the title of Sultan in Khorasan,[34] in his struggle against Transoxiana his troops had fought in the interests of Pir Muhammad b. Jahangir. It is quite possible therefore that when Khudaydad and Shaykh Nur al-Din invited Shahrukh to invade Transoxiana they expected the campaign to promote the rule of Muhammad Sultan's house. Instead Shahrukh appointed his son Ulugh Beg as governor and left for Herat.

Shahrukh did not give Ulugh Beg control over the whole of Transoxiana or limit the new governorships he established to his own line. Instead, he posed as an upholder of Temür's dispensation and where possible reproduced the governorships Temür had given out, with sons in their fathers' former places. He entrusted the regions of Tukharistan and Shadman to Muhammad Sultan b. Jahangir's son Muhammad Jahangir. Despite his earlier involvement with Shaykh Nur al-Din, Muhammad Jahangir remained close to Shahrukh until his death in 836/1433.[35] The neighboring region of Badakhshan retained its own shahs under the jurisdiction first of Amiranshah's son Ichil, and from 819/1416–17 to 821/1418–19 under Shahrukh's son Soyurghatmish.[36] Shahrukh himself remained closely involved, and it was he who organized expeditions to

[32] Yazdī, *Ẓafarnāma*, II, p. 505; Tāj al-Salmānī, *Shams*, 128–30; Ḥāfiẓ-i Abrū, *Zubdat*, 278–81.

[33] Tāj al-Salmānī, *Shams*, 111–12; Ḥāfiẓ-i Abrū, *Zubdat*, 297–300.

[34] Linda Komaroff, "The Epigraphy of Timurid Coinage: Some Preliminary Remarks," *American Numismatic Society: Museum Notes* 31 (1986), 216; M. N. Fedorov, "Klad Monet Ulugbeka i Shahrukha iz Samarkanda," *Obshchestvennye nauki v Uzbekistane*, 3 (1969), 56–57.

[35] Ḥāfiẓ-i Abrū, *Zubdat*, 315–6; Faṣīḥ Khwāfī, *Mujmal-i faṣīḥī*, vol. III, 271. Although there are several mentions of Muhammad Jahangir in the sources, Shadman is not mentioned. We know of no one else appointed there (see Ḥāfiẓ-i Abrū, *Zubdat*, 664, 872; Samarqandī, *Maṭla'*, 651).

[36] Ḥāfiẓ-i Abrū, *Zubdat*, 469–70, 586, 642–3, 690–91.

the regions during its frequent internal struggles. After 821 its shahs reported directly to Shahrukh.[37] The region of Khuttalan was likewise outside Ulugh Beg's domain.[38] The emirs who governed it are listed as Shahrukh's commanders and during the crisis of 826–27/1422–24, it was Shahrukh who took action. In 833/1429–30 Shahrukh appointed Muhammad Juki to the governorship of Khuttalan, and at his death in 848/1444–45 it passed to his son Aba Bakr.[39]

Balkh went first to Qaydu, the young son of Pir Muhammad b. Jahangir, then within a few years to Shahrukh's son Ibrahim Sultan and after 817/1414, perhaps to Soyurghatmish.[40] After 821/1418–19, when Soyurghatmish left to replace Qaydu as governor of Kabul, there is no information on who governed Balkh; it may have reported directly to the central *dīwān*.[41] Just before appointing Ulugh Beg governor of Transoxiana, Shahrukh had assigned the frontier region of Uzkand, Andijan and Kashghar to another prince, the twenty-five year old Amirak Ahmad b. ʿUmar Shaykh, a son of Shahrukh's Chinggisid wife Malikat Agha.[42] Since the area had earlier been the province of ʿUmar Shaykh, Shahrukh was continuing Temür's dispensation. This was an important province, incorporating the eastern part of the rich Ferghana Valley. Ahmad was older and more experienced than Ulugh Beg, and his appointment may have been an attempt to secure the delicate eastern border with the Chaghadayid khans.[43]

Shahrukh's attempt to appease the supporters of Jahangir's line was not successful, and although Shaykh Nur al-Din came to Samarqand on Ulugh Beg's appointment to declare his obedience, within the year he was preparing an attack from the northern borderlands. On 12 Dhuʾl-Hijja, 812/17 April, 1410 he defeated Ulugh Beg's army under Shahmalik. Shahmalik retreated

[37] Ḥāfiẓ-i Abrū, *Zubdat*, 807–8; Samarqandī, *Maṭlaʿ*, 320; Faṣīḥ Khwāfī, *Mujmal-i faṣīḥī*, vol. III, 276.

[38] The first governor mentioned is one of the local emirs, Sultan Mahmud b. Kaykhusraw Khuttalani, but quite early in Shahrukh's reign Midrab Chekü is identified as its governor (Ḥāfiẓ-i Abrū, "Majmaʿ," fol. 14a; Manz, *Rise and Rule*, 159). The position passed to his relative Nur Malik, then to his son Sultan Bayazid, mentioned as governor in 826–67/1422–24 (*Muʿizz*, fols. 92a, 133b; Ḥāfiẓ Ḥusayn Karbalāʾī Tabrīzī, *Rawḍāt al-jinān wa jannāt al-janān*, edited by Jaʿfar Sulṭān al-Qurrāʾī, 2 vols. [Tehran: Bungāh-i Tarjuma wa Nashr-i Kitāb, 1344/1965], vol. II, 240).

[39] Dawlatshāh b. ʿAlaʾ al-Dawla Samarqandī, *Tadhkirat al-shuʿarā*, edited by E. G. Browne (London: Luzac, 1901), 396; Samarqandī, *Maṭlaʿ*, 851–53, 904.

[40] Faṣīḥ Khwāfī, *Mujmal-i faṣīḥī*, vol. III, 195; Ḥāfiẓ-i Abrū, *Zubdat*, 469, 680. In 817/1414, Shahrukh appointed Ibrahim Sultan as governor of Fars; there is no statement about who took his place in Balkh, but indirect evidence suggests that it might have been added to Soyurghatmish's domains. Shahrukh's wife Malikat Agha spent the later part of her life with her son Soyurghatmish and when she died she was buried in the madrasa she had built in Balkh (Samarqandī, *Maṭlaʿ*, 751).

[41] Ḥāfiẓ-i Abrū, *Zubdat*, 690–92. Towards the end of Shahrukh's life, his emir Firuzshah was responsible for the tax administration of Balkh (Samarqandī, *Maṭlaʿ*, 793–94, 838–39.)

[42] Woods, *Timurid Dynasty*, 23.

[43] Ḥāfiẓ-i Abrū, *Zubdat*, 301, 315–16; Faṣīḥ Khwāfī, *Mujmal-i faṣīḥī*, vol. III, 271, 193; Samarqandī, *Maṭlaʿ*, 87–89.

to the mountains, leaving Samarqand undefended, and Shaykh Nur al-Din proceeded to the city to ask admittance. He was refused by the notables, who prepared to defend the city against him.[44]

Shaykh Nur al-Din also sent a messenger to Hisar-i Shadman to invite Muhammad Jahangir to his cause. According to Ḥāfiẓ-i Abrū, Muhammad Jahangir declined but Shaykh Nur al-Din was able to persuade the old emirs of Muhammad Sultan who surrounded the prince to join the opposition and bring the prince along with them. He used the youth of the princes as an inducement, stating that he planned to return to the borderlands and the emirs could thus become powerful in Samarqand. Either the appeal of Shaykh Nur al-Din's cause or the strength of his following brought other people to his side. We find among his followers Rustam b. Taghay Bugha Barlas, governor of Bukhara under Temür, and some commanders attached to neighboring steppe powers. Shaykh Nur al-Din brought Muhammad Jahangir to the gates of Samarqand, but again failed to gain admittance. Shahrukh himself now headed against him; after a defeat on 9 Rabiʿ I, 813/July 12, 1410 Shaykh Nur al-Din retreated and Shahrukh sent an expedition to plunder his lands. Hamza Suldus and other emirs in the region of Hisar-i Shadman however continued to resist and had to be put down in a separate expedition.[45]

Despite two defeats, Shaykh Nur al-Din and his party did not give up their resistance. Since he had personal ties with the eastern Chaghadayid khan, in his need Shaykh Nur al-Din turned to them. Muhammad Khan sent his brother with a sizeable army to help him attack Transoxiana. However by this time, Shaykh Nur al-Din was at odds with Khudaydad Husayni's son ʿAbd al-Khaliq, who held significant power in his region. Thus in Ramadan, 813/December, 1410–January, 1411, it was possible for Shahmalik to force Shaykh Nur al-Din to leave his lands and take refuge with the Moghuls. For a short time, the Moghul Khan continued to support Shaykh Nur al-Din and provide him with Moghul troops, but soon decided to make peace with Shahrukh who had mobilized his armies and set out towards Transoxiana on the last day of Rabiʿ I, 814/July 22, 1411.[46]

Without the support of the eastern Chaghadayids, Shaykh Nur al-Din presented a smaller threat, but it is clear that he remained a potential danger. Furthermore, Khalil Sultan had given him one of Temür's most prestigious wives, Tümen Agha. While Shahrukh approached Transoxiana with an army, Shahmalik again went to Shaykh Nur al-Din, demanding that he express

[44] Ḥāfiẓ-i Abrū, *Zubdat*, 361–67.

[45] Ibid., 361–85; Ḥāfiẓ-i Abrū, "Majmaʿ," fol. 461a.

[46] Ḥāfiẓ-i Abrū, *Zubdat*, 409–18. Even now the Moghuls remained friendly to Shaykh Nur al-Din and the marriage planned between his daughter and Muhammad Khan's brother Shamʿ-i Jahan was completed (see Mīrzā Muḥammad Ḥaydar Dughlat, *Tarikh-i Rashidi. A History of the Khans of Moghulistan*, edited and translated by Wheeler M. Thackston, *Sources of Oriental Languages and Literatures* 38, Central Asian Sources III [Cambridge, MA: Harvard University, 1996], 35).

full obedience. Shahmalik seems to have had a personal animosity against Shaykh Nur al-Din, who like him had been part of Temür's closest council, but who had now taken a different side in the succession struggle. When he found Shaykh Nur al-Din unwilling to comply immediately he arranged to have him killed by a ruse and brought his head back to Shahrukh in Samarqand, arriving there on 27 Jumadi I, 814/September 16, 1411. Shaykh Nur al-Din's brother, Amir Shaykh Hasan, sent messages of subservience and, at Shahrukh's demand, sent Temür's widow Tümen Agha to Shahrukh, who established her in Andkhud.[47] From this time on Ulugh Beg faced no serious opposition within Transoxiana. Shahrukh had successfully brought the eastern section of Temür's realm under his rule.

Once he had laid claim to the imperial city and province, Shahrukh took steps to mark his mastery of Temür's legacy and to characterize his reign as a new beginning. He entered Temür's tomb in Samarqand and removed the weapons and other non-Islamic accouterments found there. In Dhu' l-Qa'da, 813/February–March, 1411, he declared that he had abrogated the Mongolian dynastic code, the *yasa*, and reinstated the *sharīʿa*, and had wine from the taverns publicly poured onto the ground. It was also in 813/1410–11 that Shahrukh completed his first major religious complex in Herat, including a madrasa and a *khānaqāh*, and organized a ceremonial opening. During the same period Shahrukh began what became his most consistent project of patronage, the writing of history to connect his career with those of Temür and the Mongol khans. As I have argued elsewhere, Shahrukh's actions on his accession echoed those of the Ilkhan Ghazan, known both for his interest in Mongol history and for his declaration of Islam as the formal religion of the land.[48] In the years 813–14/1410–12 two court histories were written for Shahrukh, completing the story of Temür's life and chronicling the beginning of the succession struggle. Ḥāfiẓ-i Abrū, who had accompanied Temür and now became Shahrukh's court historian, wrote a continuation of Nizam al-Din Shami's *Zafarnama*, taking the story through Temür's death. At about the same time the vizier Taj al-Din Salmani, who had come to Shahrukh from Khalil Sultan, produced his history of events leading to the fall of Khalil Sultan.[49]

Having formally asserted his position as Temür's successor, Shahrukh set out to regain the region of Khorezm which had been taken over by the Jochids in Rajab, 808/December, 1405–January, 1406. The first expedition of 815/1412–13 was a humiliating failure, but at the end of the same year, after punishing his troops, Shahrukh sent out another army under Shahmalik and other great emirs which quickly succeeded. Early the next year Shahrukh

47 Ḥāfiẓ-i Abrū, *Zubdat*, 421–35.
48 Beatrice F. Manz, "Mongol History Rewritten and Relived," *Mythes historiques du monde musulman*, edited by Denise Aigle, special issue of *Revue du monde musulman et de la Méditerranée* (2001), 143–44; Samarqandī, *Maṭlaʿ*, 109.
49 Manz, "Family and Ruler," 59.

appointed Shahmalik as governor of the region. This was a politic move, as Ulugh Beg had become resentful of Shahmalik's authority and, at the age of eighteen, he was old enough to assume actual power.[50]

Once Shahrukh had united the eastern parts of Temür's realm, the logical next step was the reconquest of Azarbaijan and Iraq, which had come under the domination of the Qaraqoyunlu and the Jalayir. Shahrukh prepared for a major campaign to the west but had to divert it to deal with the threat posed to him by his nephews, the sons of ʿUmar Shaykh and Malikat Agha who held the governorships of Fars and adjacent regions. While Shahrukh had been gaining power in the east, these princes had been fighting within their realm and one of them, Iskandar, had gained sufficient power to challenge Shahrukh. Since the politics of the ʿUmar Shaykh princes presented Shahrukh's strongest internal challenge, it is worthwhile to give a brief account here.

The struggle over Fars

Temür's oldest son ʿUmar Shaykh (d. 796/1394) had been governor of Fars and had left behind many sons, several of whom were now in their early twenties. The eldest was Pir Muhammad, about twenty-five at Temür's death, and well established as governor in Shiraz. He had several brothers younger than he. Ahmad, about eighteen, remained in the eastern regions. Pir Muhammad's two closest brothers, Rustam, about twenty-three, and Iskandar, age twenty, both held governorships neighboring Pir Muhammad's. Rustam had been granted Isfahan, while Iskandar was in Hamadan, Nihavand and Lur-i Kuchik. Another brother, Bayqara, was only nine, and became politically active somewhat later. The sons of ʿUmar Shaykh had a complex relationship to Shahrukh. ʿUmar Shaykh's Chinggisid wife, Malikat Agha, was the mother of Pir Muhammad, Iskandar, and Bayqara in Fars, and Mirak Ahmad.[51] After ʿUmar Shaykh's death Malikat Agha married Shahrukh and these princes became his stepsons. It is not clear how much advantage the relationship brought them, since Malikat Agha was less close to Shahrukh and less powerful than his non-royal wife, Gawharshad.

The eldest prince, Pir Muhammad, was recognized on Temür's death by the *darugha*s of the strategic cities of Yazd and Abarquh and, according to Shahrukh's historians, he almost immediately paid homage to Shahrukh. Nonetheless, the order Temür had left in Iran soon began to fall apart. Iskandar left Hamadan and took refuge with Pir Muhammad, who installed him as governor of Yazd.[52] Pir Muhammad, Rustam and Iskandar now began to look outside at Kerman, which they tried to annex, and at

[50] Ḥāfiẓ-i Abrū, *Zubdat*, 478–81.
[51] Manz, *Rise and Rule*, 87; Woods, *Timurid Dynasty*, 20–24.
[52] Ḥāfiẓ-i Abrū, *Zubdat*, 48–51; Yazdī, *Ḥasanī*, 14.

Azarbaijan, where they joined in the struggles of Amiranshah's sons. In early Shaʿban of 809/January, 1407 they welcomed the arrival of several of the emirs who had rebelled against Shahrukh in 808/1405–06 with Sayyid Khwaja, and these men became an important part of their military support.[53]

The princes also disagreed among themselves. In 809–810/1406–08 Pir Muhammad removed Iskandar from the governorship of Yazd, repulsed an attack on Shiraz by Iskandar and Rustam, and succeeded, in his turn, in taking Isfahan. For a time, both Iskandar and Rustam left the region, so that Pir Muhammad was able to consolidate his power. By 812/1409–10 Iskandar had returned to Shiraz in a subordinate position, and he accompanied Pir Muhammad on a campaign against Kerman. In the course of the expedition Pir Muhammad was murdered by an Iranian servitor, Husayn Sharbatdar. This event marked a turning point in the career of Iskandar, who now became the most powerful figure in Fars, and he gave full rein to his ambition. On learning of the murder he hastened to Shiraz and sent his agents to Yazd, which capitulated after a siege of several months. Over the next years Iskandar tried to gain control over Isfahan, but here he was less successful. Despite repeated sieges, the city remained under the control, sometimes of other Timurid princes, primarily Rustam, and sometimes of its own population. In 814/1411–12 however Rustam murdered the city's judge, and the Isfahanis invited Iskandar to take over the city. Iskandar left an agent in Shiraz, made Isfahan his new capital, and the next year started to use the title Sultan.[54] At the same time he expanded his rule into the area of Qum and Sawa, which had remained under their own rulers. For the first time, the Timurid dynasty instituted direct rule over these cities, and Iskandar carried off the rich treasury of Qum, gathered throughout two centuries.[55]

Unlike Shahrukh, whose interests and patronage were concentrated in a relatively narrow spectrum, Iskandar was a person of broad intellectual interests and his lively ambition manifested itself in cultural production even before he could claim real regional power. The first burst came with his achievement of power in Shiraz in 812/1409–10. He gathered major religious figures at his court; we know in particular of a *majlis* including two prominent religious figures, Sayyid Sharif Jurjani and Shah Wali Niʿmat Allah. It was also at this time that Iskandar began his patronage of book production. The manuscripts created for him include albums, anthologies of scientific and historical literature, and poetry in Persian, Turkic and Arabic. Almost as soon as he took Isfahan, Iskandar made it his capital and assembled a brilliant

[53] Ando, *Timuridische Emire*, 158–59; Ḥāfiẓ-i Abrū, *Zubdat*, 131–36.

[54] Ismail Aka, "Timur'un ölümünden sonra güney-Iran'da hakimiyet mücadeleleri," in *Atsız Armağanı* (Istanbul: Ötüken Yayınevi, 1976), 3–7, 12–14; Priscilla Soucek, "Eskandar b. ʿOmar Šayx b. Timur: A Biography," *La civiltà Timuride come fenomeno internazionale*, edited by Michele Bernardini, *Oriente Moderno* XV (1996), 79–81.

[55] Yazdī, *Ḥasanī*, 14, 36–7; Ḥāfiẓ-i Abrū, *Zubdat*, 481–83.

court including religious scholars, astronomers and luminaries in other fields. He likewise undertook a major building campaign.[56]

As he began to claim the sultanate, Iskandar commissioned two histories which, like those written for Shahrukh, connected him to Temür and the Mongols. Both histories were written in 816/1413–14. One was a very brief account of Temür's rule and its aftermath, containing a short narrative describing the virtues and achievements of Iskandar's grandfather and the shortcomings of his relatives, along with a chart showing their ages, characters, and places of rule. The second was a longer and more scholarly work, the *Muntakhab al-tawarikh* of Mu'in al-Din Natanzi, a general history of mankind up through Temür's reign. In this version of his history, Natanzi omitted mention of Temür's testament in favor of Pir Muhammad, while the briefer and more informal history written for Iskandar stated that Temür had appointed him as successor.[57]

In 816/1413–14, Iskandar's ambitions brought him into direct conflict with Shahrukh. Uneasy about reports he heard from Fars, Shahrukh sent an emissary to Iskandar asking him to join his projected campaign against the Qaraqoyunlu. This move was a call to recognize his preeminence. The envoy returned to report that Iskandar was minting coins in his own name; Iskandar meanwhile prepared a campaign against Sawa and sent a letter to local rulers inviting their support against Shahrukh. As a result, Shahrukh postponed his Azarbaijan campaign and in the beginning of 817/March–April, 1414, headed against Iskandar. The decisive battle was at Isfahan, which submitted to Shahrukh after a short siege, on 3 Jumada I, 817/July 21, 1414. Iskandar fled but was captured and handed over to his brother Rustam.[58]

Shahrukh distributed the leadership of the region among several princes, leaving 'Umar Shaykh's sons with only part of their former lands. Iskandar was now out of power and his earlier holdings of Hamadan and Luristan went to his young brother Bayqara, while Rustam was reinstalled in Isfahan. Qum was entrusted to another prince, Sa'd-i Waqqas b. Muhammad Sultan. Shahrukh's son Ibrahim Sultan became governor of Fars and Shahrukh, returning through Yazd, put that city under the charge of his maternal uncle Muhammad Darwish.[59]

[56] Soucek, "Eskandar," 82–86, and Priscilla Soucek, "The Manuscripts of Iskandar Sultan: Structure and Content," in *Timurid Art and Culture*, edited by L. Golombek and M. Subtelny (Leiden, New York: Brill, 1992), 116–31; Francis Richard, "Un témoignage inexploité concernant le mécénat d'Eskandar Solṭān à Eṣfahān," *La civiltà Timuride come fenomeno internazionale*, edited by Michele Bernardini, *Oriente Moderno* XV (1996), 45–72; Basil Gray, "The School of Shiraz from 1392–1453," in *The Arts of the Book in Central Asia*, edited by Basil Gray (Paris: UNESCO, 1979), 136–38.

[57] Manz, "Family and Ruler," 60–61.

[58] Ḥāfiẓ-i Abrū, *Zubdat*, 494–506, 530–48; Soucek, "Eskandar," 81–82.

[59] Ḥāfiẓ-i Abrū, *Zubdat*, 555–58; Aḥmad b. Ḥusayn b. 'Alī Kātib, *Tārīkh-i jadīd-i Yazd*, edited by Īraj Afshār (Tehran: Intishārāt-i Ibn Sīnā, 1345/1966), 111; Ja'far b. Muḥammad al-Ḥusaynī Ja'farī, *Tārīkh-i kabīr*, St. Petersburg, Publichnaia Biblioteka im. Saltykova-Shchedrina, MS PNC 201, fol. 305b; Ja'far b. Muḥammad al-Ḥusaynī Ja'farī, *Tarīkh-i kabīr*, translated by

The princes appointed to Iran did not long remain quiet. The first to cause problems was Saʿd-i Waqqas in Qum. Bistam Chaqir, a prominent Turco-Mongolian emir from the region of Sultaniyya, defected from Qara Yusuf Qaraqoyunlu and came to Qum. Saʿd-i Waqqas put him in chains and informed Shahrukh, who scolded the prince for not giving his guest a better welcome. Receiving this reply, Saʿd-i Waqqas left with his hostage for the court of Qara Yusuf. Iskandar and Bayqara, now together in Hamadan, saw the disturbances arising from the actions of Saʿd-i Waqqas as an opportunity and made an attempt to retake Fars. Ibrahim Sultan was unable to hold Shiraz and retreated to Abarquh, so Shahrukh had to undertake a second expedition to the region.[60] He quickly restored Ibrahim Sultan to his governorship and banished Bayqara, leaving the more faithful Rustam in Isfahan.

The region of Qum was now joined to Kashan and Rayy and put under the charge of Amir Ilyas Khwaja b. Shaykh ʿAli Bahadur. The taxes of the region were to be his *soyurghal*, to be spent on the upkeep of his administration and army.[61] For about ten years the region seems to have remained fairly quiet and stable; in any case, we read little about it in the histories. Sometime before 823/1420–21, Shahrukh appointed a new governor to Yazd; this was Amir Chaqmaq Shami, who remained in Yazd for the rest of Shahrukh's reign, pursuing an active program of cultural and economic development. Chaqmaq's patronage appears to have centered around architecture, but Yazd remained a center of book production and of local history.[62]

Over the next two years, Shahrukh tightened his control over the provinces of his realm. On his return to Herat he bestowed on his son, Baysunghur, the the region of northwestern Khorasan with part of Gurgan, a region stretching from Abiward to Tus. This was not a governorship comparable to those of Fars or Transoxiana and Baysunghur seems to have spent most of his time in Herat, where he was active in administration and where the artistic patronage for which he is famous was centered.[63] In the spring of 819/1416, Shahrukh undertook an expedition against Kerman whose governor, a relative of Temür's close follower Chekü Barlas, had failed to come when summoned; he conquered the city and a little later appointed Amir Ghunashirin as governor. In the same year, he exiled several recalcitrant princes including

Abbas Zaryab, in Abbas Zaryab, "Das Bericht über die Nachfolger Timurs aus dem Ta'rīh-i kabīr des Ǧafar ibn Muḥammad al-Ḥusainī," Ph.D. dissertation, Johannes Gutenberg-Universität zu Mainz, 1960, 63. The *Tārīkh-jadīd* dates the appointment of Muhammad Darwish to 818, while the *Tārīkh-i kabīr* states it was made on return from this expedition, which ended in 817.

60 Ḥāfiẓ-i Abrū, *Zubdat*, 588–97.

61 Ibid., 606–11; Faṣīḥ Khwāfī, *Mujmal-i faṣīḥī*, vol. III, 223.

62 For book production see Gray, "School of Shiraz," 136, 140, 142.

63 Ḥāfiẓ-i Abrū, *Zubdat*, 568–73.

Ahmad b. ʿUmar Shaykh, who as governor of Andijan had shown resistance to Ulugh Beg.[64]

One more challenge remained from Shahrukh's nephews, this time from Pir Muhammad b. Jahangir's son Qaydu, whom Shahrukh had taken from Balkh and installed in Kabul. Qaydu had with him a number of his father's emirs, including the powerful Amir Buhlul Barlas, who had supported Shaykh Nur al-Din's uprising and then been forgiven. According to Ḥāfiẓ-i Abrū, the first trouble arose in 819/1416–17, when Buhlul gathered other emirs to him and proposed to put Qaydu's brother Sanjar in his place. Qaydu appealed to Shahrukh to send an army to his aid.[65] This action however did not bring peace and it seems likely that Qaydu was less than entirely loyal; he had at some point asked the Delhi ruler Khidr Khan to read the *khuṭba* in his name, a clear sign that he aimed for independent power. It seems probable that he hoped to revive his father's claims, encouraged by those of his father's emirs who remained with him. In 820/1417–18, Shahrukh learned of widespread disorders among the Hazara and other peoples of Qaydu's realm, and decided to undertake a campaign in person and to winter in the region. When he arrived in Qandahar and called for Qaydu to join him against the rebellious Hazara, Qaydu instead fled and removed his following from Kabul. Shahrukh sent emirs to negotiate with him and he agreed to come to Herat, but after a short period he headed back south planning to rejoin his followers. Shahrukh's army under Baysunghur intercepted him and returned him to Herat where he was imprisoned, and Shahrukh installed his own son Soyurghatmish in the governorship of Kabul.[66] Now all major governorships were in the hands of Shahrukh's sons and emirs.

Shahrukh's new status as absolute ruler of Temür's realm was marked by further historical works which put his reign into the framework of universal history. One was by an historian from Yazd, Jaʿfar b. Muḥammad al-Ḥusayni Jaʿfari, who in 820/1417–18 presented Shahrukh with a short world history, entitled the *Tarikh-i wasit*. In the same year Ḥāfiẓ-i Abrū completed his compilation of histories, the "Majmūʿa al-tawārīkh," in which he put together several universal and dynastic histories, including Rashid al-Din's *Jamiʿ al-tawarikh* and Shami's *Zafarnama*, with connecting narratives. Like earlier histories written for Shahrukh, this work was illustrated in a consciously archaic style mirroring the Ilkhanid illustrations of Rashid al-Din's work. In the provinces the new order likewise called for literary patronage and within two years Sharaf al-Din ʿAli Yazdi had begun to work on a history of Temür for Ibrahim Sultan in Shiraz.[67]

64 Ḥāfiẓ-i Abrū, *Zubdat*, 618–35. 65 Ibid., 637–41.
66 Ibid., 666–72, 679–92.
67 Manz, "Family and Ruler," 60; Ernst J. Grube, with Eleanor Sims, "The School of Herat from 1400 to 1450," in *The Arts of the Book in Central Asia*, edited by Basil Gray (Paris: UNESCO, 1979), 146–52.

The apogee of Shahrukh's reign

With no major internal threats remaining, Shahrukh was free to deal with the problem of the western regions, which were under the control of the Qaraqoyunlu. While he was consolidating his power in the east, Qara Yusuf Qaraqoyunlu had been increasing his, and by 822/1419–20 had brought most of the smaller rulers of northwestern Iran under his protection. The Qaraqoyunlu takeover of Azarbayjan posed two problems for Shahrukh. First of all, Qara Yusuf had killed his brother Amiranshah, and the death had to be avenged. The second issue was the symbolic importance of the region, which had formed the center of Mongol Iran. From Temür's first conquest of Sultaniyya, the dynasty had claimed the Ilkhanid inheritance, and for Shahrukh this legitimation was of particular importance because he had adopted Ilkhanid titles and imitated the acts of Ghazan Khan, who was remembered for both reimposing Islam in Iran and fostering Mongol traditions.[68] The Timurids considered Sultaniyya, the dynastic necropolis of the Ilkhans, and the nearby trading entrepot Qazwin as integral to their realm. In the beginning of 823/ January–February, 1420 therefore, Shahrukh began to plan a campaign to retake the region.

He set off from Herat on 11 Shaʿban, 823/August 21, 1420, with additional troops joining him along the way; like Temür's, Shahrukh's army included Chaghatay and Tajik forces from all the regions of his realm. This was a major campaign and most regional armies were led by the governors in person. Qara Yusuf's governor in Qazwin fled and the city submitted, but in Sultaniyya Jahanshah b. Qara Yusuf prepared for defense. From the tone of Ḥāfiẓ-i Abrū's account, it appears that Qara Yusuf was too strong a foe for comfort. As it happened, while Shahrukh headed against Sultaniyya, he learned that Qara Yusuf had died suddenly; this excellent news reached him on 11 Dhuʾl-Qaʿda, 823/November 17, 1420.[69]

Although Qara Yusuf had been ill for some time and Shahrukh's army was still quite distant, at his death on 7 Dhuʾl-Qaʿda/November 13, panic broke out. His followers abandoned his corpse where he had died, on the throne inside his tent. Members of his army plundered the tent, stripped his body of his silk clothing and his ruby earring, and left it naked on the floor. Only after two days did a sayyid from his entourage come and collect the corpse for burial. In the meantime, Qara Yusuf's family and commanders had grabbed what riches they could find and dispersed. In Sultaniyya a number of Jahanshah's commanders fled to Shahrukh, who was thus able to take the city without difficulty and to proceed triumphantly to Temür's winter pasture at Qarabagh, where he arrived on 8 Dhuʾl-Hijja, 823/December 14, 1420.

[68] Manz, "Mongol History," 141–46.

[69] Ḥāfiẓ-i Abrū, *Zubdat*, 709–26; Ismail Aka, *Mirza Şahruh ve Zamani (1405–1447)* (Ankara: Türk Tarih Kurumu Basïmevi, 1994), 115–18.

He sent his son Baysunghur to take over Tabriz.[70] While Qara Yusuf's death spared Shahrukh the necessity to face a foe possibly superior to him, it also denied him the possibility of a decisive victory over a clearly identified enemy. He was left with Jahanshah's ambitious and competing sons to bring to submission, as well as a host of local rulers who had become clients of the Qaraqoyunlu. While Shahrukh wintered in Qarabagh, numerous local rulers who had earlier been under Temür's suzerainty came to offer presents and obedience. Several Turkmen tribes and chiefs, the rulers of Shirwan, Shakki, and Georgia, and the Aqqoyunlu from Diyar Bakr were among those paying their respects, while ambassadors also arrived from more distant lands. Shahrukh cemented local ties by marrying the daughter of Aba Bakr b. Amiranshah to the ruler of Shirwan, Khalil Allah b. Shaykh Ibrahim.[71] With the spring, however, troubles arose, as local leaders sought independence and the sons of Qara Yusuf vied for power among themselves. After undertaking several expeditions against nearby fortresses Shahrukh faced the combined armies of Qara Yusuf's sons Isfand and Iskandar. The armies met in Alashgird at the end of Rajab, 824/ late July, 1421, and after a hard battle Shahrukh's forces won. This victory was sufficient for Shahrukh and, without stopping to secure the region, he went quickly through Tabriz, Sultaniyya and Qazwin to Herat, which he reached on 19 Shawwal, 824/October 17, 1421.[72]

Once Shahrukh had restored Timurid supremacy in Azarbaijan, he was the recognized ruler of the whole of the realm that had come within Temür's administration. All the provinces were now governed by people dependent on him and he controlled the dynasty and its followers. Although the Chaghatay emirs had challenged Shahrukh in the beginning of his rise to power, as his authority grew, rebellions became less frequent. We should not underestimate the skill Shahrukh displayed, though he differed from Temür in method. Shahrukh seems to have been an able commander, but what secured his success was his patience and his judgment in the timing of campaigns. He was willing to delegate power to his subordinates and to put emirs and princes in charge of campaigns that did not require the full army. During the middle period of his reign, from his first through his second Azarbaijan campaigns, this system worked very well. Only later, when the most important members of Shahrukh's family and following began to die, did serious problems arise.

Shahrukh's major instrument of power was his corps of Turco-Mongolian commanders. I have already enumerated the major emirs who had served with him while he was governor of Khorasan and have discussed the actions of those who rebelled against him. Much of his success was due to the consistent service of the other emirs attached to him. Like his father, Shahrukh built up a group of close followers through the promotion of new

[70] Ḥāfiẓ-i Abrū, *Zubdat*, 729, 732–35, 740.
[71] Ibid., 749–54, 758–60; Aka, *Mirza Şahruh*, 120.
[72] Ḥāfiẓ-i Abrū, *Zubdat*, 760–98; Aka, *Mirza Şahruh*, 118–24.

men whose lack of ties among the Chaghatay increased their attachment to his person. He seems to have collected a smaller number of such people than Temür, but those whom he did promote held very high positions.

The two followers who became most prominent, ʿAlika Kukeltash and Amir Firuzshah, do not appear in the histories of Temür's career and seem to have been attached personally to Shahrukh himself. ʿAlika is identified as the son of Aduk, but we know nothing further of his origin. He himself claimed that Temür had entrusted Shahrukh to him. His active military career began almost immediately after Temür's death; this fact and his honorific "kukeltash", meaning milk brother, suggest a strong personal tie. He appears to have been twenty-five to thirty lunar years older than Shahrukh, so it is likely that he was some sort of tutor to him. Since even in the notices of his death nothing is written of his parentage beyond his father's name, he was probably of obscure, even of servile origin.[73]

Shahrukh's other major emir, Firuzshah, was the son of Arghunshah, a commander of Turkmen provenance moderately prominent during Temür's reign and very important in the succession struggle after his death. The sources do not make it clear how Arghunshah had achieved his position. There is some evidence to suggest that he was related to an early ally of Temür's, Mubarakshah Sanjari, but in the *Shams al-husn*, Taj al-Salmani identifies him as a Turkmen slave.[74] In any case, it is notable that while Arghunshah was playing an important part in the regime of Shahrukh's opponent, Khalil Sultan, Firuzshah himself was a trusted follower of Shahrukh's, swearing fealty to him in Herat, and he remained steadfast despite his father's execution at Shahrukh's orders in 812/1409.[75] ʿAlika and Firuzshah served Shahrukh throughout the greater part of his reign. We find them listed in the "Muʿizz al-ansab" both as *amīr dīwān* and as leaders of *tümen*s in the left wing of Shahrukh's army.[76] In almost all major campaigns one or another of them was prominent in the army.[77]

Two emirs who swore allegiance to Shahrukh shortly after Temür's death, Amir Chaharshanba and Amir Farmanshaykh, seem to have originated

[73] Ando, *Timuridische Emire*, 145–46; Ḥāfiẓ-i Abrū, *Zubdat*, 14; Faṣīḥ Khwāfī, *Mujmal-i faṣīḥī*, vol. III, 288; Samarqandī, *Maṭlaʿ*, 746–47.

[74] Ando, *Timuridische Emire*, 114; Tāj al-Salmānī, *Shams*, 35–36. One should note that Taj al-Salmani was fond of ascribing slave status to Temür's emirs.

[75] Tāj al-Salmānī, *Shams*, 79; Aḥmad Ibn ʿArabshāh, *Tamerlane or Timur, the Great Amir* translated by J. H. Sanders (London: Luzac, 1936), 256; Faṣīḥ Khwāfī, *Mujmal-i faṣīḥī*, vol. III, 194; Ando, *Timuridische Emire*, 114, 150.

[76] *Muʿizz*, fols. 133a, 135b, 137a.

[77] For instance Firuzshah made up part of the Transoxiana campaign of 813/1410–11 and in 815/1412–13 was sent against Badakhshan, while ʿAlika participated in the conquest of Khorezm. Firuzshah was in the Fars expedition of 818/1415–16, while ʿAlika was in the Kerman expedition of 819/1416–17. ʿAlika wintered with part of Shahrukh's army in Astarabad in 825/1421–22 and participated in the first two Azarbaijan campaigns (Ḥāfiẓ-i Abrū, *Zubdat*, 373, 478, 597, 631, 676; Faṣīḥ Khwāfī, *Mujmal-i faṣīḥī*, vol. III, 210, 222, 226, 233, 243, 270; Samarqandī, *Maṭlaʿ*, 321.

outside the central Chaghatay elite, and we know little about their origin.[78] Two other new emirs who came from outside regions joined Shahrukh in the course of his rise to power and became pillars of his administration. These were the provincial governors Jalal al-Din Chaqmaq Shami, governor of Yazd, and Ghunashirin, governor of Kerman. The histories do not fully agree on the origin of Amir Chaqmaq; the most plausible account is that he came from the Mamluk Sultanate, fled to Asia Minor, and then joined Shahrukh with his followers sometime before 817/1414, when he is mentioned in Shahrukh's forces. His brother was also in Shahrukh's service and was killed in Azarbaijan in Jumadi I, 824/May, 1421.[79] By 823/1420 Chaqmaq was governor of Yazd where he remained through Shahrukh's reign. Chaqmaq Shami was connected personally to Shahrukh's family, particularly to Baysunghur b. Shahrukh, two of whose daughters he raised. One of these then became his wife.[80] The extent of his architectural patronage suggests that he retained a significant portion of local taxes, while accompanying Shahrukh on major campaigns with the army of Yazd.[81]

The governor whom Shahrukh appointed to Kerman, Amir Ghunashirin, held a similar position. He appears first in 810/1407–08, acting as Shahrukh's messenger to Khalil Sultan, and formed part of Shahrukh's military command over the next years. In 819/1416–17 he participated in Shahrukh's campaign against Kerman and was appointed governor of the province in 820/1417. Amir Ghunashirin's antecedents remain a mystery. His name has a Sanskrit origin, but he himself was clearly a Muslim.[82] Despite his prominence, his numerous sons active in the struggle after Shahrukh's death, and the existence of a history, the *Jamiʿ al-tawarikh-i hasani*, written by a member of his son's *dīwān*, we have no information on his parentage. His brother is mentioned once in the *Mujmal-i fasihi*, but also without mention of his antecedents.[83] Within Kerman we know little about his activities or about the structure of his government, though it seems that Kerman lost much of its fiscal independence. Nonetheless when he died the government of Kerman passed to his sons.[84]

78 Jaʿfarī, *Tārīkh-i kabīr*, 35; fol. 295a.

79 Ḥāfiẓ-i Abrū, *Zubdat*, 542, 786; Ḥāfiẓ-i Abrū, *Majmaʿ*, fol. 570b (in margins of ms); Faṣīḥ Khwāfī, *Mujmal-i faṣīḥī*, vol. III, 247. For accounts of Chaqmaq's origin, see Muḥammad Mufīd Mustawfī Bāfqī, *Jāmiʿ-i mufīdī*, edited by Iraj Afshār, 3 vols. (Tehran: Kitābfurūsh-i Asadī, 1340/1961), vol. III, 740–41, and "waqfnama," 873.

80 *Muʿizz*, fol. 147b; Mustawfī Bāfqī, *Mufīdī*, 742; Kātib, *Tārīkh-i jadīd*, 231–32, 244.

81 Kātib, *Tārīkh-i jadīd*, 97–100, 220, 243; Renata Holod-Tretiak, "The Monuments of Yazd, 1300–1450: Architecture, Patronage and Setting," Ph.D. dissertation, Harvard University, 1972, 93, 99–114; Ḥāfiẓ-i Abrū, *Zubdat*, 720 (on armies); Samarqandī, *Maṭlaʿ*, 323, 624.

82 Ḥāfiẓ-i Abrū, *Zubdat*, 104, 536, 587, 631; *Ḥāfiẓ-i Abrū*, "Majmaʿ," fol. 538b; Jean Aubin, *Deux sayyids de Bam au xve. siècle. Contribution à l'histoire de l'Iran timouride* (Wiesbaden: Franz Steiner Verlag G. M. B. H., 1956), 50–51.

83 Faṣīḥ Khwāfī, *Mujmal-i faṣīḥī*, vol. III, 247.

84 Ḥāfiẓ-i Abrū, *Zubdat*, 720; Samarqandī, *Maṭlaʿ*, 323, 624; Aubin, *Deux sayyids*, 51, 53.

A number of Chaghatay emirs chose Shahrukh's side after Temür's death and remained faithful thereafter. One of these was Yadgarshah Arlat, who belonged to the Arlat tribe of Khorasan, part of which had intermarried extensively with the dynasty during Temür's reign. Although his parentage is not given, it seems likely that Yadgarshah belonged to the branch of the Arlats related to the dynasty, since he himself later married into the Timurids.[85] He began his rise to prominence at the end of Temür's life and helped to raise Khalil Sultan to the throne but soon switched his allegiance to Temür's chosen successor, Pir Muhammad b. Jahangir, and, after his death, to Shahrukh.[86] Another emir mentioned in 807/1405 who made up part of Shahrukh's top command was Shaykh Lughman Barlas, related to Hajji Beg, former chief of the Barlas.[87]

One family particularly loyal and important during Shahrukh's early reign was that of his wife Gawharshad, daughter of Temür's follower Ghiyath al-Din Tarkhan. Ghiyath al-Din had married several daughters to Timurid princes, but Gawharshad was the most influential one and her family gathered around Shahrukh rather than other members of the dynasty.[88] Two of Gawharshad's brothers, ʿAli Tarkhan and Hasan Sufi Tarkhan, had been appointed with Shahrukh to Khorasan. They figure prominently in most of Shahrukh's early campaigns, along with four other brothers: Husayn Sufi, Sayyid Ahmad, Muhammad Sufi and Hamza. Although no one of these emirs stands out as the most powerful figure in the administration or army, together they formed much the most important family group. In 810/1407–08, Sayyid Ahmad received a land grant in Andkhud which appears to have remained his seat and that of his family.[89] His status is indicated by the fact that he had personally sent a horse to the Chinese emperor, for which he received special thanks.[90] All of these brothers performed important functions in Shahrukh's Transoxiana campaigns of 812–13/1409–11. Shahrukh sent Hasan Sufi to Khujand in 812 to fetch Khalil Sultan, and in 813 we find ʿAli leading 100 *qushun*s following after the advance guard, Muhammad Sufi in the main army with other great emirs, and Husayn Sufi sent to guard Qumis and Mazandaran during Shahrukh's absence. In

[85] Manz, *Rise and Rule*, 155–56; *Muʿizz*, fols. 102a, 121a, 126b, 140b.

[86] Tāj al-Salmānī, *Shams*, 33–35; Manz, *Rise and Rule*, 140, 155–56. Jaʿfari lists Yadgarshah among the emirs giving allegiance to Shahrukh in 807/1404–05, while Taj al-Salmani states that he was serving Pir Muhammad, but, since the princes were allied, this may not be a contradiction (Jaʿfari, *Tārīkh-i kabīr*, 35; fol. 295a).

[87] *Muʿizz*, fol. 90a; Ḥāfiẓ-i Abrū, "Majmaʿ," fol. 12b.

[88] A relatively large number of emirs active during Shahrukh's life carry the title Tarkhan, only some of whom are clearly connected to Ghiyath al-Din. For Ghiyath al-Din's descent, see Manz, *Rise and Rule*, 186, n. 31.

[89] Faṣīḥ Khwāfī, *Mujmal-i faṣīḥī*, vol. III, 177, 225; Ḥāfiẓ-i Abrū, *Zubdat*, 636.

[90] Ḥāfiẓ-i Abrū, *Zubdat*, 666; Faṣīḥ Khwāfī, *Mujmal-i faṣīḥī*, vol. III, 230.

Ramadan, 813/December, 1410–January, 1411, Hamza was sent to Sawran by Shahmalik on the occasion of Shaykh Nur al-Din's second rebellion.[91]

On Shahrukh's expeditions against the troublesome sons of ʿUmar Shaykh in Fars the sons of Ghiyath al-Din are again prominent, some in assignments requiring particular trust.[92] Shahrukh's Kerman campaign to put down the insubordinate governor Sultan Uways included Hasan and Husayn Sufi, and in 820/1417–18 Muhammad Sufi is mentioned campaigning in the Qandahar region – he was among the emirs sent to pacify Badakhshan in the same year.[93] The high position of the Tarkhan emirs is attested also in the "Muʿizz al-ansab". Two are mentioned as *amīr dīwān* under Shahrukh, apparently sequentially; these are ʿAli and Hasan Sufi.[94] Muhammad Sufi is listed as *tovachi* and as leader of a *tümen* in the center of Shahrukh's army.[95] Taken together, this family provided Shahrukh with a group of particularly trusted servitors.

By about 820/1417–18 Shahrukh had thus at his disposal a well balanced and trained military elite which he used for military, provincial and *dīwān* affairs. The largest or most central provinces were in the hands of his sons but numerous other ones were governed by emirs. As we have seen, Yazd was governed by Amir Chaqmaq and Kerman by Amir Ghunashirin. The northern regions of Iran, stretching from Qum to Sultaniyya, were under the control of Ilyas Khwaja b. Shaykh ʿAli Bahadur, although his brother Yusuf Khwaja seems also to have had some responsibility in the region.[96] Along with Gawharshad's relatives, the most active and prominent emirs included ʿAlika Kukeltash, Firuzshah, Yadgarshah Arlat, Shaykh Lughman Barlas, Farmanshaykh, Midrab b. Chekü until his death in 817/1414–15 and, after him, his nephew Ibrahim b. Jahanshah b. Chekü. Two emirs who had rebelled from Shahrukh and served the princes of Fars until their downfall held a position only slightly lower: ʿAbd al-Samad b. Hajji Sayf al-Din and Yusuf Jalil. On Shahrukh's major campaigns he quite frequently sent off separate expeditions under emirs, and important tasks were sometimes left to Shahrukh's subordinates; the conquest of Khorezm was commanded by princes and emirs, as was the pacification of Badakhshan.[97] The highest corps of emirs were named as *amīr dīwān*, and apparently served in the

[91] Faṣīḥ Khwāfī, *Mujmal-i faṣīḥī*, vol. III, 193; Ḥāfiẓ-i Abrū, *Zubdat*, 363, 373, 412.

[92] Faṣīḥ Khwāfī, *Mujmal-i faṣīḥī*, vol. III, 216, 222; Ḥāfiẓ-i Abrū, *Zubdat*, 538. Shahrukh sent Hasan Sufi to relieve the governor of Sawa, under attack by Iskandar b. ʿUmar Shaykh. When he had taken Shiraz from Iskandar he sent Muhammad Sufi, with others, to fetch Iskandar's children. Another prominent emir called Sayyid ʿAli Tarkhan died in Shiraz in 817/1414, but his relationship to the family of Ghiyath al-Din is never elucidated (Faṣīḥ Khwāfī, *Mujmal-i faṣīḥī*, vol. III, 192, 210, 218; Ḥāfiẓ-i Abrū, *Zubdat*, 420, 469, 479, 540).

[93] Ḥāfiẓ-i Abrū, *Zubdat*, 631, 671, 676; Faṣīḥ Khwāfī, *Mujmal-i faṣīḥī*, vol. III, 226, 233.

[94] *Muʿizz*, fol. 133a; Ando, *Timuridische Emire*, 139–40.

[95] *Muʿizz*, fols. 133b, 136b, 137a. The right wing contained two emirs probably related: Muhammad Ghiyath Tarkhan and Khusraw Tarkhan (*Muʿizz*, fol. 135b).

[96] This is discussed in greater detail in Chapter 3.

[97] Ḥāfiẓ-i Abrū, *Zubdat*, 478–79, 676; Faṣīḥ Khwāfī, *Mujmal-i faṣīḥī*, vol. III, 233.

administration as well as the army. They were also used to conduct negotiations and to organize the taxes of regions brought under control.[98]

The middle period of Shahrukh's reign

In the middle part of his reign, Shahrukh received valuable service from his sons. They were active not only as provincial governors and military commanders, but also in central administrative affairs, where they helped to limit the power of both emirs and viziers. Shahrukh's eldest son Ulugh Beg, governor of Transoxiana, and Ibrahim Sultan, just a few months younger and governor of Fars, remained in their provinces except for short visits to the capital – and in the case of Ibrahim Sultan, participation in Shahrukh's major campaigns. Shahrukh's fourth son Soyurghatmish served as governor of smaller regions near the capital until his appointment to the region of Kabul in 821/1418, when he was about nineteen. Two of Shahrukh's sons spent much of their time in Herat while also serving as governors of nearby provinces. The elder, Baysunghur, was only seven at the time of Temür's death but began his active career fairly soon thereafter. We find him left in charge of Herat along with senior emirs in 813/1410–11 when Shahrukh campaigned in Transoxiana. In early 818/1415, at the age of seventeen, he was given the governorship of Mazandaran and eastern Khorasan. A year or two later he was formally appointed to a position of oversight in Shahrukh's *dīwān*; this in addition to managing a *dīwān* of his own. Shahrukh's youngest surviving son was Muhammad Juki, whose active career seems to begin with the first Azarbaijan campaign in 823–24/1420–21, where he is mentioned leading troops.[99] Although ʿAbd al-Razzaq Samarqandī states that Muhammad Juki was not given access to the central *dīwān*, the same historian gives us an account of his investigation into financial irregularities.[100] Shahrukh also used his sons for special missions requiring status and finesse. Both Baysunghur and Muhammad Juki were sent on occasion to deal with difficult local rulers or frontier regions.[101]

The years following Shahrukh's first Azarbaijan campaign were the most peaceful and secure of his reign. In the 820s/1417–27 Shahrukh faced only minor pressure from border powers. When threats did arise, they were quite

98 See for example: Faṣīḥ Khwāfī, *Mujmal-i faṣīḥī*, vol. III, 242–43; Ḥāfiẓ-i Abrū, *Zubdat*, 363, 383, 515–17, 598, 670–71.

99 Ḥāfiẓ-i Abrū, *Zubdat*, 771. Before this we find him accompanying Ulugh Beg to Transoxiana, but not apparently in a military role (Ḥāfiẓ-i Abrū, *Zubdat*, 665, 705, 745).

100 Samarqandī, *Maṭlaʿ*, 793, 851–52.

101 Muhammad Juki for instance was assigned to take an army into Transoxiana when Ulugh Beg planned an expedition of which Shahrukh disapproved, and was later sent to pacify the lands of Garmsir and the Afghans (Ḥāfiẓ-i Abrū, *Zubdat*, 771; Samarqandī, *Maṭlaʿ*, 665). Baysunghur was in charge of several missions during the rebellion of prince Qaydu in 821/1418–19 and on Shahrukh's first Azarbaijan campaign (Ḥāfiẓ-i Abrū, *Zubdat*, 681–92, 736–42).

easily dealt with and in the border provinces Shahrukh's realm continued to expand at a modest rate. Ibrahim Sultan undertook several successful campaigns in Khuzistan, while Ulugh Beg led occasional expeditions against the eastern Chaghadayids and succeeded in imposing his own governor over Kashghar. In Ramadan, 825/August–September, 1422 one of the commanders of Iskandar Qaraqoyunlu raided Sultaniyya but was badly defeated in battle by its governor, Ilyas Khwaja. Shahrukh sent troops to reinforce the area.[102] Like other rulers of the period, Shahrukh had to deal with challenges in the religious sphere, in particular the messianic movements which flourished during the period. The first of these occurred in 827/1423–24 in Khuttalan, when a follower of the Kubrawi shaykh Ishaq Khuttalani declared himself *mahdī* (messiah). Shahrukh executed the aged Ishaq Khuttalani, but allowed the aspiring *mahdī*, Muhammad Nurbakhsh, to escape with a scolding and exile to central Iran.

It is just after these events, in the late 820s to 830/1426–27, that we find another spate of historical writing. It began in Fars, where from about 822/1419–20, Sharaf al-Din ʿAli Yazdi had been working on a major compilation commissioned by Ibrahim Sultan intended be a universal history from Adam through the Mongols, including a biography of Temür himself, entitled *Ẓafarnāma*. In fact, Yazdi wrote only the biography of Temür and an introduction. Just a little before Yazdi's work was finished, in 830/1426–27, Ḥafiẓ-i Abrū completed his world history, in which he incorporated Rashid al-Din's *Jamiʿ al-tawarikh* and other works, adding narrative text to connect the different parts. For the career of Temür he used the *Ẓafarnama* of Nizam al-Din Shami, with significant additions within the text. One of his additions was a genealogy of the Barlas tribe and an account of its connection to the Chaghadayid dynasty. The story was an elaborated version of the legitimation myth begun under Temür, according to which Qarachar, the Barlas chief of Chinggis Khan's time, had been assigned to Chaghatay as chief advisor of the Chaghadayid house, and had passed on this post to his descendants, down to Temür and his dynasty. An earlier version of this story had been included in the history of Muʿin al-Din Natanzi written originally for Iskandar b. ʿUmar Shaykh, probably the source for Ḥāfiẓ-i Abrū's account.[103]

The final section of Ḥāfiẓ-i Abrū's history, covering Shahrukh's reign, was dedicated to prince Baysunghur and entitled *Zubdat al-tawarikh-i Baysunghuri*. It seems likely that this dedication was in answer to the work about to come out in Fars and designed to emphasize Baysunghur's position as governor. There is little doubt that Baysunghur and Shahrukh would have

[102] Ḥāfiẓ-i Abrū, *Zubdat*, 864–65; Faruk Sümer, *Kara Koyunlular* (Ankara: Türk Tarih Kurumu Basımevi, 1967), 125–26.

[103] John Woods, "The Rise of Tīmūrīd Historiography," *Journal of Near Eastern Studies* 46, 2 (1987), 81–108, 93.

known about the work in progress, since the princes corresponded and showed great interest in each other's literary and artistic patronage. During this same year, 830/1427, Shahrukh commissioned a new version of Rashid al-Din's *Shuʿab-i panjgana*, a genealogy of the Chinggisid house; the new version, called the *Muʿizz al-ansab*, added the genealogy of the Barlas and the Timurid house. Shortly after this, by 831/1427–28, Yazdi completed his *Zafarnama*. At the beginning of the work, not included in all copies, there was an introduction giving both a genealogy of the Barlas tribe and a history of its connection to the Chaghadayid dynasty, similar to that found in Ḥāfiẓ-i Abrū. These works were the last major historical chronicles completed during Shahrukh's life, and they display Timurid legitimation in its completed form.[104]

The years from 830 to 832/1426 to 1429 brought both challenges and misfortunes. On 16 Muharram, 830/November 17, 1426, Shahrukh's son Soyurghatmish, governor of Kabul, died at the age of twenty-eight. Shortly after hearing the news, Shahrukh faced a new challenge from a religious movement. On 23 Rabiʿ I, 830/January 22, 1427, a member of the Hurufi sect, whose founder had shown political ambitions and had been executed by Amiranshah during Temür's reign, made an attempt on Shahrukh's life as he left the cathedral mosque after the Friday prayers. Shahrukh was only lightly wounded, but reacted strongly to the event. He undertook an investigation and had numerous people connected to the Hurufis executed or exiled. The level of the threat that this event posed to Shahrukh's prestige is indicated by the generosity with which he conciliated the population afterwards through the cancellation of taxes and lavish distribution of alms.[105] Later the same year, Shahrukh had to cope with a crisis caused by Ulugh Beg in Transoxiana. In 829/1425–26 Baraq, a pretender to the throne of the Golden Horde, who had been a protégé of Ulugh Beg's, laid claim to the region of Signaq and raided the area. Ulugh Beg wanted to go against him and when Shahrukh forbade the expedition he went anyway, along with his brother Muhammad Juki. Their army was badly defeated and returned to Samarqand in disorder. When he had recovered from his wound, Shahrukh came to Transoxiana and removed Ulugh Beg temporarily from his governorship.

In 831/1428, Iskandar Qaraqoyunlu plundered Timurid territories and in 832/1428–29 succeeded in taking a number of Shahrukh's western cities, including Sultaniyya. This Shahrukh could not accept, and once again he gathered an army from the Timurid provinces and marched against the Qaraqoyunlu. After winning a decisive battle at Salmas on 18 Dhuʾl-Hijja, 832/September 18, 1429, Shahrukh installed Qara Yusuf's youngest son Abu Saʿid as governor of Azarbaijan and returned to Herat. Although Abu Saʿid

104 Manz, "Family and Ruler," 64–68. 105 Ḥāfiẓ-i Abrū, *Zubdat*, 907–23.

did not long retain his governorship, rivalry within the Qaraqoyunlu provided Shahrukh several years of peace.[106]

Shifts in the balance of power

There were two separate underlying causes for the increasing difficulties which would face the regime in the 840s/1436–46 – first the growth of outside powers who posed a threat to the Timurid borders, and second, a gradual attrition in the ranks of Shahrukh's senior sons and followers. For a number of years after Shahrukh's victories in Transoxiana and Fars, we see a relatively stable group of senior commanders mentioned on almost all of his campaigns. As time went on however, the deaths of high-ranking emirs brought about a shift in the power relationships and an increasing concentration of power in the hands of relatively few men. When they died, emirs usually passed their positions on to their relatives, but the younger generation often held less power. During the 830s/1426–36 Shahrukh was able to deal effectively with the challenges confronting him, but later the balance changed and the regime was beset with increasing problems.

The earliest changes are seen in two particularly important families – those of Temür's follower Chekü and Shahrukh's wife Gawharshad. Midrab b. Chekü Barlas, son of one of Temür's earliest and most faithful followers, served loyally and prominently until his death in 817/1414. His position apparently passed on to his nephew Ibrahim b. Jahanshah b. Chekü, who played a prominent role until he was demoted for unspecified misbehavior while he was governor of Isfahan in 832/1428–29. He died about a year later.[107] From this time until the end of Shahrukh's life no members of this highly influential family appear in Shahrukh's top command, although we know that they kept their holdings in Qunduz and Baghlan, which supported a large corps of soldiers.[108] Their absence from the central positions of government presents a strong contrast to their earlier role.

The emirs related to Gawharshad remained among Shahrukh's most prominent commanders through the first Azarbaijan campaign. When Shahrukh went against the Qaraqoyunlu in 823/1420–21 he appointed Sayyid Ahmad to the highly important position of temporary governor of Khorasan, and Hasan Sufi was prominent in his army.[109] After this the relatives of Ghiyath al-Din Tarkhan appear to have declined in importance, due probably to the

[106] Faruk Sümer, "Ḳarā-Ḳoyunlu," *Encyclopaedia of Islam*, 2nd edn; Samarqandī, *Maṭlaʿ*, 320–31.

[107] Ando, *Timuridische Emire*, 127–32; Ḥāfiẓ-i Abrū, *Zubdat*, 631, 670, 676, 588, 761, 790; Faṣīḥ Khwāfī, *Mujmal-i faṣīḥī*, vol. III, 226; Jaʿfari, *Tārīkh-i kabīr*, 78.

[108] Ando, *Timuridische Emire*, 131. A more distantly related member of this family, Sultan Bayazid b. Nurmalik Barlas, listed as *amīr dīwān*, was still alive at Shahrukh's death (*Muʿizz*, fols. 92b, 93a, 132b; Hāfiẓ-i Abrū, *Zubdat*, 558; Ando, *Timuridische Emire*, 130–32).

[109] Ḥāfiẓ-i Abrū, *Zubdat*, 714; ʿAbd al-Ḥusayn Nawāʾī (ed.), *Asnād wa makātibāt-i tārīkhī-i Īrān* (Tehran: Bungāh-i Tarjuma wa Nashr-i Kitāb, 2536/1977), 200, 203; Faṣīḥ Khwāfī, *Mujmal-i faṣīḥī*, vol. III, 240, 251.

deaths of several of them, starting a few years earlier. Hamza died in Samarqand in Rabiʿ I, 819/May, 1416 and Husayn Sufi is not mentioned in the histories after 819/1416–17. ʿAli died on 22 Rajab, 820/September 4, 1417, passing his position as *amīr dīwān* to his brother Hasan Sufi, who himself died on 5 Rajab, 827/June 3, 1424.[110] It seems probable that several of these men were relatively young and left their posts to immature sons. We know that Hasan Sufi's position as head of the *dīwān* emirs passed on to his son Mihrab Tarkhan, but of Mihrab's we only know that he died in 835/1431 and that his son, Muhammad, served in the left wing of the army and died in 844/1440.[111] The one senior member of the family who remained was Muhammad Sufi Tarkhan. On Shahrukh's second Azarbaijan campaign he appears to have been left in charge of Herat, and in 835/1431–32 he was one of the emirs sent with the prince Bayqara to Mazandaran to guard against Uzbek attacks.[112] From this date until Shahrukh's death, however, we have no record of Muhammad Sufi's activities.

There is no information in the sources about other relatives of Ghiyath al-Din. One reason for the silence of the sources on the Tarkhan emirs may be the small number of major campaigns in the latter half of Shahrukh's reign, which results in less attention in the histories to the activities of emirs. It is probable however that the children of Gawharshad's brothers were too young to win themselves the influence held by their fathers and lost power to the circle of senior emirs and princes around Shahrukh. It is notable in this context that the bureaucrat and historian Fasih Khwafi, who served briefly under ʿAli Tarkhan and highlights the activities of his relatives, records little beyond the date of their deaths in the latter part of his history.[113] Another indication that the relatives of Ghiyath al-Din Tarkhan held less prominence is their apparent lack of construction activity at a time when Shahrukh's major emirs sponsored numerous buildings.[114]

It is probable that the corps of emirs under Shahrukh was becoming smaller. Since Shahrukh was appointed governor of Khorasan at the age of about twenty and was only twenty-seven at Temür's death, many of the emirs who served him during his rise to power were older than he. The majority of people listed as *dīwān* emirs in the "Muʿizz al-ansab" lived early in his reign. Most of those who died were succeeded by relatives, but some positions appear to have lapsed. There is no obvious successor to several of Shahrukh's emirs who rebelled in Shahrukh's early years – Sulaymanshah b. Daʾud, Pir Muhammad b. Pulad, and Lutf Allah b. Buyan Temür.[115] Often younger

110 Ḥāfiẓ-i Abrū, *Zubdat*, 636; Faṣīḥ Khwāfī, *Mujmal-i faṣīḥī*, vol. III, 224–25, 229, 255; Ando, *Timuridische Emire*, 139. Sayyid ʿAli died in Rabiʿ II, 825/March–April, 1422 (Faṣīḥ Khwāfī, *Mujmal-i faṣīḥī*, vol. III, 251).
111 Samarqandī, *Maṭlaʿ*, vol. II, 2, 640; Faṣīḥ Khwāfī, *Mujmal-i faṣīḥī*, vol. III, 270, 288; Ando, *Timuridische Emire*, 139.
112 Nawāʾī, *Asnād*, 219; for Mazandaran see Samarqandī, *Maṭlaʿ*, 639, and Faṣīḥ Khwāfī, *Mujmal-i faṣīḥī*, vol. III, 270.
113 Faṣīḥ Khwāfī, *Mujmal-i faṣīḥī*, vol. III, 220 and *passim*.
114 See Chapter 4.
115 "Muʿizz," fols. 132b–33a.

relatives inherited only some of the offices that their predecessor had held. For instance, while Hasan Jandar passed his *tümen* on to his son Yusuf Jalil, his place as *amīr dīwān* seems to have remained empty.[116]

It is clear then that by 830/1426–27 a large number of the emirs, powerful during Shahrukh's early career, had died and their relatives had inherited only part of their power. In the accounts of Shahrukh's later campaigns, significantly fewer emirs are mentioned than in earlier ones.[117] It is possible that the difference in the number of emirs mentioned in the "Muʿizz al-ansab" and in the histories is in part due to the character of the materials available to us.[118] Nonetheless the character of the sources probably does not account for all the change we see in Shahrukh's corp of emirs, particularly during the latter part of his reign.

The period from 832/1428–29 to the mid-840s/c. 1441–2 saw the death of many of the commanders close to Shahrukh, and an intensification of the power of those who remained. ʿAbd al-Samad b. Sayf al-Din, who had served as governor in Afghan territory and then in Isfahan, died in 835/1432.[119] Khwaja Yusuf, governor of the region of Rayy and Qum, died in 836/1432–33 and his aged father, Ilyās Khwaja b. Shaykh ʿAli Bahadur, died in 838/1434 after years of inactivity. Two members of the family remained, each with half of the former province, Khwaja Yusuf's brother Muhammad Mirum in the region of Sultaniyya and his uncle Yusuf Khwaja in Rayy.[120]

The loss of experienced commanders was problematical because the Timurid's steppe neighbors were now becoming more assertive. In early 838/fall, 1434, Shahrukh learned that Iskandar Qaraqoyunlu had begun to expand his power and attack Shahrukh's local vassals. This news triggered Shahrukh's third Azarbaijan campaign from Rabiʿ II, 838/November, 1434 to Rabiʿ II, 840/October, 1436. Iskandar retreated, allowing Shahrukh to retake Azarbaijan almost without military activity, and to install Jahanshah Qaraqoyunlu as his vassal. In 834/1430–31 the Uzbeks, newly organized under Abūʾl Khayr Khan, began to attack Shahrukh's borders in Khorezm; they

116 Ibid., fols. 132b–33a, 135b, 137a; Samarqandī, *Maṭlaʿ*, vol. II, 2, 700.

117 See for instance the accounts of the three Azarbaijan campaigns, where princes and provincial governors play an increasingly large role, while fewer regular emirs are mentioned (Ḥāfiẓ-i Abrū, *Zubdat*, 709–42; Samarqandī, *Maṭlaʿ*, 320–32, 671–75, 683–91; Faṣīḥ Khwāfī, *Mujmal-i faṣīḥī*, vol. III, 240, 242, 246, 247, 263–64, 266, 278; Abū Bakr Ṭihrānī Iṣfahānī, *Kitāb-i Diyārbakriyya*, edited by N. Lugal and F. Sümer [Ankara: Türk Tarih Kurumu Basımevi, 1962–4], 109; Jaʿfari, *Tārīkh-i kabīr*, 75, 80; fols. 310a, 313b).

118 The "Muʿizz al-ansab" was commissioned by Shahrukh in 830/1426–27 but the surviving recensions are clearly from a later date. It is possible that the coverage of the period up to the first recension is more complete than the sections added later. The major historian of Shahrukh's later reign is ʿAbd al-Razzaq Samarqandi, whose composition reveals a bias towards the ulama. We find the deaths of important emirs but little on their military activities.

119 Ḥāfiẓ-i Abrū, *Zubdat*, 671; Fasīh Khwāfī, *Mujmal-i faṣīḥī*, vol. III, 232, 270; Jaʿfari, *Tārīkh-i kabīr*, 74–5, 78; fols. 309b–10a, 312a.

120 Faṣīḥ Khwāfī, *Mujmal-i faṣīḥī*, vol. III, 270, 271, 279; Samarqandī, *Maṭlaʿ*, 629.

captured the northern part of the region in 839/1435–36, and posed a constant threat, so that every year Shahrukh sent a large army to Mazandaran to protect the border.[121] By the late 830s/1432–35 the eastern Chaghadayids had begun to gain ground on the eastern border and around 838/1434–35 they retook Kashghar. The death of two of Shahrukh's powerful sons – Baysunghur on 7 Jumadi I, 837/December 20, 1433 and Ibrahim Sultan on 4 Shawwal, 838/ May 3, 1435 – left a large gap in the power structure. Baysunghur was active in the central *dīwān* and held the strategic region of Mazandaran, important in the defense against the Uzbeks. Ibrahim Sultan governed Fars, which was the chief locus for Timurid power in central and southern Iran. Both left behind them sons who were too young to govern on their own. Ibrahim Sultan's son and successor ʿAbd Allah was only two years old.[122] The year 838/1434–35 then brought a devastating plague in Herat and Khorasan, killing a large number of people, including many of the ulama.[123]

At this time there was still no crisis within the realm, but in the 840s/1436–46, when Shahrukh was in his sixties and his most senior emirs began to die, his control was seriously shaken. The first of these deaths was that of Ghunashirin, in 840/1436. While his army and the governance of Kerman passed to his sons, notably Hajji Muhammad, early reports from the province were not favorable.[124] These tales could have reflected the actual mismanagement in the province, but may also suggest the more vulnerable position held by Ghunashirin's sons. In the next year, 841/1437–38, two of Shahrukh's most trusted followers died: Shaykh Lughman Barlas and Yadgarshah Arlat. While Shaykh Lughman's position went to his son, we hear nothing of Yadgarshah's family until after Shahrukh's death.[125] On 7 Safar, 843/July 29, 1439, came the death of another major emir, Farmanshaykh. Farmanshaykh's name appears repeatedly in the histories and in the "Muʿizz al-ansab" in positions of trust, and he had governed Herat during Shahrukh's third Azarbaijan campaign in 838/1435.[126]

As the top ranks of Shahrukh's administration thinned, the power of the remaining inner circle, most notably ʿAlika and Firuzshah, had begun to reach proportions that aroused resentment. The two emirs became symbolic of emiral power and access to the ruler.[127] We are informed that the governors of Herat did not dare dismiss the *kotwal* of the Ikhtiyar al-Din fortress, whose behavior was openly outrageous, because he was the relative of ʿAlika. This

[121] Samarqandī, *Maṭlaʿ*, 633–40, 687–88, 749–50. [122] Ibid., 652–57, 676.
[123] Ibid., 677–82; Faṣīḥ Khwāfī, *Mujmal-i faṣīḥī*, vol. III, 275–78.
[124] Aubin, *Deux sayyids*, 53; Samarqandī, *Maṭlaʿ*, 847.
[125] Samarqandī, *Maṭlaʿ*, 700, 702; Ando, *Timuridische Emire*, 170. The "Muʿizz al-ansab" lists a Baydu Arlat as leader of a *tümen* under Baysunghur but there is no evidence to link him directly to Yadgarshah (Ando, *Timuridische Emire*, 169; *Muʿizz*, fols. 136a, 137a, 144b).
[126] *Muʿizz*, fol. 136b; Samarqandī, *Maṭlaʿ*, 673, 738.
[127] Kāshifī, *Rashaḥāt*, 184; Jean Aubin, (ed.), *Matériaux pour la biographie de Shah Niʿmatullah Wali Kermani* (Tehran, Paris: Bibliothèque Iranienne, 1956), 67, 200; Muʿīn al-Dīn Zamchī Isfizārī, *Rawḍāt al-jannāt fī awṣāf madīnat Harāt*, edited by Sayyid Muḥammad Kāẓim Imām (Tehran: Dānishgāh-i Tihrān, 1338/1959), 85.

man apparently used to keep low company (*awbāsh*) and go after both women and boys. He would come ceremoniously out of the fortress to the roll of drums and proceed to the bazaar, where he would drink wine solidly for a couple of days, to the accompaniment of a continued drum fanfare. Since drums were a symbol of royal power and authority, their use in this situation seems remarkable; this story, however, is reported in ʿAbd al-Razzaq Samarqandī's history, the standard account of Shahrukh's reign. Despite his behavior, this *kotwal* was replaced in office only on his death in Jumadi I, 841/November, 1437, and then by his brother, fortunately better behaved.[128] It is interesting to note that Shahrukh's second theatrical pouring out of wine, when he emptied the wine houses of his son Muhammad Juki and his grandson ʿAlaʾ al-Dawla, occurred after this, in 844/1440–41.[129]

When ʿAlika died on 17 Jumadi I, 844/October 14, 1440 his office passed to his son Shaykh Abuʾl Fadl, who held much less influence.[130] The years that followed were difficult ones both in the provinces and in the central government and we begin to see signs of disorder. In this same year, the Uzbeks attacked Mazandaran and defeated Shahrukh's forces, killing another one of Shahrukh's important commanders, Hajji Yusuf Jalil.[131] In Central Asia, the eastern Chaghadayids were regularly plundering the region of Andijan, while the Uzbeks raided the northern borders of Transoxiana. In Fars real power had become so concentrated in the hands of ʿAbd Allah b. Ibrahim Sultan's chief advisor, Muhibb al-Din Abuʾl Khayr b. Muhammad Jazari, that the other personnel of the provincial court complained to Shahrukh.[132] In 845/1441–42 we hear of an unexplained disturbance by the prince Jalal al-Din b. Rustam, whose father had been governor of Isfahan.[133]

In the central government, 845/1441–42 was a year of strife and upheaval, involving several of the people closest to the sovereign. In Safar, 845/July, 1441, a scandal broke out in the *dīwān* which was serious enough to require Shahrukh's involvement and led first to a major investigation by Firuzshah, and then to the dismissal of the second most powerful vizier, against the will of the highest functionary of the *dīwān*.[134] During the same year, Gawharshad's preference for her grandson ʿAlaʾ al-Dawla b. Baysunghur over other descendants became so marked that her grandsons complained and Shahrukh rebuked her.[135]

The death in 846/1442 of Yusuf Khwaja b. Shaykh ʿAli Bahadur, who had taken over the defense of the region of Rayy on the death of his brother Khwaja Yusuf left a further gap in the high command and in provincial leadership.[136] The post was given to Baysunghur's son Sultan Muhammad, who used it as a

[128] Samarqandī, *Maṭlaʿ*, 701–2. [129] Ibid., 739–41. [130] Ibid., 746–7, 842. [131] Ibid., 749.
[132] Ibid., 756. [133] Ibid., 763. [134] This event is discussed in detail in Chapter 3.
[135] Samarqandī, *Maṭlaʿ*, 759. The complaint was lodged by Ulugh Beg's son ʿAbd al-Latif; we cannot be certain that the issue of succession was the major one here, but it soon became a central problem.
[136] Ando, *Timuridische Emire*, 136; Bernard O'Kane, *Timurid Architecture in Khurasan* (Costa Mesta, CA: Mazda, 1987), 185.

base for independent power.[137] The vacuum left by the deaths of most of the preeminent emirs and princes now allowed Amir Firuzshah to assume enormous control under an aging ruler, and he appears to have abused his position. In 847/1443–44 sufficient evidence of irregularities had accumulated that Shahrukh ordered his son Muhammad Juki to investigate *dīwān* affairs, and this time the investigation was aimed at Firuzshah's areas of responsibility. When Shahrukh became gravely ill in late 847 and early 848/ March–June, 1444, the news spread rapidly and brought on disturbances throughout his realm. Gawharshad pushed Firuzshah to back her choice of ʿAlaʾ al-Dawla as successor, a move which angered the other princes. When Shahrukh had recovered from his illness, the *dīwān* investigation continued and showed proof of serious problems; Firuzshah was unable to bear the disgrace, which quickly brought about his illness and death.[138] Muhammad Juki died later the same year.[139] At just about this time, Shahrukh began to hear alarming accounts of the behavior of Sultan Muhammad, governor of northern Iran. Both Sultan Muhammad and the population of his region had noticed the weakness of Shahrukh's rule and begun to consider how to improve their own positions. It was Sultan Muhammad's open rebellion in 850/1446–47 that caused the campaign on which Shahrukh died, on 25 Dhuʾl-Hijja, 850/March 13, 1447.

Conclusion

During his rise to power and his early reign, Shahrukh was able to attract and keep a group of Turco-Mongolian commanders who served him competently and loyally for many years. In the last twenty years of his life, and particularly in the last ten, however, we see progressive attrition within the corps of experienced emirs on whom he counted in the administration of army, *dīwān* and provinces. Since most offices were hereditary, the age and experience of an emir's sons at the time of his death was a crucial issue. Power within both army and administration moreover was dependent as much on the person as the office; no matter what position an emir inherited, his influence had to be won through his own efforts. The lack of major campaigns probably contributed to the problem. In a realm largely at peace and no longer expanding, young men had little opportunity to gain experience and power before they inherited the place of their fathers. Since Shahrukh, unlike his father, left details to his subordinates and interfered only on matters of importance, the change from experienced to inexperienced personnel caused serious harm. For this reason the balance of power within the top administration gradually broke down, and by the time of Firuzshah's death in 848/1444–45 abuses of power were clearly apprehended and solidly resented. The events of the years 847–49/1444–46 shook a realm which could no longer withstand such shocks.

[137] Samarqandī, *Maṭlaʿ*, 772. [138] Ibid., 793, 838–41.
[139] Ibid., 851–53. Samarqandi does not give an exact date for his death.

CHAPTER 2

Issues of sources and historiography

When we attempt to analyze the medieval Middle East we subject ourselves to severe frustration, particularly if we try to connect social structure to the political history of sovereign dynasties. For all the thousands of pages of history, biography, and geography which have come down to us, and for all their wealth of incident, the material is fragmentary, repetitious and tendentious. Historians of Iran and Central Asia are at a particular disadvantage because the detailed biographical material so useful for Mamluk history is not replicated in the Persian tradition. Biographies certainly exist, but they are usually shorter and less systematic. Furthermore, local historiographical traditions are rarely focused on the largest and most central cities. Nonetheless, we must be grateful for the existence of our sources and if we face their problems squarely we can enjoy the delights they do offer. The materials on Timurid history are plentiful, and the major ones have been well described and analyzed.[1] Instead of reviewing texts and filiations therefore, I will use this chapter to discuss some historiographical issues relevant to this inquiry and to explain how I have tried to work around the difficulties confronting me. The goal of this study, to understand the politics within and among different groups, requires a particularly careful use of the available material because the information I am seeking is not what these sources are designed to give the reader.

We can rarely find out all we wish about the people in any one group. Information provided is determined by the genre of literature in which people are discussed, and almost all texts systematically shape material in ways that can mislead the historian. As scholars have shown, medieval historians wrote history as literature, applying ideas of causation and purpose very different from those we currently use; these were moral tales, concerned with a judgment of rulers and dynastic legitimacy. Discussions of the individual personality

[1] See John Woods, "Tīmūrīd Historiography," 81–108; Shiro Ando, "Die timuridische Historiographie II: Šaraf al-Dīn ʿAlī Yazdī," *Studia Iranica* 24, 2 (1995), 219–46; Sholeh Quinn, "The *Muʿizz al-Ansāb* and *Shuʿab-i Panjgānah* as Sources for the Chaghatayid Period of History: A Comparative Analysis," *Central Asiatic Journal* 33 (1989), 229–53.

of protagonists are usually short and invariably stylized.[2] The narrative histories are the only sources which present solid chronological information and describe the activities of the dynasty and the military. These were the groups who determined much of political history and their involvement in agricultural and city life made them also a major factor in the social and economic spheres. Timurid historians do occasionally allow themselves some individual characterization of members of the dynasty, whose salient traits may receive a sentence or two. The actors beneath these men – the Chaghatay emirs – remain largely undifferentiated. We can sometimes chart the approximate course of their careers, but when it comes to even an idealized depiction of personalities, social milieu or relationships, the histories have almost nothing to say. Unlike the emirs of the Mamluk Sultanate, the Chaghatay emirs were not contenders for supreme power, and perhaps it is for this reason that they are not a subject for systematic discussion.

Most other members of the elite are memorialized primarily in biographical literature. Here we are offered almost exactly the opposite information we find in dynastic histories. Chronology and narrative play little part, while achievement, personal relationships and character take center stage. In the case of religious figures portrayal of character is idealized and the fondness for telling anecdote and the liberal use of *topoi* shape the narrative. Nonetheless, we are able to make out some aspects of the milieu of the religious classes (urban and rural), ulama and Sufi. When we come to poets and viziers, the ideal of behavior matters less and the amusement value of the anecdote more – thus, what emerges is a lively portrait of personalities and relationships. With viziers we are most fortunate, since those at the top were considered sufficiently important politically to be mentioned in narrative histories and thus we can to some extent reconstruct the chronology of their careers. For all other types of people chronological information is sadly lacking, and it is rarely possible to follow one individual reliably from youth to old age. Perhaps the greatest problem in biographical literature is its division into set categories. The way in which biographical collections are presented and the different character traits they present encourage us to see each different group as distinct and separate. Since the writer's interest lies within the profession discussed, accomplishments, family connections, and actions which relate to this profession will be highlighted, and those which do not are usually omitted. Thus, while biographies give us the fullest information we have, we must realize that they are systematically distorted.

One major obstacle to a balanced analysis of medieval society is the role that chance has played in both the writing and the preservation of source

[2] Peter Hardy, *Historians of Medieval India: Studies in Indo-Muslim Historical Writing* (London: Luzac, 1960), 18, 43, 51, 88, 118, 124; R. Stephen Humphreys, *Islamic History: A Framework for Inquiry* (Princeton: Princeton University Press, 1991), 128–47; Julie S. Meisami, *Persian Historiography to the End of the Twelfth Century* (Edinburgh: Edinburgh University Press, 1999), 280–89.

material. Historiographical traditions varied widely; some regions had a tradition of narrative history, while others produced primarily religious literature. Certain cities and regions produced historians for generation after generation, while others produced few or none for centuries together. We cannot therefore assume that the most central areas or people will be the ones most fully described. Furthermore, both histories and biographies were written by individuals who belonged not only to a certain profession, but also to a particular family and circle which determined their view of who and what mattered. The writer's personal milieu determined the people he knew and those he highlighted. All historians write at least some years after the events they describe and people still alive, or with powerful descendants, were likely to have influenced what was remembered. Like the location of historical traditions, the character and position of individual historians is the result of happenstance. The modern historian must take this into account. It is natural to infer that the people most often mentioned and those to whom important decisions are credited were those who wielded power. However, they may just as well have been those best known to the historian who happened to record the events of the period.

The first issue is what was written and what has survived to the present, and that is what I shall address first. The dynasty's needs and local historiographical traditions together influenced what histories were written and when, and their coverage has naturally determined what can be studied for this period. I will then move on to an examination of the personal networks of the major dynastic historians and how their relationships affected the picture they presented. There are also broader differences among historians, particularly between those with a strong local interest and those more exclusively focused on the central government. The information added by historians with a local perspective can help to counter the picture of a narrowly constituted power elite given by the court historians. Finally I will discuss some of the religious sources, notably the Sufi *tadhkira* literature. Here my greatest concern is the shift in viewpoint accompanying the rapid change in the Sufi *ṭarīqas* during the early Timurid period. Because my major concerns lies in the way that sources can be used together, I will not give a systematic listing of the major sources according to genre, but will introduce each source at the time that it is most fully discussed.

Geographical and social coverage

The central historian for the early part of Shahrukh's reign was Ḥāfiẓ-i Abrū, who began his career under Temür and died in 833/1430, after completing several major works for Shahrukh. Ḥāfiẓ-i Abrū appears to be careful with chronology and sober in his estimation of character and causation. For each year he chronicles the major events from the standpoint of Shahrukh's government and then summarizes events in other parts of the Timurid realm. In the early period this includes Azarbaijan, Transoxiana and Fars (with Isfahan) but after 816/1413–14 he includes Azarbaijan only when the events there directly affected the Timurids. The major focus of the history is dynastic and military; all important campaigns are described and major emirs are listed on these campaigns, but there is little about ulama or the cultural patronage of the court.

For the second part of Shahrukh's reign the fullest history is that of ʿAbd al-Razzaq Samarqandī, whose chronicle, the *Matlaʿ al-saʿdayn wa majmaʿ al-bahrayn*, was written in 875/1470. Like Ḥāfiẓ-i Abrū's work, this is a dynastic history written for the ruler and focusing particularly on the activities of the central court. On events up to 830/1426–27, Samarqandī's work is based on Ḥāfiẓ-i Abrū's history with a few additions; the rest, original Samarqandī, retains the chronicle organization of Ḥāfiẓ-i Abrū but gives greater attention to biographical materials and to *dīwān* and religious affairs.[3] Unfortunately Samarqandī did not continue to record the events of Fars and Transoxiana, so our knowledge of these areas declines after 830/1426–7.

Ḥāfiẓ-i Abrū and ʿAbd al-Razzaq Samarqandī pay scant attention to matters not related directly to the sovereign and with only these works political analysis would be difficult if not impossible. Fortunately, we have another major historical source commissioned by the dynasty which adds enormously valuable material on the dynasty and the Chaghatay emirs. This is the *Muʿizz al-ansāb fī shajarat al-ansāb*, an anonymous work written in 830/1426–27 on Shahrukh's orders. It is a detailed genealogy of the Chinggisid dynasty and the Barlas tribe, which lists wives, concubines, and officials under each member of the dynasty who held either a governorship or the sultanate. The work is solidly centered on the dynasty and their Chaghatay followers; military and court offices usually reserved for Chaghatay personnel are listed in detail, but of Persian office holders only the viziers and the *ṣadr* appear, usually without notation. The *Muʿizz al-ansab* sometimes notes dates of birth and death, relationships among emirs, and tribal affiliation. We can find out here who was responsible for the upbringing of dynastic children, a task usually entrusted to one of the sovereign's wives, the wife of a senior member of the dynasty, or an emir's wife. There are, likewise, occasional mentions of disloyalty on the part of emirs which do not appear in the histories.[4]

Fortunately for us, local historians often sought favor from dynastic patrons. Southern Iran and Khorasan had strong historiographical traditions and their historians produced several histories for the Timurids, which ostensibly covered the history of the world, but, nonetheless, bore a regional stamp;

[3] See W. Bartol'd and Muhammad Shafi, "ʿAbd al-Razzāḳ Kamāl al-Dīn b. Djalāl al-Dīn Isḥāḳ al-Samarḳandī," in *Encyclopaedia of Islam*, 2nd edn.

[4] See Ando, *Timuridische Emire*, and Quinn, "The *Muʿizz al-Ansāb*."

thus we know considerably more about these areas than most others. Since the historians from Khorasan are discussed later in the chapter I will concentrate on other local historians here.

Three historians were active in southern Iran during Shahrukh's life, all of them from Yazd. Among them they produced two histories of Yazd, centering on buildings, and several world histories. The oldest of the authors was Ja'far b. Muhammad b. Hasan Ja'fari, about whom we know very little. He was a Husayni sayyid, who seems to have begun his career under the Muzaffarid rulers of Yazd and have gone into the service of Shahrukh's governor, Amir Chaqmaq, whom he probably accompanied on Shahrukh's third Azarbaijan campaign. He was also a poet, who wrote verse for the buildings of the rulers. His best known work is the *Tarikh-i Yazd*, a discussion of the buildings and graves of Yazd, giving details of the date of construction, patron, and occupant. He also wrote two narrative histories, the *Tarikh-i wasit*, a world history to 817/1414, written about 820/1417 and dedicated to Shahrukh, and the "Tarikh-i kabir," a world history to 850/1447, written, probably, within a few years of Shahrukh's death.[5] A little later another historian, Ahmad b. Husayn b. 'Ali Katib, wrote a new and expanded version of the history of Yazd. We know almost nothing about the author, except that he states he spent most of his life in service of religious people, and he seems to have gone into the suite of the prince Sultan Muhammad b. Baysunghur on or before Shahrukh's death.[6] The third historian was Taj al-Din Hasan b. Shihab Yazdi, author of a world history known as *Jami' al-tawarikh-i hasani*, written about 855/1451. In the course of his long career, Hasan Yazdi served prince Iskandar b. 'Umar Shaykh as commander of ten men in the provincial army, then, after several years, went to Kerman, where he served as an administrator in provincial government, and after Shahrukh's death he came into the service of Sultan Muhammad.[7] Regional historians provide valuable additional information about local people and institutions, but they follow the actions of the dynasty and give little information about their regions when Shahrukh was absent and the province quiet.

One area that provides a surprising wealth of historical writing is the Caspian littoral, inhabited by a number of small dynasties which competed for power among themselves under the distant control of the Timurids. The history of Tabaristan had been written in the Mongol period and was continued in the fifteenth century by Zahir al-Din b. Nasir al-Din Mar'ashi, who lived approximately from 815/1412 to 894/1488. He was a member of the Mar'ashi dynasty of Tabaristan, but due to failed attempts at power by his father and himself, spent much of his life under the protection of the

[5] Yuri Bregel and Charles A. Storey, *Persidskaia literatura* (Moscow: Nauka, 1972), 349–50; Ja'far b. Muḥammad al-Ḥusaynī Ja'farī, *Tārīkh-i Yazd*, edited by Īraj Afshār (Tehran: Bungāh-i Tarjuma wa Nashr-i Kitāb, 1338/1960), 97, 133, 164–65, 167–68, 174, 189.

[6] Kātib, *Tārīkh-i jadīd*, 245–64. [7] Yazdī, *Ḥasanī*, 7–15, 24–35, 42, 50.

Kar-Kiya'i sayyids of Gilan. He never succeeded in gaining power and instead produced two histories, one of Gilan and one of Mazandaran and Tabaristan, leaving us a record of local dynastic struggles. These works are the most detailed local political histories we have, and also offer insight into the relationship between the center and the periphery.[8]

Even when we put together the dynastic and local histories we find ourselves with an uneven coverage of the Timurid realm, and one which depends less on the importance of the region than on the existence of local historians. For instance, we can gain quite a good understanding of Herat and its dependencies, which feature in both regional and dynastic histories. Of the central regions, the one least well represented is Transoxiana. Here there seems to have been no historical tradition which went beyond the confines of the city. Even when Transoxiana was the capital region under Temür, events were recorded only when the ruler was actually in the region and, since he spent almost all his reign on campaign, there is very little on record. In southern and central Iran, we can follow events in some detail during struggles for power which mattered to other regions, but in times of peace we hear only of a few local campaigns in Hormuz or Khuzistan. For the Caspian provinces, as I have mentioned, there is ample detail on political history. Azarbaijan, ruled almost independently by the Qaraqoyunlu, had its own set of historians, but major cities of northern Iran like Rayy, Hamadan, and Qazwin appear only when they were involved in Shahrukh's campaigns. The region of Kabul, far from the center and not providing great riches, was largely unchronicled. In this way much of the Timurid realm has remained outside the modern historian's grasp.

To examine the life of the urban and religious elite we turn to the biographical collections. Here again the Timurid period provides a rich fund of material, though it is by no means comprehensive. On ulama, scholars, and notables there are no contemporary sources beyond brief death notices, and we depend on the later historian Khwandamir, who completed his work, the *Habib al-siyar*, at the beginning of the Safavid period. For the period of Shahrukh, his text was based largely on Samarqandī but he added biographies of major urban and court figures active under each central ruler; these are uniformly short and stylized. Khwandamir also wrote a biographical work on viziers based partly on material given by Samarqandī with additional information from other sources.[9]

[8] See Charles Melville, "The Caspian Provinces: A World Apart. Three Local Histories of Mazandaran," *Iranian Studies* 33 (2000), 45–91.

[9] A. Beveridge and B. Manz, "Mīrkhwānd," *Encyclopaedia of Islam*, 2nd edn; and H. Beveridge and J. T. P. de Bruijn, "Khwāndamīr," in ibid. The article on Khwandamir incorrectly identifies him as Mirkhwand's nephew (see Ghiyāth al-Dīn Khwāndamīr, *Ḥabīb al-siyar fī akhbār afrād bashar*, edited by Muḥammad Dabīr Siyāqī, 4 vols. [Tehran: Khayyām, 1333/1955–56], vol. IV, 105, 341–42; Wheeler M. Thackston, *Habibu's-siyar, Tome Three*, *Sources of Oriental Languages and Literatures* 24, Cambridge, MA [1994], 408, 521, and Bregel and Storey, *Persidskaia literatura*, 379).

In biographical literature the regional coverage works out quite differently (though Herat remains well documented). There are two collections of biographies of viziers, both strongest on central government. The longer and more reliable one is Khwandamir's; a slightly earlier work, the *Athar al-wuzara'*, written by Sayf al-Din Hajji b. Nizam 'Uqayli during the reign of Sultan Husayn Bayqara (r.873/1469 to 911/1506), is occasionally useful on points of detail. Two collections of poets' biographies have come down to us, both strongest on the eastern section of the Timurid realm, probably because central Iran was, at this time, no longer part of the Timurid realm. The *Majalis al-nafa'is* was written by the famous poet and vizier Mir 'Ali Shir Nawa'i in 897/1491–92. His biographies are short, pithy, and concerned primarily with a judgment of the poetry produced; they contain brief anecdotes which amuse the reader while revealing the character of the poet. The other biographical collection, roughly contemporary to Nawa'i's, is the *Tadhkirat al-shu'ara* of Dawlatshah Samarqandī. Dawlatshah, whose relatives had held power in Isfahan, shows some interest in Shiraz, Isfahan and other western cities, but offers more detail on eastern poets. Nawa'i, whose father had served Abu'l Qasim Babur, brings in the poets at his court, including several from Astarabad.

For the religious sphere there are two types of source particularly useful for this project: the Sufi *tadhkira* literature and grave visitation guides. Although the *tadhkira* literature is rich, the works which are fullest on the period of Shahrukh were almost all written later – in the late fifteenth and early sixteenth centuries. For the eastern Timurid realm our sources, if late, are relatively plentiful, but for most of central and southern Iran, few hagiographies remain. For Shiraz and Isfahan, in particular, we have only incidental bits of information, quite insufficient to allow an analysis of the part that Sufis played in politics. Grave visitation manuals gained popularity in the thirteenth century and were plentiful by the Timurid period. Here again, regions and cities are unevenly served. The histories of Yazd include some information on graveyards and major mausolea. One of the most useful of such works for this book is the *Maqsad al-iqbal*, a description of the mausolea of Herat with the biographies of their inhabitants, the powers attached to them, and the etiquette of visiting them, written for Sultan Abu Sa'id in 864/1459–60, only shortly after Shahrukh's reign.[10] A similar work was written on Bukhara in the early fifteenth century by Ahmad b. Mahmud Mu'in al-Fuqara', a disciple of the *ḥadīth* scholar and shaykh, Muhammad Parsa. Since the guide was written at the beginning of the century it has almost no information on Shahrukh's reign, but it does provide background on the scholars of the city

[10] Aṣīl al-Dīn 'Abd Allāh Wā'iẓ, *Maqṣad al-iqbāl al- sulṭāniyya wa marṣad al-āmāl al-Khāqāniyya*, with *Ta'līq bar maqṣad al-iqbāl yā Risāla-i duwwum-i mazārāt-i Harāt*, by 'Ubayd Allah b. Abu Sa'īd Harawī, edited by Māyil Harawī (Tehran: Intishārāt-i Bunyād-i Farhang-i Īrān, 1351/1972–3), 9–27; Khwāndamīr, *Ḥabīb*, vol. IV, 334, 359; Thackston, *Habibu's-Siyar*, 518, 529.

and on contemporary holy sites. One other grave visitation manual is of great interest to us: the *Rawdat al-jinan wa jannat al-janan* written by Hafiz Husayn Karbala'ī Tabrizī in 990/1582. Although the *Rawdat* is organized around the graves of Tabriz, its detailed biographies, often several pages long, make it similar in many ways to the *tadhkira* literature. Karbala'i's Kubrawi affiliation and his interest in Sufi shaykhs outside of Khorasan and Transoxiana make his work a very useful counterweight to the largely Naqshbandi compilations of eastern Iran. In the case of grave manuals, Samarqand is less well served. Two guides to graves have survived, one written partly in the Timurid period, but incorporating later material, and one from the nineteenth century, but neither contains detailed information on the religious figures of the early fifteenth century.[11]

Putting our sources together, we find that the biographical literature available to us does not connect at all levels with the narrative histories, but does present information on personalities, politics, and social history. Its regional distribution overlaps with that of the narrative histories in its strong coverage of Khorasan and Herat, but southern and central Iran are less fully covered than other regions. While we have some information on the scholars in Shiraz during Iskandar b. ʿUmar Shaykh's brief rule there, we know only a little about the court patronage of his successor, Ibrahim Sultan b. Shahrukh. Transoxiana is only a little stronger in biographical literature than in narrative history. Thus we may compare regions in some aspects of history, but there is almost no area outside Herat in which all groups are well represented.

The impact of the author and his milieu

Having dealt with the factors which determined the presence or absence of information, I will turn to the question of how to evaluate the source material we do have. Histories present us not only with a particular version of events which we must test for bias, but, equally importantly, with a set of anecdotes about individuals whom the authors considered important. The connections of historians to men in power did not bring consistent flattery (at least for someone who was dead at the time of writing), but rather a greater share of attention and some privileged sources of information. Before making a judgment on the power relationships of the period we must try to understand the factors influencing the writer.

The major histories written for the central Timurid court, by Ḥāfiẓ-i Abrū, ʿAbd al-Razzaq Samarqandī, Mirkhwand, and Khwandamir, have set the accepted understanding of Timurid history. All these men were politically active and came from prominent families. Although they undoubtedly made use of government documents, their histories also contain echoes of innumerable conversations which were a source of some of their information. The

[11] See Jürgen Paul, "The Histories of Samarqand," *Studia Iranica* 22, 1 (1993), 61–92.

picture they present reflects more than the view of the person to whom the history was dedicated, and is likewise something more personal than the interpretation of a member of a certain class. Anyone who has lived in a society without a credible press knows how crucial conversation can be. If we are to understand how to read an historian, we should know whom he was most likely to talk to and if possible, where his acquaintances got their stories. We must try to uncover the broader loyalties of the authors involved – not only their careers and official positions, but also their family connections and place of origin, their religious affiliations, and their alliances among their peers.

The first historian who helped to produce Timurid history was Ḥāfiẓ-i Abrū, but unfortunately it is impossible to reconstruct his connections. He seems to have been a professional historian, living away from the court and without additional occupation as bureaucrat or religious scholar. He was born in Khwaf, educated in Hamadan, spent some time in Temür's camp, and shortly after Temür's death began writing historical works for Shahrukh. We have essentially no information on his activities once Shahrukh came to power, and since he died and was buried in his native Khwaf it is quite possible that he spent much of his time there.[12] We know more about later authors. The *Matlaʿ al-saʿdayn wa majmaʿ al-bahrayn* of ʿAbd al-Razzaq Samarqandī bears a definite personal stamp, showing the author's interest in the affairs which were close to him as a member of the ulama attached to the court. Samarqandī includes a detailed account of his embassy to India, describing the torments of seasickness and tropical heat. He tells us elsewhere about the trials he suffered at the hands of envious colleagues, and even about the discomfiture he caused the people whom he himself disliked.[13]

We can situate Samarqandī quite precisely within Herati learned society. His father, Jalal al-Din Ishaq, was *qāḍī* and *imām* at Shahrukh's court, thus part of what one might call the court ulama. In the year 841/1437–38, Samarqandī decided to try for a position at court and dedicated a textual commentary to Shahrukh, who accordingly granted him a place in his retinue.[14] In 843/1439–40, he tells us, he was criticized by other ulama of the court for having abandoned his studies too early in order to attach himself to the ruler. The response was to set up a public examination of Samarqandī in competition with another representative member of the ulama, to be held before the assembled ulama and emirs. Hajji Muhammad Farahi, chosen as competitor for Samarqandī, was a follower of the prominent *ʿālim* and Sufi shaykh Zayn al-Din Khwafi.[15] According to the author, the examination

[12] Hafiz-i Abru's full name was ʿAbd Allah b. Lutf Allah b. ʿAbd al-Rashid al-Bihdadini (F. Tauer, "Ḥāfiẓ-i Abrū," in *Encyclopaedia of Islam*, 2nd edn; Ḥāfiẓ-i Abrū, *Zubdat*, [introduction], 13–20).

[13] Samarqandī, *Maṭlaʿ*, 731–33, 764–71, 775–90, 796–830, 842–49.

[14] Ibid., 704; Faṣīḥ Khwāfī, *Mujmal-i faṣīḥī*, vol. III, 270.

[15] Wāʿiẓ, *Maqṣad*, 106–07.

resulted in his complete vindication, and certainly we find him filling court positions from this time on.[16] Samarqandī's brothers were also trained in the religious sciences. Jalal al-Din Ishaq had sent his four sons to study with the eminent scholar Shams al-Din Muhammad al-Jazari, known for knowledge of the Qur'an and *ḥadīth*.[17] ʿAbd al-Razzaq Samarqandī and his brother ʿAbd al-Wahhab were appointed emissaries to Hormuz and India in 845/1441–42; ʿAbd al-Razzaq returned in 848/1444 but his brother died on the journey.[18] In 850/1446–47 Samarqandī was sent to Gilan and shortly thereafter to Egypt.[19] Later, under Abu Saʿid, he was appointed as shaykh of Shahrukh's *khānaqāh*, a position he held at the time he wrote his history.[20]

Samarqandī shows his professional interests clearly in his writing. One type of appointment to which he pays particular attention is that of emissary to foreign rulers. What he is recording here is positions for which he was eligible, and which he may have coveted. Whereas in the *Mujmal-i fasihi*, which was written by the bureaucrat Muhammad Fasih, emissaries from abroad are often mentioned, but rarely the ulama sent by Shahrukh, in the *Matlaʿ al-saʿdayn* the ulama sent abroad are usually specifically named.[21] Samarqandī lived and worked within a group of highly placed and interconnected people, close to the court in a variety of different capacities. Like many other court ulama, Samarqandī connected his family to the religious aristocracy of Khorasan. His daughter married one of the local Husayni sayyids; their son is mentioned among the notables under Sultan Husayn Bayqara.[22] Two of Samarqandī's brothers were prominent scholars, well-connected among the religious figures respected by the dynasty and its emirs. Their careers and connections shed light on Samarqandī's choice of events and people to emphasize. One brother, Jamal al-Din ʿAbd al-Ghaffar (d. 835/1431–32), in addition to his *ijāza* from Shams al-Din Muhammad al-Jazari held *ijāza*s from two prominent Herati ulama of the time: Rukn al-Din Muhammad Khwafi and Jalal al-Din Yusuf Awbahi.[23] When Shahrukh built his madrasa and *khānaqāh* in 813/1410–11, Awbahi was one of four teachers appointed. He had been a favored student of Temür's prominent scholar Saʿd al-Din Taftazani (722/1322 to 793/1390), whose family remained influential in Herat under Shahrukh and came to hold the office of *shaykh al-islām*. Awbahi appears to have been a staunch promoter of Taftazani's works, and Khwandamir describes an inaugural lecture at the madrasa,

[16] Samarqandī, *Maṭlaʿ*, 731–34. [17] Ibid., 630–31.
[18] Ibid., 745, 775–76, 842–45. [19] Ibid., 865, 867–68.
[20] Khwāndamīr, *Ḥabīb*, vol. IV, 335; Thackston, *Habibu's-siyar*, 518; Samarqandī, *Maṭlaʿ*, 110.
[21] See for example Faṣīḥ Khwāfī, *Mujmal-i faṣīḥī*, vol. III, 204, 219, 220, 241, 249, and Samarqandī, *Maṭlaʿ*, 608, 687, 727, 792, 850, 865.
[22] Khwāndamīr, *Ḥabīb*, vol. IV, 354; Thackston, *Habibu's-siyar*, 527–28.
[23] Samarqandī, *Maṭlaʿ*, 643. Rukn al-Din Khwafi was a highly regarded scholar versed in both Sufism and the exoteric sciences, particularly *ḥadīth*, *uṣūl*, and *kalām*, and had a great following among Sufis, ulama and emirs (Khwāndamīr, *Ḥabīb*, vol. IV, 8; Thackston, *Habibu's-siyar*, 355; Samarqandī, *Maṭlaʿ*, 636–37).

in which Awbahi refuted criticism of Taftazani's marginalia by the new appointee. Shahrukh's two emirs, ʿAlika Kukeltash and Firuzshah, were present and Firuzshah praised Awbahi for his defense of his master.[24]

Samarqandī's other brother, Sharif al-Din ʿAbd al-Qahhar, was a disciple of the prominent Herat shaykh Baha' al-Din ʿUmar Jaghara'i. Shaykh Baha' al-Din was well connected among the elite, including the Chaghatay, and he spent much time in the cathedral mosque in Herat, where he talked to people of power to intercede for the poor.[25] Another person who had particularly close ties to Shaykh Baha' al-Din was Firuzshah, mentioned above in connection with Yusuf Awbahi. According to Samarqandī, it was Baha' al-Din who in 846/1442–43 suggested to Firuzshah that Shahrukh's grandson Sultan Muhammad be appointed to govern western and central Iran, a proposal that Firuzshah passed on to Shahrukh.[26] Firuzshah died before Baha' al-Din, but his sons contributed to the building of Baha' al-Din's mausoleum.[27]

When we read Samarqandī's history we should recognize his personal connections and interests – events and biographies closely connected to ʿAbd al-Razzaq's acquaintance are given greater prominence. It is not a surprise to find that the founding and staffing of Shahrukh's madrasa and *khānaqāh* is one of the events that ʿAbd al-Razzaq added to the text of Ḥāfiẓ-i Abrū's history in adapting it to the *Matlaʿ al-saʿdayn*.[28] This was the madrasa to which ʿAbd al-Razzaq's brother's teacher Jalal al-Din Yusuf Awbahi was appointed, and the author himself later held a post within the *khānaqāh*. Among the prominent personages of the city and court Baha' al-Din and Amir Firuzshah receive particular attention from Samarqandī. Shaykh Baha' al-Din is more frequently mentioned than for instance Zayn al-Din Khwafi, a man who was almost certainly of greater status.[29] Samarqandī shows the Timurid dynasty and its high functionaries eager to pay respect to Baha' al-Din. He gives a description of his departure on the pilgrimage in 844/1440–41; Shahrukh and numerous others went to see him off and requested permission to give him presents for the road, but were refused. One of the people accompanying Baha' al-Din to Mecca was Samarqandī's brother, Sharif al-Din ʿAbd al-Qahhar.[30] Samarqandī recounts several miracles (*karamāt*) connected to Baha' al-Din; he credits him for instance with the

[24] Samarqandī, *Maṭlaʿ*, 625–27; Khwāndamīr, *Ḥabīb*, vol. IV, 7–8; Thackston, *Habibu's-siyar*, 354.
[25] Kāshifī, *Rashaḥāt*, 401; ʿAbd al-Rahman b. Aḥmad Jāmī, *Nafaḥāt al-uns min ḥidrāt al-quds*, edited by Mahdī Tawḥīdīpur (Tehran: Intishārāt-i ʿIlmi, sh. 1375/1996–97), 455.
[26] Samarqandī, *Maṭlaʿ*, 772.
[27] Terry Allen, *A Catalogue of the Toponyms and Monuments of Timurid Herat* (Cambridge, MA: Agha Khan Program for Islamic Architecture at Harvard University and Massachusetts Institute of Technology, 1981), 178.
[28] Samarqandī, *Maṭlaʿ*, 109–10.
[29] In the grave visitation manual for Herat for instance, Baha' al-Din ʿUmar appears as clearly secondary to Zayn al-Din Khwafi (Wāʿiẓ, *Maqṣad*, 52, 80–81, 88–89, 90, 93–94, 105–08, 137, 139).
[30] Samarqandī, *Maṭlaʿ*, 742–43.

miraculous cure of Shahrukh's illness in 848/1444.[31] Samarqandī even suggests that Ulugh Beg's lack of respect to Baha' al-Din during the succession struggle after Shahrukh's death was one reason for his subsequent misfortunes.[32]

Samarqandī's connections to Amir Firuzshah are nowhere clearly stated, but throughout his history we find indications of special interest and a tendency to present him as closer to Shahrukh than the other leading emir, ʿAlika. His description of the 830/1426–27 attempt on Shahrukh's life is a good example. The text is considerably expanded from Ḥāfiẓ-i Abrū's account and one of the incidents ʿAbd al-Razzaq adds recounts that Shahrukh called specifically for Firuzshah, and Firuzshah's quick thinking prevented a panic.[33] Shahrukh's decision to go against Azarbaijan in 838/1434–35, which took him and his army out of Herat shortly before a devastating outbreak of the plague, was a stroke of good fortune clearly inviting explanation. It is significant that Samarqandī credits Firuzshah with promoting the campaign, while Muhammad Fasih, writing earlier, and from a different perspective, presents Shahrukh's decision to go as a sign of the ruler's divine guidance.[34] Another explanation for Samarqandī's disproportionate attention to Firuzshah and Baha' al-Din is a more pedestrian one; both of them died later than other men who held equivalent power. Samarqandī began his service at court in 841/1437–38 as a young man; Zayn al-Din Khwafi had been dead since 838/1435, and ʿAlika died within a few years, in 844/1440. Both Firuzshah and Baha' al-Din lived for some time thereafter, and it was natural that Samarqandī should extend their dominance back into the past.

We need not see Samarqandī's connections to particular people as evidence of his belonging to a specific faction. His interest in Firuzshah did not preclude criticism; Firuzshah's abuse of power is described in the *Matlaʿ al-saʿdayn*, which, indeed, is our main source about it.[35] There is however an indication of inside information. Samarqandī, several times, appears to know Firuzshah's motivation. One example is his promotion of Sultan Muhammad as governor of central and western Iran, which Samarqandī ascribes to a dream of Shaykh Baha' al-Din ʿUmar, passed on to Firuzshah who then suggested the appointment to Shahrukh. Another example is Samarqandī's statement that it was Firuzshah who chose the emissary to Egypt in 847/1443–44.[36] Samarqandī's history then is an account of Shahrukh's reign and his court seen from an individual point of view. There is no reason to deny the importance of the events or people the author emphasizes in his history; the prestige of such men as Firuzshah and Baha' al-Din is amply attested to in

[31] Ibid., 831–33. Samarqandī also describes Firuzshah's touching care for the sovereign during his illness.
[32] Ibid., 941–42.
[33] Ibid., 314–15; Ḥāfiẓ-i Abrū, *Zubdat*, 911–15; Ḥāfiẓ-i Abrū, "Majmaʿ," fols. 603a–b.
[34] Samarqandī, *Maṭlaʿ*, 671; Faṣīḥ Khwāfī, *Mujmal-i faṣīḥī*, vol. III, 278.
[35] Samarqandī, *Maṭlaʿ*, 791–95, 837–40. [36] Ibid., 792.

other sources. What is not certain is that they were the most prominent actors throughout Shahrukh's reign. We must recognize that Samarqandī's history gives a specific view of power relations, particular not only to a time, culture, and class of people, but to an individual with his own set of religious and professional relationships.

At the end of the fifteenth century the history of the Timurid dynasty was continued by Muhammad b. Khwandshah b. Mahmud, known as Mirkhwand (836–37 to 903/1433–34 to 1498), who wrote under the patronage of Mir ʿAli Shir Nawaʾi, the vizier of the last Timurid ruler, Sultan Husayn Bayqara (r. 873/1469 to 911/1506). Mirkhwand added some new information from his own sources. After his death his daughter's son, Khwandamir (c. 1475–1530 or 1542), brought the history up to his own time (it was completed under the Safavid dynasty, in about 930/1524). Since he was trained by Mirkhwand, and like him began his career under the patronage of Nawaʾi, Khwandamir's *Habib al-siyar* was intended as a completion of Mirkhwand's work. For the narrative of Shahrukh's reign both historians used Samarqandī's text, adding a few anecdotes of their own. Khwandamir's work on viziers was also based partly on material given by Samarqandī. Let us see then what these two historians added and whether their viewpoints differed sufficiently from that of Samarqandī to provide a separate and corrective point of view.

Khwandamir was closely attached to Mirkhwand, his maternal grandfather, with whom he studied. We should start the examination of political ties therefore with Mirkhwand's family. He came from an important lineage of sayyids of Transoxiana descended from Khwand Sayyid Ajall Bukhari. Mirkhwand's father, Khwandshah, went to study in Balkh and from there moved to Herat, where he became attached to Shaykh Bahaʾ al-Din ʿUmar Jagharaʾi, whose prestige remained high after Shahrukh's reign. So close was he to Bahaʾ al-Din that, according to Khwandamir, the shaykh chose him to read the prayers over his body. Khwandshah was later buried at the tomb of Bahaʾ al-Din, as was ʿAbd al-Razzaq Samarqandī's brother, Sharaf al-Din ʿAbd al-Qahhar. It is not therefore surprising that ʿAbd al-Qahhar should receive several mentions in Khwandamir's biographies.[37] It is interesting to see that the family of Saʿd al-Din Taftazani was also a connection of Khwandamir's and Mirkhwand's. We find a story about Taftazani's son told by Taftazani's great-grandson, Sayf al-Din Ahmad, and Taftazani himself is cited as the source for an anecdote about the great Husayni sayyid Sadr al-Din Yunus al-Husayni, progenitor of the family into which Samarqandī married his daughter.[38]

[37] Khwāndamīr, *Ḥabīb*, vol. IV, 58, 101–03, 105, 347; Thackston, *Habibu's-siyar*, 382–83, 406, 408, 524. The ruler Abu'l Qasim Babur helped to carry Bahaʾ al-Din's bier, on his death in 857/1453, and also financed his tomb. Bahaʾ al-Din's son Nur al-Din Muhammad was apparently much honored by Sultan Abu Saʿid.

[38] Khwāndamīr, *Ḥabīb*, vol. IV, 9, 354; Thackston, *Habibu's-siyar*, 356, 527–28.

What we find in Mirkhwand and Khwandamir then is a continuation of many of the ties which had formed Samarqandī's network. Khwandamir furthermore came from a similar professional background. His father had served the dynasty and had married into a prestigious sayyid family – that of Mirkhwand. Khwandamir, like Mirkhwand's brother, served as *ṣadr* and, like Samarqandī, he acted several times as an envoy for the dynasty.[39] If then we compare the work of Khwandamir to that of Samarqandī, we find that while Khwandamir does add new material, it apparently comes from many of the same sources. These works are linked through common networks as well as through the filiation of texts.

Even when we turn to works in other genres we find several of the same connections, not surprisingly considering that the histories are the production of a small elite close to the court. One example is the work of Isfizari, author of the *Rawdat al-jannat fi awsaf madinat Harat*, an historical geography of Herat and its region. Like many other authors, Isfizari was a bureaucrat; he served in the *dīwān* of Husayn-i Bayqara and produced a collection of correspondence as well as his *Rawdat*. The history was finished in 899/1493–94 and dedicated to Sultan Husayn Bayqara's vizier Qawam al-Din Nizam al-Mulk Khwafi.[40] Isfizari tells a story about Shams al-Din Muhammad Taftazani, told to him by one of the intimates of Taftazani's great-grandson, Sayf al-Din Ahmad, who is also mentioned as the source of one of Khwandamir's anecdotes.[41] Another personal acquaintance of Isfizari's was Samarqandī's brother, Sharif al-Din ʿAbd al-Qahhar.[42]

Amir Firuzshah and his family are well represented in the work of another historian of the late Timurid period – Dawlatshah Samarqandī, author of the *Tadhkirat al-shuʿara*, an influential collection of poets' biographies.[43] Amir Dawlatshah b. ʿAlaʾ al-Dawlat Bakhtishah was Firuzshah's cousin and began his career in military and administrative posts, then retired to devote himself to history, and finished his work in 892/1487.[44] It is clear that his background affected his interests and sources; while the entries in his collection are named after the major poets, the narrative often shifts quickly to the dynastic patron. We find anecdotes about princes and their treatment of their subordinates which do not appear elsewhere. Although Dawlatshah was born only shortly

[39] Khwāndamīr, *Ḥabīb*, vol. IV, 105; Thackston, *Habibu's-siyar*, 407; Beveridge, "K͟hwāndamīr".
[40] Isfizārī, *Rawḍāt*, editor's introduction, Va to yad.
[41] Isfizārī, *Rawḍāt*, I, 140–41; Khwāndamīr, *Ḥabīb*, vol. III, 545; Thackston, *Habibu's-siyar*, 302.
[42] Isfizārī, *Rawḍāt*, I, 114.
[43] Mīr ʿAlī Shīr Nawāʾī, *Majālis al-nafāʾis dar tadhkira-i shuʿarāʾ-i qarn-i nuhum-i hijrī, taʾlīf-i Mīr-i Niẓām ʿAlī Shīr Nawāʾī* (Persian translations from the Chaghatay original: The *Laṭāʾifnāma* of Fakhrī Harātī, and a translation by Muhammad b. Mubārak Qazwīnī), edited by ʿAlī Asghar Ḥikmat (Tehran: Chāpkhāna-i Bānk-i milli-i Īrān, 1323/1945), 108. Dawlatshah's father was Alaʾ al-Din Bakhtishah, probably the brother of Firuzshah's father Arghunshah. Although Dawlatshah claims that Bakhtishah was one of Shahrukh's closest courtiers, his name appears nowhere in the histories; it seems that for part of his life he was insane (Dawlatshāh Samarqandī, *Tadhkirat*, 337, 541).
[44] Nawāʾī, *Majālis*, 108.

before Firuzshah's death, he mentions several of Firuzshah's relatives, who were almost certainly his informants. Two of them, Firuzshah's son Nizam al-Din Ahmad and his nephew Sa'adat served under Sultan Muhammad b. Baysunghur for several years after Shahrukh's death. Dawlatshah mentions the bravery of Nizam al-Din Ahmad during the battle at which Sultan Muhammad was killed.[45] These connections explain Dawlatshah's detailed treatment of Sultan Muhammad's personality.

Corrective influences in Timurid histories

Although Timurid historians shared many connections, we are not necessarily hearing the opinions of only one political faction. Networks and factions were neither lasting nor closed, and attachment to a specific group of people did not preclude recording negative information about them. Above all, the multitude of overlapping ties among scholars and other actors made information from a variety of sources available. I will present as an example the information which Khwandamir gives about the two rival scholars of Temür's court, Sa'd al-Din Tafazani and Sayyid 'Ali Jurjani.

Sa'd al-Din Taftazani was remembered partly for his bitter rivalry with another prominent scholar at court, Sayyid 'Ali Jurjani. After the deaths of both scholars, the controversy continued as a kind of ritual debate among their students.[46] The family of Sa'd al-Din Taftazani remained in Herat and held considerable influence there during and after the reign of Shahrukh, while Jurjani returned to Shiraz after Temür's death and died in 816/1413. His son remained influential there until his death in 838/1434.[47] There are some suggestions that Jurjani was not on good terms with Shahrukh. He was highly honored in Shiraz under Iskandar b. 'Umar Shaykh at the time when Iskandar was actively opposing Shahrukh, and he had friendly relations with Shah Ni'mat Allah Wali Kirmani, who seems also to have been unfriendly towards Shahrukh.[48] Since both Khwandamir and 'Abd al-Razzaq Samarqandī were close to the family and students of Taftazani, it is interesting to find that Khwandamir's biography of Sayyid 'Ali Jurjani is highly favorable. The author states that no lesson was given without his works and that Jurjani came out the victor in most debates with Taftazani.[49] The positive assessment must be due in

[45] Samarqandī, *Tadhkirat*, 411; Kātib, *Tārīkh-i jadīd*, 255; Ṭihrānī Iṣfahānī, *Diyārbakriyya*, 296; Dawlatshāh Samarqandī, *Maṭla'*, 841.

[46] William Smyth, "Controversy in a Tradition of Commentary: the Academic Legacy of al-Sakkākī's *Miftāḥ al-'ulūm*," *JAOS* 112 (1992), 594–7; Joseph Van Ess, *Die Erkenntnislehre des 'Aḍudaddīn al-Īcī, Übersetzung und Kommentar des ersten Buches seiner Mawāqif* (Wiesbaden: Steiner, 1966), 6–7.

[47] A. S. Tritton, "al-Djurdjānī," in *Encyclopaedia of Islam*, 2nd edn; Shujā', *Anīs al-Nās*, edited by Īraj Afshār (Tehran: Bungāh-i Tarjuma wa Nashr-i Kitāb, 2536/1977), 257, 259, 325–27; Samarqandī, *Maṭla'*, vol. II, 626.

[48] Aubin, *Ni'mat*, 12–16, 86–90, 99, 180, 189–90, 318–19; Dawlatshāh Samarqandī, *Tadhkirat*, 333–35.

[49] Khwāndamīr, *Ḥabīb*, vol. III, 546–47; Thackston, *Habibu's-siyar*, 302–03.

part to Jurjani's continued eminence, but I would suggest further that if we look at Jurjani's personal network we can see how positive anecdotal material came down to Mirkhwand, who is the source of at least one of Khwandamir's stories about Jurjani. This exercise shows how differing interpretations could survive, eventually to land up in the same work and also, perhaps more importantly, how the multiplicity of ties maintained by individuals served to mitigate personal and doctrinal rivalry.

As we have seen, Samarqandī, Mirkhwand and Khwandamir all had strong ties to the families of Sa'd al-Din Taftazani and Baha' al-Din 'Umar Jaghara'i. Baha' al-Din was, in turn, friendly with several important disciples of Baha' al-Din Naqshband. When Sayyid 'Ali Jurjani lived in Samarqand he was closely associated with Baha' al-Din Naqshband's disciples 'Ala' al-Din 'Attar and Nizam al-Din Khamush. Nizam al-Din Khamush was a master of Sa'd al-Din Kashghari, whom the great Persian poet of the late Timurid period, 'Abd al-Rahman Jami, counted as his spiritual master.[50] Baha' al-Din was also in frequent and friendly contact with al-Kashghari.[51] Another person with whom Jurjani had connections was Shams al-Din Muhammad al-Jazari, from whom 'Abd al-Razzaq Samarqandī and his brothers held *ijāzas*.[52] Sayyid 'Ali Jurjani thus emerges as a person with ties in many directions. His famous controversy with Sa'd al-Din Taftazani did not define the whole of his career. In the tight and interconnected world of religious scholars personal ties united people of potentially different parties; teaching associations and friendships were likely to cut across personal rivalries.

Although the Timurid dynastic historians did not exclude information about people of opposing views, it is fortunate that we have another contemporary source which allows us to examine the workings of the government from a different perspective: the *Mujmal-i fasihi* by Fasih Ahmad Khwafi. Fasih's work gives coverage to people and institutions of local importance, many of whom were outside the view of Samarqandī and Khwandamir. His history thus allows us a more comprehensive view of society. Like 'Abd al-Razzaq, Muhammad Fasih served the Timurid rulers, but his background was quite dissimilar. While the families of 'Abd al-Razzaq, Mirkhwand, and Khwandamir apparently originated elsewhere and came to the capital to serve the dynasty,[53] Fasih Khwafi came from eastern Iran and had strong ties to Herat.[54] His history is made up of short entries, ranging from one or two lines to a paragraph, and a large proportion concerns campaigns and

[50] Kāshifī, *Rashaḥāt*, 164, 235, 244, 282, 334, 401; Wā'iẓ, *Maqṣad*, 90; Khwāndamīr, *Ḥabīb*, vol. IV, 60; Thackston, *Habibu's-siyar*, 384.

[51] Kāshifī, *Rashaḥāt*, 186–88; Samarqandī, *Maṭla'*, 742.

[52] Aubin, *Ni'mat*, 86–87.

[53] This is clear in the case of Mirkhwand. For Samarqandī and Khwandamir I am inferring it from their *nisba*s (Samarqandī, and Shirazi for Khwandamir's grandfather) and the lack of information about earlier generations of their families.

[54] Faṣīḥ Khwāfī, *Mujmal-i faṣīḥī*, vol. III, 137–38, 251; Sayf al-Dīn Ḥājjī 'Uqaylī, *Āthār al-wuzarā'*, edited by Mīr Jalāl al-Dīn Ḥusaynī Armawī (Tehran: Intishārāt-i Dānishgāh-i Tihrān, 1337/1959–60), 341.

dynastic matters or the deaths of very prominent men. Nonetheless, Fasih's work bears as strong a personal stamp as that of Samarqandī and serves as a useful counterfoil. First of all, Fasih Khwafi worked within the *dīwān* and held no religious office. What differentiates the two historians more sharply is the level at which each served. Although Fasih aspired to high office in the central *dīwān*, he achieved it for only a short period; most of his career was spent in Baysunghur's chancellery and there too he was less than fully successful. He was also in the *dīwāns* of Shahrukh's powerful in-laws, the descendants of Ghiyath al-Din Tarkhan.[55]

Fasih is particularly inclusive in recording middle-ranking offices, personnel and religious figures. We find a fairly large number of Qur'an readers, preachers and Sufis, not mentioned in other histories, and information on some madrasas founded by emirs.[56] Like Samarqandi, Fasih focuses his attention on the offices for which he himself was eligible – in this case appointments within the *dīwān*, both at the highest level and below it. While ʿAbd al-Razzaq gives full accounts of the major *dīwān* scandals, it is from Fasih Khwafi that we are able to chart the changes in the bureaucracy and occasionally learn about appointments to Baysunghur's *dīwān*.[57]

Fasih offers less direct information on his political connections than Samarqandī and Khwandamir. To evaluate his text therefore we have to work in the opposite direction: to understand his milieu, we must determine which people and institutions receive the most attention in his history. For some families both births and deaths are recorded, in others numerous deaths, including those of children, and in some only the deaths of men prominent in their own right. The pattern of recording can provide us with a guide to the relative importance Fasih ascribed to different groups and the amount of information he had about them. It is not surprising to find that Fasih gives particularly detailed information about births and deaths in his own family. His attention here however is not all inclusive. For his father's family, which originated in Bakharz, Fasih gives a genealogy showing his descent from one of the companions of the Prophet, but although Fasih's father was buried in Herat, we find out almost nothing about his family.[58] The lineage Fasih chronicles most fully is that of his mother, which, like many other prominent families from Khwaf, produced a number of viziers, and it is presumably from them that he took the *nisba* Khwafi. Fasih records almost nothing about his brothers, nephews or first cousins; the line which he

55 ʿUqaylī, *Āthār*, 341–42; Faṣīḥ Khwāfī, *Mujmal-i faṣīḥī*, vol. III, 220, 225, 228, 235, 258, 266, 271, 287, 290.
56 See for instance, Faṣīḥ Khwāfī, *Mujmal-i faṣīḥī*, vol. III, 263–64, 267, 271, 276, 278, 282, 285, 288.
57 Fasih's discussion of *dīwān* affairs will be examined in the next chapter.
58 Faṣīḥ Khwāfī, *Mujmal-i faṣīḥī*, vol. III, 137. Descent from a famous person is often recorded for others as well, though without genealogies (see Faṣīḥ Khwāfī, *Mujmal-i faṣīḥī*, vol. III, 246, 248, 255, 267).

concentrates on is that of his second cousins. It is significant that two members of this family served in the *dīwān* under Shahrukh. They may well have been the men through whom Fasih sought to enter *dīwān* service.[59]

A few other families receive special attention from Fasih and since many are neither conspicuous in other histories nor clearly connected to each other, their inclusion is probably the result of a direct connection to the author. One family is that of the sayyid and bureaucrat Zayn al-ʿAbidin Junabadi, for whom Fasih records the births of a son and three grandsons.[60] While Zayn al-ʿAbidin and his family receive mention in other histories, this fact alone cannot explain the much higher level of attention given to the family over others. Fasih's attention may well represent a common professional interest. It is significant that Zayn al-ʿAbidin and Fasih Khwafi appear to have had common enemies within the *dīwān*. We know, for instance, that Zayn al-ʿAbidin was a strong opponent of Shahrukh's early vizier, Sayyid Fakhr al-Din Ahmad, who was responsible for the exile of two of Fasih's cousins and probably for the death of one of them.[61] Neither Sayyid Zayn al-ʿAbidin nor Fasih Khwafi, moreover, seems to have been able to work well in the *dīwān* during the long tenure of Shahrukh's most successful vizier, Ghiyath al-Din Pir Ahmad Khwafi.[62]

At higher levels it is also clear that Fasih's political network was different from that of Samarqandī. First of all, Samarqandī did not like Fasih, and he recounts with apparent satisfaction a humiliation that Fasih suffered in 839/1435–36. Fasih, who "had always coveted the rank of vizier," learned of the death of one of Shahrukh's chief bureaucrats and, in the hope of securing the office for himself, he set off to join the royal camp on its way back from Azarbaijan. However the prince ʿAlaʾ al-Dawla pursued him and brought him back to Herat.[63] Samarqandī's dismissive attitude towards Fasih Khwafi was apparently shared by Khwandamir, who did not devote a separate biography to him in his *Dastur al-wuzaraʾ*, mentioning him only as the loser in a contest of witticism with a more prominent vizier.[64] Nor does Fasih's historical work win him notice by these historians.

One military family in which Fasih shows strong interest is that of ʿAlika Kukeltash, paired with Firuzshah in power and influence. Within this family

59 Ibid., vol. III, 110, 138, 149–50, 214, 276, 282.
60 Ibid., vol. III, 189, 214, 252, 253.
61 Ibid., vol. III, 149–50, 173, 194.
62 It is notable that Fasih's brief period in Shahrukh's *dīwān*, on the dismissal of Sayyid Fakhr al-Din, ended in 820/1418 when Ghiyath al-Din Pir Ahmad was appointed (Faṣīḥ Khwāfī, *Mujmal-i faṣīḥī*, vol. III, 225, 235). Sayyid Zayn al-ʿAbidin is not found serving under Ghiyath al-Din, but either he or his son served briefly again during 828–29/1424–26, when Ghiyath al-Din was temporarily dismissed, and left after Ghiyath al-Din's return (Faṣīḥ Khwāfī, *Mujmal-i faṣīḥī*, vol. III, 257, 259).
63 Samarqandī, *Maṭlaʿ*, 689.
64 Ghiyāth al-Dīn b. Humām al-Dīn Khwāndamīr, *Dastūr al-wuzarāʾ*, edited by Saʿīd Nafīsī (Tehran: Iqbāl, sh. 1317/1938–39), 357–58.

Fasih pays particular attention to the line of ʿAlika's brother, Khwaja Rasti, which provided the *kotwals* of the Ikhtiyar al-Din fortress of Herat.[65] ʿAbd al-Razzaq mentions the line only once, to give a vivid portrait of the misdeeds of ʿAlika's great-nephew as *kotwāl*.[66] While it is possible that Fasih's attention to this line simply reflects its importance in Herat, their prominence in his record, in contrast to that of Samarqandī, might suggest a personal connection.

While we can infer that Fasih belonged to a different political and social network than that of Samarqandī, we need not see these as opposing factions. We have no evidence, for instance, of enmity between ʿAlika and Firuzshah. Fasih was connected to the relatives of Shahrukh's wife Gawharshad and his coverage of their births and deaths is notably fuller than that of most other emirs. Firuzshah also seems to have had close relations with Gawharshad and her son Baysunghur. The vizier Sayyid Zayn al-ʿAbidin, to whom Fasih was attached, is mentioned with respect also by Samarqandī and Khwandamir. What we are seeing here is the work of individuals who operated within the same political world, through different, but probably not opposing, sets of political alignments.

Although local attachments obviously mattered to Muhammad Fasih, it is important to notice his lack of interest in several major figures from his own region. Most of the outstanding religious figures mentioned in the other histories are here, but several receive little emphasis. One omission is Rukn al-Din Khwafi, who died in 834/1431, and had spent much of the later part of his life in Khwaf. Rukn al-Din appears in many other sources on the period.[67] The case of Zayn al-Din Khwafi is similar. Although Fasih gives one or two biographical details and the name of Zayn al-Din's father and his son, the material offered, both biographical and genealogical, is less full than that found in several other sources. In this connection we should note that it was Ghiyath al-Din Pir Ahmad Khwafi, with whom Fasih appears to have had little connection, who built the mausoleum over Zayn al-Din's grave.[68] What we find in Fasih is the personal network of a man who had not lost his attachment to the region of his birth and who moved in circles which, though certainly elite, were neither so exalted nor so exclusively tied to Shahrukh's court as those represented by Samarqandī and Khwandamir.

65 Faṣīḥ Khwāfī, *Mujmal-i faṣīḥī*, vol. III, 236, 263, 276, 282–85.

66 Samarqandī, *Maṭlaʿ*, 701.

67 Ibid., 636; Wāʿiẓ, *Maqṣad*, 61, 78; Khwāndamīr, *Ḥabīb*, vol. IV, 8; Thackston, *Habibu's-siyar*, 355; Isfizārī, *Rawḍāt*, vol. I, 213. The omission of his death might represent a corrupt text as Khwafi does record Rukn al-Din's birth (Faṣīḥ Khwāfī, *Mujmal-i faṣīḥī*, vol. III, 71).

68 Faṣīḥ Khwāfī, *Mujmal-i faṣīḥī*, vol. III, 175, 282; Khwāndamīr, *Ḥabīb*, vol. III, 354; Thackston, *Habibu's-siyar*, 527–28.

The contribution of local histories

As I have shown, Fasih Khwafi's history differs from the central dynastic histories partly because it is the record of a man with strong local connections. Several other Timurid historians also wrote from a regional perspective, and together their works can serve to counter the narrow view of power relationships given in the major histories. Some of these works, such as the histories of Yazd or the *Rawdat al-jannat* of Isfizari, were concerned with a limited area, but there are also more general histories written by people whose major life experience lay within one region. The attention such authors bestow on local actors, their information about the origin of government officials, and their detailed discussion of regional landmarks can alter the conclusions we draw about both events and institutions.

Regionally based historians are particularly useful in elucidating the background and career path of the Timurid Iranian elite. There are numerous questions important to the understanding of these classes. It is useful to know to what extent families which produced bureaucrats or ulama also sent their members into other professions. Another issue is how new people were drawn into the *dīwān* and what backgrounds they were likely to have. These are questions which most biographical literature is not set up to answer. The most specialized and reliable source on Timurid viziers is *Dastur al-wuzara'* by Khwandamir, who combined historical knowledge with access to documents and personal anecdote. However, the biographies by Khwandamir, like most others, stress connections within the profession or to court circles; if someone's father had served the dynasty, the fact is relevant, but if his profession was different, it is less likely to be mentioned.[69] It is in just this regard that the local connections of authors can help us.

We are fortunate that the region of Khwaf, from which many viziers arose in the Timurid period, was of particular concern to several authors. Fasih Khwafi gives a detailed genealogy for himself and for his relatives within the *dīwān* to whom he was connected on his mother's side. His mother claimed descent from the famous Ghaznawid vizier Abu Nasr Mishkan and more recently from her grandfather, the warlord Majd al-Din Muhammad Mayizhnabadi Khwafi, whose father and son both served the Kartid kings.[70] Two other histories share the connection to Khwaf: Isfizari's *Rawdat al-jannat* and ʿUqayli's *Athar al-wuzara'*, both dedicated to Sultan Husayn Bayqara's vizier Qawam al-Din Nizam al-Mulk Khwafi, the son of a provincial judge from Khwaf.[71]

[69] Khwandamir gives fuller information on the origins of bureaucrats of his own period than on earlier ones. Even then however, he usually limits his information to the geographical origin and the status of the family. The only exception to this are the viziers from Simnan, whose families he appears to know better.

[70] Faṣīḥ Khwāfī, *Mujmal-i faṣīḥī*, vol. III, 110, 251.

[71] Isfizārī, *Rawḍāt*, editor's introduction, Va to yad; Beveridge, "K̲h̲wāndamīr"; Beveridge, "Mīrk̲h̲wānd."

Qawam al-Din's patronage was not Isfizari's only tie to the region; he had also served under the vizier Majd al-Din Khwafi and he mentions the *ṣadr* Qutb al-Din Muhammad Khwafi (d. 895/1489–90) as someone who favored him.[72] He cites his own father as the source of a story about a notable of the region, so it is possible that there was some family connection behind Isfizari's service with the Khwafi viziers.[73] In his discussion of Khwaf, Isfizari shows both an interest in the area and a desire to please his patron. Among the men mentioned is Muhammad Fasih whom Isfizari mentions as a good poet and historian.[74] He also gives an elaborate genealogy for his patron Qawam al-Din. Although he is silent about Qawam al-Din's immediate ancestry, he states that he was descended from Fasih's great grandfather Majd al-Din Muhammad, as well as from several other distinguished personalities of varied callings from Khwaf, and, beyond that, from most of the outstanding historical figures of eastern Iran.[75]

Sayf al-Din Hajji b. Nizam ʿUqayli was the author of a collection of biographies of viziers entitled *Athar al-wuzara'*, which predates Khwandamir's work. ʿUqayli entered government service at a young age, serving Qawam al-Din Khwafi for at least part of the time, and decided to write a book on viziers because no recent one existed. We know little else about his life. His notices of Timurid viziers are short and show puzzling inaccuracies in names, sometimes confusing personalities.[76] What makes the work useful is his addition of local information to his history, particularly his greater knowledge of the origins of viziers from eastern Iran. He provides a sympathetic biography for Fasih, perhaps not surprisingly since Fasih was related to Qawam al-Din. It is from ʿUqayli we know that Fasih, despite his *nisba*, came from Bakharz. Elsewhere he states that Temür's vizier Jalal Islam came from a military family of Tabas, about which he tells several stories, and that the infamous vizier, Sayyid Fakhr al-Din, whom Shahrukh appointed early in his reign, had become wealthy in trade.[77]

There are only a few indications of where these authors got their information. ʿUqayli gives us no information on his contacts, but Isfizari does mention some personal acquaintances. One is Amir Jalal al-Din Farrukhzad Tabasi, from the family of Jalal Islam, whose origins ʿUqayli described. Since Isfizari and ʿUqayli worked under the same patron we may here have a hint about the source of ʿUqayli's information.[78] Together Fasih, Isfizari and ʿUqayli remind us of the varied origins of families whose members entered into

[72] Isfizārī, *Rawḍāt*, vol. I, 219–20. [73] Ibid., vol. I, 199.

[74] Ibid., vol. I, 187–222; Faṣīḥ Khwāfī, *Mujmal-i faṣīḥī*, vol. III, 222.

[75] Khwāndamīr, *Dastūr*, 418; Isfizārī, *Rawḍāt*, vol. I, 200, 201, 210–11, 215–17.

[76] See for example ʿUqaylī, *Āthār*, 334, where he makes two people out of Khwaja Mahmud Shihab. Compare to Khwāndamīr, *Dastūr*, 343; see also ʿUqaylī, *Āthār*, 344 vs. Khwāndamīr, *Dastūr*, 361; Samarqandī, *Maṭlaʿ*, 752; and Faṣīḥ Khwāfī, *Mujmal-i faṣīḥī*, vol. III, 290.

[77] For Jalal Islam Tabasi, see ʿUqaylī, *Āthār*, 330–34; for Sayyid Fakhr al-Din Ahmad, see ʿUqaylī, *Āthār*, 336; for Fasih Khwafi, see ʿUqaylī, *Āthār*, 341.

[78] Isfizārī, *Rawḍāt*, vol. I, 114.

government service, and the number of occupations which might be represented within one family.[79]

The local histories of Herat by Isfizari and Fasih Khwafi are useful also in broadening our perspective in a different sphere: that of religion and the supernatural. Dynastic histories mention the most important shrines, religious institutions, and religious figures, while biographical literature gives us the lives of major shaykhs and ulama. The local histories describe many more holy people and places, some originally unconnected to any religious authority. Among the families whose births Fasih records are those of religious figures, and these may give us an indication of his spiritual loyalties. It is interesting to find that the lineages to which he gives the fullest coverage are not those of the famous shaykhs and ulama commemorated by Samarqandī, Khwandamir, and other historians. We find instead what appear to be provincial figures. These include a set of Musawi sayyids, *naqīb*s (prefects of the sayyids) of Mashhad, and the sayyids descended from Abu Ghalib Tusi, whom I have not found elsewhere.[80] The religious family to whom Fasih showed the greatest respect were shaykhs based in Sanjan in Khwaf, probably the descendants of the Chishti shaykh Rukn al-Din Mahmud, known as Shah Sanjan (d. 597). To these men, Fasih consistently gives the titles of Amir or Sultan. While Shah Sanjan's personal fame had lasted, and is shown, for example in Isfizari, his descendants were less well known.[81]

Like Fasih, Isfizari accords considerable attention to regional saints and mausolea. What is most individual in his discussion is his inclusion of natural wonders, particularly healing springs. It appears that Isfizari and his father had visited some of these and that they were widely used by the population. In one or two cases the popularity was so great that Timurid rulers found it expedient to appropriate the place by erecting a building near it. One of these was a hot spring at Awba in Herat-rud, where people went for cures.[82]

Another valuable source for the Herat region is the *Maqsad al-iqbal* by Sayyid Asil al-Din ʿAbd Allah Waʿiz (d. 883/1478–9), a grave visitation manual for the city of Herat. Sayyid Asil al-Din was a religious scholar from Shiraz who came to Herat under Abu Saʿid. The *Maqsad al-iqbāl* was written for the sultan and Asil al-Din spoke regularly at Gawharshad's mosque.[83] When we look at the people whom Asil al-Din mentions as informants, we find ourselves in familiar territory. One is Rukn al-Din Khwafi, the teacher

79 I will discuss the origins of Timurid viziers in greater detail in the next chapter.

80 Faṣīḥ Khwāfī, *Mujmal-i faṣīḥī*, vol. III, 152, 263, 272, 277, 291.

81 Ibid., vol. III, 192, 213, 252, 282. It is possible that the Taj al-Din Ahmad Sanjani who served Ghiyath al-Din Pir Ahmad as agent in Jam is the Taj al-Din Ahmad mentioned by Fasih as a member of this family. See Jalāl al-Dīn Yūsuf Ahl, *Farāyid-i ghiyāthī*, edited by Heshmat Moayyad, 2 vols. (Tehran: Foundation for Iranian Culture, 1979), vol. II, 24–25, 102, 150, 206–08.

82 Isfizārī, *Rawḍāt*, vol. I, 101–02, 105, 120, 276, 304, 355.

83 Wāʿiẓ, *Maqṣad*, 9–27; Khwāndamīr, *Ḥabīb*, vol. IV, 334, 359; Thackston, *Habibu's-siyar*, 518, 529.

of ʿAbd al-Razzaq Samarqandī's brother.[84] Another person mentioned in a way that suggests personal connection is Mawlana Shams al-Din Kusuyi (d. 863/1458–9), who was close both to Baha' al-Din ʿUmar Jaghara'i and Zayn al-Din Khwafi.[85]

Although he was of outside provenance and closely connected to the dynasty, Asil al-Din's subject was purely local and took him outside the sphere inhabited by the court elite. The *Maqsad* gives a detailed description of the mausolea and cemeteries of Herat and its environs, with short biographies of numerous inhabitants of the graves. We find here once again mention of the most important shaykhs of the Herat region at Shahrukh's time, including Zayn al-Din Khwafi, Baha' al-Din ʿUmar and Saʿd al-Din Kashghari.[86] Asil al-Din, however, does not limit his coverage to the famous, and thus provides us with a useful reminder of the variety of graves honored by the population. In the list of effective graves given by Asil al-Din, we find not only Sufis, but also rulers and popular leaders whose graves had supernatural power.[87] Like Isfizari's work, the *Maqsad* expands our view of the dynasty's relationship to religious sites. While Samarqandī reports on the honor Shahrukh paid to the major shrines at Mashhad, Bistam, and Gazurgah and on those he visited on his travels,[88] in the *Maqsad* several graves in Herat patronized or visited by Shahrukh are named. These shrines represented a variety of people and religious schools, not all of them exalted.

The local histories thus allow us to look beyond the circle of court, military, and urban elite. They may not give us a full picture of society, but we can at least see further into the connections between ruling groups and society. I have written elsewhere about the insight we can gain on the internal life of cities from the local histories of southern Iran.[89] From Isfizari, Fasih, and ʿUqayli we can gain some additional insights into the families which produced Timurid viziers; their varied provenance suggests a class that was neither fully self-perpetuating nor closed off from the rest of society. Local sources likewise reveal the breadth of the religious experience of both rulers and population. Taken together therefore, local histories indicate a closer connection of government to society and a broader distribution of power than the dynastic histories would suggest.

[84] Since Rukn al-Din died well before Abu Saʿid's reign this is puzzling, but we know that he spent time in Fars, and the connection could have occurred there (Wāʿiẓ, *Maqṣad*, 60, 74; Khwāndamīr, *Ḥabīb*, vol. IV, 8; Thackston, *Habibu's-siyar*, 355).

[85] Wāʿiẓ, *Maqṣad*, 92; Khwāndamīr, *Ḥabīb*, vol. IV, 60; Thackston, *Habibu's-siyar*, 384.

[86] Wāʿiẓ, *Maqṣad*, 52, 80–81, 88–89, 90, 93–94, 105–08, 137, 139.

[87] Ibid., 18, 40, 43, 50, 53, 57.

[88] See for instance, Samarqandī, *Matlaʿ*, 173, 184–85, 226, 290, 304–05, 318, 712, 713, 865, 874.

[89] Beatrice F. Manz, "Local Histories of Southern Iran," in *History and Historiography of Post-Mongol Central Asia and the Middle East: Studies in Honor of John E. Woods*, edited by Judith Pfeiffer and Sholeh A. Quinn (Wiesbaden: Harrassowitz, 2006), 267–81.

Problems of time and affiliation in Sufi biographical literature

Since Sufi *ṭarīqas* have received much attention from scholars during the last years their literature has been well analyzed. There are excellent studies showing the way in which texts can be used as a guide to social history or as a literary expression of the ideals held by the authors and their audience. Historians have also explored the historiographical problems which are common to the genre.[90] The inclusion of miracles and the liberal use of standard stories and *topoi* in biographical narrative call for constant caution, and there is some question about how much actual material can be extracted from these sources. As a social historian of a period in which Sufi shaykhs were important I cannot do without the biographies. I have proceeded on the principle that many incidents recounted probably did originate in actual events, and can be used with proper restraint.

Time and vantage point play an important part in shaping Sufi literature and we must take their influence into consideration when using *tadhkira* literature to analyze the role that Sufi shaykhs played in politics. Just as one estimates the importance of an individual by his or her prominence in the sources, so one often judges the influence of organizations by the power ascribed to individuals within them. One of the greatest problems we face is that most of the Sufi biographical literature on Shahrukh's period dates from the last quarter of the fifteenth century or later, when the genre became enormously popular. It was just at this time that many spiritual lineages were developing rapidly from relatively loosely organized associations to more exclusive organizations in competition with each other. The authors of later biographical collections attribute contemporary attitudes to earlier times, often portraying *ṭarīqa*s as more organized and competitive than they may actually have been.[91] They are likely also to emphasize the shaykhs of the region in which the *ṭarīqa* was strongest at their own time. Sufi communities however had been expanding their regional interests; individuals traveled to other regions and the central locus of a *ṭarīqa* sometimes shifted to a new place.

In the historiography of Sufi shaykhs, happenstance plays perhaps an even greater role than it does in narrative histories. For a *tadhkira* collection to be

[90] See Jürgen Paul, "Hagiographische Texte als historische Quelle," *Saeculum* 41, 1 (1990), 17–43; Carl W. Ernst, *Eternal Garden: Mysticism, History and Politics at a South Asian Sufi Center* (Albany, NY: State University of New York Press, 1992), 85–93; J. Mojaddedi, *The Biographical Tradition in Sufism: the Ṭabaqāt Genre from al-Sulamī to Jāmī* (Richmond, Surrey: Curzon, 2001).

[91] Devin DeWeese, "Sayyid ʿAlī Hamadānī and Kubrawī Hagiographical Traditions," in *The Legacy of Mediaeval Persian Sufism*, edited by Leonard Lewisohn (London: Khaniqahi-Nimatullahi Publications, 1992), 139–44; Jürgen Paul, *Doctrine and Organization. The Khwājagān/Nashbandīya in the first Generation after Bahāʾuddīn* (Berlin: Das Arabische Buch, 1998), 3–4. The problems of applying later characteristics onto an earlier period is discussed at length by Dina Le Gall, in *A Culture of Sufism: Naqshbandis in the Ottoman World, 1450–1700* (Albany, NY: State University of New York Press, 2005).

written and to survive, the shaykhs it commemorated had to continue to matter. The best documented shaykhs therefore are those whose disciples were later important and whose *silsila* continued to be influential. In the eastern part of the Timurid realm, the writing of Sufi biography was shaped above all by one development: the rise of the Naqshbandiyya under its shaykh Khwaja Ahrar (806–96/1404–90). There are one or two hagiographical works of the late fourteenth and early fifteenth century which cover the career of the eponymous founder of the Naqshbandiyya, Baha' al-Din Naqshband and the circle within which he lived his life,[92] but for most of our information on the shaykhs of Shahrukh's period we are dependent on later works.[93] Over the course of a long life Khwaja Ahrar became one of the most powerful figures of eastern Iran and Transoxiana, and by the late fifteenth century he had turned the Naqshbandi *ṭarīqa* into a centralized economic, religious, and political force, known for its strong connections to the dynasty and its involvement in the artisanal and agricultural spheres.

The height of Khwaja Ahrar's career coincided with the cultural efflorescence of Herat during the reign of Sultan Husayn Bayqara (r. 873/1469 to 911/1506), presided over by the vizier Mir ʿAli Shir Nawa'i and the Persian poet ʿAbd al-Rahman Jami; Nawa'i was affiliated with the Naqshbandiyya while Jami was both an adept and a close associate of Khwaja Ahrar. Two particularly influential works which have provided much of the basic information for studies of Shahrukh's period are the *Nafahat al-Uns*, a collection of biographies of shaykhs from a number of orders written by Jami in 881–83/1476–78, and the *Rashahat-i ʿayn al-hayat*, a set of biographies organized around the life and teachings of Khwaja Ahrar, written in 1504 by ʿAli b. Husayn al-Waʿiz al-Kashifi, a late disciple of Khwaja Ahrar's.[94] Although both works include shaykhs outside the Naqshbandiyya, their material is inevitably shaped by the view of their own order as central. It is important therefore to balance them with biographical literature about other groups, even when it is less full on the shaykhs of the region in question.

Several other Sufi lines were apparently well represented in Iran and Central Asia during Shahrukh's reign, but they have left us less evidence of their activities. For the Niʿmatullahi and the Kubrawi *ṭarīqa*s the early fifteenth century was a crucial time – marking for the Niʿmatullahis their establishment in southern Iran, and for the Kubrawis a permanent split. Nonetheless, the fullest and most detailed sources come from a later period and are less informative on the shaykhs active in the central Timurid areas than on

92 For these sources see Jürgen Paul, "Hagiographische Texte," 26–28; Jürgen Paul, *Die politische und soziale Bedeutung der Naqšbandiyya in Mittelasien im 15. Jahrhundert* (Berlin, New York: W. De Gruyter, 1991), 9.
93 Jo-Ann Gross and Asom Urunbaev, eds., *The Letters of Khwāja ʿUbayd Allāh Aḥrār and his Associates* (Leiden, Boston, Köln: Brill, 2002), 7–14.
94 Paul, *Naqšbandiyya*, 10.

those elsewhere.[95] Two sets of local shaykhs, the descendants of Shaykh Sayf al-Din Bakharzi in Bukhara and those of the Herati shaykh Shihab al-Din Bistami, seem to have lost prestige in the course of the fifteenth century, and we read little about their representatives during Shahrukh's reign. Nonetheless, we know from grave visitation manuals and from incidental mentions elsewhere that members of these families were still active. What we cannot tell is what role they played. Another *silsila* whose center moved out of Khorasan was the Chishtiyya, seen as having begun in Khorasan but having flourished in India.[96] There can be no doubt that from at least the fourteenth century the major weight of the Chishtiyya was in India, but this does not mean that it was inactive in Khorasan. We know from a number of non-religious sources that Chishti shaykhs were prominent in eastern Iran in the first part of the fifteenth century.[97]

The grave visitation manuals provide a counterpoint to the Naqshbandi *tadhkira* literature. One of the most useful is the *Maqsad al-iqbal*, discussed above. We find here mention of shaykhs overlooked in the local hagiographical literature, among whom are a number of Khalwati shaykhs active during Temür's and Shahrukh's period.[98] A later addition by an eighteenth-century Safavid author adds both several Chishti sayyids and numerous disciples of Zayn al-Din Khwafi, both largely ignored in the biographical literature.[99] This gives us a clue about what other spiritual affiliations were represented, but the biographies here are late and too short to provide a guide to relationships.

The prominence given to individuals and brotherhoods in biographical sources is thus a function not of their importance in their own period, but of their usefulness to later generations. The "argument from silence," never reliable, becomes quite useless under these circumstances. The late provenance of sources is an even greater problem when we attempt to understand the role of Sufi shaykhs within the politics of a given place and period. An historian tracing either the development of a *ṭarīqa* or the ideology within it can certainly be misled, but is at least looking for information which the text was written to

[95] Jean Aubin, "De Kûhbanân à Bidar: la famille niʿmatullahī," *Studia Iranica* 20, 2 (1991), 233–34; DeWeese, "Sayyid ʿAli Hamadānī," 127–36; Devin DeWeese, "The Eclipse of the Kubrawīyah in Central Asia," *Iranian Studies* 21, 1–2 (1988), 55–57. The Yasawiyya is exceptionally poor in sources, and can be reconstructed only with difficulty (see Devin DeWeese, "Sacred Places and 'Public' Narratives: The Shrine of Aḥmad Yasavī in Hagiographical Traditions of the Yasavī Ṣūfī Order, 16th–17th Centuries," *Muslim World* 90, 3–4 [2000], 355–56).

[96] B. Böwering, "Češtīya," in *Encyclopaedia Iranica*, edited by E. Yarshater (London, Boston: Routledge and Kegan Paul, 1985–2006).

[97] Shahrukh appointed a Chishti shaykh to head his new *khānaqāh* in 813/1410–11 (Samarqandī, *Maṭlaʿ*, 110). He visited the shrine at Chisht (Yūsuf Ahl, *Farāʾid-i ghiyāthī*, vol. II, 102) and, as I have shown above, Fasih Khwafi mentions a Chishti line of sayyids with particular respect.

[98] Wāʿiẓ, *Maqṣad*, 46–47, 70–71, 72, 78, 83, 89, 90.

[99] ʿUbayd Allah b. Abu Saʿīd Harawī, *Taʿlīq bar maqṣad al-iqbāl yā Risāla-i duwwum-i mazārāt-i Harāt*, edited by Māyil Harawī, in Aṣīl al-Dīn ʿAbd Allāh Wāʿiẓ, *Maqṣad al-iqbāl al-sulṭāniyya wa marṣad al-āmāl al-Khāqāniyya*. Tehran: Intishārāt-i Bunyād-i Farhang-i Īrān, 1351/1972–3, 109–15, 119–27.

provide. For both the author and the historian, individuals within the lineage are important as exemplars and transmitters. My goal however is to understand not what led to the future, but how Sufi organizations functioned at a specific time, and the individual then must be understood as a political actor. This leads to a variety of questions whose answers will not lie entirely within the literature of one *ṭarīqa*. I must ask where the individual acquired his power and influence and what role the *ṭarīqa* played in his life. Did it control him? Did it give him power? Did it do both, or neither? A number of problems which are recognized but can often be overlooked now become central. We know that many people had several different affiliations at once, or were active both as ulama and as shaykhs. Numerous affiliations are not a problem if one is tracing a line of transmission, but they are crucial if we are judging how to understand one person's actions within the society of the period. We have to be careful not to consider any one individual as representative of a given path or as belonging exclusively to one group, unless there is evidence to show that no outside forces are at work.

We must recognize also that people are not always respected during their lifetime for the same reasons that they are remembered after their deaths. To understand actions and personal power at the time we are concerned with, we must treat the major Naqshbandi sources with particular caution. To illustrate the difficulties of judging the relationship between the individual and the group, I will discuss the career of Khwaja Muhammad Parsa, a Bukharan scholar and shaykh who is remembered as one of the chief successors of Baha' al-Din Naqshband. Two well-known stories preserved in the *Rashahat-i 'ayn al-hayat* have been used by historians to illuminate the relationship of the Timurid rulership to Muhammad Parsa and the nascent Naqshbandiyya/Khwajagan as a whole. Perhaps because the incidents were preserved in a Sufi source, they have usually been interpreted within the same framework, but that may not be the best way to understand them.[100]

The first story concerns Shahrukh's rise to power and has been cited to show the support he received from the Naqshbandiyya. The *Rashahat* reports that while Khalil Sultan was ruling in Samarqand Muhammad Parsa was in friendly contact with Shahrukh and for this reason Khalil Sultan turned against him and ordered him to leave the city. Parsa obeyed briefly but soon returned and when Shahrukh sent an ultimatum to Khalil Sultan before attacking him in 811/1408–09, Muhammad Parsa read it from the minbar of the mosque, and then sent it on to Khalil Sultan.[101] If we accept this story as something based on Parsa's actions, we must examine what it means. The first question is why Muhammad Parsa was in a position to correspond with rulers and to read their edicts from the pulpit of the mosque. Was it

[100] See for example, V. V. Bartol'd, *Ulugbek*, 87, 122; Hamid Algar, "Nakshbandiyya," in *Encyclopaedia of Islam*, 2nd edn.

[101] Kāshifī, *Rashaḥāt*, 108–09.

because he was a Naqshbandi? Probably not. Baha' al-Din Naqshband had died in 1389; his disciples were only in their second generation and as far as we know there were only a few shaykhs inside Bukhara and not many outside. A new, small community of shaykhs could hardly endow its members with such standing. If we look at Parsa's other connections however, we see significant sources of power. He was a member of an established and prosperous Bukharan family which had produced several generations of ulama, particularly scholars of *ḥadīth*.[102]

Muhammad Parsa came from a family which one might expect to find among the notables of the city, and the stories about his family in the earliest biography of Baha' al-Din Naqshband, the *Anis al-talibin*, support this supposition. According to this source, Muhammad Parsa's uncle, Husam al-Din Khwaja Yusuf, was one of the outstanding ulama of Bukhara and one of the first to become a follower of Baha' al-Din. One day Baha' al-Din informed Khwaja Yusuf that he would die in the course of an insurrection and his property would pass to his nephews, including Muhammad Parsa. Some time after their conversation the city leaders of Bukhara (*ru'asā' wa ḥukkām*) were planning a rebellion against their rulers and several people, led by Husam al-Din Khwaja Yusuf, came to Baha' al-Din to ask his cooperation.[103] When the rebellion occurred, Husam al-Din was indeed killed. It is likely that this story is built around an actual occurrence. The grave manual of Bukhara states that Husam al-Din died in 768/1366–67, and it was in that year that the leaders of the Yasa'uri tribe, based near Bukhara, decided to withstand the aspiring leader of the area, Amir Husayn Qara'unas. According to the narrative sources, the population of Bukhara was active in its defense and a number were killed.[104] The author is probably using a remembered event to illustrate the prescience of Baha' al-Din. When Muhammad Parsa read Shahrukh's pronouncement from the minbar of the mosque therefore, he was almost certainly acting as a member of one of the city's leading families. It was the notables who made decisions about which ruler to support and who informed the population of the decision. Thus what we see here is the decision of the council of power holders in Bukhara to back Shahrukh, not the support of the Naqshbandiyya/Khwajagan as such.

The second story about Muhammad Parsa is also connected to his identity as a scholar of the exoteric religious sciences, particularly *ḥadīth*. The

[102] Maria Subtelny, "The Making of Bukhārā-yi Sharīf: Scholars, Books, and Libraries in Medieval Bukhara (The Library of Khwāja Muḥammad Pārsā)," in *Studies on Central Asian History in Honor of Yuri Bregel* edited by Devin DeWeese (Bloomington, Indiana: Research Institute for Inner Asian Studies, 2001), 79–111, 82–88.

[103] Ṣalāḥ al-Dīn Mubārak Bukhārī, *Anīs al-ṭālibīn wa ʿuddat al-sālikīn*, edited by Khalīl Ibrāhīm Ṣarī Ughlī (Tehran: Kayhān, 1371/1992), 67, 183–84, 229–31, 326–27. The work was written before 831/1427–28 (Paul, *Naqšbandiyya*, 9).

[104] Aḥmad b. Maḥmūd Muʿīn al-fuqarā', *Tārīkh-i mullāzāda dar dhikr-i mazārāt-i Bukhārā*, edited by Aḥmad Gulchīn Maʿānī (Tehran: Kitābkhāna-i Ibn Sīnā, 1339/1960), 56; Yazdī, *Ẓafarnāma*, vol. I, 109; Manz, *Rise and Rule*, 53, 164.

Rashahat recounts that when the preeminent *ḥadīth* expert Shams al-Din Muhammad al-Jazari came to Samarqand, some of Khwaja Parsa's enemies suggested that Parsa should be tested for the soundness of his transmission. Ulugh Beg complied, and one need hardly say that Muhammad Parsa performed brilliantly.[105] It is not easy to know how we should understand this event – assuming it happened. In the *Rashahat* the emphasis in the story is on the ability of Muhammad Parsa to foil his enemies, and it has been cited by scholars to illustrate the unfriendly relations between the Naqshbandiyya and either Ulugh Beg or Shahrukh. There is however no obvious connection to the circle of Baha' al-Din Naqshband in the actual event. Muhammad al-Jazari was the foremost expert on *ḥadīth* in the Iranian regions and his *ijāza*s are often mentioned along with those granted by Muhammad Parsa. Both were luminaries, and Muhammad al-Jazari was the greater one.[106] When al-Jazari came to Transoxiana, it would be natural for him to meet with Muhammad Parsa but it is quite possible that the question of where they should meet would have involved questions of etiquette and relative prestige. If the meeting did occur, its primary purpose was almost certainly connected to *ḥadīth* rather than mystical thought, since it was Parsa's knowledge of *ḥadīth* that attracted students to him.

Khwaja Muhammad Parsa was indeed a central person in the development of the Naqshbandi *ṭarīqa*, not because he had numerous disciples, but because he was a gifted and prolific writer; it was he who preserved the sayings of Baha' al-Din Naqshband's successor 'Ala' al-Din 'Attar and wrote treatises formulating the doctrine and practice of the order. In the long run, his Naqshbandi writings have been the most important and have given him lasting fame. During his lifetime and for some time thereafter, however, he was probably best known for his expertise in *ḥadīth* and his most famous work was almost certainly his general compendium of the religious sciences, exoteric and esoteric, entitled *Fasl al-khitab li wasl al-ahbab*.[107]

Conclusion

Taking our sources together, we still must conclude that the writing of history was an insider's business. All of the historians discussed show their connections to the circle of men close to the dynasty, while the writers of Sufi biography were almost all attached to shaykhs of power and influence. Their sources of information, particularly of anecdote, were limited largely to the men within their group. Furthermore, all authors wrote within particular genres which dictated the type of information they included and the

105 Kāshifī, *Rashaḥāt*, 106–08.

106 They are mentioned together for instance by Aḥmad Ibn 'Arabshah, *Tamerlane or Timur, the Great Amir*, translated by J. H. Sanders (London: Luzac, 1936), 312.

107 Subtelny, "The Making," 90.

meaning they ascribed to it. Nonetheless, there are significant differences among the sources, which we can usefully exploit once we have identified them. Some of these come out of the goal set by the historian; whether he is writing a universal history, a biography, or a description of local buildings and shrines. Even more important, often, are the differences among our authors which arise from chance – their particular milieus, geographical origins and personal interests, all of which influence what they knew. It is in the issue of inclusion or exclusion that the influence of personal contacts emerges most clearly. What authors set out to portray was the life of dynasty, city or region and what they created was a product of the sources available to them, both written and oral. Information found its way into a work not only systematically, but also as the author happened to know it or to care about it. Because Fasih Khwafi writes of his own ancestry, we know that he descended from a local military figure; this then applies to other members of his family serving in the *dīwān*.

Once we recognize the importance of the individual historian in determining what is included in his work, we can understand the role of chance in what we do and do not know. Fasih's middle position in the *dīwān* and his attachment to local religious figures together provide us a fund of information we would otherwise not have. On the other hand, the rise of Khwaja Ahrar just after Shahrukh's period, while it preserves information from a Naqshbandi viewpoint, has probably also helped to rob us of other points of view. If we are to judge what we do have and to use it responsibly we have to determine the factors that have influenced what was written and what has survived. Many of these factors have to do with developments outside the time period discussed; which regions have had an active historical tradition, which Sufi organizations have since risen to power.

As I have tried to show, when we combine a variety of sources, we can find ourselves balancing quite different views of society and government. While the works that one might call central – the dynastic histories written for the court, the *tadhkira* literature written for a specific *silsila* – give the impression that most power was in the hands of a few well-known men, the works of historians whose attachment to one region gave them a narrower but deeper focus can help to dispel that impression. Local grave visitation manuals fill in some of the blank spaces left by Sufi biographical literature because they include shaykhs whose *ṭariqa*s have not continued to be important in the region. With a combination of central and local sources, it is possible to gain some understanding of the breadth of power relationships across the political and religious landscape.

CHAPTER 3

Shahrukh's *dīwān* and its personnel

Under Shahrukh the chancellery and financial administration – the *dīwān* – was a significant locus for power and thus the scene of struggles for preeminence. Like other bureaucracies it had a sophisticated culture of literary and accounting skill, graft, wit and backbiting. There are several issues that deserve attention: how involved the ruler and other members of the dynasty were in administrative affairs, how power was wielded within the financial administration, and how it changed hands, and finally, how personnel were recruited and used. Another important question is how closely Chaghatay emirs worked with the fiscal bureaucrats.

From the Seljukid period on, governments in Iran usually had two separate sets of personnel; military and court offices were held by members of the Turkic military elite, while the civilian administration was staffed by Persian bureaucrats. This system did not preclude the personnel of either side from taking part in the other, and Persian viziers were sometimes important commanders. Emirs frequently attempted to influence events in the fiscal administration, which handled both their pay and their taxes.[1] Nonetheless, offices and personnel remained officially separate. In the Timurid state, the dual system continued but we cannot assume that it operated the same way. In the "Muʿizz al-ansab," which mirrors the formal organization of Timurid administration, the two sides of government are separately listed; first come the emirs, almost all of whom were Turco-Mongolian, then other offices, usually reserved for the Chaghatay, and near the end of the list we have sections for Persian scribes, Turkic scribes, and *ṣadr*s (the religious functionaries who oversaw appointments and *waqf* endowments). Listed under Persian scribes we find most of the Persian *dīwān* officials mentioned in the histories, and usually several of the men mentioned as *ṣadr* in the "Muʿizz al-ansab" also appear in narrative sources. However, the men listed as Turkic scribes are rarely mentioned elsewhere.

Scholars have provided several short descriptions of Timurid administration based primarily on materials from the late fifteenth century. There is

[1] Lambton, *Continuity and Change*, 28–68, 221–57.

general agreement that there were two separate *dīwān*s, one dealing with taxes and correspondence, staffed largely by Persian bureaucrats, and another, presumably staffed by Turks, dealing with military affairs. The exact terms used for these administrations and the range of functions each performed are difficult to determine even for Sultan Husayn Bayqara's reign. It is clear that the *dīwān-i māl* was the tax administration, while the name *dīwān-i lashgar* or *dīwān-turk* refers to the military administration. The term *dīwān-i aʿlāʾ* has been interpreted by some scholars as designating both *dīwān*s together, and by others as referring specifically to the tax administration and chancellery.[2]

It is not clear how well later analyses fit the beginning of the fifteenth century and for the period of Shahrukh it is surprisingly difficult to analyze the administrative structure and its terminology. Although events in the *dīwān* are chronicled in several histories, historians are inconsistent in their use of terms and show no interest in describing the structure of administration. The term *dīwān-i aʿlā* seems most often to denote the central administration in distinction to provincial or personal bureaucracies – thus, the first of the two meanings given above.[3] Only very occasionally do our sources mention a specialized *dīwān*; there is one mention of *dīwān-lashkar*, one of *dīwān-i lashgar wa tovachigarī*, and one or two of a *dīwān-i māl* and *dīwān-i khāṣṣa*.[4] While scholars have attributed higher standing to the Turco-Mongolian *dīwān* we have little knowledge of how it functioned. There is certainly evidence that Shahrukh and his governors had a council of emirs with whom they consulted and that membership in this council was a recognized honor, granted to high ranking Chaghatay emirs and very occasionally to an Iranian official or commander.[5] It is likely that the term *amīr dīwān* used in the *Muʿizz al-ansāb* refers to membership in this council, but its formal duties remain obscure, and I hesitate to identify it firmly with the

[2] Hans R. Roemer, *Staatschreiben der Timuridenzeit. Das Šaraf-nāmä des ʿAbdallāh Marwārīd in kritischer Auswertung* (Wiesbaden: Akademie der Wissenschaften und der Literatur, Veröffentlichungen der orientalischen Kommission, 1952), 85–87, 169; Roemer, "The Successors of Tīmūr," vol. 6, 131–32; Gottfried Herrmann, "Der historische Gehalt des 'Nāmye nāmīʾ von Ḫāndamīr," PhD dissertation, University of Göttingen, 1968, 184–91a; Ando, *Timuridische Emire*, 223–39; Maria Subtelny, "The Vaqfīya of Mīr ʿAlī Šīr as Apologia," in *Fahir Iz Armağanı II, Journal of Turkish Studies* 15 (1991), 262.

[3] Several pieces of evidence suggest that the term denoted the combined administration. In the narrative sources on Shahrukh's reign *dīwān-i aʿlāʾ* is most often used when authors refer to the central government in distinction from the provinces, and here we find the *dīwān-i aʿlāʾ* dealing with a number of different matters, which one might expect to have been assigned to separate departments. Thus we find the term in reference to the collection of taxes, the inspection of provincial administrations, and as a kind of court, investigating and punishing misbehavior both by bureaucrats and by emirs who have misbehaved in military affairs (see Samarqandī, *Maṭlaʿ*, 108, 318, 757, 850–51, 900; Marʿashī, *Tārīkh-i Ṭabaristān*, 273). If we define the *dīwān-i aʿlāʾ* as the Persian administration, we must assume that it acted as tax administration, chancellery, and as a court for military affairs, leaving little for the supposedly more important army *dīwān* to do.

[4] Samarqandī, *Maṭlaʿ*, 701; Ṭihrānī Iṣfahānī, *Diyarbakriyya*, 296, 318; Herrmann, "Der historische Gehalt," 187; Ando, *Timuridische Emire*, 224–25; Aubin, *Deux sayyids*, 72, n. 3.

[5] See for example Samarqandī, *Maṭlaʿ*, 634, 717, 758–59, 795; Kātib, *Tārīkh-i jadīd*, 250.

dīwān-i lashgar, usually thought to have dealt with army administration. While we may infer a separate military *dīwān*, we should not assume that Chaghatay personnel were limited to that side of the administration.

The historian closest to the *dīwān* was Fasih Khwafi, who spent most of his life serving within it. Fasih mentions several *dīwān*s, but the ones he distinguishes among are those serving different people: those of Baysunghur or other princes, of provinces, and of emirs. Most important figures had some administrative apparatus of their own in which they employed Persian scribes, and while the desired career path was from lower to higher, bureaucrats out of favor in the center might serve elsewhere for a time. Despite the fact that Fasih and many of his relatives served in the *dīwān* he rarely mentions a specific office, and when he refers to the main *dīwān*, calls it simply "the *dīwān* of his highness" (*dīwān-i ḥiḍrat-i aʿlāʾ-i khāqānī*). ʿAbd al-Razzaq Samarqandī, writing about the same appointments and dismissals, will sometimes use the term *dīwān-i aʿlāʾ*, but more often simply *dīwān*.[6] In general then, the word *dīwān* usually means, simply, bureaucracy or administration rather than a particular organization within government.

Personnel and property of the *dīwān*

The only administration whose history we can follow is the central tax *dīwān* and chancellery. At the head of the Persian personnel was a Persian *ṣāḥib dīwān*, usually paired with another Persian vizier of slightly less power. Both princes and Turco-Mongolian emirs also held recognized positions within the *dīwān*. Early in his rule, Shahrukh appointed his son Baysunghur to a position which is described in some histories simply as oversight and in others as the position of *amīr dīwān*.[7] There seem to have been emirs who were appointed to the position of chief emir within the central administration, and a similar position existed in provincial administrations. However, while in the provinces we usually know of only one or two such positions at a time, in the central administration there were often several. When the narrative histories mention such appointments they often use the terms *amīr dīwān* and *amīr al-umarā* interchangeably. We can see the influence of these men, and the sources indicate that they held appointed positions, but it is not clear how they fit into the bureaucracy. The biography of a *muḥtaṣib* of Abu Saʿid's time in the *Habib al-siyar* suggests a specific regional authority; the author states admiringly that the *muḥtaṣib* prevented the *amir-i tümen* of Herat from exempting any city groups from taxes or excusing them from payments they had agreed on. This passage is very suggestive and could help us to

[6] Samarqandī, *Maṭlaʿ*, 196, 670, 689, 747, 755, 839. Ḥāfiẓ-i Abrū uses the term *dīwān* (Ḥāfiẓ-i Abrū, *Majmaʿ*, fol. 7b; Ḥāfiẓ-i Abrū, *Zubdat*, 628–9.

[7] Ḥāfiẓ-i Abrū, *Zubdat*, 625–30; Khwāndamīr, *Dastūr*, 247; Faṣīḥ Khwāfī, *Mujmal-i faṣīḥī*, vol. III, 226.

understand certain *dīwān* scandals, but I have seen no evidence elsewhere for such a position.[8] It is hard to attach titles to specific offices in particular *dīwāns*.[9] The title *amīr dīwān* may well have referred both to emirs within the council surrounding the ruler and to those with responsibility in the financial administration.

It is likely that many emirs held ill-defined and overlapping administrative responsibilities. This was due partly to the problem the dynasty faced in filling offices with competent personnel while honoring the tradition of granting offices to the son of the last holder. In positions which required experience and specific skills, hereditary succession might lead to double staffing, which allowed the ruler to include both the men he was obligated to appoint and those he needed in order to achieve his goals. It is clear, for example, that two families had inherited rights over positions of command; the descendants of Temür's follower Chekü Barlas, and one branch of the descendants of Ghiyāth al-Din Tarkhan.[10] Both families retained considerable prestige from the period of Temür, during which the family of Chekü held the position of *amīr al-umarāʾ*, and the office was passed down within the family. However, as I have shown, Shahrukh chose to promote new and more dependent emirs to high positions; the two most powerful emirs in his administration were Firuzshah and ʿAlika, both of whom are described in the narrative histories as having positions of preeminent power in the administration as *amīr dīwān* or *amīr al-umarā*. Firuzshah and ʿAlika were succeeded in their positions by their sons, but ʿAbd al-Razzaq Samarqandī writes that since the two sons were young and inexperienced, Shahrukh appointed an older emir, Amir Sultanshah Barlas, to manage the *dīwān*.[11]

For an explanation of the office of supreme emir or *amīr al-umarāʾ* we might expect help from the *Muʿizz al-ansab*, usually precise in its designation of offices, but here the term *amīr dīwān* applies apparently to all emirs who were appointed to office within the administration, or at least to those who made up the central council; there are twenty-three listed under Shahrukh, several of whom were active at the same time. The "Muʿizz al-ansab" mentions the office of *amīr al-umarā* only very occasionally, and does not include it in the list of offices under each ruler.[12] We cannot therefore

[8] Khwāndamīr, *Ḥabīb*, vol. IV, 108; Thackston, *Habibuʾs-siyar*, 409. Where someone is described as *amīr-i tümen* in the *Muʿizz al-ansab*, the office is connected with command over troops (*Muʿizz*, fols. 135b–37a).

[9] For examples of provincial positions and the administrations of princes, see Samarqandī, *Maṭlaʿ*, 692–93, 699–700; Ṭihrānī Iṣfahānī, *Diyarbakriyya*, 285, 293; Kātib, *Tārīkh-i jadīd*, 266; Faṣīḥ Khwāfī, *Mujmal-i faṣīḥī*, vol. III, 255–56. For the problem of determining how many people held this position, see Ando, *Timuridische Emire*, 230–31.

[10] Ando, *Timuridische Emire*, 230–31. In these cases we can trace the inheritance of the office quite clearly (for the family of Chekü, see Yazdī, *Ḥasanī*, 40; Ḥāfiz-i Abrū, *Majmaʿ*, fol. 14a; *Muʿizz*, fols. 92b, 132b; and for the family of Ghiyath al-Din Tarkhan, see Faṣīḥ Khwāfī, *Mujmal-i faṣīḥī*, vol. III, 229; Samarqandī, *Maṭlaʿ*, 294, 640).

[11] Samarqandī, *Maṭlaʿ*, 754, 747, 841, 842.

[12] *Muʿizz*, fols. 132b–33b.

be certain what *dīwān* offices emirs held, but it is clear that some had a powerful and official position within the financial administration of Shahrukh's realm.

The *dīwān*s were not a only a conduit of wealth from population to government, but also an organization for the continued management of government property. There is frequent mention of the goods that they managed; confiscated wealth, captured households, taxes, livestock, and grain all came into the *dīwān* and sometimes remained under its management. Shahrukh for instance brought back numerous households of Turkmens after his second Azarbaijan campaign, which are referred to as *dīwān* households, and when counted numbered 10,000.[13] The prince Baysunghur greatly favored the poet Amir Shahi, descended from the Sarbadars of Sabzawar whom Temür had defeated, and to show his appreciation he negotiated the return of some of the family's properties which had been seized by the *dīwān*.[14] In the provinces the histories mention land and mills as *dīwān* property and identify officials in charge of silk production for the *dīwān*; we also hear of herds of horses belonging to it.[15]

The history of the central *dīwān*

Shahrukh's *dīwān* met the uncertainty of life after Temür in a state of upheaval. While Temür wintered in Qarabagh in 806/1403–04 he had decided to undertake a major investigation of administrative abuses throughout his realm and sent out agents to major cities, where they subjected bureaucrats to investigation and extortion. In 807/1404 Temür's wrath descended on the Herat *dīwān* in the form of Sayyid Fakhr al-Din Ahmad, appointed as inspector (*mufarrid*). Sayyid Fakhr al-Din was apparently out to ruin a lot of people and succeeded very well. Through energetic questioning and torture he and his assistant recovered two hundred *kebekī tümen*s of *dīwān* money from a variety of people. Shahrukh's chief vizier (*dīwānbekī*) Khwaja ʿAli Muhammadshah was hung up and tortured at the city gate.[16] News of Fakhr al-Din's activities spread and reached one of his enemies, Temür's bureaucrat Sayyid Zayn al-ʿAbidin Junabadi, who sent him a warning verse as he passed nearby on his way to Samarqand. Fakhr al-Din then hastened to Samarqand with the money he had extorted and succeeded in persuading Temür to exile a large number of Herati notables and functionaries to the border towns of Ashpara and Sawran. The list of people exiled suggests that Fakhr al-Din intended to empty the city of those involved with its governance, both within the government bureaucracy and outside it. The victims included five people who can be tentatively identified as Temür's former vizier Mahmud Shihab

[13] Samarqandī, *Maṭlaʿ*, 644. [14] Dawlatshāh Samarqandī, *Tadhkirat*, 247.
[15] Kātib, *Tārīkh-i jadīd*, 223; Isfizārī, *Rawḍāt*, vol. I, 124.
[16] Faṣīḥ Khwāfī, *Mujmal-i faṣīḥī*, vol. III, 149.

and his close relatives. There are also two other viziers, who were brothers, and several members of the learned class, including two pairs of fathers and sons. We find Pahlawan Hajji Zawa, head of the city patrol, his brother, a number of patrolmen, heads of quarters, and notables.[17] Fakhr al-Din's energy served him well. Temür had just dismissed and punished the vizier he had left in charge of the Samarqand *dīwān*, and now appointed Fakhr al-Din Ahmad partner to the new head of the *dīwān*, Sharaf al-Din ʿAli Simnani.[18]

After Temür's death in 807/1405, Shahrukh moved to stop some of the blood-letting. According to Muhammad Fasih, Sayyid Hasan Khwarazmi Gush Burida, the *mufarrid* whom Temür had sent to Quhistan, was killing and exiling local people and a number of sayyids had perished in the snow of the mountains while fleeing from him. Fasih reported these events to Shahrukh, who investigated Hasan and discovered that he was not a true sayyid, but had corrupted his true name, Saʿid – therefore making it possible to execute him.[19] Elsewhere Shahrukh showed less concern. It is chilling to discover that in 809/1406–07 when we first hear of the Herat *dīwān* under Shahrukh, Temür's agent Fakhr al-Din Ahmad was in charge of it, with the much less prominent ʿAli Shaqani as his subordinate partner.[20] Unlike many members of Temür's *dīwān* who came to Herat after Khalil Sultan's downfall, Fakhr al-Din had left Samarqand early to serve Shahrukh. His appointment is the more striking because he was an outsider to Shahrukh's administration and was competing with experienced and well-connected bureaucrats. He was also remarkably young – apparently in his late twenties.[21] We know little about his antecedents and connections, but according to ʿUqayli, who gives the fullest account, he was a sayyid who had been engaged in trade and amassed great wealth.[22]

In 809/1406–07 Fakhr al-Din was dislodged by two viziers who had been active during Temür's lifetime. One of these was a provincial bureaucrat,

[17] Faṣīḥ Khwāfī, *Mujmal-i faṣīḥī*, vol. III, 149–50. Shams al-Din Muhammad Simnani, who according to some sources had been head of the Herat diwan, does not appear in accounts of the purge.

[18] Ḥāfiẓ-i Abrū, "Continuation du Ẓafarnāma de Niẓāmuddīn Šāmī par Ḥāfiẓ-i Abrū," edited by F. Tauer, *Arkhiv Orientalny* VI (1934), 443–44.

[19] Faṣīḥ Khwāfī, *Mujmal-i faṣīḥī*, vol. III, 157–58. Sayyid Gush-burida is mentioned in similar terms in the hagiography of a shaykh in Quhistan (Jean Aubin, "Un santon quhistānī de l'époque timouride," *Revue des études islamiques* 35 [1967], 209–10).

[20] We do not have much information on the Herat *dīwān* during Temür's reign. In 804/1401–02, Temür sent Shams al-Din Muhammad b. ʿAli b. Yahya Simnani to Herat to take office as vizier of Khorasan; this was about the same time that he appointed Shams al-Din Muhammad's father, ʿAli Simnani, to his own vizierate (Faṣīḥ Khwāfī, *Mujmal-i faṣīḥī*, vol. III, 145; Shāmī, *Histoire des conquêtes*, vol. II, 171–72; Yazdī, *Ẓafarnāma*, vol. II, 270). The Herat personnel in the year or two after Fakhr al-Din's purge is not known.

[21] Faṣīḥ Khwāfī, *Mujmal-i faṣīḥī*, vol. III, 193–94, 229.

[22] Sayyid Fakhr al-Din Ahmad built a madrasa and *khānaqāh* in Sabzawar, and in the *Jāmiʿ al-tawārīkh-ḥasanī* he bears the *nisba* Sabzawari (Faṣīḥ Khwāfī, *Mujmal-i faṣīḥī*, 148; ʿUqaylī, *Āthār*, 336, 339; Yazdī, *Ḥasanī*, 38).

Ghiyath al-Din Salar Simnani, a forceful and ambitious man who had been active in the tax administration of Yazd during the latter years of Temür's reign.[23] The other was Sayyid Zayn al-ʿAbidin, who had already shown enmity to Fakhr al-Din in 807/1404. Ghiyath al-Din was apparently the instigator of the action, and it was he who testified against Fakhr al-Din. After only four months in office, Sayyid Zayn al-ʿAbidin was dismissed and the former *dīwān* chief, Shams al-Din Muhammad Simnani, replaced him, now holding a position secondary to that of Ghiyath al-Din Salar.[24] Ghiyath al-Din took hold actively. In his first year of office he built an *ʿīdgāh* for Herat, and we find him supervising the opening of the Fathabad canal in the region of Idwan and Tizan.[25] Unfortunately, he also attempted to assert his financial authority over Shahrukh's Chaghatay emirs at a time when their loyalty to the ruler was both fragile and badly needed. Ghiyath al-Din assessed the emirs' possessions for taxation and, according to some historians, assigned them grossly inflated values, "calling each egg a bird, each bird a sheep, each sheep a flock."[26] At the end of 810/1408, his actions brought about a rebellion by several of Shahrukh's major emirs, including sons of Temür's followers, which I described in Chapter 1. Sayyid Fakhr al-Din was not slow to profit from this event. He accused Ghiyath al-Din Salar of embezzling a large amount of money – 300 *tümens* according to the *Dastur al-wuzaraʾ* – and succeeded in proving his case. In 811/1408, while Shahrukh was campaigning in Sistan and ʿAlika Kukeltash had charge of Herat, Ghiyath al-Din and two of his agents were killed. It appears that Fakhr al-Din and the aggrieved emirs jointly engineered his downfall.[27]

Since most dramas in the bureaucracy involved charges of embezzlement, it is useful to estimate the monetary value of the sums named. This cannot be done with complete certainty, but we can achieve at least a rough understanding. It is clear that we are talking here about very large amounts. The most valuable and reliable currency during Shahrukh's reign was the *kebekī* dinar, a silver coin worth several times as much as most other dinars. A *tümen* represented 10,000 dinars.[28] It seems that currency values were fairly stable at

[23] Khwāndamīr, *Dastūr*, 343–44; Faṣīḥ Khwāfī, *Mujmal-i faṣīḥī*, vol. III, 145–46, 173; Jaʿfari, *Tārīkh-i Yazd*, 39–41; Kātib, *Tārīkh-i jadīd*, 92–93. Khwandamir dates these events to 810/1407–08. We know nothing of Ghiyath al-Din's parentage or his connection to the other Simnani viziers.

[24] Faṣīḥ Khwāfī, *Mujmal-i faṣīḥī*, vol. III, 173.

[25] Faṣīḥ Khwāfī, *Mujmal-i faṣīḥī*, vol. III, 173; T. Allen, *Catalogue*, 157.

[26] Khwāndamīr, *Dastūr*, 343–44; ʿUqaylī, *Āthār*, 336.

[27] Khwāndamīr, *Dastūr*, 344–45; ʿUqaylī, *Āthār*, 336; Faṣīḥ Khwāfī, *Mujmal-i faṣīḥī*, vol. III, 173, 183, 187. Fasih states that Shams al-Din Muhammad Tahir was appointed to the *dīwān* with Fakhr al-Din in 811/1408–09.

[28] Walther Hinz has valued the *kebekī* dinar of about 1440 at 1.95 pre-war gold marks. Walther Hinz, "The Value of the Toman in the later Middle Ages," in *Yādnāma-i Irānī-i Mīnūrskī* (Tehran: Publications of Tehran University, 1969), 90–91; E. A. Davidovich, *Istoriia denezhnovo obrashcheniia srednevekovoi Sredei Azii* (Moscow: Nauka, 1983), 33, 40, 56.

the time and we can therefore use examples from several years to estimate buying power.[29] For the *kebekī* dinar we can find several examples, all of which suggest considerable buying power. In the famine of 809/1407–08 a *mann* (2.9 kg) of wheat cost three *kebekī* dinars, considered a vastly inflated price.[30] After Shahrukh took Isfahan in 817/1414, he bestowed 100,000 *kebekī* dinars on the shrines for alms, as a gesture of goodwill after the pillage.[31] When he received and sent back the envoys who had come from India, he gave each a horse, saddle, coat and 3,000 *kebekī* dinars.[32] Though other dinars might be worth less, a *tümen* of any type was still a sizeable sum. In 808/1405 for instance, the princes besieging Kerman accepted 100 *tümen*s of Iraqi dinars (valued by Hinz at one-sixth the *kebekī* dinar) as a ransom to spare the town from being pillaged.[33] The sum of three million dinars of any denomination thus represented a very sizeable fortune for an individual.

In 811/1408 Sayyid Fakhr al-Din Ahmad regained his office, again with ʿAli Shaqani as subordinate, and he retained supremacy until 819/1416. It is not obvious how he managed to do so, since contemporary accounts of his career are uniformly hostile. According to Khwandamir, Fakhr al-Din curried favor with sayyids, ulama and other notables; nonetheless, he clearly had numerous enemies whom he persecuted freely and, in fact, we know of almost no-one whom he treated well. It seems likely that intimidation was Sayyid Fakhr al-Din's major source of power. In 812/1409–10, he was dismissed for a while from the *dīwān*, perhaps at the instigation of Sayyid Zayn al-ʾAbidin, who had returned to the *dīwān* the year before and who took over the workload in Fakhr al-Din's absence. But, after only a few weeks, Fakhr al-Din regained his post and the functionaries who had judged against him found themselves heavily fined; one, Muhammad Sagharchi, fled from the collectors (*muḥaṣṣil*s).[34] In 817/1414–15, Fakhr al-Din ordered the execution of Muhammad Fasih's cousin Khwaja Qawam al-Din Shaykh Muhammad Khwafi for an unspecified reason, and Fasih reports that, in 818/1415–16, the bureaucrat Khwaja Muʿizz al-Din Malik Simnani left Shiraz for the pilgrimage on account of Fakhr al-Din.[35]

As time went on Sayyid Fakhr al-Din's actions became increasingly outrageous. The historians relate that all people had to come as petitioners to his door and he took pleasure in keeping them waiting and turning most away without granting an audience. Eventually the feeling against him became too great for Shahrukh to ignore. According to Fasih, Fakhr al-Din's misdeeds

[29] Davidovich, *Istoriia denezhnovo*, 46; Walther Hinz, review of Jean Aubin, *Deux sayyids de Bam au xve siècle. Contribution à l'histoire de l'Iran timouride*, in *Oriens* 10, 2 (1957), 369.
[30] Faṣīḥ Khwāfī, *Mujmal-i faṣīḥī*, vol. III, 175 For the value of the *mann*, see Hinz, review of Jean Aubin, 369.
[31] Ḥāfiẓ-i Abrū, *Zubdat*, 552; Faṣīḥ Khwāfī, *Mujmal-i faṣīḥī*, vol. III, 218.
[32] Samarqandī, *Maṭlaʿ*, 849.
[33] Jean Aubin, *Deux sayyids*, 26; Hinz, review of Jean Aubin, 369.
[34] Faṣīḥ Khwāfī, *Mujmal-i faṣīḥī*, vol. III, 194.
[35] Ibid., vol. III, 214, 223.

began to emerge in 818/1415–16. Other historians begin the story in 819/1416–17, when Shahrukh returned from his final victory in Fars and appointed his son Baysunghur to supervise the *dīwān*. The implication is that he was charged with the investigation and rectification of Fakhr al-Din's abuses. Baysunghur inserted a new scribe as co-vizier; this was Ahmad Da'ud, known for his intelligence and eloquence. Ahmad Da'ud unearthed more information on Fakhr al-Din's peculiar behavior and let him know through hints that he should mend his ways. With the waning of Fakhr al-Din's power, his *dīwān* subordinates began to trust Baysunghur's intentions and to testify against their superior. As usual, Fakhr al-Din was proven to have embezzled money. His major accuser was his subordinate vizier, ʿAli Shaqani, who had suffered heavily, being threatened with dismissal if he did not pay 200 *kebeki tümen*s. It now transpired that Fakhr al-Din had instructed his functionaries to borrow large amounts from the treasury and to hand these sums over to him. As the affair became more public, the treasurer panicked and demanded the return of the money, but the borrowers put him off.[36]

For some time the affair seems to have remained within the sphere of the *dīwān*, still susceptible to rectification if the sums could be returned. However, after a while the scandal became so well known that it came to Shahrukh's attention, at which point public action was necessary. Shahrukh, following the formal laws of evidence, first punished the functionary who had actually borrowed the money, and Fakhr al-Din continued for a while as vizier. By this time, however, *dīwān* officials were openly and violently accusing the sayyid, and it became impossible for Fakhr al-Din to hold out. He accepted a debt of 200 *tümen*s, hoping to avoid further investigation. Once he had given in this far he became attackable; he was put in chains and handed over to the tax collectors. He appealed to Baysunghur without success, but Baysunghur's mother Gawharshad agreed to intercede on his behalf and persuaded Baysunghur to remove the chains. However, the tax-gatherers remained and it is at this point that Fakhr al-Din seems to have lost touch with reality. He attempted to gather the necessary money by borrowing in cash and kind on any possible pretext, convincing himself that he could achieve the whole sum and regain his position. His health however deteriorated and he died in Jumadi I, 820/June–July, 1417, not yet forty lunar years old.[37] It is hard to absolve Shahrukh from all blame in Fakhr al-Din's career. He appears to have been in Herat in 807/1404–05 during Fakhr al-Din's first purge; whether or not this happened with his consent, the character of the man was presented to him. This was the person whom he put in charge of his *dīwān* in the first years of his reign.

[36] Ḥāfiẓ-i Abrū, *Zubdat*, 625–30; Khwāndamīr, *Ḥabīb*, vol. III, 598–99; Thackston, *Habibu's-siyar*, 332; Faṣīḥ Khwāfī, *Mujmal-i faṣīḥī*, vol. III, 224, 226; Khwāndamīr, *Dastūr*, 347–52. Fasih gives the sum as 80,000 kebeki dinars; Khwandamir as 200,000.

[37] Faṣīḥ Khwāfī, *Mujmal-i faṣīḥī*, vol. III, 228–29; Khwāndamīr, *Ḥabīb*, vol. III, 599–600; Thackston, *Habibu's-siyar*, 332–33. The cause of death is given as *istisqā'* (dropsy).

With Fakhr al-Din gone, the way was open for a new power within the *dīwān*. Fakhr al-Din's second-in-command, ʿAli Shaqani, was not equipped to take full advantage. He had been in the Herat *dīwān* from 805/1402–03,[38] but did not have the strength of character to assert his authority. He had served as co-vizier to Sayyid Fakhr al-Din during both his terms of service, too cowed to refuse to do his bidding.[39] Nizam al-Din Ahmad Daʾud, competent and quick witted, was an obvious choice for successor, and indeed for a while he appears to have been chief vizier. What prevented his continued preeminence was probably the appearance of a new figure, Ghiyath al-din Pir Ahmad Khwafi, who became Shahrukh's most powerful and longest-lasting chief vizier.[40]

We know nothing of Pir Ahmad's earlier career except that he came from Khwaf and maintained a connection to his native region.[41] Fasih Khwafi gives his descent for three generations, adding some honorifics to the names of his forebears, so we may assume that he was well-born.[42] Pir Ahmad was appointed to head the *dīwān* at the end of 820/early 1418, at the expense of Ahmad Daʾud, whose dismissal he instigated.[43] With one or two short interruptions, he remained the preeminent bureaucrat until Shahrukh's death, serving with a number of partners. The historians mention him with approval as someone who respected the population, sponsored good works, and performed his duties with distinction.[44] While Sayyid Fakhr al-Din became the symbol for bureaucratic vice, Pir Ahmad figures in the sources as the powerful and active vizier, playing a role similar to that of the emirs Firuzshah and ʿAlika, mentioned in all accounts of Shahrukh's government.[45]

There were three viziers associated with Ghiyath al-Din Pir Ahmad in the *dīwān* for a significant period: Nizam al-Din Ahmad b. Daʾud Kalar, ʿAli Shaqani and Shams al-Din ʿAli Balicha Simnani, whose major terms of service probably occurred in that order.[46] In the case of all three there are indications of tensions at the beginning of the partnership that were later resolved. It seems that Pir Ahmad was able to collaborate with colleagues as long as he kept the upper hand. He was not free to choose his fellow vizier, and the

[38] Yazdī, *Ẓafarnāma*, vol. II, 372.
[39] ʿAli Shaqani seems to have remained in administration. According to Fasih, ʿAli became chief vizier for a period in 819/1416–17, but in 820/1417–18 was demoted and sent to Shiraz (Faṣīḥ Khwāfī, *Mujmal-i faṣīḥī*, vol. III, 225, 228). Açcording to the fuller, though later, story told by Samarqandī and Khwandamir, Ahmad Daʾud was appointed before the fall of Fakhr al-Din, and although ʿAli survived it, he did so in a subordinate position.
[40] Khwāndamīr, *Dastūr*, 352–53; ʿUqaylī, *Āthār*, 341; Faṣīḥ Khwāfī, *Mujmal-i faṣīḥī*, vol. III, 228; Samarqandī, *Maṭlaʿ*, 206.
[41] Khwāndamīr, *Dastūr*, 354.
[42] Faṣīḥ Khwāfī, *Mujmal-i faṣīḥī*, vol. III, 230. Ghiyath al-Din's father is referred to as *al-ṣāḥib*.
[43] Ibid., vol. III, 230; Khwāndamīr, *Dastūr*, 353.
[44] See previous footnote, also ʿUqaylī, *Āthār*, 342–43; Samarqandī, *Maṭlaʿ*, 679.
[45] For instance, Samarqandī, *Maṭlaʿ*, 724; Yazdī, *Ḥasanī*, 45; Dawlatshāh Samarqandī, *Tadhkirat*, 439.
[46] There were also other prominent viziers who shared office for a shorter time with Pir Ahmad.

appointments often displeased him; it is likely that partners were appointed with the intention of diluting the power of the chief vizier.

Ahmad b. Da'ud Kalar was probably the vizier who served with Pir Ahmad for the longest period. The terse account given by Fasih Khwafi suggests that Ahmad Da'ud was dismissed in 820/1417–18 at the instigation of Pir Ahmad, who then took over with other viziers as partners, and he places Ahmad's reappointment in 827/1423–24, suggestively, closely before Pir Ahmad's temporary dismissal in 828–9/1425–26.[47] It is likely that Ahmad Da'ud remained as associate vizier until 838/1434–35, when he was replaced by Sayyidi Ahmad Shirazi.[48] In the *Dastūr al-wuzarā'*, Khwandamir suggests that Ahmad Da'ud and Pir Ahmad shared the vizierate after the dismissal of Sayyid Fakhr al-Din, and that they were on the best of terms. He recounts a number of shared jokes involving elaborate puns on *dīwān* terms, and reports that each sent the other food when they prepared soups (*āsh*).[49] Since Fasih served in Shahrukh's *dīwān* with Ahmad Da'ud in 820/1417–18 and gives a more circumstantial account of bureaucratic appointments, his chronology should be preferred, and the joking relationship should be attributed to the later period, after Ahmad Da'ud's reappointment in 827/1423–24.

Pir Ahmad clearly had conflicts with his later co-vizier, 'Ali Shaqani, and won dominance over him. 'Ali Shaqani had remained within the administration in subordinate posts since the demotion of Fakhr al-Din Ahmad, and it is not certain when he became co-head of the *dīwān*, but the most likely occasion for his appointment is the death of Sayyidi Ahmad Shirazi in 839/1435. We know that he remained in the office until 845/1441. Khwandamir tells a vivid and humorous story about Ghiyath al-Din's subjugation of 'Ali Shaqani. Relations were so strained between the two men that their disagreements came to Shahrukh's attention and he decided to use the tension to his advantage by having each investigate the other's work. 'Ali Shaqani knew that Pir Ahmad had granted the income of a profitable village near Herat to his friend Safi al-Din b. Khwaja 'Abd al-Qadir, a man fond of jest who had played jokes on most of the people in Shahrukh's *majlis*. One can guess that Safi al-Din's antics had won him sufficient enemies to make him seem a safe target, and 'Ali Shaqani decided to start his researches with the investigation

47 Faṣīḥ Khwāfī, *Mujmal-i faṣīḥī*, vol. III, 230, 255, 257. Fasih states that Shams al-Din Muhammad b. 'Ali Simnani became Pir Ahmad's partner in 821/1418–19. Shams al-Din died in 824/1421, and we have no information about his replacement (Faṣīḥ Khwāfī, *Mujmal-i faṣīḥī*, vol. III, 247).

48 The evidence here is indirect. Fasih records Ahmad Da'ud's death in 840/1436–37, mentioning that he had been dismissed from the central *dīwān*. We know that Sayyidi Ahmad was appointed as partner to Pir Ahmad in 838/1434. Since there is no mention of any other viziers at the time, it seems likely that Ahmad Da'ud's dismissal coincided with Sayyidi Ahmad's appointment (Faṣīḥ Khwāfī, *Mujmal-i faṣīḥī*, vol. III, 281; Samarqandī, *Maṭla'*, 670).

49 Khwāndamīr, *Dastūr*, 352–53; Khwāndamīr, *Ḥabīb*, vol. IV, 2;. Thackston, *Habibu's-siyar*, 352. 'Uqaylī does not associate Ahmad Da'ud particularly with Pir Ahmad.

of his village. When ʿAli Shaqani visited, Safi al-Din was ready for him and tricked him into eating food laced with intoxicants – swearing by divorce that the dish contained no intoxicating substance and pointing to one section that was indeed without, from which he ate himself. ʿAli accordingly helped himself liberally and passed out. Safi al-Din rode off in haste to Shahrukh to report the vizier's disgraceful condition, and the equerry (*akhtaji*) whom Shahrukh sent did indeed find him in a bad state. He put him on his horse, still semi-conscious, and carried him off to court. ʿAli was not dismissed, but he was scolded and fined, and he never again stood up to Pir Ahmad.[50] After this Pir Ahmad seems to have been content with the arrangement and was not at all pleased when ʿAli Shaqani was dismissed in 845/1441.

ʿAli Shaqani's downfall made a considerable impression; we find it mentioned in the *Mujmal-i fasīhī* and described in detail by ʿAbd al-Razzaq Samarqandī, from whom Khwandamir took the story. The event was precipitated by Shams al-Din ʿAli Simnani, member of the prominent Balicha family of Simnan, who was in Shahrukh's *majlis* and much favored by the ruler. At the end of Safar, 845/July, 1441, Khwaja Shams al-Din, who had learned of irregularities in the tax collection of Jam, brought up the issue in Shahrukh's *majlis*, with Ghiyath al-Din Pir Ahmad and ʿAli Shaqani present. When Shahrukh asked for full particulars, Shams al-Din ʿAli suggested that he had evidence incriminating ʿAli Shaqani and at this point Shahrukh asked Amir Firuzshah to investigate. It is likely that the investigation of Jam came perilously close to Pir Ahmad's own interests, as he is known to have had an agent there.[51] The investigation disclosed significant abuses for which Amir ʿAli Shaqani was dismissed, on 22 Rabiʿ I, 845/August 10, 1441, and Shams al-Din ʿAli took his position the next day.[52]

This affair took place against the wishes of Pir Ahmad, who was so upset that he absented himself from the *dīwān* for several days. Shams al-Din ʿAli thought it best not to take full advantage of Pir Ahmad's discomfiture so, although he affixed his seal to documents as they came through, he sent them on to Pir Ahmad for his seal. After a few days Pir Ahmad returned out of fear of Shahrukh's displeasure.[53] Under the same year Fasih states that Ghiyath al-Din Pir Ahmad was punished at the instigation of troublemakers. He gives us no explanation, but the event suggests some threat to Pir Ahmad's power.[54] Pir Ahmad quite soon came to terms with the appointment of Shams al-Din

[50] Khwāndamīr, *Dastūr*, 358–60; Khwāndamīr, *Ḥabīb*, vol. IV, p. 3; Thackston, *Habibu's-siyar*, 352–53.
[51] Yūsuf Ahl, *Farāyid*, vol. II, 24, 102–03, 148–52, 206–08.
[52] Samarqandī, *Maṭlaʿ*, 753–54; Khwāndamīr, *Dastūr*, 361, 380–81.
[53] Samarqandī, *Maṭlaʿ*, 754–55; Khwāndamīr, *Dastūr*, 361; Faṣīḥ Khwāfī, *Mujmal-i faṣīḥī*, vol. III, 290.
[54] Faṣīḥ Khwāfī, *Mujmal-i faṣīḥī*, vol. III, 292. This story is apparently not found in all manuscripts.

ʿAli; these two viziers were still sharing the *dīwān* at the time of Shahrukh's death and remained together voluntarily for some time thereafter.[55]

What we see in the career of Pir Ahmad is the successful maintenance of power through his ability to bend others to his will, while accepting some limits on his own power. Despite his long and successful tenure in office Pir Ahmad's career was not without setbacks. Fasih Khwafi reports that he was dismissed from the *dīwān* for about a year in 828–29/1425–26 and as we have seen he suffered a blow to his power and prestige again in 845/1441.[56] There is a recurring dynamic here; the dynasty imposed its own candidate as co-vizier, choosing someone from outside the pool of clients and allies that Pir Ahmad had established for himself. Over several years, Pir Ahmad was able either to come to terms with his partner or to reduce him to a subordinate position, as he did with ʿAli Shaqani. One can guess that when a co-vizier became a close ally to Pir Ahmad he lost some of his usefulness to the dynasty and it was time to find a new person to appoint. Even if Shahrukh himself did not initiate the change of personnel he might become receptive to criticism of the incumbent.

Delegation of authority in the *dīwān*

Shahrukh sometimes exercised his authority directly and seems to have made the most important appointments, but it is hard to gauge the extent of his involvement in the workings of the bureaucracy. No source deals with this question, and the indications we can glean from various histories are inconsistent. A number of scholars have suggested that Shahrukh kept himself busy with religious exercises and left the day-to-day management of affairs to subordinates.[57] Some medieval sources certainly present this view. We find it particularly clearly in the works of Taj al-Din Hasan Yazdi and Abu Bakr Tihrani, both of whom served in provincial *dīwān*s during the latter part of Shahrukh's reign.[58]

The sources emanating more directly from the central court give a mixed picture. Appointments and dismissals in major *dīwān* posts are attributed to Shahrukh, but this could, of course, represent a formality, both of *dīwān* procedure and of historical writing.[59] When we examine accounts of the fall of Sayyid Fakhr al-Din Ahmad in 819–20/1416–18, we see indications that Shahrukh, though aware of irregularities, preferred to leave their investigation and correction to Baysunghur, interfering formally only when the scandal became too public to ignore. Elsewhere there is evidence of closer involvement in *dīwān* affairs. Khwandamir and Samarqandī both

[55] Samarqandī, *Maṭlaʿ*, 883; Kātib, *Tārīkh-i jadīd*, 252; Khwāndamīr, *Dastūr*, 361; ʿUqaylī, *Āthār*, 344.

[56] Faṣīḥ Khwāfī, *Mujmal-i faṣīḥī*, vol. III, 257, 259.

[57] See Bartol'd, *Ulugbek*, 97, and Roemer, "Successors," 104.

[58] Yazdī, *Ḥasanī*, 45; Ṭihrānī Iṣfahānī, *Diyarbakriyya*, 296–97, 316.

[59] See for instance Faṣīḥ Khwāfī, *Mujmal-i faṣīḥī*, vol. III, 257; Samarqandī, *Maṭlaʿ*, 670, 673.

occasionally mention Shahrukh's personal favor towards a vizier as a factor in his advancement, and we have seen Shahrukh's direct involvement in the events of 845/1441.[60] It seems likely then that Shahrukh maintained sufficient presence in the *dīwān* to know its personnel and either to put a halt to, or make use of, major abuses. Minor abuses seem to have been tolerated, to be used against officials when convenient.

It is by no means clear how *dīwān* responsibilities were apportioned among various groups. While it is evident that powerful viziers like Sayyid Fakhr al-Din and Ghiyath al-Din Pir Ahmad had considerable autonomy, they were not alone in running *dīwān* affairs. Princes and emirs were also intimately involved in administration, some in possession of their own *dīwān*s, and many participating formally in central administration. How much their responsibilities differed from those of the major viziers is not clear. On the death of Shahrukh's son Baysunghur his administrative responsibilities passed officially to his son ʿAlaʾ al-Dawlat, then sixteen years old.[61] When we do see princes active in the *dīwān*, they are there to correct the misdeeds of powerful figures. The role of the emirs is rather less clear. While Firuzshah's power emerges clearly, the others remain shadowy. As I have shown above, emirs were given significant responsibilities in the management of taxes, and it was Shahrukh's emirs who made it possible for Fakhr al-Din Ahmad to topple their enemy Ghiyath al-Din Salar Simnani in 811/1408. We have also seen the triumph of Firuzshah at Ghiyath al-Din Pir Ahmad's expense in 845/1441. It is telling that when Firuzshah and ʿAlika were succeeded by their young and inexperienced sons, Shahrukh found it necessary to appoint a more experienced emir in addition.

The last *dīwān* scandal of Shahrukh's reign primarily concerned emirs and princes, who figure as both accusers and accused. What probably brought it on was the overweening influence acquired by Amir Firuzshah after the deaths of Baysunghur and Amir ʿAlika Kukeltash. Firuzshah's investigation of abuses in the tax collection of Jam, to the discomfiture of Pir Ahmad Khwafi, took place about a year after ʿAlika's death. By 848/1444–45, Firuzshah's unchecked influence had become a matter of resentment and he had won further ill will through his treatment of a subordinate vizier, Sayyid ʿImad al-Din Mahmud Junabadi, whose father Zayn al-ʿAbidin has been mentioned for his enmity towards Fakhr al-Din Ahmad. ʿImad al-Din himself had a reputation for learning and enjoyed Shahrukh's personal favor. Firuzshah had insisted on giving Sayyid ʿImad al-Din the task of organizing the taxes of Balkh, despite the sayyid's reluctance and Shahrukh's belief that he should have been given a better job.[62] Although Shahrukh disapproved of the appointment, he was able to use it for his own ends. When Sayyid ʿImad al-Din left for Balkh, Shahrukh ordered him to examine the records of the last

[60] Khwāndamīr, *Dastūr*, 362; Samarqandī, *Maṭlaʿ*, 752–4. [61] Samarqandī, *Maṭlaʿ*, 665.
[62] Khwāndamīr, *Dastūr*, 362; Samarqandī, *Maṭlaʿ*, 793–94.

three years and to submit a report to the prince Muhammad Juki, who would be passing through on the way to his winter quarters.[63] At the same time, Shahrukh ordered Muhammad Juki to investigate other misbehavior by Firuzshah and his emirs in the region. The choice of Muhammad Juki was not a neutral one, as he was known to dislike Firuzshah.[64]

Shortly after this Shahrukh became gravely ill and Firuzshah agreed to swear an oath of allegiance to ʿAlaʾ al-Dawla b. Baysunghur, an act which angered Muhammad Juki still further.[65] When Shahrukh recovered and began to look into the affairs of state, the scandal of Balkh was ready and waiting for him. Sayyid ʿImad al-Din had completed his task, finding ample evidence that emirs had misappropriated funds. Muhammad Juki brought the sayyid into Shahrukh's *majlis*, with the agreement of major emirs and viziers, and there he presented the evidence. Firuzshah could not escape blame, since final responsibility for these affairs rested with him. He was too proud to accept questioning, left the *majlis*, and stayed away for several days. Shahrukh sent a messenger, reproaching him for his departure and silence, suggesting that punishment might ensue if he did not return. This was the last straw for Firuzshah, who became ill and died a few days later.[66] It is likely that the investigation into the taxes of Balkh had a dual purpose – to rectify wrongs which were large and public enough to come to Shahrukh's attention, and to put a limit on Firuzshah's excessive power. It is probably not by chance that Firuzshah's humiliation occurred only a couple of years after the blow he had given to the power and independence of Ghiyath al-Din Pir Ahmad.

What we can deduce from these stories of bureaucratic intrigues is both the strength of character necessary to succeed, and the way in which all players, from ambitious subordinates to the ruler himself, used the *dīwān*'s atmosphere of jealousy and graft to further their own ends. The standard road to advancement was the discrediting of one's predecessor and the necessary material seems always to have been at hand. For the ruler, princes, and emirs, the most effective way to check the power of a functionary was to uncover financial wrongdoing.

Nonetheless, one should not see the *dīwān* as an institution entirely devoid of moral standards. It is clear that bureaucrats were judged on their level of probity and that high levels of peculation were considered unacceptable. Likewise, the caution Shahrukh used when dismissing his *dīwān* officials, both viziers and emirs, suggests that he considered himself neither sufficiently powerful nor sufficiently above the law to punish an important official

63 While the *Dastūr al-wuzarāʾ* dates the dispatch of ʿImad al-Din to Balkh in 844/1440–41, the account in the *Maṭlaʿ-i sa dayn* places it in 847/1443–44, and adds that, in particular, it was the taxes of Delhi, forwarded via Balkh, which were in question.

64 Samarqandī, *Maṭlaʿ*, 793–95. The *Matlaʿ-i saʿdayn* and the *Dastūr al-wuzarāʾ* suggest that the move came from Shahrukh.

65 Samarqandī, *Maṭlaʿ*, 837–38.

66 Ibid., 838–40; Khwāndamīr, *Dastūr*, 363.

without firm proof of misbehavior. We should remember further that the most honest of bureaucrats might have trouble keeping accounts in order. Even in the age of the computer, accounting is a tricky science, lending itself easily to error and perhaps, for the same reason, offering temptations to graft. Two stories about viziers in the Timurid period attest to the difficulties of this job and the sacrifices it might require. In the *Tarikh-i jadid-i Yazd* we hear of a particularly virtuous vizier who, when deficits appeared in the accounts for which he was responsible, made them up out of his own money rather than through additional dues from the population. The section of Yazd for which he was responsible flourished during his tenure in office.[67] Khwandamir reports the story of Khwaja 'Ala' al-Din 'Ali Quhistani, who worked as Temür's treasurer. When accounts were audited after Temür's death, 2,000 *tümen*s were found missing and this shortfall was blamed on him. He was put in prison and his son decided to learn accounting in order to clear his father. He succeeded in showing that only 200 *tümen*s were missing, which so impressed Shahrukh that the father was cleared and the son was able to make a distinguished career in the *dīwān*.[68]

The provenance of Shahrukh's viziers

To understand the workings of the administration, we need to know who its functionaries were and how they were recruited. It is frequently observed that extended families of viziers often rose to prominence and dominated *dīwān* affairs. In the early period of Mongol rule for instance, bureaucrats of Qazwin and Simnan were paramount, while in Khorasan at the end of the Ilkhanate we find bureaucrats from Faryumad along with the descendants of Rashid al-Din and 'Ata' al-Malik Juwayni in prominent positions.[69] In discussing such bureaucratic families and how they fit into local society, we face two sets of questions. First of all, we should ask what kinds of families produced viziers and how specialized these families were: did most of their members seek employment as viziers, or were viziers members of families prominent in a number of occupations? The second question to ask concerns the importance of the geographical and family origins of Timurid viziers. A vizier's origin could play a role in his relations to other figures in the central administration and, at the same time, his career in government might well affect the economy, architecture and politics of his home territory.

The questions I have posed are complicated ones, and it is best not to assume that the answers will be simple or direct. While the common geographical provenance of viziers was in part the result of family patronage and

[67] Kātib, *Tārīkh-i jadīd*, 118. [68] Khwāndamīr, *Dastūr*, 372–76.

[69] See Jean Aubin, *Émirs mongols et viziers persans dans les remous de l'acculturation, Studia Islamica* Cahier 15 (Paris: Association pour l'avancement des études iraniennes, 1995), 22, 25, 27, 46–50, and Jean Aubin, "Le quriltay de Sultân-Maydân (1336)," *Journal asiatique* 279 (1991), 184–85.

hereditary appointment, we should not assume that identity of *nisba* and occupation signify close relationship. The habit of retaining local ties and endowing buildings in one's native place could well have led to educational and patronage networks producing large numbers of qualified and connected bureaucrats coming from the same region, but not necessarily the same family. Furthermore, while the bonds of blood and region clearly mattered, they did not preclude rivalry or even enmity among men competing for the same prizes.

It is not easy to reconstruct genealogies for Timurid bureaucrats. The standard chain seems to be two to three generations and, given the heavy use of certain popular names and honorifics within the Iranian population, this does not get us far. We can identify parents and children, or sets of brothers, and often follow the career of one family through a short dynasty. Unfortunately, the biographical collections we have for viziers are organized by dynasty and omit smaller local powers like the Karts and Muzaffarids. Between major dynasties, therefore, we are left without the links necessary to connect the lineages presented to us. When we turn to the history of places of origin, we have snapshots from selected times and places, some focused on one aspect, some on another; short collections of notable men, and perhaps some buildings.

Most bureaucrats working in the central *dīwān* under Shahrukh appear to have come from eastern or northern Iran. Several of the most prominent carried the *nisba* Simnani, many came from the region of Khwaf, and we find in lesser numbers the *nisba*s Tuni, Tusi, Junabadi, Andkhudi, and Sabzawari. I will concentrate most of my attention on those of whom we can hope to form a more collective picture – the Simnani and Khwafi viziers.

Khwaf

Although I have just complained about the sources available, I must admit that for Khwaf we possess an exceptional amount of information. It is noted in several geographies as the birthplace of an exceptional number of famous people of all types – military men, ulama, shaykhs and viziers. This is all the more striking because it was not a city but a region with numerous small centers whose relative importance varied from one period to another.[70] It appears that the diversified economy of Khwaf, which included fruit, silk and, from the Mongol period at least, the mining of iron, allowed it to support both a continuing tradition of learning and a local landowning elite with some aspirations to military power.[71] From the time of the Khwarazmshahs we find a relatively steady presence of local military powers, although we cannot

[70] Aubin, "Un santon quhistani," 191–94; C. E. Bosworth, "Khwāf," in *Encyclopaedia of Islam*, 2nd edn.

[71] Ḥamd Allāh Mustawfī, *Nuzhat al-qulūb*, edited by Guy Le Strange, *E. J. W. Gibb Memorial Series*, 23 vols., vol. XXIII (Leiden: Brill, 1915), 154, 202; Ḥāfiẓ-i Abrū, *Ḫorāsān zur Timuridenzeit*

connect them to each other. Under the Khwarazmshahs there were two important commanders from this area, Malik Shams al-Din Muhammad Anar, and Malik Zuzan, who built a magnificent palace and mosque in Zuzan.[72] Mubariz al-Din Muhammad b. Al-Muzaffar, who founded the Muzaffarid dynasty of Fars (1336–93), traced his ancestry back to Khwaf.[73] While the ancestors of the Muzaffarids had left Khwaf at the Mongol invasion, other military men remained, serving or resisting the Kartid kings.

Among the men claimed by later Khwafi dignitaries as progenitors were the famous Ghaznavid vizier Abu Nasr Mishkan al-Zuzani (d.413/1039), the Chishti shaykh Rukn al-Din Mahmud, known as Shah Sanjan (d. 597/1200–01) and the *faqīh* Mawlana Nizam al-din Mayizhnabadi, active in Herat under the Kartids and martyred by the Turks in 737/1336–37.[74] Both the places of origin given for local luminaries and the patronage of building projects show that intellectual and political activity went well beyond the confines of the regional administrative headquarters. Thus, while Ḥāfiẓ-i Abrū mentions Jezhd, Zuzan, and, perhaps, Salama as district headquarters (*qaṣaba*), we find prominent people originating from towns such as Niyazabad, Mayizhnabad, Sanjan, and Barabad.[75] Architectural patronage was also dispersed. Large buildings were erected during the Timurid period in Kharjird, a town known for the Nizamiyya madrasa built there by Nizam al-Mulk, but otherwise rarely mentioned in histories, and in Rud-i Khwaf and Rushkhwar.[76]

Numerous prominent Khwafi viziers, ulama, and shaykhs were active in Herat under Shahrukh. Since our best informant is Fasih Khwafi, we can use his family as an example of the working of genealogy and patronage. The family of Fasih Ahmad's mother produced many of the Khwafi viziers active under the Timurids. The lineage claimed descent from the vizier ʿAmid Abu Nasr Mishkan, but the man from whom lines of descent were directly drawn was Fasih's great-grandfather, Majd al-Din Muhammad Khwafi, known as Khwaja Majd. Majd al-Din is an interesting figure as progenitor of viziers and scholars. His father, Najib al-Din Ahmad, appears in Sayfi Harawi's history of Herat as a servitor of Malik Shams al-Din Kart.[77] Majd al-Din

nach dem Tārīḫ-e Ḥāfiẓ-e Abrū (verf. 817–823 h.), edited and translated by Dorothea Krawulsky, 2 vols. (Wiesbaden: Ludwig Reichert Verlag, 1982), vol. II, 37; Aubin, "Un santon quhistani," 191–94; Bosworth, "Khwāf."

72 Ḥāfiẓ-i Abrū, *Ḫorāsān*, vol. II, 37; André Godard, "Khorasan," *Āthār-e Īrān* IV (1949), 113–17. The title "malik" under the Khwarazmshahs could refer to important commanders (see Lambton, *Continuity and Change*, 38).

73 Isfizārī, *Rawḍāt*, vol. I, 188.

74 Ibid., vol. I, 205–06, 211; Lawrence G. Potter, "The Kart Dynasty of Herat: Religion and Politics in Medieval Iran," PhD dissertation, Columbia University, 1992, 135–37; Faṣīḥ Khwāfī, *Mujmal-i faṣīḥī*, vol. II, 124–25, 161–62, vol. III, 214.

75 Aubin, "Un santon quhistani," 191; Ḥāfiẓ-i Abrū, *Ḫorāsān*, vol. II, 37.

76 O'Kane, *Timurid Architecture*, 211–15, 239–45.

77 Sayf b. Muḥammad b. Yaʿqūb al-Harawī, *Tārīkh-nāma-i Harāt*, edited by Muḥammad Zubayr al-Ṣiddiqī (Calcutta: Imperial Library, 1944), 319.

Muhammad himself had greater ambitions. According to Sayfi Harawi, he ruled in Khwaf for a long time and amassed great wealth. About 714/1314–15, he gathered about a thousand fighting men (characterized as rabble: *awbāsh*), who caused trouble in Khwaf and throughout Quhistan, closing the roads to the population. He received another thousand men from the dissident Mongol prince Yasaʾur with whom he further ravaged the region. The local officials appealed to Malik Ghiyath al-Din Kart to help them.[78]

Malik Ghiyath al-Din set out first against Khwaja Majd al-Din's original fortress in Niyazabad. After several days of hard fighting he took the fortress and sent an expeditionary force against Khwaja Majd at his new fortress of Mayizhnabad. When the troops arrived and announced that the king had captured Niyazabad, Khwaja Majd appeared at the window of the gate and shouted that they were lying; all the armies of Iraq and Khorasan could not take that fortress. The king's troops brought out the captured fortress keeper of Niyazabad, a sight which shook Khwaja Majd considerably. The khwaja resisted for several days before sending out a delegation to make peace. The treaty he achieved allowed him to keep this fortress, while sending his son Jalal al-Din Muhammad to join the suite of the Kartid king.[79]

We know nothing further about Khwaja Majd al-Din's family under the Kartids, but during the Timurid period a large number of his descendants were active in and near Herat, particularly within the *dīwān*. Fasih Ahmad's mother was a granddaughter of Majd al-Din, through his son Rukn al-Din. The branch of the family apparently most active in Herat was descended from Jalal al-Din Muhammad, who had accompanied the Kartid kings. Two of Jalal al-Din's grandsons, Qawam al-Din Shaykh Muhammad and Sadr al-Din Hāmid, probably *dīwān* officials, were among the people whom Sayyid Fakhr al-Din Ahmad exiled in 807/1404.[80] These men returned, but Khwaja Qawam al-Din at least remained in Sayyid Fakhr al-Din's bad graces and was executed at his orders in 817/1414.[81] In the same year another Khwafi *dīwān* functionary, probably a member of the same family branch, died in Shiraz on *dīwān* business.[82]

During this time our author, Fasih Ahmad, was beginning his own service in the *dīwān*. The account of his career is interesting for several reasons. First of all, since he was one of several viziers from the same region we have a chance to determine whether common geographical origin led to professional alliance. Second, it allows us to follow the career of a middle-level bureaucrat.

[78] Faṣīḥ Khwāfī, *Mujmal-i faṣīḥī*, vol. III, 31–32; Sayfī, *Tārīkh-nāma-i*, 754–55.

[79] Faṣīḥ Khwāfī, *Mujmal-i faṣīḥī*, vol. III, 31–32; Sayfī, *Tārīkh-nāma-i*, 756–62.

[80] Faṣīḥ Khwāfī, *Mujmal-i faṣīḥī*, vol. III, 149–50.

[81] Ibid., vol. III, 214. They seem not to have achieved the top positions in the *dīwān*, as indeed their ancestors apparently had not under the Kart kings.

[82] Ibid., vol. III, 219, 271. This was ʿImad al-Din Muhammad the son of Mawlana Nizam al-Din Yahya Khwafi Mayizhnabadi, whom I am identifying with Mawlana Nizam al-Din Yahya b. Kamal al-Din Husayn b. Jalal al-Din Muhammad Khwafi (d. 836/1432–33).

Fasih naturally gives a fuller account of his own life than that of others; when he records that he was appointed to the *dīwān* or to the staff of a mission, he may have achieved a post which would not have deserved mention held by another person. What is certain, and is mentioned by both Fasih and others, is that he had a checkered career.

Fasih Ahmad Khwafi was born on 1 Jumadi I, 777/September 28, 1375, and we first hear of his professional activities in 807/1405. At this time he was in Zawa in Quhistan, where he states that he reported the abuses perpetrated there by Temür's agent Sayyid Hasan Gush Burida.[83] For a while Fasih served in the *dīwān* of Shahrukh's brother-in-law ʿAli Tarkhan, and from his service came into Shahrukh's.[84] It was the downfall of Sayyid Fakhr al-Din Ahmad which brought Fasih his great chance. He reports that in 819/1416–17 Shahrukh showed him favor and appointed him to the *dīwān* and that in 820/1417–18 he was one of the three people put in charge of the *dīwān* at Fakhr al-Din's dismissal, along with Ahmad Daʾud and Sayyid ʿAli Marwi. However, his success was very brief; the next year he was dismissed and Ghiyath al-Din Pir Ahmad Khwafi was appointed with other viziers.[85]

The family relationship between Fasih Ahmad and Ghiyath al-Din Pir Ahmad is not certain, but it is likely that they were second cousins. Pir Ahmad's genealogy is given for three generations: he was the son of Jalal al-Din Ishaq b. Majd al-Din Muhammad b. Fadl Allah Khwafi.[86] This does not connect him definitely to the family tree of Khwaja Majd (Majd al-Din Muhammad), whose father was Najib al-Din, but the presence of the name Majd al-Din Muhammad is suggestive, particularly as we find it borne by Pir Ahmad's brother and his son.[87] Among the known descendants of Khwaja Majd this was a frequent name and I would guess, therefore, that Pir Ahmad's great-grandfather Fadl Allah was another and probably older son of the original Majd al-Din Muhammad, and thus a brother of Jalal al-Din Muhammad and Rukn al-Din Mahmud.

Whether Ghiyath al-Din Pir Ahmad was Fasih Ahmad's cousin or merely his countryman, there is no evidence that he favored him. Indeed, Fasih seems to have been excluded from the central *dīwān* while Pir Ahmad Khwafi headed it. In 825/1422 he was sent to Kerman on *dīwān* business by Shahrukh, from whence he returned in 827/1424.[88] His next appointment, in 828/1425, was to the *dīwān* of prince Baysunghur, which he claims to have headed. But, in 836/1433, he was dismissed from Baysunghur's *dīwān*, fined and handed over to the *muḥaṣṣil*s.[89] In 839/1436, while Shahrukh was

83 Faṣīḥ Khwāfī, *Mujmal-i faṣīḥī*, vol. III, 110, 157–58.
84 Ibid., vol. III, 220.
85 Ibid., vol. III, 225, 228, 235; ʿUqaylī, *Āthār*, 341.
86 Faṣīḥ Khwāfī, *Mujmal-i faṣīḥī*, vol. III, 230, 257.
87 Ibid., vol. III, 276; Isfizārī, *Rawḍāt*, vol. I, 218–19.
88 Faṣīḥ Khwāfī, *Mujmal-i faṣīḥī*, vol. III, 251, 254.
89 Ibid., vol. III, 258, 266, 271; ʿUqaylī, *Āthār*, 341–42.

returning from Azarbaijan, Fasih Ahmad tried to get the position vacated by the death of the vizier Sayyidi Ahmad Shirazi, but was prevented by 'Ala' al-Dawla b. Baysunghur, as I described in the last chapter.[90] It is possible that Fasih was now again working for Gawharshad's relatives, since his next trial came at her hands. In Dhu'l Hijja, 843/May, 1440, she had him arrested and imprisoned.[91] 845/1441–42 is the last year reported in the *Mujmal-i fasihi* and we know nothing further about Fasih Ahmad's life. Although we have the names of his sons and several grandsons, they do not appear among notable viziers in later accounts.

Pir Ahmad Khwafi seems to have done no more for other relatives and fellow townsmen than he did for Fasih. Although Fasih and 'Abd al-Razzaq Samarqandī list Pir Ahmad's brother Majd al-Din Muhammad among the plague victims of 838/1434–35, neither mentions his occupation and there is no evidence that he was prominent in a profession.[92] No other clearly identifiable members of Pir Ahmad's or Fasih Ahmad's families figure in the history of the *dīwān* during Pir Ahmad's tenure. In Shahrukh's reign, there were several important ulama and shaykhs in Herat who bore the *nisba* Khwafi, but very few can be connected to each other or to the Khwafi viziers.[93] In the next generation, we once more find Khwafi viziers in important positions. Pir Ahmad's son, Majd al-Din Muhammad, had a distinguished career and another member of the same family was known for his skill in jurisprudence and served as *ṣadr*: this was Mawlana Qutb al-Din Muhammad Khwafi, who served under both Sultan Abu Sa'id and Sultan Husayn.[94] He is identified by Khwandamir as a member of the family of Majd al-Din Muhammad b. Pir Ahmad, who took charge of his funeral celebration.[95] His nephew and son-in-law, Khwaja Shihab al-Din Ishaq, also served as *ṣadr*.[96] Under Sultan Husayn, Isfizari's patron Qawam al-Din Khwafi, descended from Khwaja Majd, held a prominent place. His father had been *qāḍī* in Khwaf and left seeking higher office in service to the dynasty.[97] He was related to another vizier of the period, Nasir al-Din 'Imad al-Islam. There are also several other *dīwān* personnel with the *nisba* Khwafi who cannot be placed in relation to these lineages.[98]

There were thus several different families among the Khwafi viziers, some of whom were related, producing bureaucrats who apparently had little connection to those outside their immediate circle. While at the beginning

90 Samarqandī, *Maṭla'*, 689–90. 91 Faṣīḥ Khwāfī, *Mujmal-i faṣīḥī*, vol. III, 287–90.
92 Ibid., vol. III, 276; Samarqandī, *Maṭla'*, 680.
93 The Khwafi religious personnel are discussed in Chapters 6 and 7.
94 Khwāndamīr, *Dastūr*, 400, 418; Isfizārī, *Rawḍāt*, vol. I, 218.
95 Khwāndamīr, *Ḥabīb*, vol. IV, 321–22; Thackston, *Habibu's-siyar*, 511.
96 Khwāndamīr, *Ḥabīb*, vol. IV, 325; Thackston, *Habibu's-siyar*, 513.
97 Khwāndamīr, *Dastūr*, 418.
98 Isma'il Khwafi under Temür ('Uqaylī, *Āthār*, 335), Nasr al-Din Nasr Allah Khwafi (Khwāndamīr, *Dastūr*, 361–62), and Khwaja Muhammad Khwafi, probably in the *dīwān* (Faṣīḥ Khwāfī, *Mujmal-i faṣīḥī*, vol. III, 218).

of Shahrukh's career several of Fasih Khwafi's cousins descended from Jalal al-Din Muhammad b. Khwaja Majd were active in the *dīwān*, there is no mention, later in his career, of *dīwān* activities by this branch of the family. Of Pir Ahmad Khwafi's close relatives only his son appears to have held high office in the *dīwān*.

The viziers serving the dynasty in Herat remained attached to their native region, and were probably active there as well. Pir Ahmad Khwafi built a major madrasa in Kharjird.[99] His two other large monuments were a mausoleum for the shaykh Zayn al-Din Taybadi, not far from Khwaf, and one for his fellow countryman, Shaykh Zayn al-Din Khwafi, buried at Herat.[100] We do not know of any blood relationship between Pir Ahmad and Shaykh Zayn al-Din, but they may well have been connected, since they owned adjoining lands in Kharjird.[101] A congregational mosque in the village of Rushkhwar dates from the period shortly after Shahrukh's death, and another in Khwaf probably from the reign of Abu Saʿid. The minbar in the mosque at Khwaf, donated by someone called Majd al-Din Khwafi in 908/1502–03, testifies to the continued interest of the Khwafi notables in their native region.[102] While Fasih Khwafi sponsored no known building projects – his career was probably not sufficiently successful – he did remain involved in his home region. As I have written above, he suggests that he was in Quhistan when Temür's agent Sayyid Khwarazmi was active there, and he appears to have remained attached to the descendants of Rukn al-Din Mahmud Sanjani, still resident in Sanjan. What made the Khwafi viziers visible and active over the long run was their continued interest in their home territory and their willingness to invest in it, which ensured its inhabitants educational opportunities, and the possibility of useful patronage within the *dīwān*.

Simnan

The other large group of bureaucrats of common geographical origin were from Simnan, which was also known by the nickname *Dār al-wuzarāʾ*.[103] The city's viziers were particularly prominent under the Mongol Ilkhans when the best known belonged to two interrelated families, both descended from men high in the service of the Khwarazmshahs. These lineages were characterized by their intermarriage with families of religious figures and by their military

99 Godard, "Khorasan," 69–82.

100 Khwāndamīr, *Dastūr*, 354; Isfizārī, *Rawḍāt*, vol. I, 219; O'Kane, *Timurid Architecture*, 223–25.

101 "Waqfnāma-i Zayn al-Dīn Abū Bakr Khwāfī," edited by M. Muṭlaq, *Mishkāt* 22 (Spring, 1989), 194.

102 O'Kane, *Timurid Architecture*, 239–45; Ḥāfiẓ-i Abrū, *Ḫorāsān*, vol. II, 37. As O'Kane points out, the Majd al-Din Muhammad who made this contribution cannot be securely identified as the son of Pir Ahmad Khwafi, said to have died in 899/1494.

103 ʿAbd al-Rafīʿ Ḥaqīqat, *Tārīkh-i Simnān* (Tehran: Chāpkhāna-i Iṭilāʿāt, 1341/1962), 133; Khwāndamīr, *Dastūr*, 380.

activity in the service of the regime.[104] One family can be traced into the middle of the eighth century, shortly before Temür's rise to power,[105] but it does not connect directly to the Timurid viziers of Simnani origin. It appears that the end of the Ilkhans and the rise of new dynasties brought opportunities to different families, or at least to different lines within them. One less prominent lineage did bridge the two periods. There is mention of a vizier ʿIzz al-Din Tahir Simnani active in Khorasan in the late eighth century, whose grandsons ʿAli Jaʿfar and ʿAlaʾ al-Dawla served the ruler of Mazandaran. There is also mention in the Timurid sources of the death of ʿAli Jaʿfar's son in Samarqand in 812/1409–10, and of an ʿAlaʾ al-Dawla Simnani in Khalil Sultan's *dīwān*.[106]

The viziers most prominent during Temür's reign were Nizam al-Din Yahya Simnani and his children, but their relation to earlier Simnani bureaucrats is impossible to determine. Yahya may well have come into Temür's service from Ahmad Jalayir.[107] When Yahya died he was succeeded in the vizierate by his son Khwaja Masʿud, whose position was inherited by a brother Sharaf al-Din ʿAli, still serving at the time of Temür's death.[108] Sharaf al-Din ʿAli transferred from Khalil Sultan's *dīwān* to Shahrukh's, but we know almost nothing of him thereafter. His son Shams al-Din Muhammad Mushrif however had a successful career.[109] Although he was

104 The family of the viziers Jalal al-Din Mukhlis and Sharaf al-Din Muhammad (father of the Sufi shaykh ʿAlaʾ al-Dawla) married into two prominent religious lineages: the descendants of Husayn Asghar b. Zayn al-ʿAbidin and the more recent and worldly family of Saʾin al-Din, known as "*Qāḍī-i jumlaʿ-i mamālik*." This last family was the other major family of Simnani viziers, though Saʾin al-Din was executed in 700/1300 for conspiring against Rashid al-Din. It seems likely that Rukn al-Din Saʾin, vizier for the Ilkhan Abu Saʾid, was a descendant or relative of Saʾin Qadi. The coincidence of names here is striking, particularly the term *qāḍī* or *qāḍīzāda* in this line, which seems not to have actually held the office of *qāḍī* (J. Van Ess, "ʿAlāʾ al-Dawla," in *Encyclopaedia Iranica*; Faṣīḥ Khwāfī, *Mujmal-i faṣīḥī*, vol. II, 277; Ḥāfiẓ-i Abrū, *Dhayl-i jāmiʿ al-tawārīkh-i rashīdī*, edited by Kh. Bayānī, 2nd edn [Tehran: Anjumān-i Āthār-i Millī, 1350/1971–72], 162).

105 The Shams al-Din Mahmud Saʾin Qadi b. Rukn al-Din Saʾin who accompanied Pir Husayn b. Chupan to Fars where he switched to the service of Abu Ishaq Inju was almost certainly the son of the Rukn al-Din mentioned in the last footnote (Khwāndamīr, *Dastūr*, 240–42; Faṣīḥ Khwāfī, *Mujmal-i faṣīḥī*, vol. III, 17, 70–71). Shams al-Din Mahmud served as vizier, but also, significantly, led troops. Shams al-Din's son, Rukn al-Din Saʾin ʿAmid al-Mulk, born in 708/1308–09, was appointed vizier by Abu Ishaq in 747 (Faṣīḥ Khwāfī, *Mujmal-i faṣīḥī*, vol. III, 71). Rukn al-Din is probably the same as the poet Rukn al-Din Saʾin Simnani, discussed by Dawlatshah Samarqandī, who served at the courts of both Abu Ishaq Inju and Taghay Temür Khan of Khorasan (Ḥaqīqat, *Tārīkh-i Simnān*, 135; Dawlatshāh Samarqandī, *Tadhkirat*, 102, 235–36). The chain I have constructed here depends on circumstantial evidence but the confluence of names, dates and patrons seems sufficient to justify it.

106 Muḥammad b. ʿAlī b. Muḥammad Shabānkāraʾī, *Majmaʿ al-ansāb*, edited by M. H. Muḥaddith (Tehran: Amīr Kabīr, 1363/1985–86), 326; Faṣīḥ Khwāfī, *Mujmal-i faṣīḥī*, vol. III, 193–94.

107 There was a Nizam al-Din Yahya Simnani representing Sultan Ahmad in Baghdad in 784/1382–83 and, in 788/1386–87, we find Temür campaigning in Azarbaijan, leaving Yahya Simnani and others in Tabriz (Ḥāfiẓ-i Abrū, *Dhayl*, 274, 288; Faṣīḥ Khwāfī, *Mujmal-i faṣīḥī*, vol. III, 120).

108 ʿUqaylī, *Āthār*, 334–35; Faṣīḥ Khwāfī, *Mujmal-i faṣīḥī*, vol. III, 173, 195, 235; *Muʿizz*, fol. 97b.

109 For transfer from the *dīwān*, see Faṣīḥ Khwāfī, *Mujmal-i faṣīḥī*, vol. III, 194.

dismissed from Shahrukh's *dīwān* in 811/1408–09, in 812/1409–10 he was entrusted with an important mission to Sayyid Murtada of Sari and Amul. In 821/1418–19 he was appointed to share office in Shahrukh's *dīwān* with Ghiyath al-Din Pir Ahmad and, in Shahrukh's Azarbaijan campaign of 823–24/1420–21, went to Tabriz to organize the city with Baysunghur and ʿAlika Kukeltash. Finally, in 824/1421 he died in battle, as his uncle Khwaja Masʿud had done.[110] As far as I can tell, the service of the lineage of Yahya Simnani ended with Shams al-Din Muhammad's death.

During Shahrukh's reign we see the growing prominence of another Simnani family and its protégés – the Balicha. According to Khwandamir, Simnan had two great local families, the Balicha and the Bahrami. The more visible of these were the Balicha, who are mentioned with respect, as thoroughly aristocratic. The most closely related were three brothers, sons of Jalal al-Din Mahmud Balicha Simnani, a man I have not found mentioned elsewhere.[111] The son mentioned earliest is Nizam al-Din Ahmad, who was dismissed from Baysunghur's *dīwān* in 828/1425 and subsequently disappears from the histories.[112] The big advance in the fortunes of this family came with the *dīwān* scandal of 845/1441, when Nizam al-Din Ahmad's brother, Shams al-Din ʿAli Balicha, succeeded in discrediting ʿAli Shaqani and gaining the position of joint vizier. His success in doing this, against the wishes of Pir Ahmad, suggests strong patronage. Shams al-Din ʿAli remained in the *dīwān* until after Shahrukh's death, when he and Pir Ahmad repaired first to Simnan, then to Yazd. The succession struggle after Shahrukh's death was a dangerous period for all concerned, and Shams al-Din ʿAli died quite soon, probably unhappily.[113] His elder brother Wajih al-Din Ismaʿil gained prominence only after Shahrukh's death; Abuʾl Qasim Babur put him in charge of the *dīwān-i aʿlāʾ*. After Abuʾl Qasim's death he served Abuʾl Qasim's son Shah Mahmud. However, when Shah Mahmud's fortunes declined and Wajih al-Din joined the victor, Mirza Ibrahim b. ʿAlaʾ al-Dawla, his luck gave out; in 861/1456–57 he suffered imprisonment, was tortured and, shortly after, died.[114]

[110] Ḥāfiẓ-i Abrū, *Zubdat*, 327–30; Faṣīḥ Khwāfī, *Mujmal-i faṣīḥī*, vol. III, 185, 195, 235, 243, 247.

[111] The evidence connecting these men is not absolutely conclusive. Fasih identifies Nizam al-Din Ahmad as the son of Jalal al-Din Mahmud Balicha Simnani (Faṣīḥ Khwāfī, *Mujmal-i faṣīḥī*, vol. III, 258). Shams al-Din ʿAli Balicha Simnani is identified by ʿAbd al-Razzaq Samarqandī as the brother of Wajih al-Din Ismaʿil (Samarqandī, *Maṭlaʿ*, 753). Ismaʿil, in turn, is identified both by ʿUqayli and in a contemporary poem, reported by Khwandamir, as the son of Khwaja Mahmud. Khwandamir however calls Khwaja Ismaʿil "Khwaja Mahmud b. Ismaʿil," thus inverting the father-son relationship (Khwāndamīr, *Dastūr*, 364; ʿUqaylī, *Āthār*, 344; Khwāndamīr, *Habīb*, vol. IV, 59; Thackston, *Habibuʾs-siyar*, 383–84). Since ʿAbd al-Razzaq was a contemporary of Wajih al-Din Ismaʿil's, I have chosen his identification.

[112] Faṣīḥ Khwāfī, *Mujmal-i faṣīḥī*, vol. III, 258.

[113] ʿUqaylī, *Āthār*, 344; Khwāndamīr, *Dastūr*, 361; Faṣīḥ Khwāfī, *Mujmal-i faṣīḥī*, vol. III, 290; Samarqandī, *Maṭlaʿ*, 752 ff, 884; Kātib, *Tārīkh-i jadīd*, 252.

[114] Khwāndamīr, *Dastūr*, 364; Khwāndamīr, *Ḥabīb*, vol. IV, 66.

Another bureaucrat who rose to prominence during Shahrukh's reign was Muʿizz al-Din Malik Husayn b. ʿIzz al-Din Muhammad Balicha Simnani, apparently from a different branch of the Balicha family. He may have been out of favor early in Shahrukh's reign since in 818/1415–16, according to Fasih Khwafi, he left Shiraz for Mecca, due to the activities of Sayyid Fakhr al-Din. In 827/1423–24, however, he was one of three people appointed to head the *dīwān*.[115] We know that he endowed an *īwān* in the Simnan mosque in 828/1424–25, with his own money.[116] Malik Husayn is not mentioned in the central *dīwān* after this, but he continued his career in Fars. He is almost certainly the same as the Khwaja Malik Simnani mentioned in several sources, holding significant military as well as administrative responsibility. In 840/1436–37, Shahrukh sent a detachment under Khwaja Malik Simnani, Chaqmaq Shami, and Amir Ghunashirin to support his protégé in Hormuz.[117] In 845/1441–42, when the administration of Fars was in flux, Shahrukh gave its governance to Khwaja Malik and he became a member of the *jirga* of great emirs of Fars. He died in 847/1443–44.[118]

On the Bahrami family of Simnan we have very little information. One vizier active in the succession struggle after Shahrukh's death might have been a member: Khwaja Ghiyath Muhammad b. Taj al-Din Bahram Simnani, who endowed a bath in Simnan during the reign of Abuʾl Qasim Babur, in Shawwal, 856/October–November, 1452,[119] and who might be the Ghiyath al-Din Simnani whom Babur appointed to the tax administration in 855/1451–52.[120] Finally, we know of one Simnani vizier descended from an important branch of the Balicha family on his mother's side, and, on his father's from a leading Bahrami, who made his career during the disturbances after Shahrukh's death. This was Qutb al-Din Taʾus, vizier under Abuʾl Qasim Babur and chief administrator for Abu Saʿid. According to Khwandamir, Abuʾl Qasim showed him favor by bestowing Simnan on him as *soyurghal*, stipulating that no outside administrators were to set foot in the region. Qutb al-Din went on to serve Sultan Husayn Bayqara at the beginning of his reign.[121]

The lineages mentioned above are the most conspicuous, but several other *dīwān* personnel with the *nisba* Simnani were active in Timurid administration.[122] One prominent and powerful Simnani vizier, who served at the end of Temür's reign and the beginning of Shahrukh's, had already perished before this; this was Ghiyath al-Din Salar Simnani, whose career was discussed earlier in this chapter. What is interesting about Ghiyath al-Din Salar is how little we know about him, despite his wealth and prominence. Neither his father's name nor those of his sons appear in the sources. We are left

[115] Faṣīḥ Khwāfī, *Mujmal-i faṣīḥī*, III, 223, 255. [116] Ḥaqīqat, *Tārīkh-i Simnān*, 92.
[117] J. Aubin, *Deux sayyids*, 425. [118] Samarqandī, *Maṭlaʿ*, 757, 795.
[119] Ḥaqīqat, *Tārīkh-i Simnān*, 99. [120] Ṭihrānī Iṣfahānī, *Diyarbakriyya*, 325.
[121] Khwāndamīr, *Dastūr*, 380–90.
[122] See for example, Kātib, *Tārīkh-i jadīd*, 187, 227, 336; Ṭihrānī Iṣfahānī, *Diyarbakriyya*, 343.

therefore with no idea where he fits into Simnani society, although one modern Simnani family claims descent from him.[123] From the middle of the century, however, the Simnani fortunes appear to have declined, and under Sultan Husayn, after the retirement of Qutb al-Din Ta'us, Simnani viziers are not prominent. It is interesting that we find the judges of Simnan mentioned in court service under the Timurids as under the Ilkhans. In 817/1414, Shahrukh sent the *qāḍī* of Simnan, Ghiyath al-Din, to reason (unsuccessfully) with his nephew Iskandar in Shiraz and, at the end of Shahrukh's life, we find a Mawlana Jamal Islam Simnani, known as *qāḍībacha*, used again as an envoy.[124]

Although we cannot directly connect the Simnani viziers of the Timurids to those who served the Ilkhans, the careers and characteristics of the viziers we know do show significant continuities. In both periods several Simnani viziers were conspicuous in military as well as administrative roles. Shams al-Din Sa'in Qadi, under the Injuids, and Mu'izz al-Din Malik Husayn, under the Timurids, commanded significant troops, while in the Timurid period, Mas'ud b. Yahya and his nephew Shams al-Din Muhammad Mushrif died in battle. It is perhaps not by chance that both Sa'in Qadi and Malik Husayn were active in Fars, where numerous viziers were important as military commanders.[125] Since we also see Malik Husayn Simnani serving in the council of emirs in Fars, it may be that some military identity continued within the family. We also find the title or name Malik among the Simnani viziers in both the Mongol and Timurid periods – this had been used by important emirs under the Khorezmshahs, and the Simnani viziers may have used it to refer back to illustrious ancestors.[126]

It is clear also that in both the Ilkhanid and the Timurid periods some of the Simnani bureaucrats were aristocrats with a strong local power base. Khwandamir states that the Balicha and Bahrami families commanded obedience and extended protection within the Simnan region.[127] The local architectural patronage by viziers is another indication of their continued involvement, as is the longevity of local families; several twentieth-century Simnani lineages claim descent from the viziers of these periods.[128] What we do not see among the Simnani viziers is a direct continuity of lineages. It seems that by the end of the fourteenth century, several families were producing viziers; lines of power and patronage within the highest positions lasted up to four generations, and then gave way to new personnel. This

[123] Ḥaqīqat, *Tārīkh-i Simnān*, 133.
[124] Ḥāfiẓ-i Abrū, *Zubdat*, 540–41; Kātib, *Tārīkh-i jadīd*, 248; Samarqandī, *Maṭla'*, 864.
[125] For example Mahmud Haydar under Rustam b. 'Umar Shaykh (Ṭihrānī Iṣfahānī, *Diyarbakriyya*, 288, 293, 327–28), and Hafiz Razi, vizier of Iskandar b. 'Umar Shaykh (Yazdī, *Ḥasanī*, 14–15; Faṣīḥ Khwāfī, *Mujmal-i faṣīḥī*, vol. III, 251).
[126] Lambton, *Continuity and Change*, 38. [127] Khwāndamīr, *Dastūr*, 380.
[128] Ḥaqīqat, *Tārīkh-i Simnān*, 133.

pattern resembles the one found in Khwaf and probably reflects a similar method of training and recruitment.

The careers of the Timurid viziers from Khwaf and Simnan show certain similarities to those of earlier viziers under the Seljukids and Ilkhans, but also significant differences. First of all, as I have shown, we rarely see individual families maintaining a strong presence in the vizierate over a long period.[129] Instead, while the importance of their city of origin remains, the lineages themselves change. Another significant difference, perhaps connected with this last, is the lack of significant nepotism within the Timurid administration. Among the Simnani viziers there are close family relatives, but most often they replaced each other, as in the case of Sharaf al-Din ʿAli Balicha and his brother Wajih al-Din Ismaʿil. Although for a while under Temür Sharaf al-Din ʿAli Simnani and his son Shams al-Din Muhammad served concurrently in different *dīwān*s, Sharaf al-din ʿAli disappears from the histories early in Shahrukh's reign. Unlike Nizam al-Mulk under the Seljukids and the Juwaynis and Rashid al-Din under the Ilkhans, the Timurid viziers of Khwaf and Simnan do not appear to have brought large numbers of relatives with them to office. Since there was obviously a deliberate separation of the family members of emirs during the early Timurid period, it is possible that the same method was followed for high-ranking bureaucrats.

Other bureaucratic personnel

While the Khwafi and Simnani viziers were conspicuous, they did not constitute a large proportion of the *dīwān* personnel at any level. The other high-level bureaucrats – those whose antecedents we know – represent a variety of backgrounds. Under Shahrukh there was clearly a tendency for sons of *dīwān* personnel to pursue a career within the bureaucracy, but this is not surprising in a society in which occupation was often hereditary. Like other dynasties, the Timurids sometimes attracted to themselves the viziers of their defeated enemies. The historian Taj al-Din Salmani, who served in the *dīwān* under Temür and at the beginning of Shahrukh's reign, had probably served earlier under the Muzaffarids.[130] After Shahrukh's defeat of the Qaraqoyunlu in 823–4/1420–21, he appointed as *ṣāhib dīwān* Amir Jaʿfar b. Mansur, who had been *nāyib* for Qara Yusuf.[131] As we have seen, members of the Khwafi family served the Kartid kings before moving into the service of the Timurids, and

[129] For earlier practice, see Lambton, *Continuity and Change*, 301–8; Aubin, *Émirs mongols et viziers*, 22, 25, 27–28, 47–50.

[130] There is mention of a Muzaffarid envoy of that name (Tāj al-Salmāni, *Tarihnāma/Tacü's Selmânî*, edited and translated by Ismail Aka [Ankara: Atatürk Kültür, Dil ve Tarih Yüksek Kurumu, 1988], 6–7).

[131] Ḥāfiẓ-i Abrū, "Majmaʿ," fol. 561; ʿUqaylī, *Āthār*, 343. This is not the same person as Baysunghur's calligrapher; this Jaʿfar died soon after his appointment.

Yahya Simnani may well have come to Temür from the service of Ahmad Jalayir.

Despite some tendency towards hereditary office, the bureaucratic class attracted a steady stream of new people. Although scholars note the connection between some ulama and bureaucratic families, the tendency is to concentrate on connections within the bureaucratic class.[132] In this section of the chapter I will attempt to redress the balance by concentrating on families whose members followed a variety of careers. For the viziers whose antecedents we can trace, we find a variety of backgrounds and it seems clear that for an ambitious and educated man living not far from the capital, administration could be an attractive career. We should remember how many administrative jobs there were, and how many different institutions they were connected to; each provincial governor had a *dīwān*, as did important emirs. Furthermore, shrines and other organizations required scribes and financial administrators, and the training for such jobs was probably little different from that required for the central administration. Thus administration was a career open to many and embraced by men in the religious classes, by landowners, and by merchants.

Judging from the *nisba*s found among the bureaucrats of the central *dīwān* members of local families were the most likely to make a career in administration. In the provincial *dīwān*s the majority of the personnel seems to have originated within the area. We find the regions of Tus, Sabzawar, and Quhistan, for instance, repeatedly occurring in the *nisbas* of viziers of the Herat *dīwān*.[133] Some Herat viziers are specifically identified as local aristocrats. According to Sayf al-Dīn Ḥājjī ʿUqayli, Shahrukh's vizier Ahmad Da'ud came from the Shihab family of Herat.[134] Among the viziers of Sultan Husayn, who are more fully described, we find several men of high birth, such as ʿAli al-Sanaʾi, of the *ashrāf* of Bakharz who traced his lineage back to the Barmakids, Muzaffar Shabankara, of the aristocracy of Fars and Iraq, and Sayyid Zayn al-ʿAbidin, descended from prominent sayyid families on both his mother's and his father's side.[135]

The Khwafi viziers were not alone in their connection to a militarily active, landed family. Sayf al-Dīn Ḥājjī ʿUqayli gives us a vivid portrait of another vizier stemming from such a family, Jalal Islam, who served under Temür. His

[132] Lambton, *Continuity and Change*, 297; Roger M. Savory, "The Safavid Administrative System," in *Cambridge History of Iran*, vol. 6, 353.

[133] See *Muʿizz*, fols. 97b, 127a, 138a, and Yazdī, *Ḥasanī*, 38.

[134] ʿUqaylī, *Āthār*, 241. Although Sayf al-Din Ḥājjī ʿUqaylī's information is not always accurate, this identification receives support from the number of men of the Shihab family who were exiled from Herat by Sayyid Fakhr al-Din. Ahmad Daʾud was put into the *dīwān* largely to check Fakhr al-Din; if his relations had been exiled, his enmity makes sense. On the other hand, Fasih refers to Ahmad Daʾud as Kalar or Kalaʾi (Faṣīḥ Khwāfī, *Mujmal-i faṣīḥī*, vol. III, 149–50, 230, 255; Khwāndamīr, *Dastūr*, 352–53; Samarqandī, *Maṭlaʿ*, 599.

[135] Khwāndamīr, *Dastūr*, 397, 399, 446.

family came from the region of Tabas Masinan and were active in military affairs. When the family found itself in trouble, Jalal Islam fled to Herat, where one of his older relatives was *yasavul* (bodyguard or adjutant) to Malik Muʿizz al-Din Husayn Kart. Jalal Islam himself worked in the *dīwān*. From here he passed into Temür's service and rose to a high position, but he seems to have remained somewhat of an outsider. Towards the end of Temür's life he was successfully slandered, attempted suicide and, after recovering, became commander of the Tajik troops. Jalal Islam had a relative, probably his brother, called Bahramshah who was also in Temür's service as governor and *kotwal*, and was known as a poet. Bahramshah retained his attachment to Tabas, where he was buried, and even after his death some of this family remained among the Timurid elite; Isfizārī mentions one as an acquaintance.[136]

A number of viziers came from families of sayyids or ulama. This was probably due partly to the tendency for families in government service to seek out marriage alliances with local families of religious descent. I have mentioned above Sayyid Zayn al-ʿAbidin who worked in the *dīwān* of Sultan Husayn. He may well have belonged to the family of Sayyid Zayn al-ʿAbidin Junabadi, prominent in the *dīwān* during Temür's reign and at the beginning of Shahrukh's. Sayyid Zayn al-ʿAbidin profited both from his genealogy and from his religious learning; he was supposedly imprisoned by Temür and then pardoned when he presented Temür with a Qurʾan he had copied.[137] It is clear that he held lands in Junabad, since we find him entertaining Shahrukh there in 817/1414.[138] His son, Sayyid ʿImad al-Din, born in Shawwal, 817/January, 1415, served in Shahrukh's and then in Ulugh Beg's *dīwān*, and is remembered with respect for his character and learning in both exoteric and esoteric sciences.[139] It is interesting that two of the men whom Temür appointed to investigate and punish provincial *dīwān*s at the end of his career were supposedly sayyids – the false sayyid Hasan Khwarazmi, and the true sayyid Fakhr al-Din Ahmad.[140] One should remember, in this context, that the status of sayyids was taken seriously under the Timurids.[141]

The marriage connections formed between bureaucratic and religious families offered a choice of education and career to their members. A good example of the intermarriage of bureaucratic, ulama and sayyid families is

136 ʿUqaylī, *Āthār*, 330–34; Khwāndamīr, *Dastūr*, 341. For Bahramshah, see Shāmī, *Histoire des conquêtes*, vol. II, 185, and Āyat Allāh Ḥājj Shaykh Muḥammad Ḥusayn Āyatī, *Bahāristān dar tārīkh wa tarājim-i rijāl-i Qāyināt wa Quhistān* (Mashhad: Muʾassasa-i Chāp wa Intishārāt-i Dānishgāh-i Firdawsī, 1371/1992), 212.

137 ʿUqaylī, *Āthār*, 335. 138 Samarqandī, *Maṭlaʿ*, 167.

139 Khwāndamīr, *Dastūr*, 262–63; Faṣīḥ Khwāfī, *Mujmal-i faṣīḥī*, vol. III, 214; Samarqandī, *Maṭlaʿ*, 793–94, vol. II, 3, 945.

140 Faṣīḥ Khwāfī, *Mujmal-i faṣīḥī*, vol. III, 157–58; ʿUqaylī, *Āthār*, 336; Khwāndamīr, *Ḥabīb*, vol. III, 598. For other examples of viziers who were sayyids, see *Muʿizz*, fols. 133b, 138a.

141 Samarqandī, *Maṭlaʿ*, 841, 866, 943, 947; Ṭihrānī Iṣfahānī, *Diyarbakriyya*, 293, 309; Kāshifī, *Rashaḥāt*, 467.

the lineage of the historian Khwandamir. His father's family combined a tradition of religious and bureaucratic office, while on his mother's side he descended from a prestigious sayyid family, some of whose members held the office of *ṣadr*.[142] Another example of such a union of families is found in the biography of ʿAtiq Allah, who served as vizier under Sultan Husayn. He was the son of Nasir al-Din Muhammad, descended from the shaykhs of Jam, who was a *muḥtasib* under Shahrukh, and also probably related to Shihab al-Din Abu'l Makarim (d. 833/1429–30), another *muḥtasib* for Shahrukh. Nasir al-Din Muhammad married into the family of Sharaf al-Din Hajji Khwafi, who had been vizier to the Kartid kings. Since Nasir al-Din died when ʿAtiq Allah was very young, ʿAtiq Allah was brought up within his mother's family and studied accounting (*siyāq*). His career was furthered by Pir Ahmad Khwafi's son, the vizier Majd al-Din Muhammad.[143] In this way ʿAtiq Allah resembles Fasih Khwafi, who also followed the profession of his mother's family, rather than that of his father. Like Fasih Khwafi's lineage, that of Sharaf al-Din Hajji Khwafi may have had a military dimension. Sharaf al-Din's son is referred to as Amir Mubarak, and his grandson Amir Qawam al-Din Shadi, who was governor (*ḥākim*) of Khwaf, was executed for resisting the agent sent to investigate and extort taxes in 807/1404.[144]

The breadth of connection and background found among Timurid bureaucratic families can be well illustrated in the genealogy which Muʿīn al-Dīn Zamchī Isfizari gives for his patron, Qawam al-Din Nizam al-Mulk Khwafi. Isfizari's claims seem inflated, involving as they do descent from most of the important figures of eastern Iran, but a portion may be true. The relatives claimed for Qawam al-Din include the military commander and local magnate Malik Zuzan, important under the Khorezmshahs, Khwaja Majd, mentioned above as Fasih Khwafi's ancestor, the famous *faqīh* Khwaja Muhammad Mayizhnabadi of Kartid Herat, and the Chishti shaykh Shah Sanjan.[145] The relationship to Shah Sanjan could explain the privileged treatment Fasih Khwafi gives that family. Qawam al-Din also claimed to be descended from a well-known judge from Zuzan, active under the Ilkhan Muhammad Khudabanda, several sayyid lineages, numerous Sufis, including the shaykhs of Jam and Bakharz, the kings of Sistan and Badakhshan, and the Barmakid family.[146] Many of these figures had other descendants among the bureaucracy. The families mentioned here were potential sources of prestige for rising bureaucratic lineages, and they, in their turn, could benefit from a connection to men who might provide access both to the ear of the ruler and to the wealth of the *dīwān*.

[142] Beveridge and Manz, "Mīrk̲h̲wānd"; Beveridge and de Brujn, "K̲h̲wāndamīr," *Encyclopaedia of Islam*, 2nd edn; Khwāndamīr, *Ḥabīb*, vol. IV, 105; Thackston, *Habibu's-siyar*, 407.
[143] Khwāndamīr, *Dastūr*, 444–45; Khwāndamīr, *Ḥabīb*, vol. IV, 11–12; Thackston, *Habibu's-siyar*, 357; Faṣīḥ Khwāfī, *Mujmal-i faṣīḥī*, vol. III, 105.
[144] Faṣīḥ Mujmal-i fasīḥī, vol. III, 158–59. [145] Isfizārī, *Rawḍāt*, vol. I, 200–07.
[146] Ibid., vol. I, 216–17.

Conclusion

It is clear that the central bureaucracy under Shahrukh was a center of power in which Persian bureaucrats, Chaghatay emirs and Timurid princes all played an active part. It is impossible to discern exactly how the Turco-Mongolian personnel fitted into the *dīwān*, but it is safe to say that some were intimately involved and held considerable power. While the influence of individuals might vary greatly over time, all three types of people were consistently active, and if power shifted between them, this was probably a result of individual status.

Shahrukh gave considerably more latitude to his subordinates than Temür had done, and we find the *ṣāḥib dīwān* serving longer and with more authority than in Temür's time. Nonetheless, there were limits on even Ghiyath al-Din Pir Ahmad's power. He was forced to accept a partner not of his own choosing, and was several times removed from office for a short period. Neither Pir Ahmad nor his partners moreover seem to have managed to fill subordinate offices with their relatives. The *dīwān* at this period was certainly not free from graft or internal power struggles, but it seems to have been kept under reasonable control, especially after the fall of Sayyid Fakhr al-Din in 820/1417.

The bureaucratic personnel of the Timurid period formed a professional group which passed on specialized training and patronage both through family networks and through local institutions. Like the ulama, bureaucrats did not constitute a closed class separated off from the rest of society. Marriage with families of local status and a desire to grasp the opportunity of advancement brought new people into the occupation, and the duties and expertise of bureaucrats overlapped with those of other groups. Many viziers were active in military campaigns, sometimes apparently among the major commanders, and it is not therefore entirely surprising to find military men among their forebears and relatives. Even more clearly, the expertise of the bureaucrats overlapped with that of the ulama. Both religious learning and sayyid descent were considered desirable attributes for viziers, and may well have helped to protect them from the worst consequences of bureaucratic infighting. For ulama at this period, some knowledge of accounting, composition, and similar skills were not irrelevant, given the number and size of *waqf* endowments to be administered and the prevalence of the office of *ṣadr*.[147]

Bureaucrats often traveled quite widely, following rulers and avenues of power, but we find that many also exhibit a continued attachment to their home region, which often benefited materially from their patronage. It seems likely therefore that recruitment, training, and marriage alliances within the

[147] We find for instance that accounting and composition (*inshā'*) were among the accomplishments of ʿAbd al-Razzaq Samarqandī's brother ʿAbd al-Qahhar (Khwāndamīr, *Ḥabīb*, vol. IV, 102; Thackston, *Habibu's-siyar*, 406).

bureaucratic milieu occurred not only in circles active at court, but also in the provincial centers from which bureaucrats originated. This explains the numerous Khwafi and Simnani lineages we find within the Timurid bureaucracy, and the continued preeminence of the larger local group when specific lineages lost power. Just as the *dīwān* was open to the Turco-Mongolian emirs, it attracted new recruits from the Iranian landed elite whose members controlled much of local politics.

CHAPTER 4

Political and military resources of Iran

Iran and Central Asia were made up of numerous overlapping political worlds, in which for centuries power had been contested among local dynasties and cities, and such habits did not cease under central rule. When Temür conquered Iran, he called forth an imposing spectacle of submission, while leaving all but the largest regional dynasties intact.[1] Most had to provide troops for occasional campaigns; some paid regular taxes while others simply had to offer periodic expressions of submission. All had armies, usually a mix of settled Iranian soldiers, local tribes and Turco-Mongolian troops. But much of their political and military infrastructure remained in place, along with their ambitions and rivalries.

Timurid control over society radiated outward from a few major cities, and the level of governmental impact varied widely from one region to another. We can draw a hierarchy of city and regional control, starting with the capital city of Herat, largely dominated by the Timurid court, to the major provincial capitals such as Shiraz and Samarqand, ruled by princely governors heading large armies, then to the secondary capitals like Yazd and Kerman, with governors drawn from among the lesser princes and the emirs, who often came to identify closely with their region. Each governor had at his disposal a provincial *dīwān* and an army of Chaghatay soldiers. Though in theory the Chaghatay were separate from the Iranian population, in practice both the members of the dynasty and their emirs dealt directly with their subjects, whose religion, culture, and language were all part of the dynasty's heritage. When a governor took possession of his province, local people came to pay their respects and tender submission. The histories rarely explain who these men were and what level of submission they offered. We should probably identify them as the rulers of the numerous semi-independent towns, regions and tribes found throughout Iran.

Being ruled was not a passive activity. The key to the control of an area was its major cities and the decision about whether to defend a city or to submit lay largely with the local population, who participated in its defense. City

[1] Manz, *Rise and Rule*, 91.

notables had to decide which ruler to obey, and wrong decisions were expensive. Notables made their decision primarily by assessing the relative power of rival contenders, and one aspect of this power was the ruler's ability to acquire regional troops and the support of local semi-independent rulers. Cities in central regions interacted closely with the dynasty and, over the course of time, a number lost their independence and became more fully incorporated. The population of Iran continued to be active in the military sphere as well; regional armies of Iranian soldiers existed in most provinces and much of the population – local tribes, the remnants of earlier Turco-Mongolian ruling classes, peasants and city artisans – had a role to play in military campaigns. In peripheral regions, like Sistan, Khuzistan, and the Caspian littoral, local histories give us the portrait of societies in which the Timurids were a distant force, of less interest than struggles for power within families who produced more heirs than they had thrones for. Their rivalries drew in neighboring powers, both those within the Timurid realm and those outside.

The Timurids thus ruled over an armed population actively pursuing its own political aims. There was no lack of centrifugal forces within the realm, and the central ruler did not have a monopoly on force. Rule was a matter of balance among competing interests, of exemplary punishment and reward. Above all, territorial integrity depended on the opportunities that the central administration offered to local people. Scholars have pointed to the value of central government for the upper classes, dependent on trade and agriculture, but social classes and professional groups were not organized to act collectively.[2] Local elites, after all, owed their authority and thus their loyalty more to their clients than to their peers, who were as often rivals as allies. Consequently, there had to be some way in which the presence of the Timurid officials served the cause of the individuals engaged in local politics. We need to discover how central government fit into the political strategies of the men who held regional power.

In this chapter I assess the forces that worked towards dissension and fragmentation, and those that promoted cohesion. I will begin with the center – the interests of dynastic princes and emirs – then survey the structures of the provinces they ruled: the cities, regional armies, and local tribes. The later sections of the chapter deal with regional powers less fully under Timurid control. Small dynasties on the Timurid borders had relations at once with the central ruler, the provincial governors, and the outside powers, and for this reason they presented a particular challenge to Shahrukh and his governors. Finally, we will examine the politics of some largely independent dynasties, showing how local rivalries intersected with the politics of neighboring powers and Timurid government.

[2] See for example, Jean Aubin, "Comment Tamerlan prenait les villes," *Studia Islamica* 19 (1963), 89–90, and Hourani, *Arab Peoples*, 133–37.

Timurid provincial and political structure

By 821/1418–19 Shahrukh had put almost all provinces under the governorship of his own sons or close emirs. He allowed his governors considerable fiscal autonomy; it appears that taxes usually remained in the province, though practice varied.[3] Nonetheless, governors were far from independent. Part of the control Shahrukh maintained came from direct oversight and a set of recognized duties which kept governors involved in the affairs of the realm. While dynastic governors were expected to maintain control within their regions, and to expand their borders through independent campaigns, their military activities were overseen by the center. Many border powers sent regular emissaries to Shahrukh, whether or not they answered formally to the provincial governor near them, and requests for help often went directly to the center.[4] On Shahrukh's major campaigns, provinces contributed troops and in almost all cases, the governor also participated.[5] Shahrukh's sons held the largest provinces but had little power over their personal life; their most important marriages were arranged by the ruler and their older sons were usually raised by Shahrukh's wives.[6]

The system of provincial authority was far from simple, and produced numerous overlaps. Below the provincial level, some territory was distributed as land grants, the smaller called *tiyul* and the larger *soyurghal.* Such grants were probably distributions of income rather than ownership, but they were usually hereditary and some at least brought with them local authority. Shahrukh honored the grants that his father had made and was himself quite generous in giving regions in *soyurghal* to his emirs.[7] At first glance the practice seems to promote decentralization, but Shahrukh took steps to counteract the acquisition of personal power. When we look at the location of *soyurghal* holdings, we see that grants may actually have helped to prevent the concentration of regional power. Emirs usually received holdings outside the provinces in which they held official positions, and within the provinces of princes they were not attached to. It may have been for this reason that

[3] On the appointments of Baysunghur and Ilyas Khwaja the sources state that the income of the region was to remain with the governor as his *soyurghal* (Ḥāfiẓ-i Abrū, *Zubdat*, 571, 609–10). In Kerman however, when Ghunashirin became governor, the *dīwān* registers were removed to Herat (Aubin, *Deux sayyids*, 51).

[4] The dynasties of Hormuz and Badakhshan are examples (Aubin, "Les princes d'Ormuz du XIIIe au XVe siècle," *Journal Asiatique*, CCXLI [1953], 118; Ḥāfiẓ-i Abrū, *Zubdat*, 468–70, 642–43, 675–79, 807–08).

[5] The exception to this pattern was Ulugh Beg, who remained in Transoxiana.

[6] Beatrice F. Manz, "Women in Timurid Dynastic Politics," in *Women in Iran from the Rise of Islam to 1800*, edited by Lois Beck and Guity Nashat (Urbana, IL: University of Illinois Press, 2003), 122–26.

[7] Unfortunately contemporary sources used words for land grants with considerable freedom. Princes appointed as governors are quite often described as receiving the region as *soyurghal*, with no indication of what that meant (see for example Samarqandī, *Maṭlaʿ*, 904, 908; Faṣīḥ Khwāfī, *Mujmal-i faṣīḥī* III, 193, 219).

Shahrukh was willing to leave land in the possession of families of emirs even if they had rebelled against him. For example, Temür's follower Shaykh ʿAli Bahadur held the region of Mashhad/Tus and after Temür's death, in 808/1406 his son Sayyid Khwaja rebelled against Shahrukh. It seems that the family had forged local alliances, since the ruler of the nearby town of Turshiz joined the uprising.[8] Despite this rebellion, the district of Radkan, a dependency of Tus, remained in the family, passing to Shaykh ʿAli's other son Ilyas Khwaja. The family, however, did not hold any official position in the province, which was granted to Baysunghur in 817/1414. Shortly after this, in 818/1415, Ilyas Khwaja was appointed governor of a different region, stretching from Qum and Kashan to Qazwin.[9]

We see the same pattern with the family of Temür's follower Chekü Barlas, which retained its interests in the regions of Qunduz and Baghlan northeast of Herat, while holding regional offices elsewhere. This area was the seat of an important Chaghatay unit, the Boroldai *tümen*, and was a dependency of Balkh, which seems to have formed a separate governorship.[10] At the beginning of Shahrukh's reign Qunduz and Baghlan belonged to Midrab b. Chekü, whom Shahrukh appointed as governor of Fars shortly before his death in 817/1414. Qunduz and Baghlan passed to his nephew Ibrahim Sultan b. Jahanshah b. Chekü, who was also appointed to an official position elsewhere – in Isfahan. Midrab is listed under Shahrukh's office holders, while Ibrahim Sultan b. Jahanshah, after his dismissal from Isfahan, was sent to Ulugh Beg, whom he served as a *tovachi*. Ulugh Beg's governorship did not include Balkh, and he likewise had no jurisdiction over Qunduz and Baghlan.[11] Several members of Chekü's family are later mentioned holding these areas, and it is notable that most served princes unconnected with the region.[12]

Another dependency of Balkh, Shaburghan, was given to Sayyid Ahmad b. ʿUmar Shaykh as a *soyurghal* in 810/1407–08; in the same year, the governorship of Balkh was bestowed on Qaydu b. Pir Muhammad from the line of Jahangir.[13] Andkhud, near Shaburghan, was the locus of two different land holdings. Shahrukh's brother-in-law, Sayyid Ahmad b. Ghiyath al-Din Tarkhan, received a *soyurghal* in Andkhud in 810/1407, which passed to his son Ismaʾil Sufi on his death in 825/1422. Ismaʾil Sufi still held the region after

[8] Faṣīḥ Khwāfī, *Mujmal-i faṣīḥī*, vol. III, 291; Samarqandī, *Maṭlaʿ*, 42, 762–63; Ḥāfiẓ-i Abrū, *Zubdat*, 119.

[9] Ḥāfiẓ-i Abrū, *Zubdat*, 609–10. After Ilyas Khwaja's death in 838/1434–35 Radkan passed to Saʿid Khwaja's son Sayyid Yusuf (Ḥāfiẓ-i Abrū, *Ḥorāsān*, vol. II, 93; Faṣīḥ Khwāfī, *Mujmal-i faṣīḥī*, vol. III, 279; Ando, *Timuridische Emire*, 133–36).

[10] Ḥāfiẓ-i Abrū, *Zubdat*, 680; Faṣīḥ Khwāfī, *Mujmal-i faṣīḥī*, vol. III, 176, 195; Samarqandī, *Maṭlaʿ*, 87, 908.

[11] Ḥāfiẓ-i Abrū, "Majmaʿ," fol. 14a; Ḥāfiẓ-i Abrū, *Zubdat*, 558–59; *Muʿizz*, fols. 92b, 93a, 138a Ṭihrānī Iṣfahānī, Diyārbakriyya, 85; Ando, *Timuridische Emire*, 128.

[12] Ando, *Timuridische Emire*, 130–31; *Muʿizz*, fol. 93a.

[13] Faṣīḥ Khwāfī, *Mujmal-i faṣīḥī*, vol. III, 176, 193; Ḥāfiẓ-i Abrū, *Zubdat*, 192, 301, 394, 517–18.

Shahrukh's death.[14] The Sufi shaykh Amir Baraka, much favored by Temür, supposedly held the rights to the *waqf*s for the holy cities in that region, granted him by Temür.[15] Thus, although the evidence is too sparse to be conclusive, it appears that land grants were given usually outside the region in which the recipients were stationed. This practice served to prevent the formation of a regional power base for emirs and, at the same time, to dilute the power of the prince in charge of the province.

In some cases regional authority was formally divided among several people. Isfahan and its region provide a particularly strong example. After Shahrukh's final campaign against Fars, Isfahan was entrusted to his nephew Rustam, who had proven himself the least troublesome of ʿUmar Shaykh's children. After Rustam's death in 827 or 828/1423–25, governorship went to Amir Firuzshah's family; the province passed down within the family from Firuzshah's brother Khwandshah eventually to his nephew, Saʿadat b. Khwandshah.[16] During the same period, Ibrahim Sultan b. Jahanshah b. Chekü held authority in the city until he was dismissed in 833/1429–30, when his position went to another major emir, ʿAbd al-Samad, who was still in charge in 835/1431–32.[17] Another emir with a position in Isfahan was ʿAlika Kukeltash, who held the authority for tax collection (*muḥaṣṣilī*), and at his death, the post passed to his son.[18] All the emirs appointed to Isfahan were prominent, and their authority undoubtedly diluted that of the governor, Firuzshah's brother, whose formal standing in the Chaghatay elite was lower than theirs.

A similar situation existed in Khuttalan. We are informed that under Shahrukh the governorship was held by Nurmalik Barlas and then by his son Sultan Bayazid.[19] We also learn that the region was given to Muhammad Juki in *soyurghal* in 833/1429–30, and passed to his son Aba Bakr.[20] When, in 851/1447–48, Aba Bakr began to expand his holdings and plan rebellion, it was a Barlas emir who informed Ulugh Beg, sending a member of his *dīwān* as emissary.[21] What we might be seeing here is the continued presence of Nurmalik's family in Khuttalan, now part of a larger governorship held by a Timurid prince. After this Ulugh Beg bestowed the governorship on the young prince ʿAbd Allah b. Ibrahim Sultan.[22]

[14] Ando, *Timuridische Emire*, 140; Faṣīḥ Khwāfī, *Mujmal-i faṣīḥī*, vol. III, 177, 251; Ḥāfiẓ-i Abrū, *Zubdat*, 636; Ṭihrānī Iṣfahānī, *Diyārbakriyya*, 302. It seems that Sayyid Ahmad's descendants continued there, since we read in Mīr ʿAlī Shīr Nawaʾi's *Majalis al-nafāʾis* of a soldier and poet called Mawlana Tarkhani from Andkhud (Nawāʾī, *Majālis*, 41).

[15] Jürgen Paul, "Scheiche und Herrscher im Khanat Čağatay," *Der Islam* 67, 2 (1990), 302.

[16] Samarqandī, *Maṭlaʿ*, 676; Dawlatshāh Samarqandī, *Tadhkirat*, 405; Rosemarie Quiring-Zoche, *Isfahan im 15. und 16. Jahrhundert. Ein Beitrag zur persischen Stadtgeschichte* (Freiburg: Schwarz, 1980), 31–35, 117–24; Jaʿfarī, *Tārīkh-i kabīr*, 74; fols. 309b–310a.

[17] Jaʿfarī, *Tārīkh-i kabīr*, 75, 78–79; fols. 310a, 312a.

[18] *Muʿizz*, fol. 133a.

[19] *Muʿizz*, fols. 92a, 133b. The earlier masters of the region, the Khuttalani emirs, were still governors in 810/1407–08, and apparently remained there (Ḥāfiẓ-i Abrū, *Zubdat*, 189).

[20] Dawlatshāh Samarqandī, *Tadhkirat*, 396; Samarqandī, *Maṭlaʿ*, 904.

[21] Samarqandī, *Maṭlaʿ*, 904–05.

[22] Ṭihrānī Iṣfahānī, *Diyārbakriyya*, 307.

Overlapping land holdings and offices served to dilute the control of any one person or family over a given area, and probably helped to unify the realm in another way as well by ensuring that prominent emirs had interests in more than one province. Many emirs under Shahrukh had strong involvements outside the regions they held. Shahmalik, governor of Khorezm, was a major patron of the Khorezmian Sufi shaykh Husayn Khwarazmi – in addition he probably built a madrasa in Jam, and he possessed numerous *waqf*s in Mashhad, where he was buried.[23] The emirs ʿAlika and Firuzshah had widespread local interests scattered throughout Shahrukh's dominions and even beyond. ʿAlika for instance, while deeply involved in the central government, also held the governorship of Marw and Sarakhs, which he passed on to his son Shaykh Abu'l Fadl.[24] He built a pious foundation there, and both he and his son are reported visiting the region.[25] In addition, ʿAlika apparently had enormous landholdings, including some in Egypt. He was strongly interested in agriculture and planted a crop of over 1,000 *kharwār* of seed.[26] As mentioned above, he and his son also held rights to tax collection in Isfahan.

Amir Firuzshah likewise appears in connection with several areas besides Isfahan. He was granted the governorship of Abarquh near Yazd on the defeat of Iskandar b. ʿUmar Shaykh in 817/1414, and his agent remained there for much, or all, of Shahrukh's reign.[27] We also find him mentioned in connection with the taxes of Jam and Balkh. The interests in Balkh may have been part of his *dīwān* responsibilities,[28] but his connection to Jam is underlined by his architectural patronage there; he constructed a number of buildings including a mosque and a madrasa, built probably in 844/1440–41.[29] Samarqandī emphasizes the number of properties he owned throughout the realm and his patronage of sayyids in Syria, Egypt and the Holy Cities.[30] Major emirs also maintained a presence in Herat, and here we find buildings by many of the commanders of Shahrukh's period: a madrasa and mausoleum built by ʿAlika, a mosque by Shahmalik, a madrasa, mausoleum, and *khānaqāh* by Firuzshah, and a madrasa by Amir Chaqmaq of Yazd, along with buildings by other emirs.[31]

23 Ando, *Timuridische Emire*, 167; Lisa Golombek, "The Chronology of Turbat-i Shaykh Jām," *Iran, Journal of the British Institute of Persian Studies* IX (1971), 41; O'Kane, *Timurid Architecture*, 217; Lisa Golombek and Donald Wilber, *The Timurid Architecture of Iran and Turan* (Princeton, NJ: Princeton University Press, 1988), 332, 464; Devin DeWeese, "The *Kashf al-Hudā* of Kamāl al-Dīn Ḥusayn Khorezmī: A Fifteenth-Century Sufi Commentary on the *Qaṣīdat al-Burdah* in Khorezmian Turkic (Text Edition, Translation and Historical Introduction)," Ph.D. dissertation, Indiana University, 1985, 196–204.

24 *Muʿizz*, fol. 133a.

25 Faṣīḥ Khwāfī, *Mujmal-i faṣīḥī*, vol. III, 283; Samarqandī, *Maṭlaʿ*, 717.

26 Samarqandī, *Maṭlaʿ*, 746–47.

27 *Muʿizz*, fol. 133a; Yazdī, *Ḥasanī*, 40; Samarqandī, *Maṭlaʿ*, 323.

28 Samarqandī, *Maṭlaʿ*, 752, 792, 837–39.

29 Golombek, "Chronology," 28, 39–40.

30 Samarqandī, *Maṭlaʿ*, 840–41.

31 Golombek and Wilber, *Timurid Architecture*, 449–55; Terry Allen, *Timurid Herat*, Beihefte zum Tübinger Atlas des vorderen Orients (Wiesbaden: Reichert, 1983), 18–19; and Allen, *Catalogue*, 419, 450, 454, 468, 505, 597, 604.

We see then that Shahrukh's administration combined a decentralized economic structure with a governing class tied to the center but by no means detached from local society. Although both the dynasty and the standing army were foreign to the population, they were involved in many aspects of Iranian life, aspects both economic and cultural. By the time of Temür, the Chaghatay emirs were Muslim and knew Persian; by Shahrukh's reign, they had been ruling in Iran for a generation and many had developed regional attachments. What helped to prevent fragmentation was the continued involvement of governors and emirs with the Timurid realm as a whole. This was achieved in part through direct control; by the supervision of independent campaigns undertaken by princes and the participation of governors with regional armies in the campaigns undertaken by Shahrukh. The other practice that helped to maintain cohesion was Shahrukh's system of land grants and appointments, which worked against the concentration of regional power.

Politics and military activity in Iranian cities

To control their provinces, the Timurid governors relied only in part on the Chaghatay army. Equally important was the support they received from two major groups within the local population: first the notables and inhabitants of the cities, and second the regional armies. The military importance of Iranian manpower was far from negligible – indeed Iranian participation could be decisive in regional contests. It is important to note that city and regional personnel were not entirely separate; we find people of urban provenance both as commanders and as soldiers in regional armies. Nonetheless the defense of cities was a separate and particular issue, in which much of the urban population was active. In this section I shall give a sketch of the types of people who held some urban military responsibility.

Cities were ruled through the system of power sharing characterized by Marshall Hodgson as the *ayʿān-amīr* system. The state provided military protection through the governor and a garrison, and order through a bureaucracy and state involvement in local legal institutions, most notably the judiciary and market controllers. The two branches of government, local and central, are usually seen as largely separate in background and personnel. Urban affairs were organized by men with a local power base who held a variety of positions in the cities, some formal and some informal. Scholars have usually emphasized the role of the ulama as notables, since their independence in religious affairs made it possible for them to hold government appointments without coming fully under government control.[32] I suggest that the division between military and civil responsibility and between

[32] For Hodgson's discussion, see Hodgson, *Venture of Islam*, vol. II, 62–69, 112–15, and Hourani, *Arab Peoples*, 130–37.

city and state may have been less marked than the *aʿyān-amīr* dichotomy suggests.

We see the role of the city population most clearly in accounts of regional struggles, when cities had to decide whether to submit or to defend themselves. There are numerous descriptions of cities under crisis, faced either with an army outside the gates or with the recognition that the prince to whom they owed their loyalty might soon lose his throne. Along with sayyids and ulama, local bureaucrats and, occasionally merchants, who made up what one might call the higher notables, cities had heads of quarters, called variously *kadkhudā*, *kulū* or *ra'īs*. The most sensitive decisions seem to have been made by a small number of people drawn from these two groups, whom we can characterize as the city council. There were also local military commanders, *sardārs*, attached to many cities. In the list of people exiled from Herat by Sayyid Fakhr al-Din in 807/1404–05 we find an institution which probably existed elsewhere, though it is not mentioned in other sources: the head of the city patrol along with members of his force.[33] The city population, sometimes identified as artisans, sometimes as rabble, contributed manpower, though it rarely acted on its own initiative.

There was no one universal pattern of power among the cities of Iran and Central Asia. In accounts of the defense of Herat, the population of the bazaar is mentioned and usually the city judge is credited with organizing the defense.[34] In Yazd, we find mention only of the higher notables: the head judge of the city (usually in charge), some high-level bureaucrats, and one particularly wealthy merchant. Samarqand seems to have had a similar political structure and issues of defense or submission were decided largely by major religious figures. These included the *shaykh al-islām*, a judge, several members of the ulama, and a descendant of a Sufi shaykh, whose shrine was popular.[35] Isfahan had a more mixed structure of authority, in which ulama, bureaucrats, and local headmen shared power. In Shiraz, finally, we find an example of a city in which the headmen of wards or professions appear as the most prominent actors in most events, and while notables are mentioned as a group, their names are not given. The notables of both Shiraz and Isfahan were in touch with local powers in the countryside.[36]

While internal city politics usually remain obscure, we can tell that the local notables and headmen were sometimes divided among themselves. In the case

[33] Faṣīḥ Khwāfī, *Mujmal-i faṣīḥī*, vol. III, 150.

[34] Samarqandī, *Maṭlaʿ*, 953–54; Khwāndamīr, *Ḥabīb*, vol. IV, 65; Jürgen Paul, "Wehrhafte Städte. Belagerungen von Herat, 1448–1468," *Asiatische Studien/Études Asiatiques* LVIII, 1 (2004), 185–88.

[35] Ḥāfiẓ-i Abrū, *Zubdat*, 365–66.

[36] See for example Jaʿfarī, "Tārīkh-i kabīr," 59–61, 124; fols. 304a–b; Yazdī, *Ḥasanī*, 39–41; Kātib, *Tārīkh-i jadīd*, 238; Ṭihrānī Iṣfahānī, *Diyārbakriyya*, 287. The internal politics of Shiraz are discussed in the next chapter.

of the city of Khorezm, recaptured by Shahrukh in 815/1412–13 from the Golden Horde, there were two parties within the town, one favoring submission to Shahrukh and another promoting resistance.[37] Two accounts of city rebellions, one in Yazd in 798/1395–96, and one in Isfahan in 812/1409–10, show violence between opposing factions within the city, for and against the uprising.[38] Most often the issue was the choice between two contenders for regional power, and the most important question was who was likely to win. What determined the composition of the factions we cannot tell, but they were probably based partly on continuing internal rivalries for power. In some cases when the choice was between different Timurid princes, we find Chaghatay and local personnel within both factions.[39]

The next question to consider is the level of power that the city population held in decision-making. The answer here is clear; when the population and notables were in agreement, their decisions were usually decisive. Most examples concern the question of whether or not to resist an outside army. The notables met sometimes in the absence of the Chaghatay governor, but often in conjunction with him and his emirs. When the city people disagreed with the governor, it seems that their wishes usually prevailed. On several occasions cities submitted to outside powers despite the governor's desire to hold out, and sometimes the population insisted on defending the city despite reluctance on the part of the prince or governor.[40]

One reason for the weight that notables had in decision-making was the part city populations played in the defense of the city even when Chaghatay commanders were present. The class most actively involved appears to have been the craftsmen and artisans who were organized by notables, often under the leadership of the city judge or the ward headmen.[41] It is probable that the notables and population were largely responsible for the defense of the walls and towers of the city proper, while Chaghatay troops were in charge of the citadel.[42] The urban population might also be mobilized directly by the Chaghatay governor. During the struggle after Temür's death, Aba Bakr b.

[37] Ḥāfiẓ-i Abrū, *Zubdat*, 478–80.

[38] Jaʿfarī, *Tārīkh-i kabīr*, 51–2; fols. 273b–4a, 300b; Kātib, *Tārīkh-i jadīd*, 90.

[39] When Jahanshah Qaraqoyunlu took Herat in 862/1458, some notables left with the Timurid ruler, and others remained to welcome the invaders (Ṭihrānī Iṣfahānī, *Diyārbakriyya*, 351–52).

[40] I have discussed this issue in a separate article; see Beatrice Manz "Nomad and Settled in the Timurid Military," in *Mongols, Turks, and Others: Eurasian Nomads and the Sedentary World*, edited by Reuven Amitai and Michal Biran (Leiden, Boston: Brill, 2005), 425–57.

[41] See Manz, "Nomad and Settled," and Chapter 5. The military activity of the city population in Iran seems to differ from that attested to in the Mamluk Sultanate. While Mamluk city populations were sometimes used in military campaigns, they seem to have had a smaller role and to have been led by Mamluk emirs (see Ira Lapidus, *Muslim Cities in the Later Middle Ages* [Cambridge: Cambridge University Press, 1984], 159–67; Reuven Amitai, "Foot Soldiers, Militiamen and Volunteers in the Early Mamluk Army," in *Texts, Documents and Artefacts: Islamic Studies in Honor of D. S. Richards*, edited by Chase F. Robinson [Leiden, Boston: Brill, 2003], 240–46).

[42] Paul, "Wehrhafte Städte," 183–6.

Amiranshah took refuge in Kerman, where he gained sufficient popularity to pose a threat to the governor, Sultan Uways b. Edegü Barlas. Sultan Uways first called together his own emirs and had them seize and bind the followers of Aba Bakr, then he sent orders to the quarters of the city that all men between seven and seventy were to find arms and come into the fortress, where Aba Bakr remained with twenty men. This demonstration convinced Aba Bakr that he would be happier elsewhere.[43] During the struggles after Shahrukh's death, the governor of Herat called up the population for military action; they were to gather all the mounts they could find and go out of Herat after the enemy. In this case the men were unarmed and were easily dispersed.[44]

If military defense was part of the expected activities of bazaar personnel and notables, they must have had some military training. There are indications that the level of expertise varied, but it is clear that both notables and artisans could often fight competently. Two weapons were of particular utility – arrows and stones. The skilled and enthusiastic use of such weapons by people well placed on the walls could keep an army at bay for some time.[45] In assessing the probable military competence of notables, one should remember that both viziers and men of religious training often participated in campaigns. Some city judges, such as Qadi Ahmad Saʿidi of Isfahan, led troops outside the city and clearly had significant military experience. Notables originated in local families, and as I showed in the previous chapter, families might produce people of several different professions – bureaucrats, ulama, and military men – and they might also marry into military families.[46]

While Timurid histories sometimes stress the inferiority of Iranian soldiers in the field,[47] in the defense of cities the skill of Iranians is not infrequently emphasized and praised. This kind of military activity was one in which Iranian excellence was expected and accepted, and successful actions might be rewarded. After the religious notables of Samarqand led the defense of the city in the absence of its Chaghatay forces in 812/1410, Shahrukh visited the city and favored those who had participated in its defense.[48] Isfizari, listing the notable people of Khwaf, states that Mawlana Kamal al-Din Shaykh Husayn, who held the post of *muḥtasib* under Abu Saʿid, had defended Herat with great courage and skill during an attack in Abu Saʿid's reign.[49] Samarqandī describes the siege of Herat by the Turkmen prince Yar ʿAli, after Shahrukh's death, in which first the Turks and then the Tajik defenders

[43] Yazdī, *Ḥasanī*, 32. [44] Samarqandī, *Maṭlaʿ*, 953–54.

[45] See for example the siege of Kerman in 819/1416, where even numerous missile throwers were unable to make significant headway against the archers on the walls (Yazdī, *Ḥasanī*, 42–43).

[46] Manz, "Nomad and Settled," and for further examples: Amir Shahi Sabzawari (Dawlatshāh Samarqandī, *Tadhkirat*, 426–27) and Mawlana Ghiyath al-Din Jamshid Qaʾini (Khwāndamīr, *Ḥabīb*, vol. IV, 324; Thackston, *Habibuʾs-siyar*, 512).

[47] For examples see Yazdī, *Ḥasanī*, 80, 92. [48] Ḥāfiẓ-i Abrū, *Zubdat*, 379–80.

[49] Isfizārī, *Rawḍat*, 221. The biography in the *Ḥabib al-siyar*, however, does not mention military activity (Khwāndamīr, *Ḥabīb*, vol. IV, 108; Thackston, *Habibuʾs-siyar*, 409).

retreated. The situation was saved by a certain Mawlana ʿImad al-Din Mutahhar Karizi, distinguished for his skill in archery, who led his soldiers forward and held off the enemy until Ulugh Beg could send emirs to relieve the city.[50] It seems likely therefore that certain military skills important for city defense, such as archery, were practiced among the Iranian city populations and that they were recognized and rewarded by the dynasty.

It is hard to discern the organizations responsible for military training, but the sources contain tantalizing bits of information. Some Iranian military figures with the title *pahlawān* appear to have had special skills. One example of someone holding this title is Shirmard Jigardar Pahlawan, "unequaled by any Tajik on earth," who fought Iskandar b. ʿUmar Shaykh outside Isfahan, for the other Timurid princes.[51] Another was Pahlawan Muhammad Girubast wa Jandar from the region of Turshiz, who served as guardian (*kotwāl*) of the fortress Ikhtiyar al-Din.[52] We also find the title connected to the leader of the city patrol in Herat, Pahlawan Hajji Zawaʾi.[53] The historian of Gilan and Mazandaran, Zahir al-Din Marʿashi, tells a story which suggests that Shahrukh held contests of military arts in which Iranians participated. Marʿashi's relative Sayyid Fadl Allah was very skilled in archery, and at the court of Shahrukh he outdid a famous *pahlawān* of Shahrukh's who could shoot through seven iron elephants. Fadl Allah shot through nine, and received a document with the royal seal to attest to his prowess.[54]

Pahlawān is a term associated with the Iranian heroic tradition, and most of the people to whom it is applied seem to have been Iranian, though we know of one man who is identified as Qurlas, and thus presumably Turco-Mongolian.[55] The word is found in the culture of the *zurkhāna* and the fraternal tradition of *futuwwa*.[56] It is tempting to connect the use of the term and the military activities of artisans with *futuwwa* but we can do so only tentatively. Although it is attested under the Mongols and Kartids, for the early Timurid period, there is no evidence of a formal military role for *futuwwa* and scholars suggest that its earlier court and military role had disappeared.[57] The words *fityān* (singular: *fatā*) and *ayyār*, normally associated with members of *futuwwa* organizations, do not appear, and while we do

50 Samarqandī, *Maṭlaʿ*, 952–56. 51 Yazdī, *Ḥasanī*, 22.

52 Isfizārī, *Rawḍat*, 281. It is not clear whether this was under Shahrukh or Sultan Husayn.

53 Faṣīḥ Khwāfī, *Mujmal-i faṣīḥī*, vol. III, 150. 54 Marʿashī, *Tārīkh-i Ṭabaristān*, 328.

55 This man, whom Samarqandī calls the greatest *pahlawān* in Shahrukh's entourage, accompanied the prince Muhammad Juki on his expedition with Ulugh Beg against Baraq in 829–30/1425–27. Despite his prominence among the *pahlawān*, Mahmud Randani (or Dandani) is not listed in the *Muʿizz al-ansab* and he is mentioned on only one other campaign, as one of Bayunghur's men in the army chasing the rebellious Qaydu in 812/1409–10 (Samarqandī, *Maṭlaʿ*, 312; Ḥāfiẓ-i Abrū, *Zubdat*, 686).

56 Ḥusayn Wāʾiẓ Kāshifī Sabzawārī, *Futuwwatnāma-i sulṭānī*, edited by Muḥammad Jaʿfar Maḥjūb (Tehran: Intishārāt-i Bunyād-i Farhang-i Īrān, 1350/1971), 81–3, 310, 319.

57 Franz Taeschner, "Futuwwa, eine gemeinschaftbildende Idee im mittelalterlichen Orient und ihre verschiedenen Erscheinungsformen," *Schweizerisches Archiv für Volkskunde* 52 (1956), 144–47; Kāshifī Sabzawārī, *Futuwwatnāma*, 78–79.

see the similar title *ākhī*, it comes with Sufi rather than military connotations.[58] In its Sufi form however, *futuwwa* was alive; we have two treatises from the period, one by Sayyid ʿAli Hamadani (714/1314–786/1385), who passed through Transoxiana during Temür's lifetime, and one by the scholar Husayn Waʿiz Kashifi (d. 910/1504–05), active in Herat under Sultan Husayn Bayqara. The treatise of ʿAli Hamadani is largely theoretical and concerned with the Sufi appropriation of *futuwwa*, but that of Kashifi, in addition to Sufi interpretations, contains descriptions of initiation rituals and the connections of different crafts and athletic skills to *futuwwa*.[59] Among the activities Kashifi describes are a number of feats of skill like those now connected with the *zūrkhāna*, such as wrestling, stone lifting, throwing and cutting. When listing the arts involving implements, he includes several arms: the sword, shield, mace and bow. If we are to judge from the length of the entries, wrestling held particular prestige among athletic skills, while archery held pride of place among military ones.[60]

Kashifi's treatise suggests a loose organization which could include artisans, Sufis, and ulama within one framework. The emphasis on athletics, the inclusion of military skills, and the similarity of terminology to modern *zurkhāna* language suggest a culture of what might be called paramilitary arts, which could have played a role in preparing the population for active defense. Unfortunately, what we see is the ideal, and the practice must remain obscure for the Timurid period, since we lack the kind of outside source which could illuminate the actual culture of the bazaar. Probably the importance of *futuwwa* for military defense was a background one; it was an organization and ideology which helped to provide formal connections between the two classes immediately involved – the notables and the artisans – and encouraged the practice of arts useful in protecting the city. In the defense of Herat against Yar ʿAli Qaraqoyunlu in 852/1448, both Sufis and well-known artisans took part.[61] The survival of *futuwwa* might also be inferred from the popularity of shrines connected in some way to the story of Abu Muslim Khorasani, whose epic, the *Abū Muslimnāma*, became attached to the culture of *futuwwa*.[62] One of these shrines was that of Bibi Satirkuh who, with her husband, had supposedly been an *ayyār* in the service of Abu Muslim. Her grave was near

[58] See for instance, Wāʿiẓ, *Maqṣad*, 47, 54; Faṣīḥ Khwāfī, *Mujmal-i faṣīḥī*, vol. III, 266, 271; Jāmī, *Nafaḥāt*, 452.

[59] Franz Taeschner, *Zünfte und Bruderschaften in Islam. Texte zur Geschichte der Futuwwa* (Zürich, Munich: Artemis-Verlag, 1979), 262–76 (includes a translation of Hamadani's treatise); Kāshifī Sabzawārī, *Futuwwatnāma*.

[60] Kāshifī Sabzawārī, *Futuwwatnāma*, 306–20, 347–65. See also Mehdi Keyvani, *Artisans and Guild Life in the Later Safavid Period. Contributions to the Social-Economic History of Persia* (Berlin: Klaus Schwarz, 1982), 207–08.

[61] Samarqandī, *Maṭlaʿ*, 953–54.

[62] Irène Mélikoff, *Abū Muslim le "porte-hache" du Khorassan dans la tradition épique turco-iranienne* (Paris: Maisonneuve, 1962), 64–65. For the shrines, see Chapter 6.

the central bazaar and Shahrukh built both a mausoleum and a shrine there. This act could have been designed to win favor among a population important to the city in times of crisis.[63] It appears that the Timurid dynasty and its officials usually left the organization of city defense to the notables, but they probably also took steps to promote military organization and skill – up to a point – among the urban population.

The regional armies

While city artisans and notables were mobilized specifically for defense, other parts of the Iranian population were conscripted into regional armies which participated in all large campaigns and many regional ones. These troops were not as accomplished as the Chaghatay ones, but they were real soldiers – trained, armed, and equipped. The regional armies formed the basic troops of the provinces to which local tribal populations were attached, probably under their own leaders. When Shahrukh appointed his emir Ilyas Khwaja as governor of Qum for instance, he attached to him the soldiers and peasants of the region, and the regional tribes.[64] On his campaign against Kerman in 819/1416, Shahrukh's forces included what was defined as the Iranian (Tajik) army: the militias of Khorasan and the commanders (*cherīk-i khurāsānāt wa sardārān*), the armies of Sistan under its own rulers, and from Fars the militias (*cherik*) of Shiraz, Abarquh, Yazd and Isfahan (an army which the historian estimates at 40,000 foot and horse together).[65] On Shahrukh's expedition against Azarbaijan in 823/1420–21, Ilyas Khwaja joined Shahrukh with his own army and the commanders (*sardārān*) of Qum and Kashan. Many other regional armies joined at about the same time, with the governors of various regions including Simnan, Farah, Quhistan, Garmsir, Qandahar, Ghazna and Kabul, Fars, Isfahan, Yazd, Kerman, and Mazandaran.[66]

Regional armies included local commanders, some of whom were not personally connected to the troops they commanded. It seems that the position of *sardār*, often mentioned in relation to regional military formations, was usually filled by local Iranian personnel. It was held for instance by the Isfahani vizier, Mahmud Haydar, for whom it was an appointed office, and by the local commander of Warzana, ʿImad al-Din Warzanaʾi.[67] The commanders of Warzana played a significant military role in the struggles at the end of Shahrukh's life, and the fact that there was more than one such emir and that one at least was a significant architectural patron, suggests that

63 Wāʿiẓ, *Maqṣad*, 14. 64 Ḥāfiẓ-i Abrū, *Zubdat*, 609. 65 Ibid., 631.
66 Ibid., 719–20; Samarqandī, *Maṭlaʿ*, 671–73.
67 Ṭihrānī Iṣfahānī, *Diyārbakriyya*, 295, 328, and for other examples, see Faḍl Allāh Khunjī Iṣfahanī, *Tārīkh-i ʿālim-ārā-i Amīnī*, edited by John E. Woods (London: Royal Asiatic Society, 1992), 174; Yazdī, *Ḥasanī*, 46; and Kātib, *Tārīkh-i jadīd*, 238.

these were local and well established people, who may have brought their own followers into battle.[68] The histories report that the revolt of the Isfahan region against the Qaraqoyunlu in 858/1454 included headmen of districts around the city and a descendant of local lords.[69] In a number of cases, where commanders of regional armies are identified, we find among them viziers and men of religious training as well.

One important Iranian commander was Ghiyath al-Din Muhammad Hafiz Razi, who served Iskandar b. ʿUmar Shaykh as vizier, and will be discussed more fully in the next chapter. He was commander of a *tümen* of foot and horse and, judging from the description of the forces he led, it seems that his military position came not from an independent territorial base, but from his official position; his troops included the armies of Abarquh and Yazd.[70] The frequent mention of foot soldiers suggest that these were a significant part of the army, in contrast to contemporary Mamluk armies.[71] We are well informed about the army under Hafiz Razi's command because the historian Taj al-Din Hasan, author of the *Jamiʿ al-tawarikh-i hasani*, served under him as commander of a troop of ten men, and troop inspector (*tovachi*) of the footmen of Yazd. He took part in an unsuccessful campaign mounted by the sons of ʿUmar Shaykh against Azarbaijan in Dhuʾl Qaʿda, 808/April, 1406, and in the expedition that Shahrukh dispatched against Kerman in 819/1416.[72] Fortunately Hasani has left us descriptions of these campaigns, giving some insight into the army in which he served. The troops involved in the expedition to Azarbaijan included the armies of Fars, Yazd, and Abarquh, with one hundred horse and fifty foot cannoneers from Kerman. The author, as leader of ten men, describes the equipment of his troop: horse, tent, cooking pot, arms, and equipment. It is not clear whether this equipment was for each soldier or the ten together.

The armies met Aba Bakr b. Amiranshah's forces at Darguzin, north of Hamadan, and were at first successful, but when they had put their enemy to flight the army stopped fighting and began to plunder the rich baggage train. This action cannot be blamed on the Iranian commanders, since it appears that the prince Iskandar b. ʿUmar Shaykh led the movement, drawn by a particularly beautiful concubine of Aba Bakr and her equally attractive brother. He took these two and also Aba Bakr's private treasure and headed back to Yazd. Hasani gives us a picture of the riches available by listing what he himself had acquired at the time of the noon prayer: six strings of camels laden with booty, three slave girls and two male slaves (*ghulām*). Unfortunately for him and his soldiers, the battle was not yet over. Aba

[68] Ṭihrānī Iṣfahānī, *Diyārbakriyya*, 295, 327–29; Luṭf Allāh Hunarfar, "Iṣfahān dar dawra-i jānishīnān-i Tīmūr," *Hunar wa mardum* 163 (2535/1976), 7–11, 14–15.

[69] Ṭihrānī Iṣfahānī, *Diyārbakriyya*, 331–32.

[70] Yazdī, *Ḥasanī*, 14–15, 24, 30, 42; Kātib, *Tārīkh-i jadīd*, 246; Jaʿfarī, *Tārīkh-i kabīr*, 46.

[71] Amitai, "Foot Soldiers," 235–39.

[72] Yazdī, *Ḥasanī* (introduction) 11–15; (text) 2, 24, 27, 30, 36, 42, 48.

Bakr attacked again and defeated the remaining army, killing several thousand – an unusually large number. The author found himself that night among the fallen with only four of his original troop left alive, all destitute and too weak to pick up the abandoned booty on the side of the road. For seven days they remained in the mountains, living off wild plants, before reaching a city from which they could travel to Yazd.[73] The mention of booty here is instructive. The soldiers who left earlier had presumably managed to keep their plunder. We find indeed that when Aba Bakr attacked Isfahan the next year in retaliation, one of the provisions of the treaty he extorted was the return of booty.[74] If campaigns could result in significant plunder even for a minor commander, we can understand the population's willingness to fight.

Regional armies had at least basic equipment and training. In addition to the cannon, horse, and arms mentioned above, Hasani mentions the presence of four hundred and fifty missile throwers in the army of Yazd and Abarquh on Shahrukh's Kerman campaign.[75] Nonetheless, these forces were not among the crack troops of the Timurid army, and they almost certainly varied in quality. The army of Fars for instance was sent twice against Khuzistan under the leadership of a bureaucrat and religious figure, Shaykh Muhibb al-Din Abu'l Khayr b. Muhammad Jazari, who led a successful campaign in 836/1432–33, and a less successful one against a rebellious religious group, the Musha'sha', probably in 844/1441. It seems likely that Abu'l Khayr's troops were not of the highest quality, since the expedition undertaken a little later against the Musha'sha' by the Qaraqoyunlu succeeded where Abu'l Khayr had failed.[76] Another instance of apparently inferior Iranian troops occurs in the Azarbaijan campaign of 823–24/1420–21. One of Shahrukh's viziers, Khwaja Muhammad Mushrif Simnani, drove forward in battle at the head of an ill-trained contingent and was defeated and killed by the Turkmens. Fortunately the situation was saved by Chaghatay commanders and troops.[77]

We get glimpse of regional armies in Khorasan in the account of the attempted flight of Shahrukh's insubordinate nephew Qaydu from Herat in 821/1418–19. As Qaydu approached the town of Awba, east of Herat, Khwaja Nizam al-Din Shirazi, head of the armies (*amīr-i tümen*) of the region came out with people of Awba on foot and horse to harry his troops. Qaydu ambushed them and easily scattered them, since they wore no armor. However, when Qaydu reached the nearby village of Isfarz, he had less luck. Here the local troops were led by Malik Qutb al-Din, grandson of

[73] Yazdī, *Ḥasanī*, 24–31. [74] Quiring-Zoche, *Isfahan*, 20. [75] Yazdī, *Ḥasanī*, 42.

[76] Ṭihranī Iṣfahānī, *Diyārbakriyya*, 307; Ja'farī, *Tārīkh-i kabīr*, 79, 112; Shahzad Bashir, "Between Mysticism and Messianism: the Life and Thought of Muhammad Nūrbakš (d. 1464)," Ph.D. dissertation, Yale University, 1997, 38. See also de Fouchécour, " 'The Good Companion,' " 384.

[77] Samarqandī, *Maṭla'*, 257; Ḥāfiẓ-i Abrū, *Zubdat*, 790.

Malik ʿIzz al-Din of Sistan, and they killed a number of Qaydu's people.[78] Certain regions held a reputation for the bravery of their inhabitants, and it may not be chance that some of these were associated with local dynasties or people who played a part in military affairs under the Timurids.[79] What we find therefore is considerable variety in the level of the regional troops, ranging from what appear to be competent regional armies to levies from unarmed populations.

It seems likely that regional troops contained both urban people and peasants. The Khorasani troops mentioned above must have been recruited from the peasantry, since they are associated with village regions. On the other hand, we know of city dwellers who made a career in the military. I have mentioned the historian Taj al-Din Hasan above; he bears the *nisba* Yazdi, and spent most of his life in educated professions. Two other Iranians of city provenance appear as part of the military; these are the rebels Husayn and ʿAli Sharbatdar, who began their careers as druggists within the Shiraz bazaar, then served in the army under Pir Muhammad b. ʿUmar Shaykh, where they rose quickly, apparently in part through personal favor. We find them in the prince's army in the battle he fought with his brothers in the summer of 810/1407 near the meadow of Ganduman. By this time they had been raised to the status of emir and commander. Husayn had a *qushun* of cavalry and ʿAli a deputyship. Ḥāfiẓ-i Abrū states that Husayn began as a stirrup-holder (*rukubdār*) before being raised by Pir Muhammad to the rank of emir.[80]

Tribal populations

The nomads and semi-nomads of Iran enjoyed somewhat more independence than did cities and towns, but also served with the provincial armies. In the region of Rayy, Qum, and Kashan, there were tribes of Arabs, Turkmen, Baluch, Khalaj, and nomad Bedouin, listed as coming under the jurisdiction of the governor Amir Ilyas Khwaja.[81] The tribes of southern and central Iran

78 Faṣīḥ Khwāfī, *Mujmal-i faṣīḥī*, vol. III, 233–34; Ḥāfiẓ-i Abrū, "Majmaʿ," fol. 544a; Ḥāfiẓ-i Abrū, *Zubdat*, 683–84.The manuscript and published version diverge here (in the published edition, there is no mention of Malik Qutb al-Din).

79 Examples are Isfizar, where Daʾud Khitatay rebelled against Temür (Isfizārī, *Rawḍāt*, 107–12; Ḥāfiẓ-i Abrū, *Ḫorāsān*, 36), Turshiz, whose ruler joined a rebellion early in Shahrukh's reign, and which produced the Iranian *kotwāl* for the fortress Ikhtiyar al-Din (Isfizārī, *Rawḍāt*, 280–81; Samarqandī, *Maṭlaʿ*, 762), and Tabas, the birthplace of Temür's commander of Tajik troops, Jalal Islam (Isfizārī, *Rawḍāt*, 114, 327). Hafizi Abru singles out several areas in Fars known for the military prowess of their population (Ḥāfiẓ-i Abrū, *Jughrāfiyā-i Ḥāfiẓ-i Abrū*, edited by Ṣādiq Sajjādī, 3 vols. [Tehran: Bunyān-i Daftar-i Nashr-i Mirāth-i Maktūb, 1378/1999], vol. II, 119, 125, 128–32).

80 Yazdī, *Ḥasanī*, 17; Ḥāfiẓ-i Abrū, "Majmaʿ," fol. 452b; Ḥāfiẓ-i Abrū, *Zubdat*, 341. In his geography of Fars, Ḥafiz-i Abrū states that Husayn Sharbatdar commanded troops of Kurds and Lurs (Ḥāfiẓ-i Abrū, *Jughrāfiyā*, 329–30). However, these two men are not listed in the conservative "Muʿizz al-ansāb" (*Muʿizz*, fols. 102b–3a).

81 Ḥāfiẓ-i Abrū, *Zubdat*, 609.

will be discussed in the next chapter. We have little specific information about nomads in Khorasan and Transoxiana, though as a group, usually called *ḥasham*, they are also included in lists of troops and subject populations. There is mention of a Baluch chief with his tribe at Barsin, between Herat and Ghur, who stopped and questioned a dissident emir fleeing from Herat towards Qandahar, and when he could not produce a letter of safe conduct from Shahrukh, fought and defeated him.[82] In the appointment of Baysunghur b. Shahrukh to the government of Gurgan, Mashhad and surrounding regions, tribes are mentioned among the population of the province, but not named.[83] Shahrukh gathered tribes about him in his summer pasture in Badghis in 813/1410–11 and tribes are mentioned in the army of Transoxiana earlier the same year.[84] In the region of Bukhara the Turkmens and other local tribes gathered around Abu Saʿid in his successful campaign to take power from ʿAbd Allah b. Ibrahim Sultan in Jumada I, 855/June, 1451.[85] In Kerman and Sistan the sources mention several nomad populations, recruited to serve in regional armies or gathering around an aspirant for power. Near the beginning of Shahrukh's reign, when Aba Bakr b. Amiranshah was attempting to gain power at the expense of the governor of Kerman, Shaykh Uways Barlas, he was able to attract the Awghan and Jurmaʾi, who were remnants of Mongol troops, and also "Arabs" who, like Kurds, appear in numerous locations.[86] At another time we hear of Turco-Mongolian tribal contingents in this region – Qarluq and Qipchaq – but it is not clear whether these were local tribes or tribal contingents within the Chaghatay army.[87] We can infer from the above examples that the tribes living throughout Iran, in mountain, steppe, and desert, provided an additional source of manpower, sometimes under the control of the governor or ruler but potentially available for others.

The disadvantage of tribal troops was their fickle character. Iskandar b. ʿUmar Shaykh had to give up one of his sieges of Isfahan because of the desertion of a contingent of Shul troops, and in his final battle with Shahrukh, the tribes of the Isfahan region changed their allegiance.[88] We hear of Arab tribes among the troops of Kerman rebelling against the higher command during campaigns. When Aba Bakr b. Amiranshah recruited the Arab tribes in his attempt on Kerman, they first agreed to join him and then changed their

[82] Ḥāfiẓ-i Abrū, *Zubdat*, 453. [83] Ibid., 572.

[84] Ibid., 379, 394. Tribes are also mentioned in Khuttalan (Samarqandī, *Maṭlaʿ*, 904).

[85] Ṭihrānī Iṣfahānī, *Diyārbakriyya*, 310.

[86] Yazdī, *Ḥasanī*, 34. The Arabs might have been Iraqi Arabs moved to the region; Taj al-Din Hasan b. Shihab Yazdi states that Abuʾl Qasim Babur granted the use of Iraqi Arabs of Khara to a regional contestant for power after Shahrukh's death (Yazdī, *Ḥasanī*, 82–85). For Awghan and Jurmaʾi, see Manz, "Military Manpower in Late Mongol and Timurid Iran," in *L'Héritage timouride, Iran-Asie centrale-Inde XVe–XVIIIe siècles, Cahiers d'Asie centrale*, 3–4 (1997), 50–51.

[87] Yazdī, *Ḥasanī*, 90–91. [88] Ḥāfiẓ-i Abrū, *Zubdat*, 398; Samarqandī, *Maṭlaʿ*, 113.

mind.[89] When he lost his battle against Sultan Uways, his tribal army quickly scattered.[90] Thus, while such troops may have been more mobile than the regional armies from cities and agricultural regions, they were also less reliable. It is perhaps not by chance that we hear little about tribal forces on major campaigns.

When we survey the Timurids' regional subjects then, we can see that they were neither passive nor unarmed. There was considerable variation in the level of control achieved by the dynasty, but no city or region was without local leadership. In every city, including the capital, the population and notables held some power of decision and were expected to participate in their own defense. The military forces of the provinces were significant enough to make a difference on campaigns and were in part under local leadership. In some cities and regions the Timurids ruled even less directly, and here the regional dynasties played the leading role.

Independent dynasties of Iran

Timurid government represented a spectrum from relatively direct rule over central regions, under princely governors, to a hopeful fiction of suzerainty over neighboring confederations like the Qaraqoyunlu. Although in Timurid eyes the Qaraqoyunlu were subservient, they exerted constant pressure on the northwestern cities of Sultaniyya and Qazwin, and it required three major campaigns to maintain a semblance of Timurid authority. To the north the Timurids faced Chinggisid powers who nibbled at the Central Asian frontier, while intermarrying with the dynasty and sometimes providing manpower. In the south, most neighboring dynasties were small and posed only the threat of local disorder. Within the Timurid lands as well, many regions and towns were still under the control of local rulers, usually from landed families with military training and some forces at their disposal. These were dynasties which had submitted to Temür and had been confirmed in their holdings. We have no idea how many there were because we hear about them only by chance – if they rebelled and came to grief, if they were taken over by an ambitious prince, or were wooed and won by an outside rival. Such rulers paid tribute or taxes and furnished troops for major campaigns. A few made careers as commanders within the Timurid army, leaving their native lands and bringing a following along with them. They and their families might serve at court, but rarely achieved high positions in the army, and were not considered important enough to marry into the Timurid house.

Local concerns did not cease with the imposition of Timurid authority. For the largest dynasties, the question of sovereignty – of equality, or even superiority, in relation to neighboring states – might be important. Smaller powers were probably not aiming at full independence; it was necessary to

[89] Yazdī, *Ḥasanī*, 82, 84. [90] Ibid., 34.

come to an agreement with one or another power, and the major question was whether they had to pay tribute or regular taxes. In the meantime, they had other concerns. Regional magnates spent much of their time and energy enlarging their sphere of influence at the expense of other local dynasties, taking the throne of their region from the current incumbent, or if they already held the throne, keeping it safe from a covetous relative. If such dynasties inhabited a border region, they were faced with the choice of which powerful dynasty to obey. In all these undertakings, rulers were likely to gather what forces they could, and these included whatever they might be able to solicit from the Timurid dynasty, which quite frequently found itself drawn into local conflicts. Not all political initiatives ended well. The struggles for power made politics highly treacherous, offering both tempting new opportunities and increasing the dangers for local actors. If we can discern a trend after Temür's death, it is towards greater incorporation of small dynasties. In periods of confusion, magnates were likely either to overreach themselves and receive punishment, or to seek protection with the most likely pretender for power. The history of Qum presents a good example of the way cities came under Timurid control.

Qum had been controlled by local rulers from the end of the Ilkhanid period and since the city submitted voluntarily to Temür, it remained under its own dynasty.[91] Its ruler at the beginning of the ninth century was Khwaja Muhammad Qumi, who found himself on the northern edge of a lively struggle for power among the sons of ʿUmar Shaykh. In 815/1412 when Iskandar b. ʿUmar Shaykh attacked Wurujird, Muhammad Qumi became alarmed and turned to the Qaraqoyunlu, whom he incited against Iskandar. It appears that Iskandar had tried before to take Qum, and it may have been evidence of his growing strength which alarmed Muhammad. Iskandar's response was to send an army to besiege Qum. His forces took several nearby fortresses controlled by Muhammad. Iskandar's vizier, Hafiz Razi, led negotiations with the ruler's representatives and persuaded one of Muhammad's followers to betray his master and let in Iskandar's army, on the promise of appointment as tax collector. Khwaja Muhammad was executed and his nephew Amir Mahmud also died, according to some accounts by suicide since he was extremely good-looking, and an object of erotic interest to Iskandar.[92] In 817/1414–17, when Shahrukh had defeated Iskandar, Qum became the seat for the Timurid governor over the eastern part of ʿIraq-i

[91] Mudarrisī Ṭabāṭabāʾī, *Qumm dar qarn-i nuhum-i hijjrī, 801–900: faṣl az kitāb Qumm dar chahārda qarn* (Qum: Ḥikmat, 1350/1971–72), 6–14, 69–70. The men in charge of Qum in the reign of Temür and Shahrukh were descendants of the powerful Khwaja ʿAli Safi (Ṭabāṭabāʾī, *Qumm*, 71–76; Ḥāfiẓ-i Abrū, *Zubdat*, 482).

[92] Yazdī, *Ḥasanī*, 14, 35–37; Ḥāfiẓ-i Abrū, *Zubdat*, 481–83; Jaʿfarī, *Tārīkh-i kabīr*, 57–8; fol. 303a. Both the *Tārīkh-i kabīr* and *Jāmiʿ al-tawārīkh-Ḥasanī* put Iskandar's conquest of Qum in 816, and his open opposition to Shahrukh in 817, but Ḥāfiẓ-i Abrū's closeness to the events and detailed dating suggest that his version should be preferred.

ʿAjam. Nonetheless, after Shahrukh's death, we find the city defended both by its Chaghatay governor, Darwish ʿAli Mirak b. Yusuf Khwaja, and by Khwaja Nizam al-Din Yahya Qumi, presumably a local figure.[93]

The accounts of Iskandar's takeover of Qum mention another ruler: Nasr Allah Sahraʾi, ruler of the nearby town Sawa. Nasr Allah was usually unfriendly to Muhammad Qumi but now sent him military aid, out of fear that Iskandar would attack Sawa next. His help allowed the population of Qum to hold out against Iskandar's forces until the city was surrendered through treachery. Nasr Allah Sahraʾi continued to distrust Iskandar and in the winter of 816/1413–14 while Shahrukh was preparing his campaign against Fars, Nasr Allah sent a messenger to him declaring allegiance and requesting a *darugha*. When Iskandar heard he sent an army to besiege the city, but its leaders deserted to Shahrukh.[94] In 817/1414, Nasr Allah came personally to Herat to pay his respects. However, when Shahrukh headed against Azarbaijan in 823/1420–21, Nasr Allah apparently believed that Qara Yusuf Qaraqoyunlu was likely to win the contest and put coinage and *khutba* in his name. Shahrukh sent an army to take the city, but allowed Nasr Allah to retain his place. After this, we hear no more about Nasr Allah, although Sawa appears in the histories.[95] Since, as I have shown, regional populations remained important in the defense of their cities even under direct Chaghatay rule, what we see here is probably a change of status without a complete change of personnel. The families which held regional military control and the troops they led continued to exist under central rule, and it is likely that similar families provided notables and regional commanders to Isfahan, Shiraz, and other Iranian cities.

Timurids and border powers

As Timurid power shaded out and met that of other dynasties, there was an area of ambiguity in which it is hard to tell who held control at a specific time. Regions like Hamadan, Sultaniyya, and Qazwin were considered part of the Timurid realm although they were sometimes under the control of the Qaraqoyunlu, who themselves were at times, officially, vassals of the

[93] Yazdī, *Ḥasanī*, 62, 71, 81; Ṭihrānī Iṣfahānī, *Diyārbakriyya*, 326. Khwaja Nizam al-Din had earlier been in the service of Sultan Muhammad, who had used Qum as his headquarters (Ṭabāṭabāʾī, *Qumm*, 74). According to the *Muʿizz al-ansab* Yusuf Khwaja (as opposed to Ilyas Khwaja's son Khwaja Yusuf) was also governor of Qum, Rayy, and Luristan, but the narrative sources do not confirm this (*Muʿizz*, fol. 133a).

[94] Ḥāfiẓ-i Abrū, *Zubdat*, 523–28.

[95] Ḥāfiẓ-i Abrū, *Zubdat*, 564, 754–55. There are indications that the local rulers of Natanz and Tarum (in Fars) lost their independence to the sons of ʿUmar Shaykh during their struggle, though we find these cities later under men who could have been local (Jaʿfarī, *Tārīkh-i kabīr*, 48–9, 56, 122; fols. 299b, 302b). Other cities which lost independence were Isfizar (Isfizārī, *Rawḍāt*, 109–112), Turshiz (Samarqandī, *Maṭlaʿ*, 762–63; Faṣīḥ Khwāfī, *Mujmal-i faṣīḥī*, vol. III, 291–92), and Sabzawar (Dawlatshāh Samarqandī, *Tadhkirat*, 426–28).

Timurids, but at other times quite clearly counted as enemies. Rulers in border areas thus had the advantage of two powers vying for their allegiance, but the situation was not without its dangers. For the Timurid rulers, dealing with border dynasties required delicate calculation. It was desirable to obtain formal declarations of submission in order to bring other local dynasties into line. At the same time, the Timurids could not punish border vassals without fear of alienating them. What made decisions particularly difficult was that actions which benefitted the Timurid governor of the neighboring province might not be in the best interest of Shahrukh himself. The princely governors were responsible for maintaining order within their lands and for managing the security of their borders, and it was to them that the first challenge often manifested itself. On the other hand, it was Shahrukh's armies that led major campaigns abroad, and if a governor mismanaged relations with neighboring powers, Shahrukh was quick to find fault. There were several quarrels between Shahrukh and his governors over the handling of insubordinate rulers in frontier regions.

The western region was particularly tricky, and we find two local dynasties here who offer an illustration of border politics. The more prominent was the Chakirlu lineage, beginning with Chakir, a Turco-Mongolian emir serving the local Mongol Jalayirid dynasty (1336–1432), who came into the service of Temür. His position and followers passed to his son Bistam, who was among the local emirs in the service of ʿUmar b. Amiranshah when he was governor of Azarbaijan.[96] During the succession struggle after Temür's death Bistam and his family occupied eastern Azarbaijan from Ardabil to Sultaniyya. In 809/1406, the family decided to switch their allegiance to Qara Yusuf Qaraqoyunlu – a sensible choice, since he was clearly winning his struggle against the Timurid princes of Azarbaijan. The level of Chakirlu power is illustrated by Bistam's immediate appointment as *amīr al-umarāʾ* within Qara Yusuf's following. At the end of 810/1406, Bistam ventured out from his base in Ardabil to take Sultaniyya, where he installed his brother Maʿsum. Qara Yusuf put his stamp of approval on the move by naming Bistam governor (*walī*) of Iraq-i ʿAjam.[97] Bistam's conquest of Sultaniyya and Qara Yusuf's implied claim to ʿIraq-i Ajam were overt challenges to the Timurids, who counted ʿIraq-i Ajam among their territories and considered Sultaniyya, the necropolis of the Ilkhans, a city of great symbolic value.

By 815/1412–13, Bistam's relationship with Qara Yusuf had soured. The histories give no explanation for the rift but it seems likely that it was connected with a wider crisis of authority, since Qara Yusuf had to move against several other local leaders in the same year.[98] From this time the Chakirlu seem to have held themselves aloof from Qara Yusuf, while observing the growing power of both Shahrukh and his nephew Iskandar. Qara

[96] Sümer, *Kara Koyunlular*, 29; *Muʿizz*, fol. 126a. [97] Sümer, *Kara Koyunlular*, 74, 77.
[98] Ibid., 80–85, 91; Ḥāfiẓ-i Abrū, *Zubdat*, 346, 485–86.

Yusuf apparently tried to divide the family. In the beginning of 816/spring, 1413, he imprisoned Bistam's nephew, Muhammad b. Mansur, but after a month released him and granted him the regions of Ardabil and Khalkhal. Bistam himself was still in Sultaniyya, which Qara Yusuf looted, along with Qazwin, probably also part of Bistam's holding. By 817/1414, when Shahrukh was heading to Fars against Iskandar, Bistam had decided on a Timurid alliance, and sent an emissary to declare friendship.[99] At the beginning of 818/March, 1415, Qara Yusuf himself approached Shahrukh, suggesting an alliance which would grant him the region of Sultaniyya, but Shahrukh met this suggestion with reserve. It is not surprising to find Bistam soon again in Herat, declaring loyalty to Shahrukh. On Bistam's return to Sultaniyya, he found himself attacked by Qara Yusuf and, leaving his son in the fortress, he himself left for Qum, then governed by Shahrukh's great-nephew Saʿd-i Waqqas b. Muhammad Sultan.[100]

It was at this point that trouble arose among the Timurids. Saʿd-i Waqqas imprisoned Bistam and sent to Shahrukh to ask for instructions. Shahrukh replied angrily that as an ally, who held his territory with Shahrukh's permission and was seeking help, Bistam should have been met with honor. He must now be released and equipped with troops to hold his territory. Shahrukh sent an emir to see that his order was followed; he also carried a friendly letter to Bistam. Instead of obeying Shahrukh, Saʿd-i Waqqas deserted to Qara Yusuf, taking Bistam with him in chains. The histories give no explanation for his decision beyond the usual prompting by bad advisors. Probably Saʿd-i Waqqas saw his province as the next goal for the Qaraqoyunlu and, like the ruler of Qum earlier, decided that Qara Yusuf was likely to succeed. Qara Yusuf received Saʿd-i Waqqas with honor and tried to conciliate with Bistam. He freed him from captivity and sent his son with other emirs to fetch the family of Saʿd-i Waqqas from Qum. Fortunately for Shahrukh, Saʿd-i Waqqas's wife, a daughter of Amiranshah, refused to leave, seized the Turkmen emirs and killed several of Saʿd-i Waqqas's advisors. Nonetheless, other local rulers and the Timurid governors of southern and western Iran all read these events as a sign of Qara Yusuf's increasing power. There were disturbances in Qum, Kashan, and Hamadan, and ʿUmar Shaykh's sons began a series of actions which led to Shahrukh's second Fars campaign the following year.[101]

The governorship of Qum went to the emir Ilyas Khwaja b. Shaykh ʿAli Bahadur. Later in 818/late 1415, Bistam's brother Mansur, who was in Ardabil, sent Shahrukh news of Qara Yusuf and in 823/1420, when Shahrukh was moving against Azarbaijan, Bistam's other brother, Maʿsum, joined his army from the fortress of Shahriyar. On the other hand, just

[99] Ḥāfiẓ-i Abrū, *Zubdat*, 506, 522, 536; Sümer, *Kara Koyunlular*, 92.
[100] Ḥāfiẓ-i Abrū, *Zubdat*, 575–76, 587–88.
[101] Ibid., 589–92; Sümer, *Kara Koyunlular*, 96.

before this, Bistam himself was near Arzinjan, clearly in Qara Yusuf's service.[102] It seems likely therefore that the family was divided, with sections on different sides. The Chakirlu had probably lost control of Sultaniyya and Qazwin when Qara Yusuf defeated Bistam, and from this time they were limited to their more eastern territory. When they appear in Timurid histories after this, the Chakirlu *begs* number among the semi-independent powers attached to the Qaraqoyunlu.[103]

To understand Saʿd-i Waqqas' actions towards Bistam Chakirlu, we must consider both his official position and Bistam's earlier actions. First of all, Saʿd-i Waqqas was governor of Qum, a major city of the province of ʿIraq-i Ajam, and later the seat of its governance. When Bistam took Sultaniyya in 810/1412–13, he was seizing the western part of the province, and Qara Yusuf responded by naming him governor of the whole of it. The nearby powers had taken this claim seriously; Muhammad Qumi had turned to the Qaraqoyunlu rather than Shahrukh when he was threatened by Iskandar b. ʿUmar Shaykh. Furthermore, according to the *Tārīkh-i kabīr*, when Iskandar declared himself Sultan in 816/1413–14, Bistam came to pay his respects. This account need not contradict Ḥāfiẓ-i Abrū's report that Bistam declared loyalty to Shahrukh in 817/1414, since Shahrukh's expedition could well have changed Bistam's calculations. Saʿd-i Waqqas's enmity towards Bistam therefore makes sense; he was punishing a man who had conquered part of his province and given it to the Qaraqoyunlu and who had also probably supported Iskandar, from whom Shahrukh had just wrested Qum and its region. Shahrukh, on the other hand, was looking ahead to the expedition he was planning against Qara Yusuf, and the possibility of gaining Bistam's help in the campaign outweighed his past shortcomings.

A similar problem, which pitted the provincial governor against the center, arose at the end of Shahrukh's reign when Sultan Muhamad b. Baysunghur became governor of Qum and adjoining regions. Once again the issue centered around a semi-independent dynasty in the area contested between Shahrukh and the Qaraqoyunlu. The progenitor of the family, Amir Shaykh Hajji Muhammad ʿIraqi, had been one of the powerful regional commanders serving Umar b. Amiranshah in Azarbaijan during Temür's reign. However when ʿUmar was defeated by the Qaraqoyunlu and left for Khorasan, Shaykh Muhammad's son Baba Hajji did not accompany him. Baba Hajji deserted ʿUmar not from disloyalty but out of fear, and his fear was probably justified. Shortly after Temür's death, ʿUmar's chief emir, Jahanshah b. Chekü Barlas, had rebelled against ʿUmar and killed Shaykh Hajji Muhammad. ʿUmar put down the uprising and handed Jahanshah to Baba Hajji. Since the family of

[102] Ḥāfiẓ-i Abrū, *Zubdat*, 600, 738; Faṣīḥ Khwāfī, *Mujmal-i faṣīḥī*, vol. III, 240; Sümer, *Kara Koyunlular*, 106.

[103] Faṣīḥ Khwāfī, *Mujmal-i faṣīḥī*, vol. III, 263; Samarqandī, *Maṭlaʿ*, 32, 686; Sümer, *Kara Koyunlular*, 134, 139; Jaʿfarī, *Tārīkh-i kabīr*, 79; fol. 312a; Ṭihrānī Iṣfahānī, *Diyārbakriyya*, 343–47.

Chekü was one of the most powerful in Shahrukh's realm, it is not surprising that Baba Hajji, not himself a Chaghatay, should hesitate to move to Khorasan and put himself within their reach so recently after executing one of the family's most prominent members. Instead, he remained in the west and carved out a power base for himself in Hamadan, from which he continued to resist Qara Yusuf. However, he could not hold out long and after Qara Yusuf pillaged his lands in 816/1413–14 he submitted and was reconfirmed in his region.[104] Nonetheless, in 817/1414–15 Shahrukh counted Hamadan among his own territories, which he assigned along with Nihawand, Burujird, and Kurdistan to his nephew Bayqara.[105]

In the eyes of the Timurids, Baba Hajji remained one of their own, and when he failed to appear at Shahrukh's invitation after the death of Qara Yusuf in 823/1420 Shahrukh sent Baysunghur to bring him to obedience. The histories ascribe Baba Hajji's failure to appear to his continued fear of vengeance for the killing of Jahanshah b. Chekü. When Baysunghur assured him of his safety and promised to add to the lands he held, he submitted and was pardoned.[106] From this time on, Baba Hajji remained a useful vassal to the Timurids. He joined Shahrukh's second Azarbaijan campaign of 832/1429 and when Qara Yusuf's son Shah Muhammad attacked Hamadan in 838/1434–35, Baba Hajji defeated and killed him.[107] On Shahrukh's third Azarbaijan campaign, Baba Hajji was once again an active and useful participant, for which he was suitably rewarded. In 841/1437–38, he died.[108]

Despite Baba Hajji's loyalty, when Sultan Muhammad b. Baysunghur was appointed as governor of northern Iran in 846/1442–43, Baba Hajji's son Hajji Husayn was the one local ruler who refused to recognize his authority. The refusal may have been the more galling since Hajji Husayn was campaigning in Gilan at Shahrukh's request at just about this time.[109] Sultan Muhammad first sent emirs to reason with Hajji Husayn, but Hajji Husayn retained them and eventually, in 849/1445–46, Sultan Muhammad was forced to move against him. Sultan Muhammad was able to defeat Hajji Husayn's army, and when Hajji Husayn attempted to retreat into Hamadan, the city population organized themselves behind the walls with arrows and stones and refused to admit him. The Chaghatay army captured him, and Sultan Muhammad handed him over for vengeance to the sons of a man he had killed. Sultan

104 Ḥāfiẓ-i Abrū, *Zubdat*, 740–41; Faṣīḥ Khwāfī, *Mujmal-i faṣīḥī*, vol. III, 213.
105 Faṣīḥ Khwāfī, *Mujmal-i faṣīḥī*, vol. III, 218. 106 Ḥāfiẓ-i Abrū, *Zubdat*, 740–42.
107 Ja'farī, *Tārīkh-i kabīr*, 75, 77, 80; fols. 310a, 311a, 313a.
108 Ibid., 81, 86, 94, 100; fols. 314a, 316b, 321a, 325a; Ḥasan Beg Rūmlū, *Aḥsan al-tawārīkh*, edited by 'Abd al-Ḥusayn Nawā'ī (Tehran: Bungāh-i Tarjuma wa Nashr-i Kitāb, 1349/1970), 194, 212, 218, 238. The *Tarikh-i-kabir* states that Shahrukh appointed Baba Hajji's son Abu Ishaq as his successor, but the son later mentioned as ruling Hamadan is Hajji Husayn.
109 Samarqandī, *Maṭla'*, 772; Ja'farī, *Tārīkh-i kabīr*, 117; Sayyid Ẓahīr al-Dīn b. Naṣīr al-Dīn Mar'ashī, *Tārīkh-i Gīlān wa Daylamistān*, edited by Manūchihr Sutūda (Tehran: Bunyād-i Farhang-i Īrān, sh. 1347/1968–9), 246–47.

Muhammad's firmness had the desired result and other local leaders came into line. Nonetheless Shahrukh scolded Sultan Muhammad for having punished a vassal whose family had given such long and valuable service. He should have consulted Shahrukh and should have sent Hajji Husayn to Herat.[110] Here again we see that Shahrukh was willing to condone independent behavior by a provincial governor. A similar tension probably lay behind the one major disagreement between Shahrukh and Ulugh Beg, when Ulugh Beg, as governor of Transoxiana, defied Shahrukh's prohibitions and attacked the ruler of the Blue Horde, Baraq, who threatened the borders of his realm.[111]

We can see how easily provincial governors could become embroiled in the politics of their borderlands and how their decisions could affect their relations with Shahrukh. If the governor permitted insubordinate behavior to continue, he would lose prestige and face disobedience from other local leaders. Insistence on aggressive action, however, was not met with praise in the center, and it is not difficult to understand why. Shahrukh did not want to substitute open hostility for what might be definable as peace. The regions on the border, often mountain or steppe, were not easy for the Timurids to rule directly. Local rulers who could be called on to help against outside rivals were highly useful, even when they didn't meet all the usual obligations of vassalage. The actions which governors took to retain their personal authority were likely to upset the local balance and to require yet further military activity. One may also suspect that the increase in independent power and military prestige of the governor might also not always have been fully welcome to the central ruler.

Local politics and their impact

The calculations of the Chakirlu and the emirs of Hamadan, like those of the rulers of Qum and Sawa, centered around the relative power of the Timurids and their neighbors. The ability to help one or another side could bring them considerable favor, while miscalculation about who would win a contest brought misfortune. Many other local rulers were concerned primarily with the need to maintain their own positions against internal challenges. Regional politics were active and dangerous, and far from fully controlled by outside sovereign powers. Sometimes the Timurids pursued a deliberate policy of "divide and rule," but usually there was no need of outside interference to create internal divisions. For local leaders the availability of Timurid troops presented an opportunity that was hard to pass up, while for the Timurids, the offer of interference was often tempting. Engagement, however, could lead to

110 Ja'farī, *Tārīkh-i kabīr*, 117–19; Samarqandī, *Maṭla'*, 853–59.

111 Ḥāfiẓ-i Abrū, *Zubdat*, 907; Samarqandī, *Maṭla'*, 311–12. Shahrukh also objected to some of Ibrahim Sultan's border campaigns (Ḥāfiẓ-i Abrū, *Zubdat*, 805–06).

embarrassing defeat for Timurid troops fighting on difficult terrain, or to the loss of independence for a local dynasty.

We are particularly well informed about the politics of Mazandaran and Gilan due to the work of the historian Zahir al-Din b. Nasir al-Din Marʿashi. The Caspian region was under the control of several small dynasties who intermarried extensively while continually disputing borders and interfering in each other's affairs. The Marʿashi dynasty in Tabaristan and the Kar-Kiya in Gilan were both founded in the eighth century by sayyids who left large numbers of sons and grandsons to rule small territories. They were flanked by several dynasties with whom they were politically involved and the rulers of Tarum, just south of Gilan, married into the Kar-Kiya family and were frequently called in to help one or another internal faction. Between the Kar-Kiya and the Marʿashi kingdoms was the region of Larijan and Rustamdar, near Mt. Damavand, controlled during Shahrukh's reign by Malik Gayumarth of the Padusband or Rustamdari dynasty, who was involved equally in the politics of both sayyid dynasties. In Quhistan, the Murtadaʾid sayyid dynasty of Hazar Jarib intermarried with the Marʿashis.[112]

The history of the Marʿashi sayyids provides several illustrations of the way internal politics affected relationships with the Timurid state. For Shahrukh the Marʿashi dynasty mattered, both because it occupied a strategic location just north of the major route to the west and because it controlled a wealthy silk-producing region. The area was not one which the dynasty would have wanted to rule itself, since much of it was hot, humid, and wooded, thus unsuited to the lifestyle of the ruling class. The Timurid histories record the most basic information about the Marʿashi dynasty: the accession and death of the major ruler, visits to court to present messages of obedience or to request help against a rival, and indications of possible rebellion. The *Tarikh-i Tabaristan* lets us know something of the struggles that lay behind these points of confluence.

The politics of Mazandaran were lively. The dynasty's founder, Sayyid Qawam al-Din, had been active as a shaykh as well as a dynastic founder. On his death he bequeathed his realm to his ten surviving sons, leaving each a different territory, but his religious authority seems to have gone to his disciples rather than his family. The members of the religious order, referred to as *darwīsh*es, appear quite frequently under their own leadership in accounts of struggles for power, sometimes pushing the population into action, sometimes favoring a particular branch of the

112 See Yukako Goto, "Der Aufstieg zweier Sayyid-Familien am Kaspischen Meer: 'Volksislamische' Strömungen in Iran des 8/14. und 9/15. Jahrhunderts," *Wiener Zeitschrift für die Kunde des Morgenlandes*, 89 (1999); J. Calmard, "al-Marʿashī" and "Lār, Lāridjān," in *Encyclopaedia of Islam*, 2nd edn.

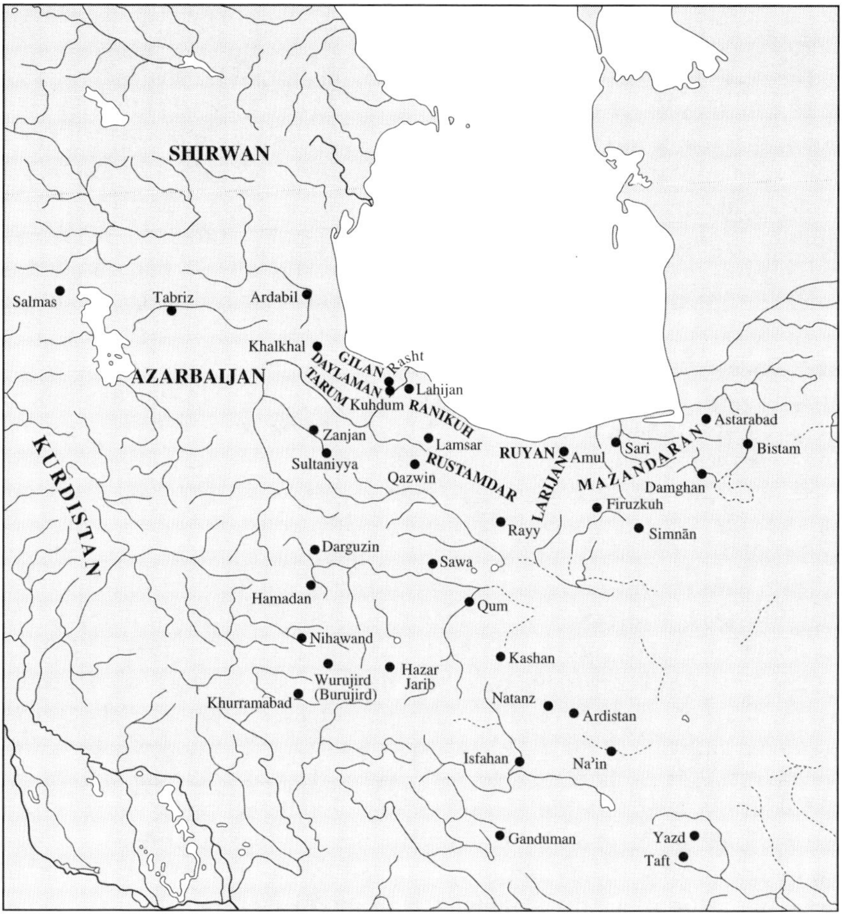

Map 2. The Caspian region and the northern Iranian provinces

family.[113] When Temür conquered the region he razed several cities, took almost all of their treasure, and massacred a number of the population, but he did not kill the sayyids themselves, whom he sent into honorable exile, while keeping one or two in his suite. Some of their lands were granted to rival dynasties and some put under Timurid governors. At the end of his life Temür returned Amul to Sayyid ʿAli b. Kamal al-Din b. Qawam al-Din, a grandson of the dynasty's founder, with one of his brothers, Ghiyath al-Din, as deputy. However, the main capital at Sari remained under Timurid rule. At Temür's

[113] Goto, "Der Aufstieg," 51–63. For the progeny of Sayyid Qawam al-Din, see Marʿashi, *Tārīkh-i Ṭabaristān*, 321–36; for the power of the *darwīsh*es, see Marʿashi, *Tārīkh-i Ṭabaristān*, 250–51, 253, 255, 276–77, 290–92.

death, further members of the dynasty began to return to the region to pursue their individual and collective claims.[114]

The year 809/1406–07 was the crucial one for the reestablishment of order in Mazandaran and also for the fortunes of the Marʿashi dynasty. The Timurid and local histories present quite different views of events. From the point of view of the Timurids, the major crisis to be faced was the rebellion of several Chaghatay emirs in western Khorasan and the support they found with the Chinggisid ruler of Astarabad, Pir Padshah b. Lughman. Shahrukh sent his forces against the coalition and defeated them; Pir Padshah fled to Khorezm and the rebellious emirs to Shiraz. After his victory, Shahrukh sent emissaries to various local dynasties to take their submission, and received the desired assurances from the sayyid at Sari.[115] In the *Tarikh-i Tabaristan* the drama is a different one. It was just at this time that the Marʿashi sayyids were returning from exile. They had had to borrow to pay for their passage home and were then held up on their way by Pir Padshah, who confiscated much of their money; this he did as a gesture of solidarity with the Timurid governor of Sari, Shams al-Din b. Jamshid. Apparently Shams al-Din had been unfriendly to Sayyid ʿAli, now in charge of Amul. The population of Sari killed Shams al-Din Jamshid and sent a message to Sayyid ʿAli saying that they intended to attack Pir Padshah. The people of Amul joined in the campaign. On their approach Pir Padshah released the sayyids he had retained, returned their goods and sent them off. This must have happened before the arrival of Shahrukh's troops, but it is likely that the army's approach influenced Pir Padshah's decision. Once the sayyids had been released, they were borne off to Sari, where they received the oath of the population. Clearly Sayyid ʿAli felt uneasy about the repercussions of the population's action, and he sent off an emissary to Shahrukh to explain the circumstances. It was presumably the answer to this embassy which the dynastic histories mention along with Timurid embassies to other local powers. Shahrukh stated that he was leaving Sari and Amul in the hands of the Marʿashi, and would overlook the murder of his governor. At this point in Shahrukh's reign, such an action was a minor infringement.[116]

However, Sayyid ʿAli continued to lead a difficult life. He had to deal at once with an unruly population, neither rich enough nor poor enough to be quiescent, a religious organization with local influence and prestige, and the demands of a large number of uncles, brothers, and cousins, all of whom could call on the testament of their revered father or grandfather. Two branches of the family appear to have held the most important territories; the children of Sayyid ʿAli's father, Kamal al-Din b. Qawam al-Din, were the inheritors of Sari, while rule over Amul belonged to the offspring of

[114] Calmard, "al-Marʿashī." [115] Ḥāfīẓ-i Abrū, *Zubdat*, 129–37.
[116] Marʿashī, *Tārīkh-i Ṭabaristān*, 245–47.

Rida al-Din b. Qawam al-Din. At the urging of the branch of Rida al-Din, Sayyid ʿAli now agreed to leave Amul and to base himself in Sari.[117]

While the ruler of Sari had the power of appointment over Amul and most people agreed that a descendant of Rida al-Din should control it, there was often disagreement about which person this should be. An alternative candidate for the post of Amul could find an ally in a pretender for the throne of Sari, thus creating a package to present to outside allies. This is what lay behind the next disturbances. Under the year 812/1409–10 Ḥāfiẓ-i Abrū and Muhammad Fasih report that Sayyid ʿAli came to Shahrukh for help against his brother Murtada, who had pushed him out with the help of Murtada's father-in-law, the ruler of Hazar Jarib.[118] According to the *Tarikh-i Tabaristan*, the challenge began with controversy over the rule of Amul. Sayyid ʿAli of Sari had prevailed upon the family of Rida al-Din to accept his candidate for Amul who proved neither a strong nor a generous governor and, after about a year, both the *darwīshes* and the population of Amul began to look towards a different son of the original Qawam al-Din, Sayyid ʿAli, known as ʿAli Amuli. Sayyid ʿAli of Sari recognized that this move had considerable backing and therefore allowed the *darwīshes* to install his uncle Sayyid ʿAli at Amul. According to the history, the *darwīshes* controlled the transfer and dominated the accession ceremony; when a member of the line of Rida al-Din attempted to speak against their candidate, they set up such a clamor that he could not be heard.[119]

The agreement was undermined by the machinations of Sayyid ʿAli Sari's brother, Sayyid Ghiyath al-Din, who had been appointed with him as deputy. Sayyid Ghiyath al-Din convinced Sayyid ʿAli Amuli that they could depose Sayyid ʿAli of Sari and put his brother Sayyid Murtada on the throne. With this proposal they pulled in support from Malik Gayumarth Rustamdari of Rustamdar and Larijan as well as the ruler of Hazar Jarib. They also sent word to the Timurid governor of Rayy stating that if they won their struggle they would come to offer service. The combined forces of the allies, the Rustamdaris, and the army of Hazar Jarib succeeded in ousting Sayyid ʿAli Sari, whose flight to Herat and request for help are documented in the major histories.[120] Shahrukh sent him off with orders that he receive help and he regained his throne. Up to this point events follow expectable lines, with few surprises to either side.

[117] Marʿashī, *Tārīkh-i Ṭabaristān*, 246–47.

[118] Ḥāfiẓ-i Abrū, *Zubdat*, 327–28; Faṣīḥ Khwāfī, *Mujmal-i faṣīḥī*, vol. III, 195.

[119] Marʿashī, *Tārīkh-i Ṭabaristān*, 248–51.

[120] Marʿashī, *Tārīkh-i Ṭabaristān*, 251–57. The *Tārīkh-i Ṭabaristān* (156) identifies the governor as Amir Sulaymanshah, but this is probably anachronistic, since Sulaymanshah had rebelled and fled to Khalil Sultan in Transoxiana in 808/1405. At the end of 812/spring 1410, Shahrukh granted ʿIraq-i ʿAjam to Khalil Sultan, but he would not have arrived at the time of these events (Marʿashī, *Tārīkh-i Ṭabaristān*, 156; Manz, *Rise and Rule*, 138–39; Ando, *Timuridische Emire*, 168; Ḥāfiẓ-i Abrū, *Zubdat*, 352–54; Faṣīḥ Khwāfī, *Mujmal-i faṣīḥī*, vol. III, 202, 207).

Timurid sources describing how Sayyid ʿAli had regained his throne in 812/1409–10 state only that he went from Herat to Mazandaran, gathered a force there, including Chaghatay soldiers, and retook his throne. It is not quite clear on what conditions Shahrukh offered help, and the uncertainty here may help to explain a minor rebellion in the year 817/1414. In his brief account of the disagreement, Ḥāfiẓ-i Abrū shows embarrassment, stating that Sayyid ʿAli had been wrongly told that Shahrukh was displeased with him and believed the story because several of his discontented relatives were always around the ruler.[121] Marʿashi's story of events in 812 provides a possible explanation for the later disagreement. According to him, the one member of the dynasty who had remained faithful to Sayyid ʿAli was another brother, the historian's father, Sayyid Nasir al-Din. Facing the plot against Sayyid ʿAli, Nasir al-Din had suggested that they immediately send to Shahrukh, offering to pay taxes in return for support. Sayyid ʿAli decided instead to meet the enemy in battle, and only after his defeat did he send Nasir al-Din to Herat. The author states that Shahrukh received Nasir al-Din immediately and sent him back with troops, assuring him that the presents he had brought were sufficient. When he and Sayyid ʿAli arrived in their land backed by a Chaghatay army however, the inhabitants told them that there was no need for a foreign army (*lashgar-i bīgāna*) since Sayyid Murtada was constantly drunk and the population had already turned against him. Sayyid ʿAli then retook his place without violence, won over the offspring of Rida al-Din, defeated Sayyid ʿAli Amuli, and returned his earlier protégé to the rule of Amul.[122]

What Marʿashi's account of the events of 812 does not explain is why after this Sayyid ʿAli found it necessary to send Nasir al-Din to Shahrukh to explain his actions and ask pardon. When Nasir al-Din arrived in Herat, the first question asked was why he had not brought the taxes. He explained that the Marʿashi sayyids were merely poor *darwīsh*es, who had returned to their plundered lands only a few years before and, since there had been constant disorder, they had no goods to send. The answer to these protestations was a reminder of the huge treasure that Temür had found in Mazandaran; it was still the same province, and must be able to afford taxes. Shahrukh retained Nasir al-Din and sent an emissary to demand taxes from Sayyid ʿAli, who returned the messenger with a rude message and his beard shaved. Shahrukh gathered an army and headed against Mazandaran, bringing along Sayyid Nasir al-Din with his feet tied to the stirrups. As it happened, on the way Shahrukh learned of raids on Transoxiana and made a face-saving agreement with Sayyid ʿAli, who sent Shahrukh his son and professions of good intentions, but no promise of taxes.[123]

[121] Ḥāfiẓ-i Abrū, *Zubdat*, 515–17. [122] Marʿashī, *Tārīkh-i Ṭabaristān*, 256–61.

[123] Ibid., 261–62; Ḥāfiẓ-i Abrū, *Zubdat*, 515–17; Faṣīḥ Khwāfī, *Mujmal-i faṣīḥī*, vol. III, 214. Marʿashi gives the date as 816, and suggests that Shahrukh himself led the army, while Ḥāfiẓ-i Abrū writes that Shahrukh sent troops.

Sayyid ʿAli Sari ruled until his death at the end of 820/early 1418. He appointed his son Sayyid Murtada to succeed him with the support of his brother Nasir al-Din. The Timurid historian Muhammad Fasih simply notes the death of the ruler and the accession of his son, but Marʿashi reports that Nasir al-Din first obtained the *bayʿat* for Sayyid Murtada from various parties within the realm, got agreement and a treaty with Malik Gayumarth of Rustamdar and Larijan, and then sent to Herat for confirmation. Here however he failed, since the court continued to demand taxes.[124] Two years later Nasir al-Din began fighting with his nephew Sayyid Murtada and when he was defeated he turned to Herat for assistance, promising that once on the throne he would pay taxes: forty *kharwār* of white and red silk a year. This was appealing to Shahrukh, who sent Firuzshah off with Nasir al-Din, following shortly thereafter himself. When they arrived, Sayyid Murtada sent his son to Firuzshah with a counteroffer of ten more *kharwār* of silk a year, and the opportunity to use his army on campaigns. When Firuzshah asked Nasir al-Din for a higher offer, he requested time to consider, and when he was refused he lost his temper and told his followers that he had made a mistake to allow a schism within the family, and that he hoped never to see another Chaghatay in his life. After writing his refusal to Firuzshah he left for Firuzkuh, near Rustamdar, and Shahrukh accepted Sayyid Murtada's offer. None of this history appears in the account of the years 822–23/1419–20 in Ḥāfiẓ-i Abrū's *Zubdat al-tawarikh*, more concerned with the threat then appearing in Azarbaijan.[125]

It seems likely that Nasir al-Din, when he was first sent to Herat, had indeed made some promise of taxes – what we cannot guess is whether he did this according to orders from Sayyid ʿAli, or on his own authority. The Timurid sources suggest that Sayyid ʿAli himself visited Herat, while Marʿashi states that Nasir al-Din was in charge of the negotiation, and that Sayyid ʿAli remained in Astarabad. Once the issue of taxes had been raised with the Herat court, Sayyid Nasir al-Din was able to use it to attempt to gain power on his own.

After this, the politics of Sari and Amul continued for some time in a similar vein, now with the rulers of Sari and Amul arguing over the apportionment of the tax between them.[126] About 840/1436–37, the author Zahir al-Din himself made an attempt at the throne in coalition with a candidate for Amul, and with the help of the *darwīsh*es. He also had the backing of Malik Gayumarth Rustamdari. In this case, it seems that the ruler, Sayyid Muhammad, did not appeal to Herat for help, but instead to Amir Hinduka, one of the Chaghatay emirs stationed in Astarabad, a man of

[124] Faṣīḥ Khwāfī, *Mujmal-i faṣīḥī*, vol. III, 230; Marʿashī, *Tārīkh-i Ṭabaristān*, 267–68.
[125] Marʿashī, *Tārīkh-i Ṭabaristān*, 273–75. [126] Ibid., 275–83, 287–303.

experience, but not of high station. We read nothing of this event in the dynastic sources.[127]

The Timurid dynastic sources give us the impression of a local history intersecting with the central government only in a few formal situations, with a rulership in a clearly inferior and dependent relationship. This picture is not necessarily untrue, but it is certainly incomplete. The local history of Tabaristan shows the complexity of local politics, and indicates that the major concern of the Marʿashi family lay with their own rivalries, and when someone needed an outside ally, he looked first to the closest neighbors, in Gilan, Lar, and Hazar Jarib, then perhaps to a Timurid governor or emir, and only after that to Shahrukh. On the other hand, it is clear that the ruler of Sari kept one eye nervously on Herat. The Timurid government on its side was not eager to undertake punitive campaigns, perhaps because the terrain was favorable to the local forces. As it happened, the internal rivalries of the Marʿashi family played to the advantage of Shahrukh, who was able to levy generous taxes without undertaking a campaign. We should however recognize that the region also posed some potential dangers to the regime. Marʿashi politics pulled in Timurid emirs and local rulers who controlled regions close to the areas of crucial importance to the Timurids – the sayyids of Hazar Jarib next to Simnan, and Malik Gayumarth just north of Rayy.

The politics of the Kar-Kiya sayyids of Gilan were in many ways similar to those of the Marʿashi dynasty, but show a greater remove from the Herat court. This was an area of mountain, marsh, and dense forest, ruled by a Zaydi Shiʿite dynasty whose feuding surpassed even that of the Marʿashis. The southern Daylaman region, famous for its soldiers, had recently become part of their realm.[128] In their political history we find little mention of the Timurid center; politicians dealt primarily with other local forces and when they wanted yet more help, appealed to the local Timurid governor. Situated on the western border of the Timurid domain, the Gilanis dealt with other border powers, and sometimes with the Qaraqoyunlu directly. Various dynasties who were vassals of the Timurids might also be pulled in. We see this quite clearly in the years 829–32/1425–29, when Shahrukh undertook his second Azarbaijan campaign. The death of the chief ruler of Gilan, Sayyid Rida Kiya, in Jumada I, 829/March–April, 1426, opened the door to internal rivalries. Malik Gayumarth Rustamdari took advantage of the confusion to pillage several regions in 830/1426–27. The next year the Gilanis retaliated, and Malik Gayumarth reacted with yet another raid in the fall of 831/1427 or 1428. The ruler of Gilan, Sayyid Muhammad, now turned outside for assistance, first to Sari and then to Shahrukh's governor at Qum, Amir Ilyas Khwaja. Both Sayyid Murtada and Ilyas Khwaja agreed to send troops, and in 832/1428–9 the combined army fought Malik Gayumarth and

[127] Ibid., 290–98. [128] Goto, "Der Aufstieg," 66–74.

defeated him.[129] What is odd about these events is that they occurred during Shahrukh's second Azarbaijan campaign, in which Malik Gayumarth took part within Shahrukh's army. On the third Azarbaijan campaign, six years later, most of these contestants were again among Shahrukh's troops.[130]

In Gilan, Timurid interference was less than successful. The embarrassment which could result from too close an involvement can be seen from the events of 845 to 846/1441–43, when enmity broke out between the two brothers who shared the rule of Gilan, Kar-Kiya Nasir in the major capital of Lahijan, and Kar-Kiya Ahmad in the city of Ranikuh. The historian Marʿashi considers Ahmad the prime mover in the quarrel, while he portrays Nasir as attempting to keep the peace. When Ahmad sent armed soldiers to the bazaar with their armor hidden under outer clothes and the ruse was discovered by Nasir's official, Nasir was persuaded to declare Ahmad innocent and to punish the official. He then asked Ahmad to spend several days with him in a show of unity to calm the population.[131] Nonetheless, strife soon broke out again, and caused so much dissension within the country that many families were split between the two sides.[132] Ahmad attempted to unseat Nasir with the help of his neighbor and father-in-law, Amir Husayn Tarumi, who had become a high-ranking emir in the Timurid army.[133] He also sent emissaries to Herat to appeal to Shahrukh for help, and, without waiting for the reply (which took five months), also sought help from Sultan Muhammad b. Baysunghur, recently appointed governor of ʿIraq-i ʿAjam. It is interesting that both Shahrukh and Sultan Muhammad agreed to support Ahmad, despite the fact that he was challenging the senior ruler. The probable explanation is his alliance with Husayn Tarumi, who had suffered serious losses in the recent campaigns against Nasir. Shahrukh sent orders that Hajji Husayn b. Baba Hajji of Hamadan, discussed above, and the governor of Qazwin, Bu Saʿid Mirum b. Ilyas Khwaja, should take troops into Gilan to support Amir Ahmad.

Timurid troops did Ahmad little good; this was not a place in which the Chaghatay could exercise their military skills to advantage. They pushed Nasir's troops back into the wilds of Daylaman, but here the enemy melted into the forest and spent the night shouting and shooting arrows at the Turks, who could not hold out in the wilderness and retreated back to Gilan proper. Their presence brought the population into an uproar and Amir Ahmad realized moreover that he could not provide for them. He apologized to

129 Marʿashī, *Tārīkh-i Gīlān*, 146–51; H. L. Rabino di Borgomale, "Les dynasties locales du Gilān et du Daylam," *Journal Asiatique* CCXXXVII, 2 (1949), 322–23. It appears that Ilyas Khwaja was not personally present at the battle.

130 Rūmlū, *Aḥsan*, 194; Jaʿfarī, *Tārīkh-i kabīr*, 81; fol. 313b.

131 Marʿashī, *Tārīkh-i Gīlān*, 225–29. 132 Ibid., 235.

133 Ibid., 230–46. Husayn Tarumi's family had had connections to the Qaraqoyunlu, but when his fortress was attacked by Timurid troops on their return from the Azarbaijan campaign in 833/1429–30, he submitted, and became enrolled among Shahrukh's senior emirs (Marʿashī, *Tārīkh-i Gīlān*, 170–71; Rūmlū, *Aḥsan*, 200; Samarqandī, *Maṭlaʿ*, 634).

Hajji Husayn and Bu Saʿid Mirum and asked them to depart with most of the army, leaving just a few commanders behind. These commanders and the local troops with them were once again attacked by Nasir's forces, and managed to find refuge in a fortress. However, the fortress keeper began to worry that they might take the fortress from him and opened the gates to Nasir's army. Most of Ahmad's officers died in battle; one commander stayed alive for a while by hiding behind a door and killing all those who came into the room, but he too eventually perished. The Turks were left alive but their goods were plundered and they were sent off to Kar-Kiya Nasir, ignominiously carrying the severed heads of their former comrades-in-arms.[134]

Ahmad went again to Qum to ask Sultan Muhammad b. Baysunghur for help. He was given a few Chaghatay emirs and succeeded in persuading Amir Husayn Tarumi to campaign again on his side. This campaign was shorter and even more disastrous. The combined forces camped in a village; the command lodged in the house of the headman (*kadkhudā*), where Ahmad settled with his family and following in the upper story, with Amir Husayn Tarumi and the Turks in the lower one. One of Ahmad's servitors went below to stable his horse and finding a column in his way, he cut it down. Unfortunately this column had supported the house, which collapsed, burying both Ahmad and his son in the rubble. Amir Ahmad was rescued but his son died and the Turks simply mounted their horses and fled. Amir Ahmad sent his son's body off to his sister for burial, but he was now in such financial straits that he had to sell a precious golden knife to pay for the funeral. He himself went to Tarum, hoping to have another son by Amir Husayn's daughter, since all his sons had died. Ahmad had no further success and was later imprisoned by his brother Nasir, who remained on the throne of Lahijan.[135] I should make it clear that the account I have given is drastically simplified; I have omitted the machinations of innumerable cousins and the exploits of the local lords of Rasht, Kuhdum, Lamsar, and many other places. The moral however is clear; in Gilan neither the Chaghatay nor those who attempted to use their aid profited from direct military interference.

The internal politics of Gilan and Mazandaran pulled in both local rulers and Timurid governors, involving the whole of the crucial northern corridor from Simnan to Sultaniyya in an unstable political web. With the fortunes of rulers within each dynasty constantly changing and rivals always looking for allies, there could be no stasis in any part of the region. Only one local ruler, Malik Gayumarth of Rustamdar, kept his throne throughout this period. For the Timurids, there might be some advantages to the promise of military intervention, but probably little to gain from an actual campaign. It was best to accept what they could gain through diplomacy and threat.

[134] Marʿashī, *Tārīkh-i Gīlān*, 247–50. [135] Marʿashī, *Tārīkh-i Gīlān*, 251–56.

Conclusion

Despite the predominant position of Chaghatays in Timurid military command, the Iranian population was neither inactive nor unimportant in the outcome of military contests. Regional armies of Iranian soldiers served in almost all campaigns, and the population of Iranian cities, both artisans and notables, regularly took part in city defense. Outside the towns, almost no province was without its local tribes of varied origin and language: Iranian, Turkic, Turkmen, Kurd, Lur, or Arab. These in turn were under their own leadership, and could gather around one or another contender for power. Most Timurid provinces were surrounded with border lands whose politics were active and complicated, and involved frequent military activity. The population of Iran was willing to sacrifice some level of autonomy or independence for the sake of protection by a competent army. The task of the Chaghatay government was to provide overarching security for the region. This was necessary not because either city or countryside was incapable of military activity, but because they were incessantly engaged in it.

Almost any kind of political power required constant effort to maintain but the resulting rivalries were not only a source of division; they could also bind the population to the central government. For almost any individual or group within the realm, the Timurid government presented an opportunity. Regional armies offered opportunities for plunder and within cities, notables worked together with Timurid officials; when a governor was pushed out, not infrequently some of the notables who owed their positions to him would leave as well. Those who had been out of power before would seek advancement from the new rulers, to whom indeed they might have opened the gates or the mountain passes.

The desire for security was less compelling for the border dynasties who always loved a good fight. What brought these regions into the orbit of larger powers was the same thing that made them separate; the practice of politics. No polity within the region could be involved only in internal politics, nor were any likely to be so devoid of internal rivalries that they presented a united front to the outside world. The Timurid ruler did hold a member of most subordinate dynasties at court as an inducement to good behavior, and thus had the means to practice a policy of divide and rule. In actual politics, as I have shown, divisions probably came more often from within small states than from action on the Timurid side. Outside powers were a crucial part of the political process, as a source of outside help for rivalries within. Political boundaries were vague, shading from members of the dynasty, to in-laws in neighboring regions, to the governors nominally in charge of their lands. As we saw in the case of the Mar'ashi dynasty, calling in help from the Timurids could result in loss of independence, and for Kar-Kiya Ahmad in Gilan, Chaghatay troops merely added to existing difficulties. Nonetheless, for the individuals involved, the temptation was impossible to resist.

CHAPTER 5

Timurid rule in southern and central Iran

The history of southern and central Iran illustrates the positive and negative sides of Timurid rule. The region was a prosperous center of agriculture, manufacture, and trade, ruled directly by Timurid governors, and its strong tax base and military manpower were important assets to the realm as a whole. The numerous histories written in this area provide valuable information about the notable class in its cities and their relations with the Timurid government. Timurid personnel often remained for long periods in one city and became closely involved with city life. Chaghatay emirs were part of the local power structure, not just as rulers, but also as builders, commercial investors and landowners. In this they resembled Mamluk emirs. The city notables on their side depended for much of their power on their local clientage, but many also served the Timurid government.

During times of peace and prosperity, the Timurids did much to win the hearts and minds of their subjects, but when central order broke down, they did just as much to lose them. For much of the time, rulers and notables cooperated in the maintenance of a healthy tax base and suitably imposing city structure. The goodwill and the habit of collaboration that the government developed through its support of the urban and agricultural economy were crucial to the maintenance of its power. As I showed in Chapter 4, during regional contests governors required the cooperation of both Turco-Mongolian military and Iranian city populations in order to hold their regions. It was just at such times, however, that the relations between rulers and cities became more difficult. Princes had limited resources and had to calculate carefully how many taxes they could levy, how many defeats they could afford, without losing the loyalty of their subjects. The city notables, who held much of the power of decision between defense and submission, had to judge which contender was likely to win and to rule with a minimum of violence and extortion. The stakes were high; for the individual – prince, commander or notable – miscalculation brought loss of position, punishment and not infrequently death, while for the city it could bring pillage or at the least a heavy ransom.

I will concentrate on the history of three cities: Shiraz, Isfahan, and Yazd. Although they were not formally in the same province, these cities were part of a common political sphere, gained and lost by the Timurid dynasty at the same time. When local power struggles broke out they were routinely contested by the same set of people. All were situated on the Iranian plateau along important trade routes but south of the northern corridor of war and trade which led from Herat to Tabriz. To the southeast lay Kerman, which was ruled by separate governors but served as a destination for campaigns of expansion.

In the first part of the chapter, I will analyze the connections between the Timurid provincial administration and the city populations of Iran, examining in particular the members of the local elite who pursued careers in financial administration. I suggest that instead of regarding local notables and government officials as separate groups, we should see them as related and often overlapping categories. The second section reviews the narrative history of the region during the struggles for power that occupied the region from Temür's death up to Shahrukh's second Fars campaign in 818/1415–16, to illustrate the dynamics of the relationship between Iranian cities and outside rulers. Finally, I will discuss the development of city structures during times of peace, showing the intimate involvement of governors and emirs in the cultural and economic life of the cities.

Local personnel in regional administration

The administration of southern Iran depended heavily on local personnel who served alongside Chaghatay emirs and the *dīwān* officials sent from outside. As I have shown, Iranian regional armies were a significant component of Timurid military strength and a number of these were led by local Iranian commanders – *sardār*s. We also find in most regional armies a few commanders of local provenance who probably led their own troops.[1] In provincial *dīwān*s likewise, local elites were strongly represented in high offices. Urban notables and central government personnel were drawn from overlapping groups of people, and were less separate than the *aʿyān-amīr* division would suggest. As we know, the ulama were often beneficiaries of government appointments. What is less often mentioned in scholarship is that members of prominent local families served as administrators; in southern Iran particularly we find numerous powerful regional viziers, some of whom, while making up part of local Timurid administration, at the same time remained part of the council of city notables.

There seems to be no clear pattern in the positions given to local personnel in distinction to those sent from the center, and neither group monopolized power. A number of bureaucrats in Iran came from other regions,

[1] Examples of emirs who appear to be local are ʿAli Isfahani and Shaykh ʿAli Dizfuli in the army of Iskandar (Ḥāfiẓ-i Abrū, *Zubdat*, 442; Faṣīḥ Khwāfī, *Mujmal-i faṣīḥī*, vol. III, 181; Yazdī, *Ḥasanī*, 16).

particularly Herat, and service in the provinces probably could be part of the career path of a bureaucrat on the way up or temporarily out of favor. Shams al-Din Muhammad Tahir for instance was dismissed from the *dīwān* in Herat in 821/1418–19 and in 828/1424–25 he arrived to serve in the *dīwān* in Yazd, where he is very favorably described.[2] In some cases such viziers represented the center; this seems to have been the case with the historian Fasih Khwafi when he spent two years in Kerman on business for Shahrukh.[3] On the other hand Fasih Khwafi's relative, killed in Shiraz in 817/1414–15, was almost certainly serving Iskandar himself, since he was executed at the time that Iskandar's governor was switching allegiance to Shahrukh.[4]

Many bureaucrats were men of high birth who served either in the city to which they were born or in nearby ones. In Yazd for instance, one of the most prominent bureaucratic families provided several generations of leading viziers; these were the reputed descendants of the Arab Banu Tamim. During the reign of Shahrukh the most important member of the family was ʿImad al-Din Masʿud, who was *ṣāḥib-dīwān*, and by the end of the period his son Diyaʾ al-Din Muhammad was also serving in the administration.[5] Iskandar b. ʿUmar Shaykh had two major viziers, Hafiz Razi, whom he hired while he was in Yazd and took with him to Shiraz and Isfahan, and Pir Husayn Tabrizi, who does not appear to have had regional affiliations. Another person who served Iskandar and later Ibrahim Sultan, probably as vizier, was Nur al-Din Kamal from Shiraz.[6] Under Rustam b. ʿUmar Shaykh in Isfahan we see the beginning of the career of Mahmud Haydar of Isfahan, who later served as chief vizier for Sultan Muhammad b. Baysunghur.[7]

Two traits stand out in the biographies of prominent viziers in this area. One is the tendency to serve in several different cities and sometimes under different princes, while remaining within the region and retaining a local power base. The other trait is their strong military capabilities. While it was not uncommon for viziers of the central administration to participate in campaigns and to lead troops, most of them seem to have been primarily bureaucrats, whose military role was only secondary. In the region we are discussing, on the other hand, most prominent viziers were also important military commanders, known as "master of the sword and pen." An

[2] Faṣīḥ Khwāfī, *Mujmal-i faṣīḥī*, vol. III, 235; Kātib, *Tārīkh-i jadīd*, 111.
[3] Faṣīḥ Khwāfī, *Mujmal-i faṣīḥī*, vol. III, 251, 254.
[4] Ibid., vol. III, 218. This is not the relative killed that year on the orders of the Herat vizier Sayyid Fakhr al-Din, mentioned in Chapter 3.
[5] Kātib, *Tārīkh-i jadīd*, 105–07, 247; Mustawfī Bāfqī, *Mufīdī*, vol. III, 162, 878; Isabel A. M. Miller, "The Social and Economic History of Yazd (c. AH 736/AD 1335 – c. AH 906/AD 1500)," DPhil thesis, University of London, 1990, 130, 136. We also find local people at a lower level. An example is Khwaja Pir Husayn Damghani, a native of the Ahristan district of Yazd, who served in the *dīwān*, during which time the people of Ahristan were well off (Kātib, *Tārīkh-i jadīd*, 118).
[6] *Muʿizz*, fol. 108a; Yazdī, *Ḥasanī*, 14–16. It appears that the *dīwān* of Ibrahim Sultan b. Shahrukh came from a number of different backgrounds; some local and some from families who served in the central *dīwān* (*Muʿizz*, fols. 142a, 142b).
[7] *Muʿizz*, fol. 105a; Ṭihrānī Iṣfahānī, *Diyārbakriyya*, 293.

examination of their lives is helpful in breaking down some of the stereotypes of separate career realms which pervade both primary and secondary literature.

The career of Hafiz Razi is a good example. Ghiyath al-Din Hafiz Razi was a native of Yazd, a learned man and a Sufi, who had memorized the Qur'an and knew seven languages.[8] His career with Iskandar began in Yazd; Hafiz Razi arrived back from a pilgrimage, became Iskandar's deputy, and later accompanied him to Shiraz and Isfahan. He is listed in the *Mu'izz al-ansab* and designated in histories as the chief vizier.[9] Hafiz Razi was also commander of a *tümen* of foot and horse, which included the regional armies of Abarquh and Yazd and also the Qushun-i Janbaz, a small force probably made up of Turco-Mongolian personnel.[10] It is clear that he enjoyed considerable influence in politics; he advised Iskandar to move against Qum, then led troops against the city and finally negotiated the surrender of its ruler, whose agent he knew personally.[11] After Iskandar's defeat and death Hafiz Razi took care to protect himself and his future career. When Shahrukh arrived in Yazd on his Fars campaign of 818/1415–16, Hafiz Razi entertained him at a magnificent feast in the madrasa he had built in Yazd while he was vizier for Iskandar. Shahrukh commissioned him to transport to the Hijaz the Ka'ba cover which the Yazd weavers produced for him. In this Hafiz Razi was not successful and he returned with the cover to Herat, where he died in Jumada I, 825/April–May, 1422. His body was returned to Yazd and buried in his madrasa.[12]

Another vizier conspicuous in administration and the military was Khwaja Jalal al-Din Mahmud Khwarazmi, who served in Shiraz under Pir Muhammad and Iskandar, moved with Iskandar to Isfahan and then returned to Shiraz to serve under Ibrahim Sultan.[13] Under Iskandar Mahmud Khwarazmi evidently held a significant military command. He was among the important commanders in two campaigns – one against Yazd in 812/1409–10 and one against the southern cities of Bam and Jiruft in 814/1411–12.[14] The fullest information we have on Khwaja Mahmud's activities comes from the histories of Yazd, where he appears to have served three times, once under each of the princes he worked for. Since the histories of the city are particularly concerned with building, it is this aspect of Khwaja Mahmud's achievements that is

[8] Yazdī, *Ḥasanī*, 14–15; Soucek, "Eskandar," 83; Aubin, *Ni'mat*, 86. He is mentioned with Sayyid 'Ali and Shah Ni'mat Allah at the mosque during Ni'mat Allah's visit to Shiraz between 1409–12.

[9] Kātib, *Tārīkh-i jadīd*, 147; *Mu'izz*, fol. 108a; Yazdī, *Ḥasanī*, 14–15.

[10] Yazdī, *Ḥasanī*, 14–15, 24, 30, 42, 46; Kātib, *Tārīkh-i jadīd*, 246.

[11] Yazdī, *Ḥasanī*, 35–36; Ja'farī, *Tārīkh-i kabīr*, 57–8.

[12] Kātib, *Tārīkh-i jadīd*, 147–49; Mustawfī Bāfqī, *Mufīdī*, vol. III, 155–57; Faṣīḥ Khwāfī, *Mujmal-i faṣīḥī*, vol. III, 251.

[13] *Mu'izz*, fols. 103a, 142a; Kātib, *Tārīkh-i jadīd*, 95, 115, 186, 201. While Mahmud Haydar served Pir Muhammad and Iskandar, he is mentioned specifically as vizier only under Ibrahim Sultan.

[14] Ḥāfiẓ-i Abrū, *Zubdat*, 345, 442; Ja'farī, *Tārīkh-i kabīr*, 51, 56; fols. 300b, 302b; Yazdī, *Ḥasanī*, 19.

reported; under each prince, he was sent to Yazd to supervise repairs and new building projects.[15]

Several viziers who served Timurid princes were also part of the city council. Two clearly had military training and seem to have served as *sardār* in their native cities. One of these was Khwaja Nur al-Din Kamal, who is mentioned among the Shiraz headmen and commanders (*kulūyān wa sardārān*) who organized the defense of the city against Pir Muhammad's murderer Husayn Sharbatdar in 812/1409–10. By 817/1414 he had joined Iskandar's service and he acted as Iskandar's agent in putting down an uprising led by the ward headmen who were pushing the city to declare for Shahrukh.[16] We find him listed as a vizier under both Iskandar and Ibrahim Sultan. It is likely that he held quite a high position, since the *Mujmal-i fasihi* states that in 820/1417–18 an official from the central *dīwān* was sent to Shiraz to investigate reports of his misconduct.[17] A minor vizier would not have elicited such interest from the center.

We know more about Mahmud Haydar, who began his career as vizier under Rustam b. ʿUmar Shaykh and later served Sultan Muhammad b. Baysunghur. He is identified as Rustam's vizier in the "Muʿizz al-ansab" and he figured prominently in the events surrounding the rebellion of Sultan Muhammad b. Baysunghur in 849–50/1445–47. Like Nur al-Din Kamal, Mahmud Haydar appears to have been among the people who made decisions for the city as a whole. He was one of several notables connected with the *dīwān* in Isfahan who were called to Herat for tax arrears and agreed to raise money from the population of Isfahan.[18] When these men failed to collect the promised sum they joined with other notables of Isfahan and appealed to Sultan Muhammad for help, thus provoking his challenge to Shahrukh.[19] Mahmud Haydar was clearly considered among those responsible for the city's action, since he was one of the men whom Shahrukh imprisoned when he moved against Sultan Muhammad in 850/1446–47.[20] After Shahrukh's death, Sultan Muhammad sent Mahmud Haydar to Isfahan with other officials to prepare for his arrival and appointed him to a high position in the *dīwān*. A little later we find Mahmud Haydar as one of the bureaucrats entrusted with the affairs of Khorasan during the period Sultan Muhammad controlled it.[21] After Sultan Muhammad's defeat and death in 855/1452 Mahmud Haydar went into the service of the victor,

[15] Kātib, *Tārīkh-i jadīd*, 95, 201, 218.

[16] Yazdī, *Ḥasanī*, 18, 40. Although Nur al-Din Kamal is not specifically identified as *sardār*, he is listed in this joint heading along with two other men both of whom were ward headmen and later acted separately from him.

[17] *Muʿizz*, fols. 108a, 142a; Faṣīḥ Khwāfī, *Mujmal-i faṣīḥī*, vol. III, 228. He is probably the Nur al-Din Muhammad Kamal who came to Yazd as tax inspector in 831/1427–28 (Kātib, *Tārīkh-i jadīd*, 226).

[18] Jaʿfarī, *Tārīkh-i kabīr*, 120. [19] Kātib, *Tārīkh-i jadīd*, 235.

[20] Ṭihrānī Iṣfahānī, *Diyārbakriyya*, 288.

[21] Kātib, *Tārīkh-i jadīd*, 246; Ṭihrānī Iṣfahānī, *Diyārbakriyya*, 293, 321.

Abu'l Qasim Babur, and once more served in Isfahan, which he was sent to organize on Babur's entry into central Iran. However, his attachment to the city was stronger than his loyalty to his new master, and only a little later we find the population of Isfahan refusing to accept Babur and coming to an agreement with Khwaja Mahmud Haydar. When the Qaraqoyunlu succeeded in taking Isfahan, they appointed him to the office of *sardār*.[22]

The careers of Nur al-Din Kamal and Mahmud Haydar show that the personnel of the city councils might become part of Timurid provincial *dīwāns*. We know too little of Nur al-Din's career to judge how his office affected the focus of his loyalty, but we know that Mahmud Haydar, after several years of succession struggle, decided to abandon the dynasty and to help to organize Isfahan against his employer, Abu'l Qasim Babur.

In Yazd several men from the city's elite served the Timurids as viziers while also making up part of the notable council; indeed in the accounts of the council of notables in Yazd viziers are always present. In 846/1442–43, the temporary governor of Yazd, Hamza Chuhra, collaborated with several people in building the *ʿidgāh* of Yazd, to which each contributed money. These men included the city judge, Sharaf al-Din Yaʿqub Qadi, a member of a rich and influential sayyid family, Amir Jalal al-Din Khidrshah, a vizier belonging to the local notables, ʿImad al-Din Masʿud of the Banu Tamim, a member of a prominent local family, who was probably then in the *dīwān* of Yazd, Mawlana Rukn al-Din Hasan, and a vizier from outside, Nasir al-Din Simnani.[23] In the struggles after Shahrukh's death, the notables of Yazd had to choose several times between various princes, and we know the names of the most important men responsible for the decision. They include once again a judge, now Yaʿqub Qadi's son, Majd al-Din Fadl-Allah Qadi, along with a member of a particularly wealthy merchant family, Khwaja Zayn al-Din ʿAli Bawardi, and two viziers, Khwaja ʿImad al-Din Masʿud and the less well-known Jalal al-Din Murshid.[24] The same viziers appear in the list of *dīwān* officials of Yazd who advised the prince Abu'l Qasim Babur to give up Yazd to his enemies.[25] When we put together the evidence from different cities, then, we can conclude that prominent viziers serving Timurid princes retained their local status and connection to city politics, and thus participated concurrently in the Chaghatay government and the city council.

Tribal and nomadic populations

The mountains of Fars and Luristan were important strongholds of nomadic and semi-nomadic populations. These people were an integral part of local politics, connected both with the city leaders and with Timurid governors.

[22] Yazdī, *Ḥasanī*, 69; Ṭihrānī Iṣfahānī, *Diyārbakriyya*, 327–28.
[23] Kātib, *Tārīkh-i jadīd*, 187; Yazdī, *Ḥasanī*, 73. [24] Kātib, *Tārīkh-i jadīd*, 265–66.
[25] Yazdī, *Ḥasanī*, 68.

Timurid princes also took advantage of regions combining pasture and inaccessible terrain by taking refuge there in times of trouble.[26] The tribesmen were a military resource as well as a constant challenge, and some control over their region was necessary for anyone controlling Fars. The most important pastoral populations were the Lur and the neighboring Shul, located on the southwestern border of Fars. The region also contained a population of Kurds. Luristan was divided into two realms under separate rulers, Lur-i Buzurg and Lur-i Kuchik; both had been incorporated as vassals by Temür, who kept hostages at his court and changed the rulership when expedient. Temür's successors continued the practice and periodically led expeditions into the territories of the kings of Lur. The Lur, Shul, and Kurds served with the armies of Timurid princes and seem to have been part of their military manpower. However, since they were not a united force, a prince might gather followers there while being resisted by local rulers. We find Shul and Kurd commanders among the men deciding how Shiraz should resist Sultan Muhammad in 850/1446, and after Shahrukh's death Sultan Muhammad gathered followers among them in his bid for power – indeed some joined him in his second attack on Shiraz, in 851/1447.[27] There is even evidence of some connection between the Shul and the Shirazi ulama.[28] Like many other tribal populations, they were not notable for their loyalty.

Several other mountain and pastoral populations are mentioned in military affairs. The Khalaj Turks who appear in various parts of Iran are mentioned on Temür's campaigns, we hear of Qashqa'i in Ganduman, not far from Isfahan, and of unnamed tribes near Isfahan.[29] The region of Abarquh, which contained desert lands, also supported some nomad populations.[30] Darabjird and Shabankara contained significant pasture and had traditionally contained nomads; the inhabitants had been famous for their depredations, but appear to have been relatively quiet at this period. A few mentions in the Timurid histories however suggest that the area remained known for its pastures and perhaps as a refuge, similar in some ways to the region of Lur. After Shahrukh retook Fars in 818/1415–16, he sent parts of his army to the pastures of Lur and of Shabankara.[31]

In addition to the pastoral populations, there were local rulers with military followings who attached their armies to those of the governor, at least when they were obedient. In 814/1411, when Iskandar moved against Kerman, he had in his army both Shaykh ʿAli Dizfuli of Khuzistan and Jalal al-Din Tarumi from the eastern edge of Fars. When Jalal al-Din died during the

[26] V. Minorsky, "Lur," "Lur-i buzurg," "Lur-i kuchik," "Shulistan, " in *Encyclopaedia of Islam*, 2nd edn. During Shahrukh's reign, the region was apparently held by Sayyidi b. ʿIzz al-Din (Manz, *Rise and Rule*, 94; Jaʿfarī, *Tārīkh-i kabīr*, 64; fol. 306a; Samarqandī, *Maṭlaʿ*, 242).

[27] Samarqandī, *Maṭlaʿ*, 980; Jaʿfarī, *Tārīkh-i kabīr*, 124–26. [28] Shujāʿ, *Anīs al-Nās*, 259.

[29] Yazdī, *Ḥasanī*, 41; Ḥāfiẓ-i Abrū, *Zubdat*, 531. [30] Miller, "History of Yazd," 116.

[31] Yazdī, *Ḥasanī*, 86; Kātib, *Tārīkh-i jadīd*, 245; Ḥāfiẓ-i Abrū, *Zubdat*, 606–07.

campaign, his brother-in-law in Tarum attempted to assert his power over the region, helped by Gurgin Lari, the ruler of the nearby town of Lar. But Iskandar's emirs moved against both regions; the sons of Gurgin Lari considered resistance, but soon opted for caution.[32] Some of these men remained part of the governors' armies, as I shall show below. The region of Khuzistan, partly under local rulers and partly under agents of the Timurid princes, remained an opportunity and a challenge, often switching its allegiance between Timurid princes and the Jalayir of Iraq.[33]

What we see in Fars then is a military and bureaucratic apparatus ruling over a complicated society which was far from powerless itself. We cannot divide population or offices into military and civil spheres, nor is it possible to divide personnel neatly between dynastic officials and local notables. The case of Mahmud Haydar shows that local Iranian bureaucrats led troops and occupied high office for the dynasty while retaining strong attachments and power in their own cities based on personal networks. Local rulers and tribes served the administration and cooperated with city populations, but also might support rivals. The governor required active cooperation from local rulers, tribal leaders and city notables. In times when the power structure was stable, this was feasible. The rulers shared with most of their subjects a common interest in peace, prosperity and order, and had the military power to chastise those who broke their contract. When the rulership of the province was called into question however, the complex web of interests and loyalties made politics difficult and dangerous for all concerned.

City leadership and the politics of calculation

Contests for rulership played themselves out largely through control of a set of key cities, with major battles in the open field. A ruler wishing to assert control either invited cities to submit willingly – if they were not strongly held by his competition – or moved against them. The major cities of Iran were walled and equipped with a citadel, and had to be taken not by assault but by siege, with periodic battles fought outside the city or on its walls. Cities were not easy to conquer and when an army entered it was almost always through some form of agreement, whether by a joint decision of the governor and notables, or the treachery of someone within the city. The cities which served as seats for governors – Shiraz, Isfahan, and Yazd – were the most crucial ones; once these were held, smaller cities and fortresses presented a lesser challenge.

The outcome of any contest depended on the strengths and the calculations of a number of different people. The Timurid candidate for power needed first of all to have a strong army with which to impress both the city population and his rival for power, who might come to relieve the city. This

[32] Ḥāfiẓ-i Abrū, *Jughrāfiyā*, vol. II, 342–44. [33] Ismail Aka, "Timurʾun ölümünden," 7–10.

meant that he had to retain the loyalty of his Turco-Mongolian followers and local troops. He had to provide either pay or booty, and above all he had to offer the prospect of success. Even this was not enough; a ruler needed also to persuade the city populations that submission and loyalty were the most advisable policy. For the city council, deciding whether or not to submit, there were two overriding considerations – first, whether the prospective ruler would be able to hold the city against rivals, and second, whether he was likely to show some respect for the welfare of the population. In times of disorder the standards applied were relatively minimal, since essentially all contenders for power taxed unmercifully and allowed their troops at least some pillage. Nonetheless, we do hear of cities reluctant to open their gates to rulers who were known for exceptionally brutal behavior.[34]

In all cities of the region urban leaders played an important role, but as I showed in Chapter 4 there were significant differences among cities in power structures. The same was true of political culture. It appears that in Yazd decisive power was held by notables from wealthy and established families, especially the chief judge, the local bureaucrats, and the top merchants, while the ward headmen and city leaders, prominent in other cities, barely appear in the histories.[35] Whether because of the power of the elite, or their harrowing experience in an earlier rebellion, the Yazdis usually tried to avoid risk in their dealings with Timurid princes. In Shiraz the most visible actors were the ward headmen, known locally as *kulū*; the presence of a butcher among these seems to argue for a bazaar provenance.[36] The politics in the city were livelier than in Yazd and the city leadership was quite often ready to take some risk in its dealing with outside powers. It is clear that the political and military prominence of ward headmen was a tradition in Shiraz, as they had played an important role in city defense in the Injuyid (c. 1313–57) and Muzaffarid (1314–93) periods. At that time, headmen of different quarters might support divergent candidates for the throne, and the victors sometimes took reprisals against the men who had opposed them in the dissenting quarters of the city. The headmen of quarters constituted an important element in the ruler's power, organizing local support and taking charge of the military defense of their own section of the walls and gates.[37] Abu Ishaq Inju (c. 1343–57) apparently so feared the military power of the Shirazis that he forbade the population of Shiraz to bear arms. The histories of the period referred

[34] This happened several times in the struggle after Shahrukh's death; see Ṭihrānī Iṣfahānī, *Diyārbakriyya*, 327–30, 344–46.

[35] The sources give prominence to the chief judges, viziers, and the wealthiest of the merchant families, but only one family of *ruʾasā* is mentioned, and then fleetingly. See, for example, Kātib, *Tārīkh-i jadīd*, 90, 108, 113, 120 (for merchants); and 91 (for the single mention of a *raʾīs*). See also, Miller, "History of Yazd," 229–30; Mustawfī Bāfqī, *Mufīdī*, vol. III, 884 (for judges); and, Mustawfī Bāfqī, *Mufīdī* , vol. III, 162, 878 (for viziers).

[36] Yazdī, *Ḥasanī*, 18; Jaʿfarī, *Tārīkh-i kabīr*, 60; fol. 304b.

[37] John Limbert, *Shiraz in the Age of Hafez: the Glory of a Medieval Persian City* (Seattle, London: University of Washington Press, 2004), 89–91.

to the people mustered by the headmen as rabble (*rindān, awbāsh, shaṭṭār*); they seem to have been feared by both local rulers and aristocrats. The Muzaffarids, who followed the Injuyids, apparently gained popularity among the upper classes by suppressing the mobs but the *kulūs* retained considerable power. They were responsible for the accession of Shah Shujaʿ in 765/1364 and they are mentioned in the account of Temür's conquest of Shiraz in 795/1393.[38]

The city in which we can most clearly discern the internal power structure is Isfahan, which, at both the beginning and the end of Shahrukh's reign, was a focal point for local power politics and was known for its contentious spirit.[39] Here the religious notables – particularly the chief judge, the viziers, and the ward headmen – were all politically and militarily active, often at odds among themselves as well as with the regime. Of all the cities in the region, Isfahan was by far the most independent and daring in its actions.

Shiraz, Isfahan, and Yazd shared a common historical legacy as centers for the Muzaffarids, an Iranian dynasty which had begun as servitors to the Mongols and established an independent realm in the middle of the fourteenth century. The Muzaffarids retained power until Temür's conquests in 787/1385–86 and are remembered as cultural patrons, who furthered the careers of such luminaries as Hafiz and Sayyid ʿAli Jurjani. They are famous likewise for their internal contentiousness, exceptional even in medieval Iran. The capital of the dynasty was at Shiraz but other major cities – Kerman, Yazd, and Isfahan – were held by separate members of the family, who incessantly fought each other and the supreme ruler. It is useful to consider that such battles were expensive to mount and that the population had to provide for the support of the armies which besieged its cities and trampled its fields.[40] During successive campaigns from 789/1387 to 795/1393, Temür reduced the Muzaffarids to vassal status and then executed most members of the dynasty. In their place he appointed his eldest son ʿUmar Shaykh as governor of Fars.

At the time of Temür's death Isfahan, Shiraz, and Yazd were controlled by ʿUmar Shaykh's sons, who continued the Muzaffarid traditions of cultural patronage and constant infighting. Just as cities differed in their political behavior, ʿUmar Shaykh's sons varied in character and in their attitude towards risk. Pir Muhammad, who held the greatest power at Temür's death, was twenty-five years old and had been governor for several years. Under Temür, he had twice been punished for suspected misbehavior and this

[38] John Limbert, "Shiraz in the Age of Hafez," Ph.D. dissertation, Harvard University, 1973, 155–58; Ḥāfiẓ-i Abrū, *Jughrāfiyā*, vol. II, 307; Yazdī, *Ẓafarnāma*, vol. I, 438 (here *kulū* and *kalāntarān-i maḥalāt*).

[39] Ibn Baṭṭūṭa, *The Travels of Ibn Baṭṭūṭa, A. D. 1325–1354*, translated by H. A. R. Gibb, 3 vols. (New Delhi: Munshiram Manoharlal, 1993), vol. II, 294–95.

[40] Peter Jackson, "Muẓaffarids," in *Encyclopaedia of Islam*, 2nd edn.

may be one reason for his relatively cautious stance during the succession struggle.[41] His marriage to a sister of Gawharshad probably also predisposed him towards alliance with Shahrukh. ʿUmar Shaykh's next son, Rustam, was about two years younger and had been active within the military for the last eight years of Temür's rule. Like Pir Muhammad, he was married to a sister of Gawharshad, and while he took part in the struggle for power within Fars, he also tended towards caution. Their younger brother Iskandar was only twenty at Temür's death and considerably more adventurous than his older brothers. In his undertakings he was able to involve a yet younger brother, Bayqara, who was only nine at the beginning of the struggle but later became an active participant.

The contest for power that erupted on Temür's death presents a vivid picture of how city and dynastic politics interconnected, and how difficult they were for all concerned. Several regional cities, including Yazd and Abarquh, were quick to declare their allegiance to Pir Muhammad as governor of Fars.[42] Some of Pir Muhammad's advisors suggested the possibility of reinstating the Muzaffarids, or of seeking a patent from the caliph in Egypt, but Pir Muhammad decided to recognize Shahrukh.[43] He set about gathering scattered regional armies and restoring their manpower to the salary rolls.[44] However, the former Muzaffarid realm had been under Timurid control for only ten years. Both the Jalayir in Iraq and the Qaraqoyunlu in Azarbaijan immediately set out to regain their old territories and to seek influence further afield. The cities and rulers of Iran therefore had a choice of overlords, and the future of the Timurids in the area probably appeared uncertain. Not all local rulers chose submission to the Timurids. One of the kings of Luristan attacked Iskandar, who was then governor of Hamadan. Iskandar felt himself further threatened by the power struggles of Amiranshah's sons, particularly by ʿUmar, who had chased out his father and was aiming at Hamadan. He therefore wrote to Pir Muhammad asking for refuge and, even after receiving a discouraging answer, left for Isfahan. It seems that he was justified in his fears since within a short time several of his emirs had deserted to ʿUmar, taking much of his treasury with them, and soon thereafter ʿUmar was indeed in Hamadan. After a month or two Pir Muhammad installed Iskandar as governor of Yazd, and the sons of ʿUmar Shaykh made peace with ʿUmar b. Amiranshah.[45]

This action did not secure calm; instead the princes of Fars became embroiled in the quarrels of Amiranshah's family. The first city of the region to suffer attack was Isfahan, and the story of its defense shows the active spirit

[41] Woods, *Timurid Dynasty*, 20; Ḥāfiẓ-i Abrū, *Jughrāfiyā*, vol. II, 317–20.
[42] Jaʿfarī, *Tārīkh-i kabīr*, 36. [43] Ḥāfiẓ-i Abrū, *Zubdat*, 44–45.
[44] Ḥāfiẓ-i Abrū, *Zubdat*, 47–48; Ḥāfiẓ-i Abrū, *Jughrāfiyā*, vol. II, 322.
[45] Ḥāfiẓ-i Abrū, *Zubdat*, 48–51; Ḥāfiẓ-i Abrū, *Jughrāfiyā*, vol. II, 322–23; Yazdī, *Ḥasanī*, 14.

of its inhabitants. Rustam b. ʿUmar Shaykh, who was governor of Isfahan, had accompanied ʿUmar against his brother Aba Bakr. First they led a successful raid on Aba Bakr's baggage train and in Dhuʾl-Qaʿda, 808/April, 1406, along with Pir Muhammad and Iskandar and the regional armies of Fars and Isfahan, undertook a full-scale battle against him.[46] They lost and Aba Bakr pursued them and attacked Isfahan in late 808–early 809/ June–July, 1406. Although Rustam was in the city at the time, the defense was led by the city judge Qadi Ahmad Saʿidi, a man of great power and considerable military skill. The soldiers mentioned defending the city are identified variously as "Iṣfahānī," "*ahl-i Iṣfahān*," and "*ahl-i shahr*." After a battle outside the city, in which the Isfahanis were defeated and about two thousand killed along with several of their commanders (*sardārān*), the sayyids and notables agreed to make peace, recognize Amiranshah, and return the booty they had seized. However when they learned that Aba Bakr planned to plunder the city, they resumed active defense. Qadi Ahmad came out to fight Aba Bakr with several notables, leading an estimated 20,000 foot soldiers and horsemen. When Aba Bakr's soldiers tried to climb the walls at the time of the Friday communal prayer the city population repulsed them under the leadership of the qadi. Finally, hearing of problems back home, Aba Bakr lifted the siege. In the "Tarikh-i kabir" where these events are chronicled in detail, Rustam b. ʿUmar Shaykh is mentioned only tangentially, unable to defend himself or to come out of the city, and Hafiz-i Abru does not mention Rustam at all. We know that he was ill a few months later so it is possible that he was already incapacitated.[47]

The prominence of Qadi Ahmad Saʿidi in the city's defense need not mean that Rustam and his emirs were uninvolved, since Qadi Ahmad was closely connected to Rustam's administration and was a member of the prince's inner circle of advisors. A year before these events, he and one of the major Chaghatay emirs, Sultanshah, had together persuaded Rustam to blind and exile another Chaghatay emir who had long served ʿUmar Shaykh's family – Amir Saʿid Barlas. They claimed that Amir Saʿid was plotting treachery, and Ḥāfiẓ-i Abrū, who tells the story, appears to agree.[48]

The next drama of Fars was caused by ʿUmar Shaykh's liveliest son – Iskandar. Not content with his governorship of Yazd, in 809/1406–07 Iskandar undertook an expedition into Kerman. When Pir Muhammad, alarmed, seized him and sent an expedition to remove his followers from

46 Ḥāfiẓ-i Abrū, *Zubdat*, 75–78; Ḥāfiẓ-i Abrū, *Jughrāfiyā*, vol. II, 323–24; Yazdī, *Ḥasanī*, 24–31. This is the campaign in which the historian Taj al-Din Hasan b. Shihab took part, described in the previous chapter.

47 Quiring-Zoche, *Isfahan*, 19–21; Jaʿfarī, *Tārīkh-i kabīr*, 39–40; fols. 296a–b; Ḥāfiẓ-i Abrū, *Zubdat*, 78–80, 178.

48 Ḥāfiẓ-i Abrū, *Zubdat*, 52. Saʿid Barlas had earlier been in Pir Muhammad's service and had denounced him to Temür (Ḥāfiẓ-i Abrū, *Jughrāfiyā*, 319).

Yazd, the prudent notables of the city handed them over without resistance.[49] Iskandar, however, escaped and joined Rustam in Isfahan. Pir Muhammad attacked, but when the inhabitants defended the city he gave up, contenting himself with breaking dams, wrecking crops, and burning houses in the surroundings to punish the population.[50] Fairly soon after this Rustam and Iskandar set out against Pir Muhammad in Shiraz. The city resisted successfully – here apparently under the active leadership of Pir Muhammad and his emirs. Although we hear of no wavering within the city itself, not all of Pir Muhammad's more distant followers remained loyal to him. Saʿid Barlas, whom Pir Muhammad had installed as his deputy in Dizful after Rustam had exiled him, now declared allegiance to Rustam, apparently bringing with him several other local governors in Khuzistan.[51] When Rustam's forces gave up the siege of Shiraz and decided instead to plunder the eastern regions of Fars, from Niriz to Darabjird, they were joined by the local ruler Gurgin Lari, whose lands were not far away.[52] This is the man who had earlier helped the rulers of Shabankara in their bid for independence.

In 810/1407–08 Pir Muhammad went after Rustam and Iskandar to exact revenge. Although his goal was Isfahan, the decisive battle was fought near the meadow of Ganduman, where Rustam and Iskandar had gone to escape the plague ravaging the city. The list of commanders in each army shows a predominantly Turco-Mongolian military, accompanied by local troops and commanders from the urban populations of Shiraz and Isfahan. In Pir Muhammad's army there were the two druggists from the Shiraz bazaar, Husayn and ʿAli Sharbatdar, who had found favor with Pir Muhammad and been raised to the status of emir and commander. In this battle, Husayn was in the left wing with the army of the Lur and Kurds.[53] Among Rustam's chief commanders was Qadi Ahmad Saʿidi of Isfahan.[54] Pir Muhammad won the battle at Ganduman and decided to pacify the Isfahanis by favor rather than force. He declared an amnesty after his victory and succeeded in attracting to his side much of the Isfahani army. After taking over the region through a combination of attraction and force he proceeded to Isfahan. The city, which was in great want, uncharacteristically offered no resistance and the prince rewarded its population by declaring tax relief. According to Ḥāfiẓ-i Abrū, Pir Muhammad was known for his control over his army and for forbidding extortion from the population.[55]

[49] Ḥāfiẓ-i Abrū, *Zubdat*, 175–77; Yazdī, *Ḥasanī*, 15–16. Ḥāfiẓ-i Abrū, in his geography, states that Pir Muhammad had disagreed with Iskandar before his expedition and had come to Yazd to confront him, but when he arrived, the notables made peace between the two brothers (Ḥāfiẓ-i Abrū, *Jughrāfiyā*, vol. II, 325).

[50] Ḥāfiẓ-i Abrū, *Jughrāfiyā*, vol. II, 326–27; Ḥāfiẓ-i Abrū, *Zubdat*, 177–78.

[51] Ḥāfiẓ-i Abrū, *Zubdat*, 181–82, 283; Ḥāfiẓ-i Abrū, *Jughrāfiyā*, vol. II, 324.

[52] Ḥāfiẓ-i Abrū, *Zubdat*, 183. [53] Ḥāfiẓ-i Abrū, *Jughrāfiyā*, vol. II, 329.

[54] Ḥāfiẓ-i Abrū, *Zubdat*, 217–19.

[55] Jaʿfarī, *Tārīkh-i kabīr*, 46–47; Ḥāfiẓ-i Abrū, *Zubdat*, 219–21.

It was unfortunate for the cities of Fars that Pir Muhammad was murdered on 3 Muharram, 812/May 18, 1409, and that the more volatile and ambitious Iskandar seized the opportunity presented. The murder took place during an expedition against Kerman, in which Iskandar was accompanying Pir Muhammad, and the perpetrator was the Shirazi commander Husayn Sharbatdar mentioned above. Husayn killed Pir Muhammad in his tent at night with a band of common soldiers. He next looked for Iskandar, planning to kill him too and when he failed to find him, he gathered other emirs, many of them Chaghatay, and led an army against Shiraz.[56]

Iskandar was in Pir Muhammad's camp when he learned of his brother's murder, and we are told he was so upset that he could not dress himself. He mounted his horse in his shirt and cap, wearing only one boot, and rushed to Shiraz intending to gather his family and flee. It was the city leaders of Shiraz who pushed for its defense. The ward headmen and local commanders met together and resisted the surrender of the city. The historian Taj al-Din Hasan names three men within this group – the ward headmen Kulu ʿAlaʾ al-Din and Sulaymanshah Qassab, and Khwaja Nur al-Din Kamal, discussed in the last section, who was probably a regional commander (*sardār*). They stated that they would not accept Husayn Sharbatdar, who, being a child of their own city, and having murdered his master, was not acceptable as ruler. They then pledged *bay'at* to Iskandar and fortified the gates and towers. When Husayn and his army arrived one of the ward headmen came to the gate and declared that the population would not admit them, and almost immediately the emirs who had joined Husayn, including many Chaghatay commanders, began to desert into the city.[57] By the time of the noon-day prayer only fifty horsemen remained with Husayn, who fled but was seized and brought back to the city. Iskandar made an example of him by shaving his eyebrows and beard, dressing him in women's clothing and displaying him to the public; then he hacked him to pieces and sent his head to Shiraz, and each hand and foot to a different city. Two other servitors who were involved in Pir Muhammad's murder also received exemplary punishment; one had stripped the clothes off the dead prince and left him naked and the other had set fire to stores of grain.[58]

Having taken – or been given – the rule of Shiraz, Iskandar lost no time in claiming power throughout the region. However, when he sent his emissary to Yazd the emirs whom Pir Muhammad had stationed there, led by the fortress keeper (*kotwāl*) Aba Bakr Khazin, refused to acknowledge Iskandar's rule.[59] Iskandar sent troops to besiege the city and for a while the city population obeyed Aba Bakr Khazin and resisted, but the notables of the city tired of the

[56] Ḥāfiẓ-i Abrū, *Zubdat*, 341–42.
[57] Yazdī, *Ḥasanī*, 17–18; Ḥāfiẓ-i Abrū, *Zubdat*, 342–45. For differences among the accounts of these events, see Manz, "Local Histories of Southern Iran."
[58] Yazdī, *Ḥasanī*, 18–19.
[59] Ḥāfiẓ-i Abrū, *Zubdat*, 345; Jaʿfarī, *Tārīkh-i kabīr*, 51; fol. 300b; Yazdī, *Ḥasanī*, 19.

siege and sent out the prominent local Sufi shaykh Farid al-Din ʿAbd al-Baqi as emissary. He made contact with Iskandar's vizier, Khwaja Mahmud Khwarazmi, who was one of the commanders on the expedition. Khwaja Mahmud, whom I discussed in the last section, was known to the notables of Yazd due to his work supervising Pir Muhammad's building projects. Together ʿAbd al-Baqi and Khwaja Mahmud went to Iskandar to plead for clemency. Iskandar met ʿAbd al-Baqi well and sent him back, but Aba Bakr refused to listen and continued the resistance. His rudeness to the shaykh met its appropriate punishment in the subsequent betrayal by his servitor Farrukhshah, who according to the local histories was the one who opened the door to Iskandar's armies. The troops took the city and killed a number of people held responsible for the resistance. We see here the caution characteristic of the Yazd notables, who rarely chose the path of resistance. In this case even the level of resistance they did condone may have been unacceptable. Sometime shortly after this it appears that Iskandar called the notables of ʿIraq and Yazd to him in Shiraz, and one of them at least, the judge Qutb al-Din Jamal Islam Masʿud, remained in Fars until he died in Darabjird in 815/1412–13.[60]

Iskandar's next goal was Isfahan, much more difficult to subjugate. Despite Pir Muhammad's clemency the city had not remained quiet. The circumstances leading to the crisis facing Isfahan in 812/1409–10 remain uncertain, since the sources relate different stories. Pir Muhammad had replaced his brother Rustam as governor with his own son, ʿUmar Shaykh, then about eight years old. ʿUmar Shaykh was unable to hold the city in the unsettled circumstances after his father's murder; either he fled before advancing troops, or he was pushed out in the course of a local rebellion. According to the "Tarikh-i kabir," when the Isfahanis heard of Pir Muhammad's murder, the commander of the Dudanga city section rallied the foot soldiers of the city and took control. Although the Chaghatay emirs put them to flight, the army sent after them joined the rebels.[61] At about the same time, Qadi Ahmad Saʿidi, on the grounds that Isfahan was empty of rulers, went to Azarbaijan to bring in the son of the former Muzaffarid ruler, Muʿtasim b. Zayn al-ʿAbidin, with troops provided by the Qaraqoyunlu. In the face of this action Iskandar set out to establish his rule by force. Although he defeated the Turkmen troops and Muʿtasim Muzaffari died in battle, Isfahan continued to resist him under the leadership of Qadi Ahmad, with the help of the city troops. After hearing that the Isfahanis were allowing in the emirs of his brother Rustam, Iskandar gave up the siege, leaving the surroundings of Isfahan in ruins.[62]

60 Jaʿfarī, *Tārīkh-i Yazd*, 151; Kātib, *Tārīkh-i jadīd*, 171, 180, 186.
61 Jaʿfarī, *Tārīkh-i kabīr*, 51; fol. 300b.
62 Quiring-Zoche, *Isfahan*, 24; Jaʿfarī, *Tārīkh-i kabīr*, 51–52; fol. 300b; Ḥāfiẓ-i Abrū, *Zubdat*, 345–49; Yazdī, *Ḥasanī*, 19.

For the next several years Isfahan remained a center of contention among the local Timurid princes, suffering yearly sieges while serving as a regional base sometimes for several princes at once. The city was under the influence of Qadi Ahmad Saʿidi, who allowed Rustam into the city and kept Iskandar's forces at bay. This changed in Dhuʾl-Hijja, 814/March–April, 1412, when Rustam, recently welcomed back to Isfahan by Qadi Ahmad, was persuaded by several of his chief emirs to use the opportunity of the Feast of the Sacrifice to kill him. The murder of Qadi Ahmad probably represents a struggle for power among the men close to Rustam, since the qadi had become involved in the politics of the Chaghatay emirs. As I have shown, he was part of Rustam's inner council and his family also appears to have entered into government service, as his brother was put in charge of the city's finances in 810/1407–08. According to the *Tārīkh-i kabīr*, there was at this time great confusion and want in Isfahan. The men encouraging Rustam against Qadi Ahmad were Asil Beg and Pir Hajji, who were among Rustam's most prominent emirs. It is possible that Amir Saʿid Barlas also played a role in Qadi Ahmad's downfall; he appears to have been back in Rustam's service at this time and was unlikely to have forgotten Qadi Ahmad's role in his earlier disgrace.[63] Rustam made no accusation against Qadi Ahmad but simply invited him to a feast, killed him and his son, and destroyed his house. The suddenness and ferocity of Rustam's action is puzzling, and it was certainly unwise. The Isfahanis turned against him and sent a messenger to Iskandar, asking him to provide a governor for the city. Although Rustam attempted to fight Iskandar, without the help of the population he could not hold out against him and he quickly left the city.[64] Iskandar made Isfahan his capital, and it is interesting to note that the first of his building projects in the city was the separation of the citadel Naqsh-i Jihan from the city.

It did not take long for Iskandar to expand his ambitions and adopt the title of Sultan. While Shahrukh was planning an attack on the Qaraqoyunlu, Iskandar began writing to rulers in neighboring regions calling for their allegiance, and he suggested to the kings of Sistan that they attack Shahrukh in Khorasan.[65] These actions brought him unfavorably to Shahrukh's attention, and thus in the beginning of 817/spring, 1414, the cities of Fars and ʿIraq-i Ajam again faced the necessity of choosing between rulers; now there was less uncertainty about the final outcome but the question of timing was tricky. In this case it was the leadership of Shiraz which displayed the greatest initiative and the main actors were the same ward headmen who had earlier been

[63] For Asil Beg and Pir Hajji, see Yazdī, *Ḥasanī*, 23; *Muʿizz*, fol. 104; Faṣīḥ Khwāfī, *Mujmal-i faṣīḥī*, vol. III, 221–22; Jaʿfarī, *Tārīkh-i kabīr*, 73; fol. 309; for Amir Saʿid Barlas, see Ḥāfiẓ-i Abrū, *Jughrāfiyā*, 331; Ḥāfiẓ-i Abrū, *Zubdat*, 349.

[64] Quiring-Zoche, *Isfahan*, 24–26; Jaʿfarī, *Tārīkh-i kabīr*, 55; fols. 302a–b; Yazdī, *Ḥasanī*, 23; Ḥāfiẓ-i Abrū, *Zubdat*, 395–99, 445–46. According to the *Tārīkh-i kabīr* Iskandar took Isfahan in 813/1410–11, but Quiring-Zoche chooses Ḥāfiẓ-i Abrū's dates, which seem more probable.

[65] Ḥāfiẓ-i Abrū, *Zubdat*, 501–05.

instrumental in securing the city for Iskandar. The upper-class city notables, not mentioned in the accounts of the attack by Husayn Sharbatdar, now also played a part. When Shahrukh first headed towards Fars in the beginning of 817/spring, 1414, the city leaders of Shiraz met together in the absence of Iskandar's governor Muhammad Sariq and decided to submit to Shahrukh. At this point, the ward headmen Kulu ʿAlaʾ al-Din and Sulaymanshah Qassab, with Khwaja Mahmud Yazdi and Sayf al-Din Kurdkhani, took matters into their own hands. They beat drums, put wood at the head of the streets, and encouraged women and children on the roofs to throw down stones and ashes, while the population called, "The city belongs to Shahrukh." They also plundered the houses of Iskandar's Turco-Mongolian officials and their dependents. Unfortunately for the pro-Shahrukh party, that very night Muhammad Sariq and Iskandar's young son Pir ʿAli arrived back in Shiraz. With Iskandar's agent Nur al-Din Kamal, they soon organized themselves, attacked the insurgents, and killed the leaders held responsible. For three days Iskandar's forces plundered houses and killed members of the population, until the sayyids and ulama persuaded them that the uprising was the work of the rabble and the population had suffered sufficiently.[66]

While the upper-class notables remain anonymous in the histories, the ward headmen are named, and they were the same people who acted in the crisis of 812/1409–10. It appears that the original decision to switch allegiance to Shahrukh was one on which all participants agreed; where the ward headmen diverged was in their quick mobilization of the population. We should perhaps be cautious in assuming that their actions went against the intentions of their notable colleagues. It is quite possible that the ward headmen served as scapegoats on the return of Iskandar's officials. The description of their followers as "rabble" might have served the same purpose, and we should note that in portraying the action against Iskandar as the impulse of an irresponsible minority, the ulama not only saved themselves but also managed to end the general punishment of the city.[67] The ward headmen involved in the incident paid with their lives, and we have no later descriptions of Timurid Shiraz which could allow us to discern whether their successors held significant power. Some time after this event Muhammad Sariq himself decided that Iskandar's fortunes were on the wane and, after consultation with the city notables, seized Iskandar's most loyal emirs, killed at least one of his *dīwān* officials, a relative of Fasih Khwafi, and sent a message of submission to Shahrukh.[68]

[66] Jaʿfarī, *Tārīkh-i kabīr*, 59–61; fols. 304a–b; Yazdī, *Ḥasanī*, 39–40. Iskandar's son Pir ʿAli is mentioned only in the *Tārīkh-i kabīr*, and according to Woods' genealogy, he died at the age of two.

[67] I have discussed epithets given to active city populations in Manz, "Nomad and Settled," 440–41.

[68] Ḥāfiẓ-i Abrū, *Zubdat*, 537–38; Faṣīḥ Khwāfī, *Mujmal-i faṣīḥī*, vol. III, 218.

A little later Turmush, Iskandar's *darugha* in Yazd, sent a message of submission to Shahrukh; he did this however in secret.[69] In the meantime Shahrukh had arrived before Isfahan with a large army. With Shahrukh's superior forces before them, some of Iskandar's emirs began to desert to Shahrukh, while local nomads likewise asked for his protection. We hear nothing about Isfahan's judge during the battle, and it is likely that the office had been robbed of some of its power. Nonetheless, the population did not lose its involvement in the fate of the city. At first they defended the walls with bows and arrows, but after failed negotiations and Iskandar's defeat in battle outside the ramparts, they invited in Shahrukh's troops, leading them up to the fortress, where Iskandar took refuge. We should note that, despite the invitation into the city, Shahrukh's troops set fire to the bazaar and spent the night in plunder before Shahrukh called them off. He then bestowed large sums of money on shrines and granted a one-third tax reduction for the year in order to aid the recovery of the region.[70] Having installed governors in the major cities of the region, he returned to Herat and his son Ibrahim Sultan became governor of Fars.

The next crisis arrived quite soon – once more provoked in part by Iskandar, who although deposed and partially blinded, remained enterprising. Taking advantage of the disturbances following Saʿd-i Waqqas' defection to the Qaraqoyunlu early in 818/spring, 1415, Iskandar persuaded his brother Bayqara to attempt to gain regional power. For Iskandar, this proved one act too many; he was captured by the Qashqaʾi nomads near Ganduman and handed over to Rustam, governor of Isfahan, who killed him and informed Shahrukh of his death. It appears nonetheless that Ibrahim Sultan had not yet established firm bonds of loyalty within Shiraz. He had arrested those of Iskandar's emirs still in the city, whose aid Iskandar and Bayqara had counted on, but these men escaped and joined Bayqara in his campaign. Ibrahim Sultan met Bayqara's forces outside the city and was defeated, in part because of the desertion of some of his forces including Masʿudshah Shul and a number of Iraqis. Ibrahim then returned to Shiraz at night, fetched his mother and some cash from the treasury and retreated to Abarquh. The notables of the city, including sayyids and judges, came out to invite Bayqara in.[71]

It seems likely that Bayqara enjoyed some support within the city, as well as from regional leaders like Masʿudshah Shul. The notables were quick to come over to him and, once in Shiraz, he rapidly organized paramilitary forces, whom Ḥāfiẓ-i Abrū unsurprisingly characterizes as rabble, thieves, and troublemakers. Bayqara also gathered an armed cavalry troop of about

[69] Jaʿfarī, *Tārīkh-i kabīr*, 61–62; fol. 305a.
[70] Quiring-Zoche, *Isfahan*, 26–30; Jaʿfarī, *Tārīkh-i kabīr*, 62–63; fols. 305a–b; Ḥāfiẓ-i Abrū, *Zubdat*, 530–38, 540–45, 550–54.
[71] Samarqandī, *Maṭlaʿ*, 180; Ḥāfiẓ-i Abrū, *Zubdat*, 591–96; Yazdī, *Ḥasanī*, 41; Jaʿfarī, *Tārīkh-i kabīr*, 64; fol. 306a.

5,000 and collected money from merchants and the population. When Shahrukh's army had arrived in Fars and was standing before the city, the Shirazis lost confidence in Bayqara and asked him to submit in order to spare the city destruction; this he agreed to do on 27 Ramadan, 818/December 1, 1415.[72] Shahrukh collected money from the city, fined a number of men and executed several emirs and viziers attached to Iskandar or Bayqara, but otherwise spared the city and handed out favors to a number of people.[73] After Shahrukh had reinstalled Ibrahim Sultan and exiled Bayqara, the region was relatively peaceful for about thirty years, with the partial exception of Isfahan. That city remained unquiet and played a crucial part in bringing on the next major challenge which faced the region: the rebellion of Sultan Muhammad b. Baysunghur in 849–50/1445–47, which will be the subject of the last chapter.

During the time we are discussing, southern and central Iran survived its share of natural disasters. It suffered rather less than most of the Middle East from the Black Death; the severe outbreaks of the plague were concentrated in Azarbaijan, Syria, and Khorasan.[74] The one outbreak of plague mentioned in our region was that of 810/1407–08 in Isfahan, where 20,000 people are said to have died.[75] In 818/1415–16 we hear of a famine in Iraq, while at the time of Sultan Ibrahim's invasion of Khuzistan in 824/1421, it was suffering from shortages due to drought.[76] The middle of the century was more difficult. In 845/1441–42 there were great rains throughout much of Iraq and Fars, leading to serious destruction – canals were damaged, a number of villages were destroyed in the southeastern regions of Shabankara and Na'in, and garden walls collapsed in Shiraz.[77] The devastation of the wars following Shahrukh's death in 850/1447 was aggravated by a general drought and famine in Iran, and in Yazd, it was compounded yet further by a disastrous flood in 860/1445–46 which destroyed many of the buildings in the southern suburbs.[78] It seems then that the timing of natural disasters in Iran coincided with the periods of greatest disorder, leaving the region relatively prosperous during the middle part of Shahrukh's reign, but intensifying the destruction of the later power struggle.

When we review the actions of cities in the face of regional power struggles, we see clear patterns emerging in the decision making of both cities and individuals. Of the princes, it was Iskandar who chose the path of adventure and for a brief time amassed considerable power, while Rustam preferred more cautious policies and in consequence lived longer. Among the cities we

[72] Ḥāfiẓ-i Abrū, *Zubdat*, 596; Jaʿfarī, *Tārīkh-i kabīr*, 65–66; fols. 305b–7a.
[73] Ḥāfiẓ-i Abrū, *Zubdat*, 602–606; Jaʿfarī, *Tārīkh-i kabīr*, 66; fols. 306a–7b.
[74] For the plague in Isfahan, see Samarqandī, *Maṭlaʿ*, 64; Jaʿfarī, *Tārīkh-i kabīr*, 47; fol. 299a. For Khorasan, see Faṣīḥ Khwāfī, *Mujmal-i faṣīḥī*, vol. III, 275–79.
[75] Jaʿfarī, *Tārīkh-i kabīr*, 47; fol. 299a.
[76] Ḥāfiẓ-i Abrū, *Zubdat*, 805–06; Jaʿfarī, *Tārīkh-i kabīr*, 73; fol. 309b.
[77] Jaʿfarī, *Tārīkh-i kabīr*, 111; fol. 330a. [78] Kātib, *Tārīkh-i jadīd*, 10, 106, 118, 157, 213.

can also see consistent differences; the notables of Yazd avoided trouble wherever possible, while the Isfahanis repeatedly initiated action, not waiting for the princes to propose it. They seem to have gone out to choose their ruler from among those available and remained loyal for as long as they found it feasible. Shiraz pursued a middle course; sometimes acting on its own when the outcome of the power struggle seemed predictable. There may well have been disagreements within the city about how bold or conservative a course to take, and the Shirazi ward headmen seem to have been the most aggressive, following an established tradition of political activism.

Behind these striking differences, however, we see one commonality: city populations rarely took action when not faced with the need to choose among contenders for power. The task of the city leaders was to ensure that the city followed the leader most likely to succeed, and the differences among cities lay in how soon they made that choice and how much risk they were willing to incur. If we look at the results of the decisions made, we see the dangers of aggressive action; the Isfahanis suffered repeated executions and massacres in retaliation for their daring. On the other hand they could reap significant rewards, and it is interesting to note that they apparently received the most generous tax relief when taken over after a struggle. Pir Muhammad, Shahrukh, and later Sultan Muhammad all offered them major exemptions, on a scale we do not hear of in other cities.

In contests for power among the princes, nothing succeeded like success, but failure was more common. Once order had broken down however, this wasn't a game one could choose not to play – the essential choice was whether to aim for a conservative policy, or to favor aggressive action in the hope of forestalling danger or achieving greater gain. No matter how cautious their actions, all cities suffered from the civil wars which accompanied changes in power. Sieges almost always brought depredations in the surrounding countryside and even compliant Yazd had to endure the passage of court and army, with the additional taxation levied to mount new campaigns. It is during crises that we learn about the power of city leaders, and it was probably at these times that their decisions had the greatest impact on regional government. During periods of peace they were also active but their interests were less starkly distinguishable from those of their Chaghatay rulers. When no wars had to be mounted, both Chaghatay and city populations could put their wealth and effort into the cities which were the focal point for the power of both groups.

Governors, emirs and notables in the life of cities

We often state that pre-modern governments were expected to oversee only the collection of taxes and the provision of military security. While central government certainly took neither full nor formal responsibility for social services, scholars have shown that the dynasty and its personnel were expected to undertake public works and that these made a significant difference to urban life. The building and repair of irrigation canals, mosques, madrasas, *khānaqāhs*, soup kitchens, cisterns, bazaars, and public baths were not demanded of the government, but they were considered part of good administration and, to a varying extent, they were provided.[79] Some works seem to have been undertaken directly by government order, while others were underwritten by individual officials with their own funds. Taxes and other extortions were often first turned into private wealth by officials and then partially returned to the public through individual charity. Within the cities, the interests of emirs, government functionaries, and notables could be quite close – not surprisingly, given the overlap in personnel between them. The building programs and cultural patronage undertaken within the cities of Fars and central Iran illustrate the background of mutual interest and collaboration which linked city elites to Timurid provincial government.

One can divide the impact of Timurid rule on urban cultural life into two spheres – that of the court and that of the city itself. Since cities are represented quite differently in our sources, we do not have the same information on all of them. For Shiraz and Isfahan we know primarily about the activities of the court, while for Yazd the opposite is true; we know little about court patronage and an exceptional amount about building projects throughout the city. The best we can achieve, therefore, is a composite picture of the relationship between the Timurid ruling stratum and the city population. What we can discover suggests that the governors and their entourage added significantly both to the intellectual life of the city and to its basic infrastructure.

Shiraz had long been a center of religious and literary culture, and continued to be so under Timurid rule. Several luminaries lived and wrote there during Shahrukh's reign. Muhammad al-Jazari, an expert in *ḥadīth* and *tafsīr*, left Samarqand after Temür's death and spent much of the rest of his life in Shiraz rather than his native Syria. It is clear that he attracted large numbers of students until his death in 833/1429.[80] Saʿd al-Din Taftazani's rival at Temür's court, Sayyid ʿAli Jurjani, also retired to Shiraz, where he was honored by Iskandar until he died in 816/1413, when the offices and emoluments he had enjoyed passed to his offspring.[81] His son was an influential figure in the city and countryside until his death in 838/1434–35.[82] Throughout Shahrukh's period, Shiraz remained a center for literature, book

[79] See, for example, Lapidus, *Muslim Cities*, 48, 68–78; Adam Sabra, *Poverty and Charity in Medieval Islam: Mamluk Egypt, 1250–1517* (Cambridge: Cambridge University Press, 2000), 4–6, 69–100.

[80] Samarqandī, *Maṭlaʿ*, 630; Ben Cheneb, "Ibn al-Dj̲azarī."

[81] Tritton, "al-Djurdjānī"; Samarqandī, *Maṭlaʿ*, 682.

[82] Jurjani's son Sayyid Muhammad was, among other things, the *mutawallī* of the Fazariyya madrasa. His stature and activities see are mentioned in the *Anīs al-Nās* (Shujāʿ, *Anīs al-Nās*, 156, 257, 259, 325–27).

production, and miniature painting.[83] Ibrahim Sultan's best known acts of patronage were his commissioning of historical works by the well-known poet and historian Sharaf al-Din ʿAli Yazdi, who seems to have remained for at least part of the time in Yazd, and a magnificently illustrated *Shahnama*, completed shortly after his death.[84] Other notable scholars and poets of Shiraz profited from the patronage of successive governors.[85]

We know little about the role the government and its personnel played outside the court and we have only rudimentary information on building programs in Shiraz. In 814/1411–12, while Iskandar based himself there, he constructed a citadel, named the Jalali fortress, surrounded by a moat.[86] Ibrahim Sultan was an active builder, remembered for the construction of a hospital, several madrasas and *khānaqāh*s. There is no information about individual buildings, except for a hospital built in 823/1420–21 and the madrasa he constructed outside the city near the tomb of Imamzada ʿAli b. Hamza b. Musa Kazim, where he was buried on his death in 838/1435.[87] Since we know that he had extensive repairs and building undertaken in Yazd, it is likely that he undertook similar programs of public works in Shiraz, but no direct evidence has survived. Despite our spotty information, we can conclude that the Timurid court contributed significantly to cultural life in Shiraz and also added to the religious and charitable institutions of the city. Certainly the city was a thriving center for religious culture during the period.

Isfahan seems to have profited less directly from Timurid rule. For two short periods the city served as a power center: under Iskandar b. ʿUmar Shaykh in 815–17/1412–15, and under Sultan Muhammad b. Baysunghur from 850–55/1447–51. Right after coming to power, in 815–16/1412, Iskandar began an aggressive building program centered around the citadel of the city. Since he intended to make Isfahan the capital of a larger realm, his projects there were more ambitious than those in Shiraz. After separating the Naqsh-i Jahan fortress from the city, he built a new fortress of baked bricks and filled the moat with water. He also constructed a palace, baths, a bazaar, a madrasa, and a hospital, while his emirs built houses for themselves.[88] It is not

[83] Jean Aubin, "Le mécénat timouride à Chiraz," *Studia Islamica* VIII (1957), 71–88; Priscilla Soucek, "Ibrāhīm Sulṭān ibn Shāhrukh," in *Iran and Iranian Studies. Essays in Honor of Iraj Afshar*, edited by Kambiz Eslami (Princeton, NJ: Zagros, 1998), 24–43; Ernst Grube, "The School of Herat," 146–78.

[84] Samarqandī, *Maṭlaʿ*, 675; Woods, "The Rise of Tīmūrid Historiography," 100–01; Thomas W. Lentz and Glenn D. Lowry, *Timur and the Princely Vision: Persian Art and Culture in the Fifteenth Century* (Los Angeles, Washington, D. C.: Los Angeles County Museum of Art, 1989), 126, 162.

[85] Faṣīḥ Khwāfī, *Mujmal-i faṣīḥī*, vol. III, 272, 277; Khwāndamīr, *Ḥabīb*, vol. IV, 334; Thackston, *Habibu's-siyar*, 518; Dawlatshāh Samarqandī, *Tadhkirat*, 366, 418, 424; Nawāʾī, *Majālis*, 19, 193; C.-H. de Fouchécour, "'The Good Companion' (*ʿAnīs al-Nās*), a Manual for the Honest Man in Shīrāz in the 9th/15th Century," in *Iran and Iranian Studies. Essays in Honor of Iraj Afshar*, edited by Kambiz Eslami (Princeton, NJ: Zagros), 1998, 42–57.

[86] Jaʿfarī, *Tārīkh-i kabīr*, 56; fol. 302b.

[87] Ibid., 79, 91; fols. 312b, 319a; Faṣīḥ Khwāfī, *Mujmal-i faṣīḥī*, vol. III, 244.

[88] Jaʿfarī, *Tārīkh-i kabīr*, 56; fol. 302b.

clear whether all these buildings were within the fortress. Iskandar Sultan likewise assembled a brilliant court, bringing religious scholars, literary figures, scientists, and writers from the whole of the region to the city. Most of these men dispersed after his fall, some, like Muhammad Jazari, to Shiraz, others to the eastern Timurid cities.[89]

For the rest of Shahrukh's reign Isfahan was a minor provincial capital, though, as far as we know, without major court patronage. The only figures whose reputation reached beyond the regional level were the religious scholars Sa'in al-Din ʿAli Turka and his nephew Afdal al-Din, neither of whom seems to have had easy relations with the dynasty. Under the governorship of Rustam Mirza and the family of Firuzshah I know of no written evidence on buildings and only one remaining structure, the Talar-i Timuri, used as the governor's palace. This building survives in altered form.[90] The buildings from the end of Shahrukh's rule, and from Sultan Muhammad's time, testify less to the activity of the governors than to the power and prestige of local notables and commanders. Two buildings, a cathedral mosque in the nearby stronghold of Warzana, built in 848/1444–45, and a winter hall added to the Friday Mosque within the city in 851/1447–48, were commissioned by the local commander ʿImad al-Din Mahmud b. Muzaffar Warzanaʾi.[91] The major surviving building commissioned by Sultan Muhammad b. Baysunghur is the mausoleum of the head (*naqīb*) of the Isfahan sayyids, Shah ʿAlaʾ al-Din Muhammad. It was erected in 852/1448 and endowed with a large *waqf*, whose administrators were the family of the sayyid.[92] The small number of Timurid buildings known in Isfahan probably indicates its lower provincial status, but we should also consider both the destruction wrought by the Qaraqoyunlu there after the departure of the Timurids, and the extensive building program of the Safavids.

The city in which we can most clearly trace patterns of construction is Yazd, which has two contemporary histories focused on the physical development of the city. We should keep in mind however that Yazd may have been atypical in a number of ways. Once the first power struggles in Fars were over, Yazd enjoyed almost thirty years of peaceful rule under Shahrukh's emir Jalal al-Din Chaqmaq who, with his wife, was a consistent and intelligent patron of arts, architecture, and public works. It is likely that Amir Chaqmaq expected to pass his governorship on to his children. We find his son Shams al-Din Muhammad active as a builder and, towards the end of Shahrukh's reign, as

89 For the personnel gathered around Iskandar Sultan at Isfahan, see Richard, "Un témoignage inexploité," 45–72; Samarqandī, *Maṭlaʿ*, 315.

90 Hunarfar, "Iṣfāhān dar dawra," 14.

91 Ibid., 7–11, 14–15. ʿImad al-Din was a commander (*sardār*) of Isfahan, mentioned serving under Sultan Muhammad (Ṭihrānī Iṣfahānī, *Diyārbakriyya*, 295).

92 Hunarfar, "Iṣfāhān dar dawra," 17–18; Jean Aubin, "Note sur quelques documents Aq Qoyunlu," in *Mélanges Louis Massignon* (Damascus: Institut Français de Damas, 1956), 135–37; Golombek and Wilber, *Timurid Architecture*, 382–83, 412–14.

deputy governor. One of his descendants was still active and powerful in the region in the late seventeenth century.[93]

Yazd was less dependent on agriculture than Shiraz or Isfahan; the region was apparently not self-sufficient in food and specialized in commerce and industry, particularly in silk and other textiles.[94] There was also a strong local confectionery industry.[95] Both notables and emirs were involved in trade, and among the common architectural projects were the building of bazaars, caravanserais, and mills.[96] It is probable that the emirs and governor drew some of their income from trade and industry, a practice which had been prevalent in the Mongol period.[97] Yusuf Jalil, who was *darugha* under Temür, built a mill which remained active throughout Shahrukh's period, and Amir Chaqmaq's wife Fatima Khatun built another, which was the closest mill to the city.[98] Muhammad Darwish, made *darugha* of the city by Shahrukh in 818/1415–16, built a caravanserai near the Mihrujird gate on the south of the city during his short tenure and Amir Chaqmaq, when he developed the Dahhuk Safali quarter outside the city, included a confectionery, caravanserai, and a bazaar containing shops with chambers.[99] Officials who came to Yazd on tax and *dīwān* business also added to the commercial structures, as did prominent local men, who often constructed bazaars near their houses and religious complexes.[100] The evidence thus suggests that almost all the wealthy elite in Yazd were involved with commerce or artisanal production and contributed to its infrastructure. However, we do not know to what extent such interest and support existed elsewhere.

In other ways, building programs in Yazd probably resembled those of other cities. Each new ruler marked his takeover with construction projects; there was a need to put one's own stamp on the city, to outdo earlier rulers.[101]

93 Miller, "History of Yazd," 135; Kātib, *Tārīkh-i jadīd*, 98, 100, 168, 201, 236, 266; Mustawfī Bāfqī, *Mufīdī* , vol. III, 265, 742, 882.

94 Quiring-Zoche, *Isfahan*, 9–10; Limbert, "Age of Hafez," 118–23, Ḥāfiẓ-i Abrū, *Jughrāfiyā*, vol. II, 110. The comment Ḥāfiẓ-i Abrū makes about the dependence on outside provisions is also found in Mustawfī's geography, though not in the *Farsnama* of Ibn Balkhī (Abu Zayd Aḥmad Ibn Balkhī, *Fārsnāma*, edited by Manṣūr Rastagār Fasāī [Shiraz: Bunyād-i Farsshināsī, 1374/1995], 287–8; Mustawfī, *Nuzhat*, 74).

95 Miller, "History of Yazd," 200–01.

96 The only other Timurid city of the period well enough documented to allow comparison is Herat, where we know of relatively little commercial building by officials. However, the difference in the type of source available may account for this impression.

97 For the involvement of Mongols in trade and industry, see Thomas Allsen, "Mongolian Princes and their Merchant Partners," *Asia Major*, 2 (1989), 83–126.

98 Kātib, *Tārīkh-i jadīd*, 98–99. 99 Ibid.; Jaʿfarī, *Tārīkh-i Yazd*, 180.

100 The famous Dar al-Fath built by Temur's tax collector Salar Simnani contained two rows of shops. Nur al-Din Kamal, *mubashir* of taxes, built shops in 831/1427–28, and Shah Nizam Kirmani built two rows of shops outside the entrance to the mosque complex (Kātib, *Tārīkh-i jadīd*, 92, 96, 111, 225). For commercial buildings by the city's elite, see, for instance, Kātib, *Tārīkh-i jadīd*, 111, 113.

101 A particularly clear expression of this is given in the account of Shahrukh's takeover of Yazd after his victory over ʿUmar Shaykh's sons (Kātib, *Tārīkh-i jadīd*, 148–49).

Yazd had been a stronghold of the Muzaffarid dynasty and the last Muzaffarid governor there, Shah Yahya, had done much to develop the city, thus setting demanding standards for the Timurid rulers who followed. The major Timurid buildings began with a new fortress, named Mubarakshah, built by Temür on the southern edge of the city after the suppression of the 798/1395–96 uprising. When Iskandar became governor of Yazd in 808/1405–06, he enlarged the city ditches and the citadel, in which he built a handsome palace.[102] After seizing and deposing Iskandar in 809/1406–07, Pir Muhammad sent Khwaja Mahmud Khwarazmi to repair and add to the city's main cathedral mosque.[103] When Shahrukh had defeated the sons of ʿUmar Shaykh in 818/1415–16, his *darugha* built a new caravanserai there.[104]

Both the central ruler and the governors of Fars commissioned building projects in Yazd and sent agents there to supervise them. While Iskandar was governor of Fars, Mahmud Khwarazmi was again in Yazd, where he repaired the buildings of Iskandar in the Cham-i Taft, a station on the way to Taft which was crucial to the city for its water supply, and he is recorded as coming for a third time, probably towards the end of Ibrahim Sultan's governorship, to undertake more extensive repairs throughout the city, including on the bazaars.[105] While Muhammad Darwish was governing Yazd, Shahrukh invested in buildings there through his tax agent, Shah Nizam Kirmani. Shah Nizam repaired the cathedral mosque inside the city and added significant improvements including an assembly hall, a storeroom, and an entrance way with a row of shops. He also enlarged and decorated one of the city's wells.[106]

From 823/1420–21, under the governorship of Amir Chaqmaq, building activity continued without the destruction and financial hardship which accompanied changes of rule. The governor and his family, Chaghatay emirs, and local members of the elite helped to repair and improve numerous buildings inside and outside the city walls and undertook significant new development in the city suburbs. We can see a number of patterns here. First, the Timurids and their servitors usually developed areas which had been favored by the Muzaffarids or by local notables. Second, in most areas, the city population and the Timurid elite were both active builders, sometimes adding separately to the same building complex.[107] There can be no doubt that the Timurid administration and its personnel made a major contribution towards the public buildings of Yazd.

[102] Kātib, *Tārīkh-i jadīd*, 92. [103] Ibid., 95.
[104] Ibid., 111. [105] Ibid., 201, 218.
[106] Ibid., 95–96, 223; Mustawfī Bāfqī, *Mufīdī*, vol. III, 157–59.
[107] My conclusions differ from those of Renata Holod-Tretiak, who posited greater separation between the Timurid rulers and the city elite, in part because the Timurids developed regions largely outside the city walls (Holod-Tretiak, "Monuments of Yazd," 128–29).

Amir Chaqmaq and his wife Bibi Fatima continued many of the undertakings of earlier rulers: the repair of palaces and administrative buildings inside the citadel, the restoration of irrigation canals, the repair of the old cathedral mosque, and the building of a *ḥammām* inside the city, along with the creation of gardens outside it. Less eminent functionaries, and a few emirs serving the dynasty, likewise contributed to public welfare. Mihtar ʿAlishah Farrash, a servitor of Amir Chaqmaq, contributed to the mosque at Musallah ʿAtiq.[108] Yusuf Chuhra b. Hajji Halabi, who served as *darugha*, and who was born in the Dahhuk Safali quarter, though his name suggests a Syrian origin, undertook several building projects in his quarter, including a madrasa and camel stable. He also built a garden for himself in the Naʿimabad region near those of other emirs.[109]

The region of Ahristan, south of the walls, had been developed by the Muzaffarids as a garden district for the dynasty and its servitors and the Timurids continued to build gardens there as well as residences for Chaghatay emirs. In addition it already had several mausolea and remained a popular burial site during Shahrukh's period.[110] Numerous canals came into this district from the uplands of Taft to the west, which made it an important location for mills, including the one built by Temür's *darugha*, Yusuf Jalil. Iskandar's *darugha*, Amir Turmush, built an addition to the local mausoleum of Mamanuk, with two domed chambers and a winter mosque, and his son, Sayyidi Ahmad Mirak, renounced his military career to live as a relatively well-to-do *darwīsh* in this area, where he built a house for his offspring at an existing mausoleum, with a public bath (*ḥammām*) and facilities for feeding travelers.[111] The quarter was not only a site for the residences of Chaghatay emirs. Two viziers of Yazdi provenance, Iskandar's vizier Hafiz Razi and Pir Husayn Damghani, who held local office under Chaqmaq, also developed the region. Hafiz Razi built a madrasa where he was buried, and Pir Husayn built a complex, including a mosque with a minaret, a grave and a *khānaqāh*, a garden, a cathedral mosque, a number of assembly halls (*jamāʿatkhānas*), a waterhouse, and a shop.[112]

The region between Ahristan and the Mihrijird gate of the city had begun to develop in the Muzaffarid period and became a major focus for building under the Timurids. The quarter was the site of several family graveyards and some commercial establishments, particularly those of the wealthy Abiwardi merchant family whose complex probably began in the early part of Timurid rule.[113] In 828/1424–25 the vizier Shams al-Din Muhammad Tahir, sent from Herat to serve in Yazd, constructed a bazaar of fifty shops in the Sararig or

[108] Kātib, *Tārīkh-i jadīd*, 118. [109] Ibid., 145, 212.
[110] Ibid., 186–87, 197. [111] Ibid., 200, 218. [112] Ibid., 118, 147.
[113] Many buildings are ascribed to Shams al-Din Abiwardi, whose son was a notable in the latter part of Chaqmaq's governorship.

Dahhuk Safali quarter just south of the gate.[114] Beginning in about 830/1426–27, Amir Chaqmaq built a large new complex there with a cathedral mosque, a madrasa, a bath, and a *khānaqāh* along with a bazaar and caravanserai. The religious buildings were supported by a sizeable *waqf*, including both land and commercial property, of which a copy has been preserved.[115] Chaqmaq's building project added considerable value to the area – providing a good bath for general use, food for the poor in the *khānaqāh*, and rooms for most of the merchants coming to the quarter in the caravanserai. Due to the restoration of the canal to this quarter, water became more freely available and the city elite added new buildings.[116] Several prominent merchants, along with other government functionaries and emirs, erected magnificent houses, commercial establishments, and religious foundations.[117]

In some other quarters it appears that the original development came from local city elites, and that emirs and government personnel continued these public projects. The Musalla ʿAtiq quarter, west of Sararig, for instance, seems to have been of particular interest to the family of the prominent sayyid Amir Shams al-Din Khidrshah; he and his son had houses and gardens here and built a mosque, with an *imām* and a *ḥāfiẓ*, a caravanserai, a stable and shop, and a waterhouse. They also repaired the older mosque built by the Musalla. Chaqmaq's servitor Mihtar ʿAlishah Farrash then contributed a platform for *muʿezzin*s to the mosque, while other government functionaries restored the nearby district of Chaharminar. Another quarter that profited from the interest of Amir Chaqmaq and his family was Sar-Ab-i Naw, east of the city, which contained the mausoleum of the local shaykh Taqi al-Din Dada and lay on the road to the village of Bundarabad where his *khānaqāh* was situated. Here the Muzaffarids had built houses and a madrasa, and in 798/1394–96 one of the local notables added a mosque; later still Fatima Khatun added a mill and a cupola.[118]

Timurid emirs and urban notables sometimes supported the same buildings. The two most important mausolea in the city, those of the Imamzada-i Maʿsum and of Taqi al-Din Dada, received additions from both groups. In one case, we know of active collaboration in the planning and funding of a building. When the emir Hamza Chuhra became governor in 846/1442–43, he collaborated with a group of notables to build an *ʿīdgāh* outside the city; each

[114] Kātib, *Tārīkh-i jadīd*, 111.

[115] Mustawfī Bāfqī, *Mufīdī*, vol. III, 871–84; Īraj Afshār, *Yādgārhā-i Yazd. Muʿarrafī-i abniyya-i tārīkhī wa āthār-i bāstānī*, 3 vols. (Yazd: Anjumān-i Āthār-i Millī, 1374/1995), vol. II, 162–83.

[116] Kātib, *Tārīkh-i jadīd*, 96–100, 220; Jaʿfarī, *Tārīkh-i Yazd*, 64, 95, 100, 180, 188–89.

[117] Kātib, *Tārīkh-i jadīd*, 108–09, 111, 113, 116, 145, 224. The major builders came from two families: the family of Khwaja Sadr al-Din Abiwardi and the Qannadi family. The only date we have for these buildings are those of 848/1444–45 for those of Burhan al-Din al-Qannadi, whose brother ʿAlaʾ al-Din also built in the area, and 840/1436–37 for a well house built by a Hajji Jan Tabrizi (Kātib, *Tārīkh-ī jadīd*, 113, 116).

[118] Kātib, *Tārīkh-i jadīd*, 98, 109–10, 117–18, 162, 225–26.

man contributed part of the necessary sum. The men he convened were the city judge, several viziers including ʿImad al-Din Masʿud, and the sayyid Jalal al-Din Khidrshah, a wealthy patron of religious institutions with strong Sufi connections.[119]

The city elite of Yazd were major patrons of architecture throughout Shahrukh's reign.[120] Although the most ambitious structures were built by governors or the agents of Timurid rulers, the greatest number of building projects mentioned are those by the notables. They were particularly active in funding mausolea and some created elaborate family complexes of gardens and houses, which often included buildings for public use and occasionally rental property.[121] This activity seems to have increased as Shahrukh's reign progressed; of the buildings whose dates are given, the largest concentration is in the 840s/1437–47.[122] Local elites built residences both in the old city and in the newer suburbs, with some gardens in Ahristan and similar districts. Here they differed from the Chaghatay emirs who built their residences either in the citadel itself or in the garden districts outside the walls.

I will describe the building programs of two families that produced prominent notables of the city: the vizieral family of ʿImad al-Din Masʿud and the merchant family of Sadr al-Din Abiwardi. Their constructions illustrate both the wealth of the Yazd elite and the community patronage which lay behind the power of notables. ʿImad al-Din Masʿud built a large house in his family's quarter near the ʿAbd al-Qadiriyya Madrasa, not far from the fortress. Next to the house he created a garden containing a pavilion with painted decoration, beside which he constructed an administration building (*dīwānkhāna*) and a large court or vestibule (*pīshgāh*), connected by a path to a mosque he

119 Kātib, *Tārīkh-i jadīd*, 227. For other building activities of Jalal al-Din Khidrshah, see Kātib, *Tārīkh-i jadīd*, 121, 171, 187, 205. On page 121 the historian mentions him in the present tense. It seems likely that Jalal al-Din was related to the sayyids Shams al-Din Muhammad Khidrshah and his son Qutb al-Din, who built in the Musallaʾ-i ʿAtiq quarter, but there is no mention of any relationship (Afshār, *Yādgārhā*, vol. I, 149–50).

120 The two doctoral dissertations written on Yazd, those of Isabel Miller and Renata Holod-Tretiak, have suggested that the notables were less wealthy and less active in building during the Timurid period than earlier. The argument is based in part on a comparison to the fourteenth-century foundations of the sayyids Rukn al-Din and his son Shams al-Din, both much larger than anything constructed by local notables of the Timurid period. One should recognize however that these sayyids had not been simply local functionaries, but administrators for a large region and closely connected to the immensely powerful vizier Rashid al-Din. Their income did not come only from Yazd, nor was their building program limited to it. In the Muzaffarid period likewise, Yazd was a center for power in a way which did not obtain for the Timurid period (Holod-Tretiak, "Monuments of Yazd," 97–99, 125–29; Miller, "History of Yazd," 216–18, 229–32; Jean Aubin, "Le patronage culturel en Iran sous les Ilkhans. Une grande famille de Yazd," *Le monde iranien et l'Islam* III [1975], 107–18).

121 Examples include the buildings of Sayyid Ghiyath al-Din ʿAli al-Husayni (Kātib, *Tārīkh-i jadīd*, 100–03) and the family of the sayyid Amir Shams al-Din Khidrshah, mentioned above (Kātib, *Tārīkh-i jadīd*, 109–11).

122 Kātib, *Tārīkh-i jadīd*, 93, 101, 106–07, 111, 113, 116–17, 119, 122, 144, 147–49, 168, 171, 187, 189, 211, 216–17, 224.

built, again with painted decoration. He went there for his five daily prayers. The mosque was completed in 845/1441–42 and had an endowment for an *imām*. In the Kuy-Pahluk or Chahar Minar district, west of the city wall, he built a reservoir of baked brick with tile decoration, including an inscription, another mosque, a mausoleum for his relatives, where the poor were fed (finished in 849/1445–46), and, finally, a madrasa, still unfinished at his death. His brother built a cistern for the use of several quarters of the city, completed in 845/1441–42, and another administration building. Finally, ʿImad al-Din's son, Diya al-Din, who also became vizier, completed his father's complex, adding several more houses and a particularly beautiful summer apartment with tile decoration, built a new public bath for women, and restored his uncle's cistern.[123] We see here a complex which allowed the family to provide hospitality and to attend to business, providing clients and petitioners with an appropriate place to wait as well as a mosque for their religious needs. In addition, they created a memorial to the family as a whole, several religious institutions, some offering charity for the poor, and finally baths and cisterns which served the public in more than one quarter of the city.

The Abiwardi family owed its position to trade and undertook an even more impressive building program, which centered on commercial services. The founder of the family, Hajji Sadr al-Din, was said to be the richest man in the city. He built several contiguous houses in the Sararig district, with a covered entryway where merchants from Yazd and other cities waited to see him every morning. In addition he provided a cistern for the use of the quarter near the house, a meeting house where the Qurʾan was recited and prayers read, and public baths for both men and women. Also in Sararig he built a caravanserai for visiting merchants, where traders from Rum and Shirwan stayed and much of the business of silk merchants was conducted, and another caravanserai in the bazaar of Sararig. His son Zayn al-Din mentioned above as a notable, repaired a mausoleum in the Ahristan district, with his brothers, he built a madrasa with a burial place for their father, and next to it a cistern.[124] Considering the wealth and the wide-ranging commercial influence of this family, it is not surprising to see one of them among the active notables.

If we look at the outside governing stratum of Yazd and at its local elite, we see two groups which had a number of common interests but also separate identities and spheres. Both Turco-Mongolian emirs and viziers from outside often served for long periods in Yazd and came to identify their interests with the city. The madrasas, mosques and *khānaqāh*s built by the Chaghatay elite provided a livelihood for the local ulama, and commercial buildings also added to the amenities of the city. The cooperation between the urban

[123] Kātib, *Tārīkh-i jadīd*, 105–07; Afshār, *Yādgārhā*, vol. II, 249–52.
[124] Kātib, *Tārīkh-i jadīd*, 109, 120, 146–47.

notables and the outside rulers can be seen in their contributions to the same quarters and the same buildings. The collaboration of the two groups in building projects and the positions created for ulama in new institutions created strong ties between local and outside personnel. On the other hand, while local and outside people developed the same quarters, the emirs do not seem to have lived inside the city except within the citadel. Emirs and members of the city elite used the same garden districts to the south of the city, but there is no record of Chaghatays building private dwellings within the city or its inner suburbs. While we see emirs and governors patronizing ulama and Sufi shaykhs, we do not see evidence of intermarriage, although the lack of information on this subject makes a firm conclusion impossible.

The close involvement of government administrators and Chaghatay emirs in the life of the cities parallels contemporary Mamluk practice. Studies of Mamluk society have emphasized the leading role of Mamluk emirs in public works, religious institutions, and commercial investment.[125] However, the economic control exercised by the Mamluk government and its emirs through monopolies and forced purchases does not seem to have existed in the Iranian cities. There are some accounts of property expropriations when a new ruler took over, and we should probably assume that the cases we hear of are a minority of those that occurred.[126] It is clear that significant commercial and agricultural property belonged to the administration and the personal property of Amir Chaqmaq and his wife, illustrated in the deed of endowment for their complex in Sararig, is certainly impressive. Some of their property came from members of the Yazd elite.[127] On the other hand, despite the economic resources held by the Timurid administration, significant economic power remained with the Iranian population. The wealth of the great merchant families indicates strength and the fact that a member of the Abiwardi family served as part of the governing council of notables upholds this impression. Thus the Chaghatay government personnel seems not to have dominated the economic life of Yazd.

Shiraz, Isfahan, and Yazd present a picture of significant development by the Timurids and their followers, which included both constructions of immediate interest to the dynasty – fortifications, citadels, and palaces – and numerous

[125] Lapidus, *Muslim Cities*, 44–78; Doris Behrens-Abouseif, "Patterns of Urban Patronage in Cairo: a Comparison between the Mamluk and the Ottoman Periods," in *The Mamluks in Egyptian Politics and Society*, edited by Thomas Philipp and Ulrich Haarmann (Cambridge: Cambridge University Press, 1998), 230; Jonathan P. Berkey, "Mamluks as Muslims: the Military Elite and the Construction of Islam in Medieval Egypt," in ibid., 163–64.

[126] When Iskandar b. ʿUmar Shaykh became governor of the city in 808/1405–06, he took new land into the citadel and we also hear that he gave a garden, formerly belonging to the Amirshahi family, to one of his servitors, Sultanshah Chuhra (Jaʿfarī, *Tārīkh-i Yazd*, 59; Kātib, *Tārīkh-i jadīd*, 92, 174). The *Tārīkh-i jadīd* also mentions the sale of some land to the regime as a petition sale in response to unjust exactions, but this refers to the Qaraqoyunlu (Kātib, *Tārīkh-i jadīd*, 207).

[127] Jaʿfarī, *Tārīkh-i Yazd*, 168; Kātib, *Tārīkh-i jadīd*, 224; Mustawfī Bāfqī, *Mufīdī*, vol. III, 876–80.

public works. In Isfahan and Yazd we see that the urban elite retained sufficient wealth to contribute significantly to the urban landscape. In times of stable government, then, Timurid rule fostered the prosperity of the cities. Unfortunately, peace could not be maintained. The disturbances beginning with Sultan Muhammad's rebellion in 849/1445–46 brought even greater hardship to Isfahan, Shiraz, and Yazd than the struggles I chronicled above. The author of the *Tarikh-i jadid-i Yazd* opens his history with a lament and a vivid description of the destruction wrought on his city by the struggle after Shahrukh's death, when the emirs and princes became petty tyrants and coveted the goods of the population.[128]

Conclusion

The history of Fars and central Iran shows a delicate balance between peace and war, good and bad government, prosperity and disaster. The region contained almost all the elements which made up Timurid government and society: the members of the dynasty and ruling elite, local nomadic and tribal populations, regional Iranian military forces, local rulers, notables, and the urban masses. These groups had more common than disparate interests. Certainly all of them profited in one way or another from peaceful conditions which allowed the advancement of agriculture and trade. Among the local populations, the one with the least stake in peace was probably the tribes, and we do find them quick to join whatever contest was going. Nonetheless, they do not appear as major predators or instigators of disorder. The lower classes of the cities and countryside might likewise get tired of paying for the luxury of others and choose the path of disorder; certainly the histories ascribe most urban disturbance to their activities, but there are few indications of significant urban unrest.

Under peaceful conditions, Timurid government was more of an advantage than a burden. In the cities they governed directly, governors and their servitors contributed significantly not only to the conditions required by the wealthy notables, in the creation of new religious posts and secure trade routes, but also to the infrastructure of city commerce and regional agriculture. This they did apparently in collaboration with the local elite. In addition, their mausolea and *khānaqāh*s dispensed free food, and baths and cisterns were provided in numerous neighborhoods, both improving the living conditions of the middle and lower classes. While the advantages were considerable, the price of Timurid overlordship was heavy and probably often unforeseeable – taxation and occasional exemplary punishments for those who got out of line. However, these were also not conditions that could be avoided under more local rulership.

128 Kātib, *Tārīkh-i jadīd*, 8–11.

With the advent of power struggles the equation changed drastically. What caused the breakdown of order was probably less ambition on the part of any one person than the difficulty of achieving and holding secure power. The men who took advantage of Temür's death were certainly ambitious for themselves, but they were probably also operating out of fear – if they did not act someone else would, to their detriment. When Iskandar left Hamadan for a career of adventure in Fars, he was facing local threats that he could not withstand. The notables of Isfahan sending off for a Muzaffarid ruler and Qaraqoyunlu troops were reacting to the danger of the kind of Timurid collapse they had seen in Azarbaijan, where conflict among Amiranshah's sons allowed the Qaraqoyunlu to take over. For those involved directly or peripherally in power struggles it was difficult to foresee who was likely to succeed, and unwise to maintain loyalty in the face of failure. The resulting fickleness lengthened regional struggles and intensified their destructiveness.

There were few people who did not suffer from these wars and, likewise, few who were either powerless or inactive. We cannot divide the population between contestants and non-contestants, nor can we identify any one group whose members consistently promoted peace. We find aggressive and daring people from all classes and groups involved in these contests: princes, emirs, local rulers, regional commanders, artisans, and ulama. What is interesting and sinister here is the unavoidable and yet voluntary participation of cities and their notables in contests for power – the increase in the power they wielded, and thus in the danger they incurred. City populations had a very considerable influence on the outcome of regional conflicts and while they could, like the Yazdis, prefer cautious action, none could remain uninvolved, unimportant, or safe. It is no wonder that the news of a ruler's illness or death struck terror into the hearts of the population.

CHAPTER 6

Political dynamics in the realm of the supernatural

In this chapter I am turning to politics of a different type from the dynamics I have been discussing. Politics in the religious sphere involved many of the same people; just as ulama and Sufi shaykhs were part of city and court politics, the ruler and his followers were active in matters of religion. In dealing with the politics of religion, I will go beyond the consideration of religious figures – Sufis and ulama – to examine the wider realm of supernatural power and its manipulation. It seems natural for men to try to experience something beyond the everyday world and to make contact with powers outside their vision. There is also a need to find intermediaries for forces which the individual cannot fully understand or control. Where in the twentieth century most people seek the help of experts, skilled in sciences beyond the understanding of most of us, earlier people sought other avenues to help and understanding. These paths were many and varied, including dreams and their interpretation, natural springs and other places considered efficacious for a variety of reasons, and men whose connection to God or to spirits gave them miraculous powers. What we now call the supernatural was at that time not a realm alien to the natural world, but an additional space from which to manipulate earthly affairs, and it was a field of action potentially open to all.

There were innumerable unseen forces and holy sites revered by the population which had no connection to organized systems of belief. Some popular practices may have been subsumed into Sufism, but many remained independent and provided a source of blessing and intercession mediated by neither shaykhs nor ulama. For lack of a better expression, I will call this kind of faith and practice popular religion, but it was not at odds with the religion of the urban ulama. The presence of the *jinn* and related magic in Islamic cosmology and law prevented a sharp demarcation between high and low religion.[1] The sources available to us suggest that we need not differentiate decisively between educated and uneducated believers; the use of

[1] P. Voorhoeve, "D̠jinn," in *Encyclopaedia of Islam*, 2nd edn.

magic formulas, the belief in the miraculous powers of unknown graves, and the value of dreams, are all well recorded in books written by the educated for the educated. The boundary between what I call popular religion and Sufism was also not sharply defined.[2] Both in personnel and in belief, there was also a large overlap between Sufis and ulama. The phrase, "learned in the exoteric and esoteric sciences," is a frequent introduction to Timurid biographical sketches. We cannot draw firm boundaries between lettered and unlettered, mystical and exoteric faith.

Local histories and grave visitation guides show how diffuse power was in the spiritual realm. Just as the government had no monopoly on armed force, so religious classes – ulama and Sufis – had no monopoly on power in the sphere of the supernatural. Numbers of other people could claim a connection to invisible powers and the respect that this brought with it. For some people this was an inherited trait, particularly for the large and important class of sayyids. It was accepted that the Prophet looked after his own, and that he was particularly likely to give counsel to his descendants. In most cities sayyids were in a recognized status group, mentioned among the notables coming out of the city to greet conquerors and other important arrivals. Families descended from famous religious scholars sometimes retained connection with a shrine or family graveyard. Others held extraordinary powers by virtue of personality and occupation: poets, *darwīsh*es and madmen, categories that sometimes overlapped, all seemed to have some access to the spirit world beyond that of the ordinary mortal. Most importantly rulers, in the Islamic world as elsewhere, were thought to rule through the favor of God and to possess special spiritual powers.

The politics of the religious sphere thus involved, in some way or another, almost all members of the population. Some men – the ruler, Sufi shaykhs, ulama – competed directly for spiritual or economic status. Others were people to be won over as disciples or patrons, and provided the necessary audience before whom contests for power or popularity were played out. It is not surprising therefore that its politics should have been constant, delicate, and complicated for all concerned. In this chapter I will start with what was on the ground: the sources of spiritual power independent of formal religion and open to all people. The next subject I address is the relationship of the religious classes, first to popular religious practice and second to rulers, who could also claim exceptional spiritual powers. Finally, I shall discuss rivalries within the religious classes, and show how they involved the broader society.

2 An example is the collection of charms and magic formulas collected in the album created for Iskandar b. ʿUmar Shaykh (Istanbul: Topkapi, MS B 411, fols. 238a, 159b; see also Lentz and Lowry, *Timur*, 148). For an excellent discussion of the issue of "popular" versus learned religion, see Ahmet Karamustafa, *God's Unruly Friends: Dervish Groups in the Islamic Later Middle Period, 1200–1500* (Salt Lake City: University of Utah Press, 1994), 1–11.

Access to the realm of the unseen

The ordinary person in the medieval Islamic world was not without independent access to the world of unseen spirits and the possibility of approaching the mysteries of God. Beyond the daily ritual of prayers and the possibility of personal invocation (*du'ā'*), there were two major avenues open to all: dreams and the visitation of graves or other holy places. In medieval Islamic thought, continued communication with the dead was not considered a matter of great difficulty – in its most basic form, grave visitation, many considered it a duty. The deceased were believed to remain in an intermediate state while awaiting the day of resurrection. During this period they were still affected by the actions of the living; prayers and alms performed for them might aid them in the Final Judgment, and in the meantime visits to their graves gave them pleasure.[3] While the living initiated contact with the dead by visiting their graves, actual communication had to come during sleep, when the soul became disassociated from the body and could unite with the souls of the dead – both to see them and to talk to them. Thus, dreams were an important conduit for communication with deceased friends and family. One common subject discussed between the living and the dead was the visitation and care of graves.[4]

The person in search of access to the supernatural might go to visit a living Sufi shaykh; their numbers were legion, and their attributes varied. This subject has been frequently discussed. There were many ways to approach the spirit world which have been less often studied and are worth describing here. Charms, amulets, and exorcism of evil spirits could be obtained by recourse to shaykhs, but also from specialists outside the religious professions, though unfortunately we have little information on these practices or the personnel who performed them.[5] People in search of help and blessing also had a variety of physical places to turn to including sites of natural power, unconnected to human agency.

The examination of holy sites illustrates the forces and concerns considered basic and powerful by the population, from the natural world and that of mythology to individual lives and the history of the community. These places were continually evolving; some may have been survivals of

[3] Johannes Pahlitzsch, "Memoria und Stiftung im Islam: Die Entwicklung des Totengedächtnisses bis zu den Mamluken," in *Stiftungen in Christentum, Judentum und Islam vor der Moderne. Auf der Suche nach ihren Gemeinsamkeiten und Unterschieden in religiösen Grundlagen, praktischen Zwecken und historischen Transformationen*, edited by Michael Borgolte (Berlin: Akademie Verlag, 2005); and Jane I. Smith, "Concourse between the Living and the Dead in Islamic Eschatological Literature," *History of Religions* 19, 3 (February, 1980), 229–31.

[4] Smith, "Concourse," 224–36.

[5] The son of Shaykh Nizam al-Din Khamush, active in Samarqand, dealt in charms and manipulation of the *jinn*, a profession which brought him into contact with royal women. Despite his father's stature, there is no indication that he was a Sufi adept (Kāshifī, *Rashaḥāt*, 196).

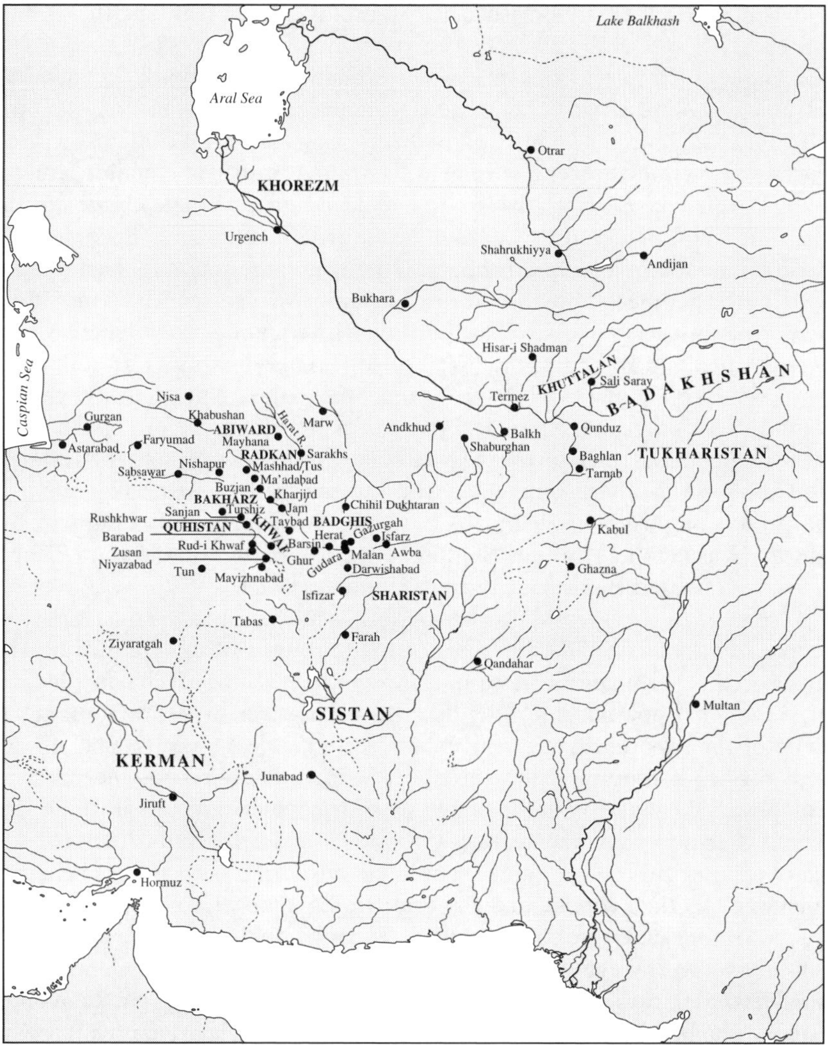

Map 3. The eastern Timurid regions

earlier religion prescribed by a class of holy people, but many were sites of power independently developed by the population at large. I will attempt to draw a kind of geography of this realm as it was portrayed by scholars who lived and wrote during the Timurid period, whose views may be taken to represent what was accepted among the educated elite. The graves and the practices they record are not described as questionable or as belonging to another more credulous class. Our sources make it clear that the attraction of smaller shrines and lesser religious figures was not confined to rural regions or to simple people, but flourished also in urban areas and among the learned classes.[6]

A number of miraculous places were distinguished purely by physical features and represented either natural wonders or locations of long-standing religious association. The historian Isfizari shows particular interest in such places and mentions several springs with healing properties, similar perhaps to those which have attracted a large clientele in Europe. One such site was the spring at Herat Rud and Awba, sought out by large numbers of people from Herat.[7] The fortress of Sharistan, near Isfizar, famous for its healing east wind, cured people with paralytic and consumptive diseases, and a mountain near Farah attracted people to a stone arch with trickling water, where wishes were granted.[8] In Bukhara, the "Well of Job" (Chashma-i Ayub), still active today, was the site of a healing spring and a tree that remained always green.[9] A number of graves mentioned in the guides have obscure origins; in some cases their names refer to the physical character of the place, for instance the Qabr-i surkh ("Red Grave"), and in other cases the name suggests that the person might come second to function. We can take as examples the Khwaja Rushana'i (Khwaja "Shining"), a grave of great fame and efficacy, or Khwaja Murad Bakhsh (Khwaja "Granter of Wishes").[10]

Access to the spirit world was available also at the mausolea of a variety of people. If we consider the numbers of any one type of miraculous grave – graves with "warm spirits" – we find those attached to Sufi shaykhs by and large the most popular and fully described. However, when we look at the realm of the supernatural as a whole, it becomes clear that the Sufi shrines were far from monopolizing the spirit world and may not indeed have represented the majority of the sacred sites from which the population sought benefit. Certainly the mausolea of well-known historical Sufis did not.

In the fifteenth century, most people saw visitation of graves as behavior sanctioned by the Prophet, and elaborate family mausolea providing regular prayer for the dead were commonplace. The introductions to grave visitation guides give several reasons to visit the graves of holy figures. Great ulama had declared that visitation was *sunna*; it was approved to visit graves of one's parents, teachers, saints and common people. *Ḥadīth* related that people who paid respect to graves would be visited after their deaths by angels. One came both to honor the dead and in the hope that when one died oneself, one would receive visits. Guides give the best days of the week to visit graves, both in

[6] See for example, Faṣīḥ Khwāfī, *Mujmal-i faṣīḥī*, vol. III, 197, 249, 252, 288; Kātib, *Tārīkh-i jadīd*, 175, 181, 184.

[7] Isfizārī, *Rawḍāt*, vol. I, 101–02.

[8] Ibid., vol. I, 109–10, 337–38. For similar examples, see ibid., 120, 303, 355; and Kātib, *Tārīkh-i jadīd*, 225.

[9] Muʿīn al-fuqarāʾ, *Mullāzāda*, 5.

[10] Other examples are Khwaja Zud Murad, and Pir Ghaybi. (Wā ʿiẓ, *Maqṣad*, 57, 59, 68, 83; Abū Ṭāhir Khwāja-i Samarqandī, *Samariyya. Dar bayān-i awṣāf-i ṭabīʿī wa mazārāt-i Samarqand*, edited by Īraj Afshār [Tehran: Farhang-i Īrān Zamīn, 1343/1965], 87).

general and for particular graves – Thursday and Friday were most auspicious for the first visit, because on these days alms and prayers for the dead would reach them sooner. On entering the burial ground, one greeted those buried there, men and women, believers and unbelievers.[11] The dead, particularly Sufis, might be aware of the state of those who visited them, especially on certain days of the week and on holy days.[12] While certain formalities are suggested for all visits, the more famous graves had particular formulas. Most of these involve religious actions – prayer and Qur'an reading – but some include other rituals such as circumambulation, or the gathering and throwing of gravel.[13]

The first duty was to the graves of one's own relatives, who could provide benefit in return. The maintenance and visitation of family graveyards could lead to a wider cult, particularly in the case of learned families who produced prominent members over several generations. In some cases, it appears that members of the family promoted the fame of their ancestors' graves. The author of the *Mullazada*, who lived in Bukhara and was descended from a prominent ulama family, describes his family's graveyard and states that many of his ancestors were people of power and had the ability to work miracles.[14] The author also mentions another family graveyard, where a descendant of the founder, visiting the grave, had told him that members of the unseen Sufi hierarchy (*abdāl*) gathered there.[15] A number of grave complexes were probably built and maintained originally as family centers, and later came to be more widely revered.

Many sacred sites, although they were graves, memorialized not individuals, but types of people who embodied virtues important to the community. Others commemorated historical dramas of particular importance or the sanctification of key aspects of human experience. One of the most prominent was the mausoleum of the forty girls, the "Chihil Dukhtaran," in Badghis near Herat, where people of the region went to seek grace; the shrine was so established that the area took its name from it.[16] Several other popular graves sanctified the plight of the weak, the lonely, or the unprotected. In death such people gained the power to attract spirits and to provide blessing. There was a Mausoleum of the Infants (Mazār-i Tiflagān), and a Mausoleum of the Maidens (Mazār-i Dukhtarān), where several young girls had gone to

[11] Mu'īn al-fuqarā', *Mullāzāda*, 10–15; Wā'iẓ, *Maqṣad*, 5–8. [12] Wā'iẓ, *Maqṣad*, 5, 8–9, 11.

[13] Wā'iẓ, *Maqṣad*, 51, 60, 68; Mu'īn al-fuqarā', *Mullāzāda*, 15; Muḥammad b. 'Abd al-Jalīl Samarqandī, *Qandiyya*, in *Dū risāla dar tārīkh-i mazārāt wa jughrāfiyā-i Samarqand*, edited by Īraj Afshār (Tehran: Mu'assasa-i Farhangī-i Jahāngīrī, 1367/1988–9), 28, 64, 82, 124. See also Christopher Taylor, *In the Vicinity of the Righteous: Ziyāra and the Veneration of Muslim Saints in late Medieval Egypt* (Leiden, Boston: Brill, 1998), 55–9, 70–78.

[14] Mu'īn al-fuqarā', *Mullāzāda*, 66.

[15] Ibid., 30–35. For the graveyard of another family of ulama, see ibid., 36.

[16] Isfizārī, *Rawḍāt*, vol. I, 145.

preserve their virtue and had perished. There was also another version of the story, but the guide's author states that contrary to what is said, the grave has great grace. In Samarqand there was a graveyard for the burial of strangers who died alone, far from their wives and children. Every week, it was believed, the good spirits of men would visit the strangers here and it was a place frequented by the people of God, where one could attain one's desires through a night vigil.[17]

When we come to the graves of identified figures credited with miraculous powers, we find several different types, symbolizing respected virtues and accomplishments. It is not surprising to find that miraculous graves attached to the person of the Prophet, the graves of sayyids, as a group, or of individual sayyids were honored. In Bukhara there were four famous graves of people supposedly buried with a hair of the Prophet. One of these, interestingly enough, belonged to someone identified as "*dihqān*," which might suggest a Persian origin.[18] The high respect accorded to learning is reflected in the powers attributed to the graves of eminent scholars and the compounds of eminent scholarly families. In Bukhara great efficacy was attributed to the Graveyard of the Seven Judges. In Samarqand, the world of learning was made clear to anyone who studied in the graveyard of the Juzjaniyan, where many ulama and authoritative jurists (*mujtahid*s) were buried.[19] The authors of guides noted ulama of all periods and often described their major achievements.[20] Graves which did not specifically have supernatural power attributed to them were visited out of respect and favored as burial places for other people of learning, since physical propinquity in death was considered a source of possible blessing.[21] Every city had several cemeteries centered around the graves of eminent scholars which enjoyed popularity among scholars over several centuries.[22]

New holy sites were continually developing, including many which commemorated the major dramas of history. The earliest years of Islamic rule are particularly strongly represented and it is clear that the establishment of Islam held continuing importance for the population. Graves of companions and relatives of the Prophet and of people involved in the Muslim conquest were popular and powerful. In Samarqand the grave of the Prophet's cousin Qutham b. ʿAbbas was the center of an important and lasting cult. His grave

17 Wāʿiẓ, *Maqṣad*, 53, 54, 56, 59; Samarqandī, *Qandiyya*, 44–45.
18 Muʿīn al-fuqarāʾ, *Mullāzāda*, 12, 56–57; Wāʿiẓ, *Maqṣad*, 55, 62, 105–06.
19 Muʿīn al-fuqarāʾ, *Mullāzāda*, 56–57; Samarqandī, *Qandiyya*, 31. For other examples, see, Muʿīn fuqarāʾ, *Mullāzāda*, 21, 28–29, 35, 36, 44, 66; and Wāʿiẓ, *Maqṣad*, 14, 18, 39, 43.
20 Muʿīn al-fuqarāʾ, *Mullāzāda*, 25, 36; and for other examples, see ibid., 28–29, 65.
21 Taylor, *In the Vicinity*, 45–46.
22 Examples are the tomb of Fakhr al-Din Razi in Herat, the Hawz-i Muqaddam and the graveyard of the family of Hafiz-i Kabir in Bukhara, and the mausoleum of the Salihin in Yazd (Wāʿiẓ, *Maqṣad*, 39, 45, 70, 74–76, 79, 89; Muʿīn al-fuqarāʾ, *Mullāzāda*, 34–36, 55–56; Kātib, *Tārīkh-i jadīd*, 170–71).

was known as the Shah-i Zinda ("Living King"), and had long been an important shrine; building there was particularly active in the eleventh and twelfth centuries, and again in the fourteenth and fifteenth. Ibn Battuta, who visited early in the fourteenth century, reported that the people of Samarqand went to the shrine on Tuesdays and Thursdays, and it was also revered by the Turco-Mongolian population, who brought offerings of livestock and money.[23] The Bukharan graves of the Prophet's companions were invented ones, as the scrupulous author of the *Tārikh-i mullāzāda* reports. He notes however the opinion of many ulama that sincere intention allowed benefit from such sites despite their false attribution.[24]

It is not surprising to find martyrs well represented among famous graves; these include individuals and groups who perished in the Islamic conquest along with some Muslims who died in the course of later events, such as the Mongol conquest. There are miracles attributed also to the graves of people credited with individual acts of courage against backsliders or heretics, and some who were martyred in unspecified circumstances.[25] Several epochs of particular emotional weight were commemorated through miracle-working graves, and the choice of event seems to vary from one place to another, reflecting the experiences of different regions. We find in Khorasan a number of effective graves connected to the ʿAbbasid revolution, in particular to the activities of Abu Muslim of Marw. There were miraculous graves of both Abu Muslim's victims and his supporters. After conquering Herat in 782/1380, Temür stopped to visit the shrine of Abu Muslim on the way to Nisa and Kalat.[26] The other person who had an important mausoleum was ʿAbd Allah b. Muʿawiyya, a member of the house of the Prophet who led a rebellion in Kufa in 744 and was later killed by Abu Muslim. His grave at Till-i Kuhandizh-Misrakh, by the old citadel of Herat, was reputedly a gathering place for spirits.[27] Three other local graves were connected to Abu Muslim, two commemorating supporters, a man and a woman, and one for someone simply killed at that time.[28] In Yazd the ʿAbbasid takeover was commemorated from a different side. Here the most important mausoleum was that of Imamzada Maʿsum, a descendant of Jaʿfar al-Sadiq who fled Baghdad after persecution by the ʿAbbasids and settled in Yazd where many of his progeny

23 Roya Marefat, "Beyond the Architecture of Death: the Shrine of the Shah-Zinda in Samarqand," PhD dissertation, Harvard University, 1991, 72, 86–89; Ibn Baṭṭūṭa, *The Travels*, vol. III, 568; Samarqandī, *Qandiyya*, 51–77.

24 Muʿīn al-fuqarāʾ, *Mullāzāda*, 16. This was a subject of controversy, see Taylor, *In the Vicinity*, 32.

25 Wāʿiẓ, *Maqṣad*, 12–13, 43–44 (Pir-i Taslim), 53 (Mazar-i shuhada), 54 (Masjid-i shuhada); Muʿīn al-fuqarāʾ, *Mullāzāda*, 39–40, 43–44; Khwāja-i Samarqandī, *Samariyya*, 63–64; Samarqandī, *Qandiyya*, 32, 46; Kātib, *Tārīkh-i jadīd*, 178, 188.

26 Shāmī, *Histoire des conquêtes*, vol. I, 84–85.

27 Wāʿiẓ, *Maqṣad*, 12–13; M. A. Shaban, *The ʿAbbāsid Revolution* (Cambridge: Cambridge University Press, 1970), 148–49. For similar examples, see Wāʿiẓ, *Maqṣad*, 56; Samarqandī, *Qandiyya*, 82.

28 Wāʿiẓ, *Maqṣad*, 14, 50, 53.

remained. Yazd also contained a memorial of a much more recent local event, namely the rebellion and siege of the city in 798/1395–96, which had provoked a famine that reportedly killed 30,000 people. The graveyard where its victims were buried held miraculous powers.[29]

Within the cosmology of Sufism, as Ibn ʿArabi and other scholars codified it, there was a hidden world of spiritual power (*wilāya*) controlled by a hierarchy of unrecognized Sufi saints. At the top was the *quṭb* or pole, who was one of four pillars (*awtād*) and seven saints who could travel as spirits while leaving behind a functioning body and mind (the *abdāl*). In addition there were holy men of great power called *afrād* who might also have one of the above functions, and numerous saints of lower rank. Although at any given time these ranks had to be filled by living shaykhs, those of the past retained stature and life in the unseen world.[30] All these saints met as spirits to consult together, and certain places were known to host them; major districts usually contained at least one such meeting place, and often there were several. It seems likely that the recognized Sufi hierarchy of saints combined in the popular imagination with other spirits, sometimes referred to by the general term *gharīb*, meaning foreign, or strange. Numerous places were frequented by such spirits.[31] According to the *Qandiyya*, they were particularly likely to gather in old mosques and cold graveyards.[32] They also congregated at a number of active mosques and miraculous graves, including those of the companions of the Prophet and some scholars of the exoteric sciences.[33] Where the *abdāl* and *gharībān* chose to appear seems to have been a matter of popular tradition rather than pronouncements from men of religion. It may also have been a phenomenon reported by people with a stake in the prestige of a certain place; I mentioned above the report of a man stating that he had met one of the *abdāl* in the graveyard of his own family.

Both natural sites and the man-made realm of graves offered the individual access to supernatural blessing without recourse to a religious figure of authority. Another even more direct access was offered by dreams. Like grave visitation, dreams offered continued communication with the dead: with relatives, teachers, and men of spiritual authority. Since the dead were still active and aware of the world, those with special spiritual powers were

[29] Kātib, *Tārīkh-i jadīd*, 151–54, 178; Jaʿfarī, *Tārīkh-i Yazd*, 166.

[30] Michel Chodkiewicz, *Le sceau des saints: prophétie et sainteté dans la doctrine d'Ibn Arabî* (Paris: Gallimard, 1986), 119–35; Éric Geoffroy, *Le Soufisme en Égypte et en Syrie sous les derniers Mamelouks et les premiers Ottomans. Orientations spirituelles et enjeux culturels* (Damascus: Institut français d'études arabes de Damas, 1995), 112–14.

[31] Geoffroy, *Le Soufisme*, 136; Leonard Lewisohn, *Beyond Faith and Infidelity: the Sufi Poetry and Teachings of Maḥmūd Shabistarī* (Richmond, Surrey: Curzon, 1995), 80.

[32] Samarqandī, *Qandiyya*, 130. Although part of the *Qandiyya* is Timurid, much of the material was added later, and it must be used with caution (Paul, "Histories of Samarqand," 75–81).

[33] Wāʿiẓ, *Maqṣad*, 58 (*gharibān* at the Masjid-i panja); Samarqandī, *Qandiyya*, 45 (good spirits of men in the strangers' cemetery), 67 (at the grave of Qutham); Muʿīn al-fuqarāʾ, *Mullāzāda*, 30 (graveyard of Satajiyya), and further, 39, 64, 70.

thought to retain them after death – if not indeed to enhance them – and thus they could offer significant help. For people closely attuned to the unseen, dreams and visions could function as a regular channel for communication with figures of the past and living people of spiritual authority. Because the ability to communicate with holy figures during sleep was an attribute of spiritual power, frequent dreams of Sufi masters or the Prophet were a mark of prestige, recorded in the biographies of shaykhs.[34] The decision about which Sufi master to follow or how to judge the relative sanctity of graves and scholars was quite frequently taken on the basis of visions.[35] The appearance of a person shortly after his death in the dreams of his acquaintance is reported as an indication of high stature.[36] In some cases people resorted to dream appearances in order to prevent the building of a dome over the grave, since this was a frequent practice frowned on by the strict ulama.[37]

The Prophet himself might appear to anyone, particularly on the performance of appropriate rites, but had an especial concern with his own descendants.[38] Sufi masters, likewise, looked after their own. This was noted of Shaykh Ahmad-i Jam (d. 536/1141), thought to have an exceptional concern for his family, even those who had not followed the Sufi path; this was one reason why the family deserved respect.[39] As is well known, dreams of future rule were a frequent part of dynastic legitimation, and within the ruling classes they were important as guides for conduct.

When we survey the realm of the supernatural in relation to mankind, we see that the population were surrounded by holy sites and phenomena offering spiritual benefits and pathways, and not necessarily dependent on shaykhs or ulama to mediate their relationship to unseen powers. The world of popular belief was not created by religious authorities – rather it was a sphere within which they worked, and attempted to establish authority. The mix of beliefs and practices was furthermore not static. The practices displayed in the Timurid period show the survival of earlier religious locations and the development of new holy sites which represented the central dramas of concern to individuals and to the community.

[34] An example is Sayyid Qutb al-Din Shirazi who saw the Prophet seventy-two times in dreams, and persuaded him to appear to others (Jaʿfarī, *Tārīkh-i Yazd*, 163–64). Jalal al-Din Bayazid Purani took intellectual problems directly to the Prophet (Khwāndamīr, *Ḥabīb*, vol. IV, 60).

[35] Monika Grönke, "Lebensangst und Wunderglaube: zur Volksmentalität im Iran der Mongolenzeit," in *XXIV. Deutscher Orientalistentag vom 26. bis 30. September 1988 in Köln: Ausgewählte Vorträge*, edited by Werner Diem and Abdoldjavad Falaturi (Stuttgart: F. Steiner, 1990), 395–96; and Isfizārī, *Rawḍāt*, vol. I, 207; Aubin, *Niʿmat*, 82–83; Wāʿiẓ, *Maqsad*, 26–27; Kāshifī, *Rashaḥāt*, 116, 182, 238, 251–52.

[36] Muʿīn al-fuqarāʾ, *Mullāzāda*, 26, 29; Wāʿiẓ, *Maqṣad*, 28, 38, 49.

[37] Kātib, *Tārīkh-i jadīd*, 168; Isfizārī, *Rawḍāt*, vol. I, 232–33.

[38] Kāshifī, *Rashaḥāt*, 325–28; Kātib, *Tārīkh-i jadīd*, 105, 159.

[39] Darwīsh ʿAlī Būzjānī, *Rawḍāt al-riyāḥīn*, edited by Hishmat Muʿayyad (Tehran: Bungāh-i Tarjuma wa Nashr-i Kitāb, 1345/1966), 44–48.

Power in the realm of spirits

The variety of contacts between humans and the spirit world could work both for and against the power of religious figures. There was widespread belief in powers existing between man and God – a world of beings interested in the actions and the condition of individual humans. The ordinary individual had points of access to this world, without the intercession of religious figures. What set Sufis and ulama apart was the possession of a body of knowledge and skills transmitted from one person to another in recognized ways. The possession of such knowledge conferred status but did not ensure control over the beliefs and practices of others. To gain prestige in the spiritual realm, they had to demonstrate superior powers of connection and to facilitate contact for others.

In the explanation of dreams, religious authorities found a natural place to work. The ability to interpret dreams authoritatively could add considerably to the prestige of a religious figure and to the size of his following and we see this gift ascribed to several prominent Timurid shaykhs. One of these was Zayn al-Din Khwafi, a major spiritual figure in Herat during Shahrukh's time. His skill was seen as a trait which increased his appeal at the expense of other shaykhs of the area.[40] Fadl Allah Astarabadi, the leader of the politically charged Hurufiyya movement was, likewise, an expert on dreams, and this skill formed an important part of his dangerous attractiveness. His book on dreams enjoyed considerable popularity. Talent in dream interpretation was also part of the attraction of some of the Nurbakhshi leaders, who built a religious movement on the mahdist claims of the shaykh Muhammad Nurbakhsh.[41]

The existence of holy places posed other opportunities and challenges. Many independently powerful sites became important for religious figures, as places whose spirits they could call upon and perhaps, through patronage, appropriate. Muslim religious figures and rulers often erected their religious buildings on sites already considered holy and thus acknowledged their power; in this way the sites kept their sanctity without threatening current religious hierarchies.[42] The stream called Juy-i Ab-i Rahmat of Samarqand was probably a place of this kind. A nineteenth-century source reports that people went there on the last day of the Persian year to perform ablutions and achieve blessing. The Timurid grave manual for the city informs us that shaykhs and ulama had agreed that this stream should be identified with the Prophetic *ḥadīth* that one of the streams of paradise was in Samarqand. A nearby mausoleum with healing water came to be identified with the prophet Daniel.[43]

[40] Kāshifī, *Rashaḥāt*, 120–21, 208; Jāmī, *Nafaḥāt*, 399, 403–04.

[41] Bashir, "Mysticism and Messianism," 48, 56, 118, 122; H. Ritter, "Die Anfänge der Ḥurūfīsekte," *Oriens* 7 (1954), 1–54.

[42] Ignaz Goldziher, "Veneration of Saints in Islam," in Ignaz Goldziher, *Muslim Studies*, translated by C. R. Barber and S. M. Stern, 2 vols. (Chicago, New York: Aldine, 1971), vol. I, 303–16.

[43] Khwāja-i Samarqandī, *Samariyya*, 34; Samarqandī, *Qandiyya*, 29.

The new sites which developed over the centuries were respected also by the religious classes, who demonstrated their authority by attesting to the relative stature of holy places. We find numerous examples of major shaykhs stating that spiritual benefit might be found in the visitation of popular sites whose qualifications might have been considered questionable, and sometimes they themselves led by example. Zayn al-Din Khwafi, for example, often visited the ancient Masjid-i Gunbad-i Khwaja Nur, saying that people of different religions had worshiped here and benefit came from it. This was a mosque near Herat situated by a healing spring and reputed to have been a holy place for four thousand years. Brave people sometimes built themselves hermitages nearby, because it required a stout heart to perform solitary exercises there. Khwafi also frequented the mausoleum of Shah Abu'l Qays, about whom no information is offered, and the powerful grave of sayyids at Imam Shish Nur (Imam "Six Lights").[44]

Another well-known shaykh, Zayn al-Din Taybadi (d. 791/1389), keeper of a shrine in northern Khorasan, attested to the power of the grave of ʿAbd Allah b. Muʾawiyya, who, as I mentioned above, had played an important part in the drama of the ʿAbbasid revolution. Since the shrine was famous as a gathering place for Sufi poles, or *quṭb*s, it could not easily be ignored. Taybadi spent a night at the mausoleum and reported that he saw no spirit higher than that of ʿAbd Allah. Another way in which the religious classes identified themselves with holy spots was to situate their graves there. Just as we find emirs and rulers choosing to be buried next to Sufi shaykhs, so we find Sufis choosing, as burial grounds, sites known for their power or prestige. In Bukhara, the particularly sacred mosque on the road to Fathabad, where many saints had seen the prophet Khidr, had become a major burial ground for Sufis, and in Herat the mausolea of Sultan Ghiyath al-Din Ghuri and Fakhr al-Din Razi were used by many ulama, along with the Mazar-i Sadat, near the Mahalla-i Tiflagan, the Abode of the Infants, and other less well-known sites.[45]

Some spots were the abode of frightening spirits, where a night vigil could be a fearsome experience. Such places offered a kind of test of courage for people seeking spiritual prestige. Two mosques mentioned in the *Maqsad al-iqbal*, the Masjid-i Panja and the Masjid-i Gunbad-i Khwaja Nur, are characterized as places in which a night vigil was "not for everyone."[46] For someone claiming spiritual credit therefore, visits served as testimony of psychological power and supernatural protection. The *Rashahat-i ʿayn al-hayat* records that, although Khwaja Ahrar had been timorous as a child, once he

[44] Wāʿiẓ, *Maqṣad*, 51–52, 58, 105–06, 155.
[45] Muʿīn al-fuqarāʾ, *Mullāzāda*, 43–44; Wāʿiẓ, *Maqṣad*, 40, 45, 51,55, 70, 75, 79. For a further example, see Khwāja-i Samarqandī, *Qandiyya*, 49. This is similar to the appropriation of graves and relics by the early Christian church (Peter Brown, *The Cult of the Saints: Its Rise and Function in Latin Christianity* [Chicago: University of Chicago Press, 1981], 31–38).
[46] Wāʿiẓ, *Maqṣad*, 51, 58. For another example, see Kātib, *Tārīkh-i jadīd*, 183.

felt his calling to the path he no longer feared graves, due to help from the spirits of Sufis. He was able even to spend the night at the grave of his ancestor Khawand Tahur, a fearsome place where strange things appeared at night and which was so frightening that people were afraid to enter it even in the daytime. For this reason, one of his enemies, trying to discredit him, hid and jumped out at him suddenly with a yell, but failed to frighten him.[47]

When we stand back and look at holy places and their use, we see that while ulama and Sufi shaykhs shared the faith and practice of the population and asserted some authority within it, they neither created nor controlled popular belief and practice. Their superior learning allowed them to serve as interpreters of dreams and to claim the authority to authenticate existing holy sites. But the world of the shrine, the miracle, the search for blessing and intercession, was a political sphere within which the religious elite had to work to achieve and maintain power.

The ruler and the supernatural

Aside from the ulama and Sufis, one other set of people were recognized as possessors and conduits of otherworldly forces: the rulers. Rather than defining the relationship between ruler and religious figures as a balance between worldly power held by the sovereign on one side and spiritual benefits controlled by religious specialists on the other, we should consider kings, Sufis and ulama as rivals and allies working within these two spheres. In both the Islamic and the Turco-Mongolian traditions, the ability to achieve and exercise power could be taken as a sign of grace, since God gave rule to those he had chosen for it. This formulation opens the door to a personal relation of the ruler with the supernatural. While the rulers of the Islamic world enjoyed no direct powers like the healing touch of European kings, some connection to the sacred was clearly important.[48] Particularly after the end of the caliphate, which had provided a genealogical link with the Prophet, claims of divine favor were often part of dynastic myths. The importance of prophetic dreams for royal legitimation has been frequently discussed.[49] On the Mongol side, access to the spirit world was part of the personal charisma of the supreme ruler.[50]

47 Kāshifī, *Rashaḥāt*, 396–98.

48 A modern example is the concept of *baraka* in Moroccan kingship. See Clifford Geertz, "Centers, Kings and Charisma," in *Culture and its Creators*, edited by J. Ben-David and T. N. Clark (Chicago, London: University of Chicago Press, 1977), 161–62.

49 See for example, Roy Mottahedeh, *Loyalty and Leadership*, 69–70; Cemal Kafadar, *Between Two Worlds: the Construction of the Ottoman State* (Berkeley, Los Angeles, London: University of California Press, 1995), 132–33.

50 See for example, Joseph Fletcher, "The Mongols: Ecological and Social Perspectives," *Harvard Journal of Asiatic Studies* 46 (1986), 34–35; Thomas Allsen, "Spiritual Geography and Political Legitimacy in the Eastern Steppe," in *Ideology and the Formation of Early States*, edited by Henri J. M. Claessen and Jarich G. Oosten (Leiden, New York, Köln: Brill, 1996), 116–18.

For Temür and his descendants connection to the supernatural and its attendant charisma were a crucial factor in holding power. Temür was credited with having direct contact with spirits, and was even said to have ascended to heaven on a ladder.[51] The claim to extraordinary psychological powers continued under Temür's successors. Several historians explicitly claimed wonders (*karāmāt*) for Shahrukh, which were close in character to some of the miracles ascribed to Sufi shaykhs. Shahrukh's decision to go to Azarbaijan on the eve of the plague in Herat was presented by the historian Fasih, writing during Shahrukh's lifetime, as a sign of divine inspiration. ʿAbd al-Razzaq Samarqandī, who served Shahrukh, relates two stories about dreams which resemble hagiographical narratives. To explain the change in relations with the Mamluk government on the accession of Sultan Chaqmaq in 842/1438, Samarqandī recounts that before his accession Chaqmaq dreamed that Shahrukh took him by the waist and sat him on the throne. When Chaqmaq indeed succeeded in taking power, he sent a friendly embassy to Shahrukh, despite contrary advice from his counselors.[52] Samarqandī benefitted personally from Shahrukh's miraculous powers. While he was in Calicut on the southwestern Indian coast he found himself in difficulties, until one night he dreamed that Shahrukh appeared riding in majesty, rubbed his face and told him not to despair. Shortly thereafter he achieved release through the embassy of a friendly ruler.[53] Dawlatshah Samarqandī recounted similar stories, one passed down from his father, who had served Shahrukh. Shahrukh supposedly knew by inspiration that Qara Yusuf Qaraqoyunlu had died, ten days before the news reached camp.[54] Comparable powers seem to have been attached to the rulers who succeeded Shahrukh. The historian Tajal-Din Hasan Gazdi credited both Shahrukh and his grandson Sultan Muhammad with *karāmāt*, and the Naqshbandi literature records the prescient dreams of Sultan Abu Saʿid.[55]

Since rulers claimed some power in the spiritual sphere, they also had to deal with other sites of spiritual power. For them, as for shaykhs and ulama, the recognition and appropriation of holy places was an important exercise. In addition to shrines, which were the center of recognized religious groups, there were places of popular appeal without what one might call an owner. I have already mentioned the shrine of the Shah-i Zinda in Samarqand, erected on the grave of the Prophet's companion Qutham ibn ʿAbbas. The popularity of the site had begun to revive in the fourteenth century and from the beginning of his reign Temür's family began to use it as a necropolis, particularly for their women. The extent to which the Timurids succeeded in associating themselves with the miraculous powers of the shrine is attested

[51] Manz, "Tamerlane and the Symbolism of Sovereignty," *Iranian Studies* 21, 1–2 (1988), 118.
[52] Samarqandī, *Maṭlaʿ*, 722–23. [53] Ibid., 785–86.
[54] Dawlatshāh Samarqandī, *Tadhkirat*, 327. He gives another example of Shahrukh's powers on the same page.
[55] Yazdī, *Ḥasanī*, 8, 10; Kāshifī, *Rashaḥāt*, 182, 519–20.

to in an elaborate story about Temür's authentication of the site by sending someone down to discover whether Qutham was still alive, contained in the composite work on Samarqand's history and graves, the *Qandiyya*.[56] Isfizari recounts several actions of Sultan Husayn which show the ruler's eagerness to build upon and control sites which attracted large numbers of people. The speedy appropriation of the supposed grave of ʿAli b. Abu Talib at Balkh is well known.[57] Sultan Husayn, like Abu Saʿid before him, erected buildings at the healing springs of Herat Rud, and at the popular pilgrimage and burial spot of Ziyaratgah near Herat.[58]

Relations between the ruler and the religious classes

The rulers' possession of spiritual powers put them in an ambiguous relationship with religious authorities. Sultans sought religious legitimation in two ways, each of which placed them in a different relation to the members of the religious classes, particularly Sufis. First of all, the ruler was the upholder of the *sharīʿa* and patron of organized religion. Secondly, he claimed legitimacy through his own connections to supernatural forces. In matters of formal religious doctrine and practice, the issue of authority had arisen during the first centuries of Islam and the ulama had won over the caliph; thus the terms on which the ulama and the ruler coexisted were fairly well settled. In the sphere of Sufism, the relationship was less well defined and there was room for competition. Scholars of Sufism have discussed the interdependence of worldly sovereignty (*salṭanat*) and spiritual authority (*wilāya*) as complementary, God-given powers.[59] Jürgen Paul depicts a competitive relationship and describes a number of spiritual duels between Temür and the Sufi shaykhs of his time, showing that Temür laid claim to a type of spiritual strength akin to theirs and some Sufis recognized him as a competitor within this realm.[60]

Several scholars have discussed the sovereign's use of Sufi patronage for legitimation. In the work cited above, Jürgen Paul has shown how Temür used spiritual recognition by Sufi shaykhs to attest to his personal charisma and fitness to rule. The opportunities and dangers involved in government legitimation through the patronage of Sufis have been well described also by

56 Khwāja-i Samarqandī, *Qandiyya*, 64–77.

57 R. D. McChesney, *Waqf in Central Asia: Four Hundred Years in the History of a Muslim Shrine, 1480–1889* (Princeton, NJ: Princeton University Press, 1991), 31–36.

58 Isfizārī, *Rawḍāt*, 83, 101–02.

59 Geoffroy, *Le soufisme*, 110–20, 135; Chodkiewicz, *Le sceau*, 111–16. See also Jo-Ann Gross, "Multiple Roles and Perceptions of a Sufi Shaykh: Symbolic Statements of Political and Religious Authority," in *Naqshbandis: Historical Developments and Present Situation of a Muslim Mystical Order*, edited by M. Gaborieau, A. Popovic and T. Zarcone (Istanbul, Paris: Isis, Institut français d'études anatoliennes d'Istanbul, 1990), 109–21.

60 Jürgen Paul, "Scheiche und Herrscher," 307–18.

Simon Digby.[61] There has been less discussion of the way in which Sufi literature uses recognition by the sovereign to demonstrate the spiritual power of shaykhs. Like secular rulers, shaykhs found outside legitimation useful.[62] Among the more straightforward uses of the ruler's prestige are the frequent mentions of favor from sultans or spiritual power over them, both seen as an attribute of a successful shaykh.[63] Buzjani, author of a biographical collection on the shaykhs of Jam, repeatedly reports the honor that rulers showed to the descendants of Shaykh Ahmad Jami and portrays both Temür and Shahrukh as disciples of the head of the shrine.[64] Many stories assert the superiority of Sufi shaykhs over worldly powers, and the authority they invoke is that of the ruler himself. The *Rashahat-i ʿayn al-hayat*, giving the biography of Hasan ʿAttar, a shaykh active during Shahrukh's reign, relates a prophecy in Hasan's youth that he would be mounted while kings were on foot about him; when Khwaja Hasan came to Khorasan, Shahrukh came to him with a mount, held his stirrup for him and then ran several steps alongside him.[65] In the case of Khwaja Ahrar, while his close relationship with Sultan Abu Saʿid may have caused some criticism, it clearly increased his standing and this is reflected in the *Rashahat*. Abu Saʿid reportedly dreamed about Khwaja Ahrar before his own accession, then recognized him on sight. On one occasion, Abu Saʿid dreamed that Khwaja Ahrar's power was such that no-one could withstand him.[66]

The ability of the sovereign to receive and understand prophetic dreams suggests that he possessed elevated spiritual abilities, and in some stories the ruler is portrayed as a visionary. We can find an example in the *Qandiyya*'s story about Temür's recognition of the graves of two shaykhs in Samarqand, those of Nur al-Din Basir and Burhan al-Din Sagharchi. The writer suggests that Temür chose Samarqand as his capital because he had heard of the miracle attendant on Sagharchi's burial there. At this point Temür paid less attention to the grave and descendants of Nur al-Din Basir, but later when he campaigned towards Iraq, he suffered a defeat and called on the spirits of saints. At the head of the spirit army he saw Nasir al-Din Basir, and thereafter he showed marked respect for his descendants.[67]

[61] Simon Digby, "The Sufi *Shaykh* and the Sultan: a Conflict of Claims to Authority in Medieval India," *Iran* XXVIII (1990), 71–81. See also, Geoffroy, *Le soufisme*, 123–24.

[62] See for a later example D. DeWeese, "*walī*. 5. In Central Asia," in *Encyclopaedia of Islam*, 2nd edn.

[63] For Timurid examples, see Kātib, *Tārīkh-i jadīd*, 194; Wāʿiẓ, *Maqṣad*, 108, 140.

[64] Būzjānī, *Rawḍāt*, 89, 99, 108–110. Būzjānī died in 929/1522–23, but he took much of his material from an earlier compilation, by another member of the same family, Shihab al-Din Abu'l Makarim, dated to 840/1436–37.

[65] Kāshifī, *Rashaḥāt*, 158–59.

[66] Ibid., 182, 519–20; Jo-Ann Gross, "Authority and Miraculous Behavior: Reflections on *Karāmāt* Stories of Khwāja 'Ubaydullāh Aḥrar," in *The Legacy of Persian Sufism*, edited by Leonard Lewisohn (London: Khaniqahi-Nimatullahi, 1992), 161–64. For other examples, see Aubin, *Niʿmat*, 44, 164, 189; and Būzjānī, *Rawḍāt*, 107–08.

[67] Samarqandī, *Qandiyya*, 119–23.

While Sufi literature uses the figure of the sovereign to increase the prestige of shaykhs, it nonetheless shows ambivalence towards the ruler. Rulers inhabited two worlds at once and held the attributes of both. Although the officials of the ruler – emirs, bureaucrats, and particularly tax officials – usually serve as the main villains, negative stories about Mongol and Timurid rulers are plentiful.[68] Some stories tell of initial lack of respect followed by a vision which enlightened the ruler; thus the ruler is at the same time a worldly oppressor and a spiritually endowed visionary. Isfizari relates a story about the accreditation of the hospice (*langar*) of the ecstatic shaykh Amir Ghiyath Sayyidzada near Badghis, which neatly illustrates both the ambivalence of the ruler's position in relation to spiritual powers and the anxiety with which rulers might view the rise of new and possibly upsetting powers. We are told that Amir Ghiyath was a beautiful stranger selling *halwā* in the bazaar, discovered by another ecstatic Sufi called Baba Akhi Mahmud Jami, who walked around attended by fierce dogs. Amir Ghiyath learned his mystical practice from Baba Akhi and, on his instructions, sought out the right place to build a hospice; he was told to look for a location where he would hear the voices of "friends," or spiritual powers. Here he settled, attracted disciples, and cultivated the land, which was very rich. Not surprisingly, the next people to arrive were the tax collectors. Amir Ghiyath sent messengers to Temür to ask for an exemption. Temür bent his magical gaze on them, and when they presented their petition he initially refused. However, almost as soon as he had spoken, he looked frightened and acceded to the request, explaining when asked that he had seen a fearsome lion attacking him.[69]

Relations between men of religion and government were no easier to reconcile in everyday life than they were in literature. It is important to remember that the politics between shaykhs and rulers not only affected their relations with each other, but also formed an important part of their competition among their peers – for the ruler in dynastic and international rivalries, and for shaykhs in status among other Sufis and the population at large. It is clear that a shaykh with good connections could be useful to students and colleagues. Yusuf Ahl, who served as scribe for the shaykhs at the shrine of Jam, and collected their correspondence under the name Farayid-i Ghiyathi, was assiduous in writing to people of influence. He dedicated his collection to Ghiyath al-Din Pir Ahmad Khwafi. He wrote to the governor of Khorezm, Ibrahim Sultan b. Shahmalik, requesting that a religious appointment be given to a friend of his and he wrote to the eminent shaykh Husayn Khwarazmi, close to Ibrahim Sultan of Khorezm.

68 See Paul, "Scheiche und Herrscher," 298; and Paul, *Naqšbandiyya*, 213–17, 237–44. See also, Kāshifī, *Rashaḥāt*, 196; Aubin, *Ni'mat*, 189, 199–201.

69 Isfizārī, *Rawḍāt*, vol. I, 136–44. For the later history of the hospice, see Khwāndamīr, *Ḥabīb*, vol. IV, 5; Thackston, *Habibu's-siyar*, 354.

Khwarazmi's response contains answers to doctrinal questions and the statement that Khwarazmi had passed on Yusuf's book to the governor. In Yusuf's letters, as well as others in the collection, we find several protestations that bad rumors spread about the writer are the result of slander by people who wished him ill.[70] The correspondence of Khwaja Ahrar and other shaykhs from a somewhat later date has been published, and here we find numerous requests on behalf of students and shaykhs connected to the writers.[71] The ability to pass on requests for help, intercession, or appointment was a source of political capital, not only for ulama but also for shaykhs.

Mutual need and competition, combined with the tricky boundaries between worldly and spiritual authority, created complicated conventions. Rulers used patronage of religious figures to prove their piety, but they had to choose the right men to honor. Shaykhs and ulama on their side found signs of respect from the ruler a valuable source of prestige, but could damage their reputation by appearing to serve worldly power, since such behavior was disapproved of. They faced the choice between losing their reputation for disinterestedness if they fully accepted the ruler's bounty, and losing their ability to function usefully as educators and protectors of the population if they removed themselves entirely from the worldly sphere.[72] Since rulers and government occupied an ambivalent moral position, there could be no perfect solution to the question of how religious figures should relate to them. Although we do find examples of religious figures who openly enjoyed the fruits of their courtly connections – one particularly worldly *ṣadr* adopted military dress – such behavior did not win approval either from historians or from the dynasty.[73] A few scholars took the opposite path and resolutely refused to serve the government, to accept gifts, or to use the buildings which officials or rulers erected for them – behavior which is reported with admiration.[74] Most people prominent enough to have contact with the ruling class chose to pursue a middle course, combining a willingness to serve government personnel with assertions of independence – refusal of gifts, care about eating food that might not be permissible, or open criticism of the ruler's behavior.

What is interesting is that admiring accounts of religious figures showing independence from rulers are often found in historical works written for members of the ruling class, like the *Tadhkira al-shuʿara* of Dawlatshah, the

[70] Yūsuf Ahl, *Farāyid-i ghiyāthī* (introduction) 21–22, (text) 102–03, 133–35, 148–52, 188, 376–78, 524–27, 545–49, 560–62.

[71] See for instance, Gross and Urunbaev, *The Letters of Khwāja ʿUbayd Allāh Aḥrār and his Associates*, 301–05, 308–09, 311, 312, 328, 330, 335–36, 340–41.

[72] For recent discussions of these tensions, see Ernst, *Eternal Garden*, 59–61, 88–89, 191–97; Paul, *Naqšbandiyya*, 45, 51–52, 208–13; and Gross, "Authority and Miraculous Behavior," 163–65.

[73] See, for example, Khwāndamīr, *Ḥabīb*, vol. IV, 16; Thackston, *Ḥābibuʾs-siyar*, 359–60.

[74] Wāʿiẓ, *Maqṣad*, 69, 73, 107; Dawlatshāh Samarqandī, *Tadhkirat*, 398–404; Khwāndamīr, *Ḥabīb*, vol. IV, 61; Thackston, *Habibuʾs-siyar*, 384. For a general discussion, see Geoffroy, *Le soufisme*, 121–22.

Rawdat al-jannat of Isfizari, and the *Habib al-siyar* of Khwandamir.[75] It is in the dynastic literature, not the hagiographical, that we find accounts of the spiritual superiority of Zayn al-Din Taybadi over Temür and his refusal to come out to meet the conqueror, forcing Temür to come to him as a supplicant. This story is first reported by Ḥāfiẓ-i Abrū, and later taken up by Isfizari and Khwandamir. These histories also report that Taybadi told Temür he welcomed the campaign against the Kartid kings because the kings had pursued their ungodly ways despite his advice, and that if Temür failed to heed him, he would turn against him as well.[76] The presence of such stories in dynastic sources need not surprise us. For rulers to profit from association with religious figures, these men had to be respected by the wider population, and for this they had to avoid too worldly a stance and too much dependence on the ruling class. Thus, it was in the interest of the ruler that the men he patronized maintain some distance from the court. When we consider Zayn al-Din Taybadi's repeated refusal to come out to meet Temür, we should keep in mind that he had earlier written recommending himself to Temür's attention.[77] The story about Taybadi's show of disrespect probably served as a useful balance, showing that he was sufficiently independent to merit respect.

While the account of Temür's meeting with Taybadi may contain significant embellishments, there is evidence that behavior of this kind bore results. It was wise for religious men close to the court to refuse at least some of what was offered them. Shahrukh chose to accept as binding the legal rulings of a jurisprudent who steadfastly refused to hold any formal office.[78] The caution shaykhs had to practice is illustrated in the career of Baha' al-Din ʿUmar Jaghara'i, who was closely connected to the ruling elite, while maintaining a very high standing in religious circles. On his departure for the pilgrimage he refused the request of Shahrukh and other great men to give him presents for the road, saying that he wished to go as a *darwīsh* and to accept nothing.[79]

One aspect of life which posed a constant challenge to the probity of religious figures was that of hospitality. For any holder of position, the entertainment of superiors, peers, and followers was a primary obligation; the ability to gather distinguished guests and to provide suitable fare was a sign of success. Both shaykhs and prominent ulama received members of the ruling classes, and receptions offered to rulers are mentioned in the *tadhkira*

[75] See Isfizārī, *Rawḍāt*, vol. I, 217; Dawlatshāh Samarqandī, *Tadhkirat*, 376–77, 421–24; Khwāndamīr, *Ḥabīb*, vol. IV, 14; Thackston, *Habibu's-siyar*, 358.

[76] Paul, "Scheiche und Herrscher," 308; Ḥāfiẓ-i Abrū, *Cinq opuscules de Ḥāfiẓ-i Abrū concernant l'histoire de l'Iran au temps de Tamerlan*, edited by F. Tauer (Prague: Éditions de l'Académie tchécoslovaque des sciences, 1959), 61–62; Isfizārī, *Rawḍāt*, vol. I, 225–27; Khwāndamīr, *Ḥabīb*, vol. III, 543; Thackston, *Habibu's-siyar*, 300–301.

[77] Aubin, "Le khanat de Čaġatai et le Khorassan (1334–1380)," *Turcica* 8, 2 (1976), 53; ʿAbd al-Ḥusayn Nawāʾī (ed.), *Asnād wa mukātabāt-i tārīkhī-i Īrān* (Tehran: Bungāh-i Tarjuma wa Nashr-i Kitāb, sh. 2536/1977), 1–3.

[78] Khwāndamīr, *Ḥabīb*, vol. IV, 11; Thackston, *Habibu's-siyar*, 356.

[79] Samarqandī, *Maṭlaʿ*, 742.

literature.[80] Sovereigns holding regular *majlis*es, or entertainments, for ambassadors required the attendance of at least some religious figures to show their patronage of religion, so men of prestige were likely to receive invitations to such occasions. For a person trying to adhere strictly to the *sunna* however the acceptance of food from rulers was problematical, given the fact that some of it would almost certainly be the fruit of oppression, or of taxes forbidden in Islamic law. Buzjani writes in the *Rawdat al-riyahin* that one of the shaykhs of Jam, Khwaja ʿAziz Allah Jami, when he traveled to Buzjan, refused to eat the food put before him because the village was crown property.[81]

To eat with a ruler therefore was an act which required justification. Those men who did accept often found ways to defend their decision – or their biographers did. The sources tell two stories about Shah Niʿmat Allah Wali and his acceptance of food from the Timurids. In one tale Temür asked why Niʿmat Allah agreed to eat with a ruler, and he answered that this was allowable because Temür liked *darwīsh*es. Another story, presumably a *topos*, relates Shahrukh's attempt to catch out Niʿmat Allah, who claimed that he always recognized forbidden food.[82] Shahrukh fed him a lamb purposely stolen from an old woman, and when he ate it without comment, crowed over him. When the matter was investigated, it turned out that the woman had been bringing the lamb to offer to Niʿmat Allah in any case, and it was therefore lawful.[83] A similar story, with a different outcome, circulated about Saʿd al-Din Taftazani at Temür's court. So great was Temür's respect for Taftazani that he made room for him on his own cushion in audiences. Khwandamir states that Saʿd al-Din ate at Temür's entertainments, a fact which bothered his son in Herat, who heard criticism about it from the local ulama. The son wrote to his father asking him to stop. Temür reportedly intercepted the letter and played a trick on the son, to whom he offered a large sum of money acquired through the illegal *tamgha* tax on trade. When Taftazani's son accepted the gift without questioning its origin, Temür revealed the stratagem and shamed him.[84]

We see from these examples how complicated were the relationships between religious figures and the members of the court. Rulers and religious figures were dependent on each other for prestige, but for both sides some distance was required to maintain the dignity of religious standing. Religious men could accept respect and could sit in seats of honor at a sultan's assembly, and, if a ruler came to visit, they were expected to entertain him suitably. On the other hand, food or gifts had to be carefully screened and it was

[80] See for example, Būzjānī, *Rawḍāt*, 110, 111. [81] Būzjānī, *Rawḍāt*, 131.

[82] This ability was frequently claimed as a sign of spiritual power. See Richard Gramlich, *Die Wunder der Freunde Gottes. Theologien und Erscheinungsformen des islamischen Heiligenwunders* (Wiesbaden: Steiner, 1987), 162–63.

[83] Aubin, *Niʿmat*, 42, 196; Dawlatshāh Samarqandī, *Tadhkirat*, 333.

[84] Khwāndamīr, *Ḥabīb*, vol. III, 545–46; Thackston, *Habibu's-siyar*, 302.

necessary to assert independence of thought and behavior. Too much distance posed other dangers. To refuse offices or gifts from the government increased the prestige of a religious figure, but one must remember that to do this, one needed something to refuse. Not to be offered favors in the first place was no help towards advancement in a competitive world.

Politics within the religious classes

The strains in the relationship between the religious classes and the court are clearly expressed in our sources; the political rivalries within the religious classes are no less clear, and they were also part of the political dynamics of the realm. Competition among the ulama formed an accepted part of city and court politics and has been frequently examined.[85] On Sufi politics, scholars have usually focused on friction between different Sufi communities, or the relations between Sufis and non-mystical ulama.[86] These were not the only tensions, nor were they necessarily the most important in the early fifteenth century, when the exclusive and competitive orders of later times had not yet developed.[87] If we are to understand the full spectrum of religious politics we must include tensions among shaykhs who shared spiritual lineage and practice, just as we do among close groups of ulama.[88] In Herat and many other cities, shaykhs of different affiliations were in close and friendly contact with each other, exchanging visits and attending each other's *majlis*es. The rivalries we perceive among them are tensions among associates, and we should not automatically ascribe them to competition between competing lineages or communities. Part of the position and status of an *ʿālim* or shaykh depended on private or *waqf* wealth, on family and *silsila* connections, or on the possession of a secure position as *mudarris, qāḍī*, or *mutawalli*. A considerable portion however came from the ability to attract followers through strength of character and power to offer spiritual and material favors.[89] Status of this kind was never secure from rivals even within a close circle – new competitors might always appear and outstanding success brought in its

[85] For example, see Anne F. Broadbridge, "Academic Rivalry and the Patronage System in Fifteenth-Century Egypt: al-ʿAynī, al-Maqrīzī, and Ibn Ḥajar al-ʿAsqalānī," *Mamluk Studies Review* III (1999), 85–107.

[86] See, for instance, Paul, *Naqšbandiyya*, 79–84; Aubin, "De Kûhbanân," 237; Devin DeWeese, "Mashāʾikh-i Turk and the Khojagān: Rethinking the Links between the Yasavī and Naqshbandī Sufi Traditions," *Journal of Islamic Studies*, 7, 2 (1996), 186–95.

[87] See DeWeese, "Mashāʾikh-i Turk," 187–99.

[88] Simon Digby has examined struggles within the Chishti community in India (Simon Digby, "*Tabarrukāt* and Succession among the Great Chishtī Shaykhs of the Dehli Sultanate," in *Delhi Through the Ages: Essays in Urban History, Culture and Society*, edited by R. E. Frykenberg [Bombay, Calcutta, Madras: Oxford University Press, 1986], 63–103).

[89] These qualities are nicely summarized by Simon Digby in "The Sufi Shaykh as a Source of Authority in Mediaeval India," in *Islam and Society in South Asia/Islam et société en Asie du sud*, edited by Marc Gaborieau (Paris: Editions de l'école des hautes études en sciences sociales, 1986) 60–61.

train jealousy and the danger of attack. What made politics in the religious sphere particularly sharp and volatile was the importance of personal loyalty and, in the case of the Sufis, something akin to love.

While the individual sought tranquility based on temporary oblivion of the outside world, the Sufi milieu was striking for its close personal connections, heightened emotions, and constant awareness of the mental state of others. The mystical discipline required contemplation, but much time was spent in company, in an atmosphere that invited comparison and competition. Sufi adepts gathered to perform the *dhikr* and *samāʿ* (listening and sometimes dancing to music), to preach, and to talk. Like rulers and other men of importance, shaykhs held their personal *majlis*es, attended by a variety of people – their own disciples, other Sufi *pīr*s, with their disciples, ulama, and lay people. There was a great deal of social visiting, with groups of shaykhs walking together to visit a colleague in his own village, and the frequent discussion of food in hagiographical writing makes it clear that hospitality was an important part of the life of a mystic. Food was expected to be fully lawful but definitely not skimpy or of poor quality. One of the wonders (*karāmāt*) recorded was the ability to guess what individual guests wanted to eat and to present them, as they entered, with the very dishes they had been longing for on their walk.[90]

The life of communal study and hospitality offered ample opportunity for shaykhs to display spiritual powers. An outstanding personality was crucial in gaining the prestige which attracted disciples and patronage. Many stories show a strong sense of theater; the display of mental powers before an audience played a significant part in personal advancement. Fasting and other ascetic practices were one way for Sufis to test and to display their piety. The practice of the *chilla* or *arbaʿīn*, a forty-day exercise of fasting and seclusion, was widespread, and those Sufis who performed the exercise under particularly harsh conditions gained prestige. The hagiographies of Shah Niʿmat Allah Wali for instance record several such exercises performed in mountains in winter, in which he sometimes consumed only snow.[91] Several of the shaykhs of Jam likewise performed forty-day fasts regularly, and Zahir al-Din Khalwati (d. 800/1397–98), in one such exercise, is said to have eaten only one meal of boiled wheat every ten days.[92]

Many powers described in hagiographical literature could be acquired only through strenuous mental training. One accomplishment that could significantly enhance one's reputation was the ability to achieve ecstacy, shown by unconsciousness to one's surroundings or occasionally by cries and moans. People of great attainments might also be able to pass on unconsciousness to

[90] Paul, *Naqšbandiyya*, 34–35; Jāmī, *Nafaḥāt*, 501–03; Būzjānī, *Rawḍāt*, 111; Kāshifī, *Rashaḥāt*, 136–37; Aubin, *Niʿmat*, 80–81, 84–85.
[91] Aubin, *Niʿmat*, 39–40, 145, 165–66, 168, 283, 313.
[92] Būzjānī, *Rawḍāt*, 109, 112, 122; Jāmī, *Nafaḥāt*, 503.

those who came into contact with them.[93] Through the training of the imagination, accomplished Sufis could visualize and communicate with people at a distance, both in their own shapes and in different, usually animal, shapes. Shams al-Din Muhammad Kusuyi, one of the shaykhs of Jam, saw some of his associates in the form of four-eyed dogs.

At the base of the Sufi path lay the close but difficult relationship between master and disciple. The attainment of the mystic's goal was achieved through deliberate training of the will and the imagination, in which the disciple was guided by a shaykh to whom he remained closely attached. The desire to undertake the quest, and the ability to succeed at it, required psychological particularities which shaykhs were trained to perceive. What made the path bearable was presumably sincere desire to attain a sense of unity with God, strong affection for the master, and the respect accorded to those who achieved spiritual transformation. Both the use of the imagination and the power of the master over the disciple were fully developed in Naqshbandi treatises, which have been the subject of several important recent works. The disciple was bound to his master first through attraction, and then by *rābiṭa*, attachment and orientation towards the shaykh. The disciple should reach the point where he could visualize the shaykh before him and communicate with the Prophet through the medium of his guide. The Sufi shaykh in his turn practiced *tawajjuh*, turning his attention on the disciple; in this way he could act on him (*taṣarruf*), transferring to his disciple the desirable qualities he himself possessed and ridding him of bad characteristics.[94] *Taṣarruf*, the ability, through imagination and will, to affect others, did not affect only disciples. Accomplished masters were able also to act on other people, whether to bring them illumination, to put them out of countenance, or to put a spiritual burden on them. *Taṣarruf* could sometimes bring even more spectacular results, such as bringing the dead to life, transferring illness from another person to oneself, or causing death or misfortune to ill-wishers – all effects frequently described in hagiographical sources.[95]

In a world in which training entailed the destruction and rebuilding of personality, insight into the psychological processes of other people was a valued quality, and many *karāmāt* of this sort are recorded. A number of

[93] Fritz Meier, "Kraftakt und Faustrecht des Heiligen," in *Zwei Abhandlungen über die Naqšbandiyya* (Istanbul: Beiruter Texte und Studien, 58, 1994), 250–53; Kāshifī, *Rashaḥāt*, 244–45; Jāmī, *Nafaḥāt*, 397.

[94] Chodkiewicz, "Quelques aspects de techniques spirituelles dans la ṭarīqa naqshbandiyya," in *Naqshbandis: Historical Developments and Present Situation of a Muslim Mystical Order*, edited by M. Gaborieau, A. Popovic and T. Zarcone (Istanbul, Paris: Isis, Institut français d'études anatoliennes d'Istanbul, 1990), 70–79; Fritz Meier, "Kraftakt," 245–51, 262–64; Fritz Meier, "Meister und Schüler im Orden der Naqšbandiyya," *Sitzungberichte der Heidelberger Akademie der Wissenschaften, phil-hist. Klasse* 2 (1995), 10–16; Paul, *Doctrine and Organization*, 34–40.

[95] Meier, "Kraftakt," 254, 260–63, 266–74.

these wonders involved guessing the thoughts of a disciple; considering the intimate and overheated atmosphere Sufis lived in, these acts are not difficult to credit. A shaykh guessed when a disciple coveted a robe just given to the shaykh himself, when one had had impure thoughts, aroused by a handsome fellow disciple or the sight of nomad women bathing, when one had been drunk or been tempted to drink. The masters made their understanding clear with a smile or a softly murmured comment.[96]

The atmosphere engendered by close personal relations and psychological influence was a charged one, and it is not hard to find traces of rivalry within Sufi communities – between shaykhs competing for influence, among disciples vying for favor or succession, even between master and disciple. Advanced disciples faced the question of who would become deputy (*khalīfa*), and it is not surprising to find that contests arose, sometimes splitting the spiritual lineage. The most dramatic of these was the division of the Kubrawiyya which I shall discuss in the next chapter.[97] Other conflicts within communities arose from the psychological stress and competition of a close community in which divine favor was mediated through earthly representatives.

There are numerous stories of trials undergone by disciples and the strains they caused – insecurity, jealousy, and despair. One particularly full account of discipleship in Herat, during the reign of Shahrukh, provides a vivid psychological portrait of an aspiring shaykh. This is the story of the early career of Shams al-Din Muhammad Ruji, who trained under Sa'd al-Din Kashghari and became the major educator of Naqshbandi disciples in Herat in the late fifteenth century.[98] Shams al-Din Muhammad was born on 14 Sha'ban, 820/September 26, 1417, to a family of traders and camel keepers in the town of Ruj near Herat. His mother had previously suffered grief at the loss of a young son and had been consoled by a dream of the Prophet, promising her a son who would live a long life and bring good fortune. Throughout Shams al-Din's childhood she told him that he was the promised child. Shams al-Din and his father had little sympathy for each other; the boy showed scant interest in the family business and spent much of his youth in solitude. Once however, he had mounted one of his father's camels without permission, and his father threw down the camel to unseat his son. Shams al-Din's mother scolded her husband for his treatment of the boy and the camel also punished him that night by rolling on him, over and over, despite the efforts of neighbors attracted by his cries. This incident impressed the local people and brought respect to the aggrieved son, Shams al-Din. With his mother Shams al-Din was very close, and it was she who taught him the prayers which could bring a dream of the Prophet. He found her one day

96 Kāshifī, *Rashaḥāt*, 172, 191, 220; Jāmī, *Nafaḥāt*, 402, 405, 502–03; Būzjānī, *Rawḍāt*, 120–22.
97 For similar problems in India in the Ni'mat Allahi and the Chishti, see Aubin, "De Kûhbanân," 253–54; and Digby, "*Tabarrukāt*."
98 Paul, *Naqšbandiyya*, 86–87.

going over these texts with her women friends, and said he would like to try them. One Thursday evening, both Shams al-Din and his mother repeated the prayers and during the night Shams al-Din dreamed that his mother took him to the Prophet, who confirmed that he was the son promised to her. When he woke up he found his mother at his bedside with a candle, having just woken from an identical dream.[99]

According to the biography in the *Rashahat-i ʿayn al-hayat*, Shams al-Din Muhammad began asking in his hometown which shaykh of Herat he should go to, and was told to go to the Friday Mosque to find Saʿd al-Din Kashghari. When Shams al-Din set off to become a disciple his mother went along, joined the community and stayed with him, rejoicing in every sign of advancement.[100] Shams al-Din was an eager and gifted disciple and, likewise, a competitive and emotional one. Kashghari had to slow him down several times – to tell him he was not ready to study Rumi's *Mathnawi*, that he should not read the Qur'an before the proper stage, that he must not practice his skill in *tawajjuh* on senior shaykhs. One night Shams al-Din saw a vision of light and, overjoyed, he spoke about it in the *majlis*. When Kashghari rebuked him for pride and dismissed him, Shams al-Din was so distraught that he spent seven or eight months wandering weeping in the fields during the day and beating his head against the floor of the mosque at night. His desperation ended when Kashghari comforted him.[101] As time went on, Shams al-Din increasingly succeeded in attaining states and visions, experiencing unconsciousness so often that it even worried him. He was once so transported that for forty days he remained in the cathedral mosque, lamenting all night and hitting his head against the pillars so that it was covered with swellings like almonds. Like many other young Sufis, he was for some time strongly attracted to a handsome fellow disciple, a circumstance which caused him great shame.[102] Despite Shams al-Din's states and his favor with his master, he remained prey to painful jealousy and when Kashghari sent him to visit another disciple, who spent his evenings bathed in supernatural light, tears of envy came to his eyes. It may not have helped that others also knew about this student, and that a local patron regularly sent him food, which he did not eat.[103]

While Shams al-Din Muhammad Ruji's discipleship is particularly fully described, numerous stories about other disciples show the psychological stress of learning the path and the desperation it could occasion. One of Khwaja Ahrar's disciples, blocked by Ahrar from performing miracles he had earlier achieved, reportedly threatened to kill either Khwaja Ahrar or himself.[104] Khwaja Ahrar's son, Muhammad Yahya, frustrated at Ahrar's refusal to grant him permission to go on the pilgrimage, repeatedly set off without permission but was always forced back by dreams of his father.[105]

[99] Kāshifī, *Rashaḥāt*, 325–28, 351. [100] Ibid., 328–31, 336. [101] Ibid., 330–35.
[102] Ibid., 336–39. [103] Ibid., 340–42. [104] Ibid., 645–46.
[105] Ibid., 581–86. For other examples, see ibid., 115, 137–39, 552–53.

We can sympathize with Sayf al-Din Khwarazmi, the unsuccessful disciple of Baha' al-din Naqshband, who lost favor because he was unable to overcome his miserliness and his attachment to worldly advantage. The incident which exemplified his faults of character was a gathering he hosted at which he failed to offer his guests sweets at the end of the meal, thus providing a meal "without a tail." After giving up the path and continuing his career in trade, he went on a journey with a caravan, and in a green meadow between Marw and Makhan, rolled in the grass, exclaiming how wonderful it was to be without a shaykh.[106]

Problems of jealousy were not limited to disciples. It is clear that exceptional accomplishments in a student could pose a problem even to an established master. We can see this in the story of the gifted and aggressive preacher Darwish Ahmad Samarqandī, who attracted enormous crowds and lost favor with his master, Zayn al-Din Khwafi, ostensibly because he quoted the poetry of the controversial shaykh Qasim al-Anwar. Khwafi banned him from preaching. According to later Naqshbandi sources, Khwaja Ahrar took him up to discountenance Khwafi and helped him to regain his audience. Soon listeners were flocking to hear him, and it wasn't long before we find Khwaja Ahrar turning against him, accusing him of talking at a level beyond his listeners.[107] It is tempting to see in this story a problem caused by too great an ability to attract attention and followers, an ability which threatened first Darwish Ahmad's recognized master and then his new patron.

An explicit case of jealousy between master and disciple is that of ʿAla' al-Din ʿAttar and his disciple Nizam al-Din Khamush. Before entering ʿAttar's service, Nizam al-Din had had considerable spiritual practice. He achieved unconsciousness early on in his life and soon became famous for his exceptional sensitivity. ʿAttar became irritated with Nizam al-Din's frequent and conspicuous states of ecstacy. During one of these he decided to bring Nizam al-Din down to earth by cooking the noodle dish known as *bughra*, which was prepared communally by throwing noodles from a tablet into a dish of broth to cook while uttering an invocation. ʿAla' al-Din put a tablet into Nizam al-Din's hand, but after one throw Nizam al-Din again became overwhelmed and the tablet fell from his hand. At this point ʿAla' al-Din gave up with good humor, saying that a person occupied by God could not be called back by people.[108]

Religious politics and the public sphere

What made contests within the religious classes part of the larger political dynamic was the fact that many were played out in public places and drew in

[106] Ibid., 136–37. [107] Ibid., 179–84.
[108] Jāmī, *Nafaḥāt*, 400. For further accounts of rivalry between these two men, see Chapter 8. For *bughra*, also connected to *futuwwa*, see Kāshifī, Sabzawārī, *Futuwwatnāma*, 311. For another example of strains between master and disciple, see Aubin, "Un santon quhistānī," 214.

people from outside, including political figures. Rivalry over prestige and the attraction of students were a visible part of city life. Students were expected to provide respectful service to senior scholars, and this could be a public and conspicuous act. ʿAbd al-Rahman Jami recollected with pride that, unlike most of his fellow students in Samarqand during Ulugh Beg's rule, he had refused to abase himself to the leading ulama. Most of the candidates of Samarqand and Herat went on foot in the train of famous scholars but Jami avoided sycophantic behavior and, as a result, received lower stipends.[109] The ideal of the student-teacher bond and its continued political importance are well illustrated by the story of Saʿd al-Din Taftazani's student Jalal al-Din Yusuf Awbahi defending Taftazani's marginal notes against criticism by a new appointee at Shahrukh's madrasa. Complimented by Amir Firuzshah for repaying his debt to his late master, Awbahi replied that if he swept the threshold with his eyelashes for a hundred years he could not discharge his obligation.[110]

While preeminent scholars enjoyed great prestige, they were likely to suffer from the jealousy of their peers. We can see this clearly with Saʿd al-Din Taftazani, as I have shown. His doctrinal views were challenged publicly during his life by the equally eminent scholar of Temür's court, Sayyid Sharif Jurjani and this rivalry was famous and long remembered.[111] His position had aroused envy and he was criticized by his colleagues for consenting to eat with Temür. Another case of jealousy is reported under Abu Saʿid, between two close colleagues who shared a common place of origin – Khwaf – and sought favor with the same emirs. The senior scholar Kamal al-Din Shaykh Husayn recommended his brilliant younger colleague, ʿIsam al-Din Da'ud Khwafi, to Sultan Abu Saʿid, first as tutor to the Sultan's son, and then as *ṣadr*. According to Khwandamir, the true reason for the recommendation was jealousy, since service to the dynasty would distract ʿIsam al-Din from his studies.[112] Contests among the ulama thus involved rulers and emirs as arbiters, audience, and agents.

Rivalry among Sufi shaykhs and their students was equally public. Although many Sufi hospices – *khānaqāh*s – were built in the Timurid period, *khānaqāh*s were not limited to Sufis, nor were they the primary locus of their activities. Mosques and madrasas are more frequently mentioned as the location for events and gatherings of importance.[113] A number of internal

[109] Kāshifī, *Rashaḥāt*, 238.
[110] Khwāndamīr, *Ḥabīb*, vol. IV, 7; Thackston, *Habibu's-siyar*, 354.
[111] Khwāndamīr, *Ḥabīb*, vol. III, 547; Thackston, *Habibu's-siyar*, 303.
[112] Khwāndamīr, *Ḥabīb*, vol. IV, 106–07; Thackston, *Habibu's-siyar*, 408–09; Isfizārī, *Rawḍāt*, vol. I, 221–2; Kāshifī, *Rashaḥāt*, 238.
[113] It is possible that the locus of activities was shifting in the fifteenth century, when Sufi learning was widespread among the ulama; this is suggested for the Mamluk regions (Geoffroy, *Le soufisme*, 93–94, 116). For the *khānaqāh*, see Th. Emil Homerin, "Saving Muslim Souls: the Khānqāh and the Sufi Duty in Mamluk Lands," *Muslim Studies Review* 3 (1999), 59–65; Lewisohn, *Beyond Faith and Infidelity*, 104–17; and also Kāshifī, *Rashaḥāt*, 119–20, 422; Jāmī, *Nafaḥāt*, 594; Aubin, *Niʿmat*, 18, 48; Karbalāʾī, *Rawḍāt*, vol. II, 214, 216, 238.

dramas took place in the cathedral mosque of Herat, where Sa'd al-Din Kashghari held his *majlis* and which was also a locus for the activities of two other prominent shaykhs, Zayn al-Din Khwafi and Baha' al-Din 'Umar Jaghara'i.[114] Shahrukh, at least at the beginning of his reign, attended public prayers here on Friday with his major emirs and retinue.[115] This was also where Shams al-Din Muhammad Ruji sat in ecstasy hitting his head against floor and pillars. The madrasas of the city were places where Sufis preached and might gather to eat. In Herat we hear particularly about the Madrasa-i Ghiyathiyya, a well-established madrasa where Khwaja Ahrar recommended that Naqshbandi shaykhs go to find food that was permissible.[116]

The bazaar, as a center for commerce and public life, served as stage and recruiting ground for the Sufi community. We learn that ecstatic shaykhs were so lost to the world around them that they walked through the bazaar unconscious of their surroundings.[117] It was also the place used by some masters to break the pride of their new disciples and cure them of their attachment to worldly status. 'Ala' al-Din 'Attar, a disciple of Baha' al-Din Naqshband who belonged to a respectable merchant family, had to go through the bazaar barefoot selling apples. When this embarrassed his brothers, 'Ala' al-Din received orders to hawk his wares right before their shop. Another disciple, hesitant to give up his madrasa studies, had to help his master, Sa'd al-Din Kashghari, carry wood through the crowds of the bazaar.[118] Any member of the city elite, or the artisan classes, would thus have been aware of activities within the Sufi community and would have made up part of the audience before which contests and trials were carried out.

I have already discussed the relationship between dynastic and Sufi politics, and will end the chapter with a discussion of how other figures, notably bureaucrats and emirs, participated in religious politics. In the hagiographies, references to holders of worldly power outside the dynasty show hostile attitudes, particularly towards tax collectors and emirs, who are most frequently mentioned. These people were representatives of worldly might, without the connection to the supernatural which helped redeem the ruler.[119] However, the existence of negative stories does not prove that Sufis in fact disdained contact with men of government. Like many displays of appropriate attitudes, these anecdotes probably served to make up for expedient practices. Exemplary stories about hostility towards emirs may be there for two reasons – first because they represent a truth, and second, because it is not the whole truth.

[114] Paul, *Naqšbandiyya*, 46, 64; Kāshifī, *Rashaḥāt*, 189; Jāmī, *Nafaḥāt*, 455. For examples in Samarqand and Bukhara, see Kāshifī, *Rashaḥāt*, 111, 124; Jāmī, *Nafaḥāt*, 501.
[115] Samarqandī, *Maṭla'*, 314, 844; Ḥāfiẓ-i Abrū, *Zubdat*, 911–12.
[116] Jāmī, *Nafaḥāt*, 405; Paul, *Naqšbandiyya*, 58; Kāshifī, *Rashaḥāt*, 187, 407, 528; Allen, *Catalogue*, 460.
[117] Jāmī, *Nafaḥāt*, 397; Kāshifī, *Rashaḥāt*, 135. [118] Kāshifī, *Rashaḥāt*, 140–41, 303–04.
[119] Paul, *Naqšbandiyya*, 213–18; Kāshifī, *Rashaḥāt*, 200, 219, 221, 539.

Many emirs were strongly involved in religious life, and were responsible for the building of mosques, madrasas, and mausolea. We know of close connections between emirs and Sufi masters and, as I have shown above, emirs were often present at religious debates. We find them also mentioned visiting shaykhs and becoming disciples.[120] There are also more general mentions of "nobles", both as disciples and simply attending *majlis*es.[121] Given the places in which prominent Sufi shaykhs preached, it would indeed have been odd if neither emirs nor other members of the elite had been present. It is clear that individual shaykhs and spiritual lineages profited considerably from the patronage of bureaucrats and emirs; the mausolea of Zayn al-Din Khwafi and Zayn al-Din Abu Bakr Taybadi were commissioned by the vizier Ghiyath al-Din Pir Ahmad Khwafi, and that of Baha' al-Din ʿUmar by the sons of Amir Firuzshah. At the shrine of Jam, the major buildings of Shahrukh's epoch were commissioned by emirs – one by Firuzshah and the other by either the governor of Khorezm, Shahmalik, or his son Nasir al-Din Sultan Ibrahim. It was not uncommon to be buried in the madrasa complex that one had built, and since graves were visited by the family, there was a continued presence of the military class. When we consider how Sufi masters competed with each other, we should consider the government elite, both Chaghatay and Persian, as part of the audience they attracted and the patrons they needed to attain the status they sought.

Conclusion

There is wide recognition of the connection between religious and political life in the medieval period, and of the importance of both Sufis and ulama to government elites. We need also to recognize that the religious realm itself depended on worldly powers – not only for appointments and patronage, but also for prestige and public recognition. Both the Perso-Islamic and the Turco-Mongolian traditions attached some supernatural powers to the person of the ruler, and this aspect of their position was recognized by the religious elite who used the ruler's reputation for supernatural abilities to attest to their own legitimacy.

The importance of the supernatural in daily life contributed to the influence of the religious elites, but it also denied them an exclusive sphere of power. Religion and spiritual power were not the concern only of the religious classes; this was a realm in which many people were active. The ordinary person might connect to the spirit world independently of any religious authority. The souls of the dead and sometimes of the living visited the individual in the form of dreams, which could sometimes be summoned through prayers and charms.

[120] Kāshifī, *Rashaḥāt*, 394, 401, 410, 471, 527, 545–47; Aubin, *Niʿmat*, 104. See also Digby, "The Sufi Shaykh as a Source of Authority," 68.
[121] Būzjānī, *Rawḍāt*, 120; Jāmī, *Nafaḥāt*, 388.

The visitation of holy sites, both graves and natural wonders, was open to all and offered a variety of blessings. These conduits were therefore points of access to political power in the supernatural sphere, and we find that contestants for power in this realm worked hard to gain and maintain a connection to them. Sufi shaykhs claimed expertise in the interpretation of dreams, and both rulers and religious authorities bestowed formal authentication on spots already holy.

The political dynamics of religious classes and government personnel was not a matter of contests played out separately among Sufis and ulama, with a ruling elite seeking religious legitimation through patronage of the religious figures who emerged on top. Politics in the two spheres were simultaneous and interconnected. Shaykhs and ulama attracted patronage from the worldly elite by demonstrating their prestige within religious circles, and they gained some of their position among their peers by showing an ability to attract members of the population, including the military and landed elite. Many religious rivalries were played out in public places – mosques, madrasas, bazaars – and their outcome often depended on a large group of followers and spectators, including members of most groups of society.

The recognition of supernatural powers in the ruler and the usefulness of recognition by government power did not prevent shaykhs and ulama from considering both ruler and governing classes as corrupting. While they gained prestige among the population and the religious classes through the patronage of the governing classes, they could lose respect by accepting benefits too freely. This is not unlike the way in which contemporary academic and artistic communities interact with government patronage. Just as it does in contemporary society, close cooperation with members of the ruling class might bring suspicion of contamination along with prestige, and had to be handled carefully with demonstrations of independence and distaste.

CHAPTER 7

The dynasty and the politics of the religious classes

For people among the religious classes, the dynasty and court circle were only one factor in advancement; they could influence, but not manage, the traditional structures of authority. The ruler might promote a specific school or tendency, but one cannot assume that he could successfully implement a program of his own. Even among those who held recognized positions – the ulama, Sufi shaykhs, and the ruler himself – religious authority was diffuse and amorphous. When we follow the lives of individuals we find that neither the formal institutions of mosque and madrasa nor the Sufi *ṭarīqa*s seem to have defined the lives of their members. Lines of alliance, loyalty and communication went across categories of all kinds, and created a space in which individuals could pursue their own careers and come to individual accommodations with government and society.

Shahrukh was one of numerous actors in the religious sphere and had to respect the status of many influential groups. As a rich capital city, Herat became a magnet for both scholars and Sufis. Probably the most prestigious ulama were the children and students of the scholars whom Temür had brought to favor. Under the Kartids, Herat had been a center of culture, and we find some personnel under Shahrukh whose antecedents go back to the ulama fostered by them. Besides scholars connected to the mosques and madrasas of the capital, there were local families who inherited religious prestige. Lineages descended from famous scholars of the past continued to enjoy respect; we hear for instance of the descendants of Ansari, Muhammad al-Ghazali, Fakhr al-Din Razi, and the caliph Abu Bakr.[1] The tomb of Imam Rida at Mashhad was a major pilgrimage goal and a locus of religious power. In addition, there were large, important and prestigious sayyid families, accorded high respect and organized under overseers, called *naqīb*s.[2] The most obvious people of independent standing were the Sufi shaykhs.

[1] Faṣīḥ Khwāfī, *Mujmal-i faṣīḥī*, 246, 255, 267; Khwāndamīr, *Ḥabīb*, vol. III, 548; vol. IV, 16, 62, 104; Thackston, *Habibu's-siyar*, 303, 359–60, 384, 407; Wāʿiẓ, *Maqṣad*, 46.

[2] Faṣīḥ Khwāfī, *Mujmal-i faṣīḥī*, vol. III, 152, 260, 263, 272, 277, 291; Khwāndamīr, *Ḥabīb*, vol. IV, 9, 105, 335, 354; Thackston, *Habibu's-siyar*, 256, 407, 518, 527–28.

Several major tomb sites and their personnel remained important over long periods: that of Ahmad of Jam, the shrine of Abu Saʿid Abiʾl Khayr at Mayhana, still kept by the shaykh's descendants, the shrine of Zayn al-Din Abu Bakr Taybadi, and many smaller sites. All these groups expected the respect of government and population alike.

In this chapter I present some of the structures and personnel of religious authority in Khorasan, assessing their relationship to each other and to the ruler. I want to examine two centers of power: the court, which might wield influence through patronage or punishment, and the Sufi communities centered around shrines or lines of transmission, which were revered by the population.

Government appointments in the religious sphere

Shahrukh was known for his strict observance of religious law, and it is worth asking how much his religious views influenced the population under him. Although the Timurids and their followers were solidly Muslim, their continued loyalty to Mongol legitimacy and the idea of the dynastic law (*yasa*) of Chinggis Khan undoubtedly gave impetus to movements for the revitalization of Islam. Shahrukh used these ideas liberally in his legitimation, and began his reign with a statement of intention to revivify Islamic law. He presented his action not as a break with Temür, but as a continuation of policies begun by the Mongol Ilkhan Ghazan Khan (r. 1295–1304) and maintained by later Turco-Mongolian rulers.[3] Since he stressed religion in his legitimation, the support of the religious classes was crucial for the success of his reign and any religious policy he might institute.

While Shahrukh was able to characterize himself as a pious ruler, achieving a definite religious policy was not a simple matter. The ruler had to respect the doctrinal currents of the time and the religious authorities among whom he lived. Religious belief at this period was diverse and, in general, accommodating, but a few aspects of practice and thought stand out. One was the widespread veneration for the descendants of the Prophet, which brought conspicuous respect to the memory of ʿAli and the other Shiʿite *imāms*. In earlier scholarship, this tendency was sometimes taken as evidence of Shiʿism – thus some dissident movements, earlier ascribed to Shiʿite belief, now require reconsideration.[4] The emphasis on the *sunna* which characterizes

[3] A. B. Khalidov and M. Subtelny, "The Curriculum of Islamic Higher Learning in Timurid Iran in the Light of the Sunni Revival under Shāh-Rukh," *Journal of the American Oriental Society* 115, 2 (1995), 15–16; Manz, "Mongol History," 141–47.

[4] B. S. Amoretti, "Religion in the Timurid and Safavid Periods," in *The Cambridge History of Iran*, vol. 6, 610–16; Aubin, "Kûhbanân," 242–43, n. 71, 244, n. 75; Shahzad Bashir, *Messianic Hopes and Mystical Visions: the Nūrbakhshīya between Medieval and Modern Islam* (Columbia, SC: University of South Carolina Press, 2003), 31–40.

the period can be seen as part of the promotion of the Prophet and his family as models of correct behavior. Extreme Sufi practices were one target of the movement. Another issue which engendered controversy was the doctrine of Ibn ʿArabi on the unity of being and God's presence in the created world. The attack on Ibn ʿArabi by the fourteenth-century Mamluk scholar Ibn Taymiyya had made his works famous, and his ideas a standard subject of debate on which all senior scholars had to take a stand.[5] However, the sharp religious controversies common in the Mamluk realm, leading the ulama to hold public trials which could result in incarceration or even execution for incorrect doctrine seem to have been rare in Timurid Iran.[6] The ulama certainly expressed disapproval of suspect ideas, but they seem rarely to have proposed serious action unless someone posed a clear political threat. In this atmosphere of restraint, rulers could not act as decisively as the Mamluk sultans sometimes did.

The ruler could hope to exercise influence over religious life in two ways: through patronage and control over religious personnel, or by attempting actually to promote a religious program affecting doctrine and observance. The most direct instrument available to Shahrukh was the imposition of administrative pressure through officials charged with religious oversight. Some offices were directly under the sovereign's control but others depended partly on heredity and local consensus. Two established offices had particular impact on the life of the city. The post of *muḥtasib*, inspector of market practice and city morality, helped to set the religious tone for the capital city, while that of *qāḍī* had a major impact on both the leadership of the ulama and the administration of justice. The Timurids sponsored two new offices involving oversight of the religious sphere, those of *shaykh al-islām* and *ṣadr*, which may have been designed to increase dynastic control over religious personnel. The examination of these positions can offer us some insight into the level of influence that Shahrukh could exert over the religious life of Herat.

Shahrukh's choice of people to fill the office of *muḥtasib* in the capital reflects his interest in the strict observance of Islamic norms. There were probably at least two high-ranking *muḥtasib*s serving together, and they seem to have been men of known accomplishment. The earliest *muḥtasib* we know of was Khwaja Shihab al-Din Abu'l Makarim (d. 833/1429–30), a man of high connections, descended from the shaykhs of Jam.[7] Jalal al-Din al-Qa'ini held the post for many years and almost certainly overlapped with

[5] Alexander Knysh, *Ibn ʿArabi in the Later Islamic Tradition: The Making of a Polemical Image in Medieval Islam* (Albany, NY: State University of New York Press, 1999), 13–14, 113–15. Two prominent scholars connected to the Timurids, al-Taftazani and his student Muhammad al-Bukhari, wrote treatises against Ibn ʿArabi's teaching (Knysh, *Ibn ʿArabi*, 163, 204–05).

[6] See Knysh, *Ibn ʿArabi*, 54–61, 127, 137.

[7] Khwāndamīr, *Ḥabīb*, vol. IV, 12; Thackston, *Habibu's-siyar*, 357. He is not the Abu'l Makarim who was administrator of the shrine at Jam during Shahrukh's period.

Abu'l Makarim. The last one we know under Shahrukh was Murtada Sahhaf, who served together with Jalal al-Din Qa'ini and continued after Qa'ini's death.[8]

The impressive qualifications of Qa'ini, the best known of Shahrukh's *muḥtasib*s, suggest that Shahrukh accorded authority to the office. He was an energetic man with connections to many prominent religious figures; he studied *ḥadīth* with Shams al-Din Muhammad al-Jazari and Muhammad Parsa, and transmitted books from ʿAbd al-Awwal al-Burhani al-Samarqandī, one of the leading jurists of Transoxiana, and from Shams al-Din Muhammad al-Taftazani, the son of the great Saʿd al-Din ʿUmar. Jalal al-Din was furthermore a disciple of the preeminent Herat shaykh Zayn al-Din Khwafi and married his son to Khwafi's daughter. One of Qa'ini's students was Jalal al-Din Yusuf b. Shams al-Din Muhammad al-Jami, a descendant of the shaykhs of Jam and the author of a collection of correspondence, the *Farayid-i Ghiyathi.*[9]

Qa'ini moved to Herat in 813/1410–11 to seek employment with Shahrukh, for whom he composed a mirror for princes with an introduction describing Shahrukh's measures for the renewal of religion. Either his own fortune or the income connected to his office allowed him to construct a madrasa in his own name.[10] It is clear that he wrote several works, mentioned among the readings in the *ijāza*s given to his students.[11] His status is further attested to by the continued prominence of his family after his death. His son held the post of *muḥtasib* under Sultan Husayn Bayqara, and in a later generation his family married into that of ʿAbd al-Razzaq Samarqandī's brother.[12]

While Shahrukh's *muḥtasib*s were prominent, it is not clear how much he and they succeeded in changing the tone of public morality. On the issue about which we have most information – drinking alcohol – they had only limited success. Qa'ini states, in his mirror for princes, that Shahrukh proclaimed the reimposition of the *sharīʿa* in Dhu'l-Qaʿda, 813/ February–March, 1411, and marked the occasion by wrecking wine houses and pouring out wine.[13] In 844/1440–41 Shahrukh staged another major attack on alcohol, by ordering Murtada Sahhaf to pour out the wine stored in the houses of Shahrukh's son Muhammad Juki and his grandson ʿAla' al-Dawla.[14] These actions however could not ensure observance. Shahrukh's

[8] Khwāndamīr, *Ḥabīb*, vol. IV, 17; Thackston, *Habibu's-siyar*, 360.

[9] Khalidov and Subtelny, "The Curriculum," 216–21; Khwāndamīr, *Ḥabīb*, vol. IV, 360; Thackston, *Habibu's-siyar*, 530.

[10] Kāshifī, *Rashaḥāt*, 340. [11] Khalidov and Subtelny, "The Curriculum," 221–22.

[12] Khalidov and Subtelny, "The Curriculum," 219; Khwāndamīr, *Ḥabīb*, vol. IV, 347; Thackston, *Habibu's-siyar*, 524.

[13] Jalāl al-Dīn Muḥammad Qā'inī, *Naṣā'iḥ-i Shāhrukhī*, Vienna, Nationalbibliothek, MS Cod. A. F. 112, fols. 1b–2a.

[14] Khwāndamīr, *Ḥabīb*, vol. IV, 17; Thackston, *Habibu's-siyar*, 360; Samarqandī, *Maṭlaʿ*, vol. II, 740. The *Maṭlaʿ* attaches this story to Jalal al-Din Qa'ini, but it is entered in the year 844/ 1440–41, well after Qa'ini's death in 838/1434–35.

elite were used to a culture in which large quantities of alcohol were consumed publicly, and several members of the dynasty were known as serious drinkers. In 819/1416–17, not long after Shahrukh's first attack on wine houses, we hear that two dissident princes he was holding in Herat spent their time drinking together and thinking bad thoughts.[15] All the histories that record the death of Shahrukh's favorite son, Baysunghur, note that he died of alcoholism.[16] As I have mentioned earlier, when ʿAlika's nephew Baba Masʿud was *kotwāl* of the fortress of Herat, he drank openly in its taverns, keeping his official drummers drumming outside their doors. At that time at least, wine cannot have been hidden. Even after the second attack on wine in 844/1440–41 one member of the dynasty, Sultan Muhammad b. Baysunghur, apparently planned to build a drinking house. When pushed to give up this idea, he drank publicly outside of Herat, though, after being confronted by Murtada Sahhaf, he repented temporarily.[17] Some of the major officials of Herat, and some serving Baysunghur and Ulugh Beg, were known for high living and public drinking.[18] Shahrukh therefore could do little more than keep alcohol away from the official activities of his own court, with occasional gestures towards wider measures.

The office of *qāḍī* was of primary importance for the city, but here the ruler's power was limited in a different way: the choice of personnel. Although the office was theoretically under the control of the *ṣadr*, it was usually hereditary and in Timurid Herat the position of chief judge was reserved for the descendants of chief judge of Kartid Herat, Jalal al-Din Mahmud Imami, who traced his lineage from the caliph Abu Bakr. There seems to have been no question about their continuance in office under Shahrukh. Jalal al-Din Mahmud's son Qutb al-Din ʿAbd Allah served as chief judge and for a while as supervisor of *waqf*s during Temür's reign and at the beginning of Shahrukh's.[19] After his death in 815/1412–13 he was succeeded by his son Sadr al-Din Muhammad, replaced probably by a nephew, Qutb al-Din Ahmad, who is known to have been *qāḍī* at the end of Shahrukh's reign.[20] After Jahanshah Qaraqoyunlu conquered Herat in 862/1458, he appointed a judge from a different family, but when the Timurids retook the city, they reinstated Qutb al-Din, and the family continued to hold the office through the Safavid conquest.[21] Thus one family of judges survived two changes of regime.

15 Samarqandī, *Maṭlaʿ*, 188. 16 Ibid., 657.

17 Khwāndamīr, *Ḥabīb*, vol. IV, 17; Thackston, *Habibu's-siyar*, 360.

18 There is an account of ʿIsam al-Din Marghinani arranging an assembly with singing girls, much disapproved of by the *muḥtasib* of Samarqand (Khwāndamīr, *Ḥabīb*, vol. IV, 35; Thackston, *Habibu's-siyar*, 369–70).

19 Khwāndamīr, *Ḥabīb*, vol. III, 548; Thackston, *Habibu's-siyar*, 303; Samarqandī, *Maṭlaʿ*, 37.

20 Faṣīḥ Khwāfī, *Mujmal-i faṣīḥī*, vol. III, 209, 275; Samarqandī, *Maṭlaʿ*, 679; Khwāndamīr, *Ḥabīb*, vol. IV, 13; Thackston, *Habibu's-siyar*, 357–58.

21 Khwāndamīr, *Ḥabīb*, vol. IV, 105, 335–36; Thackston, *Habibu's-siyar*, 408, 518–19; Samarqandī, *Maṭlaʿ*, vol. 2, 954; Ṭihrānī Iṣfahānī, *Diyārbakriyya*, 352.

The two newly created religious offices, those of *ṣadr* and *shaykh al-islām*, were more closely connected to the court. The office of *ṣadr* seems to have originated with the Kartid dynasty, and involved supervision of ranks and offices within the religious classes; officially at least, Timurid *ṣadr*s oversaw salaries, appointments, and ranks of all religious offices, as well as the functioning of *waqf* endowments and construction of religious buildings.[22] There were several *ṣadr*s at once, often one chief, and one or two subordinates.[23] The personnel in the office shows considerable continuity; a number of the men who served as *ṣadr* under Temür held office under his descendants and several sons followed their fathers into the office.[24] The *ṣadr* was paid out of the income of *waqf* endowments and, if we are to judge from the number of buildings erected by *ṣadr*s under Shahrukh, the post was lucrative. Few other ulama in Herat constructed more than their own tombs. It is likely that most *ṣadr*s were men who originated outside Herat and retained a certain distance from the political life of the city. Outside provenance would probably have been useful in an office which entailed oversight of local ulama. The office was one closely attached to the court, and *ṣadrs* sometimes also served as envoys, another potentially remunerative office.[25]

The stories related in the histories suggest that the people holding the office of *ṣadr* and other court posts affected a more worldly tone than did the judge and *muḥtasib*. The chief *ṣadr* under Shahrukh was Jalal al-Din Lutf Allah (d. 842/1438–39), who had sufficient wealth to build a madrasa outside Herat. He probably originated elsewhere since he is mentioned by both ʿAbd al-Razzaq Samarqandī and Khwandamir, but is not in the *Maqsad al-iqbal* or Fasih Khwafi's history.[26] Another *ṣadr*, Sadr al-Din Ibrahim, was from a great family of Samarqand and served Shahrukh from early in his reign until his death in 832/1428–29. Sometime after 842/1438–39, Sadr al-Din's son, Shams al-Din Muhammad Amin, took his father's place. He was a major patron of architecture, building a mosque outside Herat, and repairing two *ribāt*s at a nearby village.[27] Another family connected with the office was that of Mawlana ʿAbd Allah Lisan, a prominent philosopher at Temür's court, who married a woman descended from Fakhr al-Din Razi. Both his sons became wealthy and made full use of the good things they won in life. Jalal al-Din ʿAbd al-Rahim, who served as *ṣadr* under Baysunghur and ʿAlaʾ

[22] Gottfried Herrmann, "Zur Entstehung des Ṣadr-amtes," in *Die islamische Welt zwischen Mittelalter und Neuzeit, Festschrift für Hans Robert Roemer zum 65. Geburtstag*, edited by U. Haarmann and P. Bachmann (Wiesbaden: F. Steiner, 1979), 279–81, 293.

[23] Herrmann, "Zur Entstehung," 282. We have two lists of *ṣadr*s under Shahrukh: one in the *Muʿizz al-ansab* and one in the *Ḥabib al-siyar* (*Muʿizz*, fol. 133b; Khwāndamīr, *Ḥabīb*, vol. III, 639; Thackston, *Habibuʾs-siyar*, 351).

[24] Herrmann, "Zur Entstehung," 293–4; *Muʿizz*, fols. 138b, 142b and footnote 23.

[25] Samarqandī, *Maṭlaʿ*, 47, 86, 906, 985.

[26] Khwāndamīr, *Ḥabīb*, vol. III, 639–40; Thackston, *Habibuʾs-siyar*, 351; Samarqandī, *Maṭlaʿ*, 47, 719.

[27] Khwāndamīr, *Ḥabīb*, vol. III, 639–40, vol. IV, 326; Thackston, *Habibuʾs-siyar*, 351, 514.

al-Dawla, apparently for a time, assumed the costume and following of a military man. However, when Ulugh Beg, displeased, tested him on his learning, he answered brilliantly and escaped the consequences of his behavior. Like his father, he married a woman of the Khorasan religious aristocracy. His daughter married the son of Shahrukh's *ṣadr*, Muhammad Amin b. Sadr al-Din Ibrahim.[28] Jalal al-Din's brother, Shihab al-Din ʿAbd al-Rahman, also held a high religious post, this time in Shahrukh's service. He owned a thousand slaves and the buildings he chose to endow were a public bath and a caravanserai.[29]

The final office to be examined is the *shaykh al-islām*, which has been discussed in detail by Shiro Ando. There is little indication that this office furthered the influence of the dynasty in any direct way. It was an honorary position, involving oversight of all juridical activity, and was held during the Timurid period by the members of two families. In Samarqand the office belonged to the descendants of Burhan al-Din al-Marghinani (d. 1197), while in Herat it was passed down within the family of Saʿd al-Din Taftazani; it was held first by Taftazani's grandson, Qutb al-Din Yahya, near the end of Shahrukh's reign, and then by his son, Sayf al-Din, who was executed by the Safavids. For the period of Shahrukh, there is little information on what the office entailed, though later it seems to have had considerable authority.[30]

The promotion of the *muḥtasib*, the adoption of the *ṣadr*, and the creation of the office of *shaykh al-islām* suggest that Shahrukh wanted to attach the ulama more directly to the dynasty. How great a change his actions brought about however remains uncertain. The position of *shaykh al-islām* seems primarily to have formalized the power and status of two preeminent families. The *ṣadr*s who served under Shahrukh were clearly influential and closely tied to the government, but the sources give us little indication of how much their oversight affected the independence of the ulama. Certainly the *qāḍī* continued to be important in the creation of *waqf* endowments, which were a major factor in the control of wealth.[31]

The creation and patronage of religious institutions

Like other dynasties, the Timurids created numerous religious establishments. Such projects provided the opportunity of continued influence within

[28] Khwāndamīr, *Ḥabīb*, vol. III, 547, vol. IV, 16, 326; Thackston, *Habibu's-siyar*, 303, 359–60, 514.
[29] Khwāndamīr, *Ḥabīb*, vol. IV, 16; Thackston, *Habibu's-siyar*, 359–60; Samarqandī, *Maṭlaʿ*, 732–33.
[30] Shiro Ando, "The *Shaykh al-Islām* as a Timurid Office: a Preliminary Study," *Islamic Studies* 33, 2–3 (1994), 253–55; Khwāndamīr, *Ḥabīb*, vol. IV, 105, 348; Thackston, *Habibu's-siyar*, 408, 524.
[31] In contemporary *waqf* documents it is the local judge whose seal was first affixed to the document, followed by witnesses. See *waqfnāma*s of Muhammad Parsa ("Waqfiyya-i kitābkhāna-i Ḥiḍrat Khwāja Pārsā," Tashkent, Uzbek State Archives, Waqf collection I–323 55/14, lines 44, 54–61; "Waqfiyya-i khānaqāh-mubārak-i quṭb al-aqṭāb Ḥiḍrat Khwāja Muḥammad Pārsā," Tashkent, Uzbek State Archives, Waqf collection I–323 1291–16, l. 57; and the *waqfnāma* of Amir Chaqmaq, in Mustawfī Bāfqī, *Mufīdī*, vol. III, 883; "Waqf-nāma-i Zayn al-Dīn," 198.

the religious classes, since salaried positions were within their gift. According to Samarqandī, Shahrukh had religious scholars in his *majlis* and read books on Qur'anic commentary, *ḥadīth*, jurisprudence, and history.[32] However he displayed little of the personal favor which Temür and the next major ruler, Sultan Abu Sa'id, showed to individual scholars.[33] Most of the distinguished ulama of his period were either men of Khorasanian provenance or students of Temür's protégés. There is no evidence that Shahrukh put any particular scholar in a conspicuous position at his *majlis*, nor is it clear whether he took prominent religious figures along on his campaigns.

Since Shahrukh did not promote new religious personnel the ulama active under him show considerable continuity with Temür's reign. The prestige of three scholars Temür had brought to Samarqand, Sa'd al-Din 'Umar Taftazani, Sayyid 'Ali Jurjani, and Shams al-Din Muhammad Jazari, passed on to their offspring and students. Taftazani (722/1322 to 793/1390) had been a student of the Shafi'i and 'Ashari scholar of Fars, 'Adud al-Din 'Abd al-Rahman al-Iji, and was particularly strong at explication and synthesis, promoting a generally inclusive theology, suitable for his period.[34] Amir Sayyid Sharif al-Din 'Ali Jurjani was born in 740/1339 near Astarabad, and in 779/1377 went to Shiraz, where he established a brilliant reputation particularly in "foreign sciences."[35] Both Taftazani and Jurjani devoted part of their work to the same texts and Jurjani directly criticized Taftazani, usually on points of detail on the subject of rhetoric. I have discussed their legacy of controversy in Chapter 2.

During Shahrukh's reign, the family of Taftazani was the more prominent in the capital, since Jurjani had left Samarqand for Shiraz at Temür's death, while Taftazani's son Shams al-Din Muhammad remained in Herat.[36] Shams al-Din died in the plague of 838/1434–35, at about 80 years old, and is characterized as a prominent member of the religious establishment. Only one of Sa'd al-Din Taftazani's students is identified in the Timurid histories: Jalal al-Din Yusuf Awbahi.[37] 'Ali Jurjani apparently remained in Shiraz until his death in 816/1413. His position and honors went to his son, Shams al-Din Muhammad (discussed in Chapter 5), and when Shams al-Din died in 838/1434 in Shiraz, Shahrukh bestowed his offices on his descendants.[38] Jurjani's works continued to be influential throughout the Timurid period

[32] Samarqandī, *Maṭla'*, 705–06, 793, 876.

[33] Abu Sa'id is noted particularly for the favor he showed to Khwaja Ahrar, but he was also a patron and devotee of other religious figures (Wā'iẓ, *Maqṣad*, 92, 108, 140; Khwāndamīr, *Ḥabīb*, vol. IV, 60, 103, 105–06; Thackston, *Habibu's-siyar*, 384, 407–08).

[34] Van Ess, *Erkenntnislehre*, 6; Knysh, *Ibn 'Arabi*, 141–65. [35] Van Ess, *Erkenntnislehre*, 6.

[36] Khwāndamīr, *Ḥabīb*, vol. III, 544–46; Thackston, *Habibu's-siyar*, 301–02.

[37] Taftazani is also mentioned in *ijāza* documents among those with whom Jalal al-Din Qa'ini studied. Wā'iẓ, *Maqṣad*, 82; Samarqandī, *Maṭla'*, vol. II, 2, 679; Faṣīḥ Khwāfī, *Mujmal-i faṣīḥī*, vol. III, 275; Khalidov and Subtelny, "The Curriculum," 230.

[38] Faṣīḥ Khwāfī, *Mujmal-i faṣīḥī*, vol. III, 278; Khwāndamīr, *Ḥabīb*, vol. IV, 13; Thackston, *Habibu's-siyar*, 358. (Also given as Nur al-Din.)

and later. One of his students, Saʿd al-Din Farisi, taught at the Madrasa-i Ghiyathiyya in Herat, and is said to have had many students.[39] Another one, Mawlana Fadl Allah Laythi, was among the great ulama of Samarqand.[40]

Shams al-Din Muhammad al-Jazari was born in Damascus in 1350 and gained fame as an expert in Qurʾanic reading and *ḥadīth.* On Temür's death, al-Jazari traveled to Herat, Yazd, Isfahan, and then to Shiraz, where he remained for some time.[41] He is mentioned as being present at the inaugural lecture of al-Jajarmi at Shahrukh's madrasa in Herat, probably in 823/1420–21, and at some point during Ulugh Beg's reign he is reported visiting Samarqand.[42] He died in Shiraz on 5 Rabiʿ I, 833/December 2, 1429.[43] Among al-Jazari's students were several important scholars of Shahrukh's period, including ʿAbd al-Razzaq Samarqandī and his brothers, and Jalal al-Din Muhammad Qa'ini.[44] Two of al-Jazari's sons pursued scholarly careers outside of the Timurid realm.[45] Another son, Muhibb al-Din Abu'l Khayr, served as *ṣadr* in Shiraz under Iskandar b. ʿUmar Shaykh and Ibrahim Sultan, then went on to a political and military career.[46] Thus, throughout Shahrukh's reign, the influence of the major scholars gathered by Temür remained strong, and Shahrukh seems to have undertaken no initiatives to dislodge them.

While Shahrukh did not promote individual scholars, he and Gawharshad are known for building religious institutions. It is not easy to tell whether their appointments followed a definite program. In 813/1410–11, very shortly after taking Samarqand and establishing himself as supreme ruler, Shahrukh founded a madrasa and *khānaqāh* complex in Herat, to which he appointed four teachers whose inaugural lecture he attended. The first of these was the star student of Saʿd al-Din Taftazani, Jalal al-Din Yusuf b. Nasir al-Din Masih al-Awbahi, mentioned above. The others were Mawlana Yusuf Hallaj, Mawlana Nizam al-Din b. Pahlawan Yar Ahmad, and Nasir al-Din Lutf Allah b. ʿAziz Allah. Subtelny and Khalidov have suggested that these

39 Wāʾiẓ, *Maqṣad*, 84. 40 Nawāʾī, *Majālis*, 26, 201.

41 M. Ben Cheneb, "Ibn al-Dj̲azarī," in *Encyclopaedia of Islam*, 2nd edn; Richard, "Témoignage inexploité," 55, 59.

42 Kāshifī, *Rashaḥāt*, 106.

43 Ben Cheneb, "Ibn al-Dj̲azarī"; Khwāndamīr, *Ḥabīb*, vol. III, 548; Thackston, *Habibu's-siyar*, 303.

44 Khwāndamīr, *Ḥabīb* vol. III, 550; ibid., vol. IV, 13; Thackston, *Habibu's-siyar*, 305, 358; Samarqandī, *Matlaʿ*, 630; Khalidov and Subtelny, "The Curriculum," 219.

45 Ben Cheneb, "Ibn al-Dj̲azarī"; Carl Brockelmann, *Geschichte der arabischen Litteratur*, 2nd edn, 258–59; Aḥmad b. Muṣṭafā Tashköprüzāda, *Es-Saqâʾiq en-Noʿmânijje: enthaltend die Biographien der türkischen und im osmanischen Reiche wirkenden Gelehrten, Derwisch-Scheih̲'s und Ärzte von der Regierung Sultân ʿOt̲mân's bis zu der Sülaimân's des Grossen/von Tasköprüzâde; mit Zusätzen, Verbesserungen und Anmerkungen aus dem Arabischen übersetzt*, edited and translated by O. Rescher (Constantinople: Phoenix, 1927), 21–24; Robert D. McChesney, "Notes on the Life and Work of Ibn ʿArabshah," unpublished paper, 39.

46 *Muʿizz*, fols. 108a, 142b; Ṭihrānī Iṣfahānī, *Diyārbakriyya*, 307.

appointments formed a cornerstone of Shahrukh's policy of Sunni revival; however, we know relatively little about the beliefs and careers of the people chosen.[47] The best known is Awbahi, who is remembered for defending the marginal notes of Taftazani from the criticism of a later appointee to the madrasa, Muhammad Jajarmi. He was also a devotee of Qasim al-Anwar, a Sufi shaykh whom many considered extreme in his behavior and views, particularly on Ibn ʿArabi's theory of the unity of being. This seems an odd affiliation for a follower of Taftazani, who preached moderation in Sufism and wrote a tract against Ibn ʿArabi's views, but as I shall show, such contradictory affiliations were common.[48]

We know less about the other ulama appointed. Nasir al-Din Lutf Allah b. Khwaja ʿAziz Allah (d. 823/1420) was a well-known preacher who gave sermons at the Masjid-i Jamiʿ, and was considered accomplished in *tafsīr*.[49] Nizam al-Din ʿAbd al-Rahim b. Yar Ahmad is mentioned in the histories only in connection with his appointment to the madrasa and his death in 828/1424–25.[50] Jalal al-Din Yusuf b. Qasim Hallaj (d. 823/1420) was an accomplished scholar of *ḥadīth*, the exoteric sciences, and Sufism, and many *imām*s and teachers of Herat were his students.[51] All three men were buried in the shrine of Fakhr al-Din Razi, popular among the Herati ulama. Hallaj seems to have been replaced by his student, Shams al-Din Muhammad Jajarmi, a notable teacher, who counted ʿAbd al-Rahman Jami among his students. Jajarmi died in 864/1459–60, and was buried in the shrine of Shaykh Zayn al-Din Khwafi.[52] It was probably at his inaugural lecture that he attacked the marginal notes of Taftazani, which Awbahi defended.[53] There is little information about Shahrukh's madrasa during his lifetime, which is not surprising, since, as Jonathan Berkey has noted, madrasas are often omitted from the biographies of ulama.[54]

The next major foundation was Gawharshad's religious complex built on the outskirts of Herat, including both a madrasa and a mosque, built from 820/1417–18 to 841/1437–38. We do not know who was appointed to teach

[47] Khalidov and Subtelny, "The Curriculum," 212–13; Samarqandī, *Maṭlaʿ*, 109–10; Khwāndamīr, *Ḥabīb*, vol. IV, 6; Thackston, *Habibu's-siyar*, 354.

[48] Khwāndamīr, *Ḥabīb*, vol. IV, 7; Thackston, *Habibu's-siyar*, 354. For Taftazani's views and latitude among his students, see Knysh, *Ibn ʿArabi*, 146–53, 163–64.

[49] Khwāndamīr, *Ḥabīb*, vol. IV, 5–6; Thackston, *Habibu's-siyar*, 353–54; Wāʿiẓ, *Maqṣad*, 74; Faṣīḥ Khwāfī, *Mujmal-i faṣīḥī*, vol. III, 165, 204, 244. Fasih Khwafi gives the family the *nisba* Harati, and mentions several sons, which suggests a particular connection between them.

[50] Faṣīḥ Khwāfī, *Mujmal-i faṣīḥī*, vol. III, 258 (the name here is ʿAbd al-Rahman).

[51] Wāʿiẓ, *Maqṣad*, 75; Faṣīḥ Khwāfī, *Mujmal-i faṣīḥī*, vol. III, 244.

[52] Khwāndamīr, *Ḥabīb*, vol. IV, 7; Thackston, *Habibu's-siyar*, 354; Wāʿiẓ, *Maqṣad*, 93; Kāshifī, *Rashaḥāt*, 239.

[53] The *Ḥabīb al-siyar* states that the incident occurred some time after the initial appointments, and Jajarmi is described as the *qāʾim-i maqām* of one of the original appointees. Since Jajarmi was a favored student of Yusuf al-Hallaj, who died in 823, this would be a logical explanation of the event (Khwāndamīr, *Ḥabīb*, vol. IV, 6; Thackston, *Habibu's-siyar*, 354; Wāʿiẓ, *Maqṣad*, 58).

[54] J. Berkey, *Transmission of Knowledge in Medieval Cairo: a Social History of Islamic Education* (Princeton, NJ: Princeton University Press, 1992), 18–19.

there.[55] Another madrasa was the Ghiyathiyya, which was staffed at this time by a student of Sayyid Sharif Jurjani, Sa'd al-Din Farisi, identified as one of the foremost ulama of Herat, and a popular teacher. Like Jurjani, he had been attached to Baha' al-Din Naqshband's disciple 'Ala' al-Din 'Attar.[56] We cannot draw many conclusions from these appointments, except that Shahrukh's appointees were prominent and well connected, and that they represented some variety of viewpoint.

Outside royal foundations we know about few appointments to madrasas and mosques. The personnel in these two types of institution seems to have overlapped significantly. The teacher appointed to the madrasa of Amir 'Alika Kukeltash, Nur al-Din Nur Allah Khwarazmi (d. 838/1434–35) was also *khaṭīb* and *imām* of the cathedral mosque. He is mentioned in the *Rashahat-i 'ayn al-hayat* as one of the teachers of Shaykh Shihab al-Din Birjandi.[57] Another *mudarris* was Shams al-Din Muhammad Awhad, (d. 838/1434–35) who taught in the Baraman madrasa and was appointed in 836/1432–33 as *khaṭīb* of the mosque of Gawharshad.[58] The appointments to the cathedral mosque in Gawharshad's complex, in 836/1432–33, are mentioned more specifically. The person first chosen as *khaṭīb* was the grandson of a prominent scholar and Sufi of Herat, Shaykh Shihab al-Din Bistami or Khiyabani (d. 807/1404–05). Samarqandī writes that while the appointee, Shihab al-Din b. Rukn al-Din, gave a good sermon, it was marred by inappropriate moans and sighs. He was dismissed and replaced by Shams al-Din Muhammad b. Awhad, mentioned above as *mudarris* in the Baraman Madrasa.[59]

The fragmentary information on appointments to the posts of *mudarris* and *khaṭīb* does not allow any broad conclusions about the types of people chosen for these posts. When Shahrukh filled religious posts, he seems to have appointed the available and obvious candidates, rarely bringing in people from outside. The men chosen for the major posts were usually either of local provenance or had studied with established figures in Herat or Samarqand. One characteristic of these appointees is the number who had Sufi affiliations. This should not surprise us, given the close connection of many ulama to Sufism, but it does suggest that such affiliations were not a bar to official appointment, despite Shahrukh's quarrels with some Sufi shaykhs.

[55] T. Allen, *Timurid Herat*, 18.

[56] Wā'iẓ, *Maqṣad*, 84. This is probably not the Shams al-Din 'Ali al-Farisi mentioned in the *Habib al-siyar*, who later served Sultan Husayn. It is hard to imagine a person of that period studying with 'Ali Jurjani who died in 816/813, though it could have been done through an intermediary (Khwāndamīr, *Ḥabīb*, vol. IV, 106; Thackston, *Habibu's-siyar*, 408).

[57] Faṣīḥ Khwāfī, *Mujmal-i faṣīḥī*, 275; Wā'iẓ, *Maqṣad*, 82; Samarqandī, *Ḥabīb*, vol. IV, 13; Thackston, *Habibu's-siyar*, 358; Kāshifī, *Rashaḥāt*, 302.

[58] Faṣīḥ Khwāfī, *Mujmal-i faṣīḥī*, 275; Samarqandī, *Maṭla'*, vol. II, 647; Khwāndamīr, *Ḥabīb*, vol. IV, 13.

[59] Samarqandī, *Maṭla'*, 647; Faṣīḥ Khwāfī, *Mujmal-i faṣīḥī*, vol. III, 244; Wā'iẓ, *Maqṣad*, 45, 69, 79.

Throughout his reign, then, Shahrukh gave positions to Khorasanian personnel and ulama connected to the scholars of Temür's court. While the office of chief judge clearly remained in the hands of an established Herat family, the office of *ṣadr* was staffed largely by people connected to Temür, rather than Khorasan. Teachers, *khaṭībs*, and *muḥtasibs* appear to have been appointed from both groups. Over time, the distinction between local and imported scholars decreased, in part because the two intermarried. Given the high prestige of local ancestry, it was natural that newly arrived scholars should seek out women from Khorasanian families of religious importance. For the local families, marriage with members of the court ulama may have had considerable advantages. As I mentioned above, the father of two of Shahrukh's most prominent court ulama, Jalal al-Din ʿAbd al-Rahim and Shihab al-Din ʿAbd al-Rahman, had married into the Khorasanian aristocracy, and his son Jalal al-Din, did likewise. The son of Shahrukh's *ṣadr* Muhammad Amin, marrying the daughter of Jalal al-Din, also acquired local connections. We see similar alliances formed in the families of ʿAbd al-Razzaq Samarqandī and Ghiyāth al-Dīn b. Humām al-Dīn Khwandamir. By the end of Shahrukh's reign, a large number of the ulama and population of Herat had become closely enough attached to the Timurid dynasty to find it advisable to retreat with them before the army of Jahanshah Qaraqoyunlu.[60]

The patronage of shrines

Shahrukh was diligent in his patronage of shrines and the variety of affiliations represented suggests both political and ideological motivation. His most famous act was his rebuilding of the shrine to ʿAbd Allah Ansari at Gazurgah in 829–30/1425–27, which has been the subject of several specialized studies. Since ʿAbd Allah Ansari was a Sufi and a Hanbali famous for his adherence to the *sunna*, this could have been aimed at promoting a conservative religious revival.[61] Shahrukh further promoted the cult of Ansari by building on the grave of Ansari's teacher, Khwaja Abu ʿAbd Allah Ṭāqī (d. 416/1025–26), earlier honored by the Kartid kings. Other factors also made the shrine at Gazurgah a sensible choice for patronage. Ansari had long been considered a patron saint and protector of Herat who kept invaders away, and the area of his tomb at Gazurgah was a well-established holy spot and burial ground. Early in his reign Shahrukh had built a mosque and mausoleum at the nearby shrine of Shaykh Ismaʿil Sufi.[62] Although the cult of

[60] Ṭihrānī Iṣfahānī, *Diyārbakriyya*, 352–53.

[61] Lisa Golombek, *The Timurid Shrine at Gazur Gah*, *Royal Ontario Museum Art and Archaeology Occasional Paper* 15, c. 1969; Maria Subtelny, "The Cult of ʿAbdullāh Anṣārī under the Timurids," in *Gott ist schön und Er liebt die Schönheit/God is Beautiful and He loves Beauty*, edited by A. Giese and J. Christoph Bürgel (Berlin, New York, Paris: Peter Lang, 1994), 377–406.

[62] Wāʿiẓ, *Maqṣad*, 24, 28, 34, 60; Allen, *Catalogue*, 162, 548.

Ansari had been in decline, some of his descendants were still active and were later buried at Gazurgah, along with members of another important family, that of the chief judge, Qadi Jalal al-Din Mahmud.[63]

The other site which benefited substantially from dynastic patronage was the shrine of the eighth *imām* Rida at Mashhad, which Shahrukh visited often; he erected a palace and garden for his visits.[64] The greatest patron here was Gawharshad, who in 819–21/1416–19 built a magnificent cathedral mosque as well as a *dār al-siyāda* and a *dār al-ḥuffāẓ*. Shahrukh further built a madrasa and contributed *waqf* and gifts to the shrine, most notably a magnificent gold lamp.[65] In honoring Mashhad, Shahrukh and Gawharshad were not instituting a new policy but recognizing a shrine of growing prestige, due to the widespread reverence for the Prophet's family. Amiranshah's wife had retired here to die in 814/1411–12 and was buried at the *imām*'s shrine, and some of Shahrukh's emirs also patronized it.[66] One smaller shrine on which Shahrukh built a mosque presents an interesting contrast. This was the grave of Bibi Sitti (or Satirkuh) in the central bazaar in Herat. Bibi Satirkuh and her husband were remembered as *ʿayyārūn* who fought for Abu Muslim against the ʿAbbasids.[67] Given the popularity of Abu Muslim as patron of the *futuwwa* groups, Shahrukh may have wanted to appropriate a site already associated with miracles, which could have been a source of concern to the ruler.

Shahrukh regularly visited a number of shrines in Herat. On Thursdays he went to the shrine of Ansari, on Wednesdays, the grave of the Hanafi scholar and Sufi Abu'l Walid Ahmad al-Harawi, which had been patronized by the Kartid kings. Twice a year he visited the grave of Khwaja Majd al-Din Talib Sufi, connected with Fakhr al-Din Razi, and Mawlana Jalal al-Din Mahmud Zahid Murghabi (d. 778/1376–77), whose grave was credited with miracles. Several times a year he honored the powerful grave of Khwaja Katib, supposedly a writer of the revelation, but not listed in the books of *ḥadīth*, whose grave was reputedly the site of an earlier fire temple.[68] On his travels Shahrukh visited holy shrines, calling on the spirits of the saints for help. In this, as in his other religious observance, he both imitated and outdid Temür. The shrines he visited at Mayhana, Bistam, and Damghan, situated on the road towards the west, were established pilgrimage sites.[69]

Shahrukh's patronage thus included shrines of several different sorts. Along with those to ʿAbd Allah Ansari and Abu ʿAbd Allah Taqi comes

[63] Wāʿiẓ, *Maqṣad*, 46; Faṣīḥ Khwāfī, *Mujmal-i faṣīḥī*, vol. III, 209, 267.
[64] Ḥāfiẓ-i Abrū, *Zubdat*, 450, 692–94, 798; Samarqandī, *Maṭlaʿ*, vol. II, 41, 711.
[65] Golombek and Wilber, *Timurid Architecture*, 328–30; O'Kane, *Timurid Architecture*, 80, 82–83; Ḥāfiẓ-i Abrū, *Zubdat*, 692–94; Ḥāfiẓ-i Abrū, *Ḫorāsān*, vol. II, 95.
[66] Isfizārī, *Rawḍāt*, vol. I, 102; Ḥāfiẓ-i Abrū, *Ḫorāsān*, vol. I, 97, Ḥāfiẓ-i Abrū, *Zubdat*, 439.
[67] Wāʿiẓ, *Maqṣad*, 14. [68] Ibid., 15, 37, 45–46, 55.
[69] Samarqandī, *Maṭlaʿ*, 172, 305, 321, 632, 737, 884; Chahryar Adle, "Note sur le ʿQabr-i Šāhruhʾ de Damghan," *Le Monde iranien et l'Islam* 2 (1974), 173–82. It is possible that the edifice at Damghan was not commissioned by Shahrukh.

the shrine to the eighth *imām* in Mashhad. While honoring the *imām*s was foreign to Hanbali thought, the practice was fully acceptable at this time. There were also sites which were considered miraculous and appear to represent a more popular tradition. This was a program of conspicuous religiosity and respect for learning, Sufism, and miracle working, showing royal patronage for the sites and figures that mattered to the population.

After Shahrukh and Gawharshad, the most important patrons of religious institutions were the Chaghatay emirs, whose patronage was divided fairly evenly between Sufism and the outward religious sciences.[70] In Herat the buildings mentioned are largely mosques and madrasas, often as part of a burial complex for the emirs themselves, and the appointments we hear of are for *mudarris*. Outside however, we find buildings at the Sufi shrine in Jam, and some emirs were known to be attached to Sufi shaykhs. The most popular form of patronage was the construction of madrasa and *khānaqāh* complexes, providing both direct employment of ulama and a burial place for the founder.[71]

Of Shahrukh's emirs, the greatest patron of the religious establishment was Firuzshah, who repaired the cathedral mosque and erected several buildings along Herat's main avenue, including a madrasa and *khānaqāh*, a mosque, and also a garden (*chahārbāgh*).[72] Firuzshah clearly had a serious interest in both exoteric religion and Sufism. He is known for his patronage of the shrine of Jam, he and his descendants served as stewards for the *langar* of Amir Ghiyath in Badghis, and his sons were conspicuously devoted to Shaykh Baha' al-din 'Umar.[73] He is mentioned as being present and active at religious lectures, and Samarqandī, in his obituary, notes his generous patronage of shaykhs and sayyids.[74] Here Firuzshah appears in contrast to 'Alika Kukeltash, who seems to have been less involved in religion. One other emir had a particularly strong involvement in religious life, namely Shahmalik, governor of Khorezm, who sponsored buildings in Mashhad, where he was buried, and probably in Jam as well as Herat, and who is remembered as the patron of the great Sufi writer, Husayn Khwarazmi.[75]

Despite Shahrukh's piety and active patronage, it remains unclear whether he was promoting a specific set of doctrines. We know too little about the doctrinal views of his appointees to make firm assumptions about the teaching in the institutions that he and Gawharshad founded. What he did do however was to show his general concern with religion. Both Temür and

[70] As Bernard O'Kane has noted, Timurid princes undertook little building work in Herat under Shahrukh (O'Kane, *Timurid Architecture*, 84).
[71] I have discussed religious building programs by emirs in Herat in Chapter 4.
[72] Allen, *Catalogue*, 102, 132, 222; numbers 427, 465, 663.
[73] Kāshifī, *Rashaḥāt*, 401; Khwāndamīr, *Ḥabīb*, vol. VI, 6; Thackston, *Habibu's-siyar*, 354; Golombek, "Chronology," 28, 43. See also Chapter 2.
[74] Samarqandī, *Maṭla'*, 840–41.
[75] Golombek and Wilbur, *Timurid Architecture*, 332, 464; DeWeese, "*Kashf al-Huda*," 196–204.

Shahrukh presented an image of themselves to the public and the ulama. Temür was remembered for the brilliance of the religious personnel he collected, and Shahrukh became a shining example of personal piety and strict observance.[76] Thus, while he may not have controlled either the activities of the ulama or religious life of the city, Shahrukh's public efforts did add luster to his name.

Sufi shaykhs of Khorasan

The biographies of Sufi shaykhs are fuller than those of the ulama, and allow us to trace some internal political dynamics. Khorasan and its neighboring province, Quhistan, were hospitable territory for Sufis and during Shahrukh's reign were home to masters of many affiliations. In Herat shaykhs attended each other's assemblies, preached and taught in the congregational mosque of Herat, and visited each other's establishments, not infrequently bringing students along. Among these distinguished and charismatic men, we note differences in opinion and practice and a number of rivalries, but few lasting animosities. There were also many important shrines in Khorasan, but only one about which we have significant information: the Turbat-i Shaykh-i Jam, maintained by the descendants of Shaykh Ahmad Jami.

I will concentrate here on Jam and Herat, but it is important to remember that there was a great deal of activity beyond them. As I stated in Chapter 2, we must be aware of the role that chance plays in the creation of our source base, and thus our perceptions of status. The shaykhs of Jam had their own biographers, and one collection, the *Rawdat al-riyahin* of Darwish ʿAli Buzjani, has survived and been edited. The author was a descendant of Ahmad-i Jam and had available to him a compilation by Shaykh Abuʾl Makarim Jami, contemporary to the events described. Buzjani wrote in the early sixteenth century and was a Naqshbandi.[77] Several shaykhs of Herat are featured in the sources, partly because they were connected to the historians of the dynasty or to later biographers.[78] Above all, the people I shall discuss are conspicuous because they figure in the fullest sources we possess – those written by Naqshbandi authors of the late fifteenth to sixteenth century. One of the most influential of these was ʿAbd al-Rahman Jami, the famous poet related to the shaykhs of Jam. What we are seeing here then is two groups of

[76] See for example, Zayn al-Dīn Muḥammad Khwāfī, *Manḥaj al-rashād*, in *Īn barghā-yi pīr. Majmūʿa-i bīst athar-i chāp nāshuda-i fārsī az qalamrū-i taṣawwuf*, edited by Najīb Māyil Harawī (Tehran: Nay, 1381/2002–3), 486.

[77] Būzjānī, *Rawḍāt*, (editor's introduction), 7–17.

[78] Zayn al-Din Khwafi was the founder of a new order, and therefore worthy of notice in biographies outside of Khorasan – he was also connected through disciples to several of the authors of later sources on Sufi lives, notably ʿAbd al-Rahman Jami. Khwaja Bahaʾ al-Din ʿUmar was connected to the historians Samarqandi, Mirkhwand, and Khwandamir.

prominent Sufis who, whether or not they belonged to the same *ṭarīqa*, were in touch and important to each other. Outside of these circles there were many centers of religious power in Khorasan whose activities we can only guess at. There are some indications from Indian sources that the shaykhs at Chisht remained active.[79] When Shahrukh built his madrasa and *khānaqāh* in 813/1410–11, he appointed ʿAlaʾ al-Din ʿAli Chishti as its administrator, and, as I wrote in Chapter 6, Fasih revered shaykhs in Sanjan who were probably descendants of the Chishti shaykh Shah Sanjan (d. 1201).[80] Given the absence of later information, it seems possible that the Chishti shaykhs were indeed losing influence within elite circles, but they were undoubtedly still part of the religious picture during Shahrukh's life.

The account of politics which I present below should be seen as an example of how relationships worked, not as a full description of power structures. I have chosen a set of men whose activities have been particularly fully chronicled and this allows a deeper analysis of political dynamics than one can achieve for less well-recorded figures. There is no doubt of the prominence of the men and the circles whom I have chosen to discuss; what is uncertain is that there were no other equally important local Sufis active at this period.

In analyzing the Sufi milieu in Khorasan, I move away from the analysis of Sufi *ṭarīqa*s, and look instead at the relationships among shaykhs of different affiliations. In the Timurid realm of the early fifteenth century, organized Sufi orders like the later Naqshbandiyya under Khwaja Ahrar had not yet developed, and indeed, such a model may never have been standard.[81] The seeker of unity looked for help, inspiration and companionship through a variety of associations; we know that it was common for an aspiring Sufi to travel and study under several different shaykhs. While the propriety of changing or adding masters was sometimes questioned, it was a common practice.[82] Most senior shaykhs were considered to have a dominant loyalty to one master, but that did not prevent them from continuing associations with masters and fellow students of other spiritual lineages and some shaykhs even taught two different paths simultaneously. Under these circumstances membership in a particular spiritual lineage would not necessarily be the decisive influence on thought and action. One needs to ask what the *silsila* or *ṭarīqa* meant at that period. That it served as a genealogy and human legitimation of a set of practices and beliefs is indubitable, but what did it mean in terms of human loyalties and behavior?

[79] J. Spencer Trimmingham, *The Sufi Orders in Islam* (New York, Oxford: Oxford University Press, 1998), 64–65; Ernst, *Eternal Garden*, 62–73; Potter, "The Kart Dynasty," 94–95.

[80] Samarqandī, *Maṭlaʿ*, 110; Faṣīḥ Khwāfī, *Mujmal-i faṣīḥī*, vol. III, 192, 213, 252, 282; Khwāndamīr, *Ḥabīb*, vol. III, 385.

[81] Le Gall, *A Culture of Sufism*, 138–40, 169–72. The Niʿmatullahiyya may have been an exception.

[82] Paul, *Doctrine and Organization*, 54–60, 67.

The shaykhs of Jam

The shrine at Jam and the family that controlled it provide a good example of what a Sufi shrine could offer its keepers and the broader public. The shaykhs of Jam retained their influence over centuries, at least in part because their community remained local, centered around an hospitable shrine. The family founder, Ahmad-i Jam (d. 536/1141), wrote several didactic works which apparently had little impact; however he established a mosque and madrasa at Jam that developed into a family shrine, and he was survived by fourteen sons, who in their turn left numerous progeny.[83] He rooted his descendants in western Khorasan and Quhistan through marriage to notable families in the towns of the region, a policy followed by his descendants throughout the Mongol period.[84] Most of Shaykh Ahmad's descendants remained in Jam, Bakharz, Turshiz, and the Herat region and several of their graves were still maintained in the early sixteenth century when Buzjani wrote the *Rawdat al-riahin.*[85]

The shaykhs of Jam cultivated relations with the most powerful rulers of their times: Ahmad-i Jam with the Seljukid ruler, Sanjar, and successive descendants with the Ilkhanids, Karts, and Timurids.[86] The Turbat-i Shaykh-i Jam was crucial to the survival of the family's prestige, serving as a center for wealth and hospitality, a focus for royal and elite patronage, and a monument to the increasingly revered figure of Shaykh Ahmad. Its administration was a prize to be fought over within the family and does not seem to have remained permanently within any one branch.[87] At the time of Temür's invasion the *khānaqāh* at Jam was administered by Diya al-Din Yusuf, and he was probably *mutawallī* of the shrine as well, since he seems to have been considered the head of the family.[88] Despite patronage and marriage ties to the Kartid dynasty, the shaykh of the shrine and his cousin, the powerful vizier Muʿin al-Din Jami, actively encouraged Temür's campaign, but whether this was due to political prescience or their expressed disgust with the

[83] H. Muʾayyad, "Ahmad-e Jam," in *Encyclopaedia Iranica*; Būzjānī, *Rawḍāt*, 36, 47–8.

[84] Būzjānī, *Rawḍāt*, (for Ahmad's marriage) 51, (for those of his descendants) 73–74, 96–97, 105–06.

[85] Ibid., 60, 64, 66, 73, 79. The *khānaqāh* founded by Shaykh Ahmad's grandson in Maʿdabad remained an additional center of attraction (Būzjānī, *Rawḍāt*, 82–83, 89, 106).

[86] Potter, "The Kart Dynasty," 115–23.

[87] From Ahmad's son and successor, Burhan al-Din Nasr, the position passed to Burhan al-Din's nephew, Qutb al-Din Muhammad b. Shams al-Din Mutahhar (d. c. 647/1249–50). The next administrator we know of was his son Shihab al-Din Ismaʿil (d. 736/1335–36 or 738/1337–38), who apparently divided control between two of his sons – Fadl al-Din Ahmad, *mutawallī* of the shrine, and Shams al-Din Mutahhar, head of the *khānaqāh* (Būzjānī, *Rawḍāt*, 52, 88, 103–06). It is probable that the two positions were later reunited.

[88] Būzjānī, *Rawḍāt*, 108; Shāmī, *Histoire des conquêtes*, vol. II, 97.

godlessness of the Kartid kings, we cannot know.[89] It is uncertain who ran the shrine after Diya' al-Din Yusuf (d. 797/1394–95).[90]

The next person we can definitely identify as head of the shrine is Shihab al-Din Abu'l Makarim, born in 796/1393–94, who was in charge when Shahrukh passed through in 842/1438.[91] He was highly regarded as a scholar, writer, and Sufi, but it is not clear which branch of the family he belonged to.[92] He had excellent outside connections; on his mother's side he descended from a *naqīb* of Termez, and one of his relatives on his father's side was the highly respected Herat jurisprudent Fasih al-Din Muhammad (d. 837/1433–34).[93] Nonetheless, he seems to have had to work to make his way and acquired his position through maneuver rather than by inheritance. The *Farayid-i ghiyathi* contains a letter that Abu'l Makarim wrote to the scholar Rukn al-Din Khwafi complaining about his ill-treatment by ulama, Sufis, and the court; nowhere, he said, could he find respect, and he thought of leaving Khorasan for either Samarqand or Shiraz. He asked Rukn al-Din for his advice – undoubtedly asking for patronage, since Rukn al-Din had spent time in Shiraz and had a large following in Herat. This letter must have been written before Rukn al-Din's death in 834/1431, thus when Shihab al-Din was in his late twenties or his thirties. By 841/1437–38, he was apparently in charge of the shrine, as a recension of the *Farayid-i ghiyathi* was dedicated to him that year.[94] He died a few years later, while acting as emissary for Shahrukh to the ruler of Bengal.[95] His position passed to his son Abu'l Fath, but after this the administration of the shrine seems to have been transferred to another branch of the family.[96] It looks then as if the control of the shrine, like power in many other offices, tended to stay within one lineage for a few generations, and then pass on to another, though still within the larger family.

Management of the shrine required administrative and political ability. It is not surprising that these shaykhs cultivated cordial relations with the rulers of Khorasan, and rulers in their turn were well advised to respond. The head of the shrine Diya' al-Din Yusuf accompanied Temür on his campaign to the

[89] Potter, "The Kart Dynasty," 118–21; Aubin, "Khanat," 53.

[90] His brother Shihab al-Din ʿUmar enjoyed the favor of Amiranshah b. Temür and taught at the *khānaqāh*, but there is no direct evidence that he controlled the shrine (Aubin, "Khanat," 53, referring to Khwāndamīr, *Ḥabīb*, vol. III, 386; Būzjānī, *Rawḍāt*, 111–13.

[91] Samarqandī, *Maṭlaʿ*, vol. 2, 716.

[92] Būzjānī, *Rawḍāt*, 110–11; Khwāndamīr, *Ḥabīb*, vol. IV, 11. Abu'l Makarim's father's name, ʿAla' al-Din Abu'l Maʿali ʿAla' al-Mulk does not appear in the extant genealogies (Faṣīḥ Khwāfī, *Mujmal-i faṣīḥī*, vol. III, 138).

[93] Khwāndamīr, *Ḥabīb*, vol. IV, 11. The nature of this last relationship is unclear.

[94] Yūsuf Ahl, *Farāyid*, vol. I, 27; ibid., vol. II, 524–27. For Khwafi, see Khwāndamīr, *Ḥabīb*, vol. IV, 8; Thackston, *Habibu's-siyar*, 335.

[95] Samarqandī, *Maṭlaʿ*, 782; Khwāndamīr, *Ḥabīb*, vol. IV, 11.

[96] We find a Radi al-Din Ahmad b. Jalal al-Din managing the shrine under Abu Saʿid, succeeded by his son Jalal al-Din (Khwāndamīr, *Ḥabīb*, vol. IV, 338–39; Thackston, *Habibu's-siyar*, 520. Isfizari mentions a Murshid al-Din ʿAbd al-ʿAziz as head of the shrine in 899/1493–94 (Isfizārī, *Rawḍāt*, vol. I, 241).

Dasht-i Qipchaq, and Temür endowed two *khānaqāhs*.[97] Shahrukh in his turn stopped to visit on several of his military campaigns and was duly fêted by the shaykh. Shihab al-Din Abu'l Makarim dedicated his biographical work on the shaykhs of Jam to Shahrukh.[98] Some Timurid emirs were also closely connected to Jam, which profited particularly from Amir Firuzshah and the family of Shahmalik, governor of Khorezm.

The members of Ahmad-i Jam's family represented a variety of beliefs and practices. Abu'l Makarim's ability to produce a feast of high quality during an unexpected royal visit was counted among his *karāmāt*.[99] Another member of the family, Shaykh Shihab al-Din ʿUmar, who was the son of the powerful bureaucrat Muʿin al-Din Jami and grandson of the Kartid kings, held a low opinion of the world, and disliked associating with people of power. He preached that the world was like carrion; more than a small taste would poison you. As he lived in a time of hardship, his kitchen was open to all, but he himself was contented with little. This attitude did not prevent Amiranshah, when he was governor of Khorasan, from honoring him, nor did the shaykh fail to produce a suitable feast for his royal guest. When Amiranshah subsequently sent Shihab al-Din presents of camels, sheep, and cash, he gave them away.[100] This action was a classic gesture, which at once showed indifference towards gifts from the government and demonstrated the shaykh's ability to provide for those attached to him.

For the shaykhs of Jam, the unifying factors were family, connections, and wealth, rather than doctrine or practice. During the Timurid period they enjoyed a reputation for freedom from factionalism and zealotry.[101] Members of the family held a number of affiliations and some formed part of the circle of Baha' al-Din ʿUmar and Zayn al-Din Khwafi in Herat. The author Buzjani was a disciple of Khwaja ʿAziz Allah (d. 902/1496–97) who traced his teaching back to Saʿd al-Din Kashghari.[102] One reputed member of the family was the ecstatic and disordered Muhammad (or Mahmud) Khalwati, from whom later eastern Khalwati lines traced their lineage; the original Shaykh Ahmad, whose spirit was always concerned for his descendants, was said to have favored him.[103]

One characteristic of the Jami shaykhs was their tendency towards "Uwaysi" or spiritual discipleship. A number of people were introduced to the path by the spirit of Ahmad-i Jam.[104] The importance of the shrine's administrator,

97 Būzjānī, *Rawḍāt*, 108; Golombek, "Chronology," 28.

98 Būzjānī, *Rawḍāt*, 110–11. For Shahrukh's visits, see Ḥāfiẓ-i Abrū, *Zubdat*, 599, 715; Samarqandī, *Maṭlaʿ*, 40, 320, 713–14, 716.

99 Būzjānī, *Rawḍāt*, 110–11. ʿAbd al-Razzaq Samarqandi tells a similar story about Shahrukh's visit to the shrine in 842/1438 (Samarqandī, *Maṭlaʿ*, 716).

100 Būzjānī, *Rawḍāt*, 111–12. For examples of other ascetic Jami shaykhs, see ibid., 109, 114.

101 Jāmī, *Nafaḥāt*, 593.

102 Būzjānī, *Rawḍāt*, 124.

103 Jāmī, *Nafaḥāt*, 453. For his filiations, see Waʿiẓ, *Maqṣad*, 46–47, 72.

104 Shaykh Shams al-Din Muhammad Kusuyi, of Shahrukh's period, was called by Shaykh Ahmad. Although teachers and disciples are mentioned for Shaykh Ahmad and his immediate descendants, the number seems to decrease with time (Būzjānī, *Rawḍāt*, 78, 99, 118).

Shihab al-Din Abu'l Makarim, was demonstrated by the fact that during his life, Shaykh Ahmad's spirit took his form.[105] The same direct communication with Shaykh Ahmad was applied to shaykhs from outside the family and Shaykh Ahmad guided them into different spiritual lineages. A good example is Shihab al-Din Ahmad Birjandi (d. 856–57/1452–53). Before his birth his father had a vision of Shaykh Ahmad, who told him that he would have a son who should be named Ahmad because he would be "one of ours." The father sent his son to Herat to study the exoteric sciences with the leading lights of the city. When the young Ahmad turned to Sufism he became the disciple of Shaykh Sa'd al-Din Kashghari, who had trained with Zayn al-Din Khwafi and Nizam al-Din Khamush from the circle of Baha' al-Din Naqshband. Birjandi also appears to have served as *mudarris* in the madrasa of Khwaja 'Ali Fakhr al-Din.[106]

One famous outside devotee of Ahmad-i Jam was Zayn al-Din Abu Bakr Taybadi, remembered for his rudeness to Temür. Zayn al-Din had been educated in the exoteric sciences in Herat, then received the call from Shaykh Ahmad and spent seven years approaching his shrine barefoot while reading and meditating on the Qur'an. Since the distance between Taybad and Jam is only sixty kilometers, much of this time passed in Turbat-i Jam, where Zayn al-Din approached the tomb one step at a time. Throughout his life he remained in the service of Shaykh Ahmad's spirit and a strong supporter of the Jami shaykhs, whom he recommended to Temür's notice. Taybadi was clearly a man of great stature, important enough to receive visits from Baha' al-Din Naqshband and Temür.[107] His close association with Jam must therefore have been a significant asset. The connection between Taybad and the shaykhs of Jam seems to have been a constant; Buzjani mentions several people with the *nisba* Taybadi as disciples of Ahmad-i Jam or as sources of information.[108]

For other Sufi shaykhs, the shrine at Jam served as a welcoming and doctrinally neutral location to pursue a religious life. The restless shaykh Fakhr al-Din Luristani or Nuristani, who roamed from Egypt to Khorasan looking for suitable masters, found a congenial place there at the end of his life, and the controversial Qasim al-Anwar ended his life peacefully in a house and garden at Kharjird-i Jam. While there, he dreamed of Shaykh Ahmad Jam from whom, it is stated, he learned new truths.[109] The Jami shaykhs later

Shams al-Din Kusuyi is credited with bringing people to Sufism, but no regular disciples or *khalīfa*s of his are named (ibid., 111, 119–21). However, this trait was not uncommon among hereditary shrine lineages (D. DeWeese, "The *Tadhkira-i Bughrā-khān* and the 'Uvaysī' Sufis of Central Asia: Notes in Review of *Imaginary Muslims*," *Central Asiatic Journal*, 40, 1 [1996], 108).

105 Būzjānī, *Rawḍāt*, 109, 110; Jāmī, *Nafaḥāt*, 497.

106 Kāshifī, *Rashaḥāt*, 302–05; Wa'iẓ, *Maqṣad*, 104.

107 Jāmī, *Nafaḥāt*, 498–500; Isfizārī, *Rawḍāt*, vol. I, 225–27; ibid., vol. II, 37; Aubin, "Khanat," 53; Nawā'ī *Asnād*, 1–3; Kāshifī, *Rashaḥāt*, 97.

108 Būzjānī, *Rawḍāt*, 14, 28, 36, 40, 59.

109 Dawlatshāh Samarqandī, *Tadhkirat*, 347.

attested to miracles at his grave.[110] The shrine of Jam thus remained for centuries a locus of spiritual and economic power, remarkably independent of the personality and doctrine of its individual administrators. The emphasis on the founder, Ahmad-i Jam, as the conduit into the mystical path and the ultimate focus for personal loyalty may help to account for the family's receptiveness to a variety of teachings and its continuing adaptability to changes in political power. The shrine flourished also because it was useful; it was not only a center for the family, but also served as a refuge for shaykhs of all descriptions and as a site where the ruling elite could safely express pious generosity.

The shaykhs of Herat

While the shaykhs of Jam were outstanding for their ability to retain their position over centuries, those of Herat stood out for intellectual or philanthropic accomplishment. Several shaykhs of significant reputation made Herat their primary location and it became a center of attraction for students interested in both the exoteric sciences and Sufism. The city provides us with an excellent opportunity to analyze the political and social milieu of shaykhs who lived and taught in close proximity. Two of the senior shaykhs, Zayn al-Din Khwafi and Qasim al-Anwar, had achieved international reputations. Both men spent a significant part of their adult lives in Herat, but both also taught elsewhere. Two somewhat younger shaykhs were Baha' al-Din ʿUmar, of a Khorasanian family, and Saʿd al-Din Kashghari, who came from Samarqand. These four men had distinct spiritual lineages, leading back to figures now identified with different Sufi orders. Zayn al-Din's master ʿAbd al-Rahman al-Misri is part of the Suhrawardi *silsila*, while Qasim al-Anwar's primary master was Sadr al-Din Ardabili of the Safavid order. Baha' al-Din's spiritual lineage went back to ʿAla' al-Dawla Simnani, central to the Kubrawiyya, and Saʿd Din Kashghari first studied with the disciples of Baha' al-Din Naqshband, eponymous founder of the Naqshbandiyya. It is not at all certain however that these men, or other shaykhs of the time, saw themselves primarily as members of specific orders.

Several shaykhs seem to have had high local standing but receive less notice in the sources. One of these was Abu Yazid Purani, the disciple and successor of Zahir al-Din Khalwati. Abu Yazid formed part of the circle around Baha' al-Din and Zayn al-Din Khwafi and was known for his hospitality to other shaykhs and to members of the elite, with whom he had influence.[111] Although little is known about Khalwati shaykhs in Herat during this period, the *Maqsad al-iqbal* lists several who were linked by discipleship and they had a cemetery and *khānaqāh* in the city.[112] There were also numerous young men

[110] Jāmī, *Nafaḥāt*, 452–53, 593, 595. [111] Wāʿiẓ, *Maqṣad*, 90.
[112] Ibid., 46, 47, 72, 78, 83, 89, 90; Jāmī, *Nafaḥāt*, 503; Allen, *Timurid Herat*, 75.

who came to study in Herat, and among these was Khwaja Ahrar, who arrived about 830/1426–27, and whose biography furnishes us with valuable material. While the Herati shaykhs had a variety of formal affiliations and diverged in both practice and doctrine, we see more cooperation than rivalry among them. We know that Zayn al-Din Khwafi performed the vocal *dhikr* – apparently quite loudly – and he made the practice of the forty-day fast a cornerstone of his practice.[113] Two basic elements of later Naqshbandi practice – the silent *dhikr* and the abandonment of forty-day fasts (*chilla*) had already developed at this time, but such divergent practice was still accepted.[114] The sources mention these disparities, but they also show that personal ties developed across them.

Zayn al-Din Abu Bakr Khwafi was born in the region of Khwaf on 15 Rabiʿ I, 757/March 18, 1356 and traveled west to complete his studies. In Tabriz he reportedly attached himself to the ecstatic Kamal Khujandi, a disciple of Ismaʿil Sisi, but disliked some of his practices, particularly his fondness for contemplating young men, and therefore left for Egypt to study with Shaykh Nur al-Din ʿAbd al-Rahman Misri, from whom he received his major training and most valuable *ijāza*.[115] By 812/1409–10 he was back in Khorasan and well established; the rulers of Sistan requested him as mediator when they capitulated to Shahrukh.[116] He remained active in the region until 821/1418–19, but was living in Egypt in 822/1419–20 when he sent a cenotaph to Medina for the grave of Muhammad Parsa, with whom he was on close and cordial terms.[117] Between 825/1422 and 826/1423 he returned to Khorasan via Jerusalem and Baghdad. While he was in the west he attracted several disciples, some of whom accompanied him back to Khorasan. After his death, his spiritual lineage came to be known as the Zayniyya.[118]

When Khwaja Ahrar arrived in Herat about 830/1426–27, Zayn al-Din held a preeminent position. For most of his career Zayn al-Din lived at Ziyaratgah, often coming into the city where he is recorded as active in the cathedral mosque. In 812/1409–10 he established a *waqf*, creating a settlement in the nearby region of Gudara, which came to be called Darwishabad. This was to be administered by his family and to benefit primarily Sufis who

[113] "Waqfnāma-i Zayn al-Dīn," 189, 197. [114] Paul, *Doctrine and Organization*, 17–34.

[115] H. T. Norris, "The *Mirʾāt al-ṭālibīn*, by Zain al-Dīn al-Khawāfī of Khurāsān and Herat," *Bulletin of the School of Oriental and African Studies*, 53 (1990), 57–58; Jāmī, *Nafaḥāt*, 492–93; Leonard Lewisohn, "Muḥammad Shīrīn Maghribī," *Ṣūfī* 1 (1988), 43; Leonard Lewisohn, "A Critical Edition of the Diwan of Maghrebi," Ph.D. dissertation, School of Oriental and African Studies, University of London, 1988, 75–79. Khwafi's connection to the circle of Ibrahim Sisi is mentioned only in the sixteenth-century work of Ibn Karbalaʾi, but details from other sources corroborate it.

[116] Ḥāfiẓ-i Abrū, "Majmaʿ," fols. 450a–b; Isfizārī, *Rawḍāt*, vol. I, 329.

[117] Kāshifī, *Rashaḥāt*, 111, 174. We have a record of an *ijāza* to Darwish Ahmad Samarqandī, given in Herat in 821/1418–19.

[118] Norris, "The *Mirʿāt al-Tālibīn*," 59; Tashköprüzada, *Es-Saqâʿiq*, 37–42; Carl Brockelmann, *Geschichte der arabischen Litteratur*, vol. II, 265–66; "Waqfnāma-i Zayn al-Dīn," 188.

followed his practice along with the needy inhabitants of the immediate region.[119] Zayn al-Din was a strong follower of the Hanafi rite, *sunna* and *sharīʿa*, as well as a visionary and a skilled interpreter of dreams. While he was relatively independent of the dynasty he did not disapprove of frequenting institutions funded by government.[120] He stands out in Herat for his active recruitment of disciples, and Isfizari states that thousands of scholars were students of his.[121] His importance to the city is illustrated by the problems surrounding his burial. When he died of the plague on 2 Shawwal, 838/May 1, 1435, he was first buried in Malan, but his followers removed his body to Darwishabad. A little later he was moved to the *idgāh* of Herat, in a handsome mausoleum built by the vizier Ghiyath al-Din Pir Ahmad Khwafi. This became a burial ground for his followers and those of Saʿd al-Din Kashghari.[122]

The other outstanding shaykh in Herat during Shahrukh's early reign was the famous Qasim al-Anwar, who was born near Tabriz, according to some biographers in 757/1356. His first Sufi master was the Safavid shaykh Sadr al-Din Ardabili. After this he probably studied in Baghdad, and, like Khwafi, he apparently spent time within the circle of Shaykh Ismaʿil Sisi in Tabriz.[123] Sometime later he went to Khorasan. According to one report he went first to Nishapur, where he got in trouble with the exoteric ulama, and in 779/1377–78 he moved to Herat. We hear that he met Bahaʾ al-Din Naqshband (d. 791/1389) in Abiward, and that he attended the *majlis* of Zayn al-Din Abu Bakr Taybadi (d.791/1389). He is also reported to have spent a period of time in Samarqand before 830/1423–24.[124]

The connection of Zayn al-Din Khwafi and Qasim al-Anwar to the shaykhs of Tabriz involved them in a common network stretching across a large area and more than one generation. I will give a sketch of some of these connections here, to show how circles of influence and loyalty worked across the boundaries of spiritual lineage. Shaykh Ismaʿil Sisi was an influential shaykh identified with the Kubrawiyya; his circle has been analyzed by Leonard Lewisohn. Among the shaykhs mentioned as students of Sisi were

[119] The *waqf* was completed and registered in 830/1426–27. Khwāndamīr, *Ḥabīb*, vol. IV, 12; Thackston, *Habibuʾs-siyar*, 357; Wāʿiẓ, *Maqṣad*, 80–81; "Waqfnāma-i Zayn al-Dīn," 189–90, 197–200.

[120] Nawāʾī, *Majālis*, 28, 183; Kāshifī, *Rashaḥāt*, 328–29; Wāʿiẓ, *Maqṣad*, 81; Jāmī, *Nafaḥāt*, 497; Bernd Radtke, "Von Iran nach Westafrika: zwei Quellen für al-Ḥāǧǧ ʿUmars Kitāb rimāḥ ḥizb ar-raḥīm: Zaynaddīn al-Ḫwāfī und Šamsaddīn al-Madyanī," *Die Welt des Islams*, 35 (1995), 44–46.

[121] Isfizārī, *Rawḍāt*, vol. I, 207, 308. Shahrukh's *muḥtasib*, Jalal al-Din Muhammad Qaʾini, held an *ijāza* from him, as did the distinguished scholar Hajji Muhammad Farahi (Khalidov and Subtelny, "The Curriculum," 219; ʿUbayd Allāh Harawī, *Taʿlīq*, 106–07, 109–15). See also Wāʿiẓ, *Maqṣad*, 80, 94; Aubin, *Niʿmat*, 89; Aubin, *Deux sayyids*, 482.

[122] Jāmī, *Nafaḥāt*, 494; Khwāndamīr, *Dastūr*, 354.

[123] Jāmī, *Nafaḥāt*, 592; Karbalāʾī, *Rawḍāt*, vol. I, 335; Khwāndamīr, *Ḥabīb*, vol. IV, 10; Thackston, *Habibuʾs-siyar*, 356; Lewisohn, "Critical Edition," 15; Aubin *Niʿmat*, 37.

[124] Kāshifī, *Rashaḥāt*, 376–77, 417, 462; Jāmī, *Nafaḥāt*, 594.

the two renowned poets Kamal Khujandi and Muhammad Shirin Maghribi, as well as a less well-known shaykh called Pir Taj Gilani or Tulani. In some ways these shaykhs differed widely, notably in the question of observance of the *sunna*, for which Zayn al-Din Khwafi was famous, while Pir Taj Gilani and Qasim al-Anwar were much less strict in their observance.[125] They also diverged on their view of Ibn ʿArabi's doctrine of the unity of being, which was espoused and developed by Qasim al-Anwar, but regarded with suspicion by Khwafi.[126] Despite these differences, connections among the shaykhs continued through their careers. The rather disreputable shaykh Pir Taj Tulani studied first it appears with Ismaʿil Sisi's student Muhammad Shirin Maghribi, who sent him to his former teacher. We hear of him again when Zayn al-Din Khwafi reportedly came across him on his return from Egypt after his discipleship with Nur al-Din Misri, and lent him his fillet, which Pir Taj Gilani bore off into the tavern with him. Gilani is also blamed for having polluted the morals of Qasim al-Anwar.[127] Among the disciples of these shaykhs, some of the same connections continued. ʿAbd al-Rahim Khalwati, the son of a disciple of Muhammad Shirin Maghribi, served Muhammad Shirin, and also studied with Kamal Khujandi and Zayn al-Din Khwafi.[128] Zayn al-Din's disciple and *khalīfa* Darwish Ahmad Samarqandī is reported to have served Muhammad Shirin before he came to Zayn al-Din.[129] What we see here is the association of a group of Sufi shaykhs whose practice and beliefs differed, but who continued over their careers to maintain a connection across a considerable distance and to send students on to one another.

The positions that Qasim al-Anwar and Zayn al-Din Khwafi held in Herat reflect their differences in behavior and doctrine. Zayn al-Din was universally respected as a shaykh and scholar. Qasim al-Anwar won a large following in Herat, but the sources display ambivalence about both his ideas and his followers. On the one hand, there are suggestions that some of his teachings were considered extreme, but, on the other he is mentioned with the highest respect in both histories and hagiography, his poetry was widely admired, and he was later claimed in one way or another by three Sufi orders.[130] Whatever Qasim al-Anwar was, he was a man able to attract attention.

125 Lewisohn, "Critical Edition," 198–208; Karbalāʾī, *Rawḍāt*, vol. II, 100–01; Jāmī, *Nafaḥāt*, 492–94.

126 For Khwafi, see Zayn al-Dīn Muḥammad Khwāfī, *Manhaj al-rashād*, in *In barghā-yi pīr. Majmūʿ a-i bīst athar-i chāp nāshuda-i fārsī az qalamrū-i taṣawwuf*, edited by Najīb Māyil Harawī (Tehran: Nay, sh. 1381/2002–3), 554, 557–61.

127 Karbalāʾī, *Rawḍāt*, vol. II, 99–101; Jāmī, *Nafaḥāt*, 493–94.

128 Karbalāʾī, *Rawḍāt*, vol. I, 85–87. 129 ʿUbayd Allāh Harawī, *Taʿlīq*, 137.

130 Shah Niʿmat Allah's earliest biographer wrote that Shah Niʿmat Allah had met the child Qasim, and recommended that he go to the shaykhs of Ardabil. Later, he implies that Qasim served as a member of the Niʿmat Allahi in Herat (Aubin, *Niʿmat* [*Manāqib*], 37, 65, 80–82, 100–01). The author of the *Rashahat-i ʿayn al-hayat* suggests that, inwardly, Qasim al-Anwar was a member of the Khwajagan (Kāshifī, *Rashaḥāt*, 417). His main master was Sadr al-Din Ardabili, who connected him to the Safavid line, though he seems to have remained peripheral (Qāsim al-Anwār, *Kulliyāt*, edited by Saʿīd Nafīsī [Tehran: Kitābkhāna-i Sanāʾī, 1337/1958], 35–36).

The *Nafahat al-uns min hidrat al-quds* provides one of the earliest biographies of Qasim al-Anwar and illustrates the division of feeling about him. Jami states that his *dīwān* was full of secrets but that the *mathnawī*, variously attributed to him or to a disciple, was outside the acceptable bounds in relation to *sunna* and *sharīʿa*. In the hospice (*langar*) Qasim Anwar had set up he did not repulse adherents of questionable morals, who gathered to hear him speak of gnosis (*maʿrifat*).[131] Elsewhere there is a suggestion that Qasim al-Anwar was not strict in his observation of the *sunna*, and a member of the ulama is supposed to have left his service for that of Zayn al-Din Khwafi on that account. This should not be taken to suggest that Qasim al-Anwar was a Shiʿite since all of the shaykhs with whom he was affiliated were Sunni.[132]

Khwaja Ahrar visited Qasim regularly and the *Rashahat-i ʿayn al-hayat*, gives a favorable picture of Qasim. Here too, however, we find hints of behavior that was held against him. Khwaja Ahrar is quoted, complaining that for the followers of Qasim al-Anwar oneness (*tawḥīd*) had become a matter of going into the bazaar and looking at young boys of simple face, saying that this was the beauty of God. However the author states that Qasim al-Anwar distanced himself by saying one day, "Where have these swine of mine gone?" which showed his disapproval of their behavior.[133] One of his followers also supposedly indulged in openly licentious behavior which resulted in his dismissal.[134] We can conclude that Qasim had a large following, including young men who formed an uncomfortably compact and unmanageable group. His devotees included many of the ulama and the sons of emirs of Herat, and their youthfulness caused concern. Moreover, according to some reports, when Qasim moved around the city, he was accompanied by a large retinue and showed little of the respect for the dynasty which they considered their due.[135]

Under these circumstances it is remarkable how popular Qasim al-Anwar was with members of the religious classes. In his early years in Herat Qasim al-Anwar lived in or near the Khalwati *hazīra*, which suggests good relations, and we know also that he visited the ecstatic Ghiyath al-Din Muhammad at his *langar* in Badghis – none of the other major shaykhs are mentioned in connection with Ghiyath al-Din.[136] Many ulama and shaykhs of Herat

[131] Jāmī, *Nafaḥāt*, 593. ʿAli Shir Nawaʾi however, approved the *mathnawī* (ʿAlī Shīr Nawāʾī, *Nesāyimüʾl maḥabbe min şemāyimiʾl fütüvve*, edited by Dr. Kemal Eraslan [Ankara: Atatürk Kültür, Dil ve Tarih Yüksek Kurumu, 1996], 419).

[132] Aubin, "De Kûhbanân," 243 (including note 71); Nawāʾī, *Majālis*, 183–84.

[133] Kāshifī, *Rashaḥāt*, 453. This practice probably represents the practice of *shāhidbāzī*, the contemplation of beauty in earthly form, particularly of young boys. The contemplation of young men is also associated with other members of Ismaʿil Sisi's circle (Norris, "The *Mirʾāt al-ṭālibīn*," 58–59). For other criticism of Qasim's followers, see Kāshifī, *Rashaḥāt*, 322, 420–22, 486.

[134] Nawāʾī, *Majālis*, 8.

[135] Dawlatshāh Samarqandī, *Tadhkirat*, 346–47; Nawāʾī *Majālis*, 6, 183; Kāshifī, *Rashaḥāt*, 376, 418.

[136] For Khalwatiyya, see Jāmī, *Nafaḥāt*, 594. For Ghiyath al-Din Muhammad, see Khwāndamīr, *Ḥabīb*, vol. IV, 6; Thackston, *Habibuʾs-siyar*, 354; Qāsim al-Anwār, *Kulliyāt*, 15.

received Qasim's teachings surprisingly well. Two highly respectable members of the ulama are listed among his devotees: Hafiz Ghiyath al-Din, a specialist in *ḥadīth* counted among the distinguished ulama of Sultan Husayn Bayqara's time, and, as mentioned above, Jalal al-Din Awbahi, the student of Sa'd al-Din Taftazani appointed to Shahrukh's madrasa in 813/1410–11.[137] Nonetheless, when an adherent of the Hurufi movement attempted to kill Shahrukh in 830/1427, Qasim al-Anwar was exiled to Samarqand on the strength of a fairly tenuous connection.

Another important shaykh in Herat was the younger Baha' al-Din 'Umar Jaghara'i. He was born in Farah at an unknown date and was a disciple of his maternal uncle, Shaykh Muhammadshah Farahi, whose line of transmission went back to 'Ala' al-Dawla Simnani.[138] Shaykh Muhammadshah and his master Shaykh Shah 'Ali were major religious figures in Herat during the second half of the fourteenth century, and it was here that Baha' al-Din 'Umar was educated and had his career.[139] We do not have much information about his practice. He had been attracted at a young age and traces of ecstatic behavior remained; he was often so absorbed that he had someone stay next to him during prayers to keep track of his prostrations. His concern for correct behavior was shown in his care over the *ḥalāl* status of food and gifts. The sources suggest that he did not practice the vocal *dhikr*.[140]

Baha' al-Din 'Umar established himself just south of Herat, at Jaghara, but he came into Herat regularly and spent much time in the cathedral mosque where he talked to people of power to intercede for the poor. Indeed, he is supposed to have had a special envoy to the court on the business of the population.[141] Among his students or disciples were members of the ulama close to the court, including 'Abd al-Razzaq Samarqandi's brother and the father of the historian Muhammad b. Khwandshah b. Mahmud Mirkhwand. Amir Firuzshah's brother visited him at his house and Firuzshah accepted his advice.[142] By the time that Khwaja Ahrar arrived in Herat, Baha' al-Din was well established and Khwaja Ahrar visited him regularly.[143] Zayn al-Din Khwafi's death left Baha' al-Din as the preeminent shaykh of Herat, and later accounts of Khwafi's death suggest a kind of God-given suggestion. According to the *Habib al-siyar*, at the time of the plague of 838/1434–35

137 Kāshifī, *Rashaḥāt*, 225; Khwāndamīr, *Ḥabīb*, vol. IV, 7, 337; Thackston, *Habibu's-siyar*, 354, 519.

138 Jāmi, *Nafaḥāt*, 454–55; Isfizārī, *Rawḍāt*, vol. I, 337–38.

139 Wā'iẓ, *Maqṣad*, 70, 73, 88; Khwāndamīr, *Ḥabīb*, vol. IV, 57–58; Thackston, *Habibu's-siyar*, 382.

140 Jāmī, *Nafaḥāt*, 455–56; Kāshifī, *Rashaḥāt*, 244; Khwāndamīr, *Ḥabīb*, vol. IV, 60; Thackston, *Habibu's-siyar*, 384;.

141 Jāmī, *Nafaḥāt*, 455; Kāshifī, *Rashaḥāt*, 244, 334; Samarqandī, *Maṭla'*, vol. II, 852; Paul, *Naqšbandiyya*, 52, 58, 68–69.

142 Kāshifī, *Rashaḥāt*, 401; 'Ubayd Allāh Harawī, *Ta'līq*, 110; Jāmī, *Nafaḥāt*, 455; Khwāndamīr, *Ḥabīb*, vol. IV, 102, 105, 341; Thackston, *Habibu's-siyar*, 406, 408, 521.

143 Kāshifī, *Rashaḥāt*, 425.

the population asked Baha' al-Din to pray for relief. He refused, stating that God was clearly so angry that he would punish anyone who tried to intercede, however Khwafi accepted the population's request, prayed, and died of the disease.[144] It is after Khwafi's death that we find most of the striking incidents of honor shown to Baha' al-Din. When he left for the pilgrimage in 844/1440–41, he was accompanied by a large number of ulama and shaykhs, seen off by the powerful court scholar Shihab al-Din Lisan, and offered gifts by Shahrukh.[145] Samarqandī mentions his influence on Amir Firuzshah in the appointment of Sultan Muhammad b. Baysunghur to the governorship of ʿIraq-i ʿAjam in 846/1442–43, and his role as mediator and counselor to various princes in the succession struggle after Shahrukh's death.[146] When Baha' al-Din died in Rabiʿ I, 857/March–April, 1453, the ruler, Abu'l Qasim Babur, helped to carry the bier and ordered a mausoleum at his grave.[147] Baha' al-Din was succeeded by his son, Nur al-Din Muhammad.[148] Although we know the names of several people who were attached to him and are buried at his shrine, it is not clear that these men were full disciples, or that he gave *ijāza*s.

The presence of these four shaykhs – Zayn al-Din Khwafi, Qasim al-Anwar, Baha' al-Din ʿUmar, and Abu Yazid Purani – attracted young Sufis from a distance as well as students already studying in the city. Most aspiring disciples spent time with all these masters and, in a number of cases, it is unclear whose disciple they were. This may not have been a problem at the time, but in the later sources there are signs of embarrassment. One of the early arrivals was Saʿd al-Din Kashghari (d. 860/1456), who came to Herat from Transoxiana before 830/1426–27 and became an influential teacher. Saʿd al-Din's career presents an illustration of the difficulty of separating out personal and *ṭarīqa* attachments. In Samarqand he was a disciple of Nizam al-Din Khamush, whose line went through ʿAla' al-Din ʿAttar to Baha' al-Din Naqshband. As later Naqshbandi sources relate his life, Kashghari came to Herat on the advice of Khamush, who recommended that he go to Zayn al-Din Khwafi for the explanation of a troubling dream. Khwafi then suggested that he take the *bayʿat* to him, even though Kashghari was attached to a master still living. They agreed to wait for a sign and when Kashghari's dream clearly portended jealousy from his earlier teachers, Khwafi (without needing to be told the dream) told Kashghari that all paths led the same place, and that he could come to him for help without attaching himself formally.[149] Zayn al-Din was Herat's preeminent shaykh,

144 Khwāndamīr, *Ḥabīb*, vol. IV, 13; Thackston, *Habibu's-siyar*, 357. Samarqandī states that Khwafi had prayed without success for the end of the plague, but does not mention Baha' al-Dīn ʿUmar (Samarqandī, *Maṭlaʿ*, 678).
145 Samarqandī, *Maṭlaʿ*, 742–43. 146 Ibid., 742–43, 772, 935–36, 941, 984.
147 Khwāndamīr, *Ḥabīb*, vol. IV, 58; Thackston, *Habibu's-siyar*, 383.
148 Khwāndamīr, *Ḥabīb*, vol. IV, 105; Thackston, *Habibu's-siyar*, 408; Wāʿiz, *Maqṣad*, 88.
149 Jāmī, *Nafaḥāt*, 402–4; Kāshifī, *Rashaḥāt*, 207–08.

and it seems likely that Kashghari did become his disciple, without disassociating himself from his earlier affiliation. He is often mentioned together with Khwafi and was buried in his tomb.[150]

Accounts of younger shaykhs and students in Herat suggest that many followed several different shaykhs at once, and it was not always clear where their primary allegiance lay. The story of Shams al-Din Muhammad Kusuyi, descended from Shaykh Ahmad of Jam, shows the difficulty of choosing among masters. Kusuyi was a brilliant man, versed in outward and inward sciences, and given to visions. Early in his career he was strongly attracted and became unconscious for several days. He stated that during this time both Baha' al-Din 'Umar and Zayn al-Din Khwafi appeared in visions to teach him, and Khwafi sat on his chest performing the vocal (*jahrī*) *dhikr* with a noise like cotton being separated from its seeds. Nonetheless, he followed neither, and when a vision of Ahmad Jam appeared to him, in the guise of Shaykh Abu'l Makarim, he accepted the spirit breathed into him. Although he espoused the ideas of Ibn 'Arabi, he interpreted them in a way acceptable to all his listeners.[151] The end result was that he performed the loud *dhikr* in the manner of Zayn al-Din Khwafi, spent a great deal of time with Baha' al-Din 'Umar, and the whole of the circle I have described attended his *majlis* and applauded.[152]

With other junior shaykhs, we find a similar uncertainty. Shams al-Din Muhammad Asad is counted as a disciple of Zayn al-Din Khwafi, and the *Nafahat al-uns* recounts the story of his giving the *bay'at* to him. He also attended Baha' al-Din 'Umar and sat for forty-day exercises with him, so that people thought that he was his disciple, and, furthermore, we hear that he was much favored by the restless shaykh Fakhr al-Din Luristani (or Nuristani), who passed on to him his own robe which he wore for blessedness. Later, according to the same source, he spent much time with Sa'd al-Din Kashghari who favored him greatly.[153]

At the time that most of the biographical sources were written, the question of primary affiliation had become important, and some authors attempt to downplay the extent of cooperation among shaykhs of different affiliations. This is almost certainly the case with the portrayal of Zayn al-Din Khwafi in the Naqshbandi sources. As I have mentioned above Khwafi was on close terms with Muhammad Parsa and provided the cenotaph for his grave. Although in some of the stories above, Khwafi's use of the vocal *dhikr* is presented as a reason why some students preferred other shaykhs, there are indications that Khwafi was friendly with the followers of Baha' al-Din

150 Wā'iẓ, *Maqṣad*, 90; Khwāndamīr, *Ḥabīb*, vol. IV, 59; Thackston, *Habibu's-siyar*, 383.

151 Nawā'ī, *Nesāyim*, 319.

152 Jāmī, *Nafaḥāt*, 496–7; Būzjānī, *Rawḍāt*, 118–19; Khwāndamīr, *Ḥabīb*, vol. IV, 60; Thackston, *Habibu's-siyar*, 384.

153 Jāmī, *Nafaḥāt*, 456–57; Khwāndamīr, *Ḥabīb*, vol. IV, 61; Thackston, *Habibu's-siyar*, 384; Nawā'ī, *Nesāyim*, 296; 'Ubayd Allāh Harawī, *Ta'līq*, 114.

Naqshband and may well have shared disciples with them. It is likely that Khwaja Ahrar came to Herat in part to study with him. When Ahrar first arrived, he visited Khwafi frequently and was often present at Khwafi's teaching sessions. The *Rashahat-i ʿayn al-hayat* mentions Khwafi, in the presence of Khwaja Ahrar, giving *ijāza*s to two disciples, Khwaja ʿAbd al-Rahim Rumi and Mahmud Hisari, and sending them off to their native regions to teach.[154] It is possible that Ahrar actually attached himself to Khwafi, and that later biographies attempted to disguise the fact. The *Rashahat-i ʿayn al-hayat*, for instance, records two dreams in which Khwafi tried to attract Ahrar into his following and failed.[155]

Khwaja Ahrar's connection to Zayn al-Din Khwafi's disciples lasted beyond the death of the shaykh. A later source tells the story of one of Khwafi's western followers, ʿAbd al-Muʿti, who became well known in Mecca. The report is credited to Mahmud al-Sindi, who had studied with Zayn al-Din Khwafi, Khwaja Ahrar, and Qasim al-Anwar. When al-Sindi was in Mecca, ʿAbd al-Muʿti asked him whether he would recognize Khwaja Ahrar and indeed, Mahmud saw Ahrar during the circumambulation. This was of course a miraculous appearance, and ʿAbd al-Muʿti stated that it was a form of collaboration with Khwaja Ahrar; he had revealed the miraculous capabilities of Khwaja Ahrar to Mahmud, and Khwaja Ahrar in turn made people talk about ʿAbd al-Muʿti.[156] We find an echo of the story in the *Rashahat-i ʿayn al-hayāt* which states that Khwaja Ahrar did not perform the pilgrimage, but nonetheless had spiritual concourse with ʿAbd al-Muʿti, whom the *Rashahat* connects not with Khwafi, but with another shaykh, ʿAbd al-Qadir Yamani.[157]

Despite the evidence of lasting connections, it is unlikely that all indications of dissension between Zayn al-Din and Khwaja Ahrar are later invention. It is not surprising that friction should occur between two men who are credited with the establishment of new levels of power and organization in their orders – Zayn al-Din was the founder of a new order, the Zayniyya, and Khwaja Ahrar introduced a more organized, competitive period in the Naqshbandi. By the end of Khwaja Ahrar's life, he was showing open antipathy towards Zayn al-Din.[158] The stories told about Khwaja Ahrar's Herat years in the *Rashahat-i ʿayn al-hayat* provide a picture of what could happen with the arrival of aggressive and charismatic shaykhs within an established and relatively stable milieu. Khwaja Ahrar was not the only troublesome figure, and the two other shaykhs to consider here are the brilliant preacher, Darwish Ahmad Samarqandī, and the lightning-rod, Qasim al-Anwar.

I mentioned the successful preaching of Darwish Ahmad Samarqandī in the previous chapter. Before coming to Herat, Darwish Ahmad had reportedly traveled and studied with several shaykhs, including Khwaja

[154] Kāshifī, *Rashaḥāt*, 427. [155] Ibid., 425. [156] Tashköprüzada, *Es-Saqâʾiq*, 40–41.
[157] Kāshifī, *Rashaḥāt*, 569–70. [158] Ibid., 120–21; Harawī, *Īn barghā*, Intro., 37–38.

Muhammad Shirin and Baha' al-Din Naqshband's disciple 'Ala' al-Din 'Attar.[159] By the time that Khwaja Ahrar was in the capital, Darwish Ahmad had already received an *ijāza* from Khwafi and was enjoying great success as a preacher. He used his position to defy his teacher, both in his public preaching of Ibn 'Arabi's views and by quoting the verses of Qasim al-Anwar, and in response Zayn al-Din spoke out against him.[160] It was at this point that Khwaja Ahrar took up his cause. It seems possible that Khwaja Ahrar attempted to encourage friction between Darwish Ahmad and his master and that the later Naqshbandi sources exaggerated the extent of his success. The *Rashahat-i 'ayn al-hayat* reports that Khwaja Ahrar recounted this event as the first of his great triumphs over a rival.[161]

The greatest conflict among the shaykhs of Herat was probably that between Zayn al-Din Khwafi and Qasim al-Anwar. Given the differences between the two men, in their doctrines and their attitude towards the *sunna*, the contact forced on them by propinquity may well have been difficult. Qasim al-Anwar seems not to have been fully a member of Khwafi's own circle, but he was a person with whom many of its members were frequently in contact. Younger Sufis attended him along with Zayn al-Din Khwafi, Baha' al-Din 'Umar, and Yazid Purani.[162] Several Naqshbandi shaykhs connected to Baha' al-Din Naqshband – Hasan 'Attar, Khwaja Ahrar, and Sa'd al-Din Kashghari – seem to have been particularly close to Qasim, and we find Hasan 'Attar recommending a disciple to his service.[163] Darwish Ahmad's public use of Qasim's verses is an indication of their popularity and must have been galling to Zayn al-Din.

Khwaja Ahrar, who admired Qasim al-Anwar, reportedly saw him as a rival to Zayn al-Din Khwafi and remarked on this to Baha' al-Din 'Umar. In one of his dreams, he first saw Khwafi pointing the way to him, but he did not follow him, and shortly thereafter saw Qasim on a white horse and took the direction he pointed.[164] The *Rashahat-i 'ayn al-hayat*, written fairly late, should be treated with reserve on this subject, but other sources also suggest rivalry between the two men. In the strongly partisan account of Qasim's problems with the dynasty, written by Shah Ni'mat Allah's biographer Kirmani, there is a suggestion of collusion against Qasim by several members of the religious establishment, one of whom was called Zayn al-Din.[165] Another cause for Khwafi's opposition may have been Qasim al-Anwar's tendency to surround himself with young men. In his early years, Khwafi had

159 'Ubayd Allāh Harawī, *Ta'līq*, 137–38; Kāshifī, *Rashaḥāt*, 174.
160 Harawī, *Īn barghā*, Intro., 37.
161 Kāshifī, *Rashaḥāt*, 173–83; Paul, *Naqšbandiyya*, 80.
162 Tashköprüzada, *Es-Saqâ'iq*, 40; Wā'iẓ, *Maqṣad*, 90; Kāshifī, *Rashaḥāt*, 206, 416.
163 Kāshifī, *Rashaḥāt*, 165, 168, 425. 164 Ibid., 180, 425, 427.
165 Nawā'ī, *Majālis*, 183–84; Aubin, *Ni'mat*, (*Manāqib*), 66. The one person opposing him whose name is given in full is Nasir al-Din Kusuyi, a disciple of Zayn al-Din Taybadi and an expert in *fiqh*, who died in 828/1424–25 (Faṣīḥ Khwāfī, *Mujmal-i faṣīḥī*, vol. III, 257–58; Wā'iẓ, *Maqṣad*, 75).

apparently left the service of Kamal Khujandi because he did not like this habit in him.[166] Khwafi's dislike of Qasim al-Anwar helps to explain the repeated suggestions of objections to him among the religious establishment.

Although conflicts like the one between Khwafi and Qasim al-Anwar might be quite sharp, most rivalries among the Sufis of eastern Iran seem to have remained personal, and did not develop into lasting factional strife. Conflicts between individuals should not be interpreted as rivalries between organized groups. In this period it seems that *ṭarīqa*s were only one among several channels of influence; shaykhs trained with masters from a variety of orders and recommended their students to masters outside their own primary affiliation – if indeed they had one. While some *ṭarīqa*s were developing distinctive combinations of doctrine and practice, individual Sufis could combine the teachings of several masters and adopt the parts that suited them. The example of Zayn al-Din Khwafi is particularly striking, because he is identified with a strong program and the founding of a lasting order. Nonetheless, he studied with several shaykhs and continued to send disciples to them, or members of their circles, despite differences in practice. Khwafi rejected the contemplation of young men practiced by several of his early teachers, including Misri. His disciples in their turn varied in their acceptance of Khwafi's teaching on Ibn ʿArabi; some went beyond Khwafi and condemned even Muhammad Parsa's interpretations, while others openly favored Ibn ʿArabi's teachings on *waḥdat al-wujūd*.[167] To understand how individuals created networks of influence and affiliation, we need to look beyond the *ṭarīqas* and the master-disciple relationship, to the circles which shaykhs formed around themselves throughout their lives and which could remain in place even after their deaths.

Shahrukh and the control of religious figures

I have stressed cooperation among shaykhs and ulama and the coexistence of different doctrines and practice. Nonetheless, there were doctrines which some ulama considered unacceptable or even dangerous. There were also concerns over the level of training among ulama, the correctness of *ḥadīth* transmission and other issues – a number of which were undoubtedly fueled by jealousy. In such cases ulama and shaykhs were not averse to calling in the help of the government. These appeals brought the ruler into the religious sphere as a facilitator and a source of corrective power, though not as an authority in his own right. Shahrukh has been portrayed as inimical to Sufi shaykhs and particularly strict in acting against heterodox doctrine.[168]

[166] Lewisohn, "Critical Edition," 79. However, Misri, to whom Khwafi next attached himself, had a following of young military men.
[167] Harawī, *Īn barghā*, Intro., 39.
[168] Aubin, "Note sur quelques documents," 146–47; Bashir, *Messianic Hopes*, 65–66.

However, most occasions on which he examined scholars and shaykhs came as a result of requests by ulama, since, as ruler, he held responsibility for furthering correct religion.

The histories give several examples of royal action called forth by conflicts within the religious classes. ʿAbd al-Razzaq Samarqandī was pitted against another scholar of his own cohort when his learning was called into question by colleagues. When Hanafi jurisprudents complained about verses which Shaykh Husayn Khwarazmi had written on the pervasive presence of God, Shahrukh summoned him to Herat to be examined, but his critics could not prove their claim and he was exonerated – Khwarazmi's close attachment to the family of Shahmalik, governor of Khorezm, may have weighed in his favor.[169] The story recounted in the *Rashahat-i ʿayn al-hayat* about Ulugh Beg summoning Muhammad Parsa to Samarqand to be tested on *ḥadīth* by Muhammad al-Jazari attributes the initial impetus to criticism by jealous ulama, and whether or not it happened, the story must have been believable. An incident described by Samarqandī gives a good illustration of the way in which ulama invited the ruler into their sphere. On a visit to Mashhad, Shahrukh was approached by one of the great sayyids of Mashhad and a shaykh from the shrine of Abuʾl Khayr in Mayhana to arbitrate their quarrel. He had the army (*ordo*) judge examine the case and when the judgment went against the Mashhad sayyid, he had him beaten.[170] In acting on complaints from religious authorities, Shahrukh was fulfilling his duties as the promoter of religion.

In some cases, religious figures posed a threat to public order and called for decisive action from the ruler. There were several such incidents during the reign of Shahrukh; sometimes he acted against them on the request of religious authorities and sometimes on his own. In general Shahrukh was cautious about taking action against religious figures, since he was understandably wary of winning the ill will of any popular figure or appearing to deserve the curse of an oppressed man of religion. The awareness of danger in this regard can be seen in the government's reluctance to act against men identified as insane who claimed power or threatened the peace. The association of eccentric behavior with power in the world of the unseen made the issue a difficult one. The biographical sources record several religious madmen who spoke or acted aggressively, against whom no overt discipline was undertaken. Muhammad ʿArab of Herat for years claimed the sultanate and was ignored, but when he led an uprising in the city after Shahrukh's death, the authorities searched his house and found a large cache of arms. Since he was old and well known in the city, Abuʾl Qasim Babur, who held Khorasan, simply exiled him to Sistan where he spent his last years writing an epic poem (a *Shāhnāma*) about his own kingship.[171]

[169] Khwāndamīr, *Ḥabīb*, vol. IV, 9; Thackston, *Habibuʾs-siyar*, 355; Nawāʾī, *Majālis*, 9, 185; DeWeese, "*Kashf al-Huda*," 198, 204–05.

[170] Samarqandī, *Maṭlaʿ*, 715–16.

[171] Nawāʾī, *Majālis*, 28–29, 36, 202–03, 209, 269; Khwāndamīr, *Ḥabīb*, vol. IV, 59, 104; Thackston, *Habibuʾs-siyar*, 383, 407; Wāʿiẓ, *Maqṣad*, 93; Samaraqandī, *Maṭlaʿ*, 1098–99.

There was good reason to take religious movements seriously, since they could pose a threat to public order and to dynastic prestige. The earliest disturbance that Shahrukh had to deal with was caused by internal rivalry among the disciples of Shaykh Ishaq in Khuttalan. We have differing accounts of the event since the dynastic histories are silent and the religious sources mirror the resulting split within the Kubrawiyya. In 826/1422–23 Shaykh Ishaq Khuttalani, the chief successor of ʿAli Hamadani, recognized one of his disciples as *mahdī* and set himself up in a fort in Khuttalan. By this time Ishaq was very old and had begun to pass his duties on to his favored disciples. The man claiming to be a *mahdī*, Muhammad Nurbakhsh, had been born in Quhistan in 795/1392–93 and spent some time in Herat, where he had been encouraged to attach himself to Ishaq Khuttalani. He quickly rose in Ishaq's favor, and in 819/1416–17 began to have dreams suggesting extraordinary spiritual powers. Another disciple dreamed that he saw light descend on him from the sky, and from him it was dispersed to others on earth; as a result Ishaq gave him the epithet Nurbakhsh. However, in 822/1419 a new and ambitious disciple arrived: Sayyid ʿAbd Allah Barzishabadi, born near Tus in Shaʿban, 789/August, 1387. According to the sources from the Barzishabadi faction, Nurbakhsh's claim to be *mahdī* was accepted only reluctantly by Ishaq Khuttalani, and it was Nurbakhsh who fomented rebellion. The Nurbakhshi sources suggest that Ishaq was quick to accept the claim but Barzishabadi refused, and it was Ishaq himself who promoted the rebellion.[172]

According to the hagiographies from both sides, Barzishabadi neither accepted Nurbakhsh's claim nor joined the movement. Shahrukh was informed of what was happening and sent military force. He had the major rebels brought to Herat to be judged, and executed Ishaq as the most responsible party. Nurbakhsh was sent to Shiraz, where he was imprisoned for a while and then released. Shahrukh may have found it safer to punish the elder and more local shaykh Ishaq, while being lenient with Nurbakhsh, whose claim to *mahdī* status could have outlived him. The two scholars who have recently investigated these events have proposed political rather than doctrinal motivations for the execution of Ishaq Khuttalani. Devin DeWeese suggests that since Ishaq was connected both with the local rulers of Khuttalan and the already suspect ʿAli Hamadani, exiled by Temür, his enemies used the rebellion as a pretext to destroy him. Shahzad Bashir concludes that the political motivation behind the execution lay with Barzishabadi, who had informed the local governor of what was happening and brought in Shahrukh's troops in order to get rid of his rival.[173]

Muhammad Nurbakhsh was released on condition that he give up his claims, but according to a later source, which may exaggerate the problem,

[172] DeWeese, "Eclipse," 55, 59; Bashir, *Messianic Hopes*, 44–49; Karbalāʾī, *Rawḍāt*, 232–40.
[173] DeWeese, "Eclipse," 59; Bashir, *Messianic Hopes*, 50–54.

he was active in Luristan within a year, striking coins, reading the *khuṭba* in his own name and accepted as *mahdī* by a significant segment of the local population. Shahrukh imprisoned Nurbakhsh again in 838/1434–35 and forbade him to wear a black turban – associated with religious rebellion – or to teach any but the regular sciences. In Ramadan, 840/ March, 1437, Shahrukh arrested him once more but released him after two months. After this he went to Shirwan and Gilan, where he spent the rest of his life relatively peacefully and even achieved friendly relations with Shahrukh's immediate successors, ʿAlaʾ al-Dawla and Abuʾl Qasim Babur.[174] Since Nurbakhsh lived outside the territories the princes claimed, he no longer posed a challenge.

The next incident was more directly threatening. On 23 Rabiʿ I, 830/ January 22, 1427, a member of the Hurufi movement stabbed Shahrukh as he left the cathedral mosque after Friday prayers. He was only lightly wounded and the would-be assassin was immediately killed. The incident led to a major investigation. The people most closely connected with the attacker and those identifiable as Hurufi were executed or imprisoned (others were sent to Kerman and examined by a council of ulama). The Hurufiyya movement had been considered dangerous to the dynasty during Temür's reign, but despite action against it, some of its ideas remained popular and found their way into the poetry of the period. The assassination attempt identified the movement again as an active and dangerous force, and led to suspicion of people of possibly heterodox ideas.[175] Shahrukh took the opportunity to push Qasim al-Anwar out of the capital city. The allegations were either that a *dīwān* of Qasim al-Anwar's poems was found in the room of the man who attacked Shahrukh or that he had occasionally associated with Qasim al-Anwar. If we consider the behavior of Qasim al-Anwar's disciples and their apparent adoption of the cult of human beauty as divine, the connection made to the Hurufiyya, for whom the male face displayed the signs of God's speech, does not seem to be too far-fetched.

The activities of Muhammad Nurbakhsh also help to explain the dynasty's eagerness to exile Qasim al-Anwar. The uprising in Khuttalan had taken place only three years before this, and Nurbakhsh was active in Kurdistan at the time of the event. Moreover Qasim, in his youth, had had a dream remarkably similar to the one reported for Muhammad Nurbakhsh, which brought him the name Qasim al-Anwar ("disperser of light"), by which he was subsequently known. As I have explained, Qasim was not only attractive, but attractive to unruly people, some of them members of the Chaghatay elite, and his lack of respect towards the dynasty had caused concern. Both early and later accounts suggest that a major reason for his exile was the desire of

[174] Bashir, *Messianic Hopes*, 54–65.

[175] In Isfahan, where there had been a Hurufi uprising earlier, the scholar Saʾin al-Din ʿAli Turka was imprisoned for a period in 1427, and in Rajab, 831/April, 1428, Zayn al-Din Khwafi wrote a treatise, the *Manhaj al-rashad li nafʿal-ibad*, refuting dangerous doctrines, and warning against Sufis coming to Herat to propagate them (Khwāfī, *Manhaj* 486–87).

the dynasty to get him out of the city.[176] The disapproval of Zayn al-Din Khwafi probably helped make it possible for the dynasty to push Qasim out. Even so he was too popular to be treated harshly, so he was sent to Samarqand, where Ulugh Beg received him with honor.[177] This type of exile was an acceptable way to solve the problem of difficult personalities.[178] Qasim al-Anwar later returned to Herat, and according to some sources, gained a following, then ended his life near Jam.[179]

Later in Shahrukh's life, a similar movement caused problems both for the Timurids and for the Aqqoyunlu. This was the Mushaʿshaʿ sect in southern Iran. Like Qasim al-Anwar and Nurbakhsh, Muhammad b. Falah Mushaʿshaʿ took his *laqab* (Mushaʿshaʿ) from an image of dispersal. In this case the movement was specifically Shiʿite and militaristic. Born in the early fifteenth century in Wasit, Mushaʿshaʿ studied in Hilla with the distinguished Shiʿite theologian Sufi Ahmad b. Fahd al-Hilli (d. 841/1437–38) who favored him greatly and contracted a marriage alliance with him. However, when Mushaʿshaʿ proclaimed himself *mahdī* in 840/1436–37, al-Hilli refused to recognize him and when Mushaʿshaʿ moved to Wasit and declared his intention of conquering the world, al-Hilli apparently issued a *fatwā* for his death and asked the ruler of Wasit to carry out the sentence. The ruler moved against Mushaʿshaʿ who moved to southern Iraq, where he gathered followers among the Arab tribes. His first encounter with the Timurids was on 13 Shawwal, 844/ March 7, 1441, when he and his followers, now led partly by his son, attacked Timurid forces near Wasit. The Mushaʿshaʿ remained a source of trouble for some years, finally making peace with the Safavids.[180]

The Nurbakhshi and Mushaʿshaʿ had some traits in common, in addition to the leader's claim to be a *mahdī*. Both Nurbakhsh and Mushaʿshaʿ were favored disciples who announced their claim when their masters were old and presumably unable to control the actions of their followers. We see in both movements signs of disagreement within the group about what level of political or military actions should be taken, and how extreme a doctrine should be promulgated. In both cases, the founder of the movement went beyond the doctrinal teachings of his master.[181] We should recollect here how Qasim al-Anwar seems to have repudiated some of the actions of his followers, suggesting that he himself was not responsible for their actions. Under the circumstances it is not surprising that the dynasty and some of the ulama should have found Qasim al-Anwar, Muhammad Nurbakhsh, and Muhammad

[176] Samarqandī, *Maṭlaʿ*, 315; Dawlatshāh Samarqandī, *Tadhkirat*, 347–48; Khwāndamīr, *Ḥabīb*, vol. IV, 10; Thackston, *Habibu's-siyar*, 356.

[177] Samarqandī, *Maṭlaʿ*, 315; Thackston, *Habibu's-siyar*, 340–41; Aubin, "De Kûhbanân," 244–45.

[178] Ulugh Beg sent an insubordinate member of the religious classes to Herat, where he was well received (Khwāndamīr, *Ḥabīb*, vol. IV, 35; Thackston, *Habibu's-siyar*, 369). For further examples, see Samarqandī, *Maṭlaʿ*, 645, 866–67.

[179] Qāsim al-Anwār, *Kulliyāt*, 29; Dawlatshāh Samarqandī, *Tadhkirat*, 347; Nawāʾī, *Majālis*, 6.

[180] Bashir, "Between Mysticism," 35–41. [181] Ibid., 40.

Musha'sha' alarming. Aside from doctrinal issues, the danger of a charismatic leader with an enthusiastic following from bazaar, tribe or countryside was a very real one and not easy to counter, since the ruler did not want to risk becoming the enemy of someone who might turn out to be truly holy.

Conclusion

We see in the religious politics of Shahrukh's time an arena in which no one group or doctrinal tendency dominated. Under these circumstances the ruler might promote a program, but he also had to balance and accommodate existing trends. If we try to distinguish Shahrukh's policies from those of Temür, what appears most different is style and method rather than the doctrine or character of the religious figures favored by each ruler. Shahrukh began his independent reign with a declaration that he was restoring the *sharīʿa*, while stating that Temür had himself promoted it, and there are striking continuities in religious patronage. Under Shahrukh the students of the great figures whom Temür had brought to his court: Taftazani, Sayyid Jurjani, and Muhammad Jazari, held many of the highest positions and few new scholars were brought in from outside.

There is also similarity in the Sufi shaykhs and orders favored or punished by the two rulers. While the less well-known shaykhs patronized by Temür, notably Sayyid Baraka, have received considerable notice, his relations with the established shaykhs of Jam, Zayn al-Din Taybadi, and the circle of Baha' al-Din Naqshband were likewise cordial, and these groups also had good relations with the dynasty under Shahrukh. Almost all the Sufi groups and religious movements whom Shahrukh disapproved of had also had difficult relations with Temür. Khwaja Ishaq, executed by Shahrukh, was the disciple of ʿAli Hamadani, whom Temür is said to have exiled. The Hurufiyya, punished by Shahrukh, had been inimical towards the dynasty since Temür had ordered the execution of their founder. Another example is the Niʿmatullahi family order; Sayyid Niʿmat Allah Wali Kirmani had allegedly been pushed out of Transoxiana by Temür, and it appears that neither he nor his sons found favor with Shahrukh.[182]

What changed most significantly between Temür and Shahrukh was the style of patronage. While the sources recount numerous relations between Temür and prominent ulama, Shahrukh seems to have kept a greater distance from individuals. He combined scrupulous personal observance with the building and visitation of institutions and shrines. The shrines he chose to patronize combined his own tastes, towards a strict piety and adherence to

[182] Aubin, *Niʿmat*, 12–16. The treatise by al-Tabasi, a disciple of Shah Niʿmat Allah, suggests that Shah Niʿmat Allah tried and failed to gain influence with Shahrukh (Aubin, "De Kûhbanân," 242–43; Muḥammad Ṭabasī, *Āthār-i Darwīsh Muḥammad Ṭabasī*, edited by Īraj Afsār and Muḥammad Taqī Dānishpazhū [Tehran: Kitābkhāna-i Ibn Sīnā, 1972], 334–35).

sunna, with the sites already revered by many of his subjects, including that of Mashhad, and such local holy places as the Herati shrine of Bibi Sitti.

Among ulama and Sufis it is also difficult to find individuals or groups which represented one specific program to the exclusion of others. The students of rival figures among the ulama could all hold lucrative posts and many men retained loyalties to people of divergent views. Among the Sufi shaykhs, the members of different spiritual lineages lived in close and generally friendly contact. The two centers I have examined, the shrine at Jam and the city of Herat, both welcomed shaykhs of widely different persuasions and practice. In Herat we find a group of shaykhs sharing the education of disciples, despite divergent practices and affiliations. Their conflicts were usually a matter of personal competition or morality. One thing that is interesting is their tendency to maintain close contacts with a number of former masters and fellow disciples, and to pass them on to their own followers. The circle which formed in Herat around its senior shaykhs persisted beyond their lifetimes, despite a number of disagreements within it. In the Timurid period there were numerous institutions of authority originating from the court, like the *ṣadr* and the *shaykh al-islām*, connected to the city ulama, like the mosque or madrasa, or from the Sufi milieu, like the shrine and the *ṭarīqa*, and all were important to government and society. None of them, however, could define the shape of religious life for the individual.

CHAPTER 8

The rebellion of Sultan Muhammad b. Baysunghur and the struggle over succession

Throughout most of his rule Shahrukh provided a precious period of peace and prosperity for his subjects, but his last years were difficult. The problems which led to rebellion and then to the collapse of order on his death were those which plagued most governments of the medieval Middle East. At the center, the need to choose a successor strained relations among the royal family and their servitors. Bureaucratic corruption had grown beyond acceptable limits and efficient tax collection was hampered by abuses both at the center and in the provinces. As older and experienced governors died it became harder to retain power in the provinces and this situation was made dangerous by the constant political activity of indigenous leaders. When Shahrukh became seriously ill in 847–48/1444 disturbances arose throughout the realm, and his grandson Sultan Muhammad b. Baysunghur began a rebellion which required military action. It was on the campaign against him that Shahrukh died, and his death opened a struggle for power which brought the death of most of the major contestants and the loss of western Iran. All of these events involved several segments of the population, and, when we examine the actions and successes of Sultan Muhammad, we see a pattern of interlocking political activities involving Iranian and Turco-Mongolian leaders, dynasty and emirs, emirs and viziers. What is illustrated here is both the fragility of central government and the involvement of provincial populations in politics which affected the center. Cities and provinces feared breakdown above all, but the actions they took to gain protection helped to exacerbate the conflict they dreaded.

We are well informed about the struggles at the end of Shahrukh's reign. Sultan Muhammad attracted numerous Iranian personnel into his following, including several historians. Three major historians of Fars, Jaʿfar b. Muḥammad al-Ḥusayni Jaʿfari, who wrote the *Tarikh-i Yazd* and the *Tārīkh-i kabīr*, Ahmad b. Husayn b. Katib, author of the *Tarikh-i jadid-i Yazd*, and Taj al-Din Hasan b. Shihab Yazdi, the author of the *Jamiʿ-i tawarikh-i hasani*, all worked for Sultan Muhammad or under his jurisdiction.[1] One other major historian with connections to Sultan Muhammad was Abu Bakr Tihrani

[1] See Chapter 2.

Isfahani, who had strong ties with the notables of Isfahan.[2] We thus have a variety of viewpoints from within Sultan Muhammad's camp. Meanwhile the historian ʿAbd al-Razzaq Samarqandī served at the courts of several other contenders: ʿAbd al-Latif b. Ulugh Beg, ʿAbd al-Qasim Babur, ʿAbd Allah b. Ibrahim Sultan, and finally the successful Abu Saʿid.[3] Their histories allow us to examine the factors which led to disintegration, and the dynamics of the struggle over succession.

Problems at the center

The first place to look for dissension is within the dynasty itself. Because neither Turco-Mongolian nor Islamic traditions offered firm rules for succession, the illness or death of a ruler often unleashed a contest for power. When he died Shahrukh was almost seventy but he had apparently made no move to appoint a successor. Nonetheless, even if he was not thinking about the issue, his family and followers certainly were, and had been for some time. The death of Shahrukh's most prominent sons had left no one obvious candidate. The central contestants were the princes from the lines of Gawharshad's two elder sons.[4] Ulugh Beg, born Jumadi I, 796/March, 1394, was the only son still alive at Shahrukh's death. He had two young sons, ʿAbd al-Latif, who had been raised by Gawharshad, and ʿAbd al-ʿAziz, just becoming active in military and administrative affairs.[5] Shahrukh and Gawharshad's son Baysunghur, born in 799/1397, had enjoyed the favor of both his parents but he died before the issue of succession had become a pressing one. He left behind him three sons, who at the time of Shahrukh's death were in their twenties and ready to fight for power. The eldest, ʿAlaʾ al-Dawla, born in Jumadi I, 820/June–July, 1417 of a free wife, had been brought up at the royal court by Gawharshad. The younger brothers, Sultan Muhammad, born 821/1418, and Abu'l Qasim Babur, born on 17 Rajab, 825/July 7, 1422, were the sons of concubines and were raised elsewhere.[6] It seems likely that Shahrukh and Gawharshad had chosen the firstborn sons of their two oldest sons to groom as possible successors.

Gawharshad's son Muhammad Juki, born 24 Ramadan, 804/April 27, 1402, was considerably younger than his full brothers, and there are indications that he held a lower status.[7] While Shahrukh's other sons served as

[2] Ṭihrānī Iṣfahānī, *Diyārbakriyya*, viii–xi, 293, 325.
[3] Khwāndamīr, *Ḥabīb*, vol. IV, 335; Thackston, *Habibu's-siyar*, 518.
[4] Samarqandī, *Maṭlaʿ*, 309, 729, 878, 881. [5] *Muʿizz*, fols. 139b, 140b.
[6] *Muʿizz*, fols. 144b, 145b, 146b; Ḥāfiz-i Abrū, *Zubdat*, 643, 812; Faṣīḥ Khwāfī, *Mujmal-i faṣīḥī*, vol. III, 235. It is odd that the *Zubdat al-tawarikh*, which was dedicated to Baysunghur, should have omitted Sultan Muhammad's birth. It is given in Fasih Khwafi's history without a full date.
[7] Yazdī, *Ẓafarnāma*, vol. II, 285.

provincial governors from a young age, Muhammad Juki was granted the region of Khuttalan only in 833/1429–30.[8] He had two sons, born in 825/1422 and 831/1427, but it seems that neither was raised by Gawharshad.[9] In his adult years he played an important part in Shahrukh's major military campaigns and seems to have remained at the Herat court, often serving as a kind of troubleshooter, especially in matters concerning Transoxiana and neighboring regions.[10] According to Samarqandī, Shahrukh favored Muhammad Juki but Gawharshad kept him out of positions of power.[11] Whether or not he was actually considered for the succession, Muhammad Juki thought himself an interested party and participated in the contest for position during Shahrukh's last years. As it happened, he died before Shahrukh, in 848/1444–45.[12]

Gawharshad was involved in the question of succession and showed an active preference for her grandson ʿAlaʾ al-Dawla b. Baysunghur. Her efforts on his behalf clearly aroused opposition among Shahrukh's descendants and are consistently criticized in the dynastic histories.[13] In 845/1441, ʿAbd al-Latif returned in a huff to his father in Samarqand, complaining that Gawharshad paid attention to no prince besides ʿAlaʾ al-Dawla. Shahrukh was displeased with Gawharshad and accused her of estranging his family from him. She found it expedient to leave for a time, choosing interestingly enough to visit Samarqand, where Ulugh Beg received her well.[14] We next hear of Gawharshad's favoritism during Shahrukh's illness in 848/1444, when she persuaded Firuzshah to swear the oath of loyalty (*bayʿat*) to ʿAlaʾ al-Dawla. This time it was Muhammad Juki who was angry, both with Gawharshad and with Firuzshah.[15]

The most obvious candidate for succession was Ulugh Beg, then almost fifty-three. He quickly put himself forward after Shahrukh's death but several factors counted against him. Although he was governor of a large and important province, he had not been active in military affairs for two decades and his province suffered from constant depredations by steppe armies. Furthermore, he almost never left Transoxiana, except for short trips to Herat. Gawharshad's protégé, ʿAlaʾ al-Dawla, was much younger, but was active at the central court. On the other hand, the favoritism Gawharshad showed him had raised resentment. Ulugh Beg's son ʿAbd al-Latif, although only eighteen or nineteen and with his father still alive, was likewise close to

8 Dawlatshāh Samarqandī, *Tadhkirat*, 396; Samarqandī, *Maṭlaʿ*, 793–94, 904.

9 The *Muʿizz al-ansab* gives no information at all on the raising of Muhammad Juki's sons (*Muʿizz*, fol. 151a; Faṣīḥ Khwāfī, *Mujmal-i faṣīḥī*, vol. III, 251; Samarqandī, *Maṭlaʿ*, 319).

10 See for instance, Ḥāfiẓ-i Abrū, *Zubdat*, 906–7; Samarqandī, *Maṭlaʿ*, 324, 665, 684, 711–12, 793–95.

11 Samarqandī, *Maṭlaʿ*, 851–52.

12 Ibid., 851–53. According to these passages, Muhammad Juki's region was divided between his sons; however, in the second passage, only his son Aba Bakr is mentioned, holding Khuttalan, Arhang, and Sali Saray.

13 Manz, "Women," 132–35. 14 Samarqandī, *Maṭlaʿ*, 759. 15 Ibid., 897.

court affairs and impatient for power.[16] It is within this framework that we should evaluate Sultan Muhammad b. Baysunghur's actions at the end of Shahrukh's life.

While the members of the dynasty were beginning to jockey for future position, in the central *dīwān* struggles for power involved the princes in rivalries among viziers and emirs. Towards the end of his life, Shahrukh appears to have paid less attention to state affairs and his last years were marked by a series of financial scandals. These were probably due to both growing abuses and the desire to counter the power of two men whose power had become dangerously strong: Amir Firuzshah and the chief vizier Pir Ahmad Khwafi. The major *dīwān* events were discussed in Chapter 2 and will be reviewed only briefly here. The first major upheaval was in 845/1441, when ʿAli Shaqani, second in command within the *dīwān*, was implicated in a scandal concerning the taxes of Jam. Firuzshah was given the investigation and found him guilty. This was a major setback for Pir Ahmad Khwafi, who had established a comfortable relationship with his subordinate and had been complaining about Firuzshah's over-involvement in *dīwān* affairs. The shake-up may have been accompanied by some disciplinary action against Pir Ahmad Khwafi.[17]

By 847/1443–44, Samarqandī reports that Firuzshah had begun to abuse his position and it appears that Shahrukh decided to curb his power. At this time there were tax arrears throughout Iraq and particularly in Isfahan, which was governed by Firuzshah's family. Nothing had reached Herat from the city for several years. Shahrukh sent out an emir, Shah Mahmud Yasawul, to investigate affairs in Iraq and push for payment.[18] Although Firuzshah is not mentioned in this context, it is likely that the action was aimed in part at him. In the same year, Shahrukh ordered an inquiry into reports of irregularities in taxes administered through Balkh, which were under Firuzshah's oversight. He ordered Muhammad Juki, unfriendly to Firuzshah, to take part in the investigation.[19] The scandal broke the next year when Muhammad Juki returned to Herat – by this time the prince had yet another grudge against Firuzshah, due to his pledge of loyalty to ʿAlaʾ al-Dawla. The investigators proved graft involving emirs responsible to Firuzshah who, unable to bear the disgrace, absented himself from the court and soon died.[20] He was replaced as chief vizier in the *dīwān* by the

[16] None of the Timurid sources record the birth ofʿAbd al-Latif or ʿAbd al-ʿAziz. Since Ḥāfiẓ-i Abrū routinely reported the births of Ulugh Beg's children, it seems almost certain that ʿAbd al-Latif was born after 829/1425–26, the last year fully covered by the *Zubdat al-tawarikh*. The date of his circumcision in 840/1436–37 suggests an age, at that time, of somewhere between eight and twelve years (Faṣīḥ Khwāfī, *Mujmal-i faṣīḥī*, vol. III, 281).

[17] Samarqandī, *Maṭlaʿ*, 752; Khwāndamīr, *Dastūr*, 360; Faṣīḥ Khwāfī, *Mujmal-i faṣīḥī*, vol. III, 290, 292.

[18] Kātib, *Tārīkh-i jadīd*, 234, 237; Jaʿfarī, *Tārīkh-i kabīr*, 123.

[19] Samarqandī, *Maṭlaʿ*, 793–95; Khwāndamīr, *Dastūr*, 362.

[20] Samarqandī, *Maṭlaʿ*, 837–40.

powerful Barlas Amir Sultanshah. Once the process of investigation had begun, it gained momentum. After Firuzshah's death another abuse came to light: the fact that a number of officials of the treasury in the fortress of Ikhtiyar al-Din in Herat had been embezzling large funds. The examination of this problem uncovered yet more examples of fraud.[21] After years of relative stability, the top echelons of Shahrukh's administration were suffering a severe shakeup.

The western provinces

While dynastic and administrative rivalries contributed to Sultan Muhammad b. Baysunghur's rebellion, it was not an affair limited to the Timurid ruling elite; the local powers of Iran were also active in the movement for independence from the center. Problems had begun several years before Shahrukh's illness. The year 844/1440–41 marked the beginning of a difficult period for many of the Iranian provinces. Mazandaran suffered an Uzbek invasion and one of Shahrukh's senior emirs was killed in the battle.[22] The next year, 845/1441–42, brought devastating floods to Fars and its neighbors – Yazd, Abarquh, Isfahan, and other parts of Iraq.[23]

In Fars natural disaster was accompanied by misrule and local disorder. In 838/1435 the governorship of the province had gone to the Prince ʿAbd Allah, the two-year-old son of Ibrahim Sultan. Major responsibility was taken by Shaykh Muhibb al-Din Abuʾl Khayr, son of the famous scholar Muhammad al-Jazari.[24] Shaykh Muhibb al-Din's power and his abuse of it grew over time, and in 845/1441–42 the emirs and notables of the region wrote to Shahrukh to complain about his monopoly of administration and the suffering he was causing. This problem was not easily solved. Shahrukh dismissed Muhibb al-Din and appointed another emir, but the new appointee soon became tyrannical and died within a few months. Shahrukh now granted the position to Muʿizz al-Din Malik Simnani, who had earlier shared formal power in Shiraz. Shaykh Muhibb al-Din used his influence to get a summons to Herat, where he arrived with magnificent presents. His generosity was successful and a number of emirs and officials petitioned Shahrukh to reinstate him in the *dīwān* and to allow him to rent the taxes of Fars for 1,100 *tümen*s a year.[25] He went back to

[21] Ibid., 841–42. [22] Ibid., 749; Faṣīḥ Khwāfī, *Mujmal-i faṣīḥī*, vol. III, 289.
[23] Jaʿfarī, *Tārīkh-i kabīr*, 111; fol. 330a.
[24] Ṭihrānī Iṣfahānī, *Diyārbakriyya*, 307; Jaʿfarī, *Tārīkh-i kabīr*, 91, 95–6; fols. 319a, 321b–22a.
[25] This is the only direct mention of tax farming that I have seen in the sources.

Shiraz and soon returned to his former position.[26] However, he must have begun to abuse it again, since at the time of Shahrukh's death he was in prison in Herat.[27]

At this time Khuzistan, usually under the control of Fars, was threatened by the power of the Mushaʿshaʿ movement described in the previous chapter. When the Mushaʿshaʿ raided Huwayza, Shaykh Muhibb al-Din took an army against them but suffered a humiliating defeat; his army scattered and he had to retreat to Shushtar. What must have made the embarrassment worse was the successful campaign shortly thereafter by the Qaraqoyunlu governor of Baghdad, who pushed the Mushaʿshaʿ out of Khuzistan. Although officially a vassal, he undertook the campaign without Shahrukh's permission, and followed it with a letter of apology which Shahrukh received graciously. This event probably took place in 844/1440–41 and it is possible that it sufficiently shook Muhibb al-Din's prestige to encourage the action of the notables and emirs against him.[28] In Yazd it seems that the year 846/1442–43 also marked a crisis of leadership; the *Tarikh-i jadid-i Yazd* states that Yazd's long-term governor Jalal al-Din Chaqmaq was dismissed and replaced by someone known as Hamza Chuhra. At the time of Sultan Muhammad's movement, Chaqmaq was at Shahrukh's court.[29]

The most immediate threat to Shahrukh's power came from the northern provinces of Iran. The region from Sultaniyya to Qum was governed by Amir Yusuf Khwaja, who was probably at least in his sixties and apparently had not been providing strong leadership for some time.[30] Some of the region's cities had come under direct control only recently and politically they faced in a number of different directions. Sultaniyya was on the Turkmen border and not infrequently taken over by the Qaraqoyunlu or their vassals, while Qum and Sawa were connected to each other and sometimes also to Isfahan. Next door were the Caspian provinces of Tarum, Gilan, Rustamdar, and Mazandaran, whose active politics posed a constant challenge for any governor, and since the Timurids often succumbed to the temptation of interference, the border cities became part of the local political field. Rayy, on the frontier of Mazandaran and Rustamdar, and Qazwin, near Tarum and Gilan, were both targets for raids by local rulers. This was not a region which could afford an inactive governor.

The challenge that appeared in 845/1441–42 came from Malik Gayumarth, the ruler of Rustamdar, and it was probably not a surprise to many people in the area. Malik Gayumarth b. Bisutun had come to power

[26] Shaykh Muhibb al-Din Abu'l Khayr appears in some way to have shared power with Simnani until Simnani's death in 847/1433–34 (Samarqandī, *Maṭlaʿ*, 756–59; Faṣīḥ Khwāfī, *Mujmal-i faṣīḥī*, vol. III, 290).

[27] Samarqandī, *Maṭlaʿ*, 795–96, 893; Kātib, *Tārīkh-i jadīd*, 247.

[28] Jaʿfarī, *Tārīkh-i kabīr*, 111–13; Bashir, "Between Mysticism," 38.

[29] Kātib, *Tārīkh-i jadīd*, 227, 231.

[30] See Chapter 4.

during the reign of Temür. Shortly before Temür's death he was deposed and fled to Fars, but he regained his old position early in Shahrukh's reign.[31] For several years Malik Gayumarth gave cautious support to rulers defying Shahrukh, but after Shahrukh's victory in Fars in 817/1414–15, he accepted his rule and from that time to 845/1441–42, he appears in the major histories in the guise of a loyal vassal providing troops for the Azarbaijan campaigns.[32]

Locally Malik Gayumarth was far from inactive. He held a territory between two politically unstable regions, Gilan and Tabaristan, and his own apparently secure hold on the throne gave him ample leisure to become involved in their intrigues.[33] In 845/1441–42, when the two brothers who ruled Lahijan and Ranikuh in Gilan were fighting each other, one of them predictably appealed to Malik Gayumarth and sent him the keys to several fortresses. This contest continued for some time, drawing in powers from outside, including the governor of Sultaniyya and Qazwin. The quarrel that arose between Gayumarth and the governor Yusuf Khwaja was probably connected to it.[34]

Sometime in 845/1441–42, Yusuf Khwaja requested help from Shahrukh in his struggle with Gayumarth over border territories, and Shahrukh sent forces to help.[35] The battle was fought in difficult territory for the Timurids, who suffered a humiliating defeat during which Shahrukh's commander was killed. Yusuf Khwaja himself was probably not in the battle, but died of natural causes soon afterwards. On hearing news of the defeat Shahrukh gathered armies from his eastern provinces and set out with his major emirs. Malik Gayumarth sued for peace and was forgiven, but Shahrukh decided to appoint a new and more powerful governor. He chose Sultan Muhammad for the position and assigned him an army which included the emirs of the former governor along with two close relatives of Firuzshah.[36] The regions over which Sultan Muhammad was given authority were Sultaniyya, Qazwin, Rayy, and Qum, an area which adjoined the region of his father Baysunghur, which had been inherited by ʿAlaʾ

31 Marʿashī, *Tārīkh-i Ṭabaristān*, 49–51.

32 Ḥāfiẓ-i Abrū, *Zubdat*, 324–27, 563–64; Marʿashī, *Tārīkh-i Ṭabaristān*, 256, 263; Rūmlū, *Aḥsan*, 194; Jaʿfarī, *Tārīkh-i kabīr*, 81; fol. 313b.

33 See Marʿashī, *Tārīkh-i Ṭabaristān*, 284–87, 292–302; Marʿashī, *Tārīkh-i Gīlān*, 146–51.

34 Marʿashī, *Tārīkh-i Gīlān*, 225–50.

35 The sources disagree over early events. The *Tarikh-i Tabaristan* gives a short and garbled account, stating that Gayumarth raided a wide region including Rayy, Bistam, and Simnan (Marʿashī, *Tārīkh-i Ṭabaristān*, 51). Samarqandī writes that he had sent mountain troops against Rayy (Samarqandī, *Maṭlaʿ*, 771–72). The fullest account is in the *Tārīkh-i kabīr*, which attributes the initial aggression to Yusuf Khwaja, who contested several fortresses of Rustamdar with Gayumarth (Jaʿfarī, *Tārīkh-i kabīr*, 113). There is more agreement about subsequent events.

36 Samarqandī, *Maṭlaʿ*, 772; Jaʿfarī, *Tārīkh-i kabīr*, 113–16; Kātib, *Tārīkh-i jadīd*, 228–30. Samarqandī attributes the choice of Sultan Muhammad to Shaykh Bahaʾ al-Din ʿUmar and Firuzshah, while the *Tarikh-i jadid-i Yazd* attributes it to the emirs in general.

al-Dawla.[37] The histories make it clear that Sultan Muhammad was expected to exert his authority over the regions under him, by force if necessary.

The course of Sultan Muhammad's rebellion

When Sultan Muhammad became governor in 846/1442–43, he was about twenty-five years old, an age at which many princes had already been governor or commander for many years. It seems that Sultan Muhammad had remained with Baysunghur in his province up to his death – later we hear of him incidentally as living (and drinking) in Herat. On Baysunghur's death in 837/1433, ʿAlaʾ al-Dawla had inherited the provincial and government responsibilities, while Sultan Muhammad and his younger brother Abuʾl Qasim inherited only their shares of wealth.[38] The sketches we have of Sultan Muhammad's character portray him as brave, loyal, and generous, and a prince who showed appropriate appreciation for men of religion and learning. On the other hand, he could be quite violent when drunk. Dawlatshāh Samarqandī reports him urinating on the beard of a follower, while Ghiyath al-Din Khwandamir writes of him chasing his retainers with a sword.[39]

As governor, Sultan Muhammad moved quickly to establish his authority and the local powers were eager to recognize him, probably too eager for Shahrukh's taste. He took up residence in Qum and received delegations with tribute or gifts from adjoining areas, including Kashan, Qazwin, Sari, Isfahan, Natanz, Firuzkuh, Sultaniyya, Tarum, and Azarbaijan, many of which were not within his jurisdiction. Instead of putting the gifts in the treasury, he distributed them to gain favor.[40] He also moved to collect people around him, sending to Yazd to summon the celebrated scholar Sharaf al-Din ʿAli Yazdi; when Sharaf al-Din tried to beg off, Sultan Muhammad sent a string of camels, a litter, and the cash for the journey.[41] Sometime in 847/1443–44 Shahrukh learned of these events from his emissary Shah Mahmud Yasawul, who had visited Sultan Muhammad on his mission to enforce tax collection in Iraq. Shah Mahmud reported that Sultan

37 Samarqandī, *Maṭlaʿ*, 772. According to Dawlatshah Samarqandī, he was granted Qum, Rayy, and Nihawand up to Baghdad (Dawlatshāh Samarqandī, *Tadhkirat*, 405). According to the *Tārīkh-i kabīr*, he was originally appointed to Qum, Sultaniyya, Hamadan, Qazwin, and Rayy, and on Gayumarth's rebellion, Rustamdar was added (Jaʿfarī, *Tārīkh-i kabīr*, 116).

38 Samarqandī, *Maṭlaʿ*, 665.

39 Khwāndamīr, *Ḥabīb*, vol. IV, 17; Thackston, *Habibu's-siyar*, 360; Dawlatshāh Samarqandī, *Tadhkirat*, 405–11.

40 Jaʿfarī, *Tārīkh-i kabīr*, 116, 123; Kātib, *Tārīkh-i jadīd*, 230, 237. Abu Bakr Tihrani Isfahani names even more cities, but he may be conflating two different periods (Ṭihrānī Iṣfahānī, *Diyārbakriyya*, 317). The cities of Kashan and Natanz seem to have been part of this governorship earlier, but they are mentioned in some sources as part of Baysunghur governorship, and did not go to Sultan Muhammad (Ḥāfiẓ-i Abrū, *Zubdat*, 609–10, 720; Faṣīḥ Khwāfī, *Mujmal-i faṣīḥī*, vol. III, 223; Dawlatshāh Samarqandī, *Tadhkirat*, 351; Rūmlū, *Aḥsan*, 207).

41 Kātib, *Tārīkh-i jadīd*, 230–31; Jaʿfarī, *Tārīkh-i kabīr*, 116.

Muhammad was gaining alarming power, and Shahrukh immediately took action. He reappointed Amir Chaqmaq to Yazd and sent him to fortify the city, also ordering preparations for the defense of Shiraz and Abarquh, and he removed Qazwin and Sultaniyya from Sultan Muhammad's administration.[42] Shortly thereafter Shahrukh sent orders to the ruler of Gilan, Sayyid Nasir Karkiya, to take troops to defend the region of Qazwin from a possible attack by Sultan Muhammad; presumably he expected a raid in reprisal.[43]

At the end of 847/spring, 1444, Shahrukh was stricken with illness, and for a while incapable of action. Sultan Muhammad took advantage to expand his power. He wrote to request the presence of his sister, Payanda Sultan, who was married to the governor of Yazd, Jalal al-Din Chaqmaq. She came accompanied by Chaqmaq himself.[44] It was probably at the beginning of 849/spring, 1445, that Sultan Muhammad decided to test the loyalty of two of his new subordinates. He set off towards Firuzkuh. This action produced an expression of submission and presents from Gayumarth. Sultan Muhammad proceeded towards Hamadan, sending ahead his emir Sa'adat b. Khawandshah to talk to Hajji Husayn b. Baba Hajji. When Hajji Husayn detained Sa'adat and refused to show proper submission, Sultan Muhammad attacked and defeated him, then handed him over to his cousins to be executed, as I described in Chapter 4. This victory did a great deal to boost his prestige locally, and he now received envoys and tribute from several western regions – Hamadan, Niyawand, Wurujird, and Khurramabad. Having dealt successfully with Hajji Husayn, he turned back again to Gayumarth, who this time did resist. Sultan Muhammad won a victory, collected some wealth, sent an army to Sultaniyya, and then returned to Qum.[45]

Sultan Muhammad sent news of his victory off to Shahrukh's court, where it arrived in 849/1445, and, in reply, he received a scolding for having killed Hajji Husayn. Several other major events came in 849. Firuzshah's brother Mahmudshah, governor of Isfahan, became ill and his nephew Sa'adat got permission to leave Sultan Muhammad's service temporarily to go to his bedside. When his uncle died, Sa'adat seized the opportunity and, without asking permission from Sultan Muhammad, wrote to Shahrukh requesting

42 According to 'Abd al-Razzaq Samarqandi, Shahrukh left him the income only of Qazwin and Sultaniyya, but Abu Bakr Tihrani Isfahani states that he removed these cities from his control and left him in charge of Rayy and Qum (Samarqandī, *Maṭla'*, 795; Ṭihrānī Iṣfahānī, *Diyārbakriyya*, 318). Subsequent events suggest that Tihrani's account is the correct one.

43 Mar'ashī, *Tārīkh-i Gīlān*, 257–60. This event is described as coming after the birth of Nasir al-Din's son in 847, at the time he was heading for his *yaylaq*, thus probably late spring or early summer of 1444, early in 848.

44 Kātib, *Tārīkh-i jadīd*, 230–32; Ja'farī, *Tārīkh-i kabīr*, 116–17.

45 Kātib, *Tārīkh-i jadīd*, 232–34; Ja'farī, *Tārīkh-i kabīr*, 117–20; Ṭihrānī Isfahānī, *Diyārbakriyya*, 318; Samarqandī, *Maṭla'*, 853–9; Rūmlū, *Aḥsan*, 256–57. The *Ahsan al-tawarikh* records the victory over Hajji Husayn under the year 849.

the governorship, which he obtained.[46] It was also in 849 that the notables of Isfahan, having failed to collect enough to pay their debt to the central *dīwān*, appealed to Sultan Muhammad. Since the estrangement between Sultan Muhammad and Shahrukh was by this time well known, their appeal should be understood as an invitation to take the city from Shahrukh's control.

The role of Isfahan

Most accounts of Sultan Muhammad's actions place the moment of active rebellion at his arrival in Isfahan. He was taking over territory clearly outside his own domain and making its population his subjects. The question to pose here is why the Isfahani notables invited him. Part of the answer lies in the political culture of the city. As I showed in Chapter 5, the notables of Isfahan were exceptionally aggressive in their relations with outside powers and had a reputation as a troublesome group.[47] The city seems never to have been fully quiescent. On the death of the governor Rustam b. ʿUmar Shaykh in 827 or 828/1423–25 his emir Pir Hajji had raised Rustam's son to power and when that son died, installed another. Firuzshah then removed Rustam's people and left his own brother Khwandshah in charge.[48] In 835/1431–32 there had been a rebellion in the city, probably connected to the Hurufi movement. Amir ʿAbd al-Samad, who was stationed there, was absent at that time and his two young sons were seized and killed. When he returned he executed the perpetrators.[49] It is quite possible that the Hurufi doctrine had adherents in Isfahan. Its founder, Fadl Allah Astarabadi, had spent a number of years preaching in that region and two members of the prestigious Turka family of Isfahan, Afdal al-Din and his son Sadr al-Din, were among those whose dreams he interpreted.[50] During much of Shahrukh's period, the most prestigious scholar of Isfahan was Afdal al-Din's son, Sa'in al-Din ʿAli Turka, whose writings gave a privileged place to Hurufi doctrines. He was favored by Shahrukh early in his career, but after the Hurufi attack on Shahrukh's life, both he and his family suffered. He wrote two well-known epistles complaining about Shahrukh's treatment of him.[51]

46 Samarqandī, *Maṭlaʿ*, 858–59; Kātib, *Tārīkh-i jadīd*, 235.

47 See also, Josafa Barbaro and Ambrogio Contarini, *Travels in Tana and Persia*, translated by William Thomas and S. A. Roy, edited by Lord Stanley (London: Hakluyt Society, 1873), 72; Khunjī Isfahanī, *ʿĀlim-ārā*, 174.

48 Jaʿfarī, *Tārīkh-i kabīr*, 74; fols. 309b–10a.

49 Ibid., 79; fol. 312a; Rūmlū, *Aḥsan*, 202. According to Hasan Beg Rumlu's account, those in the fortress killed the perpetrators. Quiring-Zoche, *Isfahan*, 31–33.

50 Ritter, "Anfänge," 15, 21–22; A. Bausani, "Ḥurūfiyya," in *Encyclopaedia of Islam*, 2nd edn.

51 Quiring-Zoche, *Isfahan*, 32, 221–23; Sayyid ʿAlī Mūsawī Bihbahānī, "Iṭlāʿātī darbāra Ṣāʾin al-Dīn Iṣfahānī Khujandī maʿrūf bi Turka," in *Majmūʿa-i Khiṭābahā-i Nukhustīn-i Kungra-i taḥqīqāt-i Īrānī*, edited by Ghulāmriḍā Sutūda (Tehran: No publisher listed, 1353/1985), 262–77.

The other cause for the action of the Isfahanis was the predicament they were in. After Shahrukh's investigation into the tax arrears of Iraq, many notables of the province had been called to Herat to settle their debt. After the notables of other cities had resolved their tax issues with the central *dīwān* and had been allowed to depart, a number of the Isfahan officials still remained in Herat, apparently unable to reach an agreement. As I have mentioned, Isfahan had apparently withheld taxes completely for some time. It was probably the power of Firuzshah which had made this possible, but now he was dead and his brother Mahmudshah, governor of Isfahan, was seriously ill. The powerful current generation of the family was about to disappear.[52] The person who determined the tax owed to the *dīwān* was Khwaja Pir Ahmad Khwafi, and it is quite possible that his old rivalry with Firuzshah contributed to the difficulties of the Isfahanis. Eventually they decided to release themselves by assuming the debt personally, but when they returned home they were unable to collect the sums promised.[53] The Isfahanis, finding themselves controlled by a family whose power was likely to diminish, under a ruler seventy years old and weakened by illness, probably considered it wise to put themselves under the protection of a powerful and ambitious prince.

Sultan Muhammad was quick to take the opportunity presented to him, first sending robes and encouraging words, and then setting off himself at the end of Muharram, 850/late April, 1446. The new governor, Saʿadat, whose appeal to Shahrukh for the position showed disloyalty to Sultan Muhammad, fled at his approach. He was accompanied in his flight by one of the local ward headmen, which may suggest that the decision to invite Sultan Muhammad was not fully unanimous.[54] Sultan Muhammad arrived in Isfahan on 5 Safar, 849/May 2, 1446, declared an amnesty on taxes, and staged a magnificent feast. He erected tents and pavilions, brought in singers and musicians, scattered cash over the plain, and gave out enormous numbers of gifts – according to one history three thousand robes to the notables of the city, from judges, shaykhs and sayyids, to the ward headmen. Shah ʿAlaʾ al-Din Naqib, one of those who had written inviting him, was given authority over the whole region, and two of the men who had been in Herat and had to sign for taxes, Khwaja Mahmud Haydar and Amir Ahmad Chupan, were named to the vizierate.[55]

From this time on Sultan Muhammad left no doubt about his intention to take over the regions of Iraq-ʿAjam and Fars. He sent out messengers with letters inviting local rulers and governors to give him their loyalty, and received an enthusiastic response. The cities mentioned were both inside

[52] Kātib, *Tārīkh-i jadīd*, 235. [53] Ibid., 234; Jaʿfarī, *Tārīkh-i kabīr*, 120–21.
[54] Jaʿfarī, *Tārīkh-i kabīr*, 150; Kātib, *Tārīkh-i jadīd*, 235; Ṭihrānī Iṣfahānī, *Diyārbakriyya*, 285.
[55] Jaʿfarī, *Tārīkh-i kabīr*, 121; Kātib, *Tārīkh-i jadīd*, 235; Ṭihrānī Iṣfahānī, *Diyārbakriyya*, 285–86; Rūmlū, *Aḥsan*, 257. Since Shah ʿAlaʾ al-Din was prefect of Husayni sayyids in Isfahan, he may have been given similar authority over a larger region.

and outside the provinces originally granted to him: Hamadan, Sultaniyya, Qazwin, Qum, Rayy, Kashan, Yazd, Natanz, Ardistan, and Abarquh. Most sent back officials with presents. Even Yazd, normally very conservative in its decisions, gave a good reception to Sultan Muhammad's messenger. In this case the governor, Jalal al-Din Chaqmaq, was away and his son Shams al-Din Muhammad, along with the notables, decided to accept in his absence. Shams al-Din Muhammad went to join Sultan Muhammad along with the judge of Yazd, Mawlana Majd al-Din Fadl Allah. Sultan Muhammad's messenger to Kerman was also successful and he received a friendly message from its governor, Hajji Muhammad b. Ghunashirin.[56] Muhammad Sultan's rising star attracted people from outside Shahrukh's realm to him as well. He was joined in Isfahan by two sons of Iskandar b. Qara Yusuf Qaraqoyunlu, with their followings and wealth. Combining the armies of Isfahan, local volunteers, and the *cherik* of the region, he had an army estimated at 30,000. The one region that had refused to come over to Sultan Muhammad was Fars, and he now set out against it with his army.[57]

I have posed the question of why the Isfahanis should have invited in Sultan Muhammad when he was clearly in opposition to Shahrukh, and have suggested that we should look to political culture and circumstance for the answer. We must now ask why Sultan Muhammad received such prompt and willing support in almost all the surrounding regions, both from local notables and rulers, and from Turco-Mongolian governors like Hajji Muhammad b. Ghunashirin and Shams al-Din Muhammad b. Chaqmaq. The speed with which even conservative cities like Yazd joined Sultan Muhammad argues against the theory of a Shiʿite uprising, as suggested by some earlier scholars.[58] The most likely explanation is the obvious one: Shahrukh's age and illness and the absence of a designated successor. Although he had recovered in 848/1444, Shahrukh had not fully regained his health and was suffering a relapse when Sultan Muhammad made his move. The histories all state that he decided on the campaign despite illness.[59] If the people of Iraq and neighboring regions had to choose among the local governors for protection in the upcoming struggle, Sultan Muhammad was a logical choice. Yazd and the northeastern regions of Qazwin and Sultaniyya were governed by emirs, and in Fars the governor, ʿAbd Allah b. Ibrahim, was only thirteen, and the chief power in his realm, Shaykh Muhibb al-Din Abuʾl Khayr, was in prison for his misdeeds. ʿAlaʾ al-Dawla b. Baysunghur had inherited his father's province but it was

[56] Jaʿfarī, *Tārīkh-i kabīr*, 122; Kātib, *Tārīkh-i jadīd*, 235–6; V. V. Bartolʾd, "Novyĭ istochnik po istorii Timuridov," in *Sochineniia*, 9 vols. (Moscow: Izdatelsʾstvo Vostochnoĭ Literatury, 1963–1977), vol. VIII, 553–57.

[57] Kātib, *Tārīkh-i jadīd*, 236; Ṭihrānī Iṣfahānī, *Diyārbakriyya*, 287; Jaʿfarī, *Tārīkh-i kabīr*, 122; Samarqandī, *Maṭlaʿ*, 860.

[58] See, for example, Roemer, "Successors of Tīmūr," 137; Aubin, *Deux sayyids*, 484–85.

[59] Samarqandī, *Maṭlaʿ*, 863; Jaʿfarī, *Tārīkh-i kabīr*, 123.

distant from this region and he appears to have been concerned largely with the affairs of the central court.

Shahrukh set off against Sultan Muhammad later that year. Several histories ascribe his decision to the influence of Gawharshad, and historians have suggested a particular animosity on her part. However, it is equally possible that she took the initiative because Shahrukh was too ill to do so.[60] The danger posed by Sultan Muhammad could hardly be ignored, and Shahrukh had met his earlier challenges aggressively. Had Shahrukh not been mortally ill, he could probably have put down the rebellion with ease, since at his approach Sultan Muhammad abandoned the siege of Shiraz, then gave leave to those of his army who did not wish to stay with him, and headed off towards Luristan.

Shahrukh now undertook an action which shocked his subjects. Among those who were participating in Sultan Muhammad's expedition against Shiraz were the men who had invited him to come to Isfahan. Shahrukh's army captured most of them, took them to the town of Sawa, executed several, and imprisoned the others. Those whom Shahrukh chose to execute were the chief notables who were signatories of the letter, and most were respected men of religion. These were the judge, Imam al-Din Fadl Allah, with his nephew, Mawlana ʿAbd al-Rahman, the head of the Husayni sayyids of the city, Shah ʿAlaʾ al-Din Muhammad Naqib, along with Ahmad Chupan, who had been among those detained in Herat over taxes, and Khwaja Afdal al-Din Turka, Saʾin al-Din ʿAli Turka's nephew.[61] One other member of the ulama was implicated: the historian Sharaf al-Din ʿAli Yazdi, who supposedly told Sultan Muhammad that Shahrukh would not move against him. Sharaf al-Din ʿAli was brought before Shahrukh and questioned, but then released into the care of ʿAbd al-Latif. Shahrukh spared the population of Isfahan, and indeed exempted them from taxes in order to encourage agriculture.[62] He spent the winter in Rayy, apparently in reasonable health, but during the celebration of Nawruz on 25 Dhuʾl-Hijja, 850/March 13, 1447, he died. His death unleashed just the sort of disturbances that the city notables feared and had tried to prepare for.

The succession struggle

The people around Shahrukh announced that he was suffering from toothache, but by evening people knew the truth. It proved impossible to return Shahrukh's corpse peacefully to Herat. There was almost immediate confusion and looting in the army. Some sources state that it was begun by the common soldiers, who grabbed the mounts and weapons of their better equipped fellows, while others state that the princes present at Shahrukh's

[60] Kātib, *Tārīkh-i jadīd*, 237; Jaʿfarī, *Tārīkh-i kabīr*, 123.
[61] Ṭihrānī Iṣfahānī, *Diyārbakriyya*, 288; Rūmlū, *Aḥsan*, 259–60; Kātib, *Tārīkh-i jadīd*, 234–35, 240–42; Jaʿfarī, *Tārīkh-i kabīr*, 120–21.
[62] Samarqandī, *Maṭlaʿ*, 866–67; Kātib, *Tārīkh-i jadīd*, 240–42.

death immediately plundered army supplies before heading for the regions they controlled.[63] There is evidence that many had expected this event and planned their future actions. Gawharshad sent a messenger to inform ʿAlaʾ al-Dawla, and told ʿAbd al-Latif to inform Ulugh Beg and bring order into the army camp, which he did by executing a number of people. Gawharshad herself remained with the corpse and on the third day she and ʿAbd al-Latif set out with the central camp for Herat. However, Gawharshad's choice of ʿAbd al-Latif was not a happy one; he was young and easily moved to resentment against his elders. After a few days he decided to imprison Gawharshad and plunder her belongings with those of her relatives, who from this time became known as the "Tarkhan emirs," due to their descent from Temür's follower Ghiyath al-Din Tarkhan. With the corpse, his captive grandmother, and the major viziers, ʿAbd al-Latif continued to move east. In Damghan, the *darugha* refused to open the gates. Since the royal camp could not continue without rest and supplies, ʿAbd al-Latif had the town conquered and pillaged.[64]

It is not certain what ʿAbd al-Latif's intentions were. According to Abu Bakr Tihrani Isfahani, who was in the camp at the time of Shahrukh's death but left shortly thereafter to join Sultan Muhammad, ʿAbd al-Latif actually declared himself Sultan, backed by a large number of emirs. If this was the case, his move towards Herat was an attempt to preempt ʿAlaʾ al-Dawla's claims. However, ʿAbd al-Latif's claim to power is not recorded in other histories and it is possible that after imprisoning Gawharshad he intended to proceed to Transoxiana, where Ulugh Beg was expecting him. Father and son may well have coordinated their actions in advance. In this case ʿAbd al-Latif would have been safeguarding his father's interests against ʿAlaʾ al-Dawla and Gawharshad.[65] He did cross briefly into Transoxiana, but then changed his mind and returned to Khorasan. In Nishapur he heard that ʿAlaʾ al-Dawla had opened the treasury and asserted his own claim; he had done this, according to Samarqandī, when he heard of ʿAbd al-Latif's action against Gawharshad. ʿAlaʾ al-Dawla's troops successfully attacked ʿAbd al-Latif, who was soon deserted by most of the emirs he had attracted. They freed Gawharshad and brought her, with Shahrukh's corpse, to ʿAlaʾ al-Dawla in Jam. Now ʿAlaʾ al-Dawla declared himself sultan, returned to Herat and buried Shahrukh in Gawharshad's mausoleum. ʿAbd al-Latif had to appear before the court in disgrace and admit publicly his shameful mistreatment of his grandmother.[66] The implication of Samarqandī's account, which remained central to Timurid historiography, was that the actions of both ʿAbd al-Latif and ʿAlaʾ al-Dawla were initially defensive,

[63] Samarqandī, *Maṭlaʿ*, 878–80; Ṭihrānī Iṣfahānī, *Diyārbakriyya*, 291; Kātib, *Tārīkh-i jadīd*, 243–44.
[64] Samarqandī, *Maṭlaʿ*, 884.
[65] Ibid., 880–81, 905; Ṭihrānī Iṣfahānī, *Diyārbakriyya*, 298.
[66] Samarqandī, *Maṭlaʿ*, 885–92; Ṭihrānī Iṣfahānī, *Diyārbakriyya*, 301.

meant to forestall those of the other, and it was only Ulugh Beg who immediately aimed at the sultanate.

The history of the next several years is not an heroic tale. Few of Shahrukh's descendants survived the succession struggle and many lost their reputations along with their lives. For most princes, the first reaction was to return to their own territories and secure them – a second impulse was to enlarge them. Baysunghur's youngest son, Abu'l Qasim Babur, first set off for Khorasan from Shahrukh's camp but in Bistam he received messengers from the pre-eminent emir in Astarabad, Hinduka, inviting him to take over that region, an invitation apparently given according to prior agreement.[67] Astarabad had been connected with Baysunghur, so this action may represent a successful plan by Abu'l Qasim Babur to acquire part of his late father's domains while his brothers, Sultan Muhammad and ʿAlaʾ al-Dawla, were occupied elsewhere. The sons of Soyurghatmish set out to strengthen their hold on their father's region of Ḳabul and Ghazna.[68] Muhammad Juki's younger son Aba Bakr, who held Khuttalan, Arhang, and Sali Saray, almost immediately annexed the neighboring areas.[69] At the time of Shahrukh's death, an emissary of Jahanshah Qaraqoyunlu was passing through Sultaniyya and took the opportunity to secure it for the Qaraqoyunlu.[70]

Sultan Muhammad heard of Shahrukh's death in Hamadan and at first, not believing it, he continued to Gawrud, where the report was confirmed. He returned immediately to Qum, and many local power holders hastened to renew their allegiance.[71] One of the first to act was Jalal al-Din Chaqmaq of Yazd, married to Sultan Muhammad's sister. He was in the royal camp at Shahrukh's death and quickly left for Qum with his wife, Payanda Biki Sultan. They arrived before the prince, but the city notables opened the gates for them and he declared for Sultan Muhammad. Payanda Biki remained in Qum while Chaqmaq proceeded to Yazd, arranged to have the coinage and *khuṭba* in Sultan Muhammad's name, and then returned to Qum to pay his respects. Thus, while Chaqmaq had been unwilling to back Sultan Muhammad against Shahrukh, he now chose him over the other candidates. Other allies also hastened to Qum, including Hajji Muhammad b. Ghunashirin of Kerman, who remained with Sultan Muhammad and became one of his chief emirs. Sultan Muhammad soon made it clear that he intended to combine Iraq and Fars under his dominion. He moved to Isfahan, rewarded the notables who had survived Shahrukh's punishment and installed *darughas* in most of the cities from Kerman to Nihawand. He was also able to attract a few people from outside his region. One of the emirs whom Shahrukh had sent to persuade him into obedience went over to

[67] Samarqandī, *Maṭlaʿ*, 885–86. For Hinduka's local position, see Marʿashī, *Tārīkh-i Ṭabaristān*, 293–99.
[68] Samarqandī, *Maṭlaʿ*, 877–78, 881. [69] Ibid., 903.
[70] Ṭihrānī Iṣfahānī, *Diyārbakriyya*, 295; Rūmlū, *Aḥsan*, 277. [71] Kātib, *Tārīkh-i jadīd*, 245.

his service on Shahrukh's death, and later several men fled to him from Herat; two of these were *dīwān* or religious officials, and one was Shaykh Muhibb al-Din Abu'l Khayr, now again released from prison. Muhibb al-Din received a warm welcome in Isfahan and began pushing for another campaign against Fars, a plan that probably required little urging.[72]

Within two or three months of Shahrukh's death, most of his realm was thus parceled out into regional power blocks controlled by his descendants. At first leaders remained cautious, and when they encountered opposition in their attempts at expansion they were willing to make peace. However, even in this early period we find the ominous beginnings of financial stress, the squandering of resources and the raising of taxes.

The first aggressive action came in Transoxiana. Aba Bakr b. Muhammad Juki had taken the regions bordering Khuttalan – Balkh, Shaburghan, Qunduz, and Baghlan. These lands were inhabited by several powerful Barlas emirs who notified Ulugh Beg. Ulugh Beg removed Aba Bakr to captivity in Samarqand and crossed the Oxus to camp in Balkh, probably in late Safar, 851/early May, 1447.[73] He conferred with his great emirs and all agreed that for the moment he should make peace with ʿAlaʾ al-Dawla, who had already gathered an army and moved to block him. Meanwhile ʿAlaʾ al-Dawla heard that his brother, Abu'l Qasim Babur, was trying to expand his territories from Mazandaran into Khorasan; he had defeated some of ʿAlaʾ al-Dawla's troops in Jam and raided almost up to Herat. Under these circumstances ʿAlaʾ al-Dawla decided to accept Ulugh Beg's proposal. They agreed on a border somewhat to the south of the Oxus, putting Balkh, Maymana, Shaburghan, and other towns within Ulugh Beg's realm. ʿAbd al-Latif was to be released. ʿAlaʾ al-Dawla hastened to Mashhad and moved against Abu'l Qasim Babur, but the emirs of both princes urged them to make peace, pointing out that Ulugh Beg was aiming at conquest and that they could resist him only in alliance. Therefore they agreed to a border in Khabushan and returned to their capitals.[74] By this time it appears that many, perhaps most, of Shahrukh's emirs had chosen to join ʿAlaʾ al-Dawla, who also had with him his grandmother, the Tarkhan emirs, and the officials of the *dīwān-i aʿlāʾ*.[75] His weakness was that he held the area coveted by all other contenders for power.

Ulugh Beg stationed ʿAbd al-Latif in the border region of northern Khorasan and appointed emirs to his army. He called on the local emirs to obey ʿAbd al-Latif – these were a highly distinguished group, including the Barlas descendants of Temür's follower Chekü, in Qunduz and Baghlan, and Gawharshad's relative Ismaʿil Sufi Tarkhan b. Amir Sayyidi, who held

[72] Ibid., 244–47; Samarqandī, *Maṭlaʿ*, 886, 894. [73] Samarqandī, *Maṭlaʿ*, 851–53, 904–05.
[74] Ibid., 905–11; Ṭihrānī Iṣfahānī, *Diyārbakriyya*, 301–02.
[75] Samarqandī, *Maṭlaʿ*, 851, 888–89; Ṭihrānī Iṣfahānī, *Diyārbakriyya*, 300.

land in Andkhud.[76] The traditional lands of the Suldus tribe were also within ʿAbd al-Latif's territory, and seem to have remained the tribal base.[77] Although the region had not been under Ulugh Beg's authority during the life of Shahrukh, its Turco-Mongolian elite seem at this point to have favored him, since they had called him in to counter Aba Bakr b. Muhammad Juki's expansionism.[78]

ʿAbd al-Latif and ʿAlaʾ al-Dawla did not long remain at peace and their quarrel led to a winter campaign against Balkh by ʿAlaʾ al-Dawla, who plundered the area.[79] This action gave a pretext to Ulugh Beg, who was in any case aiming at the conquest of Khorasan, and early in 852/spring, 1448 he and ʿAbd al-Latif invaded. According to Samarqandī, ʿAlaʾ al-Dawla had agreed to recognize Ulugh Beg as sovereign and then gone back on his promise. The armies met at Tarnab, fourteen *farsakh*s from Herat. The victory went to Ulugh Beg, and ʿAlaʾ al-Dawla withdrew to Abuʾl Qasim in Astarabad. Even Gawharshad seems to have doubted ʿAlaʾ al-Dawla's ability to return, and she now took refuge with Sultan Muhammad, bringing with her the major viziers of the *dīwān-i aʿlāʾ*, many of her relatives, and a large number of troops. The population and notables of Herat welcomed Ulugh Beg. He helped himself to a considerable sum from the treasury, but seems to have tried to limit damage by his army, and chose well respected local figures to fill the posts abandoned by those who had left.[80]

Meanwhile Sultan Muhammad had used the year 851/1447–48 to consolidate and expand his power in Iran. He began to gather and equip an army, and to do this he had to raise taxes. Isfahan continued to enjoy tax relief but other regions suffered; as usual, we know most about Yazd. Despite their marriage relationship, Sultan Muhammad soon removed Amir Chaqmaq and installed one of his own followers, Amir Ahmad Janbaz Moghul. Next he summoned the city's *dīwān* officials and ordered them to collect a levy of twenty *kebekī* dinars per household from Yazd and its environs. The viziers attempted to protest, but in the end had to hand the requested sum over to the collectors from Isfahan. The same tax was levied on most of Iraq, but Kerman was exempted, perhaps because its governor Hajji Muhammad was in Sultan Muhammad's service. Sultan Muhammad's expedition against Shiraz was successful despite active resistance by both Turco-Mongolian and local troops, and he defeated the army of Fars outside of Shiraz on 25 Rajab, 851/October 5, 1447. Shiraz now became part of the Isfahan region, subordinate to its *dīwān*, and its young governor ʿAbd Allah b. Ibrahim was sent to Khorasan. Sultan Muhammad supplied his army by

[76] Ṭihrānī Iṣfahānī, *Diyārbakriyya*, 301–02; Samarqandī, *Maṭlaʿ*, 908.
[77] Manz, *Rise and Rule*, 164; Khwāndamīr, *Ḥabīb*, vol. IV, 34; Thackston, *Habibu's-siyar*, 368.
[78] Samarqandī, *Maṭlaʿ*, 904–05.
[79] Ṭihrānī Iṣfahānī, *Diyārbakriyya*, 302–03; Samarqandī, *Maṭlaʿ*, 922–24.
[80] Samarqandī, *Maṭlaʿ*, 929–44; Ṭihrānī Iṣfahānī, *Diyārbakriyya*, 303; Kātib, *Tārīkh-i jadīd*, 252.

pillaging the surrounding region and spent the winter pacifying the more recalcitrant tribes, such as the Shul, Kurds, and Khalaj.[81]

Even before the expedition to Fars, pressure from the Qaraqoyunlu was becoming a problem, and while Sultan Muhammad was in Shiraz they succeeded in taking over most of northern Iran up to Sawa. Husayn Tarumi, who had earlier joined Sultan Muhammad, now left to join the Qaraqoyunlu.[82] In the spring of 852/1448, Sultan Muhammad prepared to move against the Qaraqoyunlu with ʿAlaʾ al-Dawla, who joined him in Isfahan. Once again, caution prevailed and Sultan Muhammad allowed Gawharshad to use her close relationship to Jahanshah Qaraqoyunlu to negotiate a truce. They agreed that Jahanshah would give his daughter in marriage to Sultan Muhammad and accept Hamadan, Qazwin, and Sultaniyya as a kind of bride price.[83] These events probably took place in the summer or fall of 852/1448, a few months after Ulugh Beg's conquest of Khorasan. Sultan Muhammad was now firmly in control of Iraq and Fars, and, for a while at least, safe from Qaraqoyunlu aggression, but he had won territory at the cost of impoverishing the region. Fars had been plundered and most of the other provinces severely taxed. In Yazd and Abarquh over-taxation had brought considerable hardship. In addition to the regular tax and the capitation tax added before the Shiraz campaign, the *cherik* tax, and the payment of debts, yet more extraordinary taxes had been levied. In 853/1449 when the problem in Yazd came to Sultan Muhammad's attention, he dismissed his governor, Amir Ahmad Janbaz, ordered that no additional taxes be levied on the agricultural population, and gave administration to a new person, Shaykh Jalal al-Din Muhammad, who treated the population with greater consideration.[84]

The struggle in Khorasan

By 852/1448–49, the major contestants for power had consolidated their hold – Sultan Muhammad in Iraq and Fars, Abuʾl Qasim Babur in Mazandaran, and Ulugh Beg in an enlarged Transoxiana. After this the struggle centered around Herat and it was thus Khorasan, largely spared during Shahrukh's rise to power, which took the brunt of the fighting. During the years 852–53/1448–50, the city and region changed hands constantly. Most of the contestants based themselves elsewhere and were more than willing to despoil the capital.

The senior claimants, ʿAlaʾ al-Dawla and Ulugh Beg, quite soon lost the advantages with which they had begun. Ulugh Beg's victory over ʿAlaʾ al-Dawla in Tarnab in the spring of 852/1448 had put him in control of

81 Kātib, *Tārīkh-i jadīd*, 246–50; Samarqandī, *Maṭlaʿ*, 893–98.
82 Kātib, *Tārīkh-i jadīd*, 230, 250, 254; Ṭihrānī Iṣfahānī, *Diyārbakriyya*, 295.
83 Samarqandī, *Maṭlaʿ*, 900–02; Ṭihrānī Iṣfahānī, *Diyārbakriyya*, 295–97; Kātib, *Tārīkh-i jadīd*, 253–55.
84 Kātib, *Tārīkh-i jadīd*, 255.

Khorasan along with Transoxiana. At this time he was in the strongest position of all the contestants, but he now made the mistake which became his trademark; he moved forward before ensuring the security of his own region. He and ʿAbd al-Latif headed west to attack ʿAlaʾ al-Dawla and Abuʾl Qasim Babur, pausing to make an attempt on the fortress of ʿImad. Then Ulugh Beg headed against Bistam where, according to Samarqandī, he could have defeated the sons of Baysunghur but, before fighting, he turned back and met with ʿAbd al-Latif in Mashhad. In the middle of Ramadan, 852/mid-November, 1448, they learned that the Turkmen prince Yar ʿAli, imprisoned in a nearby fortress, had escaped and besieged Herat.[85]

This was the first time that Herat was attacked after Shahrukh's death, and its population fought bravely to defend it. Ulugh Beg's emir, Jalal al-Din Bayazid, the judge Mawlana Qutb al-Din Imama, and other notables defended the city, and both well-known artisans and Sufis took part in the fighting. Although the city population were loyal, Yar ʿAli was able to recruit soldiers from the suburbs. He sent a small party across the ditch to the fortification breastwork, at which most of the defenders – Turk and Tajik alike – fled the area, which was held reportedly only through the bravery of a certain Mawlana ʿImad al-Din Mutahhar Karizi. After a few days, the defending army was strengthened by a small troop of Ulugh Beg's emirs and it succeeded in holding off Yar ʿAli's troops for seventeen days, until Ulugh Beg could arrive and put Yar ʿAli's army to flight.[86]

Ulugh Beg rewarded the city's defenders, but on learning that Yar ʿAli had received help from the suburban population, he loosed his army on the countryside for three days to punish them. The soldiers made numerous arrests and failed to show respect even for places of religion. This happened just before the feast ending Ramadan, and the population of Herat thus encountered the festival in dire want. Samarqandī leaves us in no doubt about his judgment on Ulugh Beg's behavior; he writes that on the day of the festival a naked *darwīsh* whose clothes had been plundered jumped out before Ulugh Beg's horse and cried out, "Oh, just King, you gave a good festival to the *darwīsh*es, may your life and fortune be long!"[87]

At just this time, Ulugh Beg learned that the Uzbek army had taken advantage of his absence to raid up to Samarqand and pillage its environs. They had even destroyed his famous palace of Chinese porcelain. When ʿAbd al-Latif arrived from Mashhad, retreating from the advance of Abuʾl Qasim Babur, Ulugh Beg entrusted Herat to him and hastened home. He took with him Shahrukh's corpse to bury in Samarqand, and also artisans and many of the rarities which Shahrukh had collected in Herat. Samarqand was probably to be restored to its position as capital. Abuʾl Qasim Babur was quick to press his advantage. He intercepted and defeated Ulugh Beg's forces, won booty and prisoners, and headed on for Herat. Ulugh Beg on his side continued to

[85] Samarqandī, *Maṭlaʿ*, 947–51. [86] Ibid., 956–58. [87] Ibid., 957–59.

the Oxus and built a bridge across it for his army but was attacked by the Uzbeks. It was only with difficulty that he managed to bring the remnants of his army back to Bukhara. There he remained for the winter, sending Shahrukh's corpse to Samarqand to be buried in Temür's mausoleum.[88]

Over the next months Herat played host to a bewildering number of conquerors. Abu'l Qasim Babur sent several emirs ahead of his army and when they arrived ʿAbd al-Latif, after only fifteen days of rule, abandoned the city. Abu'l Qasim's emirs took over and then proceeded to squeeze the population. After a few days, the Turkmen Yar ʿAli returned and started a siege. A group of Heratis allowed his soldiers in and Abu'l Qasim's men fled into the Ikhtiyar al-Din fortress. After a day or two they abandoned it, carrying with them a large amount of wealth.[89] Yar ʿAli enjoyed the rule of Herat for about twenty days, and we are told that the population suffered little from him because his time and attention were devoted to drinking. This behavior made reconquest easy for Abu'l Qasim Babur, one of whose servitors had gone over to Yar ʿAli and now restored himself to Abu'l Qasim's favor by giving Yar ʿAli narcotics in his wine. In Dhu'l-Hijja, 852/February, 1449 Abu'l Qasim's forces entered through the gate, then captured and executed Yar ʿAli. This event ushered in a relatively long period of uninterrupted rule for Herat – eight or nine months – since Abu'l Qasim was not pushed out until Ramadan, 853/October–November, 1449.

At the time that Abu'l Qasim retook Herat, he and ʿAlaʾ al-Dawla were still together, though there seems to have been little doubt about who was in charge. Once in Herat, Abu'l Qasim apparently found ʿAlaʾ al-Dawla's presence awkward, and so first granted him a *soyurghal* in Tun and then decided to imprison him with his son Ibrahim.[90] ʿAlaʾ al-Dawla never regained the advantage he had held, but he remained a threat partly because of continued support from the population of Khorasan and partly because of Gawharshad's favor and her continued power.

The end of Shahrukh's line in Transoxiana

Ulugh Beg was the senior prince and had been the earliest to put forward a sustained claim to the sultanate. He was probably the first of Shahrukh's successors to mint money in his own name; we have coins from him as sultan from both Samarqand and Herat.[91] However, he was unable to return to Khorasan to press his claim and passed the rest of his reign in Transoxiana. There he was undone not by stronger contestants for power but by the enmity of his son ʿAbd al-Latif and his inability either to maintain order or to command loyalty within his own province. The histories portray the duel of father and son as something decreed by fate, an end recognized and

[88] Ibid., 957–63. [89] Ibid., 964. [90] Ibid., 964–69. [91] Komaroff, "Timurid Coinage," 220.

forwarded by the two men involved.[92] Ulugh Beg had alienated ʿAbd al-Latif by denying him appropriate credit or financial reward for the conquest of Khorasan.[93] As we have seen, ʿAbd al-Latif was quick to act on his grudges; he had shown his anger at Gawharshad during Shahrukh's life and acted on it afterwards. Ulugh Beg had spent twenty years largely immersed in scientific interests and after more than thirty years as governor, he was one of the least experienced commanders in the field. The campaigns he undertook in his bid to take over the Timurid sultanate show a disregard for dangers not immediately before him and a surprising carelessness in dealing with people, his two sons most particularly.

After ʿAbd al-Latif retreated from Herat, Ulugh Beg suggested that he return to the region of Balkh. Here he began to gather people around him specifically to oppose his father, and there was sufficient unhappiness with Ulugh Beg to provide him a large following. According to Abu Bakr Tihrani Isfahani, it was the Barlas and Tarkhan emirs who encouraged ʿAbd al-Latif to rebel, even though a year earlier the Barlas had called in Ulugh Beg against Aba Bakr. To enhance his local popularity, ʿAbd al-Latif abrogated the *tamgha* tax on trade which Ulugh Beg had been collecting. He protected his rear by informing Abu'l Qasim Babur that he would block any attempt by Ulugh Beg to take Khorasan.[94]

ʿAbd al-Latif's opposition became so open that Ulugh Beg had no choice but to move against him; this happened probably in the early summer of 853/1449. The two armies faced each other across the Oxus for several months. Ulugh Beg's army included the forces of prince ʿAbd Allah b. Ibrahim Sultan, to whom he had granted Khuttalan as *soyurghal*, and with ʿAbd Allah came a number of the emirs who had been attached to him in Fars.[95] The armies occasionally skirmished and in most cases ʿAbd al-Latif's army won. As the standoff wore on, Ulugh Beg's emirs became so restless that he feared they might seize him and hand him over to ʿAbd al-Latif. In the meantime, Samarqand was in the care of ʿAbd al-ʿAziz, whose arrogance alienated the population. Ulugh Beg for some time tried to propitiate his emirs with promises, while sending threatening messages to ʿAbd al-ʿAziz to bring him to order.

The situation developed into a crisis with an attempt on Samarqand by the Timurid prince Abu Saʿid, a descendant of Amiranshah who was in Ulugh Beg's service and had probably been stationed near the northern borders. He left Ulugh Beg's army on the Oxus to attack Samarqand with his followers, a group of Arghun tribesmen from the steppe border. ʿAbd al-ʿAziz took refuge in the citadel and called for help. Ulugh Beg headed north with his army and Abu Saʿid retreated, but ʿAbd al-Latif pressed his advantage and pursued his

92 Samarqandī, *Maṭlaʿ*, 972. 93 Ibid., 944; Dawlatshāh Samarqandī, *Tadhkirat*, 364.
94 Samarqandī, *Maṭlaʿ*, 969–72; Ṭihrānī Iṣfahānī, *Diyārbakriyya*, 304–05.
95 Samarqandī, *Maṭlaʿ*, 985; Ṭihrānī Iṣfahānī, *Diyārbakriyya*, 307.

father, who had to meet his army in the suburbs of Samarqand. Ulugh Beg was defeated, deserted even by the great Barlas emir Sultanshah and his son, and he found the gates of Samarqand closed against him by one of his own emirs, Miranshah Qaʾuchin. In this case we hear nothing about the actions of notables or the city population. When Ulugh Beg retreated to the border fort, Shahrukhiyya, he met the same reception and was thus forced to return to Samarqand to give himself up. ʿAbd al-Latif now committed the crime that did much to tarnish the reputation of Shahrukh's line. He appointed a Chinggisid as khan and had him judge Ulugh Beg "according to the *sharīʿa.*" When the predictable judgment had been pronounced he allowed Ulugh Beg to begin the pilgrimage and had him murdered on the way, on 8 or 10 Ramadan, 853/October 25 or 27, 1449. He also did away with his brother, ʿAbd al-ʿAziz.[96] The Timurid histories present Ulugh Beg's killing as a serious crime. As a royal patron and scholar prince he had achieved high respect and most histories portray him as Shahrukh's successor in office.

It is clear that Ulugh Beg had lost his realm in part through the disaffection of his emirs. During the disturbances of the next years, as the Turco-Mongolian emirs played an increasingly important part in politics, they too began to quarrel and to kill each other. On the day that Ulugh Beg lost Samarqand several emirs who remained loyal to him, including both Barlas and Tarkhan, had discovered Amir Sultanshah Barlas and his son going to join ʿAbd al-Latif and killed them. Shortly after coming to power, ʿAbd al-Latif summoned and executed these men on the suspicion of plotting against him.[97] ʿAbd al-Latif ruled for about six months before being killed in his turn on 25 Rabiʿ I, 854/May 8, 1450, by a group probably including both emirs and notables, who then sent to Balkh to invite ʿAbd Allah b. Ibrahim Sultan to take the throne.[98]

Discussing the brief reign of Sultan ʿAbd Allah which followed, Tihrani Isfahani states that he ruled justly. However, the emirs he had brought with him from Shiraz were hungry for power and unwilling to share it with local men. One should remember that ʿAbd Allah had succeeded his father in 838/1435, at the age of two, and his emirs were used to a governor controlled by those around him. Until shortly before Shahrukh's death, power had been monopolized by Shaykh Muhibb al-Din Abuʾl Khayr, who had remained in Shiraz. It is not hard to understand why ʿAbd Allah's emirs were intent on holding on to the powers they had recently gained. They were both angry and jealous when ʿAbd Allah chose one of Ulugh Beg's emirs,

[96] Samarqandī, *Maṭlaʿ*, 985–92; Ṭihrānī Iṣfahānī, *Diyārbakriyya*, 306; Khwāndamīr, *Ḥabīb*, vol. IV, 34; Thackston, *Habibu's-siyar*, 368–69.

[97] Samarqandī, *Maṭlaʿ*, 992; Ṭihrānī Iṣfahānī, *Diyārbakriyya*, 302.

[98] According to Taj al-Din Hasan Yazdi this was done by the notables and sayyids of Samarqand, while Khwandamir attributes the decision to the emirs; ʿAbd al-Razzaq Samarqandī mentions both (Yazdī, *Ḥasanī*, 55–56; Khwāndamīr, *Ḥabīb*, vol. IV, 42–43; Thackston, *Habibu's-siyar*, 374; Samarqandī, *Maṭlaʿ*, 1003–05).

Ibrahim b. Eyegü Temür, to oversee his finances. First they had Ibrahim imprisoned on the charge of favoring Ulugh Beg's surviving son, ʿAbd al-Rahman, and then had both him and ʿAbd al-Rahman killed. On learning of this a number of important emirs of Ulugh Beg's army, who had already left for Hisar-i Shadman, decided to continue into Khorasan where some of them joined the prince ʿAlaʾ al-Dawla, recently escaped from Abuʾl Qasim Babur.[99]

The news of defections from Sultan ʿAbd Allah reached the prince Abu Saʿid, who gathered support in Bukhara from some notables and surrounding populations, among which Turkmen tribes are mentioned; the people of this region apparently had also suffered from the oppression of the Shirazi emirs. Abu Saʿid was defeated on his first attempt, but as the abuses of ʿAbd Allah's emirs and extortionate taxation by his chief vizier, Khwaja ʿAtaʾ Allah Shirazi, continued, increasing numbers of emirs defected to Abu Saʿid. He gained reinforcements from the Jochid Abuʾl Khayr Khan, attacked, captured, and killed ʿAbd Allah on 21 or 22 Jumadi I, 855/June 21 or 22, 1451, and took power in Samarqand.[100]

When Shahrukh's line was replaced by Abu Saʿid in Transoxiana, it was less a case of winning than of losing – one prince after another lost the loyalty of the emirs and notables, needed to maintain power. At the time of Shahrukh's death, Ulugh Beg and his sons still had their backing, and when Ulugh Beg took Herat he was able to attract powerful men like Sultanshah Barlas into his service. By the time that he and ʿAbd al-Latif opposed each other, some of his followers were turning against him and part of the notable class in Bukhara was willing to back Abu Saʿid. Both the emirs and the notables of Samarqand plotted against ʿAbd al-Latif, and Ulugh Beg's emirs soon abandoned the service of ʿAbd Allah. There is no reason to believe that these men made their choices lightly; they had spent their life in service to the Timurid dynasty as had their fathers before them. Like the populations of the cities, the emirs could not afford to be on the losing side of a struggle, and had to choose the most likely winner in order to survive. Furthermore, ʿAbd al-Latif's murder of both his father and his brother – deliberate acts, outside of battle – were considered highly reprehensible and made his own murder and that of ʿAbd Allah easier to justify.

The sons of Baysunghur

For several years Abu Saʿid left the succession struggle to the sons of Baysunghur, who based their power in the Iranian provinces of the realm. Unfortunately for the population of Iran, Sultan Muhammad and Abuʾl Qasim Babur were quite evenly matched. Both enjoyed support in their own provinces, but neither proved capable of extending his control permanently

[99] Ṭihrānī Iṣfahānī, *Diyārbakriyya*, 309–10. [100] Ibid., 310–15.

into outside areas. In their struggle, as in Transoxiana, we see increasingly independent action by Turco-Mongolian emirs who began to rebel or desert their masters. The notables and population of the cities also began to assert themselves as their situation worsened.

Abu'l Qasim Babur had taken power in Herat at the beginning of 853/1449 and declared himself sultan. He was spared concern about attack from Transoxiana by the message of ʿAbd al-Latif promising protection from Ulugh Beg. At the same time he bought security by offering submission to his brother Sultan Muhammad in Rabiʿ I, 853/April–May, 1449. He then undertook a punitive campaign against Sistan, as Shahrukh had done at a similar period during his career. The campaign was short and successful but Abu'l Qasim encountered other problems at home, most notably the insurrection of his powerful emir Hinduka, who had opposed his expedition. Hinduka went off to Astarabad, his original base of power. Abu'l Qasim sent two emirs against him; one was killed, but the other brought back Hinduka's head. ʿAbd al-Razzaq Samarqandī hints that before this Abu'l Qasim's emirs had begun to become insubordinate and had been kept in check only by Hinduka; we may here be seeing the signs of disagreement among them.[101] At the same time Abu'l Qasim succeeded in taking the fort of ʿImad, where ʿAlaʾ al-Dawla had stored a large treasure trove. This success, however, was offset by the simultaneous escape of ʿAlaʾ al-Dawla, who fled first to Ghur and then to Sistan. When Babur pursued him, he retreated to Yazd, within Sultan Muhammad's jurisdiction.[102]

At this point Sultan Muhammad began to look towards Khorasan. He had restored some semblance of order and prosperity to his own region, if we can judge from the experience of Yazd and Abarquh. He had both Gawharshad and ʿAlaʾ al-Dawla with him and they apparently encouraged him to attempt the conquest of the capital. His emirs also promoted the idea. He was further pushed in this direction by the recalcitrance of some of the local rulers, notably Gayumarth Rustamdari and the Atabek of Luristan. Both refused to obey a mere governor, saying that they owed obedience only to a sultan who controlled the capital. Sultan Muhammad therefore sent emirs to Kerman and Yazd, ordering them collect dues, gather an army, and set off for Khorasan with the new governor of Yazd, Shaykh Jalal al-Din Muhammad. Sultan Muhammad himself took the northern route through Simnan and Damghan. Both of Sultan Muhammad's armies received a warm welcome along their way and accepted the voluntary submission of numerous towns. Sultan Muhammad now sent a message to Abu'l Qasim inviting submission, but Abu'l Qasim prepared to resist. When the two armies met near Jam on 13 Ramadan, 853/October 30, 1449, Sultan Muhammad defeated his brother and headed for Herat. Abu'l Qasim

[101] Samarqandī, *Maṭlaʿ*, 974–77 [102] Ibid., 977–79; Kātib, *Tārīkh-i jadīd*, 256.

retreated north towards Marw and then Nisa, pillaging as he went, and then began again to collect armies.

Sultan Muhammad sent ahead a representative with a letter to the notables and emirs of Herat; it was well received and when he arrived he took care to reward and conciliate with the population.[103] He also showed respect to Shaykh Baha' al-din 'Umar, with whom he consulted regularly. Like Abu'l Qasim Babur, he was nervous about ʿAlaʾ al-Dawla's continued support in the region, and so sent him off to govern Kabul.[104] ʿAbd al-Latif, who had just taken power in Samarqand, sent a message expressing the hope that both Sultan Muhammad's conquest of Khorasan and his own takeover of Transoxiana would be blessed, and Sultan Muhammad sent a friendly answer, apparently not wishing to make an issue of Ulugh Beg's fate.[105] In organizing his administration, Sultan Muhammad combined the new with the old. His chief emir was his close advisor, Hajji Muhammad b. Ghunashirin, formerly governor of Kerman. According to Samarqandī, Hajji Muhammad was not fully competent to run the administration and Pir Ahmad Khwafi was attached to him as partner. Despite this precaution, Hajji Muhammad was ruthless in his extortions from the population and other government officials were powerless to stop him.[106]

While disaffection grew among the Khorasanians under Sultan Muhammad, Abu'l Qasim gathered forces in the northwestern regions of the province. Sultan Muhammad prepared to move against him, sending a force ahead under Hajji Muhammad. The advance guard met and fought Babur's army on 3 Rabiʿ II, 854/May 16, 1450, a battle in which Hajji Muhammad was defeated and killed. When Sultan Muhammad approached with the rest of the army, Abu'l Qasim retreated, but Sultan Muhammad was reluctant to pursue him. At this point he learned that ʿAlaʾ al-Dawla had profited from his absence to return and take over Herat with the help of its population. Sultan Muhammad's prospects in Khorasan began to look dim and several of the powerful Tarkhan emirs who had joined him with Gawharshad plotted to seize him. He discovered the conspiracy and fled with a few followers to Yazd.[107]

Despite his earlier attempt to foster economic recovery, Sultan Muhammad used his time in Yazd to collect capitation and trade taxes. He heard that the prince Khalil Sultan b. Muhammad Jahangir, whom he

[103] Kātib, *Tārīkh-i jadīd*, 256–60; Ṭihrānī Iṣfahānī, *Diyārbakriyya*, 318–19; Samarqandī, *Maṭlaʿ*, 979–83.

[104] Kātib, *Tārīkh-i jadīd*, 259. In 855/1451 ʿAlaʾ al-Dawla gained the support of the Arlat tribe, with whom he had marriage ties, for another attempt at the throne (Khwāndamīr, *Ḥabīb*, vol. IV, 47; Thackston, *Habibu's-siyar*, 376). There was also an attempted uprising in his favor organized by a *darwīsh* in 860/1455–56 (Samarqandī, *Maṭlaʿ*, 1098–99; Nawāʾī, *Majālis*, 28–29, 203).

[105] Samarqandī, *Maṭlaʿ*, 985. [106] Ibid., 994–96.

[107] Kātib, *Tārīkh-i jadīd*, 260–61; Ṭihrānī Iṣfahānī, *Diyārbakriyya*, 321–22; Samarqandī, *Maṭlaʿ*, 996 ff.

had appointed to govern Shushtar, had taken over Shiraz and killed Shaykh Muhibbal-Din. Sultan Muhammad fought and defeated him, then once again he sent his *muḥaṣṣil*s throughout Iraq to collect extra taxes.[108] Hajji Muhammad b. Ghunashirin was now dead, so in the first months of 855/ February–March, 1451 Sultan Muhammad went down to Kerman to collect its wealth. According to the historian Taj al-Din Hasan b. Shihab Yazdi, Sultan Muhammad's action was the result of slander against Ghunashirin's family by emirs earlier denied power. The prince chose to believe the slanderers and confiscated the wealth that the family had amassed over thirty years. As governor Sultan Muhammad appointed a follower of his own, Sayyid Mirak Shirwani, who had risen from a low station. It is likely that one of Sayyid Mirak's primary duties was to raise cash, since we hear that he and his administration immediately began to extort additional taxes from the population.[109]

While Sultan Muhammad reestablished his hold over his central territories, Abu'l Qasim Babur headed for Herat and on his approach ʿAlaʾ al-Dawla retreated to Balkh. Even in the absence of ʿAlaʾ al-Dawla, Abu'l Qasim was unable to take Herat's fortress by force, and after a long siege was allowed in by the commander of the citadel only after he had sworn in the presence of two religious figures, Baha' al-Din ʿUmar and Amir Nasir al-Din Qurʾaysh, that he would permit no harm to the population. The caution shown by the fortress keeper on this occasion contrasts with the earlier willingness of cities to submit to members of the dynasty.[110] ʿAlaʾ al-Dawla made an unsuccessful attempt against Samarqand and then another try at Herat, but this too failed and Abu'l Qasim had him blinded in punishment.[111] Instead of remaining in Herat, Abu'l Qasim returned to Astarabad, where he apparently had an established court.[112]

It was Sultan Muhammad who took the lead in the next attack, even though it appears that Abu'l Qasim was willing to rule in his name. However, when the two armies met near Astarabad on 15 Dhu'l-Hijja, 855/January 9, 1452, Sultan Muhammad met defeat. According to Dawlatshah b. ʿAlaʾ al-Dawla Samarqandī, his emirs had sworn loyalty to him before the battle, but most deserted in the course of the fighting.[113] He was brought before Abu'l Qasim who followed the new Timurid fashion and had him killed. Like the killing of Ulugh Beg, this fratricide was criticized by Timurid historians.[114]

[108] Kātib, *Tārīkh-i jadīd*, 262. The taxes levied on Yazd are named, but those levied on Iraq appear to have been extra taxes and forced gifts: "*naʿl-i bahā wa nithār wa pishkash.*"
[109] Yazdī, *Ḥasanī*, 58–62, 71–76; Kātib, *Tārīkh-i jadīd*, 262; Aubin, *Deux sayyids*, 427–28.
[110] Thackston, *Habibu's-siyar*, 373.
[111] Yazdī, *Ḥasanī*, 57; Ṭihrānī Iṣfahānī, *Diyārbakriyya*, 309–16. ʿAlaʾ al-Dawla's expedition to Transoxiana occurred shortly before ʿAbd Allah's defeat and execution by Abu Saʿid on 22 Jumadi I, 855/June 22, 1451.
[112] See Dawlatshāh Samarqandī, *Tadhkirat*, 428–29; Nawāʾī, *Majālis*, 43.
[113] Dawlatshāh Samarqandī, *Tadhkirat*, 410–11.
[114] Kātib, *Tārīkh-i jadīd*, 262–63; Ṭihrānī Iṣfahānī, *Diyārbakriyya*, 324–25; Yazdī, *Ḥasanī*, 62–67; Thackston, *Habibu's-siyar*, 375–76.

The Timurid loss of central Iran

Although Abu'l Qasim Babur had now destroyed his greatest rival, he was not able to take over Sultan Muhammad's territories and within a short time the central and western provinces of Iran were in the hands of the Turkmen dynasties. There were two major reasons for the Timurid failure to hold Iran against the Qaraqoyunlu. One was the independence of Isfahan, whose notables were not willing to trust the enemy of their former protector, and the other was the erosion of support among the population due to continued financial extortion.

Immediately after Abu'l Qasim's victory, the situation in Iraq and Fars looked promising for him. Sultan Muhammad's emirs had scattered to various regions and were not notably successful in maintaining loyalty. Amir Moghul Janbaz, who had earlier been in charge of milking Yazd, returned there, gathered the notables, fortified the city and got in stores. However, when Babur approached and Amir Moghul prepared to resist, the notables of Yazd refused to hold out, saying that Babur had a legal claim to the region. This decision was backed by two particularly powerful figures somewhat apart from the usual administration of the city: Sharaf al-Din ʿAli Yazdi and Amir Nur al-Din Niʿmat Allah, the local Niʿmat Allahi shaykh. When Babur arrived the notables and ulama came out in force to greet him. With them came the former governor, Chaqmaq Shami, who offered rich presents and was rewarded with a renewal of his governorship. Babur in return treated the city well and appointed overseers (*darugha*) to each quarter to prevent destruction. After consulting frequently with Sharaf al-Din ʿAli Yazdi and granting him the suburb Taft as *soyurghal*, he proceeded to Shiraz, which also submitted. His emissary to Sayyid Mirak Shirwani in Kerman met with a good reception and the coinage and *khuṭba* of Kerman were put into his name. Several of the emirs and administrators who had formerly served Sultan Muhammad now came into the service of Abu'l Qasim, including some of the pillars of Sultan Muhammad's administration like the Isfahani vizier and commander Khwaja Mahmud Haydar.[115]

The problem for Abu'l Qasim Babur lay with Isfahan and neighboring cities. The Qaraqoyunlu were well positioned to take advantage, encouraged by several of Sultan Muhammad's senior emirs who chose to serve them rather than Abu'l Qasim.[116] Amir Pirzad Bukhari, who had been *darugha* of Nihawand and later of Isfahan under Sultan Muhammad, seems to have headed directly for Hamadan and entered the service of Jahanshah Qaraqoyunlu along with his brother, ʿAbd al-Rahman.[117] Amir Shaykhzada Qush Ribati, who had been Sultan Muhammad's governor in Sawa, went to

[115] Kātib, *Tārīkh-i jadīd*, 263–64; Yazdī, *Ḥasanī*, 68–70; Khwāndamīr, *Ḥabīb*, vol. IV, 46; Thackston, *Habibu's-siyar*, 376.
[116] Yazdī, *Ḥasanī*, 81. [117] Kātib, *Tārīkh-i jadīd*, 245, 246, 264; Yazdī, *Ḥasanī*, 68, 69.

Isfahan and took it over. Shaykhzada distributed robes to the notables but for the rest of the population he instituted a harsh rule, demanding that all inhabitants, except the ulama, shave their beards. After a few days the population was in an uproar and attacked the walls of the fortress, succeeding in making holes in it. Shaykhzada then left to join the Qaraqoyunlu, and control went to a member of a local sayyid family, Amir Zayn al-ʿAbidin Mir-i Miran.[118]

Instead of heading towards Rayy to block the Qaraqoyunlu, Abu'l Qasim decided to avoid the route which Sultan Muhammad had taken and where supplies were depleted, and instead set out towards Yazd and Shiraz. Even this route produced too little for his army, as the population was hiding their stores and the local powers had decided to withhold grain to drive up the price. Abu'l Qasim therefore ordered his armies to seize grain wherever they could find it; they invaded houses and took whatever they could unearth.[119] Meanwhile, the Qaraqoyunlu aimed for Qum and Sawa. According to the *Habib al-siyar*, the governors whom Abu'l Qasim appointed to the region, Amir Shaykh ʿAli Bahadur in Sawa and Amir Darwish ʿAli in Qum, had immediately begun a regime of harsh taxation, most particularly Shaykh ʿAli Bahadur, who had not governed in this region before. As a result, a group of Sawa notables appealed to the Turkmen armies already in the region, who were thus able to seize Shaykh ʿAli without difficulty. This conquest presents a contrast to the Turkmen attempt to take the city while Sultan Muhammad was alive, when it held out successfully under Shaykhzada.[120] Qum held out longer, but after appeals for reinforcements had been ignored by Abu'l Qasim's emirs, the city submitted to the Qaraqoyunlu.[121]

One reason for Abu'l Qasim's inability to hold Qum and Sawa was his failure to win the cooperation of Isfahan. As usual, the Isfahanis asserted their right to choose among contenders for power, and preferred to attach themselves to the Qaraqoyunlu. Abu'l Qasim clearly considered himself in charge of the city, since he sent off several officials to govern it: Amir Muhammad Khudaydad with Pahlawan Husayn Diwana as *darugha*, Ghiyath al-Din Simnani as tax collector, and as vizier the Isfahani notable Mahmud Haydar, who had served Sultan Muhammad and was now with Abu'l Qasim.[122] The *Tarikh-i jadid-i Yazd* however reports that the Isfahanis were afraid of Abu'l Qasim and did not submit to him. Thus, when he came to the region to gather an army to send against the Qaraqoyunlu siege of Qum, the city refused to contribute troops.[123] After the Qaraqoyunlu took Qum the Isfahanis sent one of the headmen to invite them in. Abu'l Qasim dispatched an army against them but the Isfahanis came to an agreement with his vizier

[118] Ṭihrānī Iṣfahānī, *Diyārbakriyya*, 325. [119] Rūmlū, *Aḥsan*, 307–08.
[120] Kātib, *Tārīkh-i jadīd*, 248, 251; Thackston, *Habibu's-siyar*, 376.
[121] Kātib, *Tārīkh-i jadīd*, 265; Ṭihrānī Iṣfahānī, *Diyārbakriyya*, 326.
[122] Ṭihrānī Iṣfahānī, *Diyārbakriyya*, 325; Yazdī, *Ḥasanī*, 69.
[123] Kātib, *Tārīkh-i jadīd*, 264–65.

Mahmud Haydar, barricaded the city streets against the troops and waited for the Turkmen. Abu'l Qasim's other agents in Isfahan, Husayn Diwana and Khwaja Ghiyath al-Din Simnani, left the city on Abu'l Qasim's approach, fearing harm from the city population.[124]

Yazd and Shiraz were less adventurous than Isfahan, but faced with continuing Timurid extortion and the growing success of the Qaraqoyunlu, they also switched sides. When it became clear to Abu'l Qasim that he could not hold the regions of Qum and Isfahan, he retreated to Yazd, where the inhabitants saw the arrival of his army with well-founded trepidation. Those who could retreat into the city did so, and for three days the troops remained outside, plundering several quarters. Then Abu'l Qasim headed off to Khorasan, handing control of Yazd to Khalil Sultan b. Muhammad Jahangir, who declared safety for the province, but then decided to attempt the conquest of Fars, as he had done under Sultan Muhammad. To gather the necessary funds, he assigned a huge sum to be collected from the notables of the region, graded according to wealth. He paid no attention to the administrators who argued that the sum was well beyond what they could raise. Having squeezed the region unmercifully he left the grandson of Jalal al-Din Chaqmaq in charge and departed to attempt the conquest of Fars, taking with him the taxes, the armies and several of the notables of the city. These included the men who probably constituted the highest city council: the chief judge, Majd al-Din Fadl Allah, two viziers, Khwaja ʿImad al-Din Masʿud and Khwaja Jalal al-Din Murshid, and the enormously wealthy merchant Khwaja Zayn al-Din ʿAli Bawardi. On Khalil Sultan's approach to Shiraz, Abu'l Qasim Babur's governor retreated to Kerman and Khalil Sultan was welcomed into the city by its notables. This happened in Ramadan, 856/September, 1452.[125]

A week after Khalil Sultan's arrival, the Shirazis learned that the Turkmen army was heading towards them. Khalil Sultan fled towards Kerman but the notables he had brought from Yazd remained and both they and the Shiraz notables welcomed the Qaraqoyunlu and told them of the plight of the population of Fars and the suffering of the notables of Yazd. The Yazd notables who were in Shiraz wrote to their junior colleagues at home advising that the city surrender to the Turkmen; if they did otherwise, they would be doing harm to the population. This letter was signed by all the major notables. When the letter arrived in Yazd, the Timurid governor and officials departed, leaving the city in the hands of the notables, headed by Mawlana Jalal al-Din Muhammad, to await the Qaraqoyunlu arrival.[126] The Qaraqoyunlu conquest of Iran was not final, due in part to their rapacity and brutality, which turned the population against them. Nonetheless, the

[124] Ṭihrānī Iṣfahānī, *Diyārbakriyya*, 325–29.
[125] Kātib, *Tārīkh-i jadīd*, 265–66; Aubin, *Deux sayyids*, 434.
[126] Kātib, *Tārīkh-i jadīd*, 266–67.

Timurids were never again able to regain the central Iranian cities for more than a short period.

Conclusion

The experience of the Timurid realm at the end of Shahrukh's reign illustrates both the weakness of central rule and the reason that it was so greatly desired. In the case of the Timurids, the major threat to peace came from rivalry within the dynasty, but the struggle was more than dynastic; it included the politics of emirs, local rulers, and city notables as well. All of these groups were necessary for the success of a dynastic claimant, and since they were particularly active in times of crisis, their goals entered into the politics of succession. The struggle was complicated by opposing tendencies – for loyalty and for pragmatism, for regionalism and for centralization.

The Timurid realm consisted of several separate political regions, which show clearly in the succession struggle. After the deaths of both Temür and of Shahrukh, the polity broke down into sections: Azarbaijan and western Iraq, southern and central Iran, including Fars, Yazd, Isfahan, and Qum, the Caspian region, Khorasan, and Transoxiana. Each area had its own political life, revolving around several major cities, prominent families, and local landed powers. The princes who governed, and the emirs who served under them, were not removed from the local politics; they owned land and commercial enterprises, sponsored institutions, and made use of local bureaucrats and armies. Each region also provided administrative and military personnel from the local population, and these men might serve several different rulers in a number of cities, while remaining within the area.

The political programs of local people contributed significantly to the difficulty of the succession struggle. In times of insecurity city notables were eager to find a powerful protector and terrified of finding themselves on the losing side. It was natural to turn first to a prince with local connections. Fear brought many cities to show support to Sultan Muhammad, even during Shahrukh's lifetime, and thus encourage him in his rebellion. Although they became connected to those who governed them, city notables were unlikely to remain loyal through a long succession struggle. A major cause for switching allegiance was the sense of mistreatment. Repeated extortion and unjust taxation was considered reason to abandon loyalty to a ruler who was not fulfilling his responsibilities towards the population. Local military power holders faced the same choices but had more to gain. When they came into the service of an outside ruler, they often used their position to counsel campaigns which suited their own purpose. Thus Shaykh Abu'l Khayr b. Muhammad Jazari joined Sultan Muhammad and encouraged him to go against Shiraz, whose emirs and administrators had denounced him to Shahrukh. Husayn Tarumi, once he had chosen to go over to Jahanshah Qaraqoyunlu, encouraged him to attack Timurid territories, as did the emirs of Sultan Muhammad who joined him later, and all were useful guides and counselors in the conquest of territories with which they were well acquainted.

The princes were in a difficult situation. There was continued interest in preserving the larger polity, and therefore to gain full power within one region, one needed control over the center or at least a firm alliance with someone who had it. Nonetheless, the contestants for power depended heavily on the support of their own provinces and had trouble expanding their power beyond them. This difficulty was exacerbated by the tendency of princes, their emirs, and the administrators who served them to treat new provinces like conquered territory to be exploited. Ulugh Beg's plunder of the Herat region contributed to his loss of prestige in that region, and when Sultan Muhammad ruled in Khorasan, he and his chief emir, Hajji Muhammad of Kerman, also oppressed the population. The "Shirazi" emirs and administrators of ʿAbd Allah b. Ibrahim Sultan cost him the support of the population of Transoxiana, and led directly to Abu Saʿid's victory. The experience of Shahrukh's descendants highlights the skill Shahrukh himself had shown during his own rise to power.

Despite frequent switches of allegiance, it would be wrong to discount political loyalty among most segments of the population. At the beginning of the struggle most emirs remained faithful to the princes they served and to the dynasty. City populations likewise often welcomed Timurids and opposed people from outside; a prime example is the population of Herat who accepted members of the dynasty without resistance, but organized to oppose the Turkmen prince Yar ʿAli. In the long run however, all members of society faced danger if they remained loyal to a losing ruler. For emirs this could mean execution, as it did for several servitors of Ulugh Beg, killed by ʿAbd al-Latif, and those of Sultan Muhammad, killed by Abuʾl Qasim Babur. Furthermore, since a protracted internal struggle required more taxation than the population could comfortably provide, loyalty to the ruler of the region could bring severe impoverishment. The Timurid princes attempted to spare their own regions at the beginning of the struggle, but by the end they seized money and goods wherever they could find them. Under these circumstances, almost any outsider could look better than the current ruler.

Conclusion

At the end of the book I pose the same two questions I began with and suggest some answers. How did a society with diffuse power structures and few legal corporate entities remain stable despite frequent breakdowns of order? How could a government without the monopoly of force control a large and heterogeneous society over wide territories?

The cohesion of society through periods of turmoil has been attributed to the strength of the groups which made it up: the extended family or tribe, the city quarters, the ulama buttressed by a self-conscious identity and, at a later date, the Sufi *ṭarīqa*s. There can be no doubt that these institutions contributed to social cohesion, but we still need to ask how they did so. Group solidarity itself cannot explain their strength because there was dissension within all communities. Furthermore, most groups overlapped with others with whom their interests could diverge. For the city elite there were several levels of belonging: family and quarter, then profession – as merchant, Sufi shaykh, *ʿālim*, or bureaucrat.[1] Professional groups themselves overlapped significantly. Sufi shaykhs were also members of the ulama, viziers and members of the ulama might also be part of the army, and a single family might well produce Sufis of different affiliations, ulama, bureaucrats, and even military men.

Politics in Iran at this period were not organized according to profession, ideology, or class, but rather among shifting factions which included members of different groups. In the medieval Middle East even more than in most pre-modern societies, the centrality of personal alliance required individuals to establish relationships with people above and below them who were outside their immediate lineages. While clientship was in theory permanent, the alliances formed in factional politics were often changed and required agility of speech and action. Many bonds within a profession took the form of patron-client relationships: teacher and student, shaykh and disciple, senior and junior bureaucrat. However, both in the learned professions and among the Sufi orders it was usual to have more than one teacher and to seek out the

[1] Mottahedeh, *Loyalty and Leadership*, 105–22.

most celebrated masters available. Thus, any active member of the elite, and many within the middle classes, were likely to have multiple affiliations. With such a large number of group memberships and attachments, it would be difficult indeed to avoid some conflict of loyalty. This situation was perhaps not a bad thing. It might create uncertainty, but it also gave people freedom of action; they could choose which ties to put first, which to honor and which to disregard.

To understand how politics worked, one must look at the individual and his relation to the various groups of which he was a member. Most classes and groups were important and powerful, but not because of cohesion; as I have shown internal rivalry could be as strong as rivalry with outsiders. Certainly one could always go to one's family or to other members of one's profession in search of help – but that does not mean that one was certain to find it. Fasih Khwafi chose his mother's *nisba* rather than his father's and followed the bureaucratic profession of her relatives, but although he was probably related to Pir Ahmad Khwafi he was apparently unable to find employment within the central *dīwān* while Pir Ahmad was running it. While the urban notables certainly had a common interest in the welfare of their city, they also had ties to different quarters and different outside powers, and often disagreed about how to react to outside danger.

What made professional and family associations important and durable was their usefulness; they provided the framework necessary for the advancement of individuals. At base, power was an individual achievement – it was what one person could make out of a variety of affiliations which sometimes went across the boundaries between military and civil affairs and between the religious and governmental spheres. In no sphere could power easily be inherited, in part because neither the political system nor the *sharī'a* recognized the principle of primogeniture. The history of the Timurids and most other dynasties shows that rulership could not simply be bequeathed; it also had to be won. One could inherit the possibility of holding the sultanate, but one almost always had to fight for the actual position. The same was undoubtedly true of many positions of power within society. It was certainly an advantage to be born into a powerful family, but significant prestige only came to some individuals within it. While many posts were inherited there were usually more sons than offices and few appointments provided a secure position or a clear set of duties. The power of an office depended heavily on the men who held it. Most people who succeeded in gaining a position of preeminence had more than one single source of strength; it was the combination of affiliations that set an individual apart.

We can take as examples a number of people of prominence who have appeared in these pages. Two of the Sufis of Herat illustrate how individuals enhanced their status by combining a variety of loyalties and affiliations. While he was alive, Zayn al-Din Khwafi was probably the most respected shaykh in Herat. His major affiliation went back to Shihab al-Din

Suhrawardi, but there is no indication that his preeminence was related to the popularity of Suhrawardi teachings in Khorasan – no major *khānaqāh*, graveyard, or particular group of people is associated with the line at the time of Khwafi. Shaykh Zayn al-Din had chosen to travel and study with prominent ulama as well as a variety of famous shaykhs and had retained his contacts with them; this, along with his writings and his teaching abilities, was what gave him particular status and is mentioned repeatedly in the literature. His continued travels and his ability to attract students to Herat from the western regions clearly added to his prestige at home. It is likely that he combined scholarly eminence with wealth and high family connections; as I suggested, he may have been related to the vizier Ghiyath al-Din Pir Ahmad Khwafi who built him a handsome mausoleum that became the burial place of numerous distinguished mystics. His personal wealth also allowed him to build a *khānaqāh* in Darwishabad, where his disciples continued his teaching.

Zayn al-Din's colleague, Baha al-Din ʿUmar Jaghara'i, combined a different set of skills and connections. In his case the religious credentials came largely from his family, which had been active and influential in the region for some time. Like Zayn al-Din he seems to have attracted devotees, but he did not apparently produce a great number of disciples. His position was inherited by his son and we hear of no outside *khalīfa*s. What distinguished him was his close relations to emirs and to the dynasty which he used apparently for the good of the population. The biography given in ʿAbd al-Rahman b. Ahmad Jami's *Nafahat al-uns* gives this activity a prominent place and, as I have shown, Baha' al-Din is mentioned quite frequently in the dynastic histories. It is clear that in the succession struggle after Shahrukh's death the competing princes attempted to win his approbation. Ulugh Beg's failure to do so is mentioned, along with Baha' al-Din's prediction of a bad end for him.[2]

For a shaykh to have the ear of the dynasty and the elite might compromise him in the opinion of the pure-minded, but for most of his colleagues it almost certainly increased his standing. We have no way of knowing exactly what Bahaʾ al-Din requested from those in power, but he is reputed to have influenced government appointments and it is clear that a shaykh with good connections could be useful not only to the population, but also to his own students and colleagues. Shaykh Abuʾl Makarim Jami, before he became head of the shrine of Jam, wrote to a senior shaykh asking for help finding employment and stated that he had attempted to find help from the religious figures at the court of Shahrukh but had failed. The ability to pass on requests for help or intercession was a significant source of political capital, not only to ulama, but also to shaykhs.

[2] Samarqandī, *Maṭlaʿ*, 935, 941, 984; Khwāndamīr, *Ḥabīb*, vol. IV, 58; Thackston, *Habibu's-siyar*, 383.

When we turn to a more worldly sphere and examine the position of urban notables we find a similar variety of occupations and ties. The history of southern and central Iran provides particularly good examples. In Yazd we see viziers serving in the Chaghatay governor's *dīwān* while also being counted among the city notables. These were men who came from distinguished local bureaucratic families, whose combination of wealth, local standing, and service to successive regimes won them prominence. The most striking example of the combination of powers is Qadi Ahmad Saʿidi of Isfahan, discussed in Chapter 5. Qadi Ahmad came from an old scholarly lineage of Isfahan and Shiraz, which was one of the families traditionally considered for the position of judge.[3] While most judges helped to arrange city defense few were as active in military command as Qadi Ahmad, who led troops to fight outside the city and participated as commander in the army of the prince Rustam b. ʿUmar Shaykh. The combination of these two roles, along with his strong personality, made Qadi Ahmad, for some years, the decisive voice in Isfahan. He added further to his influence by becoming part of the inner circle of Rustam among his top Chaghatay emirs. In the turbulent situation of Iran these positions, and the level of power they brought, were dangerous. Qadi Ahmad was murdered, partly perhaps because he had meddled in the politics of the Chaghatay emirs. We should note however, that the murder was a bad mistake; when the city population learned that Rustam had killed Qadi Ahmad they immediately turned against him.

Many of the people I have mentioned combined positions in spheres of potential opposition. Shaykh Bahaʾ al-Din ʿUmar was connected with emirs, princes, other shaykhs, and, we assume, with the local people for whom he petitioned; he was thus attached to the worldly and the otherworldly, the oppressor and the oppressed. Qadi Ahmad Saʿidi and the viziers of Yazd were at once part of the city council, which decided which Timurid prince or Chaghatay emir to allow into the city, and direct servitors of the government they might decide to turn against. Such tensions could sometimes cause a crisis, as they did for Qadi Ahmad. Accounts of the surrender of a city often mention several local officials leaving with the outgoing government, and we can guess that these were the men whose association with the Chaghatay administration was too strong to permit service to another regime. The positions they left were open for those who embraced the newcomers. For many others, like Shaykh Bahaʾ al-Din and the viziers of Yazd, the system worked more smoothly.

In the cities of Iran it is not always easy to distinguish local notables and commanders from central government personnel. Jürgen Paul has divided the notable, intermediary class into three categories: those bound primarily to the state, those requiring both state appointment and local consensus – like headmen and judges – and those whose support was primarily

[3] Quiring-Zoche, *Isfahan*, 230–31.

local.[4] However, individuals do not fit into only one category throughout their careers. How should one classify Hafiz Razi, who originated in Yazd and served Iskandar b. ʿUmar Shaykh as vizier and commander in Yazd, Shiraz and Isfahan? There is no doubt of his local roots, but his service was with the Chaghatay, in several different cities. We see Khwaja Nur al-Din Kamal, probably a local commander (*sardār*) in Shiraz, first as one of the council of people who refused to open the city to Husayn Sharbatdar and pushed Iskandar b. ʿUmar Shaykh to take control of the city. A few years later, on Shahrukh's invasion, we find him as Iskandar's agent helping to punish the men he had earlier consulted with, and he subsequently served as vizier for Iskandar and Ibrahim Sultan. The Isfahani Mahmud Haydar moved the other way; he served several princes as vizier, but in the end chose to side with the Isfahanis when they refused to cooperate with his new master, Abuʾl Qasim Babur. Later he was a *sardār* under the Qaraqoyunlu. Another interesting local figure is Husayn Tarumi, from the region adjoining Gilan. He joined Shahrukh in 834/1430–31 and became enrolled among his emirs. When Sultan Muhammad became governor Husayn joined his service and participated in his attack on Shiraz. He ranked among Sultan Muhammad's senior emirs, even for a while in charge of Isfahan, until he found Jahanshah Qaraqoyunlu advancing east and left to join him.[5] While in service to the Timurids and the Qaraqoyunlu he continued his activities as a local ruler, connected as he was to the Kar-Kiya sayyids of Gilan and deeply involved in their politics.

When we consider the individuals involved, such actions make good sense; these men were looking out for their own interests as best they could. If we want to fit them into the *amīr-aʿyān* system of distinct spheres, we have to be willing to blur the edges. For provincial administrations we cannot posit a government personnel truly separate from the city population; it is clear that local elites served in the *dīwāns* of the governors and some also campaigned along with Chaghatay armies. Since close association with the central government brought access to money and favor, which could be passed on to followers, service was likely to enhance their local position. The multiplicity of conflicting allegiances prevented the formation of separate and warring communities, and thus promoted the cohesion of society as a whole. At the same time, the active practice of politics that such a system required helped to attach society as a whole to the ruling elite.

The issue of politics brings us to the second question: how did the government maintain its control? Iran had a heterogeneous society in which both political capital and military capability were widely diffused. Cities and regions had the potential ability to decide their own fates and to separate from the center, and if the ruler was to stay in control he required the active consent of local forces. Shahrukh maintained power for forty years, and even

[4] Paul, *Herrscher, Gemeinwesen, Vermittler*, 144–45.
[5] Samarqandī, *Maṭlaʿ*, 634; Jaʿfarī, *Tārīkh-i kabīr*, 116, 125; Rūmlū, *Aḥsan*, 278.

the regions he lost remained under the rule of Turkic military dynasties. Local power holders must therefore have found the central government useful in some way.

In the case of local rulers the use of the central government is easy to discern. The shahs of Badakhshan and the rulers of Hormuz regularly brought in Timurid troops when they felt themselves threatened. The politics of Gilan and Mazandaran provide more complex examples of local opportunism. In those regions there were inevitably several potential candidates for any position of power. While ambitious men could find a following within their own area, they often looked outside for reinforcements – first to their neighbors, then to the nearest Timurid governor, and finally to the court at Herat. The person on the throne also sought allies in his struggle to keep it, and here he was very likely to appeal to the central government. I have shown how Sayyid Nasir al-Din Marʿashi offered taxes in return for Shahrukh's help in gaining the throne. This particular project backfired, but in a number of cases the Timurids did prove helpful. In any case, the temptation to involve them seems to have been irresistible.

For larger cities, and the professional classes as a whole, the primary advantage of central government might be security, but for the individual who was politically active the central government also offered tools for gaining and keeping a position of power. It is important to recognize the extent to which the local and central political activity was interdependent. Governors could not hold their cities without the participation of the notables and often rewarded them for their services. There were numerous reasons why notables were likely to forge close contacts with the provincial governor and his administration. The notable relied for his power on clients within his own class and among those below him. These were the men whom he could muster when necessary, sometimes on his own business and sometimes in the defense of the city. The professions of notables – ulama, shaykhs, merchants, and bureaucrats – were ones for which government favor was helpful. Favors and wealth received by service to the central government could be used to strengthen one's local position. For both notables and other segments of the population, regional armies, staffed with local commanders and personnel, were a further possible source of wealth and employment.

Like other notables, Sufi shaykhs could use their connections to the regime to grant favors to junior colleagues and students. In a more general way they referred to the ruler and his connection to the supernatural to give legitimacy to their own position. The image of the powerful ruler honoring an otherworldly shaykh was flattering to both Sufis and the ruler, and was thus maintained and elaborated almost equally in religious and dynastic literature. For the ulama, favor with the ruler and the Chaghatay emirs was clearly one road to advancement. Connection to the court could equally well facilitate action against one's competitors, and numerous surviving letters complaining of slander suggest that such action was a frequent occurrence.

The ruler was important to the religious classes in another way as well; as an arbiter and a force to ensure that religious controversies remained within acceptable limits. Intractable disputes, like the one between the shaykh and the *naqīb* of Mashhad, could be brought to the ruler for judgment. More importantly, the existence of the ruler gave religious figures a tool to use against those whose ideas were considered unacceptable. Husayn Khwarazmi was brought to Herat on the instigation of local scholars, but was exonerated. In other cases, such as the Mushaʿshaʿ, the danger to doctrine coincided with potential danger to government and society and led to military action.

The central government thus was a source of money, employment, status, and military manpower, which might be converted into political capital within one's own region or profession. This statement would be true of any society and government, but it was particularly marked in the medieval Middle East because of the informality of institutions and the resulting insecurity of individual power, which had to be maintained through continued effort. This was a society exceptionally active politically at many levels – from the artisans of the city to the members of the dynasty. Whatever their official attitude towards the ruler and his military following, the members of almost all groups found a use for them when competing for advancement within their own sphere. In using the central government they helped to legitimize it and to further its influence.

If the central government was crucial in the functioning of society at numerous levels, then we must ask how the social fabric remained so stable despite frequent political breakdowns. I suggest that despite suffering and danger, periods of confusion increased the power of religious and city associations. For almost any individual, a succession struggle was highly dangerous, and threatened impoverishment at the very least. For many city notables and local rulers it brought ruin and death, but it did so in part because the struggle increased their political importance. As I have shown, it was almost impossible for urban notables or local rulers to remain uninvolved in a regional contest, and the decisions they had to make were central for all levels of government. Choosing which prince to favor was the most important responsibility of city notables. Their decisions directly affected both the population of the city and the outcome of the struggle as a whole. During normal times the semi-independent ruler of a city or small region did not have the power to challenge a major dynasty, but changing sides in a struggle could make a real difference, both because it removed manpower and because it might lead to other desertions. Thus, military struggles were both the hour of peril and the hour of glory for city leaders.

To a somewhat lesser extent, the same was true for the religious classes. Scholars have remarked that Sufi shaykhs gained importance during early Mongol rule, in part because they were able to offer social services which the government no longer provided. The ulama likewise controlled numerous institutions offering help to the population, and they were furthermore the group from which most city notables were recruited. Both ulama and Sufis were frequently used as mediators, intercessors, and envoys in times of conflict, partly no doubt because of their prestige, and partly because they could not be killed lightly. In the periods of breakdown and regional struggle which punctuated the middle periods of Iranian history, agriculture, trade, and the population suffered, but the institutions underlying them gained importance. Thus, when a new dynasty capable of creating a cohesive state arose it was welcomed, and it was based on a social system close to that of the one before it.

Bibliography

Primary Sources

Aubin, Jean, ed. *Matériaux pour la biographie de Shah Niʿmatullah Wali Kermani*. Tehran, Paris: Bibliothèque Iranienne, 1956.

Barbaro, Josafa and Ambrogio Contarini. *Travels in Tana and Persia*. Trans. William Thomas and S. A. Roy. Ed. Lord Stanley. London: Hakluyt Society, 1873.

Bukhārī, Ṣalāḥ al-Dīn Mubārak. *Anīs al-ṭālibīn wa ʿuddat al-sālikīn*. Ed. Khalīl Ibrāhīm Ṣarī Ughlī. Tehran: Kayhān, 1371/1992.

Būzjānī, Darwīsh ʿAlī. *Rawḍāt al-riyāḥīn*. Ed. Hishmat Muʿayyad. Tehran: Bungāh-i Tarjuma wa Nashr-i Kitāb, 1345/1966.

Dughlat, Mīrzā Muḥammad Ḥaydar. *Tarikh-i Rashidi. A History of the Khans of Moghulistan*. Ed. and trans. Wheeler M. Thackston. 2 vols. Cambridge, MA: Harvard University Press, 1996.

Faṣīḥ Khwāfī, Aḥmad b. Jalāl al-Dīn. *Mujmal-i faṣīḥī*. Ed. Muḥammad Farrukh. 3 vols. Mashhad: Bāstān, 1339/1960–61.

Gross, Jo-Ann and Asom Urunbaev, ed. and trans. *The Letters of Khwāja ʿUbayd Allāh Aḥrār and his Associates*. Leiden, Boston, Köln: Brill, 2002.

Ḥāfiẓ-i Abrū. *Cinq opuscules de Ḥāfiẓ-i Abrū concernant l'histoire de l'Iran au temps de Tamerlan*. Ed. F. Tauer. Prague: Editions de l'Académie tchécoslovaque des sciences, 1959.

– "Continuation du Ẓafarnāma de Niẓāmuddīn Šāmī par Ḥāfiẓ-i Abrū." Ed. F. Tauer. *Arkhiv Orientalny* VI (1934), 429–66.

– *Dhayl-i jāmiʿ al-tawārīkh-i rashīdī*. Ed. Kh. Bayānī. 2nd edn. Tehran: Anjumān-i Āthār-i Millī, 1350/1971–72.

– *Ḫorāsān zur Timuridenzeit nach dem Tārīḫ-e Ḥāfiẓ-e Abrū (verf. 817–823 h.)*. Ed. and trans. Dorothea Krawulsky. Vol. I, edition and introduction. Vol. 2, translation. (*Beihefte zum tübinger Atlas des vorderen Orients*, Reihe B, Nr. 46). Wiesbaden: Ludwig Richert Verlag, 1982.

– *Jughrāfiyā-i Ḥāfiẓ-i Abrū*. Ed. Ṣādiq Sajjādī. 3 vols. Tehran: Bunyān-i Daftar-i Nashr-i Mirāth-i Maktūb, vol. I, 1375/1997, vols. II and III, 1378/1999.

– *Majmaʿ al-tawārīkh*. Istanbul: Süleymaniye Library. MS Fatih 4371/1.

– *Majmūʿa al-tawārīkh*. Istanbul: Damad Ibrahim Pasha. MS 919.

– *Zubdat al-tawārīkh*. Ed. Sayyid Kamāl Ḥājj Sayyid Jawādī. 2 vols. Tehran: Nashr-i Nay, 1372/1993.

Harawī, Najīb Māyil, ed. *Īn barghā-yi pīr. Majmūʿa-i bīst athar-i chāp nāshuda-i fārsī az qalamrū-i taṣawwuf*. Tehran: Nay, 1381/2002–3.

al-Harawī, Sayf b. Muḥammad b. Yaʿqūb. *Tārīkh-nāma-i Harāt*. Ed. Muḥammad Zubayr al-Ṣiddiqī. Calcutta: Imperial Library, 1944.

Harawī, ʿUbayd Allah b. Abu Saʿīd. *Taʿlīq bar maqṣad al-iqbāl yā Risāla-i duwwum-i mazārāt-i Harāt*: see under Wāʿiẓ, Aṣīl al-Dīn ʿAbd Allāh. *Maqṣad al-iqbāl*.

Ibn ʿArabshāh, Aḥmad. *Tamerlane or Timur, the Great Amir*. Trans. J. H. Sanders. London: Luzac, 1936.

Ibn Balkhī, Abu Zayd Aḥmad. *Fārsnāma*. Ed. Manṣūr Rastagār Fasāī. Shiraz: Bunyād-i Farsshināsī, 1374/1995.

Ibn Baṭṭūṭa. *The Travels of Ibn Baṭṭūṭa, A. D. 1325–1354*. Trans. H. A. R. Gibb. 3 vols. New Delhi: Munshiram Manoharlal, 1993.

Isfizārī, Muʿīn al-Dīn Zamchī. *Rawḍāt al-jannāt fī awṣāf madīnat Harāt*. Ed. Sayyid Muḥammad Kāẓim Imām. Tehran: Dānishgāh-i Tihrān, 1338/1959.

Jaʿfarī, Jaʿfar b. Muḥammad al-Ḥusaynī. *Tārīkh-i kabīr*. St. Petersburg, Publichnaia Biblioteka im. Saltykova-Shchedrina, MS PNC 201. (references given to folios refer to this MS)

– *Tārīkh-i kabīr*. Trans. Abbas Zaryab. In Abbas Zaryab. "Das Bericht über die Nachfolger Timurs aus dem Taʾrīh-i kabīr des Ǧafar ibn Muḥammad al-Ḥusainī." Ph.D. dissertation, Johannes Gutenberg-Universität zu Mainz, 1960.

– *Tārīkh-i Yazd*. Ed. Īraj Afshār. Tehran: Bungāh-i Tarjuma wa Nashr-i Kitāb, 1338/1960.

Jāmī, ʿAbd al-Raḥman b. Aḥmad. *Nafaḥāt al-uns min ḥiḍrāt al-quds*. Ed. Mahdī Tawḥīdīpūr. Tehran: Intishārāt-i ʿIlmī, 1375/1996–97.

Karbalāʾī Tabrīzī, Ḥāfiẓ Ḥusayn. *Rawḍāt al-jinān wa jannāt al-janān*. Ed. Jaʿfar Sulṭān al-Qurrāʾī. 2 vols. Tehran: Bungāh-i Tarjuma wa Nashr-i Kitāb, 1344–49/1965–70.

Kāshifī, Fakhr al-Dīn ʿAlī b. Ḥusayn Wāʾiẓ. *Rashaḥāt-i ʿayn al-ḥayāt*. Ed. ʿAlī Aṣghar Muʿīniyān. Tehran: Bunyād-i Nīkūkārī-i Nūriyānī, 2536/1977.

Kāshifī Sabzawārī, Ḥusayn Wāʾiẓ. *Futuwwatnāma-i sulṭānī*. Ed. Muḥammad Jaʿfar Maḥjūb. Tehran: Intishārāt-i Bunyād-i Farhang-i Īrān, 1350/1971.

Kātib, Aḥmad b. Ḥusayn b. ʿAlī. *Tārīkh-i jadīd-i Yazd*. Ed. Īraj Afshār. Tehran: Intishārāt-i Ibn Sīnā, 1345/1966.

Khunjī Iṣfahānī, Faḍl Allāh. *Tārīkh-i ʿālim-ārā-i amīnī*. Ed. John E. Woods. London: Royal Asiatic Society, 1992.

Khwāfī, Zayn al-Dīn Muḥammad. *Manhaj al-Rashād*. In *Īn barghā-i pīr. Majmūʿa-i bīst athar-i chāp nāshuda-i fārsī az qalamrū-i taṣawwuf*. Ed. Najīb Māyil Harawī. Tehran: Nay, 1381/2002–03, 472–579.

Khwāja-i Samarqandī, Abū Ṭāhir. *Samariyya. Dar bayān-i awṣāf-i Ṭabīʿī wa mazārāt-i Samarqand*. Ed. Īraj Afshār. Tehran: Farhang-i Īrān Zamīn, 1343/1965.

Khwāndamīr, Ghiyāth al-Dīn b. Humām al-Dīn. *Dastūr al-wuzarāʾ*. Ed. Saʿīd Nafīsī. Tehran: Iqbāl, 1317/1938–39.

– *Ḥabīb al-siyar fī akhbār afrād bashar*. Ed. Muḥammad Dabīr Siyāqī. 4 vols. Tehran: Khayyām, 1333/1955–56.

– *Ḥabīb al-siyar fī akhbār afrād bashar*. Trans. Wheeler M. Thackston. In Wheeler M. Thackston. *Habibu's-siyar. Tome Three*. 2 vols. Cambridge, MA: *Sources of Oriental Languages and Literatures* 24, 1994.

Marʿashī, Sayyid Ẓahīr al-Dīn b. Naṣīr al-Dīn. *Tārīkh-i Gīlān wa Daylamistān*. Ed. Manūchihr Sutūda. Tehran: Bunyād-i Farhang-i Īrān, 1347/1968–9.

– *Tārīkh-i Ṭabaristān wa Rūyān wa Māzandarān*. Ed. Muḥammad Ḥusayn Tasbīḥī. Tehran: Sharq, 1966.

Mīrkhwānd, Muḥammad b. Khwāndshāh b. Maḥmūd. *Rawḍāt al-ṣafā fī sīrat al-awliyā wa'l mulūk wa'l khulafā'*. 10 vols. Tehran: Markaz-i Khayyām Pīrūz, 1338–39/1960.

Mu'īn al-Fuqarā', Aḥmad b. Maḥmūd. *Tārīkh-i mullāzāda dar dhikr-i mazārāt-i Bukhārā*. Ed. Aḥmad Gulchīn Ma'ānī. Tehran: Kitābkhāna-i Ibn Sīnā, 1339/1960.

Mu'izz al-ansāb fī shajarat al-ansāb. Paris: Bibliothèque Nationale. MS 67.

– London: British Library MS Or. 467. (Where not otherwise specified, references are to Paris MS.)

Musawī, Muḥammad b. Faḍl Allāh. *Tārīkh-i khayrāt*. Istanbul, Turhan Hadica Sultan, MS 224.

Mustawfī, Ḥamd Allāh. *Nuzhat al-qulūb*. Ed. Guy Le Strange. E. J. W. Gibb Memorial Series. Vol. 23. Leiden: Brill, 1915.

Mustawfī Bāfqī, Muḥammad Mufīd. *Jāmi'-i mufīdī*. Ed. Īraj Afshār. 3 vols., Tehran: Kitābfurūsh-i Asadī, 1340/1961 (includes "waqfnāma").

Naṭanzī, Mu'īn al-Dīn. *Extraits du Muntakhab al-tavārīkh-i Mu'īnī (Anonyme d'Iskandar)*. Ed. Jean Aubin. Tehran: Khayyām, 1336/1957.

Nawā'ī, 'Abd al-Ḥusayn, ed. *Asnād wa mukātabāt-i tārīkhī-i Īrān*. Tehran: Bungāh-i Tarjuma wa Nashr-i Kitāb, 2536/1977.

Nawā'ī, Mīr 'Alī Shīr. *Majālis al-nafā'is dar tadhkira-i shu'arā'-i qarn-i nuhum-i hijrī, ta'līf-i Mīr-i Niẓām 'Alī Shīr Nawā'ī (Persian translations from the Chaghatay original: The* Latā'ifnāma *of Fakhrī Harātī, and a translation by Muhammad b. Mubārak Qazwīnī)*. Ed. 'Alī Asghar Ḥikmat. Tehran: Chāpkhāna-i Bānk-i milli-i Irān, 1323/1945.

– *Nesāyimü'l maḥabbe min şemāyimi'l fütüvve*. Ed. Dr. Kemal Eraslan. Ankara: Atatürk Kültür, Dil ve Tarih Yüksek Kurumu, 1996.

Qā'inī, Jalāl al-Dīn Muḥammad. *Naṣā'iḥ-i Shāhrukhī*. Vienna, Nationalbibliothek, MS Cod. A. F. 112.

Qāsim al-Anwār. *Kulliyāt*. Ed. Sa'īd Nafīsī. Tehran: Kitābkhāna-i Sanā'ī, 1337/1958.

Rūmlū, Ḥasan Beg. *Aḥsan al-tawārīkh*. Ed. 'Abd al-Ḥusayn Nawā'ī. Persian Text Series. Vol. 41. Tehran: Bungāh-i Tarjuma wa Nashr-i Kitāb, 1349/1970.

Samarqandī, 'Abd al-Razzāq. *Maṭla' al-sa'dayn wa majma' al-baḥrayn*. Ed. Muḥammad Shafī'. 2 vols. Lahore: Kitābkhāna-i Gīlānī, 1360–68/1941–49.

Samarqandī, Dawlatshāh b. 'Alā' al-Dawla. *Tadhkirat al-shu'arā*. Ed. E. G. Browne. London: Luzac, 1901.

Samarqandī, Muḥammad b. 'Abd al-Jalīl. *Qandiyya*. In *Dū risāla dar tārīkh-i mazārāt wa jughrāfiyā-i Samarqand*. Ed. Īraj Afshār. Tehran: Mu'assasa-i Farhangī-i Jahāngīrī, 1367/1988–89.

Shabānkāra'ī, Muḥammad b. 'Alī b. Muḥammad. *Majma' al-ansāb*. Ed. M. H. Muḥaddith. Tehran: Amīr Kabīr, 1363/1985–86.

Shāmī, Niẓām al-Dīn. *Histoire des conquêtes de Tamerlan intitulée Ẓafarnāma, par Niẓāmuddīn Šāmī*. Ed. F. Tauer. Prague: Oriental Institute, 1937 (vol. I), 1956 (vol. II). (Volume II contains additions made by Ḥāfiẓ-i Abrū.)

Shujā', *Anīs al-Nās*. Ed. Īraj Afshār. Persian Text Series, 45. Tehran: Bungāh-i Tarjuma wa Nashr-i Kitāb, 2536/1977.

Shūshtarī, Qāḍī Sayyid Nūr Allāh. *Kitāb-i mustatāb-i majālis al-mū'minīn*. Tehran: Kitābfurūshī-i Islāmīya, 1377/1998–99.

Ṭabasī, Muḥammad. *Āthār-i Darwīsh Muḥammad Ṭabasī*. Ed. Īraj Afshār and Muḥammad Taqī Dānishpazhū. Tehran: Kitābkhāna-i Ibn Sīnā, 1972.

Tāj al-Salmānī. *Šams al-ḥusn: eine Chronik vom Tode Timurs bis zum Jahre 1409 von Tāǧ al-Salmānī*. Ed. and trans. Hans Robert Roemer. Wiesbaden: F. Steiner, 1956.

– *Tarihnāma/Tacü's Selmânî*. Ed. and trans. Ismail Aka. Ankara: Atatürk Kültür, Dil ve Tarih Yüksek Kurumu, 1988.

Tashköprüzāda, Aḥmad b. Muṣṭafā. *Es-Saqâ'iq en-No'mânijje: enthaltend die Biographien der türkischen und im osmanischen Reiche wirkenden Gelehrten, Derwisch-Scheiḫ's und Ärzte von der Regierung Sultân 'Otmân's bis zu der Sülaimân's des Grossen/von Tašköprüzâde; mit Zusätzen, Verbesserungen und Anmerkungen aus dem Arabischen übersetzt*. Ed. and trans. O. Rescher. Constantinople: Phoenix, 1927.

Thackston, Wheeler, ed. and trans. *A Century of Princes: Sources on Timurid History and Art*. Cambridge, MA: Aga Khan Program for Islamic Architecture at Harvard University and the Massachusetts Institute of Technology, 1989.

Ṭihrānī Iṣfahānī, Abū Bakr. *Kitāb-i Diyārbakriyya*. Eds. N. Lugal and F. Sümer. Ankara: Türk Tarih Kurumu Basımevi, 1962–64.

'Uqaylī, Sayf al-Dīn Ḥājjī b. Niẓām. *Āthār al-wuzarā'*. Ed. Mīr Jalāl al-Dīn Ḥusaynī Armawī. Tehran: Intishārāt-i Dānishgāh-i Tihrān, 1337/1959–60. (In many catalogues, the name is spelled 'Aqīlī.)

Wā'iẓ, Aṣīl al-Dīn 'Abd Allāh. *Maqṣad al-iqbāl al-sulṭāniyya wa marṣad al-āmāl al-Khāqāniyya*. With *Ta'līq bar maqṣad al-iqbāl yā Risāla-i duwwum-i mazārāt-i Harāt*, by 'Ubayd Allah b. Abu Sa'īd Harawī. Ed. Māyil Harawī. Tehran: Intishārāt-i Bunyād-i Farhang-i Īrān, 1351/1972–73.

"Waqfiyya-i khānaqāh-mubārak-i quṭb al-aqṭāb Ḥiḍrat Khwāja Muḥammad Pārsā." Tashkent: Uzbek State Archives. Waqf collection I–323, 1291–16. (Listed as 1291/13 in uncorrected catalogue.)

"Waqfiyya-i kitābkhāna-i Ḥiḍrat Khwāja Pārsā." Tashkent: Uzbek State Archives, Waqf collection I–323, 55/14.

"Waqfnāma-i Zayn al-Dīn Abū Bakr Khwāfī." Ed. Maḥmūd Fāḍil Yazdī Muṭlaq. *Mishkāt* 22 (Spring, 1989), 187–200.

Yazdī, Sharaf al-Dīn 'Alī. *Ẓafarnāma*. Ed. Muḥammad 'Abbāsī. 2 vols. Tehran: Amīr Kabīr, 1336/1957.

Yazdī, Tāj al-Dīn Ḥasan b. Shihāb. *Jāmi' al-tawārīkh-ḥasanī*. Eds. Ḥusayn Mudarrisī Ṭabāṭabā'ī and Īraj Afshār. Karachi: Mu'assasa-i Taḥqīqāt-i 'Ulūm-i Āsiyā-i Miyāna wa Gharbī-i Dānishgāh-i Karāchī, 1987.

Yūsuf Ahl, Jalāl al-Dīn. *Farāyid-i ghiyāthī*. Ed. Heshmat Moayyad. Tehran: Foundation for Iranian Culture, 1977 (vol. I), 1979 (vol. II).

Secondary Sources

Adle, Chahryar. "Note sur le 'Qabr-i Šāhruh' de Damghan." *Le Monde iranien et l'Islam* 2 (1974): 173–85.

Afshār, Īraj. *Yādgārhā-i Yazd. Mu'arrafī-i abniyya-i tārīkhī wa āthār-i bāstānī*. Yazd: Anjumān-i Āthār-i Millī 1374/1995.

Aka, Ismail. *Mirza Şahruh ve Zamani (1405–1447)*. Ankara: Türk Tarih Kurumu Basımevi, 1994.

– "Timur'un ölümünden sonra güney-Iran'da hâkimiyet mücadeleleri." *Atsız Armağanı*. Istanbul: Ötüken Yayınevi, 1976: 3–15.

Allen, Terry. *A Catalogue of the Toponyms and Monuments of Timurid Herat.* Cambridge, MA: Agha Khan Program for Islamic Architecture at Harvard University and Massachusetts Institute of Technology, 1981.
– *Timurid Herat.* Beihefte zum Tübinger Atlas des vorderen Orients. Wiesbaden: Reichert, 1983.
Allsen, Thomas. *Culture and Conquest in Mongol Eurasia.* Cambridge: Cambridge University Press, 2001.
– "Mongolian Princes and their Merchant Partners." *Asia Major* 2 (1989).
– "Spiritual Geography and Political Legitimacy in the Eastern Steppe." In *Ideology and the Formation of Early States.* Eds. Henri J. M. Claessen and Jarich G. Oosten. Leiden, New York, Köln: Brill, 1996.
Amitai, Reuven. "Foot Soldiers, Militiamen and Volunteers in the Early Mamluk Army." In *Texts, Documents and Artefacts: Islamic Studies in Honor of D. S. Richards.* Ed. Chase F. Robinson. Leiden, Boston: Brill, 2003.
Amoretti, B. S. "Religion in the Timurid and Safavid Periods." In *The Cambridge History of Iran.* 8 vols. vol. 6, Eds. Peter Jackson and Lawrence Lockhart, Cambridge: Cambridge University Press, 1986: 610–55.
Ando, Shiro. *Timuridische Emire nach dem Muʿizz al-ansāb. Untersuchung zur Stammesaristokratie Zentralasiens im 14. und 15 Jahrhundert.* Berlin: K. Schwarz, 1992.
– "Die timuridische Historiographie II: Šaraf al-Dīn ʿAlī Yazdī." *Studia Iranica* 24, 2 (1995): 219–46.
– "The *Shaykh al-Islām* as a Timurid Office: a Preliminary Study." *Islamic Studies* 33, 2–3 (1415/1994): 253–80.
Aubin, Jean. "Comment Tamerlan prenait les villes." *Studia Islamica* 19 (1963): 83–122.
– "De Kûhbanân à Bidar: la famille niʿmatullahī." *Studia Iranica* 20, 2 (1991): 233–61.
– *Deux sayyids de Bam au xve siècle. Contribution à l'histoire de l'Iran timouride.* Wiesbaden: Steiner Verlag G. M. B. H., 1956. (Akademie der Wissenschaften und der Literatur, *Abhandlungen der Geistes- und sozialwissenschaftlichen Klasse* 7, 1956.)
– *Émirs mongols et vizirs persans dans les remous de l'acculturation. Studia Islamica.* Cahier 15. Paris: Association pour l'avancement des études iraniennes, 1995.
– "Le khanat de Čaġatai et le Khorassan (1334–1380)." *Turcica* 8, 2 (1976): 16–60.
– "Le mécénat timouride à Chiraz." *Studia Islamica* VIII (1957): 71–88.
– "Note sur quelques documents Aq Qoyunlu." In *Mélanges Louis Massignon.* Damascus: Institut Français de Damas, 1956.
– "Les princes d'Ormuz du XIIIe au XVe siècle." *Journal Asiatique* CCXLI (1953): 77–137.
– "Le patronage culturel en Iran sous les Ilkhans. Une grande famille de Yazd." *Le monde iranien et l'Islam* III (1975): 107–18.
– "Le quriltai de Sultân-Maydân (1336)." *Journal asiatique* 279 (1991): 175–97.
– "Un santon quhistānī de l'époque timouride." *Revue des études islamiques* 35 (1967): 185–216.
Āyatī, Āyat Allāh Ḥājj Shaykh Muḥammad Ḥusayn. *Bahāristān dar tārīkh wa tarājim-i rijāl-i Qāyināt wa Quhistān.* Mashhad: Muʾassasa-i Chāp wa Intishārāt-i Dānishgāh-i Firdawsī, 1371/1992.
Bartol'd, V. V. "Novyĭ istochnik po istorii Timuridov." In *Sochineniia.* 9 vols. Moscow: Isdatels'stvo Vostochnoĭ Literatury, 1963–1977: vol. VIII, 546–74.
– "Khronologiia praviteleĭ vostochnoĭ chasti Chagataĭskogo ulusa (liniia Tugluk-Timur-khana)." In *Vostochnyĭ Turkestan i Srednaia Aziia. Istoriia, kul'tura, sviazi.* Ed. B. A. Litvinskiĭ. Moscow: Nauka, 1984: 156–64.

– *Ulugbek i ego vremia*. In *Sochineniia*. 9 vols. Moscow: Nauka, 1964: vol. II, pt. 2, 25–177.

Bashir, Shahzad. "Between Mysticism and Messianism: the Life and Thought of Muḥammad Nūrbaḵš (d. 1464)." PhD dissertation, Yale University, November, 1997.

– *Messianic Hopes and Mystical Visions: the Nūrbakhshīya between Medieval and Modern Islam*. Columbia, SC: University of South Carolina Press, 2003.

Behrens-Abouseif, Doris. "Patterns of Urban Patronage in Cairo: a Comparison between the Mamluk and the Ottoman Periods." In *The Mamluks in Egyptian Politics and Society*. Eds. Thomas Philipp and Ulrich Haarmann. Cambridge: Cambridge University Press, 1998: 224–34.

Berkey, Jonathan P. "The Mamluks as Muslims: The Military Elite and the Construction of Islam in Medieval Egypt." In *The Mamluks in Egyptian Politics and Society*. Eds. Thomas Philipp and Ulrich Haarmann. Cambridge: Cambridge University Press, 1998: 163–73.

– *The Transmission of Knowledge in Medieval Cairo: a Social History of Islamic Education*. Princeton, NJ: Princeton University Press, 1992.

Bihbahānī, Sayyid ʿAlī Mūsawī. "Iṭṭilāʿātī darbāra Ṣāʾin al-Dīn Iṣfahānī Khujandī maʿrūf bi Turka." In *Majmūʿa-i Khiṭābahā-i Nukhustīn-i Kungra-i taḥqīqāt-i Īrānī*. Ed. Ghulāmriḍā Sutūda. Tehran: No publisher listed, 1353/1985: 262–77.

Bregel, Iuriĭ and Charles A. Storey. *Persidskaia literatura*. Moscow: Nauka, 1972.

Broadbridge, Anne F. "Academic Rivalry and the Patronage System in Fifteenth-Century Egypt: al-ʿAynī, al-Maqrīzī, and Ibn Ḥajar al-ʿAsqalānī." *Mamluk Studies Review* III (1999): 85–107.

Brockelmann, Carl. *Geschichte der arabischen Litteratur*. 2nd edn. 2 vols. and supplement. Leiden: Brill, 1943–49.

Brown, Peter. *The Cult of the Saints: Its Rise and Function in Latin Christianity*. Chicago: University of Chicago Press, 1981.

Cahen, Claude. *Mouvements populaires et autonomisme urbain dan l'Asie musulmane du moyen âge*. Leiden: Brill, 1959.

Chamberlain, Michael. *Knowledge and Social Practice in Medieval Damascus*. Cambridge: Cambridge University Press, 1994.

Chodkiewicz, Michel. "Quelques aspects de techniques spirituelles dans la ṭarīqa naqshbandiyya." In *Naqshbandis: Historical Developments and Present Situation of a Muslim Mystical Order*. Eds. M. Gaborieau, A. Popovic, and T. Zarcone. Istanbul, Paris: Isis, Institut français d'études anatoliennes d'Istanbul, 1990: 69–82.

– *Le sceau des saints: prophétie et sainteté dans la doctrine d'Ibn Arabî*. Paris: Gallimard, 1986.

Davidovich, E. A. *Istoriia denezhnogo obrashcheniia srednevekovoĭ Sredneĭ Azii*. Moscow: Nauka, 1983.

DeWeese, Devin. "The Eclipse of the Kubravīyah in Central Asia." *Iranian Studies* 21, 1–2 (1988): 45–83.

– "The *Kashf al-Hudā* of Kamāl al-Dīn Ḥusayn Khorezmī: A Fifteenth-Century Sufi Commentary on the *Qaṣīdat al-Burdah* in Khorezmian Turkic (Text Edition, Translation and Historical Introduction)." PhD dissertation, Indiana University, 1985.

– "The Mashāʾikh-i Turk and the Khojagān: Rethinking the Links between the Yasavī and Naqshbandī Sufi Traditions." *Journal of Islamic Studies* 7, 2 (1996): 180–207.

– "Sacred Places and 'Public' Narratives: The Shrine of Aḥmad Yasavī in Hagiographical Traditions of the Yasavī Ṣūfī Order, 16th–17th Centuries." *Muslim World* 90, 3–4 (2000): 353–76.

– "Sayyid 'Alī Hamadānī and Kubrawī Hagiographical Traditions." In *The Legacy of Mediaeval Persian Sufism*. Ed. Leonard Lewisohn. London: Khaniqahi-Nimatullahi Publications, 1992: 121–57.

– "The *Tadhkira-i Bughrā-khān* and the 'Uvaysī' Sufis of Central Asia: Notes in Review of *Imaginary Muslims*." *Central Asiatic Journal* 40, 1 (1996): 87–127.

Digby, Simon. "The Sufi *Shaykh* and the Sultan: a Conflict of Claims to Authority in Medieval India." *Iran* 28 (1990): 71–81.

– "The Sufi Shaykh as a Source of Authority in Mediaeval India." In *Islam and Society in South Asia/Islam et société en Asie du sud*. Ed. Marc Gaborieau. Paris: Éditions de l'école des hautes études en sciences sociales, 1986: 57–77.

– "*Tabarrukāt* and Succession among the Great Chishtī Shaykhs of the Delhi Sultanate." In *Delhi Through the Ages: Essays in Urban History, Culture and Society*. Ed. R. E. Frykenberg. Bombay, Calcutta, Madras: Oxford University Press, 1986: 63–103.

Encyclopaedia Iranica. Ed. E. Yarshater. London, Boston: Routledge and Kegan Paul, 1985–2006.

Encyclopaedia of Islam. Eds. H. A. R. Gibb et al. 2nd edn. Leiden: Brill, c. 1960–2003.

Ernst, Carl W. *Eternal Garden: Mysticism, History and Politics at a South Asian Sufi Center*. Albany, NY: State University of New York Press, 1992.

Fedorov, M. N. "Klad monet Ulugbeka i Shakhrukha iz Samarkanda." *Obshchestvennye nauki v Uzbekistane* 3 (1969): 53–57.

Fletcher, Joseph. "The Mongols: Ecological and Social Perspectives." *Harvard Journal of Asiatic Studies* 46 (1986): 11–50.

Fouchécour, C.-H. de. " 'The Good Companion' (*'Anīs al-Nās*), a Manual for the Honest Man in Shīrāz in the 9th/15th Century." In *Iran and Iranian Studies. Essays in Honor of Iraj Afshar*. Ed. Kambiz Eslami. Princeton, NJ: Zagros, 1998: 42–57.

Geertz, Clifford. "Centers, Kings and Charisma." In *Culture and its Creators*. Eds. J. Ben-David and T.N. Clark. Chicago, London: University of Chicago Press, 1977: 150–71.

Geoffroy, Éric. *Le soufisme en Égypte et en Syrie sous les derniers Mamelouks et les premiers Ottomans. Orientations spirituelles et enjeux culturels*. Damascus: Institut français d'études arabes de Damas, 1995.

Godard, André. "Khorasan." *Āthār-i Īrān* IV (1949): 7–150.

Goldziher, Ignaz. "Veneration of Saints in Islam." In Ignaz Goldziher. *Muslim Studies*. Trans. C. R. Barber and S. M. Stern. 2 vols. Chicago, New York: Aldine, 1967–1971: vol. I, 209–38.

Golombek, Lisa. "The Chronology of Turbat-i Shaykh Jām." *Iran, Journal of the British Institute of Persian Studies* IX (1971): 27–44.

– *The Timurid Shrine at Gazur Gah. Royal Ontario Museum of Art and Archaeology Occasional Paper* 15. c. 1969.

Golombek, Lisa and Donald Wilber. *The Timurid Architecture of Iran and Turan*. Princeton, NJ: Princeton University Press, 1988.

Goto, Yukako. "Der Aufstieg zweier Sayyid-Familien am Kaspischen Meer: 'volksislamische' Strömungen in Iran des 8/14. und 9/15. Jahrhunderts." *Wiener Zeitschrift für die Kunde des Morgenlandes* 89 (1999): 45–84.

Gramlich, Richard. *Die Wunder der Freunde Gottes. Theologien und Erscheinungsformen des islamischen Heiligenwunders*. Wiesbaden: Steiner, 1987.

Gray, Basil. "The School of Shiraz from 1392–1453." In *The Arts of the Book in Central Asia*. Ed. Basil Gray. Paris: UNESCO, 1979: 121–45.
Grönke, Monika. "Lebensangst und Wunderglaube: zur Volksmentalität im Iran der Mongolenzeit." In *XXIV. Deutscher Orientalistentag vom 26. bis 30. September 1988 in Köln: Ausgewählte Vorträge*. Eds. Werner Diem and Abdoldjavad Falaturi. Stuttgart: F. Steiner, 1990: 391–99.
Gross, Jo-Ann. "Authority and Miraculous Behavior: Reflections on *Karāmāt* Stories of Khwāja ʿUbaydullāh Aḥrār." In *The Legacy of Persian Sufism*. Ed. Leonard Lewisohn. London: Khaniqahi-Nimatullahi Publications, 1992: 159–71.
– "Multiple Roles and Perceptions of a Sufi Shaikh: Symbolic Statements of Political and Religious Authority." In *Naqshbandis: Historical Developments and Present Situation of a Muslim Mystical Order*. Eds. M. Gaborieau, A. Popovic, and T. Zarcone. Istanbul, Paris: Isis, Institut français d'études anatoliennes d'Istanbul, 1990: 109–21.
Grube, Ernst J. with Eleanor Sims. "The School of Herat from 1400 to 1450." In *The Arts of the Book in Central Asia*. Ed. Basil Gray. Paris: UNESCO, 1979: 146–78.
Ḥaqīqat, ʿAbd al-Rafīʿ. *Tārīkh-i Simnān*. Tehran: Chāpkhāna-i Iṭṭilāʿāt, 1341/1962.
Hardy, Peter. *Historians of Medieval India: Studies in Indo-Muslim Historical Writing*. London: Luzac, 1960.
Herrmann, Gottfried. "Der historische Gehalt des 'Nāma-ye nāmī' von Ḫwāndamīr." Ph.D. dissertation, University of Göttingen, 1968.
– "Zur Entstehung des Ṣadr-amtes." In *Die islamische Welt zwischen Mittelalter und Neuzeit, Festschrift für Hans Robert Roemer zum 65. Geburtstag*. Eds. U. Haarmann and P. Bachmann. Wiesbaden: F. Steiner, 1979: 278–95.
Hinz, Walther. Review of Jean Aubin, *Deux sayyids de Bam au XVe siècle. Contribution à l'histoire de l'Iran timouride*. *Oriens* 10, 2 (1957): 168–70.
– "The Value of the Toman in the later Middle Ages." In *Yādnāma-i Īrānī-i Mīnūrskī*. Tehran: Publications of Tehran University, 1969.
Hodgson, Marshall G. S. *The Venture of Islam*. 3 vols. Chicago, London: Chicago University Press, 1974.
Holod-Tretiak, Renata. "The Monuments of Yazd, 1300–1450: Architecture, Patronage and Setting." PhD dissertation, Harvard University, 1972.
Homerin, Th. Emil. "Saving Muslim Souls: the Khānqāh and the Sufi Duty in Mamluk Lands." *Muslim Studies Review* 3 (1999): 59–83.
Hourani, Albert. *A History of the Arab Peoples*. New York: MJF Books, 1991.
Humphreys, R. Stephen. *Islamic History: A Framework for Inquiry*. Princeton: Princeton University Press, 1991.
Hunarfar, Luṭf Allāh. "Iṣfahān dar dawra-i jānishīnān-i Tīmūr." *Hunar wa mardum* 163 (2535/1976): 6–18.
Jackson, Peter. *The Delhi Sultanate. A Political and Military History*. Cambridge: Cambridge University Press, 1999.
Kafadar, Cemal. *Between Two Worlds: The Construction of the Ottoman State*. Berkeley, Los Angeles, London: University of California Press, 1995.
Karamustafa, Ahmet T. *God's Unruly Friends: Dervish Groups in the Islamic Later Middle Period, 1200–1500*. Salt Lake City: University of Utah Press, 1994.
Keyvani, Mehdi. *Artisans and Guild Life in the later Safavid Period. Contributions to the Social-economic History of Persia*. Berlin: Klaus Schwarz, 1982.

Khalidov, A. B. and Maria E. Subtelny. "The Curriculum of Islamic Higher Learning in Timurid Iran in the Light of the Sunni Revival under Shāh-Rukh." *Journal of the American Oriental Society* 115, 2 (1995): 210–36.

Knysh, Alexander D. *Ibn 'Arabi in the Later Islamic Tradition: The Making of a Polemical Image in Medieval Islam*. Albany, NY: State University of New York Press, 1999.

Komaroff, Linda. "The Epigraphy of Timurid Coinage: Some Preliminary Remarks." *American Numismatic Society: Museum Notes* 31 (1986): 207–32.

Lambton, Ann K. S. *Continuity and Change in Medieval Persia. Aspects of Administrative, Economic and Social History, 11th–14th Century*. Albany, NY: Bibliotheca Persica, 1988.

Lancaster, William. *The Rwala Bedouin Today*. Cambridge: Cambridge University Press, 1981.

Lapidus, Ira. *A History of Islamic Societies*. Cambridge: Cambridge University Press, 1988.

– *Muslim Cities in the Later Middle Ages*. Cambridge: Cambridge University Press, 1984.

Le Gall, Dina. *A Culture of Sufism: Naqshbandis in the Ottoman World, 1450–1700*. Albany, NY: State University of New York Press, 2005.

Lentz, Thomas W. "Painting at Herat under Baysunghur ibn Shahrukh." PhD dissertation, Harvard University, 1985.

Lentz, Thomas W. and Glenn D. Lowry. *Timur and the Princely Vision: Persian Art and Culture in the Fifteenth Century*. Los Angeles, Washington, D.C.: Los Angeles County Museum of Art (Arthur M. Sackler Gallery), 1989.

Lewisohn, Leonard. *Beyond Faith and Infidelity: the Sufi Poetry and Teachings of Maḥmūd Shabistarī*. Richmond, Surrey: Curzon, 1995.

– "A Critical Edition of the Diwan of Maghrebi." PhD dissertation, School of Oriental and African Studies, University of London, 1988.

– *A Critical Edition of the Divan of Muhammad Shirin Maghribi*. Tehran: Mu'assasa-i Intishārāt-i Islāmī, 1993.

– "Muḥammad Shīrīn Maghribī." *Ṣūfī* 1 (1988): 40–46.

Limbert, John. "Shiraz in the Age of Hafez." PhD dissertation, Harvard University, 1973.

– *Shiraz in the Age of Hafez: the Glory of a Medieval Persian City*. Seattle, London: University of Washington Press, 2004.

Manz, Beatrice F. "Family and Ruler in Timurid Historiography." In *Studies on Central Asian History in Honor of Yuri Bregel*. Ed. D. DeWeese. Bloomington: Research Institute for Inner Asian Studies, Indiana University, 2001: 57–78.

– "Local Histories of Southern Iran." In *History and Historiography of Post-Mongol Central Asia and the Middle East: Studies in Honor of John E. Woods*. Eds. Judith Pfeiffer and Sholeh A. Quinn. Wiesbaden: Harrassowitz, 2006: 267–81.

– "Military Manpower in Late Mongol and Timurid Iran." *L'Héritage timouride, Iran-Asie centrale-Inde XVe–XVIIIe siècles, Cahiers d'Asie centrale* 3–4 (1997): 43–56.

– "Mongol History Rewritten and Relived." *Mythes historiques du monde musulman*. Ed. Denise Aigle. Special issue of *Revue du monde musulman et de la Méditerranée* (2001): 129–49.

– "Nomad and Settled in the Timurid Military." In *Mongols, Turks, and Others: Eurasian Nomads and the Sedentary World*. Eds. Reuven Amitai and Michal Biran. Leiden, Boston: Brill, 2005: 425–57.

– *The Rise and Rule of Tamerlane*. Cambridge: Cambridge University Press, 1989.

– "Tamerlane and the Symbolism of Sovereignty." *Iranian Studies* 21, 1–2 (1988): 105–22.

– "Women in Timurid Dynastic Politics." In *Women in Iran from the Rise of Islam to 1800*. Eds. Lois Beck and Guity Nashat. Urbana, Chicago: University of Illinois Press, 2003: 121–39.

Marefat, Roya. "Beyond the Architecture of Death: the Shrine of the Shah-Zinda in Samarqand." PhD dissertation, Harvard University, 1991.

McChesney, Robert D. "Notes on the Life and Work of Ibn ʿArabshah." Unpublished paper.

– *Waqf in Central Asia: Four Hundred Years in the History of a Muslim Shrine, 1480–1889*. Princeton, NJ: Princeton University Press, 1991.

Meier, Fritz. "Kraftakt und Faustrecht des Heiligen." In *Zwei Abhandlungen über die Naqšbandiyya*. Istanbul: Beiruter Texte und Studien, 58, 1994.

– *Meister und Schüler im Orden der Naqšbandiyya*. Heidelberg: *Sitzungberichte der Heidelberger Akademie der Wissenschaften, phil-hist. Klasse* 2, 1995.

Meisami, Julie S. *Persian Historiography to the End of the Twelfth Century*. Edinburgh: Edinburgh University Press, 1999.

Mélikoff, Irène. *Abū Muslim le "porte-hache" du Khorassan dans la tradition épique turco-iranienne*. Paris: Maisonneuve, 1962.

Melville, Charles. "The Caspian Provinces: A World Apart. Three Local Histories of Mazandaran." *Iranian Studies* 33, 1–2 (2000): 45–91.

Miller, Isabel A. M. "The Social and Economic History of Yazd (c. AH 736/AD 1335 – c. AH 906/AD 1500)." PhD thesis, University of London, January, 1990.

Mojaddedi, J. *The Biographical Tradition in Sufism: the Ṭabaqāt Genre from al-Sulamī to Jāmī*. Richmond, Surrey: Curzon, 2001.

Mottahedeh, Roy P. *Loyalty and Leadership in an Early Islamic Society*. Princeton, NJ: Princeton University Press, 1980.

Norris, H. T. "The *Mirʾāt al-Ṭālibīn*, by Zain al-Dīn al-Khawāfī of Khurāsān and Herat." *Bulletin of the School of Oriental and African Studies* 53 (1990): 57–63.

OʾKane, Bernard. *Timurid Architecture in Khurasan*. Costa Mesta, CA: Mazda, 1987.

Pahlitzsch, Johannes. "Memoria und Stiftung im Islam: Die Entwicklung des Totengedächtnisses bis zu den Mamluken." In *Stiftungen in Christentum, Judentum und Islam vor der Moderne. Auf der Suche nach ihren Gemeinsamkeiten und Unterschieden in religiösen Grundlagen, praktischen Zwecken und historischen Transformationen*. Ed. Michael Borgolte. Berlin: Akademie Verlag, 2005: 71–94.

Paul, Jürgen. *Doctrine and Organization. The Khwājagān/Naqshbandīya in the First Generation after Bahāʾuddīn*. ANOR 1. Berlin: Das Arabische Buch, 1998.

– "Hagiographische Texte als historische Quelle." *Saeculum* 41, 1 (1990): 17–43.

– *Herrscher, Gemeinwesen, Vermittler: Ostiran und Transoxanien in vormongolischer Zeit*. Beirut: F. Steiner, 1996.

– "The Histories of Samarqand." *Studia Iranica* 22, 1 (1993): 69–92.

– *Die politische und soziale Bedeutung der Naqšbandiyya in Mittelasien im 15. Jahrhundert*. Berlin, New York: W. De Gruyter, 1991.

– "Scheiche und Herrscher im Khanat Čaġatay." *Der Islam* 67, 2 (1990), 278–321.

– "Wehrhafte Städte. Belagerungen von Herat, 1448–1468." *Asiatische Studien/Études Asiatiques* LVIII, 1 (2004): 163–93.

Potter, Lawrence G. "The Kart Dynasty of Herat: Religion and Politics in Medieval Iran." PhD dissertation, Columbia University, 1992.

Quinn, Sholeh A. "The *Muʿizz al-Ansāb* and *Shuʿab-i Panjgānah* as Sources for the Chaghatayid Period of History: A Comparative Analysis." *Central Asiatic Journal* 33 (1989): 229–53.

Quiring-Zoche, Rosemarie. *Isfahan im 15. und 16. Jahrhundert. Ein Beitrag zur persischen Stadtgeschichte*. Freiburg: Schwarz, 1980.

Rabino di Borgomale, H. L. "Les dynasties locales du Gîlân et du Daylam." *Journal Asiatique* CCXXXVII, 2 (1949): 301–50.

Radtke, Bernd. "Von Iran nach Westafrika: zwei Quellen für al-Ḥāǧǧ ʿUmars Kitāb rimāḥ ḥizb ar-raḥīm: Zaynaddīn al-Ḫwāfī und Šamsaddīn al-Madyanī." *Die Welt des Islams* 35 (1995): 37–49.

Richard, Francis. "Un témoignage inexploité concernant le mécénat d'Eskandar Solṭān à Eṣfahān." *La civiltà Timuride come fenomeno internazionale*. Ed. Michele Bernardini, *Oriente Moderno* XV (1996): 45–72.

Ritter, Helmut. "Die Anfänge der Ḥurūfīsekte." ("Studien zur Geschichte der Islamischen Frömmigkeit," II). *Oriens* 7 (1954): 1–54.

Robinson, Chase F. *Islamic Historiography*. Cambridge: Cambridge University Press, 2003.

Roemer, Hans R. *Staatschreiben der Timuridenzeit. Das Šaraf-nāmä des ʿAbdallāh Marwārīd in kritischer Auswertung*. Wiesbaden: Akademie der Wissenschaften und der Literatur, Veröffentlichungen der orientalischen Kommission, 1952.

– "The Successors to Tīmūr." In *The Cambridge History of Iran*. 8 vols. Cambridge: Cambridge University Press, vol. VI, Eds. Peter Jackson and Lawrence Lockhart, 1986: 98–145.

– "Tīmūr in Iran." In *The Cambridge History of Iran*. 8 vols. Cambridge: Cambridge University Press, vol. VI, Eds. Peter Jackson and Lawrence Lockhart, 1986: 42–97.

Sabra, Adam. *Poverty and Charity in Medieval Islam: Mamluk Egypt, 1250–1517*. Cambridge: Cambridge University Press, 2000.

Savory, Roger M. "The Safavid Administrative System." In *The Cambridge History of Iran*. 8 vols. Cambridge: Cambridge University Press, vol. VI, Eds. Peter Jackson and Lawrence Lockhart, 1986: 351–72.

Sayılı, Aydin. *Ghiyath al-Din al-Kashi's Letter on Ulugh Bey and the Scientific Activity in Samarqand; Ulug Bey ve semerkanddeki ilim faaliyeti hakkında Giyasüddin Kâşî'nin mektubu*. Ankara: Türk Tarih Kurumu Basımevi, 1960.

Shaban, M. A. *The ʿAbbasid Revolution*. Cambridge: Cambridge University Press, 1970.

Shoshan, Boaz. "The 'Politics of Notables' in Medieval Islam." *Asian and African Studies* 20 (1986): 179–215.

Smith, Jane I. "Concourse between the Living and the Dead in Islamic Eschatological Literature." *History of Religions* 19, 3 (February, 1980): 224–36.

Smyth, William. "Controversy in a Tradition of Commentary: the Academic Legacy of al-Sakkākī's *Miftāḥ al-ʿulūm*." *Journal of the American Oriental Association* 112 (1992): 589–97.

Soucek, Priscilla. "Eskandar b. ʿOmar Šayx b. Timur: A Biography." *La civiltà Timuride come fenomeno internazionale*. Ed. Michele Bernardini, *Oriente Moderno* XV (1996): vol. I, 73–87.

– "Ibrāhīm Sulṭān ibn Shāhrukh." In *Iran and Iranian Studies. Essays in Honor of Iraj Afshar*. Ed. Kambiz Eslami. Princeton, NJ: Zagros, 1998: 24–43.

– "The Manuscripts of Iskandar Sultan: Structure and Content." In *Timurid Art and Culture*. Eds. L. Golombek and M. Subtelny. Leiden, New York: Brill, 1992: 116–31.

Subtelny, Maria. "The Cult of 'Abdullāh Anṣārī under the Timurids." In *Gott is schön and Er liebt die schönheit/God is Beautiful and He loves Beauty*. Eds. Alma Giese and J. Christoph Bürgel. Festschrift in Honor of Annemarie Schimmel. Bern, Berlin, New York: Peter Lang, 1994.

– "The Making of Bukhārā-yi Sharīf: Scholars, Books, and Libraries in Medieval Bukhara (The Library of Khwāja Muḥammad Pārsā)." In *Studies on Central Asian History in Honor of Yuri Bregel*. Ed. Devin DeWeese. Bloomington, Indiana: Research Institute for Inner Asian Studies, 2001: 79–111.

– "The *Vaqfīya* of Mīr 'Alī Šīr Navā'ī as Apologia." *Fahir Iz Armağanı II, Journal of Turkish Studies* 15 (1991): 257–86.

Sümer, Faruk. *Kara Koyunlular*. Ankara: Türk Tarih Kurumu Yayınlarından, 1967.

Ṭabāṭabā'ī, Mudarrisī. *Qumm dar qarn-i nuhum-i hijrī, 801–900: faṣl az kitāb Qumm dar chahārda qarn*. Qum: Ḥikmat, 1350/1971–72.

Taeschner, Franz. "Futuwwa, eine gemeinschaftbildende Idee im mittelalterlichen Orient und ihre verschiedenen Erscheinungsformen." *Schweizerisches Archiv für Volkskunde* 52 (1956): 122–58.

– *Zünfte und Bruderschaften in Islam*. Texte zur Geschichte der Futuwwa. Zürich, Munich: Artemis-Verlag, 1979.

Taylor, Christopher S. *In the Vicinity of the Righteous: Ziyāra and the Veneration of Muslim Saints in late Medieval Egypt*. Leiden, Boston: Brill, 1998.

Trimmingham, J. Spencer. *The Sufi Orders in Islam*. New York, Oxford: Oxford University Press, 1998.

Van Ess, Josef. *Die Erkenntnislehre des 'Aḍudaddīn al-Īcī, Übersetzung und Kommentar des ersten Buches seiner Mawāqif*. Wiesbaden: Steiner, 1966.

Woods, John E. "The Rise of Tīmūrīd Historiography." *Journal of Near Eastern Studies* 46, 2 (1987): 81–108.

– *The Timurid Dynasty, Papers on Inner Asia*. Bloomington: Indiana University, 1990.

– "Timur's Genealogy." In *Intellectual Studies on Islam, Essays Written in Honor of Martin B. Dickson*. Eds. Michel M. Mazzaoui and Vera B. Moreen. Salt Lake City: University of Utah Press, 1990: 85–126.

– "Turco-Iranica II: Notes on a Timurid Decree of 1396/798." *Journal of Near Eastern Studies* 43, 4 (1984): 331–37.

Index

Abā Bakr b. Amīrānshāh, Mīrzā 18–19, 35, 119–20, 124–25, 127, 157
Abā Bakr b. Muḥammad Juki, Mīrzā 26, 115, 247, 259, 260–61
Abā Bakr Khāzin, *kotwāl* 159–60
Abarquh 29, 32, 116, 123, 124, 125, 149, 152, 156, 163, 249, 253, 256, 268
ʿAbbasid revolution 185, 189
ʿAbd al-ʿAzīz b. Ulugh Beg, Mīrzā 246, 248, 265–66
ʿAbd al-Khāliq b. Khudāydād Ḥusaynī 27
ʿAbd Allāh b. Ibrāhīm Sulṭān, Mīrzā 46, 47, 115, 127, 246, 249, 256, 261, 265, 266–67, 270, 275
ʿAbd Allāh b. Muʿawiyya, also shrine of 185, 189
ʿAbd Allāh Lisān, Mawlānā 213
ʿAbd al-Laṭīf b. Ulugh Beg 47, 246–47, 248, 257, 269, 275
  in succession struggle 246, 263–68
ʿAbd al-Muʿṭī, shaykh 236
ʿAbd al-Qādiriyya Madrasa, *see* Yazd
ʿAbd al-Raḥmān b. Ulugh Beg 267
ʿAbd al-Raḥmān, brother of Pīrzād Bukhārī 271
ʿAbd al-Raḥmān (nephew of Qāḍī Imām al-Dīn Faḍl Allāh) 257
ʿAbd al-Ṣamad b. Ḥājjī Sayf al-Dīn, emir (d. 835/1432) 22, 23, 24, 39, 45, 115, 254
ʿAbd al-Wahhāb b. Jalāl al-Dīn Isḥāq, *see* Samarqandī, ʿAbd al-Wahhāb
abdāl 183, 186
Abiward 230
Abīwardī family of Yazd 171, 175
Abīwardī, Ḥājjī Ṣadr al-Dīn 172, 173–74
Abīwardī, Shams al-Dīn 171
Abīwardī, Zayn al-Dīn b. Ṣadr al-Dīn 174
Abū Bakr, caliph 208, 212
Abū Isḥāq b. Bābā Ḥājjī 134
Abū Isḥāq Inju (r.1343–57) 101, 154
Abūʾl Khayr Khan Uzbek (r. 1429–68) 45, 267
Abūʾl Qāsim Babur b. Baysunghur, Mīrzā 61, 102–03, 127, 150–51, 239, 241, 246, 252, 262–65, 267–73, 275, 280
  relation to religious figures 234
Abū Muslim (Khorasani, of Marw) 122, 185, 220
Abū Muslimnāma 122
Abū Nar Mishkān (Ghaznavid vizier) 68
Abū Saʿīd, Ilkhan (r. 1317–35) 101
Abū Saʿīd, Sulṭān (r. 1451–69) 55, 58, 61, 81, 99, 100, 103, 120, 127, 191–93, 204, 215, 225, 246, 265, 267, 270, 275
  relation to religious figures 215
Abū Saʿīd b. Abīʾl Khayr (shrine, Mayhana) 209, 239
Abū Saʿīd b. Qara Yusuf Qaraqoyunlu 42
Afghanistan 40, 45
afrād 186
agriculture 85, 95, 169, 171, 194
  promotion 116
  destruction 2, 263, 275
Aḥmad b. ʿUmar Shaykh, Mīrzā (d. 828/1435) 23, 26, 29, 32
Aḥmad Chupan 255, 257
Aḥmad Dāʾūd, vizier, *see* Kalar, Aḥmad Dāʾūd
Aḥmad Jalayir, Sulṭān 101, 106
Aḥmad-i Jām, Shaykh (Zhinda Pil; d. 536/1141) 187, 224, 226–28, 235
Aḥmad Jānbāz Moghul, emir 261–62, 271
Aḥrār, Khwāja ʿUbayd Allāh (d. 896/1490) 2, 73, 78, 189, 193, 195, 202, 203, 205, 215, 223, 229, 232, 233, 236–37
Ahristān district, *see* Yazd
ākhī 122
ʿAlāʾ al-Dawla b. Baysunghur, Mīrzā (d. 865/1460) 47, 48, 66, 92, 93, 99, 211, 213, 241, 246–48, 251, 252, 256, 267, 269, 270
ʿAlāʾ al-Dīn Bakhtishāh 62
ʿAlī b. Abū Ṭālib (shrine at Mazar-i Sharif) 192, 209
ʿAlī b. Kamāl al-Dīn b. Qawām al-Dīn Mar ʿashī, Sayyid (Sayyid ʿAlī Sārī) 137–41

'Alī b. Qawām al-Dīn Mar'ashī, Sayyid ('Alī Āmulī) 139–40
'Alī Iṣfahānī 147
'Alī Muḥammadshāh 83
'Alī Ṣafī 129
'Alī Tarkhan b. Ghiyāth al-Dīn Tarkhan, emir 22, 38–39, 44, 98
'Alīka Kukeltash b. Aduk, emir (d. 844/1440) 36, 39, 46–47, 60, 66–67, 82, 85, 92, 102, 115, 116, 212
  madrasa, *see* Herat
  relations with religious classes 59, 221
amīr (title) 70
amīr al-umarā' 81–82, 131
amīr dīwān 23, 36, 39, 43, 44, 45, 81–82
Amīr Baraka 115, 243
Amīr Ja'far b. Manṣūr, *ṣāḥib dīwān* 105
Amīr Nāṣir al-Dīn Qur'aysh 270
Amīr Shāhī 83, 175
Amīr Zayn al-'Abidīn Mīr-i Mīrān, sayyid 272
Amīrak Aḥmad, *see* Aḥmad b. 'Umar Shaykh
Amīrānshāh b. Temür (d. 810/1408) 17, 18–19, 34, 119, 226
  descendants of 14, 17, 24, 30, 132, 156, 177, 225, 265
amīr-i tümen 81, 125
Amul 138–41
Anār, Malik Shams al-Dīn Muḥammad 96
Anatolia 7, 9
Andijan 24, 26, 33, 47
Andkhud 28, 38, 95, 114, 115, 261
Ando, Shiro 214
Anīs al-ṭālibīn wa 'uddat al-sālikīn, of Ṣalā al-Dīn Mubārak Bukhārī 76
Anṣārī, 'Abd Allāh, shaykh (d. 481/1089) 208
  shrine 219–20
Aqqoyunlu 35, 242
Aqtemür 22
Arab (tribes in Iran) 126–27, 145, 242
arba'īn (*see also chilla*) 199
Ardabil 131–32, 231
Ardabīlī, Ṣadr al-Dīn, shaykh 228, 230, 231
Ardistān 256
Arghunshāh, emir 36, 62
Arghun tribe 265
Arhang 247, 259
Arlat tribe 38, 269
artisans 2, 10, 118, 119, 122, 123, 263, 282
Arzinjān 133
Ashpara 83
ashrāf, *see* sayyids
Aṣīl Beg, Amīr 161
Aṣīl al-Dīn 'Abd Allāh Wā'iẓ, sayyid (d. 883/1478–79) 70–71
Astarabad 36, 55, 138, 141, 259, 261, 268, 270
Astarābādī, Faḍl Allāh 188, 254
'Atā' Allāh Shīrāzī, vizier 267
Āthār al-wuzarā' of Sayf al-Dīn Ḥājjī b. Niẓām 'Uqaylī 68–69
'Atīq Allāh 108
'Attār, 'Alā' al-Dīn, shaykh (d. 802/1399–1400) 64, 203, 205, 218, 234, 237
'Attār, Khwāja Ḥasan b. 'Alā' al-Dīn, shaykh (d. 826/1423) 193, 237
Awba 70, 125, 182
Awbahī, Jalāl al-Dīn Yūsuf 58–59, 204, 215, 216–17, 233
awbāsh 47, 97, 155
Awghān 127
'ayān-amīr system 3–4, 117, 147, 280
'ayyār, *'ayyārūn* 121, 122
Azarbaijan 14, 18–19, 29, 34–35, 52, 54, 124, 131, 141, 156, 160, 164, 177, 251, 252, 274
  first campaign 37, 40, 42, 43, 102, 123, 125, 130
  second campaign 44, 83, 134, 142–43
  third campaign 46, 53, 60, 134, 143
'Azīz Allāh, *see* Jāmī, 'Azīz Allāh

Bābā Ākhī, *see* Jāmi, Bābā Ākhī
Bābā Ḥājjī b. Shaykh Ḥājjī Muḥammad 'Irāqī 133–34
Bābā Mas'ūd, nephew of Amīr 'Alīka 212
Badakhshan 25, 36, 39, 108, 113, 281
Badghis 127, 183, 194, 232
Baghdad 8, 101, 185, 229, 230, 250, 252
Baghlan 22, 43, 114, 260
Bahrāmī family of Simnān 102, 103–04
Bahrāmshāh, relative of Jalāl Islām 107
Bākharz 65, 69, 106, 108, 224
Bākharzī, Sayf al-Dīn, Shaykh 74
Bālīcha family of Simnān 90, 102–03, 104
Bālīcha Simnānī, Jalāl al-Dīn Maḥmūd 102
Bālīcha Simnānī, Mu'izz al-Dīn Malik Ḥusayn (d. 847/1433) 86, 103, 104, 249, 250
Bālīcha Simnānī, Niẓām al-Dīn Aḥmad b. Jalāl al-Dīn Maḥmūd 102
Bālīcha Simnānī, Shams al-Dīn 'Alī b. Jalāl al-Dīn Maḥmūd 88, 102
Bālīcha Simnānī, Sharaf al-Dīn 'Alī b. Jalāl al-Dīn Maḥmūd 90, 105
Bālīcha Simnānī, Wajīh al-Dīn Ismā'īl b. Jalāl al-Dīn Maḥmūd 102, 105
Balkh 20, 26, 92–93, 114, 116, 192, 248, 260, 265, 266, 270
  governance 26, 33
  religious classes and activity 61
Balūch 126, 127
Bam 149
Banū Tamīm, tribe 148, 151
Barābād 96
baraka 183–84
Baraka, Amīr, *see* Amīr Baraka
Barāmān madrasa, *see* Herat
Baraq of Blue Horde 42, 121, 135

Barlas tribe 41, 43, 52, 115, 260, 265, 266
Barmakids 106, 108
Barsīn 127
Barzishābādī, Sayyid ʿAbd Allāh 240
Bashir, Shahzad 240
Baṣīr, Nūr al-Dīn, shaykh 193
Bāwardī, Khwāja Zayn al-Dīn ʿAlī 151
Baydu Arlat 46
Bayqarā b. ʿUmar Shaykh, Mīrzā (d. 826/1423) 29, 31–32, 44, 134, 156, 163–64
Baysunghur b. Shāhrukh, Mīrzā (d. 837/1423) 33, 35, 37, 40, 46, 81, 83, 87, 91–92, 98, 102, 114, 127, 134, 212, 213, 246, 251, 252
  his *dīwān* 102
  governorship 32, 113, 252
  patronage 32, 41, 65–65, 105
  sons of 263, 267
bazaar 47, 118, 120, 121, 122–23, 143, 154, 163, 171, 194, 205
Bedouin 126
Berkey, Jonathan 217
Bībī Fāṭima, wife of Amīr Chaqmaq 168–69, 172
Bībī Satirkuh, *see* Bībī Sitti
Bībī Sitti, mosque of 122, 220, 244
Birdi Beg, emir, brother of Shaykh Nūr al-Dīn 21
Birjandī, Shihāb al-Dīn Aḥmad, shaykh (d. 856–57/1452–53) 218, 227
Bisṭām b. Chakir, emir 32, 131–33
Bisṭām, city 71, 220, 251, 259, 263
Bisṭāmī, Shihāb al-Dīn b. Rukn al-Dīn 218
Bisṭāmī, Shihāb al-Dīn (d. 807/1404–05) 74, 218
blessing, *see baraka*
Blue Horde (also called White Horde) 24, 135
Bū Saʿīd Mīrum b. Ilyās Khwāja, emir 143–44
bughra (food) 203
Buhlūl Barlas, Amīr 33
Bukhara 27, 127, 182, 183, 189, 205, 264
  Chashma-i Ayūb 182
  city notables 267
  family of Ḥāfiẓ-i Kabīr 184
  graves 184–85
  Hawḍ-i Muqaddam 184
  religious classes and activity 55, 74, 75–76
Bukhārī, Khwānd Sayyid Ajall 61
al-Bukhārī, Muḥammad 210
Bundarābād, *see* Yazd
burial
  of emirs 189, 220, 221
  of ruler and dynasty 28, 189, 220, 263
  of Ṣūfīs 189, 230, 235
  of ulama 220
Burujird 134
Būzjān 197
Būzjānī, Darwīsh ʿAlī (d. 929/1522–23) 193, 197, 222, 224

Calicut 191
caliphate 8, 156, 190
cathedral mosque or Friday mosque, *see individual cities*
Central Asia 4, 5, 7, 8, 47, 49, 73
Chaghadai, son of Chinggis Khan 8
Chaghadayid dynasty, *see* eastern Chaghadayid khanate
Chaghatay, ethnic group 8, 15, 22, 36, 59, 111, 114, 117, 119, 120, 123, 134, 140, 159, 206, 241
Chahārminār district, *see* Yazd
Chahārshanba, emir 36
Chakir, emir 131
Chakirlu lineage 131–33, 135
Cham-i Taft, *see* Yazd
Chaqmaq Shāmī, Jalāl al-Dīn, emir 32, 39, 53, 103, 116, 171, 175, 250, 253, 256, 259, 261, 271, 273
  building activity, *see also* Yazd 37
  cultural patronage 168–72
  origins 37
Chaqmaq, Sulṭān, Mamluk (r. 842–57/1438–53) 191
Chashma-i Ayūb, *see* Bukhara
Chekü Barlas, emir (d. 785–86/1383–84), family of 32, 43, 82, 114, 133, 260
cherik 123, 256
chilla 199, 229, 235
China 9, 11, 16, 38
Chinggis Khan 7, 8, 9, 14, 41, 209
Chinggisid family 8, 9, 10, 17, 42, 52, 138, 266
  marriage into 9, 10, 17, 26, 27
Chisht 108
Chishtī, ʿAlāʾ al-Dīn ʿAlī, shaykh 201, 223
Chishtiyya 74, 198, 223
cities 6
  building activity by notables 151, 168
  city patrol 118, 121
  defense 76, 111–12, 119, 120, 122–23, 130, 146, 150–51, 152, 153–65, 261, 263, 271–73
  government 2, 268, 273
  notables 6, 54, 76, 83–84, 111–12, 117–119, 123, 146–51, 165, 267, 268, 272, 273, 274–75, 277, 279, 281
  rebellions 124, 162
commercial structures 169
commercial activity 83, 136, 172
currency (value) 85, 87, 94, 261

Dahūk Safalī quarter, *see* Yazd
Damascus 216
Damavand (mountain) 136
Damghan 220, 258, 268
Dāmghānī, Pīr Ḥusayn vizier 148
Daniel (Prophet) 188
Dārābjird 152, 158, 160
Dār al-Fatḥ, *see* Yazd

Darguzīn 124
darughas 29, 130, 163, 169, 170, 171, 258, 259, 271, 272
darwīsh 136, 137–42, 171, 179, 196, 197, 263, 269
Darwīsh 'Alī Mīrak b. Yūsuf Khwāja, emir 130, 272
Darwīshābād 229, 230, 278
Dastūr al-wuzarā' of Khwāndamīr 66, 68, 85, 89
Da'ūd Khiṭaṭāy 126
Dawlatshāh, *see* Samarqandī, Dawlatshāh b. 'Alā' al-Dawla Bakhtishāh
Daylamān 142, 143
Delhi 17, 93
Delhi Sultanate 7, 10, 11, 33
DeWeese, Devin 240
dhikr 199
  silent 229
  vocal (*jahrī*) 229, 233, 235
Digby, Simon 192
dīwān 12, 39, 40, 44, 46, 47, 48, 52, 62, 65–66, 78, 79–110, 148, 248–49, 255, 257, 260, 277
  dīwān-i a'lā' 80, 102, 260, 261
  dīwān-i khāssa 80
  dīwān-i lashgar 80–81
  dīwān-i lashgar wa tovachigarī 80
  dīwān-i māl 80
  dīwān-turk 80
  dīwānbeki 83
  dīwāns of emirs 115
  provincial 37, 82, 147, 150, 154, 279, 280, *see also individual cities*
  wrongdoing 47, 48, 83, 85, 87, 90, 92, 93, 248–49
Ḍiyā' al-Dīn Muḥammad b. 'Imād al-Dīn vizier 148, 174
Diyar Bakr 35
Dizful 158
Dizfulī, Shaykh 'Alī 147, 152
dreams 180, 186–88, 193, 201–02, 236, 237, 240, 241
  for dynastic legitimation 187, 190–91
  interpretation 230, 234
  of the Prophet 201–02
Dūdanga, *see* Iṣfahān

eastern Chaghadayid khanate 10, 24–25, 26, 27, 46, 47
Edigü Barlas, emir 22
Egypt 8, 58, 60, 116, 156, 227, 229, 231
emirs 3, 45, 116, 248–49, 265–67, 271, 274–75
emirs, Turco-Mongolian 13–15, 35, 36, 50, 52, 79–83, 85, 92, 103, 113–15, 119, 141, 142, 147, 160, 162, 163, 175–76, 251, 260–61, 268
  architectural patronage 44, 65, 116, 123, 167, 169, 206, 221
  involvement in dīwān 109
  land holdings 113–15
  local attachments 116–17, 146, 165
  relations with religious classes 175, 194, 205–07, 221

Faḍl al-Dīn Aḥmad 224
Faḍl Allāh, Sayyid (Mar'ashī) 121
Fakhr al-Dīn Aḥmad, Sayyid, vizier (d. 820/1417) 66, 69, 83, 84, 85, 88, 91–92, 97, 98, 106, 107, 109, 118, 148
famine 164, 186
Farah 123, 182, 233
Farahī, Ḥājjī Muḥammad 57, 230
Farahī, Muḥammadshāh, shaykh 233
Farayid-i Ghiyāthī of Yūsuf Ahl 194, 211, 225
Farīd al-Dīn 'Abd al-Bāqī, shaykh 160
Fārisī, Sa'd al-Dīn 216, 218
al-Fārisī, Shams al-Dīn 'Alī 218
Farmānshaykh, emir 36, 39, 46
Farrukhshāh 160
Fars 18, 23, 24, 47, 96, 106, 123, 126, 151–67, 249–50, 251, 255–56, 259–60, 262, 271, 273, 274
  dīwān 103, 249
  emirs 161, 249–50, 265, 266, 275
  governorship 18, 26, 29–32, 40, 46, 114, 163
  historiography 41, 52
  regional armies 124, 125, 157, 261
  Shāhrukh's campaigns against 36, 39, 43, 115, 130, 132, 147, 149
Faryumad 94
Faṣīḥ al-Dīn Muḥammad (d. 837/1433–34) 84, 225
Faṣīḥ Khwāfī, *see* Khwāfī
Faṣl al-khiṭāb li waṣl al-aḥbāb of Muḥammad Pārsā 77
Fatḥābād canal, *see* Herat
Fatḥābād (near Bukhara) 189
Fāṭima Khātun *see* Bībī Fāṭima
Fazāriyya, *see* Shiraz
Ferghana Valley 26
Firuzkuh 23, 141, 252, 253
Fīrūzshāh (Jalāl al-Dīn) b. Arghunshāh, emir (d. 848/1444–45) 36, 39, 46, 48, 67, 82, 116, 141, 204, 206, 247–49, 251, 254
  building activity 221
  in *dīwān* 47, 48, 90, 92–93
  historiography on 59–60, 62
  relations with religious classes 59–60, 116, 221, 226, 233–34
  relatives 115, 168, 206, 221, 233, 251, 253
fityān 121
futuwwa 121–22, 203, 220

Gandumān 152, 158–63
Garmsir 40, 123
Gawharshād 22, 29, 38–39, 43–44, 67, 87, 156, 216, 260, 261, 262, 264–65, 268, 269
  building 216, 217, 220, 221

Gawharshād (cont.)
political activity 13, 47, 48, 216, 219–20, 246–47, 257
relatives, *see* Ghiyāth al-Dīn Tarkhan
Gawrud 259
Gayūmarth b. Bīsutūn Rustamdārī, Malik 136, 139, 141–43, 144, 250–51, 252, 253, 268
Gazurgāh, *see* Herat
Georgia 35
gharīb, *gharībān* 186
al-Ghazālī, Muḥammad 208
Ghazan Khan (Ilkhan, r. 1295–1304) 28, 34, 209
Ghazna 123, 259
Ghiyāth al-Dīn Kart, Malik 97
Ghiyāth al-Dīn Alī al-Ḥusaynī, sayyid 173
Ghiyāth al-Dīn Ghūrī, Sulṭān (mausoleum) 189
Ghiyāth al-Dīn, *qāḍī* 104
Ghiyāth al-Dīn Kamāl al-Dīn b.Qawām al-Dīn Mar'ashī, Sayyid 138, 139
Ghiyāth al-Dīn Muḥammad Sayyidzāda, Amīr, shaykh 194, 232
Ghiyāth al-Dīn Tarkhan 38, 99
relatives of 38, 43–44, 65, 67, 82, 258, 261
Ghiyāth Sayyidzāda, *langar* of 221
Ghunashirin, emir (d. 840/1436) 37, 39, 46, 103, 270
Ghur 127, 268
Gilan 54, 58, 134, 136, 142, 145, 241, 250–53, 280, 281
Gīlānī or Tūlānī, Pīr Tāj 231
Golden Horde 10, 42, 119
governors 2, 25–26, 52, 153, 271
governors of cities 22, 23, 24, 26, 27, 30, 32, 34, 43, 107, 108, 111, 117, 119, 123, 130, 132, 134, 138, 139, 151, 155, 156, 158, 252, 253, 272, 281
building 151
cultural patronage 32, 37
governors of provinces 23, 29–33, 37, 40, 41, 42, 45, 47, 113, 115, 130, 131–35, 142, 151, 194, 246, 247, 252, 254, 265, 270, 279
cultural and architectural patronage 116, 150, 155
relation with ulama 174–75
graveyards, grave visitation 55–56, 71, 171, 179–86
Gudāra 229
Gurgan 32, 127
Gurgīn Lārī 153, 158
Gūsh Burīda, sayyid, *see* Khwārazmī, Ḥasan Gūsh Burīda

Ḥabīb al-siyar fī akhbār afrād bashar of Khwāndamīr 54, 61, 81, 196, 233, 272
ḥadīth 55, 58, 76–77, 166, 182, 188, 211, 215, 217, 220, 233, 238, 239
Ḥāfiẓ Ghiyāth al-Dīn 233
Ḥāfiẓ Razi, *see* Razi, Ghiyāth al-Dīn Muḥammad Ḥāfiẓ
Ḥāfiẓ-i Abrū 27, 28, 33, 34, 41–42, 51–52, 56, 57, 59, 60, 96, 126, 133, 139, 140, 157, 158, 163, 196
Ḥājjī Beg 38
Ḥājjī Ḥusayn b. Bābā Ḥājjī b. Shaykh Ḥājjī Muḥammad 'Irāqī 134–35, 143, 253
Ḥājjī Muḥammad b. Ghunashirin, emir 32, 46, 256, 259, 261, 269–70, 275
Ḥājjī Sayf al-Dīn, emir 21
Ḥājjī Yūsuf Jalīl, emir 47
ḥākim (pl. *hukkām*) 76, 108
al-Hallāj, Jalāl al-DīnYūsuf (d. 823/1420) 216–17
Hamadan 29, 31, 32, 54, 57, 124, 130, 132, 134–35, 143, 156, 177, 252, 253, 256, 259, 262, 271
Hamadānī, Sayyid 'Alī (714/1314–786/1385) 122, 240, 243
Ḥamza b. Ghiyāth al-Dīn Tarkhan, emir (d. 819/1416) 38–39, 44
Ḥamza Chuhra 151, 172, 250
Ḥamza Suldus, emir 27
Ḥanafī *madhhab* 220, 230, 239
Ḥanbalī *madhhab* 219, 221
al-Harawī, Abū'l Walīd Aḥmad 220
Ḥasan Jāndār, emir 22, 24, 45
Ḥasan Ṣūfī Tarkhan b. Ghiyāth al-Dīn Tarkhan, emir (d. 827/1424) 22, 38–39, 43–44
ḥasham 127
Hazār Jarīb 136, 139, 142
Hazāra 33
heads of quarters 83–84, 118, 119, 124, 150, 159, 161–62, 165, 255, 272, *see also ra'is*; *kulū*
Herat 25, 32, 33, 36, 40, 60, 81, 141–42, 147, 149, 171, 242, 247, 252, 255, 257, 281, 282
Barāmān madrasa 218
bazaar 220, 232
building in 28, 116, 169
cathedral mosque 42, 59, 202, 205, 217, 218, 221, 222, 229, 233
city defense 263, 264, 270
city notables 261, 263, 269
Gawharshād's complex 70, 217–18, 258
Gāzurgāh 71, 219–20
governance 40, 46, 106
Herātīs 106, 118, 148, 182, 264, 269, 270, 275
historiography 54, 55, 56, 64, 70–71, 96–97, 127, 188
holy places 185, 189
'Īdgāh 85, 230
Ikhtiyār al-Dīn fortress 46, 67, 121, 126, 249, 264
madrasa of 'Alīka Kukeltash 218
madrasa of Khwāja 'Alī Fakhr al-Dīn 227
Madrasa-i Ghiyāthiyya 205, 216, 218

plague 46, 191, 230, 233, 234
qāḍī of 212, 219
religious classes 96, 204, 208, 210–19
Shāhrukh's *khānaqāh* 58, 59, 74, 216, 223
Shāhrukh's madrasa 58, 59, 204, 216–17
in succession struggle after Shāhrukh's death 119, 120, 239, 258, 260, 262–65, 268–70, 275
Sufi shaykhs 59, 74, 201, 218, 222, 228–36, 240, 241, 242, 244, 277–78
during Temür's reign 83, 84
ulama 58, 61, 108, 122, 208, 232
Herāt-rūd 182, 192
Hilla 242
al-Hillī, Aḥmad b. Fahd (d. 841/1437–38) 242
Hinduka, emir 141, 259, 268
Hisar-i Shadman 21, 27, 267
Ḥiṣarī, Maḥmūd 236
history, history writing 10, 11, 13, 17, 23, 28, 31, 33, 41–42, 49–78, 215
Hodgson, Marshall G. S. 3–4
Holod, Renata 170
Hormuz 54, 58, 103, 113, 281
Hourani, Albert 3–4
Ḥurūfiyya 42, 188, 233, 241, 243, 254
Ḥusām al-Dīn Khwāja Yūsuf 76
Ḥusayn Asghar b. Zayn al-ʿĀbidīn 101
Ḥusayn Qaraʾunas, Amīr 76
Ḥusayn Sharbatdār, *see* Sharbatdār, Ḥusayn
Ḥusayn Ṣūfī b. Ghiyāth al-Dīn Tarkhan, emir 38, 44
Ḥusayn Ṭārumī, Iranian emir, *see* Ṭārumī, Ḥusayn
al-Ḥusaynī, Ṣadr al-Dīn Yūnus, sayyid 61
Huwayza 250

Ibn ʿArabī 210, 217, 231, 235, 237, 238
Ibn ʿArabshāh, Aḥmad 77
Ibn Baṭṭūṭa 185
Ibn al-Jazarī, *see* al-Jazarī
Ibn Taymiyya 210
Ibrāhīm b. ʿAlāʾ al-Dawla, Mīrzā 102, 264
Ibrāhīm b. Eyegü Temür, emir 266
Ibrāhīm (Sulṭān) b. Jahanshāh b. Chekü, emir (d. c. 833/1429–30) 39, 43, 114, 115
Ibrāhīm Sulṭān b. Shāhmalik, emir 194, 206
Ibrāhīm Sulṭān b. Shāhrukh, Mīrzā (d. 838/1435) 24, 26, 33, 40, 41, 46, 56, 135, 148, 149–50, 163–64, 216, 280
building activities 170
cultural and artistic patronage 167
Ichil b. Amīrānshāh, Mīrzā 25
Idwān 85
ijāza 58, 64, 77, 211, 215, 229, 230, 234, 236, 237
al-Ījī, ʿAḍūd al-Dīn ʿAbd al-Raḥmān (d. 756/1355) 215
Ikhtiyār al-Dīn fortress, *see* Herat
Ilangir b. Abā Bakr b. Amīrānshāh 24
Ilkhanate 8, 34, 94, 100–01, 104–05, 129, 131, 224–25
Ilyās Khwāja b. Shaykh ʿAlī Bahādur, emir (d. 838/1434–35) 32, 39, 41, 45, 113, 114, 123, 126, 132, 142
ʿImād fortress 263, 268
ʿImād al-Dīn Maḥmūd b. Zayn al-ʿĀbidīn Junābādī, sayyid 92, 93, 107
ʿImād al-Dīn Masʿūd, Khwāja, vizier 148, 151, 173–74, 273
ʿImād al-Dīn Muṭahhar Kārīzī, Mawlānā 121
imām (prayer leader) 57, 174, 217, 218
Shiʿite 209, 221
Imām al-Dīn Faḍl Allāh, *qāḍī* 257
Imām Riḍā, mausoleum at Mashhad 208, 220–21
Imāmī, Jalāl al-Dīn Maḥmūd, *qāḍī* 212
burial 220
Imāmī, Quṭb al-Dīn ʿAbd Allāh b. Jalāl al-Dīn Maḥmūd, *qāḍī* 212
Imāmī, Quṭb al-Dīn Aḥmad, *qāḍī* 212, 263
Imāmī, Ṣadr al-Dīn Muḥammad b. Quṭb al-Dīn ʿAbd Allāh 212
Imāmzada ʿAli b. Ḥamza b. Mūsā Kāẓim (tomb of) 167
Imāmzada-i Maʿṣūm mausoleum, Yazd 172, 185
India 57, 58, 74, 86, 191, 201
Injuyid dynasty (1313–57 A.D.) 104, 154–55
intoxicants 28, 47, 90, 211–12, 252, 264
Iran 4–9, 49, 261, 280
Iran, eastern 55, 64, 69–71, 73, 95, 108
Iran, northern 39, 53, 95, 112, 250–53, 262, 274
Iran, south and central 41, 59, 146–76, 242, 271–74, 279–80
city notables 154–55
governorships 14, 156, 166–76
historiography 52–53, 54, 55, 56
power struggle after Temür's death 29–32
Iran, western 34–35, 59, 245
Iranian landed elite 3, 68, 69, 78, 94, 120, 124, 126, 128, 144, 147–51, 213, 279
Iraq 8, 19, 29, 106, 153, 160, 164, 248, 249, 252, 255, 256, 259, 261, 270, 271, 274
Iraqis 163
regional armies 97, 127
Iraq-i ʿAjam 23, 129, 131, 133, 139, 143, 161, 255
Isfahan 52, 55, 116, 127, 146, 148–52, 164, 166–69, 216, 248, 249, 250, 252, 274
building in 161, 167, 175–77
cathedral mosque 168
dīwān 150, 161, 255
Dūdanga 160
governance 29–32, 43, 45, 47, 55, 114, 115, 157, 161, 255
Iṣfahānīs 30, 157, 158, 160, 161, 163, 246, 259, 271–73
Naqsh-i Jahān citadel 161, 167

Isfahan (cont.)
political structure 118–19, 120–21, 124–25, 130
regional armies 123, 157, 158, 168, 256
religious personnel and activity 168, 241, 255
and Sulṭān Muḥammad 254–57, 259, 261, 271
Tālār-i Tīmūrī 168
Isfand b. Qara Yūsuf Qaraqoyunlu 35
Isfarz 125
Isfizar 126, 130, 182
Isfizārī, Muʿīn al-Dīn Zamchī 62, 68, 107, 108, 120, 182, 194, 196, 230
Isḥāq Khuttalānī 41, 240, 243
Iskandar b. Qara Yūsuf Qaraqoyunlu 35, 41, 42, 45
sons of 256
Iskandar b. ʿUmar Shaykh, Mīrzā (d. 818/1415) 29, 32, 39, 53, 121, 124, 127, 129–30, 147, 148–50, 152, 158, 171, 177, 216, 280
building activities 31, 104, 170, 175
character 13, 164
patronage 30–31, 41, 56, 63, 166–68, 179
rise to power and defeat 131, 133, 164
Islamic law, *see sharīʿa*
Ismāʿīl Ṣūfī b. Sayyid Aḥmad Tarkhan, emir 114
Ismāʿīl Ṣūfī Tarkhan b. Amīr Sayyidi, emir 260
Ismāʿīl Ṣūfī, shaykh (shrine of) 219
ʿIzz al-Dīn, Malik 125

Jaʿfar al-Ṣādiq 185
Jaʿfarī, Jaʿfar b. Muḥammad al-Ḥusaynī 33, 53, 245
Jaghāra 233
Jaghāraʾī, Bahāʾ al-Dīn ʿUmar, shaykh (d. 857/1453) 59, 61, 64, 196, 205, 206, 222, 226, 228, 233–35, 237, 251, 269, 270, 278–79
mausoleum of 234
relations with emirs and dynasty 59–60, 61, 221, 278
Jaghāraʾī, Nūr al-Dīn Muḥammad b. Bahāʾ al-Dīn ʿUmar 61, 71, 234
Jahān b. Uch Qara 24
Jahāngīr b. Temür 16, 17
Jahāngīr b. Temür, line of 14, 20, 24, 25, 26, 114
Jahānmalik b. Malikat, emir 22, 24
Jahānshāh b. Chekü Barlas, emir 133–34
Jahānshāh b. Qara Yūsuf Qaraqoyunlu 34, 45, 119, 212, 219, 259, 262, 271, 274, 280
al-Jājarmī, Shams al-Dīn Muḥammad (d. 864/1459–60) 216, 217
Jalāl al-Dīn ʿAbd al-Ghaffār, *see* Samarqandī, Jalāl al-Dīn ʿAbd al-Ghaffār
Jalāl al-Dīn ʿAbd al-Raḥīm b. ʿAbd Allāh Lisān, *ṣadr* 213–14, 219
Jalāl al-Dīn Bāyazīd, emir 263
Jalāl al-Dīn b. Rustam b.ʿUmar Shaykh, Mīrzā 47
Jalāl al-Dīn Isḥāq, father of ʿAbd al-Razzāq Samarqandī, *see* Samarqandī
Jalāl al-Dīn Luṭf Allāh, *ṣadr* (d. 842/1438–39) 213
Jalāl al-Dīn Muḥammad 97, 262, 268, 273
Jalāl al-Dīn Mukhliṣ, vizier 101
Jalāl al-Dīn Murshid, vizier 151, 273
Jalāl Islām 69, 106–07, 126
Jalālī fortress, *see* Shiraz
Jalayir tribe 153, 156
Jalayirid dynasty (1336–1432) 18, 19, 29
Jam 70, 90, 116, 224, 242, 248, 258, 260
Jam, shaykhs of 108, 193, 197, 199–200, 210–11, 222, 224–28
relations with Timurids 224–26, 243–44
Jam, shrine of 194, 206, 209, 221, 222–23, 224–28, 278
administration 224–26
Jāmī, Abūʾl Fatḥ b. Shihāb al-Dīn Abūʾl Makārim 225
Jāmī, Aḥmad, shaykh, *see* Aḥmad-i Jām
Jāmī, ʿAlāʾ al-Dīn Abūʾl Maʿālī ʿAlāʾ al-Mulk 225
Jāmī, ʿAzīz Allāh (d. 902/1496–97) 197, 226
Jāmī, Bābā Ākhī Maḥmūd 194
Jāmī, Burhān al-Dīn Naṣr b. Aḥmad 224
Jāmī, Diyāʾ al-Dīn Yūsuf (d. 797/1394–95) 224–25
Jāmī, Jalāl al-Dīn b. Raḍī al-Dīn Aḥmad b. Jalāl al-Dīn 225
Jāmī, Jalāl al-Dīn Yūsuf b. Shams al-Dīn Muḥammad 211
Jāmī, Muʿīn al-Dīn, vizier 224
Jāmī, Murshid al-Dīn ʿAbd al-ʿAzīz 225
Jāmī, Nūr al-Dīn ʿAbd al-Raḥmān (d. 898/1492) 64, 73, 204, 217, 222, 232
Jāmī, Quṭb al-Dīn Muḥammad b. Shams al-Dīn Muṭahhar 224
Jāmī, Raḍī al-Dīn Aḥmad b. Jalāl al-Dīn 225
Jāmī, Shihāb al-Dīn (d. 736/1335–36 or 738/1337–38) 224
Jāmī, Shihāb al-Dīn Abūʾl Makārim 193, 222, 225–27, 235, 278
Jāmī, Shihāb al-Dīn ʿUmar b. Muʿīn al-Dīn 225, 226
Jāmiʿal-tawārīkh-i Ḥasanī of Tāj al-Dīn Ḥasan b. Shihāb Yazdi 37, 53, 124, 245
Jāmiʿal-tawārīkh of Rashīd al-Dīn 33, 41
al-Jazarī, Shams al-Dīn Abūʾl Muḥammad (d. 833/1429) 10, 58, 64, 77, 166, 168, 211, 216, 239, 243, 249
Jerusalem 229
Jezhd 96
jirga 103
Jiruft 149
Jochi, son of Chinggis Khan 8, 9, 28
judge, *see qāḍī*
Junābād 95, 107

Junābādī, Zayn al-'Ābidīn, Sayyid 66–67, 83, 85, 86, 92, 107
Jurjānī, Sayyid 'Alī (Sayyid-i Sharīf) (d. 816/1413) 10, 30, 63–64, 149, 155, 166, 204, 215, 218, 243
Jurjānī, Shams al-Dīn Muḥammad b. 'Ali, Sayyid 166, 215
Jurma'ī 127
Juwaynī, 'Atā' al-Malik, descendants of 94

Kabul 14, 17, 24, 26, 33, 40, 42, 54, 123, 259, 269
kadkhudā 118, 144
Kālār, Niẓām al-Dīn Aḥmad b. Dā'ūd, vizier 87, 88, 89, 98, 106
Kalat 185
Kamāl al-Dīn Shaykh Ḥusayn of Khwaf 120, 204
karāmāt 191, 194
  graves 71, 183–86, 220–21
  rulers 60, 191
  shaykhs 59, 193, 199, 200, 202, 226, 228, 236
Karizī, Mawlānā 'Imād al-Dīn Muṭahhar 263
Kār-Kiyā Aḥmad (of Ranikuh) 143–44, 145
Kār-Kiyā Nāṣir (of Larijan) 143–44, 253
Kār-Kiyā'ī sayyids 53, 136, 142–44, 280
Kartid dynasty 68, 96–97, 105, 108, 121, 196, 208, 212, 213, 219, 220, 224, 226
Kashan 32, 114, 123, 126, 132, 252, 256
Kashghar 26, 41, 46
Kashgharī, Sa'd al-Dīn, Shaykh 71, 201, 205, 226–27, 228–30, 234–35, 237
Kāshifī, Ḥusayn Wā'iẓ (d. 910/1504–05) 73, 122
Kātib, Aḥmad b. Ḥusayn b. 'Alī 53, 245
Kerman 19, 53, 86, 111, 120, 123, 127, 147, 152, 155, 241, 256, 259, 261, 268, 269, 270, 271, 273
  dīwān 98, 113, 148
  governorship 22, 37, 39, 46
  Shāhrukh's campaign 32, 36, 39, 124, 125
  and sons of 'Umar Shaykh 18, 29, 30, 157, 159
Khabushan 260
khaghan 8, 10
Khalaj 126, 152, 262
Khalidov, A. B. 216
khalīfa (Ṣūfī) 201, 227, 231, 278
Khalīl Allāh b. Shaykh Ibrāhīm, ruler of Shirwan 35
Khalīl Sulṭān b. Amīrānshāh, Mīrzā 17, 20–21, 24–25, 27, 28, 36, 37, 38, 75, 84, 101, 139
Khalīl Sulṭān b. Muḥammad Jahāngīr, Mīrzā 269, 273
Khalkhāl 132
Khalwatī, 'Abd al-Raḥīm 231
Khalwatī, Muḥammad (or Maḥmūd) 226
Khalwatī, Ẓahīr al-Dīn, shaykh (d. 800/1397–98) 199, 228
Khalwatiyya 74, 226–28, 232
khan 7, 20, 21, 266
khānaqāh 11, 28, 204, 224, 225
Khānzāda 16, 17, 220
Khara 127
Kharjird 96, 100
Kharjird-i Jām 227
Khawānd Ṭahūr, grave of 190
Khiḍr (Prophet) 189
Khiḍr Khan, Delhi Sultan (r. 817/1414 to 824/1421) 33
Khiḍrshāh, Amīr Jalāl al-Dīn, sayyid 151, 172, 173
Khiḍrshāh, Amīr Shams al-Dīn, sayyid 172, 173
Khiḍrshāh, Quṭb al-Dīn b. Shams al-Dīn Muḥammad 173
Khitay Bahadur 22
Khiyabānī, Shihāb al-Dīn, *see* Bisṭāmī
Khorasan 14, 17, 19, 20, 22, 24, 25, 32, 35, 38, 40, 43, 46, 84, 94, 97, 101, 123, 127, 134, 150, 164, 185, 261, 262, 269, 273, 274, 275
  armies 126
  historiography 52–53, 56
  landed families 58
  religious classes 209–19
  after Shāhrukh's death 258, 262–65
  Ṣūfī shaykhs 74, 222–38
Khorezm (province) 9, 28, 39, 138, 239
Khorezm (city) 36, 45, 116, 119
Khudāydād, emir 21, 24–25
Khujand 38
Khujandī, Kamāl, shaykh 229, 231, 238
Khurramabad 253
Khusraw Tarkhan 39
khuṭba 33, 130, 241, 259, 271
Khuttalan 26, 41, 115, 127, 240, 241, 247, 259, 260, 265
Khuttalānī, Isḥāq, *see* Isḥāq Khuttalani
Khuzistan 41, 54, 112, 152–53, 158, 164, 250
Khwaf 57, 65, 68, 95, 105, 108, 120, 204, 229
  ulama from 99
  viziers from 65, 68, 95–100, 105, 108, 110
Khwāfī, Aḥmad b. Jalāl al-Dīn Faṣīḥ 58, 60, 67, 74, 81, 85, 86, 87, 88–89, 91, 103, 139, 191, 213, 246, 277
  career 64–71, 78, 97–100, 108, 223
  family 86, 96, 148, 162
Khwāfī, Amīr Mubārak b. Sharaf al-Dīn Ḥājjī 108
Khwāfī, Faḍl Allāh
Khwāfī, Ghiyāth al-Dīn Pīr Aḥmad b. Jalāl al-Dīn Isḥāq, vizier 66, 67, 70, 85, 88, 89, 92, 93, 98–100, 102, 109, 194, 206, 230, 248, 255, 269, 277–78
Khwāfī, 'Imād al-Dīn Muḥammad b. Niẓām al-Dīn Yaḥyā (d. 817/1414–15) 97
Khwāfī, 'Iṣām al-Dīn Dā'ūd 204
Khwāfī, 'Ismā'īl 99

Khwāfī, Jalāl al-Dīn Isḥāq b. Majd al-Dīn Muḥammad 98
Khwāfī, Jalāl al-Dīn Muḥammad b. Majd al-Dīn Muḥammad 100
Khwāfī, Majd al-Dīn (alive in 908/1502–03) 100
Khwāfī, Majd al-Dīn Muḥammad, brother of Ghiyāth al-Dīn Pīr Aḥmad Khwāfī (d. 838/1434–35) 99
Khwāfī, Majd al-Dīn Muḥammad b. Pīr Aḥmad (d. 899/1494) 69, 99
Khwāfī, Majd al-Dīn Muḥammad Māyizhnābādī (Khwāja Majd) 68, 69, 70, 96–97, 98, 99, 108
Khwāfī, Najīb al-Dīn Aḥmad (father of Majd al-Dīn Muḥammad Khwāfī) 96, 98
Khwāfī, Naṣr al-Dīn Naṣr Allāh (d. 845/1441–42) 99
Khwāfī, Niẓām al-Dīn Yahyā b. Kamāl al-Dīn Ḥusayn b. Jalāl al-Dīn Muḥammad 97
Khwāfī, Niẓām al-Dīn Yahyā Mayizhnābādī 97
Khwāfī, Qawām al-Dīn Niẓām al-Mulk (d. 903/1498) 62, 68, 99, 108
Khwāfī, Qawām al-Dīn Shaykh Muḥammad (d. 817/1414–15) 86, 97
Khwāfī, Quṭb al-Dīn Muḥammad, *ṣadr* (d. 895/1489–90) 69, 99
Khwāfī, Rukn al-Dīn b. Majd al-Dīn Muḥammad 97, 98
Khwāfī, Rukn al-Dīn Muḥammad (d. 834/1430–31) 58, 67, 70, 71, 225
Khwāfī, Ṣadr al-Dīn Ḥāmid 97
Khwāfī, Zayn al-Dīn Abū Bakr Muḥammad, shaykh (d. 838/1435) 57, 59, 60, 67, 71, 74, 100, 188, 189, 203, 205, 206, 211, 222, 226–38, 241, 242, 277–78
Khwāfī, Zayn al-Dīn, mausoleum 217
Khwāja Kātib (shrine) 220
Khwāja Rastī, brother of ʿAlīka Kukeltash 67
Khwājagān, *see* Naqshbandiyya
Khwāja Yūsuf b. Ilyās Khwāja 45, 47
Khwāndamīr, Ghigāth al-Dīn 54, 56, 61–62, 63–64, 68, 85, 86, 87, 88, 89–90, 91, 94, 99, 102, 103, 104, 108, 196, 197, 204, 213, 222, 252
  family 219
Khwāndshāh, emir, brother of Fīrūzshāh 115, 254
Khwāndshāh (father of Mīrkhwānd) 61
Khwārazmī, Ḥasan Gūsh Burīda, sayyid 84, 98, 100, 107
Khwārazmī, Ḥusayn, shaykh 116, 194–95, 221, 239, 282
Khwārazmī, Jalāl al-Dīn Maḥmūd, vizier 149, 160, 170
Khwārazmī, Nūr al-Dīn Nūr Allāh (d. 838/1434–35) 218–19
Khwārazmī, Sayf al-Dīn 203
Khwārazmshāhs 95–96, 100, 104, 108
Kirmānī, ʿAbd al-Razzāq 237
Kirmānī, Shāh Niẓām 169, 170
kotwāl 46, 47, 67, 107, 121, 126, 159, 212, 270
Kubrawiyya 41, 56, 73, 201, 228, 230, 240
Kufa 185
Kuhdum 144
kulūʾ, pl. *kulūyān* 118, 150, 154–55
Kulūʾ ʿAlāʾ al-Dīn 159, 162
Kurdistan 134
Kurdkhani, Sayf al-Dīn 162
Kurds 126, 127, 145, 152, 158, 262
Kūsūyī, Nāṣir al-Dīn 237
Kūsūyī, Shams al-Dīn, shaykh (d. 863) 71, 200, 226–27

Lahijan 251
Lamsar 144
Lancaster, William 6
langar 194, 232
Lār (Caspian) 142
Lār (Fars) 153
Larijan 136, 139, 143–44
Laythī, Faḍl Allāh 216
Lewisohn, Leonard 230
Lur (people) 126, 145, 152, 158
Lur-i Buzurg 152
Lur-i Kuchik 29, 152
Luristan 31, 130, 151–52, 156, 241, 257
  atabeg 268
Luristānī or Nūristānī, Fakhr al-Dīn, shaykh 227, 235
Luṭf Allāh b. Buyan Temür, emir 44

Maʿdābād 224
madrasa of Khwāja ʿAlī Fakhr al-Dīn, *see* Herat
Madrasa-i Ghiyāthiyya, *see* Herat
Maghribī, Muḥammad Shīrīn, shaykh 231, 236
mahdī 41, 188, 240–41, 242
Maḥmūd, Amīr, nephew of Khwāja Muḥammad Qumī 129
Maḥmūd Ḥaydar, vizier 104, 123, 148, 149, 150–51, 153, 255, 271, 272–73, 280
Maḥmūd Shihāb 83
Maḥmūd Yazdī 162
Maḥmūdshāh b. Arghunshāh 253, 255
Majālis al-nafāʾis of Mīr ʿAlī Shīr Nawāʾī 55
Majd al-Dīn Faḍl Allāh, *qāḍī* (of Yazd) 273
Majd al-Dīn Faḍl-Allāh Qāḍī b. Yaʿqūb Qāḍī 151, 256
Majd al-Dīn Ṭālib Ṣūfī (shrine) 220
"Majmūʿa al-tawārīkh" of Ḥāfiẓ-i Abrū 33
Makhan 203
Malan 230
malik 104
Malik Zūzan 96, 108

Malikat Agha 26, 29
Malikat, emir 22
Māmānūk mausoleum, *see* Yazd
Mamluk Sultanate 8, 9, 11, 12, 37, 119, 146, 175, 204, 210
armies 124
Sultans 9, 50
Manhaj al-rashād li naf'al-ibād of Zayn al-Dīn Khwāfī 241
Manṣūr b. Chakir, Amīr 132
Maqṣad al-iqbāl of Sayyid Aṣīl al-Dīn 'Abd Allāh Wa'iẓ (d. 883) 55, 70–71, 74, 189, 213
Mar'ashī dynasty of Tabaristan 53, 136–42, 145
Mar'ashī, Ẓahīr al-Dīn b. Naṣīr al-Dīn 136, 140, 141, 143
al-Marghīnānī, Burhān al-Dīn (d. 1197) 214
al-Marghīnānī, 'Isām al-Dīn b. 'Abd al-Malik 212
marriage
dynasty 10, 15, 17, 21, 22, 23, 35, 37, 38, 52, 113, 132, 156, 259, 262
Iranian elites 61, 62, 101
regional rulers 136, 139, 144
religious classes 58, 100, 107, 175, 211, 214, 219, 224, 242
Marw 116, 203, 269
Marwī, Sayyid 'Alī 98
Mashhad/Tus 71, 114, 127, 221, 239, 244, 260, 263
dār al-ḥuffāẓ 220
dār al-siyāda 220
Masjid-i Gunbad-i Khwāja Nūr 189
masjid-i jāmi', *see* cathedral mosque
Mas'ūdshāh Shūl 163
Ma'ṣūm b. Chakir, Amīr 131, 132
Maṭla' al-sa'dayn wa majma' al-baḥrayn of 'Abd al-Razzāq Samarqandī 52, 57–62
mausoleums and mausoleum complexes 11, 71, 176, 182–87, 221, 224, 230
Mawlānā Tarkhānī 115
Mayhana 220
Māyizhnābād 96, 97
Māyizhnābādī, Muḥammad, *faqih* 108
Mayizhnābādī, Niẓām al-Dīn (d. 737/1336–37) 96
Maymana 260
Mazandaran 22, 38, 40, 44, 46, 47, 54, 123, 136, 144, 249, 250, 260, 262, 281
Mazār-i Dukhtarān 183
Mazār-i Sādāt 189
Mazār-i Tiflagān 183, 189
Mecca 59, 236
Medina 229
merchants 2, 118, 151, 154, 164, 273, 281
Midrāb b. Chekü Barlas, emir 22, 26, 39, 43, 114
Miḥrāb Tarkhan b. Ḥasan Ṣūfī Tarkhan, emir 44
Mihrījird gate, *see* Yazd
Mihtar 'Alīshāh Farrāsh 171, 172
military 4, 5, 9, 10, 11, 15, 22, 34, 35, 80, 113, 117, 128, 140, 257, 280
cavalry 124, 125, 149, 157, 163
Chaghatay command 14, 15–16, 43–45, 125, 260
foot soldiers 124, 149, 157, 160
Iranian commanders 15, 30, 53, 69, 79, 95, 104, 107, 117, 120–21, 123–26, 128, 133, 143, 147, 148–51, 158, 159, 279–80
local Turco-Mongolian troops 20, 22, 114, 123, 127, 149, 154, 156, 158
regional armies 9, 32, 34, 36, 37, 43, 53, 111–12, 117, 123–28, 145, 147–53, 251, 256, 268, 272, 273, 281
Mīr 'Alī Shīr Nawā'ī, *see* Nawā'ī, Mīr 'Alī Shīr
miracles, *see karāmāt*
Mīrak Shirwānī, sayyid 270, 271
Mīrānshāh Qa'uchin 266
Mīrkhwānd, Muḥammad b. Khwāndshāh b. Maḥmūd 54, 56, 61–62, 64, 222, 233
Mishkān, 'Amīd Abū Naṣr (d. 413/1039) 96
al-Miṣri, Nūr al-Dīn 'Abd al-Raḥmān 228, 229, 231, 238
Moghuls, *see* eastern Chaghadayids
Mongols 12, 31, 155, 194
Mongol conquest 7–10, 96–97, 185
Mongol Empire 10, 11, 14, 28, 94, 95, 97, 121, 169
Mongol tradition 9, 10, 34, 209
Mottahedeh, Roy 2, 3
Mubārakshāh citadel, *see* Yazd
Mubārakshāh Sanjarī 36
Mubāriz al-Dīn Muḥammad b. al-Muẓaffar 96
mudarris 198, 218, 221, 227
mufarrid 83, 84
Muḥammad (Prophet) 179, 182, 184, 187, 190, 209, 220
Muḥammad, sayyid (of Gilan) 142
Muḥammad Amīn b. Ṣadr al-Dīn Ibrāhīm 214, 219
Muḥammad 'Arab of Herat 35, 239
Muḥammad b. Manṣūr, nephew of Bistam Chakirlu 132
Muḥammad b. Miḥrāb Tarkhan b. Ḥasan Ṣūfī Tarkhan, emir 44
Muḥammad Darwīsh, maternal uncle of Shāhrukh 31, 169, 170
Muḥammad Ghiyāth Tarkhan 39
Muḥammad Gīrubast wa Jāndār, Pahlawān 121
Muḥammad Jahāngīr b. Muḥammad Sulṭān, Mīrzā 17, 20, 21, 25, 27
Muḥammad Juki b. Shāhrukh, Mīrzā 26, 40, 42, 47, 48, 93, 115, 121, 211, 246–48
Muḥammad Khan, Chaghadayid 25, 27
Muḥammad Khan, Eastern Chaghadayid 27

Muḥammad Khudābanda, *see* Öljeitü
Muḥammad Khudāydād, emir 272
Muḥammad Mar'ashī, sayyid 141
Muḥammad Mīrum b. Ilyās Khwāja, emir 45
Muḥammad Nūrbakhsh, shaykh 41, 240–42
Muḥammad Pārsā, shaykh 55, 75–77, 211, 229, 235, 238, 239
Muḥammad Sāriq 162
Muḥammad Ṣūfī b. Ghiyāth al-Dīn Tarkhan 38–39, 44
Muḥammad Sulṭān b. Jahāngīr 16–17, 20, 21, 22, 25, 27
Muḥammad Yahyā b. 'Ubayd Allāh Aḥrār 202
Muḥibb al-Dīn Abū'l Khayr b. Muḥammad Jazarī 47, 125, 216, 249–50, 256, 260, 266, 270, 274
muḥtasib 81, 108, 120, 210, 212, 213, 214, 219, 230
Mu'īn al-Fuqarā', Aḥmad b. Maḥmūd 55
Mu'izz al-Dīn Pīr Ḥusayn Kart, Malik (r. 1332–70) 107
Mu'izz al-ansāb fī shajarat al-ansāb 15, 23, 36, 39, 42, 44, 45, 52, 79–80, 82, 121, 149, 150
Mujmal-i faṣīḥī of Aḥmad b. Jalāl al-Dīn Faṣīḥ Khwāfī 37, 58, 64, 90, 99, 150
mujtahid 184
Multan 17
Muntakhab al-tawārīkh of Mu'īn al-Dīn Naṭanzī 31
Murghābī, Jalāl al-Dīn Maḥmūd Zāhid (d. 778/1376–77) 220
Murshid, Jalāl al-Dīn, vizier
Murtaḍā b.Kamāl al-Dīn Mar'ashī
Murtaḍā'id sayyid dynasty of Hazār Jarīb 136
Musallā 'Atīq, *see* Yazd
Musawī sayyids 70, 239
Musha'sha' movement 125, 242, 250, 282
Musha'sha', Muḥammad b. Falāḥ 242–43
Mu'taṣim b. Zayn al-'Ābidīn Muẓaffar (Muzaffarid) 160
mutawallī 166, 198, 224
Muẓaffar Shabānkāra'ī 106
Muzaffarid dynasty (1314–93 A.D.) 53, 95, 96, 105, 154–55, 160, 170–71, 173, 177

Nafaḥāt al-uns min ḥiḍrāt al-quds, of 'Abd al-Raḥmān Jāmī 73, 232, 235, 278
Na'in 164
Na'īmābād region, *see* Yazd
Naqsh-i Jahān citadel, *see* Iṣfahān
naqīb 70, 208, 225, 282
Naqshband, Bahā' al-Dīn, shaykh (d. 791/1389) 64, 73, 75–76, 77, 203, 205, 218, 227, 228, 230, 234, 235, 237, 243
Naqshbandiyya 56, 73, 75–77, 78, 191, 200, 201, 203, 205, 222, 223, 228–29, 231, 234, 235, 236–37
Nāṣir al-Dīn b. Kamāl al-Dīn Mar'ashī, Sayyid 140–41, 281
Nāṣir al-Dīn 'Imād al-Islām, vizier 99
Nāṣir al-Dīn Lutf Allāh b. 'Azīz Allāh (d. 823/1420) 216–17
Nāṣir al-Dīn Muḥammad, *muḥtasib* 108
Nāṣir Kārkiyā, Sayyid 253
Natanz 130, 252, 256
Naṭanzī, Mu'īn al-Dīn 31, 41
natural disasters 164, 249
Nawā'ī, Mīr 'Alī Shīr 55, 61, 73, 232
Nihawand 29, 134, 252, 259, 271
Ni'mat Allāh, Shāh Walī, shaykh 30, 63, 149, 197, 199, 201, 231, 237, 243, 271
Ni'matulāhiyya 73, 223, 231, 243, 271
Nīrīz 158
Nisa 185, 269
Nishapur 230, 258
Niyawand 253
Niyāzābād 96–97
Niẓām al-Dīn 'Abd al-Raḥīm b. Pahlawān Yār Aḥmad (d. 828/1424–25) 216–17
Niẓām al-Dīn Aḥmad b. Fīrūzshāh, emir 63
Niẓām al-Dīn Khāmūsh, shaykh 64, 180, 203, 227, 234
Niẓām al-Mulk 96, 105
nomads 5, 8, 10, 11, 14, 15, 18, 126, 151–52, 163
nomads, regional armies 152
Nūr al-Dīn Kamāl 148, 150–51, 159, 162, 169, 280
Nūrbakhsh, Shaykh Muḥammad 188
Nūrbakhshiyya 188
Nūristānī, Fakhr al-Dīn, *see* Luristānī
Nūrmalik Barlas, emir 26, 115

Öljeitü Muḥammad Khudābanda (Ilkhan, r. 1304–16) 108
Ottoman dynasty 7, 9, 11, 12
Oxus river 260, 264, 265

Padusband dynasty, *see* Rustamdārī
pahlawān 121
Pahlawān Ḥājjī Zawa
Pahlawān Ḥusayn Dīwāna 272–73
Paul, Jürgen 3, 192, 193
Pāyanda Biki Sulṭān bt. Baysunghur 253, 259
Persian elite, *see also* Tājik 13, 184
Persian language 1, 10, 30, 117
Pīr' 'Alī b. Iskandar b. 'Umar Shaykh 162
Pīr Ḥājjī, emir 161, 254
Pīr Ḥusayn b. Chupan 101
Pīr Muḥammad b. Jahāngīr, Mīrzā 14, 17, 20, 25, 38
Pīr Muḥammad b. Pulad, emir 22, 23, 44
Pīr Muḥammad b. 'Umar Shaykh 2, 23, 29–30, 126, 149, 155–60, 165, 170
Pīr Pādshāh b. Lughmān 138

Pīrzād Bukhārī, emir 271
plague 46, 60, 99, 158, 164
poets 50, 55, 62, 69, 115, 167, 179, 203
prayer 180, 183, 201
Prophet (*see* Muḥammad)
punishment 28, 80, 248, 263
  of city notables 118, 150, 162, 257
  of emirs 22, 24, 36, 266, 275
  of Iranian military 159
  of local rulers 108, 134
  of princes 136, 258, 266, 270
  of religious figures 41, 42, 233, 240–42
  of viziers 83, 84, 85, 86, 87, 90, 93–94, 99, 102
Pūrānī, Abū Yazīd, shaykh 228, 234, 237
Pūrānī, Jalāl al-Dīn Bāyazīd 187

qāḍī 30, 68, 99, 108, 198, 210, 214, 255
  in city defense 118, 119, 157, 163, 213
  in city government 154–55, 160, 163, 257
  court service 57, 101, 104, 239
al-Qā'inī, Jalāl al-Dīn Abū Muḥammad 210, 211, 215, 216, 230
Qandahar 33, 39, 123, 127
Qandiyya of Muḥammad b. 'Abd al-Jalīl Samarqandī 186, 192, 193
Qannadī family of Yazd 172
Qannadī, 'Alā' al-Dīn 172
Qannadī, Burhān al-Dīn 172
Qara Yūsuf Qaraqoyunlu (r. 791/1389–802/1400, 809/1406–823/1420) 32, 34–35, 105, 130, 131–34, 191
  sons of 35
Qarabagh 34, 83
Qarachar Barlas, Amīr 41
Qaraqoyunlu 18, 19, 29, 31, 34, 42, 43, 45, 54, 105, 124, 125, 128, 129, 130, 142, 143, 151, 156, 160, 161, 163, 168, 175, 177, 250, 259, 262, 271–73, 280
Qarluq 127
Qashqa'i, tribe 152, 163
Qāsim al-Anwār, shaykh 203, 217, 227, 228, 230–33, 236, 237, 241–42
Qa'uchin 22
Qawām al-Dīn Mar'ashī, Sayyid 136
Qaydu b. Pīr Muḥammad b. Jahāngīr, Mīrzā 20, 24, 26, 33, 40, 114, 121, 125–26
Qazwin 34, 35, 54, 94, 114, 128, 130, 132, 133, 143, 250–53, 256, 262
Qipchaq tribe 127
Quhistan 84, 97, 98, 100, 106, 123, 136, 222, 224, 240
Quhistānī, 'Alā' al-Dīn 'Alī 94
Qum 30, 31–32, 39, 45, 114, 123, 126, 129–30, 132–33, 135, 142, 144, 149, 252, 253, 256, 259, 272–73, 274
  city notables 259
Qumī, Muḥammad, Khwāja 129–30, 133
Qumī, Niẓām al-Dīn Yahyā 130
Qumis 38, 250–53
Qunduz 22, 43, 114, 260
Qur'ān commentary, *see tafsīr*
Qurlas 121
Qushun-i Jānbāz 149
quṭb (Sufi term: "pole") 186, 189
Quṭb al-Dīn, Malik, of Sistan 125
Quṭb al-Dīn Jamal Islām Mas'ūd 160
Qutham b. 'Abbās (shrine) 184, 186, 191

rābita 200
Radkan 23, 114
ra'īs 76, 118, 154, *see also kulū'*; heads of quarters
Randānī, Maḥmūd (or Maḥmūd Dandānī) 121
Ranikuh 143, 251
Rashaḥāt-i 'ayn al-ḥayāt, of Fakhr al-Dīn 'Alī b. Ḥusayn Kāshifī 73, 75, 77, 189, 193, 202, 218, 236–37, 239
Rashīd al-Dīn Hamadānī 94, 101, 105, 173
Rasht 144
Rawḍāt al-jannāt fī awṣāf madīnat Harāt, of Mu'īn al-Dīn Zamchī Isfizārī 62, 68, 195
Rawḍāt al-jinān wa jannāt al-janān of Ḥāfiẓ Ḥusayn Karbalā'ī Tabrīzī 56
Rawḍāt al-riyāḥīn of Darwīsh 'Alī Būzjānī 197, 222, 224
Rayy 23, 32, 45, 47, 54, 126, 130, 142, 250, 251, 252, 253, 256, 257, 272
Rāzī, Fakhr al-Dīn (mausoleum) 184, 189, 208, 213, 220
Rāzī, Ghiyāth al-Dīn Muḥammad Ḥāfiẓ 104, 124, 129, 148–49, 171, 280
rebellions 269
rebellions, religious 240, 241
  cities 76, 119, 170, 239, 254
  emirs 16, 22–24, 26–28, 39, 85, 114, 133, 138
  princes 48, 115, 265
  regional rulers 126
  tribes 151–52
religious classes 2, 6, 10, 50, 53, 55–56
  military activities 120, 124, 279
religious movements 41, 42, 239–43
ribāṭs 213
Riḍā al-Dīn b.Qawām al-Dīn Mar'ashī 138–39, 140
Riḍā Kiyā, Sayyid (d. 1426) 142
ru'asā', *see ra'īs*
Rud-i Khwaf 96
Rūj 201
Rūjī, Shams al-Dīn Muḥammad, shaykh 201–02, 205
Rukn al-Dīn, sayyid 173
Rukn al-Dīn Ḥasan, Mawlānā 151
Rukn al-Dīn Maḥmūd, known as Shāh Sanjān (d.1200–01) 70, 96, 100, 108, 223

Rukn al-Dīn Ṣā'in 101
Rukn al-Dīn Ṣā'in ʿAmīd al-Mulk b. Shams al-Dīn 101
rukubdār 126
ruler 2–3, 5
ruler, central relation with religious classes 13, 192–97, 207, 241
  death of 2, 34
  majlis 30, 197
  and supernatural 188, 190
rulers, regional 6, 25, 32, 34, 35, 40, 111–12, 113, 114, 128–45, 152, 161, 249, 252–54, 268, 274–75, 281, 282
Rum 174
Rūmī, ʿAbd al-Raḥīm 236
Rushkhwār 96, 100
Rustam b. Sulaymānshāh, emir 23
Rustam b. Taghay Bugha Barlas, emir 27
Rustam b. ʿUmar Shaykh, Mīrzā 29–32, 104, 115, 148, 150, 156–58, 164, 168, 254, 279
  son of 254
Rustamdar 136, 139, 141, 250, 251, 252
Rustamdārī dynasty 136

Saʿādat b. Khwāndshāh, emir 63, 115, 253, 255
Sabzawar 83, 84, 95, 106
Saʿd-i Waqqāṣ b. Muḥammad Sulṭān, Mīrzā 31–32, 132–33, 163
ṣadr 52, 62, 69, 79, 99, 108, 109, 195, 210, 212, 213–14, 219, 244
Ṣadr al-Dīn Ibrāhīm, *ṣadr* 213
Ṣadr al-Dīn Yūnus al-Ḥusaynī, sayyid, *see* al-Ḥusaynī
Safavid dynasty 54, 61, 168, 212, 214, 231
Ṣafawiyya 228
Ṣafī al-Dīn b. Khwāja ʿAbd al-Qādir 89–90
Sāgharchī, Muḥammad 86
Sāgharchī, Shaykh Burhān al-Dīn (mausoleum of) 193
Ṣaḥḥāf, Murtaḍā 211–12
ṣāḥib dīwān 81, 105, 109, 148
Ṣaḥrāʿi, Naṣr Allāh 130
Saʿīd Barlas, emir 157, 161
Ṣāʿidi, Qāḍī Aḥmad 120, 157, 160–61, 279–80
Ṣā'in al-Dīn *(qāḍī)* 101
Salama 96
Sali Saray 247, 259
Salmānī, Tāj al-Dīn 28, 36, 105
Salmas 42
salṭanat 192
samāʿ 199
Samarqand 7, 17, 20, 25, 26, 27, 28, 42, 44, 56, 75, 83–84, 111, 118, 120, 184–85, 188, 191, 193, 204, 205, 207, 213, 239, 247, 260, 263, 269, 270
  city defense 266
  city notables 266
  dīwān 84, 267
  Jūy-i Āb-i Raḥmat 188
  Shāh-i Zinda 185, 191
  sufi shaykhs 228, 230, 233, 234
  ulama 212, 214, 215, 216, 218, 225
Samarqandī, ʿAbd al-Awwal al-Burḥānī 211
Samarqandī, ʿAbd al-Razzāq
  career and family 57–62, 63–64, 71, 121, 211, 216, 219, 222, 233, 234, 239, 246
  history 45, 47, 52, 54, 56, 64–67, 70, 81, 88, 90, 91, 99, 102, 120, 191, 213, 215, 221, 239, 247, 248, 258, 263, 268, 269
Samarqandī, ʿAbd al-Waḥḥāb b. Jalāl al-Dīn Isḥāq 58
Samarqandī, Darwīsh Aḥmad, shaykh 203, 229, 231, 236–37
Samarqandī, Dawlatshāh b. ʿAlā' al-Dawla Bakhtishāh 55, 62, 101, 252, 270
Samarqandī, Jalāl al-Dīn Isḥāq (father of ʿAbd al-Razzāq) 57, 58
Samarqandī, Jamāl al-Dīn ʿAbd al-Ghaffār b. Jalāl al-Dīn Isḥāq (d. 835/1431–32) 58
Samarqandī, Sharaf al-Dīn ʿAbd al-Qahhār b. Jalāl al-Dīn Isḥāq 59, 61, 62, 109
al-Ṣāna'ī, ʿAlī, vizier 106
Sanjan 70, 96, 223
Sanjānī, Tāj al-Dīn Aḥmad 70
Sanjar, Sulṭān (r. 1118–57) 224
Sanjar b. Pīr Muḥammad, Mīrzā 33
Sar-Āb-i Naw district, *see* Yazd
Sarakhs 116
Sararīg quarter, *see* Dahūk Safalī *under* Yazd
Sarbadars 83
sardār 118, 123, 147, 150, 151, 157, 168, 280
Sari 22, 23, 136, 137–42, 159, 252
Sawa 30, 31, 39, 130, 135, 250, 257, 262, 271, 272
Sawran 39, 83
Sayf al-Dīn Aḥmad, *see* Taftazānī
Sayfī Harawī 96
Sayyid Aḥmad b. Ghiyāth al-Dīn Tarkhan, emir 38, 43, 89, 114, 115
Sayyid Aḥmad b. ʿUmar Shaykh, Mīrzā 114
Sayyid ʿAlī Āmulī, *see* ʿAlī b. Qawām al-Dīn Marʿashī, Sayyid
Sayyid ʿAlī Sārī, *see* ʿAlī b. Kamāl al-Dīn
Sayyid ʿAlī Tarkhan 39
Sayyid Khwāja b. Shaykh ʿAlī Bahadur, emir 22, 23, 30, 114
Sayyid Murtaḍā of Sari and Amul 102, 141
Sayyid Yūsuf b. Saʿīd Khwāja 114
Sayyidī Aḥmad Mīrak b. Turmush 171
Sayyidī b. ʿIzz al-Dīn 152
sayyids 34, 61, 62, 70, 84, 86, 107, 118, 136, 151, 162, 163, 172, 179, 184, 189, 208, 255, 266, 272
  Ḥusaynī sayyids 53, 58, 61, 106–08, 255
Seljukid dynasty 79, 105, 224
Shabankara 106, 152, 158, 164

Shaburghan 114, 260
Shādī, Amīr Qawām al-Dīn Ḥusayn, *ḥākim* of Khwaf 108
Shadman 25
Shāh Abū'l Qays (mausoleum) 189
Shāh ʿAlāʾ al-Dīn Muḥammad Sayyid, *naqīb* 168, 255
Shāh ʿAlāʾ al-Dīn Muḥammad, sayyid (mausoleum) 168
Shāh ʿAlī, shaykh 233
Shāh Maḥmūd b. Abū'l Qāsim Babur, Mīrzā 102, 259–60
Shāh Maḥmūd Yasawul, emir 248, 252
Shāh Muḥammad b. Qara Yūsuf Qaraqoyunlu 134
Shāh Shujāʿ Muẓaffarī, *see* Shujāʿ Muẓaffarī
shāhidbāzī 232
Shāhmalik, emir 20, 25, 26, 27–29, 39, 116, 206, 221, 226, 239
Shāhnāma 167
Shahriyār fortress 132
Shāhrukh 5, 7, 10, 11, 13, 14, 248
  building 170, 216, 219–20
  burial 258
  consolidation of power 28–33
  dīwān affairs 81, 84, 89–94, 109
  final illness and death 48, 253
  as governor of Khorasan 21–22
  issue of succession 48, 93, 246–48
  karāmāt 60, 191
  legitimation 28, 41–42, 209
  literary patronage 11, 28, 33, 41–42, 52, 53, 57, 226
  relations with governors 113, 252–53
  religious policy 28, 71, 123, 196, 205, 209–22, 238–44, 254
  rise to power 20, 21–28
  and Sufi shaykhs 59, 76, 226, 233, 240–42, 243
Shāhrukhiyya 266
Shakki 35
Shamʿ-i Jahān Khan, eastern Chaghadayid 27
Shams al-Dīn ʿAlī Bālīcha Simnānī, *see* Bālīcha Simnānī
Shams al-Dīn b. ʿAbbās, emir 21
Shams al-Dīn b. Jamshid, governor of Sari 138
Shams al-Dīn b. Rukn al-Dīn 173
Shams al-Dīn b. Uch Qara, emir 23
Shams al-Dīn Kart, Malik (1245–78) 96
Shams al-Dīn Maḥmūd Ṣāʾin Qāḍī b. Rukn al-Dīn Ṣāʾin 101
Shams al-Dīn Muḥammad Amīn b. Ṣadr al-Dīn, *ṣadr* 213
Shams al-Dīn Muḥammad Asad, shaykh 235
Shams al-Dīn Muḥammad Awḥad, (d. 838/1434–35) 218
Shams al-Dīn Muḥammad b. ʿAlī Jurjānī, *see* Jurjānī, Shams al-Din Muḥammad
Shams al-Dīn Muḥammad b. Jalāl al-Dīn Chaqmaq 168, 256
Shams al-Dīn Muḥammad Mushrif, *see* Simnānī
Shams al-Dīn Muḥammad Ṭāhir, vizier 85, 148, 171
Shams al-Dīn Ṣāʾin, *qāḍī* (under Injuids) 104
Shams al-ḥusn of Tāj al-Salmānī 36
Shaqānī, ʿAlī 84, 86, 87–88, 248
Sharaf al-Dīn ʿAbd al-Qahhār, *see* Samarqandī, Sharaf al-Dīn ʿAbd al-Qahhār
Sharaf al-Dīn ʿAlī Yazdī, *see* Yazdī, Sharaf al-Dīn ʿAlī
Sharaf al-Dīn Ḥājjī Khwāfī, vizier 108
Sharaf al-Dīn Muḥammad, vizier 101
Sharaf al-Dīn Yaʿqūb, *qāḍī* 151
Sharbatdār, ʿAlī 126, 158
Sharbatdār, Ḥusayn 30, 126, 150, 158–59, 162, 280
sharīʿa 3, 9, 13, 28, 209, 211, 230, 232, 243, 266, 277
Sharistan 182
Shaykh Abū'l Faḍl b. ʿAlīka Kukeltash, emir 47, 116
Shaykh ʿAlī Bahadur, emir 23
Shaykh ʿAlī Bahadur, emir under Abū'l Qāsim Babur 114, 272
shaykh al-islām 58, 118, 210, 213, 214, 244
Shaykh Ḥājjī Muḥammad ʿIrāqī, emir 133
Shaykh Ḥasan, emir 28
Shaykh Lughmān Barlas, emir 38, 39, 46
Shaykh Nūr al-Dīn, emir 21, 24–25, 26–28, 33, 39
Shaykhzāda Qush Ribāṭī, Amīr 271–72
Shihāb al-Dīn ʿAbd al-Raḥmān b. ʿAbd Allāh Lisān 214, 219, 234
Shihāb al-Dīn Abū'l Makārim, *muḥtasib* (d. 833/1429–30) 108, 193, 210–11
Shihāb al-Dīn Bisṭāmī, Shaykh
Shihāb al-Dīn Isḥāq, Khwāja 99
Shihāb family 106
Shiʿism 209, 232, 242, 256
Shīr ʿAlī b. Uch Qara 23
Shiraz 11, 29, 33, 39, 55, 56, 63, 88, 111, 118, 123, 130, 138, 146, 148–50, 153–55, 158, 169, 175–76, 240, 249, 253, 257, 261, 266, 270, 271, 273, 274, 280
  bazaar 126, 158
  building activity 167
  dīwān 97, 148, 162
  Fazāriyya madrasa 166
  hospital of Ibrāhīm Sulṭān 167
  Jalālī fortress 167
  literary and artistic patronage 166
  Shīrāzīs 154–55, 158, 162, 163, 273
  ulama 152, 166, 225

Shīrāzī, Niẓām al-Dīn 125
Shīrāzī, Sayyid Quṭb al-Dīn 187
Shīrāzī, Sayyidī Aḥmad 89, 99
Shīrmard Jigardār, Pahlawān 121
Shirwan 35, 174–76, 241
shrines 11, 185, 209, 219–21
Shuʿab-i panjgāna of Rashīd al-Dīn 42
Shujāʿ Muẓaffarī, Shāh (r. 765/1364–786/1384) 155
Shūl (people) 127, 152, 262
Shushtar 250, 270
Signaq 42
silsila 73, 74, 78, 198, 223
Simnan 100, 102–05, 123, 142, 251, 268
  building activities 103
  viziers from 68, 85, 94, 95, 100–05, 110, *see also* Bālīcha Simnānī
Simnānī, ʿAlāʾ al-Dawla, grandson of ʿIzz al-Dīn Ṭāhir 101
Simnānī, ʿAlāʾ al-Dawla, shaykh 101, 228, 233
Simnānī, ʿAlī Jaʿfar, grandson of ʿIzz al-Dīn Ṭāhir 101
Simnānī, Ghiyāth al-Dīn (under Abūʾl Qāsim Babur) 103, 272–73
Simnānī, Ghiyāth al-Dīn Sālār (d. 811/1408) 84–85, 92, 103, 169
Simnānī, Ghiyāth Muḥammad b. Tāj al-Dīn Bahrām, vizier 103
Simnānī, ʿIzz al-Dīn Ṭāhir 101
Simnānī, Jamāl Islām, Qāḍībacha 104
Simnānī, Masʿūd b. Niẓām al-Dīn Yahyā, Khwāja 101, 104, 105
Simnānī, Muʿizz al-Dīn Malik, *see* Bālīcha Simnānī
Simnānī, Niẓām al-Dīn Yahyā 101–02
Simnānī, Quṭb al-Dīn Ṭāʾus, vizier 103–04
Simnānī, Rukn al-Dīn Ṣāʾin, poet, *see* Rukn al-Dīn Ṣāʾin ʿAmīd al-Mulk
Simnānī, Shams al-Dīn Muḥammad b. ʿAlī 84, 85, 89, 105
Simnānī, Shams al-Dīn Muḥammad Mushrif b. Sharaf al-Dīn ʿAlī 84, 101–02, 104, 125
Simnānī, Sharaf al-Dīn ʿAlī b. Niẓām al-Dīn Yahyā 84, 101–02, 105
al-Sindī, Maḥmūd 236
Sīsī, Ismāʿīl, shaykh 229–32
Sistan 19, 85, 108, 112, 123, 127, 161, 229, 239, 268
soyurghal 23, 32, 103, 113–14, 115, 264, 265, 271
Soyurghatmish b. Shāhrukh, Mīrzā 25, 26, 33, 40, 42
  sons of 259
Subtelny, Maria 216
Ṣūfī shaykhs 3–5, 11, 50, 70, 72–78, 95, 108, 118, 122, 136, 139, 141, 149, 178–207, 217, 222–38, 241, 255, 263, 283
  circles 223, 228–38
  internal relations 198, 236–38
  majlis 198–99, 202, 205, 206, 230, 235
  masters and disciples 199, 200–03, 223, 234–36, 238
  relation to rulers 59, 75, 192–98, 207, 241, 243, 278, 281
  relations with emirs 59
Suhrawardī, Shihāb al-Dīn 277
Suhrawardiyya 228, 278
Sulaymānshāh b. Dāʾūd Dughlat, emir 22, 23, 44, 139
Sulaymānshāh Qaṣṣāb. *kulūʾ* 159, 162
Suldus tribe 261
sulṭān (title), sultanate 25, 30, 70, 133, 161, 239, 258, 268
Sulṭān Bāyazīd b. Nūrmalik Barlas, emir 26, 43, 115
Sulṭān Ḥusayn Bayqarā (r. 1470–1506) 58, 61, 62, 68, 73, 80, 99, 103–04, 106–07, 121, 122, 192, 211, 218
Sulṭān Maḥmūd b. Kaykhusraw Khuttalānī 26
Sulṭān Muḥammad b. Baysunghur, Mīrzā 53, 59, 63, 130, 150, 152, 164, 165, 167–68, 191, 212, 245–46, 248, 251, 252, 262, 267–71, 272, 273, 274–75, 280
  appointment as governor 47–48, 60, 133–35, 143, 234, 251
  dīwān 269
  rebellion 150, 176, 249, 252–57
  after Shāhrukh's death 259–62
Sulṭān Uways b. Edegü Barlas, emīr, governor of Kerman 39, 120, 127–28
Sultaniyya 32, 34, 35, 39, 41, 42, 45, 128, 130, 131–33, 250–53, 256, 259, 262
Sulṭānshāh, emir 157
Sulṭānshāh Barlas, emir 82, 249, 266, 267
Sulṭānshāh Chuhra 175
sunna 182, 197, 209, 217, 219, 230, 231, 232, 243
supernatural places 56, 70, 180–87, 188–90
Syria 116, 164, 166, 171

Tabaristan 53–54, 136–42, 251
Tabas (Masinan) 69, 107, 126
Tabasī, Jalāl al-Dīn Farrukhzād, emir 69
al-Tabasī, Muḥammad 243
Tabriz 11, 35, 101, 102, 229–30
Tabrīzī, Ḥāfiẓ Ḥusayn Karbalāʾī 56
Tabrīzī, Ḥājjī Jān 172
Tabrīzī, Pīr Ḥusayn, vizier 148
tadhkira 51, 55, 72–77, 78, 196
Tadhkirat al-shuʿarā of Dawlatshāh b. ʿAlāʾ al-Dawla Samarqandī 55, 62, 195
tafsīr 166, 215
Taft 170, 271, *see also* Yazd
Taftazānī, family of 61, 197, 211, 214, 215
Taftazānī, Quṭb al-Dīn Yahyā (grandson of Saʿd al-Dīn) 214

Taftazānī, Sa'd al-Dīn 10, 58, 63–64, 197, 204, 210, 215, 216, 217, 233, 243
Taftazānī, Sayf al-Dīn Aḥmad b. Quṭb al-Dīn Yahyā 61, 62, 214
Taftazānī, Shams al-Dīn Muḥammad b. Sa'd al-Dīn 62, 211
Taghay Temür Khan 101
Tāj al-Dīn Salmānī, *see* Salmānī, Tāj al-Dīn
tājik 120, 123, 126, 263
Tālār-i Tīmūrī, *see* Isfahan
Tamerlane, *see* Temür
tamgha, *see* taxes
Ṭaqī, Abū 'Abd Allāh (d. 416/1025–26) (grave) 219, 220
Ṭaqī al-Dīn Dādā, shaykh 172
  mausoleum 172
Tārīkh-i jadīd-i Yazd of Aḥmad b. Ḥusayn Kātib 94, 176, 245, 272
Tārīkh-i kabīr, of Ja'far al-Ḥusaynī Ja'farī 53, 133, 157, 160, 161, 245
Tārīkh-i mullāzāda dar dhikr-i mazārāt-i Bukhārā of Aḥmad Mu'īn al-Fuqarā' 183, 185
Tārīkh-i Ṭabaristān wa Rūyān wa Māzandarān of Sayyid Ẓahīr al-Dīn Mar'ashī 136, 138, 139
Tārīkh-i wāsiṭ of Ja'far b. Muḥammad al-Ḥusaynī Ja'farī 33
Tārīkh-i Yazd of Ja'far b. Muḥammad al-Ḥusaynī Ja'farī 53, 245
ṭarīqa 5, 11, 51, 72, 77, 78, 208, 223, 234, 238, 244
Tarkhan emirs 38, 44, 260, 265, 266, 269, *see also* Ghiyāth al-Dīn Tarkhan, relatives of
Tarnab 261
Tarum (Fars) 130, 153
Tarum (s. of Gilan) 136, 144, 250–52
Ṭārumī, Ḥusayn, Iranian emir 143–44, 262, 274, 280
Ṭārumī, Jalāl al-Dīn (of eastern Fars) 152
taṣarruf 200
tawajjuh 200, 202
tax, taxation 2, 6, 10, 24, 32, 40, 42, 79, 80, 81, 85, 90, 92–93, 103, 111, 113, 115, 116, 128–29, 140–41, 146, 150, 154, 165, 169, 176, 197, 248, 260, 261–62, 267, 269, 270, 271, 272, 273, 274, 275, 281
  capitation tax 262, 269
  cherik tax 262
  tax collectors 86, 87, 98, 129, 170, 194, 270, 272
  tax collection 115, 116, 150, 249, 252, 254, 255, 257
  tax exemptions 158, 163, 165, 194, 255, 257
  trade tax: *tamgha* 197, 265, 269
Taybad 227
Taybādī, Zayn al-Dīn, shaykh (d. 791/1389) 100, 196, 227, 230, 237, 243
  mausoleum 100, 189, 206, 209
Temür 1, 7, 9–11, 94
  building 170, 225
  cultural interests 10–11
  death 2
  karāmāt 191, 192, 193–94
  Mongol tradition 10–12
  political organization 14–15, 16–17, 22, 83–84, 94, 101, 103, 105–06, 107, 111, 129, 131, 137, 155
  relations with Sufi shaykhs 226, 243
  testament 17, 20, 21
  and ulama 197, 212, 213, 215, 222, 243
Termez 225
Ṭihrānī Iṣfahānī, Abū Bakr 91, 245, 252, 265, 266
Till-i Kuhandizh-Miṣrakh (shrine of 'Abd Allāh b. Mu'awiyya) 185
Timurid dynasty 1, 2, 7, 10–12, 13–21, 40, 50, 52, 58
  building 166
  building by princes 221
  princes 92, 109, 146, 148, 151, 212, 248–49
  and religious classes 168, 204
  shrine visitation 71
Tizan 85
Tokhtamish 9
tovachi 23, 39, 124
Transoxiana 21, 22, 36, 40, 43, 73, 77, 122, 127, 247, 260, 262–68, 269, 270, 274, 275
  historiography 52, 54, 56
  religious classes 211, 243
  Shāhrukh's takeover 23, 24–25, 27–28, 38
  in struggle after Shāhrukh's death 258
  under Ulugh Beg 40, 42, 47, 113, 135, 140
tribes 126–28
  Chaghatay 15, 261
  local, non-Chaghatay 127, 145, 176, 262
Tukharistan 25
Tūlānī, Pīr Tāj, *see* Gīlānī
Tümen Agha 27, 28
*tümen*s, command of 15, 16, 23, 24, 39, 43, 45, 46, 124, 149
Tun 264
Tūnī 95
Turbat-i Shaykh-i Jām, *see* Jām, shrine of
Turco-Mongolian culture and population 10, 15, 185, 190, 209, 246, 261
  elite 7, 13
Turka family of Isfahan 254
Turka, Afḍal al-Dīn 254
Turka, Afḍal al-Dīn b. Ṣadr al-Dīn (d. 850/1446) 168, 257
Turka, Ṣadr al-Dīn b. Afḍal al-Dīn 254
Turka, Ṣā'in al-Dīn 'Ali b. Afḍal al-Dīn (d. 835/1432) 168, 241, 254
Turkic language 10, 30
Turkic scribes 79–80
Turkmen 35, 36, 126–27, 145, 267

Turks 8, 11, 120, 143–44, 263
Turmush, *darugha* 163, 171
Turshiz 114, 121, 224
Tus 95, 106, 240
Ṭūsī, Abū Ghālib 69, 70
Ṭūsī, Naṣīr al-Dīn 11

Uch Qara 23, 24
ulama 4, 5, 45, 50, 52, 54, 57–59, 68, 86, 95, 109, 117, 122, 147, 162, 178–79, 182, 183, 184, 188, 189, 192, 204, 210–19, 272, 282–83
  building activity 211, 213–14
  burial and graves 183
  internal relation 77, 198, 244
  military 216
  relation to rulers 195–98, 207, 238–39, 241, 242, 279, 281–82
  relations with Ṣūfī shaykhs 217–18, 232–33
Ulugh Beg b. Shāhrukh, Mīrzā 23, 24, 26, 29, 33, 40, 41, 42, 107, 113, 114, 115, 121, 135, 204, 214, 216, 242, 246, 247, 262, 266, 269, 275
  appointment to Transoxiana 25, 26, 40
  artistic patronage 263
  murder of 270
  relation to religious classes 60, 77, 239, 278
  after Shāhrukh's death 262
Ulus Chaghatay 15
ʿUmar b. Amīrānshāh, Mīrzā 19, 131–33, 156
ʿUmar Shaykh b. Pīr Muḥammad b. ʿUmar Shaykh, Mīrzā 160
ʿUmar Shaykh b. Temür, Mīrzā 26
  sons of 14, 18, 22, 23, 29, 39, 124, 129, 130, 132, 155
ʿUqaylī, Sayf al-Dīn Ḥājjī b. Niẓām 68–69, 71, 84, 102, 106
Uwaysī discipleship 226
Uzbeks 10, 44, 45, 46, 47, 249, 263
Uzkand 24, 26

viziers 40, 50, 52, 54–55, 61, 68, 79–110, 154, 194, 248–49, 272, *see also dīwān*
  building activities 100, 103, 104, 149
  military activities 103, 109, 120, 123, 125, 148–51
  regional viziers 147, 279
  relations to the Ṣūfīs 205–07

waqf 11, 79, 109, 115, 168, 172, 198, 212–13, 214, 229
Warzana 123
Warzana, cathedral mosque 168
Warzanaʾī, ʿImād al-Dīn Maḥmūd b. Muẓaffar 123, 168
Wasit 242
wilāya 186, 192
women 21, 96, 180, 191, 201
Wurujird 129, 253

Yādgārshāh Arlat, emir 38, 39, 46
Yahyā b. Muḥammad Sulṭān, Mīrzā 20
Yahyā Muẓaffar, Shāh (r. 789/1387–795/1393) 170
Yamānī, ʿAbd al-Qādir, shaykh 236
Yār ʿAlī Turkmen 120, 263–64, 275
yasa 28, 209
Yasaʾur 97
Yasaʾurī tribe 76
yasavul 107
Yasawiyya 74
Yazd 29–32, 37, 39, 53, 68, 85, 94, 111, 116, 118–19, 123, 146, 148, 150, 153, 158, 163, 173, 185–86, 216, 249, 250, 252–53, 256, 259, 261–62, 268, 270, 271, 273, 274, 279–80
  ʿAbd al-Qādiriyya Madrasa 173
  Ahristān district 148, 171, 172, 174
  bazaar 169, 170
  building activity 168–75; by emirs 170–73; by governor 170; by merchants 171–72, 175; by notables 169, 170; by viziers 151, 171
  Bundarābād 172
  cathedral mosque 170, 171
  Chahār Minār quarter 172, 174
  Cham-i Taft 170
  citadel 173
  city notables 256, 271, 273
  commercial activity 169, 174
  Dahūk Safalī Quarter or Sararīg 169, 171–72, 174, 175
  Dār al-Fatḥ 169
  dīwān 148–51, 169, 171, 261
  fortress Mubārakshāh 170
  gardens 171–73, 175
  governor 156, 168, 171, 261, 262
  hammāms 171
  ʿīdgāh 151, 172
  Imāmzada-i Maʿsūm mausoleum
  judges 151, 273
  Māmānūk mausoleum 171
  mausoleum complexes 172, 174
  mausoleum of Ṣaliḥīn 184
  Mihrījird gate 169, 171
  Musallā ʿAtīq 171, 172, 173
  Muẓaffarids in 170–71, 172
  Naʿīmābād 171
  Sar-Āb-i Naw 172
Yazdī, Sharaf al-Dīn ʿAlī 33, 41–42, 167, 252, 257, 271
Yazdī, Tāj al-Dīn Ḥasan b. Shihāb 53, 91, 124–25, 126, 159, 191, 245, 270
Yūsuf Ahl 194–95
Yūsuf b. Sulaymānshāh, emir 22
Yūsuf Chuhra b. Ḥājjī Ḥalabī 171
Yūsuf Jalīl, *darugha* 169, 171

Yūsuf Jalīl b. Ḥasan Jāndār 24, 39, 45
Yūsuf Khwāja b. Shaykh ʿAlī Bahādur, emir 39, 45, 47, 130, 251

Ẓafarnāma of Niẓām al-Dīn Shāmī 28, 33, 41
Ẓafarnāma of Sharaf al-Dīn ʿAlī Yazdī 41, 42
Ẓahīr al-Dīn b. Naṣīr al-Dīn Marʿashī 53, 121
Zawa 98
Zāwaʾī, Pahlawān Ḥājjī 84, 121
Zaydi Shiʿites 142
Zayn al-ʿĀbidīn, Sayyid 106
Zayn al-Dīn ʿAlī Bāwardī 151, 273
Zayniyya 229, 236
Ziyāratgāh 192, 229
Zubdat al-tawārīkh-i Bāysunghurī of Ḥāfiẓ-i Abrū 41, 141, 246
zūrkhāna 121–22
Zuzan 96, 108
Zūzan, Malik, *see* Malik Zūzan

Cambridge Studies in Islamic Civilization

Other titles in the series

Popular Culture in Medieval Cairo
Boaz Shoshan

Early Philosophical Shiism
The Ismaili Neoplatonism of Abū Yaʿqūb al-Sijistāni
Paul E. Walker

Indian Merchants and Eurasian Trade, 1600–1750
Stephen Frederic Dale

Palestinian Peasants and Ottoman Officials
Rural Administration around Sixteenth-century Jerusalem
Amy Singer

Arabic Historical Thought in the Classical Period
Tarif Khalidi

Mongols and Mamluks
The Mamluk-Īlkhānid War, 1260–1281
Reuven Amitai-Preiss

Hierarchy and Egalitarianism in Islamic Thought
Louise Marlow

The Politics of Households in Ottoman Egypt
The Rise of the Qazdağlis
Jane Hathaway

Commodity and Exchange in the Mongol Empire
A Cultural History of Islamic Textiles
Thomas T. Allsen

State and Provincial Society in the Ottoman Empire
Mosul, 1540–1834
Dina Rizk Khoury

The Mamluks in Egyptian Politics and Society
Thomas Philipp and Ulrich Haarmann (eds.)

The Delhi Sultanate
A Political and Military History
Peter Jackson

European and Islamic Trade in the Early Ottoman State
The Merchants of Genoa and Turkey
Kate Fleet

Reinterpreting Islamic Historiography
Harun al-Rashid and the Narrative of the ʿAbbāsid Caliphate
Tayeb El-Hibri

The Ottoman City between East and West
Aleppo, Izmir, and Istanbul
Edhem Eldem, Daniel Goffman and Bruce Masters

A Monetary History of the Ottoman Empire
Sevket Pamuk

The Politics of Trade in Safavid Iran
Silk for Silver, 1600–1730
Rudolph P. Matthee

The Idea of Idolatry and the Emergence of Islam
From Polemic to History
G. R. Hawting

Classical Arabic Biography
The Heirs of the Prophets in the Age of al-Maʾmūn
Michael Cooperson

Empire and Elites after the Muslim Conquest
The Transformation of Northen Mesopotamia
Chase F. Robinson

Poverty and Charity in Medieval Islam
Mamluk Egypt, 1250–1517
Adam Sabra

Christians and Jews in the Ottoman Arab World
The Roots of Sectarianism
Bruce Masters

Culture and Conquest in Mongol Eurasia
Thomas T. Allsen

Revival and Reform in Islam
The Legacy of Muhammad al-Shawkani
Bernard Haykel

Tolerance and Coercion in Islam
Interfaith Relations in the Muslim Tradition
Yohanan Friedmann

Guns for the Sultan
Military Power and the Weapons Industry in the Ottoman Empire
Gábor Ágoston

Marriage, Money and Divorce in Medieval Islamic Society
Yossef Rapoport

The Empire of the Qara Khitai in Eurasian History
Between China and the Islamic World
Michal Biran

Domesticity and Power in the Mughal world
Ruby Lal

Power, Politics and Religion in Timurid Iran
Beatrice Forbes Manz